REFERENCE
808.85
S967s
1966-80
P9-BJT-254
[redacted]
For Reference
Not to be taken from this room

SPEECH INDEX

An Index to Collections of World Famous Orations and Speeches for Various Occasions

Fourth Edition

Supplement, 1966-1980

by

CHARITY MITCHELL

JOHN TAGGART HINCKLEY LIBRARY
NORTHWEST COLLEGE
POWELL, WY 82435
WITHDRAWN

The Scarecrow Press, Inc.
Metuchen, N.J., & London 1982

Library of Congress Cataloging in Publication Data

Mitchell, Charity.
Speech index.

Rev. ed. of: Speech index. Fourth edition supplement / by Roberta Briggs Sutton and Charity Mitchell. 1972-1977.
Includes indexes.
1. Speeches, addresses, etc.--Indexes. 2. Orations--Indexes. 3. American orations--Indexes. I. Sutton, Roberta Briggs. Speech index. Fourth edition supplement. II. Sutton, Roberta Briggs. Speech index. 4th ed. III. Title.
AI3.S85 1966 Suppl. 2 081 81-23282
ISBN 0-8108-1518-4 AACR2

Copyright © 1982 by Charity Mitchell

Manufactured in the United States of America

Dedicated to

Roberta Briggs Sutton

CONTENTS

Preface vii

List of Books Indexed: Key to Symbols ix

Index to Speeches 1

Selected List of Titles 427

PREFACE

This supplement cumulates the 1966-1970 and 1971-1975 supplements to the fourth edition of Roberta Sutton's Speech Index. It also includes speeches in books published between 1975 and 1980 and in earlier publications listed in the Library of Congress Subject Catalog between 1970 and 1980. It indexes 115 titles (176 volumes) published mostly between 1966 and 1980.

The Speech Index is an index to monographs; periodicals have not been included. For speeches published in Vital Speeches and other periodicals, the Readers' Guide and other periodical indexes should be consulted.

Each title was indexed for speeches only. Small selections have been excluded. The List of Books Indexed indicates the coverage of the indexing of each title. Since many editors of anthologies do not state whether they have used a speech in its entirety or have just included selections, extracts are not indicated. It would be extremely difficult to ascertain the completeness of each speech except by comparing each speech word for word with the complete works of each orator. To help the user identify speeches, the date and place of the presentation of the speech is included, if known, in the author entry for books indexed in the last two supplements.

To ensure that as far as possible all the entries for one speech are listed together, cross-references have been made from variant titles to the title which was first indexed. A speech appearing only once is entered as stated in the source.

Some speeches are known better by title than by orator; therefore there is a selective title listing with an explanation at the end of the main index.

The following sources were checked as authorities for subject headings: Library of Congress Subject Headings, 7th--9th editions; Readers' Guide; and the Social Sciences Index. Names were checked in the National Union Catalog, British Museum Catalogue, OCLC, various Who's Who books, and the Dictionary of National Biography. Some subject headings have been changed to bring them into line with current Library of Congress practice.

LIST OF BOOKS INDEXED

KEY TO SYMBOLS

*Books with this symbol have been indexed for speeches only.

ACC	The accused and the accusers; the famous speeches of the eight Chicago anarchists in court. Introduction by Leon Stein and Philip Taft. New York, Arno, 1969. (American labor)
ALA	Aly, Bower and Lucile F. American short speeches; an anthology selected and edited by Bower Aly and Lucile Folse Aly. New York, Macmillan, 1968.
ALS	Aly, Bower and Lucile F. Speeches in English. New York, Random House, 1968.
AND	Andrews, James R. A choice of worlds; the practice and criticism of public discourse. New York, Harper & Row, 1973. *
ANN	Annals of America. Chicago, Encyclopaedia Britannica, 1970. 20 vol. *
ARN	Arnold, Carroll C. Criticism of oral rhetoric. Columbus, Ohio, Charles E. Merrill Pub. Co., 1974. *
ARS	Arnold, Carroll C. The speaker's resource book. 2d ed. Glenview, Ill., Scott, Foresman and Co., 1966. *
BA	Baird, Albert Craig, comp. Representative American speeches, 1965-1980. 15 vols. New York, H. W. Wilson, 1965-1980.
BAAE	Baird, Albert Craig Essentials of general speech communication. 4th ed. New York, McGraw-Hill, 1973. *
BAAGB	Baird, Albert Craig General speech communication. 4th ed. New York, McGraw-Hill, 1971. *

BAD Bagnall, Joseph
Depression dialogue. Dubuque, Iowa, W. C. Brown, 1965. *

BAP Barrett, Harold
Practical methods in speech. 2d ed. New York, Holt, 1968. *

BAPR Barrett, Harold
Practical methods in speech. 3rd ed. San Francisco, Rinehart Press, 1973. *

BAPRR Barrett, Harold
Practical uses of speech communication. 4th ed. New York, Holt, 1977. *

BAS Barker, Thoburn V.
Speech; its structure and composition. New York, American Book Co., 1968.

BEN Benedict, Stewart H.
Famous American speeches. New York, Dell, 1967.

BLY Blyton, Gifford
Speaking out: 2 centuries of Kentucky orators, by Gifford Blyton and Randall Capps. Winston-Salem, N. C., Hunter Pub. Co., 1977.

BNH Bolding, Amy
Handy introduction and replies and other helps for speakers. Grand Rapids, Michigan, Baker Book House, 1968. *

BON Bolding, Amy
New welcome speeches. Grand Rapids, Michigan, Baker Book House, 1971.

BOORA Boorstin, Daniel J., ed.
American primer. Chicago, University of Chicago Press, 1966. 2 volumes. *

BOS Bolding, Amy
Simple welcome speeches and other helps. Grand Rapids, Michigan, Baker Book House, 1968. * (Indexed for speeches or parts of speeches only.)

BOSC Bosmajian, Haig A. and Hamida Bosmajian
Rhetoric of the Civil Rights Movement. New York, Random House, 1969. *

BOSR Bosmajian, Haig A.
Rhetoric of the speaker: speeches and criticism. Boston, D. C. Heath and Co., 1967. *

BOST Bosmajian, Hamida
This great argument: the rights of women, edited by Hamida Bosmajian and Haig Bosmajian. Reading, Mass., Addison-Wesley Pub. Co., 1972. *

BREWE Brewer, David J.
World's best orations. Metuchen, N.J., Mini-Print Corporation, 1970 rep. of 1901. 10 vols. in 2.

BREWW Brewer, Robert S.
Winning FFA speeches; principles of speech preparation and presentation, by Robert S. Brewer and Dan B. Curtis. Danville, Ill., Interstate Printers & Publishers, 1976.

BRN Brandes, Paul Dickerson
The rhetoric of revolt. Englewood Cliffs, N.J., Prentice-Hall, 1971. *

BRP Braden, Waldo W.
Public speaking: the essentials. New York, Harper, 1966. * (Indexed for speeches and suggestions for preparation of types of speeches.)

BRR Brockway, Thomas P., ed.
Language and politics. Boston, D. C. Heath and Co., 1965. *

BRYF Bryant, Donald C.
Fundamentals of public speaking, by Donald C. Bryant and Karl R. Wallace. 5th ed. Englewood Cliffs, N.J., Prentice-Hall, 1976. *

BRYH Bryant, Donald C., ed.
Historical anthology of select British speeches edited by Donald C. Bryant, Carroll C. Arnold, Frederick W. Haberman, Richard Murphy, and Karl R. Wallace. New York, Ronald Press Co., 1967.

BRYO Bryant, Donald C.
Oral communication: a short course in speaking, by Donald C. Bryant and Karl R. Wallace. 4th ed. Englewood Cliffs, N.J., Prentice-Hall, 1976. *

BURT Burton, Arthur
Mr. Toastmaster: the basic principles of better listening-thinking-talking through effective public speaking. New York, William-Frederick Press, 1967. *

CAPB Capp, Glenn Richard
Basic oral communication. 3rd ed. Englewood Cliffs, N.J., Prentice-Hall, 1971. *

CAPG Capp, Glen R.
Great society; a sourcebook of speeches. Belmont, California, Dickenson Pub. Co., 1967.

CLAYP Clarke, William
Political orations, from Wentworth to Macaulay. London, W. Scott, 1889. (The Camelot series)

COG Connor, W. Robert
Greek orations. Ann Arbor, University of Michigan Press, 1966.

CROCK Crocker, L. G.
Rhetorical analysis of speeches. Boston, Allyn, 1967.

CUB Culp, Ralph Borden.
Basic types of speech. Dubuque, Iowa, Wm. C. Brown Co., 1968. (Speech communication series)*

CUR Current, Richard N., ed.
Reconstruction (1865-1877). Englewood Cliffs, N.J., Prentice-Hall, 1965. *

CURM Curry, Horace C.
Masterpieces in Philippine oratory and lessons in public speaking, edited by Horace C. Curry in collaboration with T. Uewaki. Manila, Novel Publishing Co., 1970. Reprint of the 1939 ed. *

DAVF Davis, David Brion
The fear of conspiracy. Ithaca, N.Y., Cornell University Press, 1971. *

ECH Echoes from the South; comprising the most important speeches, proclamations and public acts emanating from the South during the late war. Westport, Conn., Negro Universities Press, 1970. (Reprint of 1866 edition.)*

EHN Ehninger, Douglas
Principles and types of speech communication, by Douglas Ehninger, Alan H. Monroe, and Bruce E. Gronbeck. 8th ed. Glenview, Ill., Scott, Foresman, 1978. *

EMP Emerson, Rupert, ed.
Political awakening of Africa, edited by Rupert Emerson and Martin Kilson. Englewood Cliffs, N.J., Prentice-Hall, 1965. *

ERP Ericson, Jon L.
Public speaking as dialogue. Dubuque, Iowa, Kendall/Hunt, 1970. *

FON Foner, Philip S.
The voice of Black America, major speeches by Negroes in the United States, 1797-1971. New York, Simon and Schuster, 1972.

FRIP Frisch, Morton J.
The political thought of American statesmen. Edited by Morton J. Frisch and Richard G. Stevens. Itasca, Ill., F. E. Peacock Publishers, 1973. *

GRG Graham, John
Great American speeches, 1898-1963. Texts and studies. New York, Appleton-Century-Crofts, 1970. *

HAW Hawken, Henry A.
Trumpets of glory: Fourth of July orations, 1786-1861. Granby, Conn., Salmon Brook Historical Society, 1976.

HNWM Hobbs, Herschel H.
More welcome speeches and emergency addresses for all occasions. Grand Rapids, Mich., Zondervan Publishing House, 1968.

HNWSN Hobbs, Herschel
New welcome speeches. Grand Rapids, Michigan, Zondervan Publishing House, 1975.

HOR Horn, Francis H.
Go forth, be strong: advice and reflections from commencement speakers. Carbondale, Southern Illinois University Press, 1978.

HOW Howe, Daniel Walker
The American Whigs. New York, Wiley, 1973. *

HURD Hurd, Charles
A treasury of great American speeches. New and revised edition. Selected by Charles Hurd. Revised and edited by Andrew Bauer. New York, Hawthorn Books, 1970.

HURH Hurd, Charles
A treasury of great American speeches. Selected by Charles Hurd. New ed., rev. by Andrew Bauer. New York, Hawthorn Books, 1970.

HURS Hurst, Charles G.
Effective expression, by Charles G. Hurst and Lewis H. Fednerson. Columbus, Ohio, Merrill, 1966.

JAE Jackman, Sydney W., ed.
English reform tradition, 1790-1910. Magnolia, Mass., P. Smith, 1967. *

JAM Jamieson, Kathleen M.
Critical anthology of public speeches. Palo Alto, Calif., Science Research Associates, 1978.

JEF Jeffrey, Robert Campbell
Speech. New York, Harper, 1971. *

JEFF Jeffrey, Robert Campbell
Speech. 2nd ed. New York, Harper & Row, 1975. *

JON Jones, Phyllis M.
Salvation in New England; selections from the sermons of the first preachers. Edited by Phyllis M. Jones and Nicholas R. Jones. Austin, Univ. of Texas Press, 1977.

KEO Kendall, H. Bruce and Stewart, C. J.
On speech and the speakers. New York, Holt, 1968. *

LAA Lafeber, Walter
America in the cold war. New York, Wiley, 1969. (Problems in American History series.)*

LINR Linkugel, Wil A.
Contemporary American speeches. 2d ed. Belmont, Calif., Wadsworth Publishing Company, 1969.

LINRS Linkugel, Wil A.
Contemporary American speeches. 3rd ed. Belmont, Calif., Wadsworth Publishing Company, 1972.

LINRST Linkugel, Wil A.
Contemporary American speeches. 4th ed. Dubuque, Iowa, Kendall/Hunt Pub. Co., 1978.

LINS Linsley, William A.
Speech criticism: methods and materials. Dubuque, Iowa, William C. Brown Company, 1968. *

LYI Lyle, Guy R. and Guinagh, Kevin.
I am happy to present. 2d ed. New York, H. W. Wilson Co., 1968.

MAC McCroskey, James C.
Introduction to rhetorical communication. Englewood Cliffs, N.J., Prentice-Hall, 1968. *

MACR McCroskey, James C.
An introduction to rhetorical communication. 2nd ed. Englewood Cliffs, N.J., Prentice-Hall, 1972. *

MACS McIntyre, W. David
Speeches and documents on New Zealand history, ed. by W. David McIntyre and W. J. Gardner. Oxford, Clarendon Press, 1971. *

MAES Maestas, John A.
Contemporary native American address. Provo, Utah, Brigham Young University, 1976.

MCA McLeod, A. L.
Australia speaks; an anthology of Australian speeches. Sydney, Wentworth Press, 1969.

MCB McBath, James H.
British public addresses, 1828-1960. Edited by James H. McBath and Walter R. Fisher. Boston, Houghton Mifflin, 1971.

MDT Mathews, Donald G.
Agitation for freedom. New York, Wiley, 1972. *

MDV Matson, Floyd W., ed.
Voices of crisis: vital speeches on contemporary issues. New York, The Odyssey Press, 1967.

MDYG May, Derwent, ed.
Good talk: an anthology from BBC radio. New York, Taplinger Publishing Company, 1969.

MILS Miller, Melvin H.
Special occasion speeches. Skokie, Illinois, National Textbook Company, 1965. * (Indexed for suggestions on preparation of types of speeches for various occasions.)

MONS Morais, John Victor, ed.
Selected speeches; a golden treasury of Asian thought and wisdom. Kuala Lumpur, Printed by Rajiv Printers, 1967.

MONSA Morais, John Victor, ed.
Selected speeches; a golden treasury of Asian thought and wisdom. New ed. Petaling Jaya, Malaysia, 1971.

MOP Monroe, Alan Houston
Principles of speech communication. 6th ed. Glenview, Ill., Scott, Foresman, 1969. *

MOPR Monroe, Alan H.
Principles of speech communication, by Alan H. Monroe and Douglas Ehninger. 7th brief ed. Glenview, Ill., Scott, Foresman, 1975. *

MUS Mudd, C. S.
Speech; content and communication. 2d ed. San Francisco, Chandler, 1969.

NOB Nobel Prize Library
New York, Alexis Gregory, 1971. 20 vol. *

NOL Nobel Lectures
Literature, 1901-1967. Edited by Horst Frenz. Amsterdam, Elsevier, 1969. *

NOLC Nobel Lectures
Chemistry, 1901-1970. Amsterdam, Elsevier, 1966-1972. 4 vols. *

NOLM Nobel Lectures
Physiology or medicine, 1901-1970. Amsterdam, Elsevier, 1967-1972. 4 vols. *

NOLP Nobel Lectures
Peace, 1901-1970. Edited by Frederick W. Haberman. Amsterdam, Elsevier, 1972. 3 vols. *

NOLPH Nobel Lectures
Physics, 1901-1970. Amsterdam, Elsevier, 1967-1972. 4 vols. *

OE O'Neill, Daniel Joseph
Speeches by Black Americans. Encino, Calif., Dickenson Publishing Company, 1971.

OLIS Oliver, Robert T., ed.
Selected speeches from American history, edited by Robert T. Oliver and Eugene E. White. Boston, Allyn and Bacon, 1966.

PAE Painter, Margaret
Educator's guide to persuasive speaking. Englewood Cliffs, N.J., Prentice-Hall, 1966. *

PAF Parsons, Lucy Eldine (Gonzalez)
Famous speeches of the eight Chicago anarchists. New York, Arno, 1969. (Mass violence in American History series). Reprint of 1910.

POC Potter, David and Thomas, Gordon L.
Colonial idiom. Carbondale, Southern Illinois University Press, 1970. (Landmarks of rhetoric and public address)

PRS Prochnow, Herbert V.
Successful toastmaster by Herbert V. Prochnow and Herbert V. Prochnow, Jr. New York, Harper

and Row, 1966. * (Indexed for complete speeches only.)

REID Reid, Loren Dudley, 1905- .
Speaking well. 3d ed. New York, McGraw-Hill, 1977. *

REIR Rein, Irving J.
Relevant rhetoric: principles of public speaking through case studies. Free Press, 1969.

Representative American speeches see Baird, Albert Craig, comp. Representative American speeches.

ROD Rollins, Alfred B., Jr., ed.
Depression, recovery, and war: 1929-1945. New York, McGraw-Hill, 1966. (Documentary History of American life, vol. 7)*

SAG Saunders, A. N. W.
Greek political oratory. Harmondsworth, Penguin, 1970.

SCHW Schrier, William, ed.
Winning Hope College orations, 1941-1966. Holland, Hope College, 1966.

SIN Singer, Aaron
Campaign speeches of American Presidential candidates, 1928-1972. New York, Ungar, 1976.

SMHR Smith, Arthur L.
Rhetoric of Black revolution. Boston, Allyn and Bacon, 1969.

SMHV Smith, Arthur L.
The voice of Black rhetoric: selections, edited by Arthur L. Smith and Stephen Robb. Boston, Allyn and Bacon, 1971.

STAT State of the Union Messages of the Presidents from Washington to Johnson. Introduction by Arthur Schlesinger, Jr. Robert Hector Publishers, 1966. 3 volumes.

STOT Stewart, Charles J.
On speech communication; an anthology of contemporary writing and messages. New York, Holt, Rinehart and Winston, 1972. *

STRM Strother, David B., ed.
Modern British eloquence. New York, Funk and Wagnalls, 1969.

TAC Tacey, William S.
Business and professional speaking. 2nd ed. Dubuque, Iowa, Brown, 1975. *

THOMS Thomas, William B.
Shall not perish; nine speeches by three great Americans; selected and edited by William B. Thomas. Copenhagen, Gyldendal, 1968.

USINAU United States. 91st Congress, 1st Session, House Document 142
Inaugural addresses of the Presidents of the United States from George Washington, 1789 to Richard Milhous Nixon, 1969. Washington, D.C., United States Govt. Print. Off., 1969.

USINAUG United States. 93rd Congress, 1st Session, House Document 93-208
Inaugural addresses of the Presidents of the United States from George Washington, 1789 to Richard Milhous Nixon, 1973. Washington, United States Govt. Print. Off., 1974.

VER Verderber, Rudolph F.
The challenge of effective speaking. 2nd ed. Belmont, Calif., Wadsworth Publishing Company, 1973. *

VERD Verderber, Rudolph F.
The challenge of effective speaking. 3rd ed. Belmont, Calif., Wadsworth Publishing Company, 1976. *

VI Vietnam War: Christian perspectives, ed. by Michael P. Hamilton. Grand Rapids, Eerdmans, 1967. *

WALE Wallack, Morton A.
Eulogies. New York, Jonathan David, 1965.

INDEX TO SPEECHES

Abbott, Lyman
Cure for anarchism. ANN 12:441.

Abbott, Robert S.
A message to youth (Chicago, August 5, 1931). FON:778

Abdul Kadir bin Yusof
Now is the era of real awakening in Southeast Asia (New Delhi, January, 1971). MONSA:351
The role of attorney-general, Malaysia (Kuala Lumpur, May 25, 1970). MONSA:354
We cannot afford to fail this time to meet aspirations of people (Kuala Lumpur, Oct. 22, 1970). MONSA:361

Abdul Rahman, Tunku
"All the earth is my homeland." MONS:31
Basis of our unity. MONS:41
Big challenges ahead. MONS:25
Break with Singapore. MONS:19
Can ASEAN meet the challenge of the 70's? (Cameron Highlands, Dec. 16, 1969). MONSA:61
Concept of Malaysia becomes a reality. MONS:12
Dato Onn-a great leader. MONS:33
English language must continue. MONS:7
Face the future with faith and without fear (Aug. 30, 1970). MONSA:55
Fight for Merdeka. MONS:1
Lest we forget (at unveiling ceremony of National monument in Kuala Lumpur). MONS:34
Our university; pledge to nation (installation speech as Chancellor of University of Malaya). MONS:28
Soul of our nation. MONS:36
These truths to remember (Kuala Lumpur, May 15, 1970). MONSA:68
Tunku's recipe for success: how to get things done (Kuala Lumpur, Oct. 27, 1970). MONSA:67
Warning to trade unions. MONS:45
What Abraham Lincoln said: Tunku's pledge to people of Malaysia (Petaling Jaya, Dec. 26, 1969). MONSA:65
What the Commonwealth means (response to welcome address by British Prime Minister). MONS:22

ABDUL RAHMAN, TUNKU
Thuraisingham, E. E. S. C.
The prince of sportsmen. MONSA:187

Abdul Rahman Putra, Tunku (Prince) See Abdul Rahman, Tunku

Abelard, Pierre
Divine tragedy. BREWE 1:23
Last entry into Jerusalem. BREWE 1:22
Resurrection of Lazarus. BREWE 1:20

Abernathy, Ralph David
The Kerner report, promises and realities (Georgetown University, March 5, 1969). FON:1145

ABOLITION MOVEMENT See Slavery in the United States

ABORTION
Lonnquist, K.
Ghosts. LINRST:176

Abzug, Bella Savitsky
A new kind of Southern strategy (Nashville, Tenn., Feb. 12, 1972). BA 1971-72:37

ACADEMIC DEGREES See Acceptance speeches--Degrees, Academic; Presentation speeches-Degrees, Academic

ACADEMIC FREEDOM See Teaching, Freedom of

ACCEPTANCE SPEECHES
Ford, G. R.
Acceptance speech. BA 1973-74:193
King, Mrs. M. L., Jr.
We need to be united. FON:1169
Quezon, M. L.
On Spain's contribution to the Philippines. CURM:24

---- DEGREES, ACADEMIC
Churchill, W. L. S.
Sinews of peace (speech at Fulton, Missouri). ANN 16:365; MCB:541
Humphrey, H. H., Jr.
Open door (21st anniversary of Churchill's "Iron Curtain" speech). LINR:236
Kennedy, J. F.
Intellectual and the politician. BAP:285; LINR:236
Romulo, C. P.
The mind of a new commonwealth. CURM:267
Sampson, E. S.
Choose one of five. MOP:386
Stevenson, A. E.
Today's most fateful fact (accepting honorary degree of Doctor of Laws). OLIS:272
Washington, B. T.
Address delivered at the Harvard Alumni dinner in 1896. HURH:144

---- GIFTS
Acceptance of a gift (3 examples). BNH:87
Suggestions for preparation of a speech accepting a gift or an award. MILS:10
Suggestions for preparation of acceptance speeches. With examples of. PAE:181

---- JOURNALISM AND JOURNALISTS
Gallagher, W.
Upon acceptance of the 1967 William Allen White Foundation Award for Journalistic Merit. JEF:327; JEFF:311

---- MEDALS
Glenn, J. H.
Accepting the Distinguished Service Medal (outline of speech). CUB:65

---- MILITARY COMMISSIONS
Washington, G.
Acceptance of military commission. POC:164

---- NOMINATIONS
Bryan, W. J.
Imperialism (accepting Democratic nomination for Presidency, 1900). ANN 12:345
Dewey, T. E.
Acceptance speech, Chicago, Illinois, June 28, 1944. SIN:205
Acceptance speech, Philadelphia, Pennsylvania, June 24, 1948. SIN:229
Eisenhower, D. D.
Acceptance speech, Chicago, Illinois, July 11, 1952. SIN:242
Acceptance speech, San Francisco, California, August 23, 1956. SIN:265
Ford, G. R.
Republican National Convention acceptance speech. LINRST:349
Goldwater, B. M.
Extremism in defense of liberty (accepting nomination for presidency, July 17, 1964). MAC:251; MACR:292; MDV:115; SIN:337
Hoover, H. C.
Acceptance speech, Constitution Hall, Washington, D.C., August 11, 1932. SIN:88
Accepting the nomination for presidency. SIN:4

Humphrey, H. H., Jr.
Acceptance speech, Chicago, Illinois, August 29, 1968. SIN:372
Johnson, L. B.
Acceptance speech, Atlantic City, New Jersey, August 27, 1964. SIN:329
Kennedy, J. F.
New frontier. CAPG:8; HURH:353; SIN:298
Landon, A. M.
Acceptance speech, Topeka, Kansas, July 23, 1936. SIN:136
McGovern, G.
Acceptance speech, Miami Beach, Florida, July 14, 1972. SIN:408
Nixon, R. M.
Acceptance speech: Miami Beach, Florida, August 8, 1968. SIN:356
Acceptance speech, Miami Beach, Florida, August 23, 1972. SIN:392
It is time to speak up for America. SIN:307
Roosevelt, F. D.
Acceptance of renomination for the presidency, June 27, 1936. SIN:125
Acceptance speech, Chicago, Illinois, July 2, 1932. SIN:68
Acceptance speech on renomination for president, July 20, 1944. SIN:194
Acceptance speech via radio to convention, Washington, D.C., July 19, 1940. SIN:156
Smith, A. E.
Acceptance speech, Albany, New York, August 22, 1928. SIN:34
Stevenson, A. E.
Acceptance speech, Chicago, Illinois, August 17, 1956. SIN:282
Agrees to run for President. ANN 17:196; BEN:123; GRG:96; HURH:302; LINS:345; SIN:251
Truman, H. S.
Acceptance speech, Democratic Party National Convention. OLIS:262; SIN:220
Willkie, W. L.
Acceptance speech. ANN 16:27; SIN:171

---- REWARDS (PRIZES)

Agnon, S. Y.
Acceptance [of the Nobel Prize for Literature, 1966]. NOB 1:5; NOL:614
Andrić, I.
Acceptance [of the Nobel Prize for Literature, 1961]. NOB 1:121; NOL:565
Asturias, M. A.
Acceptance [of the Nobel Prize for Literature, 1967]. NOB 2:7; NOL:626
Benitez, J.
Acceptance [of the Nobel Prize for Literature for Juan Ramón Jiménez, 1956]. NOB 10:7; NOL:517
Bergson, H.
Acceptance [of the Nobel Prize for Literature, 1927]. NOB 2:273; NOL:246
Bjórnson, B. M.
Acceptance [of the Nobel Prize for Literature, 1903]. NOB 3:81; NOL:16
Blough, R. M.
Response to an introduction on an occasion when he is given an award. PRS:129
Briand, A.
Acceptance [of the Nobel Prize for Peace, Dec. 10, 1926]. NOLP 2:3
Brown, J. E.
Acceptance [of the Nobel Prize for Literature for Eugene Gladstone O'Neill, 1936]. NOB 19:131; NOL:336
Buck, P.
Acceptance [of the Nobel Prize for Literature, 1938]. NOB 3:157; NOL:359
Bunin, I. A.
Acceptance [of the Nobel Prize for Literature, 1933]. NOB 3:291; NOL:314
Camus, A.
Acceptance [of the Nobel Prize for Literature, 1957]. NOB 4:7; NOL:524
Chamberlain, J.
Acceptance [of the Nobel Prize

for Peace for 1925, Dec. 10, 1926]. NOLP 1:394

Churchill, Sir W. L. S.
Acceptance [of the Nobel Prize for Literature, 1953]. NOB 4:183; NOL:493

Dawes, C. G.
Acceptance [of the Nobel Prize for Peace for 1925, Dec. 10, 1926]. NOLP 1:399

DuGard, R. M.
Acceptance [of the Nobel Prize for Literature, 1937]. NOB 14:9; NOL:348

Edberg, R.
Acceptance [of the Nobel Prize for Peace for Dag Hammarskjöld, Dec. 10, 1961]. NOLP 3:248

Eliot, T. S.
Acceptance [of the Nobel Prize for Literature, 1948]. NOB 5:267; NOL:435

Eucken, R.
Naturalism or idealism? NOL:74

Faulkner, W.
On accepting the Nobel Prize, exhorts the young writers of the world. ALA:125; ANN 17:33; ARS:52; BOORA 2:988; GRG:86; HURH:291; MOPR:379; NOB 19:7; NOL:444

France, A.
Acceptance [of the Nobel Prize for Literature, 1921]. NOB 6:93; NOL:181

Galbraith, J. K.
On history, political economy, and Vietnam. BA 1975-76:78

Gallagher, W.
Upon acceptance of the 1967 William Allen White Foundation Award for Journalistic Merit. BA 1966-67:148; JEF:327; JEFF:311

Gide, A.
Acceptance [of the Nobel Prize for Literature, 1947]. NOB 7:7; NOL:426

Hamsun, K. P.
Acceptance [of the Nobel Prize for Literature, 1920]. NOB 9:123; NOL:170

Hauptmann, G. J. R.
Acceptance [of the Nobel Prize for Literature, 1912]. NOB 8:7; NOL:122

Hemingway, E.
Acceptance [of the Nobel Prize for Literature, 1954]. NOB 9:7; NOL:501

Huber, M.
Acceptance [of the Nobel Prize for Peace for the International Committee of the Red Cross, 1944, Dec. 10, 1945]. NOLP 2:293

Jensen, J. V.
Acceptance [of the Nobel Prize for Literature, 1944]. NOB 8:263; NOL:400

Johnson, L. B.
Vietnam: the struggle to be free (on accepting National Freedom award). BA 1965-66:11

Kawabata, Y.
Acceptance speech [for the Nobel Prize for Literature, 1968]. NOB 11:7

Kellogg, F. B.
Acceptance and banquet speech for the Nobel Prize for Peace, 1929 (Dec. 10, 1930). NOLP 2:79

Kissinger, H. A.
America's permanent interests. BA 1975-76:48

Labouisse, H. R.
Acceptance [of the Nobel Prize for Peace, Dec. 10, 1965]. NOLP 3:362

Lagerkvist, P. F.
Acceptance [of the Nobel Prize for Literature, 1951]. NOB 10:205; NOL:469

Lagerlöf, S. O. L.
Acceptance [of the Nobel Prize for Literature, 1909]. NOB 10:283; NOL:94

Lawrence, D. L.
Speaker of the year award. TAC:227

Laxness, H. K.
Acceptance [of the Nobel Prize for Literature, 1955]. NOB 12:7; NOL:508

Lewis, S.
The American fear of literature. ANN 15:62; BEN:208; BOORA 2:824; NOL:278

Linowitz, S. M.
Let candles be brought. BA 1976-77:149

Luce, C. B.
Optimism about the future. BA 1979-80:168

Luthuli, A. J.
Africa and freedom. MDV:79; NOLP 3:217

MacArthur, D.
Farewell to the cadets (accepting Sylvanus Thayer award for service to his nation, West Point, May 12, 1962). LINR:264; LINRS:283; LINRST:357; MDV:20; MUS:332

McNamara, R. S.
Searching for new solutions to poverty. BA 1976-77:91

Mann, T.
Acceptance [of the Nobel Prize for Literature, 1929]. NOB 12:225; NOL:263

Mathias, C. M.
The First Amendment: freedom and responsibility. BA 1977-78:134

Mauriac, F.
Acceptance [of the Nobel Prize for Literature, 1952]. NOB 13:7; NOL:481

Mistral, G.
Acceptance [of the Nobel Prize for Literature, 1945]. NOB 14:170; NOL:408

Osborne, L.
Acceptance [of the Nobel Prize for Peace for Cordell Hull, Dec. 10, 1945]. NOLP 2:318

Peirce, H. H. D.
Acceptance [of the Nobel Prize for Peace for Theodore Roosevelt, Dec. 10, 1906]. NOLP 1:99

Perse, S.
Acceptance [of the Nobel Prize for Literature, 1960]. NOB 20:7; NOL:556

Pirandello, L.
Acceptance [of the Nobel Prize for Literature, 1934]. NOB 20:77; NOL:324

Quasimodo, S.
Acceptance [of the Nobel Prize for Literature, 1959]. NOB 20:285; NOL:537

Royster, V. C.
What the people grant, they can take away. BA 1978-79:191

Russell, B. A. W.
What desires are politically important? NOL:452

Sachs, L. N.
Acceptance [of the Nobel Prize for Literature, 1966]. NOB 16:5; NOL:619

Schmedeman, A. G.
Acceptance [of the Nobel Prize for Peace for Woodrow Wilson, 1919, Dec. 10, 1920]. NOLP 1:294

Seferis, G.
Acceptance [of the Nobel Prize for Literature, 1963]. NOB 17:5; NOL:582

Sienkiewicz, H.
Acceptance [of the Nobel Prize for Literature, 1905]. NOL:45; NOB 17:183

Stanton, F.
Remarks on government regulation of broadcasting (accepting Printers' Ink gold medal). MDV:277

Steinbeck, J.
Acceptance [of the Nobel Prize for Literature, 1962]. NOB 19:205; NOL:575

Suggestions for preparation of a speech accepting a gift or award. MILS:10

Torata, Count de
Acceptance [of the Nobel Prize for Literature for Jacinto Benavente, 1922]. NOL:191

Truman, H. S.
Campaign speech, Harlem, New York, October 29, 1948. SIN:226

Undset, S.
Acceptance [of the Nobel Prize for Literature, 1928]. NOB 18:167; NOL:255

Vallotton, H.
Acceptance [of the Nobel Prize for Literature for Hermann Hesse, 1946]. NOB 9:237; NOL:416

Wauters, C. C. M. A.
Acceptance [of the Nobel Prize for Literature for Maurice Maeterlinck, 1911]. NOL:114

Yalow, R. S.
"Let us join hands, hearts and minds." BA 1977-78:181

Yeats, W. B.
Acceptance [of the Nobel Prize for Literature, 1923]. NOB 18:263; NOL:199

ACETIC ACID
Lynen, F.
The pathway from "activated acetic acid" to the terpenes and fatty acids. NOLM 4:103

Acheson, Dean G.
Ethics in international relations today. ARS:229
Marshall Plan; relief and reconstruction are chiefly matters of American self-interest. LAA:55
North Atlantic Pact. ANN 16:587
Strategy of freedom. ANN 17:42

ACHIEVEMENT See Success

ACKNOWLEDGMENTS See Acceptance speeches; Thanks

Acton, Harold See Sykes, C., jt. auth.

Adams, Charles Francis, 1807-1886
States and the Union. BREWE 1:25

Adams, Charles Francis, Jr., 1835-1915
Battle of Gettysburg. BREWE 1:31

Adams, E. J.
These are revolutionary times. (Charleston, S. C., March 19, 1867). FON:342

Adams, John
First annual address. STAT 1:40
Fourth annual message. STAT 1:52
Inaugural address. BREWE 1:39; USINAU:7; USINAUG:7
On the Boston Massacre. BREWE 1:45; POC:108
Second annual address. STAT 1:44
Speech in defence of the soldiers. Same as his On the Boston Massacre
Third annual message. STAT 1:49

ADAMS, JOHN
Everett, E.
Adams and Jefferson. HURH:64
Webster, D.
Eulogy on Adams and Jefferson. BREWE 10:3848
Wirt, W.
Death of Jefferson and Adams. BREWE 10:3905

Adams, John Quincy
Declaration and the Constitution. Same as his Jubilee of the Constitution (50th)
First annual message (Dec. 6, 1825). ANN 5:185; HOW:11; STAT 1:232
Fourth annual message. STAT 1:278
Fourth of July oration, 1828. HAW:94
Inaugural address. ANN 5:138; USINAU:47; USINAUG:47
Jubilee of the Constitution (50th). ANN 6:470; BREWE 1:85
Life and character of Lafayette. BREWE 1:79
On participating in a congress of American nations. ANN 5:188
Oration at Plymouth (commemoration of the landing of the Pilgrims). (Plymouth, Mass., Dec. 22, 1802). HURH:51
Oration at Plymouth (commemoration of the landing of the Pilgrims). BREWE 1:65
Policy for internal improvements. Same as his First annual message
Second annual message. STAT 1:249
State of the Union Message. Same as his First annual message
"Think of your forefathers and of your posterity." Same as his Oration at Plymouth (commemoration of the landing of the Pilgrims)
Third annual message. STAT 1:264

Adams, Samuel
American independence. BREWE 1:94; HURH:31
"We have no other alternative than independence." Same as his American independence

Addams, Jane
Foreign-born children in the primary grades. ANN 12:130
"...one who has looked through the confusion of the moment and has seen the moral issue involved." Same as her Washington's birthday
Washington's birthday (Chicago, Feb. 23, 1903). HURH:163

ADDAMS, JANE
Koht, H.
Presentation [of the Nobel Prize for Peace to Jane Addams and Nicholas Murray Butler, Dec. 10, 1931]. NOLP 2:125

Adler, Kurt
Diene synthesis and related reaction types (Nobel Lecture, Dec. 12, 1950). NOLC 3:267

ADLER, KURT
Fredga, A.
Presentation [of the Nobel Prize for Chemistry to Otto Paul Hermann Diels and Kurt Adler, Dec. 12, 1950]. NOLC 3:255

Adler, Morris
Rare spirit. WALE:3

Adrian, Edgar Douglas
The activity of the nerve fibres (Nobel Lecture, Dec. 12, 1932). NOLM 2:293

ADRIAN, EDGAR DOUGLAS
Liljestrand, G.
Presentation [of the Nobel Prize for Physiology or Medicine to Sir Charles Scott Sherrington and Edgar Douglas Adrian, Dec. 12, 1932]. NOLM 2:273

ADULT EDUCATION See Education, Adult

ADVERTISING
Myers, N. J.
Moppet manipulation. ARS:123
Rokeach, M.
Images of the consumer's changing mind on and off Madison Avenue. ARS:115

Aelfric
Sermon on the sacrifice on Easter-Day. BRYH:14

Aelred, Saint
Farewell. BREWE 1:110
On manliness. BREWE 1:113
Sermon after absence. BREWE 1:111

Aeschines
Against Ctesiphon. BREWE 1:114; COG:120
Debate on the crown. Same as his Against Ctesiphon

AFRICA
Bacon, L.
Plea for Africa. HAW:60
Blyden, E. W.
Africa's service to the world. EMP:26
The African problem and the methods of its solution. FON:540
Casely-Hayford, J. E.
Leadership and African cooperation. EMP:49
Houphouet-Boigny, F.
French Africa and the French Union. EMP:73
Johnson, J. W.
Africa at the Peace Table and the descendants of Africans in our American democracy. FON:730
Legum, C.
Pan-Africanism, the Communists, and the West. ARS:255
Luthuli, A. J.
Africa and freedom. MDV:79; NOLP 3:217
Nkrumah, F. N. K.
African history through African eyes. EMP:22
Freedom and unity as Africa's salvation. EMP:145
Palmer, J.
Africa: continent of change. LINRS:33
New Africa: continent of change. LINR:32
Pitt, W., 1759-1806
Indicts the slave trade and

foresees a liberated Africa. BREWE 8:3208; CLAYP:138; JAE:12; STRM:91
Robeson, P.
Anti-imperialists must defend Africa. FON:833

AFRICA, SOUTH See South Africa

AFTER DINNER SPEECHES
Burton, S.
You (male) should wear long hair. BAS:200 (outline only)
Clemens, S. L.
Horrors of the German language. BEN:204
"The ladies." BEN:201
New England weather. HURH:128
Curtis, G. W.
Liberty under the law. BAS:141 (outline only); LINS:249
Dear Old Dad. BURT:172
Executive. BURT:27
Frustrated toastmaster. BURT:160
Good old days. BURT:158
Grady, H. W.
New South (speech to the New England Society). ANN 11:240; BAS:121 (outline only); BOORA 1:465; LINS:254
Hazlitt, W.
On wit and humor. BREWE 7:2449
Hypochondriac. BURT:106
Investor. BURT:175
Landis, F.
Witty after-dinner speech on Will Hayes. LYI:224
Police. BURT:32
Schurz, C.
Old world and the new. HURH:135
Sickness. BURT: 7
Suggestions for the preparation of an after-dinner speech. MILS:13
What makes Sammy laugh? BURT:60

AGE See Old age; Youth; Youth-Adult relationship

Agnew, Spiro
Address before the Midwest Regional Republican Committee. BA 1969-70:59
Responsibility and television news. Same as his Television news coverage; network censorship
Television news coverage; network censorship (Des Moines, Iowa, Nov. 13, 1969). ARN:367; BRYF:467; ERP:153; LINRS:191; LINRST:221; MACR:331; STAT:274
Television news media. Same as his Television news coverage; network censorship
Thoughts on broadcast journalism. Same as his Television news coverage; network censorship
Vice President Agnew on televised news. Same as his Television news coverage; network censorship

AGNEW, SPIRO
Stanton, F.
Reply to the Vice President. STOT:282

Agnon, Shmuel Yosef
Acceptance [of the Nobel Prize for Literature, 1966]. NOB 1:5; NOL:614

AGNON, SHMUEL YOSEF
Österling, A.
Presentation [of the Nobel Prize for Literature to Shmuel Yosef Agnon and Leonie Nelly Sachs, 1966]. NOB 1:3; NOB 16:3; NOL:611

AGRICULTURAL ADMINISTRATION - UNITED STATES
Truman, H. S.
First annual message. STAT 3:2900

AGRICULTURAL INNOVATIONS
Howell, W.
A new century in agriculture. BREWW:211
Morrison, H. C.
In the pursuit of excellence. BREWW:61

AGRICULTURAL LAWS AND LEGISLATION See Agriculture

AGRICULTURAL RESEARCH
Grass, F.

The sky's the limit.
BREWW:115

AGRICULTURE
Benson, E. T.
Price supports and farm surpluses. ANN 17:383
Blizzard, E.
Not just a farmer.
BREWW:49
Borah, W. E.
Western farming and the tariff. ANN 15:28
Brooks, T. J.
Antitrust laws as applied to farmers. ANN 13:331
Cobden, R.
Effects of protection in agriculture. MCB:189
Effects of Corn Laws in agriculture. STRM:246
Coolidge, C.
Vetoing the farmer: Nonplanning as a way of life.
ANN 14:568
Cram, R. A.
What is a free man?
ANN 15:498
Davidson, G.
Farmer, heal thyself!
BREWW:165
Herink, R.
A succession of goals.
BREWW:141
Ivens, M.
I still believe in the future of farming. BREWW:195
Lincoln, A.
Labor, education, and the American farmer. ANN 9:121
Madison, J.
Agriculture and conservation.
ANN 4:503
Madrid, S.
I am proud to be a part of it.
BREWW:153
Mathias, T.
Is agriculture on its way out?
BREWW:64
May, C.
The American farmer.
LINSR:117
Muench, A.
Rural families and welfare.
ANN 15:462
Price, S.
Agriculture--the real answer to starvation. BREWW:161
Roosevelt, F. D.
Fireside chat: AAA and NRA, July 24, 1933. ANN 15:210
Roosevelt, T.
Seventh annual message.
STAT 3:2240
Roper, B.
A fable come true.
BREWW:201
Smith, E. R.
United we stand, divided we fall. BREWW:134
Stratton, T.
Agriculture--America's greatest tool. BREWW:109
Wallace, H. A.
Declaration of interdependence.
ANN 15:220
New Farm Act--balanced abundance for farm and city.
BAD:37
Pigs and pig iron. ANN 15:336
Wilson, W.
First annual message.
STAT 3:2544

---- EDUCATION - MALAYSIA
Aziz, U.
Scientific concepts of external aid for agricultural education.
MONSA:161

---- EXPERIMENTATION
Morse, D.
Lab farms in vocational agriculture. BREWW:144

AGRICULTURE AS A PROFESSION
Morelli, L.
Vocational agriculture, the FFA, and our free enterprise system. BREWW:78
Morse, D.
Lab farms in vocational agriculture. BREWW:144
Spray, C.
A new crisis in agriculture.
BREWW:71

Ahmad, Ungku Omar See Ungku Omar Ahmad

Ahmad bin Mohamed Ibrahim See Ibrahim, Ahmad M.

Aiken, Frederick A.
Defense of Mrs. Mary E. Surratt.
BREWE 1:120

Aiken, George D.
Either impeach ... or get off his back. (Washington, D. C., Nov. 7, 1973). BA 1973-74:66

AIR - POLLUTION
Schalliol, G.
Strangler. LINR:246; LINRS:260; LINRST:298

Akerman, J.
Presentation [of the Nobel Prize for Physiology or Medicine to Alexis Carrel, Dec. 11, 1912]. NOLM 1:437

Akintola, Samuel Ladoke and others (A. T. Balewa)
Nigeria debates self-government. EMP:65

ALASKA
Roosevelt, T.
Annual message, December 6, 1905. STAT 2:2105
Seward, W. H.
Promise of Alaska. ANN 10:193

Alatas, Syed Hussein
Sheep and lions in trade unions (Johore Bharu, Oct. 22, 1970). MONSA:179 selections
Universities: discrepancy between ideal and reality takes alarming turn (Kuala Lumpur, Aug., 1970). MONSA:177

Albert, Carl See Burger, W. E., jt. auth.

Albertus Magnus, bp. of Ratisbon
Blessed dead. BREWE 1:149
Meaning of the crucifixion. BREWE 1:147

ALCOHOLISM
Karos, P. A.
Haven of the defeated. ARS:148

Alconcel, Douglas
Aquaculture--an answer to the food crisis. BREWW:88

Aldrin, Edwin E. See Armstrong, Neil, jt. auth.

Alfvén, Hannes
Plasma physics, space research and the origin of the solar system (Nobel Lecture, Dec. 11, 1970). NOLPH 4:306

ALFVEN, HANNES
Gustafsson, T.
Presentation [of the Nobel Prize for Physics to Hannes Alfvén and Louis Néel, Dec. 11, 1970]. NOLPH 4:303

ALICYCLIC COMPOUNDS
Wallach, O.
Alicyclic compounds. NOLC 1:178

ALIEN AND SEDITION LAWS, 1798
Alien, J. and others
Debate on the Sedition Act. ANN 4:53
Dickerson, M.
Alien and Sedition Acts of the Adams administration. BREWE 5:1836
Gallatin, A.
Constitutional liberty and executive despotism. BREWE 6:2209
Livingston, E.
On the Alien Bill. ANN 4:49
Marshall, J.
Address on constitutionality of Alien and Sedition Laws. FRIP:99

Allen, Ethan
Call to arms (1861). BREWE 1:150

Allen, James
The Naval Defence Bill, 1908 (New Zealand House of Representatives, Sept. 30, 1908). MACS:270 sel.

Allen, John and others (A. Gallatin)
Debate on the Sedition Act. ANN 4:53

Alphand, Hervé
Responds to introductions. PRS:159; 198

ALSCHULER, ALFRED S.
Shulman, C. E.
Alfred S. Alschuler. WALE:299

Alsop, John
Responds to an introduction. PRS:154

Altgeld, John Peter
Children of toil. ANN 11:445
Choice before labor-organization or annihilation. Same as his Children of toil

Alunan, Rafael R.
Mindanao, the land of promise (University of the Philippines, Dec. 7, 1937). CURM:108

Alvarez, Luis W.
Recent developments in particle physics (Nobel Lecture, Dec. 11, 1968). NOLPH 4:241

ALVAREZ, LUIS W.
Friesen, S. V.
Presentation [of the Nobel Prize for Physics to Luis W. Alvarez, Dec. 11, 1968]. NOLPH 4:239

Aly, Bower
Remarks on Jefferson Day. BAP:273

AMERICA See United States

AMERICAN COLONIZATION SOCIETY
Blyden, E. W.
The African problem and the methods of its solution. FON:540

AMERICAN INDIAN MOVEMENT
Bellecourt, V.
American Indian Movement. MAES:66
Trudell, J.
Commitment. MAES:83
Wilson, D.
Real Indian leaders condemn A. I. M. MAES:63

AMERICAN LEGION
Stevenson, A. E.
Speech to the American Legion, August 27, 1952. BEN:129

AMERICAN WAY See United States - Economic policy

AMERICANISM See Citizenship; National characteristics - American; Nationalism - United States

AMERICANS FOR INDIAN OPPORTUNITY
Harris, L.
American Indian education and pluralism. MAES:96

AMERICANS IN FOREIGN COUNTRIES
Kuiper, D. R.
"You're an American, aren't you?" SCHW:186

Ameringer, Oscar
Overproduction and underconsumption. ANN 15:129

Ames, Fisher
Jay Treaty. BREWE 1:156
On the British Treaty. Same as his Jay Treaty

AMMONIA
Bosch, C.
The development of the chemical high pressure method during the establishment of the new ammonia industry. NOLC 2:197
Haber, F.
The synthesis of ammonia from its elements. NOLC 1:326

ANAPHYLAXIS
Richet, C. R.
Anaphylaxis. NOLM 1:473

ANARCHISM AND ANARCHISTS
Abbott, L.
Cure for anarchism. ANN 12:441
Goldman, E.
Anarchy vs. patriotism. HURH:166
Lawson, J.
The remedy for anarchy. FON:639
Sanford, E. T. and others
Gitlow v. New York: opinion for the court and dissenting opinion. ANN 14:476

---- See also Chicago Haymarket Square Riots

Andelson, Robert V.
Campus unrest; the erosion of excellence. (Union Academy, Dadeville, Ala., May 29, 1970). LINRS:204

Anderson, Carl David
The production and properties of positrons (Nobel Lecture, Dec. 12, 1936). NOLPH 2:365

ANDERSON, DILLON
Tweed, H.
Presents Dillon Anderson. LYI:125

Andino, Judy and others (Gary Pandora, Karen Brown, Jerry Pursley)
How can the government best protect the American consumer? EHN:462; MOPR:387

Andrić, Ivo
Acceptance [of the Nobel Prize for Literature, 1961]. NOB 1:121; NOL:565

ANDRIC, IVO
Österling, A.
Presentation [of the Nobel Prize for Literature to Ivo Andrić, 1961.] NOB 1:117; NOL:562

Andrus, Cecil D.
The inaugural address (governor of Idaho). (Boise, Idaho, January 4, 1971). BA 1970-71:137

Angell, Norman
Peace and the public mind (Nobel Lecture for 1934, June 12, 1935). NOLP 2:153

ANGELL, NORMAN
Lange, C. L.
Presentation of the Nobel Prize for Peace, 1933, to Norman Angell, Dec. 10, 1934. NOLP 2:147

ANIMAL HUSBANDRY See Agriculture

ANIMALS
Hughes, T.
Capturing animals. MDYG:191

---- See also Monkeys

Anjain, John
Speech before the Senate Committee on Energy and Natural Resources, June 16, 1977. JAM:12

Annerstedt, Claes
Presentation [of the Nobel Prize for Literature to Selma Ottiliana Lovisa Lagerlöf, 1909]. NOB 10:279; NOL:90

ANNIVERSARIES
Adams, J. Q.
Jubilee of the Constitution (50th). ANN 6:470; BREWE 1:85
Aly, B.
Remarks on Jefferson Day. BAP:273
Beecher, H. W.
Success of American democracy (anniversary of attack on Fort Sumter). OLIS: 191
Brown, H. A.
Dangers of the present. BREWE 2:685
One century's achievement (Valley Forge centennial). BREWE 2:683
Burger, W. E.
Bicentennial of American independence. BA 1976-77:185
Choate, R.
On American nationality (82nd anniversary of American independence). ANN 9:54
Church, B.
Boston Massacre oration (third anniversary). POC:255
Clay, C. M.
The man died, but his memory lives. BLY:109
Constitution, right or wrong (outline of speech celebrating Constitution Day). CUB:80
Douglass, F.
I denounce the so-called emancipation as a stupendous fraud. FON:520
Elizabeth II, Queen of England

Toast to President Ford and to the American people. JAM:22

Everheart, W. E.
We hold these truths. BA 1975-76:27

Ford, G. R.
Toast to Queen Elizabeth. JAM:21

Frankfurter, F.
The Zeitgeist and the Judiciary. FRIP:3 40

Fuller, Z.
Tree of liberty (George Washington Birthday address). ANN 5:355

Gannon, A. I.
A Catholic college, yesterday and tomorrow. HOR:78

Graham, W. F.
Our bicentennial. BA 1975-76:34

Hancock, J.
Boston Massacre. BRN:26; HURH:24
Boston Massacre oration (third anniversary). BREWE 6:2393; POC:262

Harper, F. E. W.
Address at the centennial anniversary of the Pennsylvania Society for Promoting the Abolition of Slavery. FON:430

Howard, J. A.
"... our sacred honor." BA 1975-76:9

Hughes, C. E.
150th anniversary of the First Congress. HURH:237

Hugo, V. M.
On the centennial of Voltaire's death. BREWE 7:2550

Humphrey, H. H., Jr.
Open door (21st anniversary of Churchill's "Iron Curtain" speech). LINR:236

Hunt, E. L.
Lincoln's rhetorical triumph at Cooper Union (centennial speech). BA 1969-70:189

Johari, M. K.
Malaysian Brothers (diamond jubilee of Y. M. C. A. of Kuala Lumpur). MONS:150

Johnson, L. B.
As the days dwindle down. BA 1972-73:138

Kerr, C.
Urban-grant university (centennial meeting of City College). BA 1967-68:86

Kirk, G.
Responsibilities of the educated man (at centennial of University of Denver). LINR:143

Langston, J. M.
Equality before the law (anniversary of adoption of Fifteenth Amendment). FON:409

Lee Kuan Yew
Brighter future for all peoples of Singapore if.... MONSA:239

Lewis, W. D.
Founder's Day remarks. BAS:164 (outline only)

McGill, R. E.
Meaning of Lincoln today (centennial of Lincoln's speech at Cooper Institute). LINS:360

McGill, W. J.
Science and the law. BA 1977-78:83

Mayhew, J.
Discourse on the anniversary of the death of Charles I. ANN 1:481; POC:508

Oppenheimer, J. R.
Prospect in the arts and sciences (at Columbia University bicentennial anniversary celebration). HURH:319; HURS:211

Potter, H. C.
Washington and American aristocracy (100th anniversary of Washington's first inauguration). BREWE 8:3225

Quincy, J., 1772-1864
At the second centennial of Boston. BREWE 9:3272

Razak, T. A.
UMNO'S twentieth milestone (20th anniversary of United Malay National Organization). MONS:53

Reed, T. B.
Immortality and good deeds (semi-centennial of Girard College). BREWE 9:3307

Sandburg, C.
On Lincoln (at 150th anniversary of Lincoln's birth). GRG:101; HURH:347

Sayre, F. B.
The tall ships.

BA 1976-77:181
Schrier, W.
Address to the 60th Anniversary Oratorical Banquet, March 1, 1957. SCHW:226
Seward, W. H.
Fourth of July oration, 1840. HAW:183
Smith, G.
Lamps of fiction (at centenary of Sir Walter Scott). BREWE 9:3465
Suggestions for preparation of the anniversary speech. MILS:5
Toh Chin Chye
The beginnings of the city state and its achievement. MONSA:288
Urey, H. C.
Science and society (at 100th anniversary Academic Convocation of Cooper Union for the Advancement of Science and Art). ARS:78
Webster, D.
Plymouth oration. BREWE 10:3846
Wiesner, J. B.
Science in the affluent society (centennial celebration of National Academy of Sciences). ANN 18:186
Young, O. D.
How we meet ourselves (semi-centennial of Hendrix College). HURH:227

---- See also Birthdays; Commemorative addresses. Also names of special days, e.g. Fourth of July

---- GOLDEN
McNally, J.
"Terrible beauty is born" (golden jubilee of St. Joseph's Novitiate and silver jubilee of Rev. Brother Michael in Penang). MONS:334

---- SILVER
McNally, J.
"Terrible beauty is born" (golden jubilee of St. Joseph's Novitiate and silver jubilee of Rev. Brother Michael in Penang). MONS:334

ANNOUNCEMENTS
Announcements of things to come. (10 examples). BNH:88
Suggestions for preparation of announcements. With examples of. PAE:183
Trumbull, L.
Announcing the death of Douglas. BREWE 9:3654

ANNUAL ADDRESSES See Anniversaries; Also under names of United States Presidents

Anselm, Saint
Sea of life. BREWE 1:168

Anspach, Charles L.
Responds to an introduction. PRS:138

Anthony, Susan B.
Enfranchisement of women. (New York, 1873). HURH:123
"The only question left to be settled now is: Are women persons?"--Same as her Enfranchisement of women

ANTHONY, SUSAN B.
Holtzman, E.
In celebration of the inauguration of the Susan B. Anthony coin. BA 1979-80:174

ANTI-AMERICAN PROPAGANDA See Propaganda, Anti-American

ANTI-BALLISTIC MISSILES SYSTEM See Guided missiles - Defenses

ANTI-TRUST LAWS See Trusts, Industrial

ANTONY, MARK
Cicero, M. T.
Fourth Philippic. BREWE 3:1201

APATHY
Estep, P. M.
Apathy. ARS:164

Appleton, Sir Edward Victor
The ionosphere (Nobel Lecture, Dec. 12, 1947). NOLPH 3:79

APPLETON, SIR EDWARD VICTOR
Hulthén, E.
Presentation [of the Nobel Prize for Physics to Sir Edward Victor Appleton, Dec. 12, 1947]. NOLPH 3:75

Appling, Howell, Jr.
Responds to an introduction. PRS:144

APPRECIATION See Thanks

AQUACULTURE
Alconcel, D.
Aquaculture--an answer to the food crisis. BREWW:88

Aquino, Benigno S.
The Church and the State must never mix! (National Assembly, April 26, 1938). CURM:129

ARAB COUNTRIES - 20TH CENTURY
Eagleton, T. F.
1977: year of opportunity in the Middle East? LINRST:124

ARCHIAS
Cicero, M. T.
For the poet Archias. BREWE 3:1189

ARCHITECTURE
Banham, R.
Fourth monument. MDYG:216
Sullivan, L.
Characteristics and tendencies of American architecture. ANN 11:40
Young architect. ANN 12:385
Wright, F. L.
Art and the machine. ANN 12:409
On architecture. HURH:241

ARGON
Rayleigh, J. W. S.
The density of gases in the air and the discovery of argon. NOLPH 1:90

ARGUMENTATIVE SPEAKING See Debates and debating

ARISTOCRACY
Deniehy, D. H.
On the Constitution Bill. MCA:26

ARIZONA
Taft, W. H.
Veto of Arizona Enabling Act. ANN 13:272

Arm, Milton
Vial of fragrant ointment. WALE: 13

ARMAMENTS See Disarmament; Munitions

ARMED FORCES DAY
Welcome to military personnel. HNWM:25

ARMISTICE DAY See Unknown soldier; Veterans Day

Armstrong, Lebbeus
Masonry proved to be a work of darkness (1830). (New York, 1830). DAVF:82

Armstrong, Neil and others (Neil Armstrong and Michael Collins)
Moon rendezvous. (Congress, Sept. 16, 1969). BAAGB:404

ARMY
Pulteney, W.
Against standing armies. BREWE 8:3244

---- See also Armed Forces Day; Conscription; Soldiers; Also Names of countries, subhead Army, e.g. United States - Army

ARMY APPROPRIATION ACT
Hayes, R. B.
Veto of the Army Appropriation Act. ANN 10:449

Arnold, Carroll C.
Speech as a liberal study. ARS:2

Arnold, Matthew
Literature and science. (Cambridge Univ., June 14, 1882). MCB:388

ARNOLD, MATTHEW
Holmes, O. W.
Introduces Matthew Arnold. LYI:44

Arnold, Thomas
Realities of life and death. BREWE 1:173

Arnoldson, Klas Pontus
World referendum (Nobel Lecture, Dec. 10, 1908). NOLP 1:175

ARNOLDSON, KLAS PONTUS
Løvland, J. G.
Presentation [of the Nobel Prize for Peace to Klas Pontus Arnoldson, Dec. 10, 1908]. NOLP 1:173

Arrhenius, Svante August
Development of the theory of electrolytic dissociation (Nobel Lecture, Dec. 11, 1903). NOLC 1:45
Presentation of the Nobel Prize for Physics for 1921 to Albert Einstein, July 11, 1923. NOLPH 1:482
Presentation [of the Nobel Prize for Physics to Niels Bohr, Dec. 11, 1922]. NOLPH 2:3

ARRHENIUS, SVANTE AUGUST
Törnebladh, H. R.
Presentation [of the Nobel Prize for Chemistry to Svante August Arrhenius, Dec. 11, 1903]. NOLC 1:43

ART AND ARTISTS
Cousin, V.
Eloquence and the fine arts. BREWE 4:1419
Dondero, G. A.
Modern art shackled to communism. DAVF:302
Gladstone, W. E.
Commercial value of artistic excellence. BREWE 6:2283
Morris, W.
Art, wealth, and riches. BRYH:422
Oppenheimer, J. R.
Prospect in the arts and sciences (at Columbia University bicentennial anniversary celebration). HURH:319; HURS:211
Wright, F. L.
Art and the machine. ANN 12:409

---- See also Negro artists

Arthur, Chester A.
First annual message. STAT 2:1424
Fourth annual message. STAT 2:1492
Inaugural address. BREWE 1:180
Second annual message. STAT 2:1452
Third annual message. STAT 2:1474

Ascoli, Max
Scarcity of ideas. ARS:201

ASEAN DECLARATION
Abdul Rahman, T.
Can ASEAN meet the challenge of the 70's? MONSA:61

Ashley, Leonard R. N.
A guided tour of gobbledygook. REID:408

Ashmore, Harry Scott
Presents J. William Fulbright. LYI:205

ASIA
Goh Keng Swee
Elite combat party (Communist Party). MONS:394
Some delusions of the decade of development. MONS:385
Lee Kuan Yew
Democratic socialism under stress in Asia. MONS:345
Lim Kim San
Three major problems of developing countries. MONS:412
Muhammad Ghazali bin Shafie
Malaysia and the Asian perspective. MONS:222
Rajaratnam, S.
Asia's unfinished revolution. MONS:425

---- See also Malaysia; Singapore

---- INDUSTRIES
Rajaratnam, S.

Asia needs the spirit of Sisphyus to succeed. MONSA:303

---- SOUTHEASTERN
Abdul Kadir bin Yusof
Now is the era of real awakening in Southeast Asia. MONSA:351
Lee Kuan Yew
Problems of leadership. MONS:371
Muhammad Ghazali bin Shafie
Power politics and nation-building (Malaysia). MONS:232
Narayanan, P. P.
Role of trade unions in South-East Asia. MONS:295
Rahman, Dr. I. bin A.
New era of regional cooperation. MONS:103
Razak, T. A.
Crucial cross-roads of history. MONS:64
Most unfortunate of conflicts. MONS:69

---- FOREIGN RELATIONS
Razak, T. A.
Hopes and anxieties of the countries of Southeast Asia. MONSA:47

Asquith, Herbert Henry See Oxford and Asquith, Herbert Henry, 1st Earl of

ASSER, TOBIAS MICHAEL CAREL
Løvland, J. G.
Presentation [of the Nobel Prize for Peace to Tobias Michael Carel Asser, Dec. 10, 1911]. NOLP 1:233

ASSETS See Success

ASSOCIATIONS See Club speeches

Aston, Francis William
Mass spectra and isotopes (Nobel Lecture, Dec. 12, 1922). NOLC 2:7

ASTON, FRANCIS WILLIAM
Söderbaum, H. G.
Presentation [of the Nobel Prize for Chemistry to Francis William Aston, Dec. 12, 1922]. NOLC 2:3

ASTRONOMY
Rittenhouse, D.
Oration, &c. POC:142

Asturias, Miguel Angel
Acceptance [of the Nobel Prize for Literature, 1967]. NOB 2:7; NOL:626

ASTURIAS, MIGUEL ANGEL
Österling, A.
Presentation [of the Nobel Prize for Literature to Miguel Angel Asturias, 1967]. NOB 2:3; NOL:624

Atcitty, Thomas E.
The future is at hand. MAES:160

Atcitty, Wilbur R.
Remarks. MAES:38

Athanasius, Saint
Divinity of Christ. BREWE 1:182

ATHENS
Hypereides
Funeral oration. COG:210
Isocrates
Panegyric. COG:27; SAG:99
Lysias
Funeral orations. COG:9
Pericles
On those who died in the war. ARS:191; BAS:133 (outline only); BREWE 8:3169; SAG:33

---- See also Greece, Ancient

ATHLETICS
Welcome and introduction of coach of athletic team at awards banquet. HNWM:34

---- See also Sports

Atkinson, Harry
Proposal for a National Insurance scheme, 1882 (New Zealand House of Representatives, July 10, 1882). MACS:186 sel.

Atkinson, Henry and others (Sir George Grey)
The abolition of the provinces, 1876 (New Zealand House of Representatives, Sept. 19, 1876). MACS:111 sel.

ATLANTA RIOTS, 1906
Washington, B. T.
We must be a law-abiding and law-respecting people. FON:652

ATLANTIS
DeBeer, G.
Atlantis. MDYG:272

ATOMIC AGE
Van Voorst, B.
Clock. SCHW:74

ATOMIC BOMB
Truman, H. S.
Announcement of the first use of the atomic bomb. ANN 16:334

ATOMIC ENERGY
Anjain, J.
Speech before the Senate Committee on Energy and Natural Resources, June 16, 1977. JAM:12
Baruch, B. M.
International control of atomic energy. ANN 16:360; HURH:279
Eisenhower, D. D.
International control of atomic power for peaceful purposes. ANN 17:211
Nixon, R. M.
Campaign speech, Toledo, Ohio, October 27, 1960. SIN:319

ATOMIC POWER See Atomic energy

ATOMIC WARFARE
Hatfield, M. O.
If we fall down in the land of peace. BA 1979-80:67
Hiatt, H. H.
Prevention of the last epidemic. BA 1979-80:56
Kennedy, J. F.
Step toward peace. ANN 18:192
McNamara, R. S.
Nuclear strategy. ANN 18:527
Wald, G.
Generation in search of a future. BA 1968-1969:33

ATOMIC WEAPONS AND DISARMAMENT
Carter, J.
Our common responsibility and our common challenge. BA 1977-78:59

ATOMIC WEIGHTS
Richards, T. W.
Atomic weights. NOLC 1:280

ATOMS
Bohr, N.
The structure of the atom. NOLPH 2:7
Hertz, G.
The results of electron-impact tests in the light of Bohr's theory of atoms. NOLPH 2:112
Siegbahn, K. M. G.
The x-ray spectra and the structure of the atoms. NOLPH 2:81
Stark, J.
Structural and spectral changes of chemical atoms. NOLPH 1:427

Attlee, Clement R.
A common endeavour. Same as his Speech in Commons on the United Nations charter.
The Labour programme. (BBC Broadcast, June 5, 1945). MCB:471
Speech in Commons on the United Nations charter. (Jan. 10, 1946). MCB:536

---- See Baldwin, S. B., jt. auth.

Attwood, Thomas
Chartist movement. JAE:68

Aubert, Jean-Marie
Vietnam and world peace. VI:104

AUCKLAND RIOT, 1932
Lee, J. A.
The Auckland Riot, 1932. MACS:312 sel.

Augustine, Saint
On our Lord's prayer. BREWE 1:188

AUSTRALIA
Evatt, H. V.

Australia and the United Nations charter. MCA:161
Payne, J. R.
Australia and the Vietnam War. VI:75

---- COLONIES
Parkes, H.
New constellation. MCA:37

---- CONSTITUTION
Deakin, A.
For the Federal Constitution. MCA:84

---- FOREIGN RELATIONS - UNITED STATES
Curtin, J.
We are fighting mad. MCA:154

---- IMMIGRATION AND EMIGRATION See Immigration and emigration - Australia

---- POLITICS AND GOVERNMENT
Deniehy, D. H.
On the Constitution Bill. MCA:26
Hughes, W. M.
Australian Judas. MCA:125

---- See also Labor Party (Australia)

AUTHORS AND AUTHORSHIP
See Literature; Poetry and poets

AUTOBIOGRAPHY
Cutforth, R.
Illuminations. MDYG:35

AUTOMOBILE DRIVERS
Lorge, B.
Great auto rally (outline). REIR:93

AUTOMOTIVE INDUSTRY AND TRADE
Cole, E. N.
Two myths and a paradox. BA 1971-72:93
Curtice, H.
Automotive research at General Motors. ANN 17:379

AUXILIARIES See Club speeches

Avebury, John Lubbock, 1st Baron
Hundred best books. BREWE 7:2820

AWARDS See Acceptance speeches - Rewards (Prizes); Presentation speeches - Rewards (Prizes)

Axelrod, Julius
Noradrenaline: fate and control of its biosynthesis (Nobel Lecture, Dec. 12, 1970). NOLM 4:444

AXELROD, JULIUS
Uvnäs, B.
Presentation [of the Nobel Prize for Physiology or Medicine to Julius Axelrod, Ulf Von Euler, and Bernhard Katz, Dec. 12, 1970]. NOLM 4:441

Ayer, A. J. and others (R. Kee; O. Todd)
What are philosophers for? MDYG:101

Aziz, Ungku
Languages: anguish and confusion (Univ. of Malaya). MONSA:167
Scientific concepts of external aid for agricultural education (Copenhagen, July 28-Aug. 8, 1970). MONSA:161

Azmi, Bin Haji Mohamed
Duty of a lawyer. MONS:97

- B -

Babbidge, Homer D.
On thinking big (Univ. of Connecticut, May 18, 1975). HOR:121

BABIES See Children

BACCALAUREATE ADDRESSES
Brewster, K., Jr.
Due process radicalism. HOR:37
Heuss, J.
Introduction to baccalaureate

sermon. PRS:55
Lindsley, P.
Dangers of a sectarian college. ANN 5:310
Pusey, N. M.
Thanksgiving and entreaty, a President's valedictory. HOR:26

BACHELORS
Long live the bachelors. BURT:71

BACKACHES
Ragan, D. O.
Backaches. MOP:366; MOPR:358

Backhouse, Margaret A.
The international service of the Society of Friends (Nobel Lecture, Dec. 12, 1947). NOLP 2:380

Bacon, Francis, Viscount of St. Albans
Against dueling. BREWE 1:199; BRYH:96
Upon the motion of subsidy (November 15, 1598 speech). BRYH:90

Bacon, Leonard
Plea for Africa (Boston, July 5, 1824). HAW:60
Sermon from Mark XII, 34 (Boston, July 4, 1824). HAW:57

Bacon, Wallace A.
Language and the lived world (Knoxville, Tenn., April 18, 1977). BA 1976-77:174
The seacoast of Bohemia: truth in literature (Washington, Dec. 2, 1977). BA 1977-78:170

BACTERIA
Jacob, F.
Genetics of the bacterial cell. NOLM 4:148

BACTERIAL DISEASES
Domack, G. J. P.
Further progress in chemotherapy of bacterial infections. NOLM 2:490

BAECK, LEO
Dreyfus, A. S.
Leo Baeck. WALE:207

Bajer, Fredrik
The organization of the Peace Movement (Nobel Lecture, 1908, May 18, 1909). NOLP 1:190

BAJER, FREDRIK
Løvland, J. G.
Presentation [of the Nobel Prize for Peace to Fredrik Bajer, Dec. 10, 1908]. NOLP 1:188

Baker, Richard
Crime of Mrs. Douglass in teaching colored children to read. ANN 8:224

Balch, Emily Greene
Toward human unity or beyond nationalism (Nobel Lecture for 1946, April 7, 1948). NOLP 2:333

BALCH, EMILY GREENE
Jahn, G.
Presentation of the Nobel Prize for Peace to Emily Greene Balch, Dec. 10, 1946. NOLP 2:325

Baldwin, H. C. See Warner, A. J., jt. auth.

Baldwin, James
The American dream is at the expense of the American Negro. FON:1012

Baldwin, Roger S.
Executive prerogative in foreign policy. ANN 7:423

Baldwin, Stanley Baldwin, 1st Earl of Bewdley
Goodwill in industry. (H. of Commons, March 6, 1925). MCB:243; STRM:433
Industrial peace. Same as his Goodwill in industry

---- and others (Edward VIII; C. Attlee; A. Sinclair; W. L. S. Churchill; J. Maxton; W.

Gallacher; G. Buchanan; C. Stephen; W. Thorne; J. Simon; A. Chamberlain)
Debate in the House of Commons on the abdication of Edward VIII. BRYH:491

Balewa, Sir Aubbaker Tafawa See Akintola, S. L., jt. auth.

Ball, George W.
Issue in Vietnam. BA 1965-66:43

Ball, John
Bondmen and freemen: address to the rebels at Blackheath. BRYH:42
Let us go to the King. Same as his We have the pain and travail
Speech at the Peasants' rising. Same as his Bondmen and freemen: address to the rebels at Blackheath
We have the pain and travail. BRYH:42

Ballance, John
The 1890 election: the opposition case (Wanganui, Sept. 23, 1890). MACS:201 selections
A land tax of a halfpenny in the pound on land exceeding £500 in value, 1878 (New Zealand House of Representatives, Aug. 6, 1878). MACS:184 selections

BALLOT See Blacks - Politics and suffrage; Elections; Women - Suffrage

BALZAC, HONORE DE
Hugo, V. M.
Oration on Honoré de Balzac. BREWE 7:2546

Bancroft, George
Fourth of July oration, 1826. (Northampton, Mass., July 4, 1826). HAW:75

Banham, Reyner
Fourth monument. MDYG:216

BANK OF THE UNITED STATES, 1816-1836 See Banks and banking

BANKRUPTCY
Webster, D.
For a uniform bankruptcy law. ANN 6:561

Banks, Nathaniel P. See Butler, B. F., jt. auth.

BANKS AND BANKING
Benton, T. H.
Against the United States Bank. ANN 5:430; BREWE 2:425
Clay, H.
Bank and the power of the executive. ANN 6:46
Crockett, D.
Fourth of July oration, 1834. HAW:136
Jackson, A.
Fifth annual message. STAT 1:373
Fourth annual message. STAT 1:358
Seventh annual message. ANN 6:164; STAT 1:415
Sixth annual address. STAT 1:389
Veto message of July 10, 1832. ANN 5:524
La Follette, R. M.
A small group of men hold in their hands the business of this country (1908). DAVF:200
Lee, H. H. S.
Great Institution (Central Bank of Malaya). MONS:164
Peel, R.
Bank charter--the currency. STRM:213
Robinson, R.
A Jacksonian attack on monopoly (1834). DAVF:69
Tyler, J.
Second annual message. STAT 1:581
Van Buren, M.
First annual message. STAT 1:472
Webster, D.
For the Bank Renewal Bill. ANN 5:535

---- MALAYSIA
Ismail bin Mohammed Ali
The central Bank--the "financial conscience" of the government. MONSA:189

BANQUETS See After dinner speeches; Announcements; Club speeches; Toastmasters; Also types of speeches e. g. Introductions; Toasts; Welcoming addresses, etc. Also types of banquets e. g. Fathers and sons; Mothers and daughters

Banting, Frederick Grant
Diabetes and insulin (Nobel Lecture for 1923, Sept. 15, 1925). NOLM 2:50

BANTING, FREDERICK GRANT
Sjöquist, J.
Presentation [of the Nobel Prize for Physiology or Medicine for 1923 to Frederick Grant Banting and John James Richard Macleod, 1925]. NOLM 2:45

BAPTIST CHURCH See Church

BAR See Law and lawyers

Barany, Robert
Some new methods for functional testing of the vestibular apparatus and the cerebellum (Nobel Lecture for 1914, Sept. 11, 1916). NOLM 1:500

Barbour, James
Treaties as supreme laws. BREWE 1:209

Bard, George M.
Introduces Alexander Rorke, Jr. PRS:69
Introduces Arthur Godfrey. PRS:45
Introduces Dr. Deane W. Malott, President of Cornell University. PRS:115
Introduces Dr. Henry A. Kissinger. PRS:124
Introduces George Ratterman. PRS:62
Introduces Gilbert W. Fitzhugh. PRS:17
Introduces Walter W. Heller, chairman of the President's Council of Economic Advisers. PRS:33
Introduces William F. Buckley, Jr., columnist. PRS:57

Bardeen, John
Semiconductor research leading to the point contact transistor (Nobel Lecture, Dec. 11, 1956). NOLPH 3:318

Barger, Robert Newton
Theology and amnesty. (Peoria, Ill., Nov. 11, 1973). BA 1973-74:177

Bark, Dale R.
World food crisis. BREWW: 219

Barkla, Charles Glover
Characteristic Röntgen radiation (Nobel Lecture for 1917, June 3, 1920). NOLPH 1:392

Barkley, Alben W.
Record of Democratic Party. (Philadelphia, July 12, 1948). BLY:233

Barlow, Earl J.
Education on Indian terms. MAES:90
If a man loses something; address at the 5th annual state Indian Education Conference, College of Great Falls, Montana, April 3, 1975. MAES:343
Multicultural education: its effective management. MAES:110

Barlow, Joseph
Unfinished revolution. ANN 3:90

Barnard, Daniel D.
American experiment in government. ANN 6:353
The social system. (House of Convocation of Trinity College, Hartford, Conn., 1848). HOW:106

Barnard, Sir John See Walpole, R., jt. auth.

Barnave, Antoine Pierre Joseph Marie
Commercial politics. BREWE 1:221
Representative democracy against majority absolutism. BREWE 1:218

Barnett, Ferdinand L.
Race unity. (Nashville, Tenn., May 6-9, 1879). FON:461

Barton, Bruce
Which knew not Joseph (New York, 1923). BRYF:554; BRYO:228

Barton, Derek H. R.
The principles of conformational analysis (Nobel Lecture, Dec. 11, 1969). NOLC 4:298

BARTON, DEREK H. R.
Fredga, A.
Presentation [of the Nobel Prize for Chemistry to Derek H. R. Barton and Odd Hassel, Dec. 11, 1969]. NOLC 4:295

Barrett, B. F.
The unreasonable prejudices against people of color in Philadelphia. (Philadelphia, Sept. 23, 1866). FON:337

Barrow, Isaac
Slander. BREWE 1:224

Baruch, Bernard M.
Choice between the quick and the dead. Same as his International control of atomic energy
International control of atomic energy (United Nations, June 14, 1946). ANN 16:360; HURH:279
"We are here to make a choice between the quick and the dead." Same as his International control of atomic energy (June 14, 1946)

Barzun, Jacques
Place and the price of excellence. ARS:28

Basil the Great, Saint
On a recreant nun. BREWE 1:235

BASIL THE GREAT, SAINT
Gregory of Nazianzur
Eulogy on Basil of Baesarea. BREWE 6:2336

Basov, Nikolai G.
Semiconductor lasers (Nobel Lecture, Dec. 11, 1964). NOLPH 4:89

BASOV, NIKOLAI G.
Edlén, B.
Presentation [of the Nobel Prize for Physics to Charles H. Townes, Nikolai G. Basov, and Alexander M. Prochorov, Dec. 11, 1964]. NOLPH 4:55

Bates, Darrell
Bride-price. MDYG:59

Bathurst, Henry See Walpole, R., jt. auth.

Baxter, Richard
Unwillingness to improve. BREWE 1:242

BAY OF PIGS See United States - Foreign relations - Cuba

Bayard, James Asheton
Commerce and naval power. BREWE 1:262
Federal Judiciary. BREWE 1:249

Bayard, Thomas F.
Plea for conciliation in 1876. BREWE 1:265

Beaconsfield, Benjamin Disraeli, 1st Earl of
Against democracy for England. BREWE 1:296
Against repeal of the Corn Laws. Same as his Third reading of the Corn Importation Bill
Assassination of Lincoln. BREWE 1:295
Conservative and liberal principles. Same as his Meaning of conservatism
Conservative versus liberal. Same as his Meaning of conservatism
Meaning of conservatism (Crystal Palace, London, June 24, 1872). BREWE 1:309; BRYF:534; MCB:431
Reform Bill of 1867 (Edinburgh

speech, October 29, 1867). STRM:296
Third reading of the Corn Importation Bill (H. of Commons, May 15, 1846). BRYH:371; MCB:211
Tory democracy. JAE:139

BEACONSFIELD, BENJAMIN DISRAELI, 1st EARL OF
Gladstone, W. E.
On Lord Beaconsfield. BREWE 6:2291

Beadle, George Wells
Genes and chemical reactions in Neurospora (Nobel Lecture, Dec. 11, 1958). NOLM 3:587

BEADLE, GEORGE WELLS
Caspersson, T.
Presentation [of the Nobel Prize for Physiology or Medicine to George Wells Beadle, Edward Lawrie Tatum, and Joshua Lederberg, Dec. 11, 1958]. NOLM 3:583

BEATNIKS
Brown, J. M.
"Beat" generation. HURH:341

Beaudin, John A.
Testimony to the Senate Education Committee May 6, 1975 at the State Capitol concerning Senate Bill 145. MAES:245

BEAUTY, PERSONAL
Flaxman, J.
Physical and intellectual beauty. BREWE 6:2167

Becker, Arie
To make a commonplace wondrous. WALE:15

BECKETT, SAMUEL
Gierow, K. R.
Presentation address [of the Nobel Prize for Literature to Samuel Beckett, 1969]. NOB 3:3

Becquerel, Antoine Henri
On radioactivity, a new property of matter (Nobel Lecture, Dec. 11, 1903). NOLPH 1:52

BECQUEREL, ANTOINE HENRI
Törnebladh, H. R.
Presentation [of the Nobel Prize for Physics to Antoine Henri Becquerel, Pierre Curie and Marie Sklodowska-Curie, Dec. 11, 1903]. NOLPH 1:47

Bede (The Venerable)
Meeting of mercy and justice. BREWE 1:340
On the nativity of St. Peter and St. Paul. BRYH:9
Sermon for any day. BREWE 1:343
Torments of hell. BREWE 1:344

Beecher, Henry Ward
Effect of the death of Lincoln. BREWE 1:365
"Hold each other in true fellowship. Same as his On fellowship
Liverpool speech, October 16, 1863. LINS:229
On fellowship. (Plymouth, Mass., Nov. 18, 1869). HURH:118
Raising the flag over Fort Sumter. BREWE 1:347
Success of American democracy (anniversary of attack on Fort Sumter). OLIS:191

Beecher, Lyman
A plea for the West. (Delivered several times, 1835). HOW:133

BEERNAERT, AUGUSTE MARIE FRANÇOIS
Løvland, J. G.
Presentation [of the Nobel Prize for Peace to Auguste Marie François Beernaert, Dec. 10, 1909]. NOLP 1:211

Begin, Menachem See Carter, J., jt. auth.

BEHAVIOR
Getting along with difficult people. BURT:109
Nies, N.
Warrior and the woman. SCHW:10
Roosevelt, T.

Strenuous life. BEN:189; HURH:150
Wycliffe, J.
Rule for decent living. BREWE 10:3918

Behring, Emil Adolf Von
Serum therapy in therapeutics and medical science (Nobel Lecture, Dec. 12, 1901). NOLM 1:6

BEHRING, EMIL ADOLF VON
Mörner, K. A. H.
Presentation [of the Nobel Prize for Physiology or Medicine to Emil Adolf Von Behring, Dec. 12, 1901]. NOLM 1:3

Bekesy, Georg Von
Concerning the pleasures of observing, and the mechanics of the inner ear (Nobel Lecture, Dec. 11, 1961). NOLM 3:722

BEKESY, GEORG VON
Bernhard, C. G.
Presentation [of the Nobel Prize for Physiology or Medicine to Georg Von Bekesy, Dec. 11, 1961]. NOLM 3:719

Belhaven, John Hamilton, 2d Baron
Plea for the national life of Scotland. BREWE 1:371

Bell, David E.
Responds to introduction. PRS:94

Bell, Francis H. D.
The defence of the Empire in the Great War (July 12, 1917). MACS:273 selections

Bell, Griffin B.
Notes on the situation: a critique (Lawrence, Kan., Jan. 25, 1979). BA 1978-79:93

Bell, John
Against extremists, North and South. BREWE 1:384
Trans-continental railroads. BREWE 1:390

Bellecourt, Vernon
American Indian Movement. MAES:66

Belloc, Hilaire See Shaw, G. B., jt. auth.

BELMONT, ELEANOR ROBSON
Lamont, T. W.
Presents Eleanor Robson Belmont. LYI:23

Beloff, Max
Americanisation of British intellectual life. MDYG:114

Belson, Richard S.
What really counts. WALE:18

BENAVENTE, JACINTO
Hallström, P.
Presentation [of the Nobel Prize for Literature to Jacinto Benavente, 1922]. NOB 2:179; NOL:186
Torata, Count de
Acceptance [of the Nobel Prize for Literature for Jacinto Benavente, 1922]. NOL:191

Benchley, Robert C.
Treasurer's report. (New York, 1930). HURH:211

Benedict, Donald L.
Remarks in Chicago on urban imperatives. BA 1967-68:78

Benezet, Louis T.
Acceleration or direction? BA 1966-67:105
The educator's leap of faith (Hebrew Union College, Los Angeles, June 13, 1969). HOR:107

Benham, William J.
An Indian education resources center. MAES:114

Benitez, Jaime
Acceptance [of the Nobel Prize for Literature for Juan Ramón Jiménez, 1956]. NOB 10:7; NOL:517

Benjamin, Judah Philip
Farewell to the Union.

BREWE 1:399
Slavery as established by law. BREWE 1:406

Bennett, John C.
Issue of peace: the voice of religion. BA 1965-66:142

Bennett, Robert
The fall and rise of Indian sovereignty. MAES:11

BENNY, JACK
Jessel, G.
Presents Jack Benny. LYI:30

Benson, Ezra Taft
Price supports and farm surpluses. ANN 17:383

Benton, Thomas Hart
Against the United States Bank. ANN 5:430; BREWE 2:425
Mischiefs of a national bank. Same as his Against the United States Bank
Political career of Andrew Jackson. BREWE 2:411
There is East; there is India. BREWE 2:429

BENTON, THOMAS HART
Blair, F. P.
Character and work of Benton. BREWE 2:509
Deathbed of Benton. BREWE 2:514

Benton, William
For the expulsion of Senator McCarthy. ANN 17:108

Bergius, Friedrich
Chemical reactions under high pressure (Nobel Prize for Chemistry for 1931, May 21, 1932). NOLC 2:244

BERGIUS, FRIEDRICH
Palmaer, W.
Presentation [of the Nobel Prize for Chemistry for 1931 to Carl Bosch and Friedrich Bergius, May 21, 1932]. NOLC 2:189

Bergson, Henri
Acceptance [of the Nobel Prize for Literature, 1927]. NOB 2:273; NOL:246

BERGSON, HENRI
Hallström, P.
Presentation [of the Nobel Prize for Literature to Henri Bergson, 1927]. NOB 2:267; NOL:242

Bergstrand, H.
Presentation [of the Nobel Prize for Physiology or Medicine to Max Theiler, Dec. 11, 1951]. NOLM 3:347

Bergstrom, S.
Presentation [of the Nobel Prize for Physiology or Medicine to Konrad Bloch and Feodor Lynen, Dec. 11, 1964]. NOLM 4:75

BERI-BERI
Eijkman, C.
Antincuritic vitamin and beriberi. NOLM 2:199

Berkeley, William
Speech to the Virginia House of Burgesses. POC:169

Berle, Adolf A., Jr.
Emerging common law of free enterprise. ANN 16:573

BERLIN QUESTION, 1945-
Kennedy, J. F.
Berlin crisis. THOMS:22
Ich bin ein Berliner. ALA:129; AND:79; LINR:294; LINRS:293

Bernard, Saint
Advice to young men. BREWE 2:433
Against luxury in the Church. BREWE 2:434
On the Canticles. BREWE 2:435
Preaching the Crusade. Same as his Why another crusade
Second crusade. Same as his Why another crusade
Why another crusade? BAS:43 (outline only); BREWE 2:432

Bernard, Sir Francis
Speech to the Council and House of Representatives. POC:227

Bernhard, C. G.
Presentation [of the Nobel Prize for Physiology or Medicine to Georg Von Bekesy, Dec. 11, 1961]. NOLM 3:719

Presentation [of the Nobel Prize for Physiology or Medicine to Ragnar Granit, Haldan Keffer Hartline, and George Wald, Dec. 12, 1967]. NOLM 4:251

Bernstein, Leonard
American musical comedy. KEO:274
World of jazz. (Telecast: October 16, 1955). ARN:320; ARS:67

Berrien, John M.
Conquest and territorial organization. BREWE 2:436
Effect of the Mexican conquest. BREWE 2:439

Berryer, Pierre Antoine
Censorship of the press. BREWE 2:443

Bersin, Alan
Open letter to my middle-aged father. REIR:215

Bertonneau, Arnold
Every man should stand equal before the law. (Boston, April 12, 1864). FON:303

Besdin, Abraham R.
Life's struggle. WALE:20

Bethe, Hans Albrecht
Energy production in stars (Nobel Lecture, Dec. 11, 1967). NOLPH 4:215

BETHE, HANS ALBRECHT
Klein, O.
Presentation [of the Nobel Prize for Physics to Hans Albrecht Bethe, Dec. 11, 1967]. NOLPH 4:211

Betjeman, John <u>See</u> Sykes, C., jt. auth.

Bevan, Aneurin
Change the direction of the war. (H. of Commons, July 2, 1942). MCB:524
National Health Service Bill. STRM:445

Beveridge, Albert J.
In support of an American empire. Same as his Philippine question
March of the flag. ANN 12:198; BOORA 2:622; GRG:14; LINS:276
Philippine question. ANN 12:336; BRR:29
Philippines are ours forever. Same as his Philippine question
Taste of empire. Same as his March of the flag

Bevin, Ernest
Testimony at the "Docker's Inquiry." STRM:423

Bial, Morrison D.
Light from the stones. WALE:21

BIBLE
Damiani, P.
New Testament history as allegory. BREWE 4:1606

BIBLE SCHOOLS <u>See</u> Religious education

BICENTENNIAL SPEECHES <u>See</u> Anniversaries

Biddle, Nicholas
Princeton commencement address. (Sept. 30, 1835). HOW:123

Bigelow, Jacob
Future of the arts and sciences. ANN 4:449

BILE
Wieland, H. O.
The chemistry of the bile acids. NOLC 2:94

Bilheimer, Robert S.
Christian conscience and the Vietnam War. VI:15

BILL OF RIGHTS (UNITED STATES) <u>See</u> United States - Constitution

Billings (District Judge)
Labor and the antitrust laws. Same as his United States v. Workingmen's Amalgamated

Council of New Orleans, 1893
United States v. Workingmen's Amalgamated Council of New Orleans, 1893. ANN 11:435

Billington, Ray A.
Cowboys, Indians, and the land of promise: the world image of the American frontier (San Francisco, Aug. 22, 1975). BA 1975-76:176

Bingham, John A.
Against the assassins of President Lincoln. BREWE 2:445

---- See also Butler, B. J., jt. auth.

Binney, Barnabas
Valedictory oration. POC:51

BIOLOGICAL RESEARCH
Tatum, E. L.
A case history in biological research. NOLM 3:602

BIOLOGY
Delbrück, M.
A physicist's renewed look at biology--twenty years later. NOLM 4:404

Birenbaum, William M.
Time for reconstruction. BA 1969-70:154

Birkenhead, Lord See Sykes, C., jt. auth.

BIRKETT, SIR NORMAN
Daniels, J.
Presents Sir Norman Birkett. LYI:135
Lusty, R.
Presents Sir Norman Birkett. LYI:54

BIRTHDAYS
Holmes, O. W., Jr.
"Live-I am coming:" response to birthday greeting. GRC:48; HURH:215

Bishop, Joey
Responds to introduction (when substituting for Sir Cedric Hardwicke). PRS:119

Bismarck, Otto von
Plea for imperial armament. BREWE 2:456

Bittner, John R.
The news media and campus unrest. (Indiana Speech Association meeting - Indianapolis, Oct. 4, 1969). STOT:290

Bjorklund, Jan
Nice people. EHN:158; MOPR:246

Bjørnson, Bjørnstjerne Martinus
Acceptance [of the Nobel Prize for Literature, 1903]. NOL:16; NOB 3:81
Introduction [presenting the Nobel Prize for Peace to Bertha von Suttner, 1905, April 18, 1906]. NOLP 1:81

BJØRNSON, BJØRNSTJERNE MARTINUS
Wirsen, C. D. af
Presentation [of the Nobel Prize for Literature to Bjørnstjerne Martinus Bjørnson, 1903]. NOL:14; NOB 3:77

Black, Hugo L.
Need to share what we have. ROD:75
United States v. Lovett, Watson, and Dodd: opinion for the court. ANN 16:404

---- and others (F. Frankfurter, F. Murphy, R. H. Jackson)
Korematsu v. United States: opinion for the court and dissenting opinion. ANN 16:234

---- See also Brennan, W. J., Jr., jt. auth; Jackson, R. H., jt. auth.

Black, Jeremiah Sullivan
Corporations under eminent domain. BREWE 2:471

BLACK ARTISTS
Hansberry, L.
A challenge to artists. FON:954

BLACK AUTHORS
Hughes, L.
Negro writers have been on the blacklist all their lives. FON:916
Killens, J. O.
White liberals and the Black revolution. FON:1001

BLACK-ENGLISH DIALECTS
Taylor, O. L.
African origins of Black English. JEF:443

BLACK MUSLIMS
Little, M.
Prospects for freedom. SMHV:250

BLACK NATIONALISM
Little, M.
Black revolution. SMHV:235
Prospects for freedom. SMHV:250

BLACK PANTHER PARTY
Cleaver, E.
Farewell address. SMHV:284
Political struggle in America. SMHR:166
Revolution in the white mother country and national liberation in the black colony. FON:1101
Hulett, J.
We've decided to stop begging. FON:1019
Newton, H. P.
The transformation of the Black Panther Party. FON:1182
Seale, B.
Free Huey. MACR:322; SMHR:175

BLACK PANTHERS
Garry, C. R.
In defense of Huey Newton. ERP:161

BLACK POWER
Brown, H. R.
The Third World and the ghetto. FON:1088
Carmichael, S.
Black power. FON:1033; SMHV:264
Power and racism. BOSC:101
Speech at Morgan State College, January 16, 1967. BOSC:109
Clark, K. B.
The present dilemma of the Negro. FON:1091
Cleaver, E.
Revolution in the white mother country and national liberation in the black colony. FON:1101
Forman, J.
Black manifesto. FON: 1156; OE:235
Karenga, M. R.
The Black community and the university; a community organizer's perspective. LINRS:255
Killens, J. O.
White liberals and the black revolution. FON:1001
King, M. L., Jr.
Where do we go from here? FON:1068
McKissick, F. B.
Speech at the National Conference on Black Power, July 21, 1967. BOSC:127; FON:1065
Simmons, B.
As time runs out. LINRS:251

BLACK STUDENTS
Carmichael, S.
Speech at Morgan State College, January 16, 1967. ARN:343; BOSC:109

BLACK SUFFRAGE See Blacks - Politics and suffrage

Blackett, Patrick Maynard Stuart
Cloud chamber researches in nuclear physics and cosmic radiation (Nobel Lecture, Dec. 13, 1948). NOLPH 3:97

BLACKETT, PATRICK MAYNARD STUART
Ising, G.
Presentation [of the Nobel Prize for Physics to Patrick Maynard Stuart Blackett, Dec. 13, 1948]. NOLPH 3:93

BLACKS
Abbott, R. S.
A message to youth. FON:778

Baldwin, J.
The American dream is at the expense of the American Negro. FON:1012
Barnett, F. L.
Race unity. FON:461
Blyden, E. W.
The African problem and the method of its solution. FON:540
Breitman, G.
Myths about Malcolm X: another view. LINR:120
Brockett, J. A.
Reply to Grady. ANN 11:250
Brown, D. P.
The state of the country from a Black man's point of view. FON:617
Brown, E. E.
Importance of race pride. FON:514
Brown, J.
Don't terrorize--but organize. BRYF:495
Browne, R. S.
A case for separation. FON:1121
---- and others
Separation or integration: which way for America? BA 1968-69:143
Bruce, J. E.
Negro plea for organized resistance to white men. ANN 11:214; FON:536
Bryant, M. E.
How shall we get our rights? FON:510
Clark, K. B.
The present dilemma of the Negro. FON:1091
Cleage, A.
Myths about Malcolm X. LINR:108
Costley, W.
A plan for a defense movement. FON:640
Davis, B. J.
The Negro people on the march. FON:902
Delany, M. R.
Advice to ex-slaves. FON:318
Douglas, S. A.
Reply to Lincoln at Chicago, July 9, 1858. ANN 9:4; BAS:45 (outline only); OLIS:133
Douglass, F.
The abilities and possibilities of our race. FON:326
The claims of the Negro ethnologically considered. FON:144
Color line in America. ANN 10:584; FON:491
I denounce the so-called emancipation as a stupendous fraud. FON:520
"Men of color, to arms!" OE:49
There is a better day coming. CUR:173
What the Black man wants. MDT:175
DuBois, W. E. B.
Behold the land. FON:837
Shall the Negro be encouraged to seek cultural equality? FON:772
The value of agitation. FON:663
Evers, C.
We are going to make it better for Blacks and Whites. FON:1167
Farmer, J.
The "Movement" now. FON:1040
---- and others
Debate at Cornell University, March 7, 1962. BOSC:59; OE:248
Feldmann, M. H.
Eyes of the whole world. SCHW:156
Florence, F.
Meaning of Black power. SMHR:161
Ford, J. W.
The right of revolution for the Negro people. FON:800
Fortune, T. T.
It is time to call a halt. FON:556
Garvey, M.
The principles of the Universal Negro Improvement Association. FON:748; OE:103; SMHV:100
We are mostly subject peoples all over the world. FON:790
Graham, D. A.
Some facts about Southern lynchings. FON:613
Green, J. P.
These evils call loudly for

redress. FON:499
Greener, R. T.
Emigration of colored citizens from the southern states. FON:466
Grimke, A. H.
Shame of America, or the Negro's case against the Republic. FON:764
Hamilton, W.
A defense of the Negro. FON:26
Why a Negro convention is necessary. FON:56
Hayden, L.
Deliver us from such a Moses. FON:334
Holland, J. H.
Options along the pathway of community involvement. HOR:8
Holly, J. T.
The Negro race, self-government and the Haitian revolution. FON:169
Hood, W. R.
Uncle Tom is dead! FON:843
Hope, J.
We are struggling for equality. FON:594
Hughes, L.
Negroes speak of war. FON:787
Humphreys, B. G.
Justice but not equality for the Negro. ANN 9:626
James, D.
"Given time we'll get it together." BA 1974-75:135
Johnson, M. W.
Faith of the American Negro (at Harvard commencement). FON:742
Jones, W. N.
Why Negroes should support the Communists. FON:785
Jordan, V. E., Jr.
The Black agenda for the 1980s. BA 1979-80:87
The Black and Jewish communities. VERD:273
Under the hammer: freedom, justice, and dignity. LINRST:215
Kane, A.
Glory of notoriety. REIR:223
King, M. L., Jr.
"I have a dream." AND:50; ANN 18:156; ARS:154; BRR:78; CAPG:83; FON:971; GRG:117; HURH:366; LINR:290; LINRS:289; LINRST:362; LINS:379; MAC:247; MACR:288; MDV:156; MUS:336; OE:152; OLIS:289; SMHV:182; THOMS:94
Nonviolence and social change. OE:157
Where do we go from here? FON:1068
Little, M.
To young people. FON:1004
Lynch, J.
Colored men standing in the way of their own race. FON:316
McDuffie, G.
Natural slavery of the Negro. ANN 6:191
McGowan, E. D.
Stop the foes of Negro freedom. FON:860
McKissick, F. B.
Speech at the National Conference on Black Power, July 21, 1967. BOSC:127; FON:1065
Miller, K.
The Brownsville affair. FON:654
Morris, C. S.
The Wilmington massacre. FON:604
Pennington, J. W. C.
The position and duties of the colored people. FON:271
Pickens, W.
Kind of democracy the Negro race expects. FON:601
Pinchback, P. B. S.
The whole race must protest. FON:596
Powell, A. C.
Can any good thing come out of Nazareth? FON:1027; SMHR:154
Randolph, A. P.
The crisis of the Negro and the Constitution. FON:816
March on Washington address. OE:113
The task of the Negro people. FON:807
Remond, C. L.
Rights of colored citizens in

travelling. ANN 7:74; FON:72
Rustin, B.
A way out of the exploding ghetto. FON:1078
Sampson, B. K.
To my white fellow citizens. FON:347
Smith, J. M.
On the fourteenth query of Thomas Jefferson's Notes on Virginia. FON:215
Spottswood, S. G.
The Nixon administration's anti-Negro policy. FON:1173
Steffens, G.
Law of the land. SCHW:132
Stephens, A. H.
On the Confederate Constitution. ECH:77
Tilton, T.
The Negro: a speech. MDT:161
Trotter, W. M.
How I managed to reach the Peace Conference. FON:740
Turner, H. M.
How long? How long, O Heaven? FON:445
Justice or emigration should be our watchword. FON:561
Reasons for a new political party. FON:504
Walters, A. and others
Two contrasting Black voices. FON:611
Washington, B. T.
Address at the opening of the Atlanta Exposition. ANN 12:9; BAPRR:255; BAS:77 (outline only); BRYF:492; FON:577; LINS:263; OE:82; SMHV:94
There is still much to be done. FON:707
We must be a law-abiding and law-respecting people. FON:652
Watkins, W. J.
Our rights as men. FON:130
Weaver, R. C.
Negro as an American. MDV:162; SMHV:129
White, G. H.
Defense of the Negro race. FON:635
I raise my voice against one of the most dangerous evils in our country. FON:624
Wilkins, R.
Keynote address to the NAACP annual convention, Los Angeles, July 5, 1966. OE:166; AND:101
Williams, F.
Duty of colored men in the present national crisis. FON:281
Williams, P.
A tribute to Captain Paul Cuffe. FON:28
Young, W. M., Jr.
A strategy for the seventies: unity, coalition, negotiation. STOT:331

---- See also Black Panther Party; Black Power; Civil Rights; Civil Rights Act (1866); Civil Rights Act of 1964; Discrimination; Emancipation Proclamation; Integration; National Association for the Advancement of Colored People; Race problems; Segregation; Segregation, Resistance to; Segregation in education; Slavery in the United States; Voting Rights Law of 1965. Also headings under this subject

---- ECONOMIC CONDITIONS
Bond, J.
A new movement and a new method. FON:1161

---- EDUCATION
Baker, R.
Crime of Mrs. Douglass in teaching colored children to read. ANN 8:224
Grisham, G. N.
The functions of the Negro scholar. FON:599
Smith, C. S.
The fallacy of industrial education as the solution of the race problem. FON:607

---- HISTORY
Clarke, J. H.
The meaning of Black history. FON:1138

---- POLITICS AND SUFFRAGE
Adams, E. J.

These are revolutionary times. FON:342
Bertonneau, A.
Every man should stand equal before the law. FON:303
Bruce, B. K.
Speech delivered in March, 1876 when it became necessary for the Senate to introduce a resolution appointing a committee to investigate election practices in Mississippi. ANN 10:350
DuBois, W. E. B.
Politics and industry. FON:673
Gray, W. H.
Justice should recognize no color. FON:353
Holmes, O. W., Jr.
Nixon v. Herndon: opinion for the court. ANN 14:534
Johnson, L. B.
Voting Rights Law of 1965--a victory for freedom. CAPG:97
King, M. L., Jr.
Give us the ballot--we will transform the South. FON:919
Langston, J. M.
Equality before the law. FON:409
Little, M.
The ballot or the bullet. AND:135; FON:985; REIR:47; SMHV:214
Miller, T. E.
A plea against the disfranchisement of the Negro. FON:582
Morton, O. P.
Reasons for Negro suffrage. BREWE 8:3079
Stevens, T.
Radical view of reconstruction. BREWE 9:3529; CUR:58
Still, W.
A defense of independent voting. FON:398
Taylor, G. E.
Revolution by the ballot. FON:647
Tilden, S. J.
Negro suffrage. ANN 10:122
Turner, H. M.
I claim the rights of a man. FON:357
Wears, I. E.
The Ku Klux of the North. FON:378

---- UNEMPLOYED See Unemployed - Blacks

BLACKS AS BUSINESSMEN
DuBois, W. E. B.
Politics and industry. FON:673
Goodloe, J. W.
A Black-operated firm. VER:253

BLACKS AS SOLDIERS
Campbell, J. P.
Give us equal pay and we will go to war. FON:300
Cornish, D. T.
A warrior against fate. BA 1975-76:207
Green, A. M.
Let us take up the sword. FON:249
Johnson, J. W.
Africa at the Peace Table and the descendants of Africans in our American democracy. FON:730
Miller, G. F.
They are all heroes. FON:719

BLACKS IN AFRICA
Bruce, J. E.
Reasons why the colored American should go to Africa. FON:459

BLACKS IN THE PERFORMING ARTS
Robeson, P.
The Negro artist looks ahead. FON:849

Blaine, James Gillespie
"He trod the wine-press alone."
Same as his Life and character of J. A. Garfield
Life and character of J. A. Garfield (Washington, Feb. 27, 1882). BREWE 2:482; HURH:137

BLAINE, JAMES GILLESPIE
Ingersoll, R. G.
Nominating Blaine. BREWE 7:2578; HURH:154

Blair, Austin
Military government.
BREWE 2:504

Blair, Francis Preston
Character and work of Benton.
BREWE 2:509
Deathbed of Benton.
BREWE 2:514
On the 15th Amendment.
BREWE 2:516

Blake, Eugene Carson
Ecumenism and peace.
VI:132

Blakely, Robert J.
Presents Stephen Hayes Bush.
LYI:77

Bland, Richard P.
Parting of the ways.
BREWE 2:530

Blizzard, Eddie
Not just a farmer. BREWW:49

Bloch, Felix
The principle of nuclear induction (Nobel Lecture, Dec. 11, 1952).
NOLPH 3:203

BLOCH, FELIX
Hulthén, E.
Presentation [of the Nobel Prize for Physics to Felix Bloch and Edward Mills Purcell, Dec. 11, 1952].
NOLPH 3:199

Bloch, Konrad
The biological synthesis of cholesterol (Nobel Lecture, Dec. 11, 1964). NOLM 4:78

BLOCH, KONRAD
Bergstrom, S.
Presentation [of the Nobel Prize for Physiology or Medicine to Konrad Bloch and Feodor Lynen, Dec. 11, 1964]. NOLM 4:75

BLOOD
Landsteiner, K.
On individual differences in human blood. NOLM 2:234

---- DISEASE
Zimmerman, R.
Mingled blood. ARS:98; LINR:199

Blough, Roger M.
Responds to an introduction on an occasion when he is given an award. PRS:129

Blue, Brantley
Thinking out loud (American Indian Prayer Breakfast Group, August 20, 1976). MAES:419

Blue Spruce, George
Needed: Indian health professionals.· MAES:171

Blumenschein, Carl M.
Introduces Smith Hempstone.
PRS:23

Blyden, Edward Wilmot
The African problem and the methods of its solution. (Washington, D. C., Jan. 19, 1890). FON:540
Africa's service to the world.
EMP:26

Bocobo, Jorge C.
Love of country (University of the Philippines, June 7, 1937).
CURM:149

BOER WAR See South African War, 1899-1902

Bohr, Niels
The structure of the atom (Nobel Lecture, Dec. 11, 1922).
NOLPH 2:7

BOHR, NIELS
Arrhenius, S. A.
Presentation [of the Nobel Prize for Physics to Niels Bohr, Dec. 11, 1922]. NOLPH 2:3

Boissier, Leonard L.
Some aspects of the mission of the International Committee of the Red Cross (Nobel Lecture, Dec. 11, 1963). NOLP 3:301

Bolinbroke, Henry Saint-John, 1st Viscount
Misfortune and exile.

BREWE 2:541
Patriotism. BREWE 2:550

Bolton, Thomas
Oration (burlesque of Warren's second Boston Massacre oration). POC:301

Bonaventura, Saint
Life of service. BREWE 2:552

Bond, Julian
A new movement and a new method. (New York-Lexington Democratic Club Annual Dinner - May, 1969). FON:1161

Bonner, James See Sevareid, E., jt. auth.

BONUS BILL, 1816
Madison, J.
On the commerce clause. ANN 4:462

Böök, Fredrik
Presentation [of the Nobel Prize for Literature to Thomas Mann, 1929]. NOB 12:221; NOL:260

BOOK REVIEWS
Crooks, J.
Defense of "The death of a President." REIR:182
Suggestions for preparation of book reviews. PAE:190

BOOKS AND READING
Gallup, G.
Mass information or mass entertainment. ANN 17:215

---- See also Booksellers and Bookselling; Literature

BOOKSELLERS AND BOOKSELLING
Textbooks and all that: an inquiry into the operation of the college bookstore (outline). CUB:28
You get what you ask for (outline of speech). CUB:31

BOOMS See Business cycles

Boorstin, Daniel J.
Beginnings (Washington, Nov. 9, 1976). BA 1976-77:138
Dissent, dissension and the news. BA 1967-68:125; JEF:187; JEFF:181; LINR:203
An historian adapts his introduction to an audience of journalists. Same as his Dissent, dissension and the news

Booth, Arch N.
Responds to an introduction. PRS:146

Borah, William E.
League of Nations. (Washington, Nov. 19, 1919). HURH:190
"Peace upon any other basis than rational independence ... is fit only for slaves." Same as his League of Nations
Release of political prisoners. ANN 14:405
Western farming and the tariff. ANN 15:28

BORDET, JULES
Petterson, A.
Presentation [of the Nobel Prize for Physiology or Medicine to Jules Bordet, 1919]. NOLM 1:519

Borlaug, Norman Ernest
The green revolution, peace, and humanity (Nobel Lecture, Dec. 11, 1970). NOLP 3:454

BORLAUG, NORMAN ERNEST
Lionaes, A.
Presentation [of the Nobel Prize for Peace to Norman Ernest Borlaug, Dec. 10, 1970]. NOLP 3:445

Born, Max
The statistical interpretation of quantum mechanics (Nobel Lecture, Dec. 11, 1954). NOLPH 3:256

BORN, MAX
Waller, I.
Presentation [of the Nobel Prize for Physics to Max Born and Walther Bothe, Dec. 11, 1954]. NOLPH 3:253

BORROMEO, ANDRES
Malcolm, G. A.
Judge Andres Borromeo did his duty! CURM:183

Borsch, Reubin A.
Introduces Irish Deputy Prime Minister William Norton. PRS:41
Introduces Selwyn Lloyd, former British Secretary of State for Foreign Affairs. PRS:39

Bosch, Carl
The development of the chemical high pressure method during the establishment of the new ammonia industry (Nobel Lecture for 1931, May 21, 1932). NOLC 2:197

BOSCH, CARL
Palmaer, W.
Presentation [of the Nobel Prize for Chemistry for 1931 to Carl Bosch and Friedrich Bergius, May 21, 1932]. NOLC 2:189

Bosley, Harold
Is God really dead? BA 1965-66:157

Bosman, Robert A.
Witch hunt. SCHW:128

Bossuet, Jacques Benigne, bp.
Funeral oration over the Prince of Condé. BREWE 2:557

BOSTON
Hale, E. E.
Boston's place in history. BREWE 6:2355
Mather, C.
"Boston Ebenezer." POC:395
Quincy, J. 1772-1864
At the second centennial of Boston. BREWE 9:3272

BOSTON MASSACRE, 1770
Adams, J.
On the Boston Massacre. BREWE 1:45; POC:108
Bolton, T.
Oration (burlesque of Warren's second Boston Massacre oration). POC:301
Church, B.
Boston Massacre oration (third anniversary). POC:255
Hancock, J.
Boston Massacre. BRN:26; HURH:24
Lovell, J.
Boston Massacre oration. POC:231
Quincy, J., 1744-1775
Defence of British soldiers, 1770. BREWE 9:3269; POC:25
Rock, J. S.
I will sink or swim with my race. FON:203
Thatcher, P.
Boston Massacre oration, March 5, 1776. POC:272
Warren, J.
Boston Massacre (March 5, 1772). ANN 2:211; POC:237
Oration on the Boston Massacre (March 5, 1775). POC:245

BOSTON TEA PARTY, 1773
Quincy, J., 1744-1775
"Let us look to the end." POC:295

Bothe, Walther
The coincidence method (Nobel Lecture, 1954). NOLPH 3:271

BOTHE, WALTHER
Waller, I.
Presentation [of the Nobel Prize for Physics to Max Born and Walther Bothe, Dec. 11, 1954]. NOLPH 3:253

Boucher, Jonathan
Civil liberty and nonresistance. ANN 2:343; POC:552

Boudinot, Elias
Mission of America. BREWE 2:581

Bourdaloue, Louis
Passion of Christ. BREWE 2:581

BOURGEOIS, LEON VICTOR AUGUSTE
Buen, A. J.
Remarks [presenting the Nobel

Prize for Peace to Leon Victor Auguste Bourgeois, Dec. 10, 1920]. NOLP 1:304

Bourguiba, Habib
Responds to an introduction. PRS:136

Boutwell, George Sewall
President Johnson's "High crimes and misdemeanors." BREWE 2:604

Bovet, Daniel
The relationships between isosterism and competitive phenomena in the field of drug therapy of the autonomic nervous system and that of the neuromuscular transmission (Nobel Lecture, Dec. 11, 1957). NOLM 3:552

BOVET, DANIEL
Uvnäs, B.
Presentation [of the Nobel Prize for Physiology or Medicine to Daniel Bovet, Dec. 11, 1957]. NOLM 3:549

Bowdoin, James
Encouragement of knowledge. ANN 2:540

Bowen, William G.
Commitment to scholarship and research (Washington, March 7, 1979). BA 1978-79:41

BOY SCOUTS
Welcome to Boy Scout troop (or Boys' Brigade). HNWM:49

BOYCOTTING
Parnell, C. S.
At Ennis (boycotting defined and defended). MCB:296; STRM:346

Boyd Orr, John
Science and peace (Nobel Lecture, Dec. 12, 1949). NOLP 2:415

BOYD ORR, JOHN
Jahn, G.
Presentation [of the Nobel Prize for Peace to Lord Boyd Orr of Brechin, Dec. 10, 1949]. NOLP 2:407

BOYS' BRIGADE
Welcome to Boy Scout troop (or Boys' Brigade). HNWM:49

Bozeman, Mike
Soil--America's lifeblood. BREWW:85

Brackenridge, Henry M.
Vindication of civil rights for Jews. ANN 4:552

BRADEEN, JOHN
Rudberg, E. G.
Presentation [of the Nobel Prize for Physics to William Shockley, John Bardeen and Walter Houser Brattain, Dec. 11, 1956]. NOLPH 3:315

Brademas, John
Eulogy for Robert Kennedy (June 9, 1968). JAM:43

Braden, Waldo W.
Has TV made the public speaker obsolete? EHN:309; MOPR:360

Bradlaugh, Charles
Appeal for justice. JAE:142

Bradley, Joseph P. and others (J. M. Harlan)
Civil rights cases: opinion for the court and dissenting opinion. ANN 10:577

Bragg, Lawrence
Art of talking about science. MOP:358

Bragg, William Lawrence
The diffraction of x-rays by crystals (Nobel Lecture for 1915, Sept. 6, 1922). NOLPH 1:370

Brandeis, Louis Dembitz
Ashwander rules. ANN 15:350
Business as a profession. ANN 13:342

Curse of bigness. BOORA 2:759
Danger of inaction: dissenting opinion for the Supreme Court on New State Ice Co. v. Liebmann, 1931. ROD:73
Law and the laboring classes. ANN 13:23

---- See Sutherland, G., jt. auth.

Brandli, Wilbur
Taps and reveille. SCHW:30

Branting, Karl Hjalmar
Fraternity among nations (Nobel Lecture for 1921, June 19, 1922). NOLP 1:324

Brattain, Walter Houser
Surface properties of semiconductors (Nobel Lecture, Dec. 11, 1956). NOLPH 3:377

BRATTAIN, WALTER HOUSER
Rudberg, E. G.
Presentation [of the Nobel Prize for Physics to William Shockley, John Bardeen and Walter Houser Brattain, Dec. 11, 1956]. NOLPH 3:315

Braun, Carl Ferdinand
Electrical oscillations and wireless telegraphy (Nobel Lectures, Dec. 11, 1909). NOLPH 1:226

BRAUN, CARL FERDINAND
Hildebrand, H.
Presentation [of the Nobel Prize for Physics to Guglielmo Marconi and Carl Ferdinand Braun, Dec. 11, 1909]. NOLPH 1:193

Bray, Charles W.
De-mystifying anti-Americanism (Washington, Jan. 17, 1980). BA 1979-80:38

Breckenridge, John C.
Dred Scott decision, December 1859. BREWE 2:615
Removal of the United States Senate. (Washington, 1858). BLY:122

Breitman, George
Myths about Malcolm X: another view. LINR:120

Brennan, William J., Jr.
Baker v. Carr: opinion for the Supreme Court. ANN 18:130
Conciliation between the press and the law (Newark, N.J., Oct. 17, 1979). BA 1979-80:119

---- and others (H. Black and W. O. Douglas)
Ginzburg et al. v. United States: opinion for the court and dissenting opinion. ANN 18:350

Brewer, David J.
In Re Debs: opinion for the court. ANN 12:18
Independent judiciary as the salvation of the nation. ANN 11:423

Brewster, Kingman, Jr.
The decade of shortcuts. (Yale University, Sept. 11, 1972). BA 1972-73:176
Due process radicalism (Yale College, June 7, 1970). HOR:37

Briand, Aristide
Acceptance of the Nobel Prize for Peace, Dec. 10, 1926. NOLP 2:3

BRIAND, ARISTIDE
Nansen, F.
Speech at Award Ceremony presenting Nobel Prize for Peace to Aristide Briand and Gustav Stresemann, Dec. 10, 1926. NOLP 2:3

Bridgman, Percy Williams
General survey of certain results in the field of high-pressure physics (Nobel Lecture, Dec. 11, 1946). NOLPH 3:53

BRIDGMAN, PERCY WILLIAMS
Lindh, A. E.
Presentation [of the Nobel Prize for Physics to Percy Williams Bridgman, Dec. 11, 1946]. NOLPH 3:53

Bright, John
The angel of death. Same as his Russia: negotiations at Vienna, House of Commons, February 23, 1855
Morality and military greatness (Birmingham, Oct. 29, 1858). BREWE 2:637; MCB:23
On punishment of death. BRYH:398
On the foreign policy of England. Same as his Morality and military greatness
Russia: negotiations at Vienna, House of Commons, February 23, 1855. AND:61
Trent affair. STRM:271
Will the United States subjugate Canada? BREWE 2:620

Bristol, George Digby, 2d Earl of
Army in domestic politics. BREWE 5:1865
Grievances and oppressions under Charles I. BREWE 5:1861

BRITISH COMMONWEALTH See Commonwealth of Nations

BRITISH EMPIRE See Great Britain

Brockett, Joshua A.
Reply to Grady. ANN 11:250

Bronowski, Jacob
Protest-past and present. BA 1969-70:119

Brooke, Edward W.
The cause of civil rights. (Boston, 1967). FON:1058
Crisis in the two-party system (Boston, Jan. 5, 1966). BA 1965-66:170; SMHV:143
Responsibilities inherent in a constitutional democracy. (Milwaukee, Wisc., Feb. 27, 1974). BA 1973-74:74

Brooks, Edward
Report on Vietnam and East Asia. BA 1966-67:23

Brooks, Phillips, Bp.
Character of Abraham Lincoln. BREWE 2:644
Lincoln as a typical American. Same as his Character of Abraham Lincoln
Power over the lives of others. BREWE 2:651

Brooks, Preston S.
Assault on Sumner. BREWE 2:654

Brooks, Sidney H.
God's grief. WALE:23

Brooks, T. J.
Antitrust laws as applied to farmers. ANN 13:331

Brorby, Melvin
Introduces Arnold J. Toynbee, professor, author and historian of Great Britain. LYI:86

BROTHERLINESS
Men's brotherhood (for laymen's group). HNWM:23

Brougham and Vaux, Henry Peter Brougham, 1st Baron
Against Pitt and war with America. BREWE 2:661
Closing argument for Queen Caroline. BREWE 2:665
Present state of the law (1828). STRM:153
Speech on Parliamentary reform. Same as his Supports the Reform Bill
Supports the Reform Bill. BRYH:322

BROUN, HEYWOOD
Nizer, L.
Presents Heywood Broun. LYI:105

Brown, Benjamin Gratz
Prophecy. BREWE 2:675

Brown, D. P.
The state of the country from a Black man's point of view. (New England Conference of the African Episcopal Church, August, 1899). FON:617

Brown, Edmund G.
State of the state address (Jan. 7, 1976). JAM:13
Proposals for change: an in-

augural address (Sacramento, Calif., Jan. 8, 1979). BA 1978-79:103

BROWN, EDMUND G.
Zumwalt, E.
Introduction to Edmund G. Brown, Jr. JAM:33

Brown, Edward Everett
Importance of race pride. (National League of Boston, March 5, 1888). FON:514

BROWN, GEORGE ALFRED
Cavanagh, J. P.
Presents George Alfred Brown. LYI:203

Brown, H. Rap
Colonialism and revolution. Same as his The Third World and the ghetto.
The Third World and the ghetto (Detroit, Oct., 1967). FON:1088; SMHV:304

Brown, Harrison S.
Science, technology, and world development. ARS:83
Social responsibility of science. BAP:280

Brown, Henry Armitt
Dangers of the present. BREWE 2:685
One century's achievement (Valley Forge centennial). BREWE 2:683
Plea of the future. BREWE 2:686

Brown, Henry B. and others (J. M. Harlan)
Plessy v. Ferguson: opinion for the court and dissenting opinion. ANN 12:92

Brown, James
Don't terrorize--but organize. (1968). BRYF:495

Brown, James E.
Acceptance [of the Nobel Prize for Literature for Eugene Gladstone O'Neill, 1936]. NOB 19:131; NOL:336

Brown, Joan and others (Peggy Way and Helen Fannings)
Liberation struggle generates tension on race, sex issues. BOST:265

Brown, John
Courtroom speech. Same as his Last speech at Charleston, West Virginia
'I feel no consciousness of guilt." Same as his Last speech at Charleston, West Virginia
Last speech at Charleston, West Virginia (Nov. 2, 1859). ALA:21; ANN 9:143; BOS:44; HURH:103
To free the slaves. Same as his Last speech at Charleston, West Virginia

BROWN, JOHN
Garrison, W. L.
On the death of John Brown. BREWE 6:2238
Moore, S.
A Southern response to John Brown and black republicanism (1859). DAVF:146
Phillips, W.
John Brown and the spirit of "59." BREWE 8:3181
Roosevelt, T.
New nationalism (at dedication of John Brown Memorial Park, Osawatomie, Kansas). ANN 13:250; BOORA 2:711
Thoreau, H. D.
Plea for Captain John Brown. ANN 9:136

Brown, John Mason
"Beat" generation. (Groton, Mass., 1958). HURH:341
'I am sick and tired of the snivelers, the defeated and the whiners." Same as his "Beat" generation

Brown, Karen <u>See</u> Andino, Judy

Brown, Millard
Famine: a reality, not just a threat. BREWW:168

Brown, William Wells
Slavery as it is, and its influence upon the American people.

(Salem, Mass. Female Anti-slavery Society, Nov. 4, 1847). FON:90

Browne, Robert S.
A case for separation. (Plenary Session of the National Jewish Community Relations Advisory Councils, June 30, 1968). FON:1121

---- and others (B. Rustin)
Separation or integration: which way for America? BA 1968-69:143

Brownlow, William Gannaway
Grape shot and hemp. BREWE 2:690
Value of the American Union. BREWE 2:690

Bruce, Blanche K.
A call for a change in our Indian policy. (Washington, April 7, 1880). FON:471
Negro hopes for assimilation. Same as his Speech delivered in March, 1876, etc.
Speech delivered in March, 1876 when it became necessary for the Senate to introduce a resolution appointing a committee to investigate election practices in Mississippi. ANN 10:350

Bruce, John E.
Negro plea for organized resistance to white men (Oct. 5, 1889). ANN 11:214; FON:536
Organized resistance is our best remedy. Same as his Negro plea for organized resistance to white men
Reasons why the colored American should go to Africa. (Philadelphia, Oct. 1877). FON:459

Brunsting, Lucille
Kid dreams. SCHW:49

Bryan, William Jennings
Cross of gold (Chicago, 1896). ANN 12:100; BAS:50 (outline only); BEN:52; BOORA 2:575; BREWE 2:694; HURH:147; LINS:268; OLIS:207
Imperialism (accepting Democratic nomination for Presidency, 1900). ANN 12:345
Naboth's Vineyard. GRG:11
Paralyzing influence of imperialism. Same as his Imperialism (accepting Democratic nomination for Presidency, 1900)
"You shall not crucify mankind upon a cross of gold." Same as his Cross of gold

BRYAN, WILLIAM JENNINGS
Depew, C. M.
Presents William Jennings Bryan. LYI:227

Bryant, M. Edward
How shall we get our rights? (Selma, Ala., Dec. 4, 1887). FON:510

Bryant, William Cullen
Greatness of Burns. Same as his To the Burns Club
To the Burns Club. BREWE 2:702

BRYCE, JAMES
Choate, J. H.
Presents James Bryce. LYI:237

Brzezinski, Zbigniew
Our China policy in a wider context (Washington, Jan. 15, 1979). BA 1978-79:150

Buchan, John
Novel and the fairy tale. ARS:54

Buchanan, Colin
Planning and public opinion. MDYG:130

Buchanan, David
Eulogy of Garibaldi. MCA:78

Buchanan, George See Baldwin, S. B., jt. auth.

Buchanan, James
First annual message. STAT 1:942
Fourth annual message. ANN 9:209; STAT 1:1025
Impending disruption of the Union.

Same as his Fourth annual message
Inaugural address.
BREWE 2:707; USINAU:111; USINAUG:111
Second annual message.
STAT 1:969
Third annual message.
STAT 1:1001

Buchanan, John G.
Presents Augustus N. Hand.
LYT:133

Buchner, Eduard
Cell-free fermentation (Nobel Lecture, Dec. 11, 1907).
NOLC 1:103

BUCHNER, EDUARD
Mörner, K. A. H.
Presentation [of the Nobel Prize for Chemistry to Eduard Buchner, Dec. 11, 1907]. NOLC 1:99

Buchwald, Art
Parody of political speeches (Washington Post, Jan. 13, 1976). JAM:27

Buck, Pearl
Acceptance [of the Nobel Prize for Literature, 1938].
NOB 3:157; NOL:359
The Chinese novel (Nobel lecture, Dec. 12, 1938).
NOL:361

BUCK, PEARL
Hallström, P.
Presentation [of the Nobel Prize for Literature to Pearl Buck, 1938].
NOB 3:149; NOL:354

Buckley, F. R.
La Folle epoque. MDYG:181

Buckley, James
The Equal Rights Amendment: the legislative aspect (Washington, March 22, 1972). LINRST:271

Buel, David, Jr. See Sanford, N., jt. auth.

Buen, A. J.
Remarks [presenting the Nobel Prize for Peace to Leon Victor Auguste Bourgeois, Dec. 10, 1920]. NOLP 1:304

BUILDINGS, DEDICATION OF See Dedication addresses, subheads Buildings; Churches, Cornerstones, Libraries

Buisson, Ferdinand Edouard
Changes in concepts of war and peace (Nobel Lecture, 1927, May 31, 1928). NOLP 2:35

BUISSON, FERDINAND EDOUARD
Stang, F.
Presentation of the Nobel Prize for Peace to Ferdinand Edouard Buisson and Ludwig Quidde, Dec. 10, 1927. NOLP 2:29

Bulkeley, Peter
City set upon a hill. ANN 1:211
The gospel-covenant (1638 or 1639). JON:30

Bulkley, William L.
Race prejudice as viewed from an economic standpoint. (National Negro Conference-1909).
FON:680

Bullock, Hugh
Presents Lester B. Pearson.
LYI:207

Bunche, Ralph J.
Barriers of race can be surmounted. CAPG:66
Human relations in world perspective. (Dillard University - spring 1954). FON:882
Some reflections on peace in our time (Nobel Lecture, Dec. 11, 1950). NOLP 2:443

BUNCHE, RALPH J.
Jahn, G.
Presentation of the Nobel Prize for Peace to Ralph Johnson Bunche, Dec. 10, 1950.
NOLP 2:435

BUNDY, McGEORGE
Martin, C.

Presents McGeorge Bundy. LYI:88

Bunin, Ivan Alekseevich
Acceptance [of the Nobel Prize for Literature, 1933]. NOB 3:291; NOL:314

BUNIN, IVAN ALEKSEEVICH
Hallström, P.
Presentation [of the Nobel Prize for Literature to Ivan Alekseevich Bunin, 1933]. NOB 3:285; NOL:309

Bunting, James E.
The pay is good. (California State Univ., Hayward). BAPR:364; BAPRR:271

Bunting, Mary Ingraham
Their questions (Amherst College, May 28, 1965). HOR:93

Bunyan, John
Heavenly footman. BREWE 2:716

BUREAUCRACY
Bell, G. B.
Notes on the situation: a critique. BA 1978-79:93

---- UNITED STATES
Hart, G.
Big government: real or imaginary? LINRST:100

Burger, Warren E.
How long can we cope? (Washington, Sept. 21, 1978). BA 1978-79:81
State of the Judiciary. (St. Louis, Mo., Aug. 10, 1970). BA 1970-71:13

---- and others
Bicentennial of American independence (Washington, July 2, 1976). BA 1976-77:185

Burges, Tristam
Supreme Court. BREWE 2:729

Burgess, W. Randolph
Presents Paul H. Douglas. LYI:231

Burke, Edmund
Against coercing America. Same as his Conciliation with America
Age of chivalry. BREWE 2:817
Conciliation with America (March 22, 1775). ALS:29 (with analysis); ANN 2:312; BREWE 2:806; CLAYP:50; STRM:39
Declining the poll. Same as his On declining the election at Bristol, September 9, 1780
Marie Antoinette. Same as his Age of chivalry
On conciliation with the colonies. Same as his Conciliation with America
On declining the election at Bristol, September 9, 1780. BRYH:243
Principle in politics: speech at Bristol, previous to the election, 1780 (defends his Parliamentary conduct). BREWE 2:812; BRYH:211
Speech on moving resolutions for conciliation with the American colonies, March 22, 1775. Same as his Conciliation with America
To his Constituents. Same as his Principle in politics: speech at Bristol, previous to the election, 1780 (defends his Parliamentary conduct)

Burke, Yvonne Brathwaite
"Aspirations ... unrequited." (Los Angeles, March 10, 1975). BA 1974-75:143

Burlingame, Anson
Massachusetts and the Sumner assault. BREWE 2:820

Burnet, Sir Frank Macfarlane
Immunological recognition of self (Nobel Lecture, Dec. 12, 1960). NOLM 3:689

BURNET, SIR FRANK MACFARLANE
Gard, S.
Presentation [of the Nobel Prize for Physiology or Medicine to Sir Frank Macfarlane Burnet and Peter Brian Meda-

war, Dec. 12, 1960].
NOLM 3:685

Burns, John L.
Responds to an introduction.
PRS:150

BURNS, ROBERT
Bryant, W. C.
To the Burns Club.
BREWE 2:702
Emerson, R. W.
Memory of Burns. HURH:106

BURR, AARON
Randolph, E.
In defence of Aaron Burr, 1807. BREWE 9:3284
Wirt, W.
Burr and Blennerhasset (at trial of Burr).
BREWE 10:3908

Burrows, John Lansing
Opposition to the theater in time of war. ANN 9:402

Burstein, Abraham
Power of memory. WALE:25

Burton, Steven
You (male) should wear long hair. BAS:200 (outline only)

Bush, George
Views of US foreign policy in the future (Washington, Jan. 25, 1979).
BA 1978-79:159

BUSH, STEPHEN HAYES
Blakely, R. J.
Presents Stephen Hayes Bush. LYI:77

BUSH, VANNEVAR
Trippe, J. T.
Presents Vannevar Bush.
LYI:177

Bushnell, Horace
Dignity of human nature.
BREWE 3:825

BUSINESS
Abdul Rahman, T.
Tunku's recipe for success: how to get things done.
MONSA:67
Berle, A. A., Jr.
Emerging common law of free enterprise. ANN 16:573
Brandeis, L. D.
Business as a profession.
ANN 13:342
Carpenter, C. U.
Justification of big business.
ANN 13:327
Goodman, S. J.
Raising the fallen image of business. BA 1973-74:160
McGraw, H. W.
Business's responsibility in an information society.
BA 1977-78:121
Marshall, J.
Trustees of Dartmouth College v. Woodward: opinion for the Supreme Court. ANN 4:522
Moorehead, J. R.
Plight of small business.
ANN 13:322
Roosevelt, F. D.
What the New Deal has done for business (campaign speech in Chicago, October 14, 1936).
ANN 15:379
Sulzberger, A. O.
Business and the press: is the press anti-business? EHN:387
Taylor, F. W.
On scientific management.
BOORA 2:740

BUSINESS CYCLES
Grant, U. S.
Sixth annual message.
STAT 2:1275

BUSINESS DEPRESSION See Business cycles; United States - Economic conditions

BUSINESS ETHICS
Marcus, S.
Can free enterprise survive success? BA 1975-76:152

BUSING See School integration

Buteyn, Donald P.
Invisible abutments. SCHW:44

Butler, Benjamin F.
"Article Ten," (Impeaching A. Johnson). BREWE 3:832

---- and others (R. P. Spalding; N. P. Banks; S. Shellabarger; J. Mullins; W. E. Robinson; J. A. Bingham; H. Maynard; G. W. Woodward)
Congressional debate on Haiti and Santo Domingo, January 13, 1869. ANN 10:143

Butler, Joseph
Government of the tongue. BREWE 3:842

Butler, Joseph T. See Lodge, H. C., jt. auth.

Butler, Nicholas Murray
Presents Wilbur L. Cross. LYI:97
Radio address (Nobel Lecture, Dec. 12, 1931). NOLP 2:136

BUTLER, NICHOLAS MURRAY
Koht, H.
Presentation [of the Nobel Prize for Peace to Jane Addams and Nicholas Murray Butler, Dec. 10, 1931]. NOLF 2:125

BUYING AND MARKETING See Business; Sales talks and salesmanship

Butz, Earl Laver
Feast or famine: the key to peace. (Des Moines, Dec. 10, 1974). BA 1974-75:81

BYRNES, JAMES F.
Fraser, L.
Presents James F. Byrnes. LYI:218

- C -

Cadbury, Henry J.
Quakers and peace (Nobel Lecture, Dec. 12, 1947). NOLP 2:391

Cadwell, Darius
Oration (Andover, Ohio, July 4, 1847). HAW:319

Caesar, Caius Julius
On the conspiracy of Catiline. BREWE 3:846

Cahill, Daniel W.
Last judgment. BREWE 3:851

Caird, John
Art of eloquence. BREWE 3:855

Calhoun, John C.
Against general resolutions on foreign affairs. ANN 7:336
Compromise of 1850. Same as his On the slavery question
Danger of abolitionist petitions (February, 1837). ANN 6:346
Denouncing Andrew Jackson. BREWE 3:919
Either slavery or disunion. Same as his On the slavery question
Force Bill. BREWE 3:866
"... the greatest and gravest question that ever can come under your consideration: how can the Union be preserved?" Same as his On the slavery question
Individual liberty. BREWE 3:925
On internal improvement, 1817. ANN 4:457
On territorial expansion. ANN 7:87
On the slavery question (Washington, March, 1850). ANN 8:16; HURH:77; OLIS:93
Replying to Henry Clay (from 'Independent treasury debate"). BREWE 3:921
Roadways and waterways. Same as his On internal improvement, 1817
Self-government and civilization. BREWE 3:924

---- See also Niles, J., jt. auth.

Califano, Joseph A.
Federal support of science and medicine (Ann Arbor, Mich., Dec. 18, 1977). BA 1977-78:99
A tribute to the man of the people (Washington, Nov. 1, 1977). BA 1977-78:197

CALIFORNIA
Polk, J. K.

Fourth annual message.
STAT 1:731
Seward, W. H.
On the admission of California to the Union. ANN 8:29

---- BUDGET
Brown, E. G., Jr.
Proposals for change: an inaugural address.
BA 1978-79:103

---- ECONOMIC CONDITIONS
Brown, E. G.
State of the state address.
JAM:13

---- POLITICS AND GOVERNMENT
Brown, E. G.
State of the state address.
JAM:13

Calvin, John
Necessity for courage.
BREWE 3:928

Calvin, Melvin
The path of carbon in photosynthesis (Nobel Lecture, Dec. 11, 1961).
NOLC 3:618

CALVIN, MELVIN
Myrbäck, K.
Presentation [of the Nobel Prize for Chemistry to Melvin Calvin, Dec. 11, 1961].
NOLC 3:615

CAMBODIA
Nixon, R. M.
Cambodia. LINRS:236

Cambon, Pierre Joseph
Crisis of 1793. BREWE 3:931

CAMBRIDGE UNIVERSITY
D'Ewes, S.
Antiquity of Cambridge.
BREWE 5:1818

CAMPAIGN FUNDS
Nixon, R. M.
Apologia. MAC:258; MACR:269; REIR:191

CAMPAIGN SPEECHES
Attlee, C. R.
The Labour programme.
MCB:471
Ballance, J.
The 1890 election: the opposition case. MACS:201 selections
Barkley, A. W.
Record of Democratic Party.
BLY:233
Beveridge, A. J.
March of the flag. ANN 12:198; BOORA 2:622; GRG:14; LINS:276
Brougham and Vaux, H. P. B.
Against Pitt and war with America. BREWE 2:661
Bryan, W. J.
Naboth's Vineyard. GRG:11
Buchwald, A.
Parody of political speeches.
JAM:27
Carter, J.
Speech at the Martin Luther King, Jr. Hospital. JAM:25
Chisholm, S.
Economic injustice in America today. BA 1971-72:27
Churchill, Sir W. L. S.
The Conservative programme.
MCB:464
Coates, J. G.
The 1925 election: the Coates campaign. MACS:307 sel.
Cockran, W. B.
An answer to William J. Bryan.
BREWE 4:1339
Costley, W.
A plan for a defense movement.
FON:640
Coughlin, C. E.
Money changers in the temple.
ANN 15:388
Dewey, T. E.
Acceptance speech, Chicago, Illinois, June 28, 1944.
SIN:205
Acceptance speech, Philadelphia, Pennsylvania, June 24, 1948.
SIN:229
Campaign speech, Des Moines, Iowa, September 20, 1948.
SIN:232
Corporate state not an American system (campaign speech, October 7, 1944). ROD:333
Opening campaign speech in Philadelphia (Sept. 7, 1944).
SIN:210
Douglas, S. A.

Fifth joint debate at Galesburg, October 7, 1858. ANN 9:22
Lincoln-Douglas joint debate at Alton, October 15, 1858. ANN 9:30
Opening speech of Lincoln-Douglas debate, Ottawa, August 21, 1858. ANN 9:8
Reply to Lincoln at Chicago, July 9, 1858. ANN 9:4; BAS:45 (outline only); OLIS:133
Reply to Lincoln, Freeport, August 27, 1858. ANN 9:17; BREWE 5:1912; HURH:94
Reply to the Jonesboro speech. ANN 9:20

Eisenhower, D. D.
Acceptance speech, Chicago, Illinois, July 11, 1952. SIN:242
Acceptance speech, San Francisco, California, August 23, 1956. SIN:265
Campaign speech, Cleveland, Ohio, October 1, 1956. SIN:275
Crusade for peace. ANN 17:199

Ford, G. R.
Presidential remarks with question-and-answer session. BA 1975-76:133
Republican National Convention acceptance speech. LINRST:349
The third presidential debate. BA 1976-77:30

Gladstone, W. E.
Campaign speech (at Perth, December 1, 1879). BRYH:415

Goldwater, B. M.
Campaign speech, Washington, D.C., October 21, 1964. SIN:345
Extremism in defense of liberty (accepting nomination for presidency, July 17, 1964). MAC:251; MACR:292; MDV:115; SIN:337
Why we must be stronger militarily. BAS:92 (outline only); LAA:8

Harding, H. F.
Matter of doubt and grave concern. BA 1968-1969:121

Hoover, H. C.
Acceptance speech, Constitution Hall, Washington, D.C., August 11, 1932. SIN:88
Accepting the nomination for presidency. SIN:4
Against the proposed New Deal (October 31, 1932). ANN 15:188
Campaign speech, Madison Square Garden, New York City, October 31, 1932. SIN:103
In defense of tradition (Detroit, 1932). ROD:39
Speech at New York City, October 22, 1928. ANN 14:595; BOORA 2:803: SIN:21

Humphrey, H. H., Jr.
Acceptance speech, Chicago, Illinois, August 29, 1968. SIN:372
Campaign speech, Salt Lake City, Utah, September 30, 1968. SIN:380

Johnson, L. B.
Acceptance speech, Atlantic City, New Jersey, August 27, 1964. SIN:329
Campaign speech, Washington, D.C., October 7, 1964. SIN:334

Jordan, B. C.
Keynote address to the Democratic National Convention. BA 1976-77:11; JAM:7; LINRST:334

Kennedy, J. F.
New frontier. CAPG:8; HURH:353; SIN:298
Religion in government. ANN 17:589; SIN:303

Landon, A. M.
Acceptance speech, Topeka, Kansas, July 23, 1936. SIN:136
Action challenged. ROD:162
Campaign speech, New York City, October 29, 1936. SIN:145
Federal and family finances. BAD:62

Lemke, W.
Introduction of the aims of the Union Party of the United States. BAD:117

Lincoln, A.
First joint debate at Ottawa, August 21, 1858. ANN 9:11
Lincoln-Douglas joint debate at

Alton, October 15, 1858. ANN 9:26
Reply to Douglas at Chicago. OLIS:150
Second joint debate at Freeport, August 27, 1858. ANN 9:15; BREWE 7:2785
Speech at Charleston, September 18, 1858. ANN 9:21
Speech at Galesburg, October 7, 1858. ANN 9:23
Speech at Jonesboro, September 15, 1858. ANN 9:19
McGovern, G.
Acceptance speech, Miami Beach, Florida, July 14, 1972. SIN:408
Campaign speech, Washington, D.C., August 5, 1972. SIN:413
Muskie, E. S.
Election eve address. STOT:262
Nixon, R. M.
Acceptance speech, Miami Beach, Florida, August 8, 1968. SIN:356
Acceptance speech, Miami Beach, Florida, August 23, 1972. SIN:392
Bridges to human dignity. LINR:255
Campaign speech, radio broadcast, September 19, 1968. SIN:366
Campaign speech, Toledo, Ohio, October 27, 1960. SIN:319
Campaign speech, White House, Washington, D.C., November 2, 1972. SIN:402
It is time to speak up for America. SIN:307
---- and others.
Opening statements: the fourth debate. GRG:106
Percy, C. H.
Chicagoan goes South. BA 1956-66:106
Reagan, R.
Time for choosing. CAPG:48
Roosevelt, F. D.
Acceptance of renomination for the presidency, June 27, 1936. SIN:125
Acceptance speech, Chicago, Illinois, July 2, 1932. SIN:68
Acceptance speech on renomination for president, July 20, 1944. SIN:194
Acceptance speech via radio to convention, Washington, D.C., July 19, 1940. SIN:156
Action defended (campaign speech, October 31, 1936). ROD:168
Address to the Commonwealth Club, September 23, 1932. ANN 15:158; ROD:31; SIN:77
American business is moving ahead. BAD:1
Call for federal responsibility (October 13, 1932). ANN 15:185
Campaign speech, Chicago, Illinois, October 14, 1936. SIN:129
Campaign speech, Cleveland, Ohio, November 2, 1940. SIN:164
Facing Communism: the true conservative is liberal. BAD:15
Opening campaign speech at dinner of International Brotherhood of Teamsters. LINS:330; SIN:198
Philosophy of social justice through social action (campaign speech in Detroit October 2, 1932). ARS:135
Republican leadership and national defense. ANN 15:379
What the New Deal has done for business (campaign speech in Chicago, October 14, 1936). ANN 15:379
Roosevelt, T.
Issues of the coming election. ANN 11:170
Smith, A. E.
Acceptance speech, Albany, New York, August 22, 1928. SIN:34
Campaign speech, Oklahoma City, Sept. 20, 1928. SIN:52
Religion and politics. HURH:209
Stevenson, A. E.
Acceptance speech, Chicago, Illinois, August 17, 1956. SIN:282
Agrees to run for President. ANN 17:196; BEN:123; GRG:96; HURH:302; LINS:345; SIN:251
Campaign speech, Academy of Music, Brooklyn, New York,

October 31, 1952. SIN:255
Campaign speech, Minneapolis, Minnesota, September 29, 1956. SIN:288
The speaker seeks a favorable hearing. JEF:189; JEFF:182
Speech to the American Legion, August 27, 1952. BEN:129
Tilden, S. J.
Negro suffrage. ANN 10:122
Truman, H. S.
Acceptance speech, Democratic Party National Convention. OLIS:262; SIN:220
Campaign speech, Harlem, New York, October 29, 1948. SIN:226
Willkie, W. L.
Acceptance speech. ANN 16:27; SIN:171
Campaign speech, St. Louis, Missouri, October 17, 1940. SIN:183
Consensus established. ROD:174
Wilson, W.
Fear of monopoly. ANN 13:356
New call to duty. ALA:77
What is progress? BEN:62
Zumwalt, Elmo
Introduction to Edmund G. Brown, Jr. JAM:33

Campbell, Alexander
Mind the master force. BREWE 3:935

Campbell, Bill
On the banks of the Wabash (Purdue Univ., 1966). KEO:226; STOT:266

Campbell, J. P.
Give us equal pay and we will go to war. (Baltimore, Feb. 29, 1864). FON:300

Camus, Albert
Acceptance [of the Nobel Prize for Literature, 1957]. NOB 4:7; NOL:524

CAMUS, ALBERT
Österling, A.
Presentation [of the Nobel Prize for Literature to Albert Camus, 1957]. NOB 4:3; NOL:522

CANADA
Bright, J.
Will the United States subjugate Canada? BREWE 2:620
Laurier, W.
Canada, England and the United States in 1899. BREWE 7:2737
Macdonald, J. A.
On the treaty of Washington. BREWE 8:2891
Prerogative and public right. BREWE 8:2895
Mackintosh, J.
Canada and the autonomy of British colonies. BREWE 8:2909
Quincy, J., 1772-1864
Against the conquest of Canada. BREWE 9:3274
Stevenson, A. E.
Today's most fateful fact (accepting honorary degree of Doctor of Laws). OLIS:272
Thompson, D.
Hitler's plans for Canada and the United States. HURH:257

CANALS
Adams, J. Q.
Fourth of July oration, 1828. HAW:94
Clinton, D.
Address at the Licking Summit near Newark, Ohio. HAW:119
Wolcott, O.
Address at state line between Southwick, Massachusetts and Granby, Connecticut, July 4, 1825. HAW:122

CANCER
Fibiger, J. A. G.
Investigations on Spiroptera carcinoma and the experimental induction of cancer. NOLM 2:122
Huggins, C. B.
Endocrine-induced regression of cancers. NOLM 4:235
Rous, P.
The challenge to man of the neoplastic cell. NOLM 4:220

CANDIDATES
Burke, E.

On declining the election at Bristol, September 9, 1780. BRYH:243
Nixon, R. M.
Apologia (Television, Sept. 23, 1952). MAC:258; MACR:269; REIR:191

Canning, George
Christianity and oppression. BREWE 3:944
England in repose. BREWE 3:941
Hate in politics. BREWE 3:946

CAPILLARIES
Krogh, A.
A contribution to the physiology of the capillaries. NOLM 1:536

CAPITAL AND LABOR See Industrial relations

CAPITAL PUNISHMENT
Bright, J.
On punishment of death. BRYH:398
Darrow, C.
Against capital punishment. BEN:149
Robespierre, M.
Against capital punishment. BREWE 9:3326

CAPITALISM
Carlat, Janice
Green parrot. LINR:46
Carleton, William G.
Effective speech in a democracy. ARS:5
Carlyle, Thomas
Edinburgh address. Same as his Inaugural address at Edinburgh
Debs, E. V.
The issue. LINR:46
Fortune, T. T.
The present relations of labor and capital. FON:506
Friedman, M.
The future of capitalism. LINRST:243

Capp, Al
Is this your university? (Franklin Pierce College, Rindge, N. H., April 27, 1969). STOT:297

CARBOHYDRATES
Haworth, W. N.
The structure of carbohydrates and of vitamin C. NOLC 2:414

CARBON
Calvin, M.
The path of carbon on photosynthesis. NOLC 3:618

CARDIAC CATHETERIZATION
Forssmann, W. T. O.
The role of heart catheterization and angiocardiography in the development of modern medicine. NOLM 3:506
Richards, D. W.
The contributions of right heart catheterization to physiology and medicine, with some observations on the physiopathology of pulmonary heart disease. NOLM 3:513

Cardozo, Francis L.
Break up the plantation system. (Charleston, S. C.-Constitutional Convention of South Carolina, 1868). FON:350

CARDUCCI, GIOSUE
Wirsén, C. D. af
Presentation [of the Nobel Prize for Literature to Giosué Carducci, 1906]. NOB 5:3; NOL:48

Carlat, Janice
Green parrot (Univ. of Kansas, 1967). LINR:46; LINRS:59

Carlyle, Thomas
Heroic in history. BREWE 3:962
Inaugural address at Edinburgh. BREWE 3:951

Carmichael, Stokely
Black power (Univ. of California, Berkeley, Nov. 16, 1966). FON:1033; SMHV:264
Power and racism. BOSC:101
Speech at Morgan State College, January 16, 1967. ARN:343; BOSC:109

Carnot, Lazare N. M.
Against imperialism in France. BREWE 3:967

CAROLINE AMELIA ELIZABETH, CONSORT OF GEORGE IV, KING OF GREAT BRITAIN
Brougham and Vaux, H. P. B.
Closing argument for Queen Caroline. BREWE 2:665

Carpenter, C. U.
Justification of big business. ANN 13:327

Carpenter, Edna
We are involved in the world food crisis. BREWW:223

Carpenter, Liz
Faces and voices of American women (Houston, Nov. 19, 1977). BA 1977-78:184

Carpenter, Matthew Hale
In favor of universal suffrage. BREWE 3:978
Louisiana Returning Board. BREWE 3:976
Replying to the Grand Duke Alexis (response to Duke's toast "To the President of the United States"). BREWE 3:974

Carrel, Alexis
Suture of blood-vessels and transplantation of organs (Nobel Lecture, Dec. 11, 1912). NOLM 1:442

CARREL, ALEXIS
Akerman, J.
Presentation [of the Nobel Prize for Physiology or Medicine to Alexis Carrel, Dec. 11, 1912]. NOLM 1:437

Carson, Alexander
Glories of immortality. BREWE 3:981

Carson, Sir Edward See Oxford and Asquith, Herbert Henry Asquith, 1st Earl of, jt. auth.

Carson, Hampton L.
American liberty. BREWE 3:985

Carstairs, Paddy See Sykes, C., jt. auth.

Carter, Jimmy
Address to the citizens of the world. Same as his Inaugural address
Energy address to the nation (April 18, 1977). EHN:327
Energy and the national goals (Washington, July 15, 1979). BA 1979-80:76
Energy problems (Washington, April 18, 1977). BA 1976-77:117
Fireside chat: unity on U. S. goals (Washington, Feb. 2, 1977). LINRST:340
The inaugural address (Washington, Jan. 20, 1977). BA 1976-77:18; JAM:38
Inauguration address. (Atlanta, Ga., Jan. 12, 1971). BA 1970-71:142
My good friend Hubert Humphrey (Washington, Dec. 2, 1977). BA 1977-78:200
Our common responsibility and our common challenge (New York, Oct. 4, 1977). BA 1977-78:59
Speech at the Martin Luther King, Jr. Hospital. (Los Angeles, June 1, 1976). JAM:25
Universal declaration of human rights (Washington, Dec. 6, 1978). BA 1978-79:52

---- and others (Anwar El-Sadat and Menachem Begin)
Announcing the Camp David accords (Washington, Sept. 17, 1978). BA 1978-79:142

---- See Ford, G. R., jt. auth.

CARTER, JIMMY
Moore, P.
A biblical faith for a president. BA 1976-77:24

Carty, John J.
Pure science and industrial research. ANN 14:9

CASABLANCA CONFERENCE
Roosevelt, F. D.

Address at the annual gathering of the White House Correspondents' Association, February 12, 1943. ANN 16:130

Casely-Hayford, Joseph Ephraim
Leadership and African cooperation. EMP:49

Caspersson, T.
Presentation [of the Nobel Prize for Physiology or Medicine to George Wells Beadle, Edward Lawrie Tatum, and Joshua Lederberg, Dec. 11, 1958]. NOLM 3:583
Presentation [of the Nobel Prize for Physiology or Medicine to Hermann Joseph Muller, Dec. 12, 1946]. NOLM 3:149

Cass, Lewis
American progress and foreign oppression. BREWE 3:989

---- and others (J. C. Jones)
Suitability of moral declaration in foreign policy. ANN 8:167

Cassin, Rene-Samuel
The charter of human rights (Nobel Lecture, Dec. 11, 1968). NOLP 3:394

CASSIN, RENE-SAMUEL
Lionaes, A.
Presentation of the Nobel Prize for Peace to René-Samuel Cassin, Dec. 10, 1968. NOLP 3:385

Castelar, Emilio
In the Camp Santo of Pisa. BREWE 3:1003
Plea for Republican institutions. BREWE 3:998

Castro, Fidel
Cuba is no longer an American colony. LAA:127 (Summary)
Give me liberty or give me death! (Civic Plaza, Havana, May 1, 1960). BRN:136

CATALYSIS
Ostwald, W.
On catalysis. NOLC 1:150

CATHODE RAYS
Lenard, P. E. A. V.
On cathode rays. NOLPH 1:105

CATHOLIC CHURCH See Roman Catholic Church

CATHOLICS IN THE UNITED STATES
Kennedy, J. F.
Religion in government. ANN 17:589; SIN:303
Smith, A. E.
Campaign speech, Oklahoma City, Sept. 20, 1928. SIN:52

Catiline
Before defeat in battle. Same as his To his soldiers
To his soldiers. BAS:37 (outline only)

CATILINE
Caesar, C. J.
On the conspiracy of Catiline. BREWE 3:846
Cato, M. P.
Against the accomplices of Catiline. BREWE 3:1007
Cicero, M. T.
First oration against Catiline. BREWE 3:1159
Second oration against Catiline. BREWE 3:1171

Cato, Marcus Porcius, known as Uticensis
Against the accomplices of Catiline. BREWE 3:1007

CATO, MARCUS PORCIUS, KNOWN AS UTICENSIS
Cicero, M. T.
Cato and the Stoics. BREWE 3:1182

Catt, Carrie Chapman
Political parties and women voters (Chicago, Feb. 14, 1920). BRYF:506

CATTLE
Fishburn, P.
Land of cattle, land of America. BREWW:105
Hayes, K.
Crossbreeding beef cattle: progress or regression? BREWW:214

CATTO, OCTAVIUS V.
Wears, I. C.
The Ku Klux of the North.
FON:378

Catton, Bruce
Response to introduction.
PRS:88

CATTON, BRUCE
Shull, M. A.
Presents Bruce Catton.
LYI:203

Cavanagh, Jerome P.
Presents George Alfred Brown.
LYI:203

Caveny, Charles C.
Greets Joey Bishop, substituting for Sir Cedric Hardwicke.
PRS:118
Introduces David E. Bell, director of the Bureau of the Budget. PRS:92
Introduces Dr. George W. Beadle, chancellor of the University of Chicago.
PRS:50
Introduces Dr. Jonas E. Salk.
PRS:88
Introduces Henry J. Taylor, former United States Ambassador to Switzerland.
PRS:25
Introduces Leonard E. Read.
PRS:98
Introduces Ogden Nash.
PRS:106
Introduces Robert E. Brooker, president of Whirlpool Corporation. PRS:9
Introduces Senator John G. Tower of Texas. PRS:111
Introduces Senator Kenneth B. Keating. PRS:27

Cavour, Camillo Benso, Conte di Rome and Italy.
BREWE 3:1012

Cecil, Robert
The future of civilization (Nobel Lecture for 1937, June 1, 1938). NOLP 2:246

CECIL, ROBERT
Lange, C. L.
Presentation of the Nobel Prize for Peace to Viscount Cecil of Chelwood, Dec. 10, 1937.
NOLP 2:235

Cecil of Salisbury, Robert Arthur Talbot Gascoyne-Cecil, 3d Marquis See Salisbury, R. A. T. G.-C.

Cederblom, J. E.
Presentation [of the Nobel Prize for Chemistry to Sir William Ramsay, Dec. 12, 1904].
NOLC 1:65
Presentation [of the Nobel Prize for Physics to Lord Rayleigh, Dec. 12, 1904]. NOLPH 1:87

CELEBRATIONS See Anniversaries

CELL NUCLEI
Kossel, A.
The chemical composition of the cell nucleus. NOLM 1:394

CELL PHYSIOLOGY
Ehrlich, P.
Partial cell functions.
NOLM 1:304

Celler, Emanuel See Griffiths, Martha W.

CELLS
Lwoff, A.
Interaction among virus, cell, and organism. NOLM 4:186
Monod, J.
From enzymatic adaptation to allosteric transitions.
NOLM 4:188

CENSORSHIP
Agnew, S.
Television news coverage; network censorship. ARN:367; BRYF:467; ERP:153; LINRS:191; LINRST:221; MACR:331; STAT:274
Berryer, P. A.
Censorship of the press.
BREWE 2:443
Brennan, W. J., Jr. and others
Ginzburg et al. v. United States: opinion for the court and dissenting opinion.
ANN 18:350

Krug, J. F.
In defense of liberty: extremism and other vices. BA 1975-76:193
Royer-Collard, P. P.
Against press censorship. BREWE 9:3347
Stanton, F.
Reply to the Vice President. STOT:282
Woolsey, J. M.
Opinion December 6, 1933 (Ulysses case-freedom of reading). ANN 15:236

CENSURE See Prosecution

CENTENNIAL CELEBRATIONS
See Anniversaries

CENTRAL INTELLIGENCE AGENCY
Donovan, W. J.
Call for a Central Intelligence Agency. ANN 16:391

CENTRIFUGES
Svedberg, T.
The ultracentrifuge. NOLC 2:67

CEREBELLUM
Barany, R.
Some new methods for functional testing of the vestibular apparatus and the cerebellum. NOLM 1:500

Cerenkov, Pavel Aleksejevič
Radiation of particles moving at a velocity exceeding that of light, and some of the possibilities for their use in experimental physics (Nobel Lecture, Dec. 11, 1958). NOLPH 3:423

CEYLONESE IN MALAYSIA
Thuraisingham, E. E. S. C.
Call to Ceylonese to have one and only loyalty to rulers of Malaysia. MONSA:185

Chadwick, James
The neutron and its properties (Nobel Lecture, Dec. 12, 1935). NOLPH 2:339

CHADWICK, JAMES
Pleijel, H.
Presentation [of the Nobel Prize for Physics to James Chadwick, Dec. 12, 1935]. NOLPH 2:333

CHAFFEE, ROGER B.
Sevareid, E.
Eulogy for the astronauts. MOP:189

Chain, Ernst Boris
The chemical structure of the penicillins (Nobel Lecture for 1945, March 20, 1946). NOLM 3:110

CHAIN, ERNST BORIS
Liljestrand, G.
Presentation [of the Nobel Prize for Physiology or Medicine to Sir Alexander Fleming, Ernst Boris Chain, and Sir Howard Walter Florey, Dec. 11, 1945]. NOLM 3:77

CHAIRMEN See Officers, presiding; Toastmasters; Toasts

Challemel-Lacour, Paul Amand
Humboldt and the Teutonic intellect. BREWE 3:1018

Chalmers, Thomas
Use of living. BREWE 3:1025
War and truth. BREWE 3:1024
When old things pass away. BREWE 3:1023

Chamberlain, Sir Austen See Baldwin, S. B., jt. auth.

Chamberlain, Daniel Henry
Present hour in South Carolina (inaugural address of would-be governor). CUR:158

Chamberlain, Joseph
Acceptance [of the Nobel Prize for Peace for 1925, Dec. 10, 1926]. NOLP 1:394
Empire and home rule. (Birmingham, May 15, 1903). MCB:60; STRM:387
Imperial preference. Same as his Empire and home rule
Imperial union and tariff reform.

Same as his Empire and home rule
Manhood suffrage. Same as his Megaphone and manhood suffrage
Megaphone and manhood suffrage. BREWE 3:1026

CHAMBERLAIN, JOSEPH
Nansen, F.
Speech at Award Ceremony [presenting the Nobel Prize for Peace to Joseph Austen Chamberlain and Charles Gates Dawes for 1925, Dec. 10, 1926]. NOLP 1:383

Chamberlain, Owen
The early antiproton work (Nobel Lecture, Dec. 11, 1959). NOLPH 3:489

CHAMBERLAIN, OWEN
Hulthén, E.
Presentation [of the Nobel Prize for Physics to Emilio Gino Segrè and Owen Chamberlain, Dec. 11, 1959]. NOLPH 3:487

Chambers, Merritt M.
Higher education who should pay? CAPG:125

Champion, George
Consensus complex vs. the free market. BA 1965-66:187

Chandler, A. B.
Address to the General Assembly, Frankfort, Kentucky, April 20, 1936. BLY:258

Chandler, Marvin
Introduces Roscoe Drummond. PRS:122
Quest for peace. SCHW:180

Chandler, Zachariah
On Jefferson Davis. BREWE 3:1030

Chaney, Fannie Lee
Ben is going to take his big brother's place. (New York, 1965). FON:1017

CHANEY, JAMES
Chaney, F. L.
Ben is going to take his big brother's place. FON:1017

Channing, William Ellery
Attack on orthodox Calvinism. Same as his Unitarian Christianity
Man above the state. BREWE 3:1032
Unitarian Christianity. ANN 4:544

Chapin, Edwin Hubbell
Peaceful industry. BREWE 3:1037
Rectitude higher than morality. BREWE 3:1040
Scientia Liberatrix. BREWE 3:1039
Source of modern progress. BREWE 3:1038
Sovereignty of ideas. BREWE 3:1036

Chapman, John Ray
Coatesville. ARS:163

Chapuisat, Edouard
The activity of the International Committee of the Red Cross during the War, 1939-1945 (Nobel Lecture for 1944, Dec. 11, 1945). NOLP 2:295

CHARACTER
Moody, D. L.
On Daniel and the value of character. BREWE 8:3057

CHARITIES
Winthrop, J.
Modell of Christian charity. BOORA 1:10

CHARLES I, KING OF ENGLAND
Mayhew, J.
Discourse on the anniversary of the death of Charles I. ANN 1:481; POC:508

CHARTISM
Attwood, T.
Chartist movement. JAE:68

CHASE, HARRY WOODBURN
Nizer, L.

Presents Harry Woodburn Chase. LYI:91

CHASE, ILKA
Mulroy, T. R.
Presents Ilka Chase. LYI:17

Chase, Salmon P.
Thomas Jefferson and the colonial view of manhood rights. BREWE 3:1044
Three great eras. BREWE 3:1056

---- and others (J. R. Giddings)
Opposition to the Kansas-Nebraska Bill (January 1854). ANN 8:251

CHASE, SAMUEL
Harper, R. G.
Defending Judge Chase. BREWE 6:2425

Chateaubriand, François Auguste René, Viscomte de
Has one government the right to intervene in the internal affairs of another? BREWE 3:1060

Chatham, William Pitt, 1st Earl of See Pitt, W., 1708-1778

Chauncy, Charles
Caveat against enthusiasm. POC:488
Good news from a far country (repeal of Stamp Act). BREWE 3:1090

Cheek, James E.
A promise made, a promise to keep: Whitney Young and the nation. (Washington, D. C., March 19, 1971). BA 1970-71:131

CHEMICAL BONDS
Hassel, O.
Structural aspects of interatomic charge-transfer bonding. NOLC 4:312
Mulliken, R. S.
Spectroscopy, molecular orbitals, and chemical bonding. NOLC 4:131

CHEMICAL COMPOUNDS
Werner, A.
On the constitution and configuration of higher-order compounds. NOLC 1:256

CHEMICAL EQUILIBRIUM
Hoff, J. H. V.
Osmotic pressure and chemical equilibrium. NOLC 1:5

CHEMICAL REACTIONS
Eigen, M.
Immeasurably fast reactions. NOLC 4:170

CHEMISTRY
Nernst, W. H.
Studies in chemical thermodynamics. NOLC 1:353
Pauling, L. C.
Modern structural chemistry. NOLC 3:429

CHEMOTHERAPY
Bovet, D.
The relationships between isosterism and competitive phenomena in the field of drug therapy of the autonomic nervous system and that of the neuromuscular transmission. NOLM 3:552

CHEROKEE INDIANS
Marshall, J.
Cherokee Nation v. State of Georgia: opinion for the Supreme Court. ANN 5:427
Swimmer, R. O.
Cherokee history. MAES:314

Chertoff, Mordecai S.
Benjamin A. Lichter. WALE:205
Go thou in peace. WALE:27

CHESAPEAKE & OHIO CANAL
Adams, J. Q.
Fourth of July oration, 1828. HAW:94

Chesterfield, Philip Dormer Stanhope, 4th Earl of
Against revenues from drunkenness and vice. BREWE 3:1095

Chesterton, Gilbert Keith See Shaw, G. B., jt. auth.

Cheves, Langdon
In favor of a stronger navy. BREWE 3:1101

CHEVRILLON, ANDRE
Phelps, W. L.
Presents André Chevrillon. LYI:52

Chew, Samuel
Speech, &c. POC:77

Chiang, Mei-Ling (Sung) Mme. Chiang Kai Shek
Japan is first U. S. foe. CROCK:46

CHICAGO - WORLD'S COLUMBIAN EXPOSITION, 1893
Depew, C. M.
Columbian oration. BREWE 5:1769

CHICAGO HAYMARKET SQUARE RIOTS
Engel, G.
Address at trial, Chicago, October 7-9, 1886. ACC:43; PAF:37
Fielden, S.
Address at trial, Chicago, October 7-9, 1886. ACC:49; PAF:41
Fischer, A.
Address at trial, Chicago, October 7-9, 1886. ACC:36; PAF:32
Lingg, L.
Address at trial, Chicago, October 7-9, 1886. ACC:39; PAF:34
Neebe, O.
Address at trial, Chicago, October 7-9, 1886. ACC:29; PAF:28
Parsons, A. R.
Address at trial, Chicago, October 7-9, 1886. ACC:90; PAF:65
Schwab, M.
Address at trial, Chicago, October 7-9, 1886. ACC:24; PAF:25
Spies, A.
Address at trial, Chicago, October 7-9, 1886. ACC:1; ANN 11:117; PAF:11

CHICANOS See Mexicans in the United States

Chiel, Samuel
Seder of life. WALE:29

Chifley, Joseph Benedict
Things worth fighting for. MCA:166

CHILD LABOR
Cobbett, W.
Factory Bill (1833). STRM:191
Roesch, G. F.
Constitutionality of a New York child labor law: opinion for the court. ANN 12:571
Shaftesbury, A. A. C.
Employment of children. JAE:81

CHILDREN
Geiman, C. K.
Are they really "unteachable"? LINR:94
Jones, J. L.
"Let's bring back Dad": a solid value system. LINRST:254
Kingsley, C.
Human soot: address at Liverpool in behalf of the Kirkdale Ragged Schools. BREWE 7:2645
Myers, N. J.
Moppet manipulation. ARS:123
Nixon, R. M.
Remarks at the White House Conference on Children. BA 1970-71:37
Stowe, L.
Children, peanuts-and you. MOP:263

CHILDREN'S DAY
Children on Children's Day (welcome address). HNWM:15
Welcome to mothers on Children's Day. HNWM:7

CHILDREN'S RIGHTS
Lonnquist, K.
Ghosts. LINRST:176

Chillingworth, William
False pretenses. BREWE 3:1106

CHINA
Clemens, S. L.

Public Education Association. GRG:21
Cushing, C.
England and America in China. BREWE 4:1583
McKinley, W.
Fourth annual message. STAT 2:1971

CHINESE IN MALAYSIA
Tan Siew Sin
Malays and Chinese must co-exist. MONSA:85
The role of M.C.A. and the loyalty of Malaysian Chinese. MONSA:78

CHINESE IN THE UNITED STATES
Meade, E. R.
Chinese immigration to the United States. ANN 10:386

CHINESE LITERATURE
Buck, P.
The Chinese novel. NOL:361

Chino, Wendell
Indian affairs--what has been done and what needs to be done. BA 1969-70:179

Chisholm, Shirley
Economic injustice in America today (Newark College of Engineering, April 15, 1972). BA 1971-72:27
In support of the Equal Rights Amendment (Washington, Aug. 10, 1970). BOST:243; EHN:364; MOPR:372
It is time for a change (March 26, 1969-Congress). FON:1152
It is time to reassess our national priorities. BA 1968-1969:68
Representative Shirley Chisholm speaks in support of the Equal Rights Amendment. Same as her In Support of the Equal Rights Amendment
Women in politics (Houston, Feb. 9, 1973). BA 1972-73:79

Chiu Ban It
Be strong and of good courage (enthronement sermon). MONS:456

CHIVALRY
Burke, E.
Age of chivalry. BREWE 2:817

CHLOROPHYLL
Fischer, H.
On haemin and the relationships between haemin and chlorophyll. NOLC 2:165

Choate, Joseph Hodges
Bench and bar. (New York, Dec. 22, 1880). HURH:133
Farragut. BREWE 3:1109
Presents James Bryce. LYI:237
"You cannot live without lawyers, and certainly you cannot die without them." Same as his Bench and bar

Choate, Rufus
Books and civilization in America. BREWE 3:1120
Heroism of the early colonists. Same as his Puritan and Spartan heroism
Necessity of compromises in American politics. BREWE 3:1127
On American nationality (82nd anniversary of American independence). ANN 9:54
Preservation of the Union. (Boston, Mass., 1850). HURH:80
Puritan and Spartan heroism. BREWE 3:1135
State and mental culture. ANN 7:235
"There are influences that never sleep." Same as his Preservation of the Union

CHOIRS <u>See</u> Music and musicians

CHOLESTEROL
Bloch, K.
The biological synthesis of cholesterol. NOLM 4:78

CHRISTIAN ETHICS
Winthrop, J.
Modell of Christian charity. BOORA 1:10

CHRISTIANITY
Canning, G.
Christianity and oppression. BREWE 3:944

Unitarian Christianity.
ANN 4:544
Dix, J. A.
Christianity and politics.
BREWE 5:1883
Ethelbert
Coming of Christianity.
BRYH:3
Hare, J. C.
Children of light.
BREWE 6:2402
Nation, C. A.
Spiritual authority for my Christian work. BLY:183
selections
Newman, J. H., Cardinal
Christianity and scientific investigation. MCB:361
Ockenga, H. J.
Evangelical Christianity.
ANN 16:115
Parker, T.
Transient and permanent in Christianity. LINS:178
Shepard, T.
The parable of the ten virgins. JON:133
Söderblom, N.
The role of the church in promoting peace (Nobel Lecture, Dec. 11, 1930).
NOLP 2:93
Thomas, J. B.
"Light of the world."
SCHW:110
Vander Werf, N.
Mistaken enemy. SCHW:171
Van Tatenhove, J. E.
Echo or a voice? SCHW:115

CHRISTIANITY AND ECONOMICS
Herron, G. D.
Christianity and the use of private property.
ANN 12:226

CHRISTMAS
Christmas prayer. BNH:75
Paul VI
Key to peace. BAS:150
(outline only)

CHROMATOGRAPHY
Martin, A. J. P.
The development of partition chromatography. NOLC 3:359
Synge, R. L. M.
Applications of partition chromatography. NOLC 3:374

Chrysostom, John, Saint, Patriarch of Constantinople
Avarice and usury.
BREWE 3:1141
Blessing of death.
BREWE 3:1138
Heroes of faith. BREWE 3:1139

Church, Benjamin
Boston Massacre oration (third anniversary). POC:255

Church, Frank
Foreign policy and the generation gap (St. Louis, Dec. 3, 1970).
BA 1970-71:49
Rediscovering America (San Francisco, Oct. 20, 1975).
BA 1975-76:124
War without end. BA 1969-70:27
The yen to make a mark with the dollar (Provo, Utah, Dec. 12, 1978). BA 1978-79:168

CHURCH
Bernard, Saint
Against luxury in the Church.
BREWE 2:434
Korteling, M.
Renascence. SCHW:39
Parker, T.
Critique of American churches.
ANN 7:486
Welcome to Baptist Training Union officers (Christian Endeavor, etc.). HNWM:27
Welcome to church officials (Deacons, Stewards, Elders, etc.). HNWM:26
Welcome to guest speaker at a stewardship banquet (3 examples). HNWM:60
Welcome to new Christians (3 examples). HNWM:62
Welcome to new church member by transfer. HNWM:63
Welcome to new members of church staff and family.
HNWM:64
Welcome to visitors at church service (3 examples).
HNWM:52
Welcome to visitors at Men-of-the-Church dinner (3 examples).
HNWM:39

---- See also Dedication addresses - Churches

CHURCH AND STATE
Colman, B.
Piety and duty of rulers to comfort and encourage the ministry of Christ. POC:142
Grant, U. S.
Separation of church and school. ANN 10:365
Harris, J. G.
The prayer amendment. BA 1971-72:143
Henry, J.
On religion and elective office. ANN 4:239; BOORA 1:220
Kahn, R. I.
Vote against prayer and for God. KEO:300
Madison, J.
Civil and religious functions of government. ANN 4:287
Wilkinson, H. C.
How separate should government and God be? LINR:98

---- PHILIPPINE ISLANDS
Aquino, B. S.
The Church and the State must never mix! CURM:129

CHURCH COLLEGES
Stendahl, K.
Faith that enlivens the mind. BA 1976-77:168

Churchill, Lord Randolph Henry Spencer
Administration of Chips. STRM:355
Age of action. BREWE 3:1144
Financial reform: the administration of "Chips." Same as his Administration of Chips
Gladstone's Egyptian inconsistencies. BREWE 3:1148
"Trust the people" speech. (Birmingham, April 16, 1884). MCB:441

---- See also Sykes, C., jt. auth.

Churchill, Sir Winston Leonard Spencer
Acceptance [of the Nobel Prize for Literature, 1953]. NOB 4:183; NOL:493
Address to Congress, December 26, 1941. ALS:223; AND:120; ARN:301; BRR:51; CROCK:29; JEF:190; JEFF:184
Be ye men of valour. (BBC Broadcast, May 19, 1940). MCB:495
"Blood, sweat and tears." (H. of Commons, May 13, 1940). ALA:99; MCB:493
Blood, toil, tears, and sweat. Same as his "Blood, sweat and tears"
A British prime minister addresses Congress. Same as his Address to Congress, December 26, 1941
The Conservative programme. (BBC Broadcast, June 4, 1945). MCB:464
Dunkirk. (H. of Commons, June 4, 1940). MCB:498
Government policy (October 5, 1938 speech). STRM:468
Iron curtain. Same as his Sinews of peace
Never in the field of human conflict. (H. of Commons, Aug. 20, 1940). MCB:514
On the Munich Agreement (October 5, 1938). BRYH:521
Parliament in the air raids (September 17, 1940 speech). STRM:481
Sinews of peace (Westminster College, Fulton, Missouri, March 5, 1946). ANN 16:365; MCB:541
Solemn hour (May 19, 1940 broadcast). BRYH:534
"Their finest hour." (H. of Commons, June 18, 1940). MCB:506

---- See also Baldwin, S. B., jt. auth.

CHURCHILL, SIR WINSTON LEONARD SPENCER
Clemens, S. L.
Presents Winston Churchill. LYI:198
Menzies, R. G.
Eulogy of Churchill. MCA:151
Siwertz, S.
Presentation [of the Nobel Prize for Literature to Sir Winston Leonard Spencer Churchill, 1953]. NOB 4:177; NOL:488
Stevenson, A. E.
Address at the memorial serv-

ice for Sir Winston Churchill. LINR:305; LINRS:307; LINRST:373
Truman, H. S.
Presents Winston Churchill. LYI:211
Vincent, J.
Churchill's early achievements. MDYG:50

Cicero, Marcus Tullius
Catiline's departure. Same as his Second oration against Catiline
Cato and the Stoics. BREWE 3:1182
Crucifixion of Gavius. Same as his First oration against Verres
First oration against Catiline. BREWE 3:1159
First oration against Verres. BREWE 3:1174
For the poet Archias. BREWE 3:1189
Fourth Philippic. BREWE 3:1201
Second oration against Catiline. BREWE 3:1171
Supernatural justice. BREWE 3:1178

CITIES AND TOWNS
Benedict, D. L.
Remarks in Chicago on urban imperatives. BA 1967-68:78
Church, F.
Rediscovering America. BA 1975-76:124
Dinwoodie, S. D.
Inner city--our shame. ARS:216
Ely, R. T.
Needs of the city. ANN 11:234
Kingsbury, F. J.
In defense of the city. ANN 12:61
Lindsay, J. V.
Reality and rhetoric. BA 1967-68:79
Olmsted, F. L.
Unplanned growth of cities. ANN 10:224
Stevenson, A. E.
City--a cause for statesmanship. ARS:219
Stuart, J. D.
What can I do that matters? BRYF:512
Thani Nayagam, X.
Town versus gown. MONS:183
Whitney, F. L.
Total redevelopment of cities. ANN 18:338
Wilson, W. H.
Interaction of country and city. ANN 14:4
Young, W. M., Jr.
Crisis of the city: the danger of the ghetto. BA 1966-67:82; OE:177; SMHV:160

CITIZEN ACTION See Local government - citizen participation

CITIZENSHIP
Curtis, G. P.
Public duty of educated men. ALS:179
Farber, W. O.
Changing concepts of public service. ARS:208
Gardiner, R. K.
Citizenship and political liberalism. EMP:106
Marshall, D. S.
Duty of citizens. MONS:448
Warren, E.
Perez v. Brownell: dissenting opinion. ANN 17:499

---- See also Suffrage

---- NEW ZEALAND
Parry, W. E.
New Zealand citizenship, 1948. MACS:294 sel.

CIVIL DISOBEDIENCE See Government, Resistance to

CIVIL LIBERTY See Democracy; Liberty; United States - Economic policy

CIVIL RIGHTS
Barrett, B. F.
The unreasonable prejudices against people of color in Philadelphia. FON:337
Brackenridge, H. M.
Vindication of civil rights for Jews. ANN 4:552
Bradley, J. F. and others
Civil rights cases: opinion for the court and dissenting opinion. ANN 10:577

Brooke, E. W.
The cause of civil rights. FON:1058
Bruce, J. E.
Negro plea for organized resistance to white men. ANN 11:214
Carter, J.
Universal declaration of human rights. BA 1978-79:52
Cassin, R. S.
The charter of human rights (Nobel Lectures, Dec. 11, 1968). NOLP 3:394
Chase, S. P.
Thomas Jefferson and the colonial view of manhood rights. BREWE 3:1044
Collins, L.
Rout the forces of hate. ARS:157
Cushing, C.
Primordial rights of the universal people. BREWE 4:1577
Douglass, F.
Color line in America. ANN 10:584; FON:491
Dunn, O. J.
We ask an equal chance in the race of life. FON:355
Eisenhower, D. D.
Federal Court orders must be upheld. ANN 17:457
Farmer, J. and others
Debate at Cornell University, March 7, 1962. BOSC:59; OE:248
Goldberg, A. J.
Human rights and détente. BA 1977-78:71
Gregory, D.
Let your son fight for freedom. FON:981
Grimke, F. J.
Equality of rights for all citizens, black and white, alike. FON:668
Hannah, J. A.
Civil rights and the public universities. BA 1965-66:93
Hatcher, R. G.
Which is the path of change? FON:1110
James, D.
"Given time we'll get it together." BA 1974-75:135
Johnson, L. B.
Address to a Joint Session of Congress, March 15, 1965. AND:81; BOORA 2:919; CROCK:164; MDV:144; REIR:143
Voting Rights Law of 1965--a victory for freedom. CAPG:97
Jordan, V. E., Jr.
Blacks and the Nixon administration: the next four years. BA 1972-73:39
Survival. BA 1971-72:49
Katzenbach, N.
Civil Rights Act of 1964: respect for law. CAPG:88
Kennedy, J. F.
Negro and the American promise. ANN 18:152
Special message to the Congress on Civil Rights. THOMS:50
Kennedy, R. F.
Law Day address--University of Georgia. CAPG:73; THOMS:120
King, M. L., Jr.
'I have a dream." AND:50; ANN 18:156; ARS:154; BRR:78; CAPG:83; FON:971; GRG:117; HURH:366; LINR:290; LINRS:289; LINRST:362; LINS:379; MAC:247; MACR:288; MDV:156; MUS:336; OE:152; OLIS:289; SMHV:182; THOMS:94
I see the promised land. FON:1108
A long way to go. SMHV:188
Nonviolence and social change. OE:157
Where do we go from here? FON:1068
Lewis, J.
We are in a serious revolution. FON:975
Little, M.
Black revolution. SMHV:235
Macdonald, J. A.
Prerogative and public right. BREWE 8:2895
McGill, W. J.
Simple justice and existential victims. BA 1978-79:23
Marshall, T.
In praise of the sit-in strikes. FON:930
The legal attack to secure civil rights. OE:123
Muhammad, E.
We must have justice.

FON:969
Nixon, R. M.
Bridges to human dignity. LINR:255
Patterson, W. L.
"Free by '63." FON:924
Percy, C. H.
Chicagoan goes South. BA 1965-66:106
Price, J. C.
The race problem stated. SMHV:78
Randolph, A. P.
March on Washington address. OE:113
Rowan, C. T.
New frontiers in racial relations. OE:201
Russell, R. and others
Pro's and con's of civil rights. BRR:73
Steffens, G.
Law of the land. SCHW:132
Stephens, A. H.
Civil rights in the Confederacy. ANN 9:493
Truman, H. S.
Campaign speech, Harlem, New York, October 29, 1948. SIN:226
Civil Rights, February 2, 1948. ANN 16:510
Vance, C. R.
Human rights and the foreign policy. BA 1976-77:127
Warren, E.
Brown et al v. Board of Education of Topeka et al: opinion for the court. ANN 17:253; BOORA 2:904
---- and others
Miranda v. Arizona: opinion for the court and dissenting opinion. ANN 18:427
Weaver, R. C.
Negro as an American. MDV:162
Wilkins, R.
Keynote address to the NAACP annual convention, Los Angeles, July 5, 1966. AND:101; BOSC:89; OE:166
Young, W. M., Jr.
Crisis of the city: the danger of the ghetto. BA 1966-67:82; OE:177; SMHV:160
The social revolution: challenge to the nation. FON:961
A strategy for the seventies: unity, coalition, negotiation. STOT:331

---- See also Free speech; Liberty of the press; Negroes; Religious liberty; Segregation in education

---- RUSSIA
Griffin, R. P.
When freedom dies in its sleep. BA 1978-79:60

CIVIL RIGHTS ACT (1866)
Elliott, R. B.
Civil Rights Bill. FON:384; OE:55
Johnson, A. and others
Debate on civil and states' rights. ANN 10:11
Rapier, J. T.
Civil Rights Bill. FON:418

CIVIL RIGHTS ACT OF 1964
Katzenbach, N.
Civil Rights Act of 1964: respect for law. CAPG:88
Wallace, G. C.
Civil Rights Bill: fraud, sham and hoax. MDV:175

CIVIL SERVICE
Arthur, C. A.
First annual message. STAT 2:1424
Second annual message. STAT 2:1452
Burger, Warren E.
How long can we cope? BA 1978-79:81
Cleveland, G.
First annual message (first term). STAT 2:1514
Hayes, R. B.
First annual message. STAT 2:1334
Fourth annual message. STAT 2:1395
Schurz, C.
Necessity and progress of Civil Service reform. ANN 11:493

---- MALAYSIA
Suffian bin Hashim
Important factors for ensuring

efficient, loyal public service. MONSA:132
Tan Slew Sin
The need for dedicated service by civil servants. MONSA:89 selections

CIVIL SERVICE REFORM
Bell, G. B.
Notes on the situation: a critique. BA 1978-79:93

CIVILIZATION
Calhoun, J. C.
Self-government and civilization. BREWE 3:924
Choate, R.
Books and civilization in America. BREWE 3:1120
Guizot, F. P. G.
Civilization and the individual man. BREWE 6:2344
Pennings, B.
New men for a new world. SCHW:153

Claesson, S.
Presentation [of the Nobel Prize for Chemistry to Lars Onsager, Dec. 11, 1968]. NOLC 4:269

Clark, Champ
Courage of leadership. BREWE 3:1207

Clark, Edwin M.
Responds to an introduction. PRS:139

Clark, Kenneth B.
Beyond the dilemma. BA 1969-70:168
The present dilemma of the Negro. (Second Carter G. Woodson Memorial Luncheon, Greensboro, N. C., Oct. 14, 1967). FON:1091

Clark, Peter H.
Socialism: the remedy for the evils of society. (Cincinnati, July 22, 1877). FON:451

Clark, Thomas C.
Sheppard v. Maxwell, warden: opinion for the court. ANN 18:402

CLARK, THOMAS C.
Lewe, J. C.
Presents Thomas C. Clark (Attorney General of the United States). LYI:137

Clarke, John Henrik
The meaning of Black History. (Jewish Currents Conference - New York, Feb. 15, 1969). FON:1138

CLASS DAY ADDRESSES See Commencement addresses; Farewell addresses; Valedictory addresses; Welcoming addresses

Clay, Cassius Marcellus
America as a moral force. BREWE 3:1213
Aspirations for the Union. BREWE 3:1212
The man died, but his memory lives. (Yale College, Feb. 22, 1832). BLY:109
Rhapsody. BREWE 3:1211

Clay, Clement C., Sr.
Subtreasury Bill of 1837. BREWE 3:1216

Clay, Henry
Against the growing power of the executive. ANN 6:565
American industry, 1824. ANN 5:114
American system (U.S. Senate, Feb. 2nd, 3rd, 6th, 1832). BREWE 4:1249; HOW:32
Bank and the power of the executive. ANN 6:46
Compromise of 1850 (Washington, Feb. 5 & 6, 1850). ANN 8:1; BREWE 4:1273; HURH:83; OLIS:66
Compromise resolutions. Same as his Compromise of 1850
Dictators in American politics (Washington, April 30, 1834). BLY:33; BREWE 4:1224
Emancipation of South American Republics. ANN 4:488; BREWE 4:1240
Expunging Resolution.

BREWE 4:1233
For a vigorous prosecution of the war. Same as his On the War of 1812
Free trade and seamen's rights. BREWE 4:1264
Greek Revolution. BREWE 4:1268
In favor of a paternal policy of internal improvements. BREWE 4:1260
Internal improvements and the power of Congress. ANN 4:482
"Let us look to our country and our cause, elevate ourselves to the dignity of pure and disinterested patriots." Same as his Compromise of 1850 (February 5 & 6, 1850 speech)
Manufacturing and a protective tariff. ANN 4:612
Noblest public virtue. BREWE 4:1271
On the Seminole War. BREWE 4:1236
On the War of 1812. ANN 4:327
Protective tariff. Same as his American industry, 1824
Recognition for Latin American governments. Same as his Emancipation of South American Republics
Sixty years of sectionalism. Same as his Compromise of 1850
Slavery and expansion, May 13 and May 21, 1850. ANN 8:36
System of real reciprocity. ANN 5:392

CLAY, HENRY
Crittenden, J. J.
Henry Clay and the nineteenth-century spirit. BREWE 4:1472

Clay, Laura
Laws of the states affecting women. (Women's Club of Central Kentucky, ca. 1894). BLY:199

CLAY COMPROMISE See Slavery in the United States

Clayton, John M.
Clayton-Bulwer treaty and expansion. BREWE 4:1283
Justice the supreme law of nations. BREWE 4:1290

Cleage, Albert
Myths about Malcolm X. LINR:108

Cleaver, Eldridge
Farewell address (San Francisco, Nov. 22, 1969). SMHV:284
Meditation on the assassination of Martin Luther King, Jr. (April, 1968). OE:229
Political struggle in America. SMHR:166
Revolution in the white mother country and national liberation in the black colony. (Richmond, Calif., March 16, 1968). FON:1101

Clemens, Jeremiah
Cuba and "manifest destiny." BREWE 4:1292

Clemens, Samuel Langhorne
Accident insurance--etc. MUS:291
Horrors of the German language. BEN:204
"The ladies." BEN:201
New England weather. (New York, Dec. 22, 1876). HURH:128
Presents Henry M. Stanley. LYI:117
Presents Joseph B. Hawley. LYI:148
Presents Winston Churchill. LYI:198
Public Education Association. GRG:21
"There is a sumptuous variety about the New England weather that compels the stranger's admiration--and regret." Same as his New England weather

Cleon
Democracies and subject colonies. Same as his On the punishment of the Mytileneans
On the punishment of the Mytileneans. BREWE 4:1298

CLERGY
Edwards, J.
Farewell-sermon. POC:443
Introductions for evangelists (19 examples). BNH:13
Introductions for ministers (16 examples). BNH:9
Reply to an introduction by a former pastor (4 examples). BNH:82
Stoddard, S.
Defects of preachers reproved. POC:430
Tennent, G.
Danger of an unconverted ministry. POC:469
Welcome to a new pastor and family (2 examples). BNH:49
Welcome to guest minister at church service (4 examples). HNWM:59
Welcome to minister as speaker at a civic club (3 examples). HNWM:43
When a pastor has to say goodbye (2 examples). BNH:83
Words by a young man about to be ordained as a minister. BNH:90

Cleveland, Grover
American interests in the Cuban Revolution. Same as his Fourth annual message (second term)
Controversy over Hawaii (against annexation). ANN 11:480
First annual message (first term). STAT 2:1514
First annual message (second term). STAT 2:1736
First inaugural address. BREWE 4:1301; USINAU:149; USINAUG:149
Fourth annual message (first term). STAT 2:1598
Fourth annual message (second term). ANN 12:119; STAT 2:1824
On tariff revision. ANN 11:154; STAT 2:1587
Second annual message (first term). STAT 2:1555
Second annual message (second term). STAT 2:1762
Second inaugural address. USINAU:163; USINAUG:163
Skeptical view of pension legislation. ANN 11:90
Surplus revenues and the tariff. Same as his On Tariff revision
Third annual message (first term). Same as his On Tariff revision
Third annual message (second term). STAT 2:1794

Clevenger, Theodore
To have lived without reason. (Baylor University, 1951). CAPB:373

Clifford, Clark M.
We must renew our confidence. (Philadelphia, Nov. 1, 1972). BA 1972-73:109

Clinton, De Witt
Address at the Licking Summit near Newark, Ohio, July 4, 1825. HAW:119
Against the military spirit. BREWE 4:1309
Federal power and local rights. BREWE 4:1306

CLOTHING AND DRESS
MacColl, R.
Borrowed plumage. MDYG:174
Wesley, J.
On dressing for display. BREWE 10:3880

CLOUD CHAMBER
Blackett, P. M. S.
Cloud chamber researches in nuclear physics and cosmic radiation. NOLPH 3:97

CLUB SPEECHES
Bryant, W. C.
To the Burns Club. BREWE 2:702
Nine examples of brief thanks to special committees. BNH:46
Welcome to new members in civic club (3 examples). HNWM:46

Coates, Dandeson
Missionary opposition to the New Zealand Company (House of Lords Committee on New Zealand, May 14, 1838). MACS:4 selections

Coates, J. Gordon
The 1925 election: the Coates

campaign (Christchurch, Oct. 13, 1925). MACS:307 sel.
Support for the Singapore Naval Base, 1927 (New Zealand House of Representatives, Sept. 21, 1927). MACS:278 selections

Cobb, Howell
"Fifty-four forty or fight." BREWE 4:1317
Speech of Howell Cobb, at Atlanta, Georgia, May 22. ECH:182

Cobbett, William
Factory Bill (1833). STRM:191
Man on the tower (defending himself against a charge of libel). BREWE 4:1321

Cobden, Richard
Effects of Corn Laws in agriculture. STRM:246
Effects of protection in agriculture. (H. of Commons, March 13, 1845). MCB:189
Free trade with all nations. BREWE 4:1326
Need for improved education. JAE:124
Small states and great achievements. BREWE 4:1336

COBDEN, RICHARD
Palmerston, H. J. T.
On the death of Cobden. BREWE 8:3131

Cockcroft, Sir John Douglas
Experiments on the interaction of high-speed nucleons with atomic nuclei (Nobel Lecture, Dec. 11, 1951). NOLPH 3:167

COCKCROFT, SIR JOHN DOUGLAS
Waller, I.
Presentation [of the Nobel Prize for Physics to Sir John Douglas Cockcroft and Ernest Thomas Sinton Walton, Dec. 11, 1951]. NOLPH 3:163

Cockran, William Bourke
An answer to William J. Bryan. BREWE 4:1339

Coffin, William Sloane, Jr.
Vietnam: a sermon. VI:64

Coffman, Lotus Delta
Adult education for the unemployed. ANN 15:98

Coke, Edward
Prosecuting Sir Walter Raleigh. BREWE 4:1348

Cole, Albert L.
Responds to introduction. PRS:97

Cole, Edward N.
Two myths and a paradox. (Warren, Michigan, Feb. 10, 1972). BA 1971-72:93

Colepeper, John, 1st Baron
Against monopolies. BREWE 4:1494

Coleridge, John Duke Coleridge, 1st Baron
Sacredness of matrimony. BREWE 4:1355

Coles, Robert
A "larger vision" of the humanities (Washington, Oct. 18, 1977). BA 1977-78:163

Colfax, Schuyler
Confiscation of rebel property. BREWE 4:1361

COLLECTIVISM
Hoover, H. C.
Road to freedom. ANN 15:384
Welch, R.
More stately mansions (1964). DAVF:327

COLLEGE EDUCATION See Colleges and universities; Education, Higher; Knowledge, Theory of; Learning and scholarship

COLLEGE STUDENTS See Students

COLLEGES AND UNIVERSITIES
Birenbaum, W. M.
Time for reconstruction. BA 1969-70:154
Crosby, G. A.
The uses of adversity.

BA 1976-77:156
Damrin, D. E.
The James Scholars and the university. BRYF:528; BRYO:243
Hannah, J. A.
Civil rights and the public universities. BA 1965-66:93
Henry, D. D.
Perceptions of the university. HOR:70
Horner, M. S.
Opportunity for educational innovation. BA 1972-73:184
Karenga, M. R.
The Black community and the university; a community organizer's perspective. LINRS:255
Kerr, C.
Urban-grant university (centennial meeting of City College). BA 1967-68:86
Lewis, W. D.
Founder's Day remarks. BAS:164 (outline only)
Lindsley, P.
Dangers of a sectarian college. ANN 5:310
McGill, W. J.
Requiem for Joe College. BA 1969-70:139
Norton, E. H.
In pursuit of equality in academe: new themes and dissonant chords. BA 1976-77:65
Randolph, J.
Japanese "Lunchbox" universities. REIR:15
Reinert, P. C.
America, America, how does your garden grow? HOR:82
Reston, J.
Remarks at the Centennial Charter Day Convocation, the Ohio State University, March 22, 1970. BAAE:285
Shaw, G. B.
Universities and education. KEO:237
Sutton, P. M.
Liberal arts in an agricultural college. ANN 11:18
Tappan, H. P.
Call for a secularized university. ANN 9:79
Turner, J. B.
Industrial university for Illinois. ANN 8:157
Washington, G.
Eighth annual message. ANN 3:604; STAT 1:31

---- See also Education, Higher; Educators; Students. Also names of universities, e.g. Dartmouth College; Harvard University; Oxford University; University of Malaya

---- AUSTRALIA
Wentworth, W. C.
For the University Bill. MCA:17

---- ENTRANCE REQUIREMENTS
Howe, H. II
Changing the pecking order. BA 1967-68:111

---- MALAYSIA
Alatas, S. H.
Universities: discrepancy between ideal and reality takes alarming turn. MONSA:177
Hamzah Sendut
Some new approaches to university education. MONSA:168
Suffian bin Hashim
University should slow down: call to education planners (Univ. of Malaya, June 20, 1970). MONSA:144

---- SINGAPORE
Toh Chin Chye
The role of the university in a multi-racial society. MONSA:291

Collins, LeRoy
Rout the forces of hate. ARS:157

Collins, Michael See Armstrong, Neil, jt. auth.

COLLOIDS
Zsigmondy, R. A.
Properties of colloids. NOLC 2:45

Colman, Benjamin
Piety and duty of rulers to comfort and encourage the ministry of Christ. POC:412

COLONIALISM
Romulo, C. P.
Bandung address.
CROCK:141

COLONIZATION
Cotton, J.
God's promise to his plantations. ANN 1:107

---- NEW ZEALAND
Vogel, J.
Colonization by public works and immigration.
MACS:42 sel.

COLOR PHOTOGRAPHY
Lippmann, G.
Colour photography.
NOLPH 1:186

COMBUSTION
Semenov, N. N.
Some problems relating to chain reactions and to the theory of combustion.
NOLC 3:487

COMMEMORATIVE ADDRESSES
Adams, J. Q.
Oration at Plymouth (commemoration of the landing of the Pilgrims).
BREWE 1:65; HURH:51
Chapman, J. R.
Coatesville. ARS:163
Frankfurter, F.
John Marshall and the judicial function, September 22, 1955. FRIP:353
Suggestions for preparation of commemorative speech.
MILS:3

COMMENCEMENT ADDRESSES
Alunan, R. R.
Mindanao, the land of promise. CURM:108
Andelson, R. B.
Campus unrest; the erosion of excellence. LINRS:204
Babbidge, H. D.
On thinking big. HOR:121
Benezet, L. T.
The educator's leap of faith.
HOR:107
Biddle, N.
Princeton commencement address. HOW:123
Brandeis, L. D.
Business as a profession.
ANN 13:342
Brown, J. M.
"Beat" generation. HURH:341
Bunche, R. J.
Barriers of race can be surmounted. CAPG:66
Bunting, M. I.
Their questions. HOR:93
Califano, J. A.
Federal support of science and medicine. BA 1977-78:99
Curtis, G. W.
Public duty of educated men.
ALS:179
Dewey, T. E.
Public service. ANN 16:471
Eisenhower, M. S.
A new historical perspective, interdependence. HOR:157
Gannon, A. I.
A Catholic college, yesterday and tomorrow. HOR:78
Goheen, R. F.
Sorting it out. HOR:21
Golden, J. L.
Moments to remember (commencement address-John Glenn High School). BRP:236
Graduates at commencement time.
HNWM:16
Hammarskjöld, D.
Values of nationalism and internationalism (Stanford University commencement address).
HURS:206
Hancher, V. M.
Art of contemplation.
CROCK:132
Hartzog, G. B., Jr.
Finding America.
BA 1972-73:194
Henry, D. D.
Perceptions of the university.
HOR:70
Hesburgh, T. M.
The problems and opportunities on a very interdependent planet.
HOR:142
Service to others.
BA 1979-80:180
Holland, J. H.
Options along the pathway of community involvement.
HOR:8
Howard, J. A.

The new furies: skepticism, criticism, and coercion. LINRST:146
Johnson, L. B.
Great Society (commencement address at University of Michigan). ANN 18:216; CAPG:15; MDV:108; MUS:135
Johnson, M. W.
Faith of the American Negro (at Harvard commencement). FON:742
Keeney, B. C.
Afterword: how to make a commencement speech. HOR:165
Kemeny, J. G.
An optimist looks at America's future. HOR:128
Valedictory to the graduates. HOR:2
Kennedy, J. F.
Intellectual and the politician. BAP:285; LINR:267
Toward a strategy of peace. KEO:312; MDV:2
Kerr, C.
The independent spirit. HOR:114
Perspectives on the prophets of doom. HOR:34
King, M. L., Jr.
The American dream. FON:933
Lippmann, W.
Our world today. MDV:26
McGill, W. J.
Requiem for the counterculture: problems of a new student generation. HOR:66
Manley, A. E.
Charge to the graduates. HOR:6
Meyerson, M.
The ivory tower of Babel. HOR:99
Moos, M.
Restoring the tidemarks of trust. BA 1973-74:148
Ness, F. W.
Freedom and the labyrinth. HOR:87
Odegaard, C. E.
Bridging the generation gap, the march downtown. HOR:42
Paradox (outline of commencement speech). CUB:91
Perkins, J. A.
Bridging the generation gap, how the New Deal became today's establishment. HOR:56
Pogrebin, L. C.
Commencement address. TAC:242
Powell, A. C.
Can any good thing come out of Nazareth? FON:1027; SMHR:154
Rainer, J. C.
Institute of American Indian Arts Commencement exercises, Friday, May 21, 1976. MAES:219
Reinert, P. C.
America, America, how does your garden grow? HOR:82
Roosevelt, F. D.
Italy enters this war. ANN 16:8
Rowan, C. T.
Commencement address (at Howard University, June 5, 1964). HURS:216
Russwurm, J. B.
The condition and prospects of Haiti. FON:33
Sampson, E. S.
Choose one of five. MOP:386; REID:398
Sanford, T.
After Vietnam, a new United States foreign policy. HOR:132
Spencer, S. R., Jr.
A call for new missionaries. BA 1971-72:172
Stevenson, A. E.
Trained intelligence: education and womanpower (Radcliffe College commencement address). MDV:205
Suggestions for preparation of commencement address. MILS:5
Thibeault, M. L.
The hazards of equity. VERD:265
Vargas, J. B.
The role of the army. CURM:98
Weicker, L. P., Jr.
Be a flake ... on behalf of somebody or something. BA 1979-80:187
Wells, H. B.
Charge to the graduates.

HOR:3
White, R.
The educated man in the age of Aquarius. BAAE:271
Wilson, L.
Education for adequacy. HOR:16
Wilson, W.
New call to duty. ALA:77

COMMERCE
Barnave, A. P. J. M.
Commercial politics. BREWE 1:221
Bayard, J. A.
Commerce and naval power. BREWE 1:262
Morgenthau, H., Jr.
Roosevelt monetary program. BAD:23

COMMON LAW See Law and lawyers

COMMONWEALTH OF NATIONS
Lee Kuan Yew
The moral for Commonwealth members and Britain. MONSA:259
A new relevance and a fresh validity for Commonwealth. MONSA:272
Macmillan, H.
"The wind of change." MCB:75

COMMUNICATION
Ashley, L. R. N.
A guided tour of gobbledygook. REID:408
Bacon, W. A.
Language and the lived world. BA 1976-77:174
Bittner, J. R.
The news media and campus unrest. STOT:290
Goldhaber, G. M.
Organizational communication. LINRST:44
Lundy, R. F.
World divided by three (politics, science, and religion). MONS:489
McGraw, H. W.
Business's responsibility in an information society. BA 1977-78:121
Nail, W. A.
What did you say? VER: 272
Oliver, R. T.
Culture and communication. ARS:19

COMMUNICATION IN SCIENCE
Root, T. C.
The failure of scientists to communicate. BA 1977-78:110

COMMUNICATIONS SATELLITES
Stasheff, E.
What will the satellites say? KEO:262

COMMUNION
Frelinghuysen, T.
Revivalist sermon. ANN 1:344

COMMUNISM
Bosman, R. W.
Witch hunt. SCHW:128
Davis, A.
I am a black revolutionary woman. FON:1177
Dondero, G. A.
Modern art shackled to communism. DAVF:302
Eisenhower, D. D.
State of the Union (January 9, 1958). STAT 3:3076
Ford, J. W.
The right of revolution for the Negro people. FON:800
Goh Keng Swee
Elite combat party (Communist Party). MONS:394
Some delusions of the decade of development. MONS:385
Goldwater, B.
Total victory in the Cold War. ANN 18:42
Why we must be stronger militarily. BAS:92 (outline only); LAA:8
Harriman, W. A.
Challenges to peace and freedom. ANN 18:328
Hoover, J. E.
Menace of the Communist Party. ANN 16:451
Jones, W. N.
Why Negroes should support the Communists. FON:785
Legum, C.
Pan-Africanism, the Communists, and the West. ARS:255
McCarthy, J. R.

Annual Kansas Day Republican banquet speech. BOSR:53
Communists in the State Department. ANN 17:16
A conspiracy of blackest infamy (1951). DAVF:304
Muhammad Ghazali bin Shafie
Malaysia and the Asian perspective. MONS:222
Power politics and nation-building (Malaysia). MONS:232
Roosevelt, F. D.
Facing Communism: the true conservative is liberal. BAD:15
Truman, H. S.
Veto of the Internal Security Act. ANN 17:35
Vander Werf, N.
Mistaken enemy. SCHW:171
Youngdahl, L.
United States v. Lattimore. ANN 17:300

---- See also Russia

---- GUATEMALA
Dulles, J. F.
Why the Arbenz government was overthrown in Guatemala. LAA:117

---- RUSSIA
Dulles, J. F.
Containment or liberation? ANN 17:204

COMMUNIST PARTY OF AMERICA
Dondero, G. A.
Communism in our schools (1946). DAVF:296
Jackson, R. H.
The Communist Party is a secret conclave. DAVF:282
To secure the existing order against revolutionary radicalism (1950). DAVF:294

COMPROMISE (ETHICS)
Watterson, H.
The compromises of life. BLY:158

COMPROMISE OF 1850 See Slavery in the United States

Compton, Arthur Holly
X-rays as a branch of optics (Nobel Lecture, Dec. 12, 1927). NOLPH 2:174

COMPTON, ARTHUR HOLLY
Siegbahn, K. M. G.
Presentation [of the Nobel Prize for Physics to Arthur Holly Compton and Charles Thomson Rees Wilson, Dec. 12, 1927]. NOLPH 2:169

COMPUTERS
Sargent, F. W.
The computer and civil liberties. BA 1973-74:141

Conant, James Bryant
Education for a classless society. ANN 16:22
Responds to an introduction. PRS:153
Role of the state in education. CAPG:131
Science and spiritual values. ARS:88

CONDE, LOUIS II DE BOURBON
Boussuet, J. B.
Funeral oration over the Prince of Condé. BREWE 2:557

CONDUCT OF LIFE See Behavior; Character; Charities; Conscience; Courage; Ethics; Honesty; Justice; Life; Love; Man; Patience; Patriotism; Success; Truthfulness and falsehood

CONFEDERATE STATES OF AMERICA
Davis, J.
Final exhortation to the Confederate people. ANN 9:557
Inaugural address of 1861. ANN 9:238; BREWE 5:1656; ECH:137
Stephens, A. H.
Civil rights in the Confederacy. ANN 9:493
On the Confederate Constitution. BREWE 9:3517; ECH:77
Toombs, R.
Robert Toombs' address, to the people of Georgia. ECH:103

CONFERENCE SPEECHES See Congresses and conventions; Debates and debating

CONFLICT OF GENERATIONS See Youth-adult relationship

CONFORMATIONAL ANALYSIS
Barton, D. H. R.
The principles of conformational analysis. NOLC 4:298

CONGRATULATIONS
Brief words of congratulations on special occasions (9 examples). BNH:92

CONGRESSES AND CONVENTIONS
Suggestions for preparation of reports on conventions. PAE:188

Conkling, Roscoe
Against Senator Sumner. BREWE 4:1374
Nomination of U. S. Grant for a third term. BREWE 4:1366
Stalwart standpoint. BREWE 4:1369

Connally, Thomas T. and others (C. Glass)
Censure of Senator Nye. BRR:69

Connolly, Cyril See Sykes, C., jt. auth.

Connor, John T.
Impact on the American economy of the Vietnamization program. BA 1969-70:47

CONSCIENCE
Leenhouts, T.
Men of conscience. SCHW:119
Morgan, C., Jr.
Time to speak. KEO:308

CONSCRIPTION
Cry on the campus. BURT:102
Howarth, D.
2S Draft deferment should be retained. REIR:130
Mannix, D.
Case against conscription. MCA:134
Webster, D.
Against conscription. ANN 4:355
Wirtz, W. W.
Address at Catholic University of America. BA 1966-67:177

CONSERVATION OF NATURAL RESOURCES
Dubos, R.
Theology of the earth. BA 1969-70:83
Hill, J. J.
Natural wealth of the land and its conservation. ANN 13:153
Madison, J.
Agriculture and conservation. ANN 4:503
Roosevelt, T.
Annual message, December 6, 1904. STAT 2:2105
Eighth annual message. STAT 3:2296
Fifth annual message. ANN 13:1; STAT 3:2144
First annual message. ANN 12:433; STAT 2:2014
"I took the Canal Zone." STAT 2:2073
Public domain: the people's heritage. ANN 13:161
Seventh annual message. STAT 3:2240
Schurz, C.
Need for a rational forest policy. ANN 11:200

CONSERVATISM
Coolidge, C.
Have faith in Massachusetts (on being elected President of Massachusetts Senate). BOORA 2:752

CONSERVATIVE PARTY (GREAT BRITAIN)
Beaconsfield, B. D.
Meaning of conservatism. MCB:431
Churchill, Lord R. H. S.
Trust the people speech. MCB:441
Churchill, Sir W. L. S.
The Conservative programme. MCB:464

---- See also Great Britain - Politics and government

Constant, Benjamin
Free speech necessary for good government. BREWE 4:1376

CONSTANT, PAUL HENRY BENJAMIN
Løvland, J. G.
Presentation [of the Nobel Prize for Peace to Baron d'Estournelles de Constant, Dec. 10, 1909]. NOLP 1:216

CONSTITUTION See Names of countries with the subhead Constitution e.g. United States - Constitution

CONSUMER PROTECTION
Andino, J.
How can the government best protect the American consumer? EHN:462; MOPR:387
Crichton, J.
Consumer protection: what Johanna won't read. BA 1965-66:210
Franklin, B. H.
Consumer safety and health. BA 1978-79:133
Nader, R.
Meet the press. BA 1971-72:79

CONSUMERS
Morrison, H. C.
In the pursuit of excellence. BREWW:61
Spray, C.
Consumer education: the farmer's responsibility. BREWW:67

CONTEST SPEECHES
Alconcel, D.
Aquaculture--an answer to the food crisis. BREWW:88
Bark, D. R.
World food crisis. BREWW:219
Bjorklund, J.
Nice people. EHN:158; MOPR:246
Blizzard, E.
Not just a farmer. BREWW:49
Bozeman, M.
Soil--America's lifeblood. BREWW:85
Brown, M.
Famine: a reality, not just a threat. BREWW:168
Carpenter, E.
We are involved in the world food crisis. BREWW:223
Davidson, G.
Farmer, heal thyself! BREWW:165
Depta, M.
Aims and purposes of the FFA. BREWW:157
Dunlap, D. E.
The world needs our help. BREWW:98
Edwards, L.
Libbing. BRYF:489
Ferguson, V.
Women in agriculture. BREWW:122
Fishburn, P.
Land of cattle, land of America. BREWW:105
Francis, H.
Our three goals. BREWW:131
Gould, J. C.
My responsibility as an agricultural citizen. BREWW:147
Grappe, A.
The age of food. BREWW:112
Grass, F.
The sky's the limit. BREWW:115
Harrison, R.
Leadership--a goal for us all. BREWW:150
Hayes, K.
Crossbreeding beef cattle: progress or regression? BREWW:214
Herink, R.
A succession of goals. BREWW:141
Hirschler, P.
How to beautify your farm. BREWW:124
Holt, R.
The second dust bowl. BREWW:137
Howell, W.
A new century in agriculture. BREWW:211
Ivens, M.
I still believe in the future of

farming. BREWW:195
Kermicle, J.
Bridging the gap. BREWW:94
Kubicek, K.
Global crisis. BREWW:128
Lipton, J.
Land preservation in the Northeast. BREWW:75
Lucas, M.
The waste of our precious farmland. BREWW:102
McKinney, S. M.
Soils--our basic natural resources--the key to man's survival. BREWW:187
Madrid, S.
I am proud to be a part of it. BREWW:153
Mathias, T.
Is agriculture on its way out? BREWW:64
Meyer, S.
What leadership means to me. BREWW:171
Morelli, L.
Vocational agriculture, the FFA, and our free enterprise system. BREWW:78
Morgan, M.
Building a better rural community today for a better agriculture tomorrow. BREWW:198
Morrison, Howard C.
In the pursuit of excellence. BREWW:61
Morse, D.
Lab farms in vocational agriculture. BREWW:144
Neal, J.
DDT: friend or foe? BREWW:183
Palovesik, S.
Ripples of hope. BREWW:179
Price, S.
Agriculture--the real answer to starvation. BREWW:161
Rindo, J. P.
Life, librium, and the pursuit of happiness. LINRST:230
Roper, B.
A fable come true. BREWW:201
Rush, W.
Feeding the hungry world. BREWW:91
Slabach, D.
Five hundred miles south. BREWW:208
Smith, E. R.
United we stand, divided we fall. BREWW:134
Spray, C.
Consumer education: the farmer's responsibility. BREWW:67
A new crisis in agriculture. BREWW:71
Stratton, R. D.
Food: a world crisis. BREWW:81
Stratton, T.
Agriculture--America's greatest tool. BREWW:109
Trafton, C.
The moral dimensions of the world food problem. BREWW:206
Warren, P.
Bring forth the children. BRYF:485; MOPR:368
Wivell, C. A.
World hunger: a question of rights. BREWW:119
Wright, T.
"Viva la Huelga." BREWW:174

CONVERSATION
Griswold, A. W.
On conversation--chiefly academic. CROCK:75

CONVOCATION ADDRESSES
Dickey, J. S.
Betrayal of idealism (convocation address). BA 1967-68:136
Gallaher, B. G.
Memorial convocation address (on Martin Luther King, Jr.). BA 1967-68:169
Okpara, M. I.
Progress without tears: address at convocation, University of Nigeria. EMP:138

Conwell, Russell Herman
Acres of diamonds (Philadelphia, 1925). ANN 11:271; BEN:159; HURH:202
"Money is power and you ought to be reasonably ambitious to have it." Same as his Acres of diamonds

Cook, Joseph
Ultimate America.
BREWE 4:1381

Coolidge, Calvin
Destiny of America. ANN 14:409
Fifth annual message.
STAT 3:2710
First annual message.
STAT 3:2642
Fourth annual message.
STAT 3:2690
Have faith in Massachusetts (on being elected President of Massachusetts Senate).
BOORA 2:752
Inaugural address.
USINAU:215; USINAUG:215
Intervention in Nicaragua.
ANN 14:519
Second annual message.
STAT 3:2655
Sixth annual message.
STAT 3:2727
Third annual message.
STAT 3:2669
Veto of the McNary-Haugen Bill. Same as his Vetoing the farmer: Nonplanning as a way of life
Vetoing the farmer: Nonplanning as a way of life.
ANN 14:568

COOLIDGE, CALVIN
Rogers, W.
Nominating Calvin Coolidge.
BAP:298; BAPR:366

Cooper, Lady Diana See Sykes, C., jt. auth.

COOPERATION
Casely-Hayford, J. E.
Leadership and African cooperation. EMP:49
Everett, E.
Universal and uncoerced cooperation. BREWE 6:2115

Copely, James S.
Responds to an introduction.
PRS:152

Corbin, Francis
Answering Patrick Henry.
BREWE 4:1394

Cordiner, Ralph J.
Responds to an introduction.
PRS:137

Cori, Carl Ferdinand and others (Gerty Theresa Cori-Radnitz)
Polysaccharide phosphorylase (Nobel Lecture, Dec. 11, 1947). NOLM 3:186

CORI, CARL FERDINAND
Theorell, H.
Presentation [of the Nobel Prize for Physiology or Medicine to Carl Ferdinand Cori, Gerty Theresa Cori-Radnitz, and Bernardo Alberto Houssay, Dec. 11, 1947]. NOLM 3:179

Cori-Radnitz, Gerty Theresa See Cori, Carl Ferdinand

CORI-RADNITZ, GERTY THERESA
Theorell, H.
Presentation [of the Nobel Prize for Physiology or Medicine to Carl Ferdinand Cori, Gerty Theresa Cori-Radnitz, and Bernardo Alberto Houssay, Dec. 11, 1947]. NOLM 3:179

CORN LAWS
Beaconsfield, B. D.
Third reading of the Corn Importation Bill. BRYH:371; MCB:211
Cobden, R.
Effects of Corn Laws in agriculture. STRM:246
Effects of protection in agriculture. MCB:189
Peel, R.
On the repeal of the Corn Laws. BREWE 8:3148; JAE:102

Cornish, Dudley T.
A warrior against fate (Pittsburg, Kansas, Nov. 16, 1975).
BA 1975-76:207

CORPORATIONS
Black, J. S.
Corporations under eminent domain. BREWE 2:471

CORRUPTION See Civil service; Crime and criminals; Elections - Corrupt practices; Watergate

CORTISONE
Hench, P. S.
The reversibility of certain rheumatic and nonrheumatic conditions by the use of cortisone or of the pituitary adrenocorticotropic hormone. NOLM 3:311
Kendall, E. C.
The development of cortisone as a therapeutic agent. NOLM 3:270

Corwin, Thomas
Against dismembering Mexico. Same as his War with Mexico
War with Mexico. (Senate, Feb. 11, 1847). HOW:203; BREWE 4:1405

COSMIC PHYSICS
Powell, C. F.
The cosmic radiation. NOLPH 3:144

COSMIC RAYS
Hess, V. F.
Unsolved problems in physics: tasks for the immediate future in cosmic ray studies. NOLPH 2:360

Costley, William
A plan for a defense movement. (San Francisco, Sept. 1902). FON:640

Costo, Rupert
Indian history--fact or fiction. MAES:321

Cotton, John
Divine right to occupy the land. Same as his God's promise to his plantations
God's promise to his plantations. ANN 1:107
A treatise of the covenant of grace (Boston, 1630's). JON:48
Viall I: the powring out of the seven vials or An exposition, with an application of the 16th Chapter of Revelation. POC:363
The way of life (1627-1630). JON:121

Coughlin, Charles E.
The menace of the World Court (1935). (Radio address, Jan. 27, 1935). DAVF:249
Money changers in the temple. ANN 15:388

Coulter, Thomas H.
Introducing Marguerite (Maggie) Higgins to the Executives' Club of Chicago. LYI:113

COUNTRY LIFE See Rural life

COURAGE
Calvin, J.
Necessity for courage. BREWE 3:928
Leenhouts, T.
Men of conscience. SCHW:119

Cournand, André Frederic
Control of the pulmonary circulation in man with some remarks on methodology (Nobel Lecture, Dec. 11, 1956). NOLM 3:529

COURNAND, ANDRE FREDERIC
Liljestrand, G.
Presentation [of the Nobel Prize for Physiology or Medicine to André Frederic Cournand, Werner Theodor Otto Forssmann, and Dickinson Woodruff Richards Jr., Dec. 11, 1956]. NOLM 3:501

COURTS
Brewer, D. J.
Independent judiciary as the salvation of the nation. ANN 11:423
Burger, W. E.
State of the Judiciary. BA 1970-71:13
Roosevelt, T.
Eighth annual message. STAT 3:2296
Thomson, T. J. B.
Spirit of humanity (opening of Federal Court of Malaysia). MOND:285
Warren, E.
Federal court congestion. ANN 17:487

---- See also Law and lawyers; Also names of courts e.g. United States - Supreme Court

---- PHILIPPINE ISLANDS
Osias, C.
Justice and separation of powers. CURM:190
Yamzon, V.
The lawyer shall never retreat. CURM:323

Cousin, Victor
Eloquence and the fine arts. BREWE 4:1419
Foundations of law. BREWE 4:1428
Liberty an inalienable right. BREWE 4:1426
True politics. BREWE 4:1431

COWARDICE
Davies, S.
Curse of cowardice. ANN 2:23; POC:534

Cox, Archibald
Can the dream survive? (Boston, Mass., July 4, 1979). BA 1979-80:157
Creative in law and government. (Amherst, Mass., Jan. 22, 1974). BA 1973-74:49

Cox, Harvey See Sevareid, E., jt. auth.

Cox, Samuel Sullivan
Against the ironclad oath. BREWE 4:1436
Sermon on the Mount. BREWE 4:1446
Stephen A. Douglas and his place in history. BREWE 4:1449

Coxe, Tench
Prospects for American manufacturing. ANN 3:196

Cragg, Richard T.
Introduces Judge Lester H. Loble of Juvenile Court of Helena, Montana. PRS:38
Presents Chet Huntley. LYI:109
Presents Cyril Northcote. LYI:45

Cram, Ralph Adams
What is a free man? ANN 15:498

Cramer, John See Sanford, N., jt. auth.

Cranmer, Thomas
Against the fear of death. BREWE 4:1458
Forgiveness of injuries. BREWE 4:1459
Speech at the stake. BREWE 4:1455; BRYH:60

Crary, Daniel R.
Plague of people. LINR:220

Crawford, Frederick C.
Jobs, freedom, and opportunity. ANN 16:132

Crawford, William Harris
Issue and control of money under the Constitution. BREWE 4:1462

CRAWLEY, SIR FRANCIS
Waller, E.
Tyrant's plea, necessity (impeaching Justice Crawley). BREWE 10:3709

CREATION
Helmholtz, H. L. F.
Mystery of creation. BREWE 7:2465

CREDIT
Witherspoon, J.
Public credit under the Confederation. BREWE 10:3912

Cremer, William Randal
The progress and advantages of international arbitration (Nobel Lecture for 1903, Jan. 15, 1905). NOLP 1:46

CREMER, WILLIAM RANDAL
Løvland, J. G.
Welcome [presenting the Nobel Prize for Peace, 1903, to William Randal Cremer, Jan. 15, 1905]. NOLP 1:45

Crichton, John
Consumer protection: what Johanna won't read. BA 1965-66:210

Crick, Francis Harry Compton
On the genetic code (Nobel Lecture, Dec. 11, 1962). NOLM 3:811

CRICK, FRANCIS HARRY COMPTON
Engström, A.
Presentation [of the Nobel Prize for Physiology or Medicine to Francis Harry Compton Crick, James Dewey Watson, and Maurice Hugh Frederick Wilkins, Dec. 11, 1962]. NOLM 3:751

CRIME AND CRIMINALS
Barry, R.
Sentencing of "Ned" Kelly. MCA:74
Bingham, J. A.
Against the assassins of President Lincoln. BREWE 2:445
Chew, S.
Speech, &c. POC:77
Darrow, C.
Crime and criminals. ARS:142
Izenbart, L.
Real criminal. SCHW:101
Marvin, R.
Man's other society. MOP:377
Murphy, P. V.
What the police expect of the citizenry. BA 1970-71:122
Roosevelt, T.
Sixth annual message. STAT 3:2194
Stanmeyer, W. A.
Urban crime: its causes and control. LINRST:303
Why go second class? (Outline of speech to persuade City of Del Norte it should establish a Juvenile Court). CUB:42
Woodmason, C.
You are to take these free booters and desperadoes. POC:548

CRIMEAN WAR, 1853-1856
Bright, J.
Russia: negotiations at Vienna, House of Commons, February 23, 1855. AND:61
Lyndhurst, J. S. C.
Russia and the Crimean War. BREWE 7:2842

Crispi, Francesco
At the unveiling of Garibaldi's statue. BREWE 4:1467
Socialism and discontent. BREWE 4:1469

CRITICISM
Howard, J. A.
The new furies: skepticism, criticism, and coercion. LINRST:146

Crittenden, John Jordan
Against warring on the weak. BREWE 4:1477
Compromise resolutions. Same as his On the Crittenden Compromise
Henry Clay and the nineteenth century spirit. BREWE 4:1472
On the Crittenden Compromise. ANN 9:221; BLY:71
Speech on his resolution. Same as his On the Crittenden Compromise
Union at any price. ANN 9:246

Crittenden, Thomas T.
Trade and commerce for the southwestern states. ANN 11:16

Croarkin, Walter
Presents Frank F. Rosenthal. LYI:165
Presents William David O'Brien. LYI:163

Crockett, David
Fourth of July oration, 1834 (Philadelphia, July 4, 1834). HAW:136
Raccoon in a bag. BREWE 4:1482

Crockett, George W.
Racism in the law. (Wayne State Univ., Detroit, Oct. 15, 1968). FON:1131

Cromwell, Oliver
Address to Parliament, September 4, 1654. BRYH:144
Debating whether or not to become King of England. BREWE 4:1485
On the dissolution of Parliament (First Protectorate Parliament). (Jan. 22, 1655). CLAYP:14
Speech on the dissolution of the First Protectorate Parliament, January 22, 1655. Same as his On the dissolution of Parliament (First Protectorate Parliament)
Speech to the First Protectorate Parliament. Same as Address to Parliament, September 4, 1654

CROMWELL, RICHARD
Vane, H.
Against Richard Cromwell. BREWE 10:3684

Cronbach, Abraham
Of Earth, earthy and of Heaven, heavenly. WALE:30

Crooks, John
Defense of "The death of a President." REIR:182

Crosby, Glenn A.
The uses of adversity (Pullman, Wash., March 8, 1976). BA 1976-77:156

CROSS, WILBUR L.
Butler, N. M.
Presents Wilbur L. Cross. LYI:97

Crosswaith, Frank R.
The Negro labor committee. (March 6, 1952). FON:857

CRUCIFIXION
Albertus Magnus
Meaning of the crucifixion. BREWE 1:147

Crummell, Alexander
The Black woman of the South: her neglects and her needs. (Ocean Grove, N. J., August 15, 1883). FON:479

CRUSADES
Bernard, Saint
Why another crusade? BAS:43 (outline only); BREWE 2:432

CTESIPHON
Aeschines
Against Ctesiphon. BREWE 1:114; COG:120

CUBA
Castro, F.
Cuba is no longer an American colony. LAA:127
Give me liberty or give me death! BRN:136
Clemens, J.
Cuba and "manifest destiny." BREWE 4:1292
Cleveland, G.
Fourth annual message (second term). ANN 12:119; STAT 2:1824
Garnet, H. H.
A plea in behalf of the Cuban revolution. FON:380
Giddings, J. R.
Slavery and the annexation of Cuba. BREWE 6:2258
Lodge, H. C.
For intervention in Cuba. ANN 12:85
McKinley, W.
First annual message. ANN 12:161; STAT 2:1858
Second annual message. STAT 2:1881
Third annual message. STAT 2:1922

---- See also United States - Foreign relations - Cuba

CUFFE, PAUL
Williams, P.
A tribute to Captain Paul Cuffe. FON:28

Cullman, Howard S.
Presents Roger L. Stevens. LYI:29

Culpeper, John See Colepeper, John

CULTURAL RELATIONS
Thayer, R. H.
America's cultural relations abroad. ANN 17:545

CULTURE
Choate, R.
State and mental culture. ANN 17:545
Huxley, T. H.
Science and culture. MCB:376
Oliver, R. T.
Culture and communication. ARS:19
Tan Siew Sin
Meeting place of cultures. MONS:115
Thomas, D.
Life among the culture vultures. ANN 17:239
Young, O. D.
How we meet ourselves (semi-centennial of Hendrix College). HURH:227

Curie, Marie
Radium and the new concepts in chemistry (Nobel Lecture, Dec. 11, 1911). NOLC 1:202

CURIE, MARIE
Dahlgren, E. W.
Presentation [of the Nobel Prize for Chemistry to Marie Sklodowska Curie, Dec. 11, 1911]. NOLC 1:199
Harding, W. G.
Presents Marie S. Curie. LYI:179
Törnebladh, H. R.
Presentation [of the Nobel Prize for Physics to Antoine Henri Becquerel, Pierre Curie and Marie Sklodowska-Curie, Dec. 11, 1903]. NOLPH 1:47

Curie, Pierre
Radioactive substances, especially radium (Nobel Lecture for 1903, June 6, 1905). NOLPH 1:73

CURIE, PIERRE
Törnebladh, H. R.
Presentation [of the Nobel Prize for Physics to Antoine Henri Becquerel, Pierre Curie and Marie Sklodowska-Curie, Dec. 11, 1903]. NOLPH 1:47

Curran, John Philpot
Against pensions. BREWE 4:1543
Diversions of a Marquis. BREWE 4:1539
England and English liberties--in the case of Rowan. BREWE 4:1546
Farewell to the Irish Parliament. BREWE 4:1552
For Peter Finnerty and free speech. BREWE 4:1537
In the case of Justice Johnson--Civil liberty and arbitrary arrests. BREWE 4:1499
Liberties of the indolent. BREWE 4:1550
On government by attachment. BREWE 4:1557

CURRENCY See Money

CURRENCY QUESTION See Silver

Curtice, Harlow
Automotive research at General Motors. ANN 17:379

Curtin, John
We are fighting mad. MCA:154

Curtis, Benjamin Robbins
Defense of President Johnson. BREWE 4:1563

Curtis, George William
Duty of the American scholar. ANN 8:411
Eulogy on Wendell Phillips. BREWE 4:1571
His sovereignty under his hat. BREWE 4:1570
Liberty under the law. BAS:141 (outline only); LINS:249
Public duty of educated men. ALS:179
Puritan principle: liberty under law. Same as his Liberty under the law
Wendell Phillips as a history-maker. Same as his Eulogy on Wendell Phillips

Curzon of Kedleston, George and others (Earl of Halsbury, Marquess of Landsdowne, Viscount Morley, and Earl of Rosebery)
Debate on the Parliament Bill. (H. of Lords, August 9-10, 1911). MCB:169

Cushing, Caleb
England and America in China.
BREWE 4:1583
Extermination of the Indians.
BREWE 4:1584
Primordial rights of the universal people.
BREWE 4:1577

CUSTER, GEORGE A.
Tanner, B. T.
The Sioux's revenge.
FON:443

Cutforth, René
Illuminations. MDYG:35

CYCLOTRON
Lawrence, E. O.
The evolution of the cyclotron.
NOLPH 2:430

Cyprian, Saint, Bp. of Carthage
Unshackled living.
BREWE 4:1588

Cyril, Saint, Bp. of Jerusalem
Infinite artifices of nature.
BREWE 4:1594

- D -

D-DAY See World War, 1939-1945 - Campaigns - Western front

Dabney, Virginius
Facts and the founding fathers.
(Williamsburg, Va., Feb. 8, 1975). BA 1974-75:168

Dahlgren, E. W.
Presentation [of the Nobel Prize for Chemistry to Marie Sklodowska Curie, Dec. 11, 1911]. NOLC 1:199
Presentation [of the Nobel Prize for Physics to Wilhelm Wien, Dec. 11, 1911].
NOLPH 1:271

DAKOTA INDIANS
Tanner, B. T.
The Sioux's revenge.
FON:443

Dale, Sir Henry Hallett
Some recent extensions of the chemical transmission of the effects of nerve impulses (Nobel Lecture, Dec. 12, 1936).
NOLM 2:402

DALE, SIR HENRY HALLETT
Liljestrand, G.
Presentation [of the Nobel Prize for Physiology or Medicine to Sir Henry Hallett Dale and Otto Loewe, Dec. 12, 1936].
NOLM 2:397

Dale, James
Rehearsing with George Bernard Shaw. MDYG:44

DALEN, NILS GUSTAF
Söderbaum, H. G.
Presentation [of the Nobel Prize for Physics to Nils Gustaf Dalen, 1912]. NOLPH 1:293

Dallas, George M.
Pennsylvania idea.
BREWE 4:1599

Dam, Henrik
The discovery of vitamin K, its biological functions and therapeutical application (Nobel Lecture for 1943, Dec. 12, 1946).
NOLM 3:8

Damiani, Peter, Saint
New Testament history as allegory.
BREWE 4:1606
Secret of true greatness.
BREWE 4:1605

Damrin, Dora E.
The James Scholars and the university (Univ. of Illinois, Dec. 4, 1964). BRYF:528; BRYO:243

DAMS
Brandeis, L. D.
Ashwander rules. ANN 15:350
Roosevelt, F. D.
President reminds Congress of the comprehensive program of the Tennessee Valley Authority.
BAD:21

Daniel, John Warwick
Dedication of the Washington

monument. BREWE 4:1608
Was Jefferson Davis a traitor? BREWE 4:1615

Daniels, Josephus
Presents Sir Norman Birkett. LYI:135

Danton, George Jacques
Against imprisonment for debt. BREWE 5:1628
Education, free and compulsory. BREWE 5:1629
Freedom of worship. BREWE 5:1631
How can France be saved? (National Convention, Salle du Manege, Paris, March 27, 1793). BRN:56
Let France be free. BREWE 5:1626
Squeezing the sponge. BREWE 5:1631
To dare again, ever to dare. BREWE 5:1625

D'Arcy, Martin See Sykes, C., jt. auth.

Darrow, Clarence
Against capital punishment. BEN:149
Crime and criminals. ARS:142
Defense of Richard Loeb and Nathan Leopold. (Chicago, 1924). HURH:196
"I am pleading that we overcome cruelty with kindness and hatred with love." Same as his Defense of Richard Loeb and Nathan Leopold
To the jury; self-defense. GRG:31

DARTMOUTH COLLEGE
Marshall, J.
Trustees of Dartmouth College v. Woodward: opinion for the Supreme Court. ANN 4:522
Plumer, W.
State control of Dartmouth College. ANN 4:420
Webster, D.
Dartmouth College case. ANN 4:477; BREWE 10:3860

Dato Azmi See Azmi, Bin Haji Mohamed

Dato David S. Marshall See Marshall, David Saul

Dato Sir Clough Thuraisingham See Thuraisingham, Ernest Emmanuel Sir Clough

DAUGHTERS OF THE AMERICAN REVOLUTION
Roosevelt, F. D.
Immigrants and revolutionists. ALA:93

Davenport, John
Responds to an introduction. PRS:155
The saint's anchor-hold (1661). JON:147

David, John K.
Responds to an introduction at a Newcomen Society dinner. PRS:151

Davidson, Gregg
Farmer, heal thyself! BREWW:165

Davies, Samuel
Curse of cowardice. ANN 2:23; POC:534

Davis, Angela
I am a black revolutionary woman. (Dec., 1970 and Jan. 5, 1971-2 statements). FON:1177
The legacy of George Jackson. (August, 1971). FON:1191

Davis, Benjamin J.
The Negro people on the march. (New York, June 23, 1956). FON:902

Davis, Chester R.
Presents Will Durant. LYI:56

Davis, David
Ex parte Milligan, 1866: opinion for the court. ANN 10:31
On appeal from the caucus. BREWE 5:1634

Davis, George R.
Vietnam War: a Christian perspective. VI:46

Davis, Henry Winter
Constitutional difficulties of reconstruction. BREWE 5:1647
Reasons for refusing to part company with the South. BREWE 5:1642

Davis, Jefferson
Against Clay and compromise. BREWE 5:1660
Announcing the secession of Mississippi. Same as his On withdrawing from the Union
Final exhortation to the Confederate people. ANN 9:557
"If you will have it thus, we will invoke the God of our fathers." Same as his On withdrawing from the Union
Inaugural address in 1861. ANN 9:238; BREWE 5:1656; ECH:137
Message to Congress, April 29, 1861. ANN 9:259
On withdrawing from the Union (Washington, Jan. 21, 1861). BAS:71 (outline only); BREWE 5:1651; ECH:72; HURH:109
Speech of President Davis at Richmond, June 1st, 1861. ECH:146
War message. Same as his Message to Congress, April 29, 1861

DAVIS, JEFFERSON
Chandler, Z.
On Jefferson Davis. BREWE 3:1030
Daniel, J. W.
Was Jefferson Davis a traitor? BREWE 4:1615

Davis, John W.
Presents Lester B. Pearson. LYI:220

Davis, Ossie
Malcolm was our manhood, our living black manhood. (Harlem, Feb. 27, 1965). FON:1010

Davis, Samuel H.
We must assert our rightful claims and plead our own cause. (Buffalo, N.Y., August 15-19, 1843). FON:77

Davisson, Clinton Joseph
The discovery of electron waves (Nobel Lecture, Dec. 13, 1937). NOLPH 2:387

DAVISSON, CLINTON JOSEPH
Pleijel, H.
Presentation [of the Nobel Prize for Physics to Clinton Joseph Davisson and George Paget Thomson, Dec. 13, 1937]. NOLPH 2:387

Davitt, Michael
Ireland a nation, self-chartered and self-ruled. BREWE 5:1666

Dawes, Charles Gates
Acceptance [of the Nobel Prize for Peace, 1925, Dec. 10, 1926]. NOLP 1:399

DAWES, CHARLES GATES
Nansen, F.
Speech at Award Ceremony [presenting the Nobel Prize for Peace to Joseph Austen Chamberlain and Charles Gates Dawes for 1925, Dec. 10, 1926]. NOLP 1:383

Dawes, Henry Laurens
Tariff Commission of 1880. BREWE 5:1671

Dawson, Mathew
My profession. (Baylor University). CAPB:363

Day, James E.
Introduces G. Keith Funston, president New York Stock Exchange. PRS:10
Introduces John L. Lewis, American Labor leader. LYI:61

DAY, JAMES R.
Milburn, J. G.
Presents James R. Day. LYI:90

Day, William R. See McKenna, J., Jt. auth.

Dayton, William L.
Arraigning President Polk.
BREWE 5:1676
Issues against slavery forced by the Mexican War.
BREWE 5:1679

DDT
Neal, J.
DDT: friend or foe?
BREWW:183

Deakin, Alfred
For a white Australia.
MCA:88
For the Federal Constitution.
MCA:84

DEAKIN, ALFRED
Hughes, W. M.
Australian Judas. MCA:125

Dean, Vera Micheles
Minds of the non-western world.
ARS:234

DEATH
Albertus Magnus.
Blessed dead. BREWE 1:149
Arnold, T.
Realities of life and death.
BREWE 1:173
Chrysostom, J.
Blessing of death.
BREWE 3:1138
Cranmer, T.
Against the fear of death.
BREWE 4:1458
Everybody dies. BURT:178
Trumbull, L.
Announcing the death of Douglas. BREWE 9:3654

DEATH OF GOD THEOLOGY
Bosley, H.
Is God really dead?
BA 1965-66:157

DEBATES AND DEBATING
Eliezer, C. J.
Democratic societies and debating societies.
MONS:262
Ford, G. R.
The third presidential debate.
BA 1976-77:30
Goodman, J. B.
Broadcast journalism: serving the democratic process.
BA 1976-77:52
Klayton, R. J.
Bureau of Forests and Waters should control pests by biological means rather than pesticides. BAS:188 (outline only)
Macios, M. A.
Model studies of structural design and construction should be conducted prior to the building of structure rather than on the site studies made after the completion of the project.
BAS:193 (outline only)
Suggestions for group discussion.
PAE:192
Weicker, L. P.
Televised debates.
BA 1976-77:61
Zwerling, J. C.
Federal Government should continue its present housing program for low-income groups rather than change to the proposed rent subsidy plan.
BAS:196 (outline only)

DeBeer, Sir Gavin
Atlantis. MDYG:272

DeBow, James D. B.
That feeling of hostility. CUR:52

DeBroglie, Louis
The wave nature of the electron (Nobel Lecture, Dec. 12, 1929). NOLPH 2:244

DE BROGLIE, LOUIS
Oseen, C. W.
Presentation [of the Nobel Prize for Physics to Louis-Victor de Broglie, Dec. 12, 1929].
NOLPH 2:241

Debs, Eugene V.
Capitalism and socialism. Same as his The Issue
"I am prepared to receive your sentence." Same as his On receiving sentence
The issue. ANN 13:137
On receiving sentence. (Chicago, Sept. 1918). HURH:183

DEBS, EUGENE V.
Brewer, D. J.

In Re Debs: opinion for the court. ANN 12:18

DEBTS
Danton, G. J.
Against imprisonment for debt. BREWE 5:1628

Debye, Petrus Josephus Wilhelmus
Methods to determine the electrical and geometrical structure of molecules (Nobel Lecture, Dec. 12, 1936). NOLC 2:383

DEBYE, PETRUS JOSEPHUS WILHELMUS
Westgren, A.
Presentation [of the Nobel Prize for Chemistry to Petrus Josephus Wilhelmus Debye, Dec. 12, 1936]. NOLC 2:379

DECISION-MAKING
Rusk, D.
Formulating foreign policy. ANN 18:20

DEDICATION ADDRESSES
Dedication of a musical instrument. BNH:65
Greetings to people on day of dedication. BOS:67
Quirino, E.
Commemorating a national event. CURM:239
Suggestions for preparation of a speech of dedication. MILS:7

---- BRIDGES
Roosevelt, F. D.
Quarantining the aggressors. ANN 15:502; BEN:93; BOORA 2:847; ROD:263

---- BUILDINGS
Brennan, W. J., Jr.
Conciliation between the press and the law. BA 1979-80:119
Califano, J. A.
A tribute to the man of the people. BA 1977-78:197
Cornish, D. T.
A warrior against fate. BA 1975-76:207
Curtice, H.
Automotive research at General Motors. ANN 17:379
Dedication services of a building. BNH:61
Dedication services of a Christian home. BNH:59
Dedications of a building. BOS:61
Holmes, O. W., Jr.
Path of the law. BOORA 2:593
Lee Kuan Yew
Lesson we have to learn (opening new Science Tower at University of Singapore). MONS:361
Livingston, H. J.
Responds to an introduction and speaks briefly at the dedication of a new manufacturing plant. PRS:130

---- CEMETERIES
Lincoln, A.
Gettysburg address. See Lincoln, A. Gettysburg address

---- CHURCHES
Appreciation on a day of dedication (3 examples). BNH:68
Dedication of a Christian home. BOS:59
Dedication of a pastor's study and church office. BNH:66
Greetings to people on day of dedication (2 examples). BNH:67
Hildebert of Lavardin
Rebecca at the well. BREWE 7:2502

---- CORNERSTONES
Roosevelt, T.
Man with the muck-rake. ARS:102; GRG:24; HURH:291; LINS:283; OLIS:217
Seward, W. H.
Prosperity and education. ANN 6:140

---- EXHIBITIONS
Washington, B. T.
Address at the opening of the Atlanta Exposition. ANN 12:9; BAPRR:255; BAS:77 (outline only); BRYF:492; FON:577; LINS:263; OE:82; SMHV:94

---- LIBRARIES
Dedication of a library (2 examples). BNH:64
Dedications of a library. BOS:64
Nixon, R. M.
Campus revolutionaries. BAAGB:386

---- MONUMENTS
Abdul Rahman, T.
Lest we forget (at unveiling ceremony of National monument in Kuala Lumpur). MONS:34
Blair, F. P.
Deathbed of Benton. BREWE 2:514
Daniel, J. W.
Dedication of the Washington monument. BREWE 4:1608
Douglass, F.
Address for the unknown dead. ALA:51
Oration in memory of Abraham Lincoln (at unveiling of Freedman's monument, Washington, D.C.). FRIP:242
Evangelista, T.
The needs of a nation. CURM:160
McKinley, W.
American patriotism (at dedication of Cuyahoga County Soldiers' and Sailors' monument in Cleveland). BREWE 8:2899
Grant (at dedication of Grant monument in New York City). BREWE 8:2905
Webster, D.
Bunker Hill monument. BREWE 10:3828; HURH:62; LINS:145

---- MUSICAL INSTRUMENTS
Dedications of a musical instrument. BOS:65

---- PARKS
Roosevelt, T.
New nationalism (at dedication of John Brown Memorial Park, Osawatomic, Kansas). ANN 13:250; BOORA 2:711

---- PASTOR'S STUDY
Dedications of a pastor's study and church office. BOS:66

---- SCULPTURE
Haydon, H.
Testimony of sculpture. MOP:384

---- STATUES
Blair, F. P.
Character and work of Benton. BREWE 2:509
Choate, J. H.
Farragut. BREWE 3:1109
Crispi, F.
At the unveiling of Garibaldi's statue. BREWE 4:1467
Depew, C. M.
Unveiling the Statue of Liberty. BREWE 3:1782

DEFEAT
Houston, S.
On his defeat as a Union candidate. BREWE 7:2530

DEFECTORS, POLITICAL
Ward, E. J.
Petrov case. MCA:196

DEFENSE, SPEECHES OF
Adams, J.
On the Boston Massacre. BREWE 1:45; POC:108
Aiken, F. A.
Defense of Mrs. Mary E. Surratt. BREWE 1:120
Andocides
On the mysteries. SAG:61
Bernard, F.
Speech to the Council and House of Representatives. POC:227
Brougham and Vaux, H. P. B.
Closing argument for Queen Caroline. BREWE 2:665
Brown, J.
Last speech at Charleston, West Virginia. ALA:21; ANN 9:143; BOS:44; HURH:103
Burke, E.
Principle in politics: speech at Bristol, previous to the election, 1780 (defends his Parliamentary conduct). BREWE 2:812; BRYH:211
Cicero, M. T.
For the poet Archias.

BREWE 3:1189
Cobbett, W.
Man on the tower (defending himself against a charge of libel). BREWE 4:1321
Cranmer, T.
Speech at the stake. BREWE 4:1455; BRYH:60
Crooks, J.
Defense of "The death of a President." REIR:182
Curran, J. P.
England and English liberties --in the case of Rowan. BREWE 4:1546
In the case of Justice Johnson--civil liberty and arbitrary arrests. BREWE 4:1499
Curtis, B. R.
Defence of President Johnson. BREWE 4:1563
Darrow, C.
Defense of Richard Loeb and Nathan Leopold. HURH:196
To the jury; self-defense. GRG:31
Debs, E. V.
On receiving sentence. HURH:183
Demosthenes
On the crown. BREWE 5:1686; COG:151
Deseze, R.
Defending Louis XVI. BREWE 5:1811
Dexter, S.
"Higher law" of self-defense. BREWE 5:1825
Emmet, R.
Protest against sentence as a traitor. BREWE 6:2030
Engel, G.
Address at trial, Chicago, October 7-9, 1886. ACC:43; PAF:37
Erskine, T.
Free speech and fundamental rights: defense of Tom Paine. BREWE 6:2069; CLAYP:166
Homicidal insanity (J. Hadfield). BREWE 6:2058; BRYH:294
In defense of Thomas Hardy. BREWE 6:2066
Speech in behalf of John Stockdale. BREWE 6:2050
Evarts, W. M.
Weakest spot in the American system (defense at impeachment of A. Johnson). BREWE 6:2082
Fielden, S.
Address at trial, Chicago, October 7-9, 1886. ACC:49; PAF:41
Fischer, A.
Address at trial, Chicago, October 7-9, 1886. ACC:36; PAF:32
Garry, C. R.
In defense of Huey Newton. ERP:161
Gibbons, J.
Defense of the Knights of Labor. ANN 11:131
Grattan, H.
Invective against Corry. BREWE 6:2330
Hamilton, W.
A defense of the Negro. FON:26
Hampden, J.
Patriot's duty defined: against own impeachment. BREWE 6:2385
Harper, R. G.
Defending Judge Chase. BREWE 6:2425
Harrison, T.
Speech on the scaffold. BREWE 6:2421
Holborne, R.
In defense of John Hampden. BREWE 7:2524
Houston, S.
His defense at the Bar of the House. BREWE 7:2532
Johnson, L. B.
A president defends his policies by argument from authorities. JEF:331; JEFF:316
Kamin, L.
Defense of the Jew. CAPB:366
Langston, C. H.
Should colored men be subject to the pains and penalties of the Fugitive Slave Law? FON:208
Lewis, D.
His speech on the scaffold. BREWE 7:2772
Lingg, L.
Address at trial, Chicago, October 7-9, 1886. ACC:39;

PAF:34
Logan, John, Chief of the Mingoes
On the murder of his family. ALA:9; BOORA 1:62; BREWE 7:2569
Luther, M.
Before the Diet of Worms. BREWE 7:2829
MacArthur, D.
Defends his conduct of the war in Korea. ALS:243; ANN 17:79; ARS:279; BAS:82 (outline only); BEN:113; BOSR:22; GRG:88; HURH:293; HURS:214; LINS:337
Mackintosh, J.
In behalf of free speech: on the trial of Jean Peltier accused of libelling Napoleon Bonaparte. BREWE 8:2919
Mirabeau, H. G. R.
Against the charge of treason. BREWE 8:3039
More, T.
Speech when on trial for life. BREWE 8:3062
Morse, W. L.
Rejoiner to Joseph Alsop's attack. BRR:72
Verbiage of defense and attack. BRR:71
Neebe, O.
Address at trial, Chicago, October 7-9, 1886. ACC:29; PAF:28
Nixon, R. M.
Apologia. MAC:258; MACR:269; REIR:191
Parsons, A. R.
Address at trial, Chicago, October 7-9, 1886. ACC:90; PAF:65
Phillips, W.
Murder of Lovejoy. ALS:161; HURH:74
Quincy, J., 1744-1775
Defence of British soldiers, 1770. BREWE 9:3269; POC:95
Raleigh, W.
Speech on the scaffold. BREWE 9:3280; BRYH:104
Randolph, E.
In defence of Aaron Burr, 1807. BREWE 9:3284
Robespierre, M.
Defense from the charge of tyranny. BREWE 9:3341
His defense of terrorism. BREWE 9:331
Rumbold, R.
Against booted and spurred privilege. BREWE 9:3352
Sacco, N. and Vanzetti, B.
Proclaim their innocence. ALA:85; ANN 14:527
Schwab, M.
Address at trial, Chicago, October 7-9, 1886. ACC:24; PAF:25
Sidney, A.
Governments for the people and not the people for government (scaffold speech). BREWE 9:3454
Socrates
On being declared guilty. BAS:67 (outline only); BREWE 9:3493
Spies, A.
Address at trial, Chicago, October 7-9, 1886. ACC:1; ANN 11:117; PAF:11
Strafford, T. W.
Defense before the House of Lords. BREWE 9:3540; BRYH:131
Talfourd, T. N.
Queen against Moxon-Shelley as a blasphemer. BREWE 9:3565
Taylor, F. W.
On scientific management. BOORA 2:740
Tooke, J. H.
On the "Murders at Lexington and Concord" (at his trial for libel). BREWE 9:3633
Vane, H.
At his trial for high treason. BREWE 10:3685
Walpole, R.
On patriots (at motion to dismiss him from Council). BREWE 10:3724
White, G. H.
Defense of the Negro race. FON:635
Zola, E.
Appeal for Dreyfus. BAS:110 (outline only); BREWE 10:3931

DeGaulle, Charles
France: the third world power. MDV:38

DeGeer, G.
Presentation [of the Nobel Prize for Chemistry to Walther Hermann Nernst, 1920, Dec. 12, 1921]. NOLC 1:349

DEGREES, ACADEMIC See Acceptance speeches - Degrees, Academic

Delany, Martin Robinson
Advice to ex-slaves. (St. Helena Island, South Carolina, July, 1865). FON:318

Delbrück, Max
A physicist's renewed look at biology--twenty years later (Nobel Lecture, Dec. 10, 1969). NOLM 4:404

DELBRÜCK, MAX
Gard, S.
Presentation [of the Nobel Prize for Physiology or Medicine to Max Delbrück, Alfred D. Hershey, and Salvador E. Luria, Dec. 10, 1969]. NOLM 4:401

DELEDDA, GRAZIA
Schück, H.
Presentation [of the Nobel Prize for Literature to Grazia Deledda, 1926]. NOB 5:117; NOL:232

De Leon, Daniel
Aims of socialism. ANN 12:106
Political power of labor. ANN 13:19

DEMENTIA PARALYTICA
Wagner-Jauregg, J.
The treatment of dementia paralytica by malaria inoculation. NOLM 2:159

Demmert, William G.
Tribal chartered education. MAES:156

DEMOCRACY
Barnave, A. P. J. M.
Representative democracy against majority absolutism. BREWE 1:218
Beaconsfield, B. D.
Against democracy for England. BREWE 1:296
Beecher, H. W.
Success of American democracy (anniversary of attack on Fort Sumter). OLIS:191
Brooke, E. W.
Responsibilities inherent in a constitutional democracy. BA 1973-74:74
Cleon
On the punishment of the Mytileneans. BREWE 4:1298
Desmoulins, C.
Live free or die. BREWE 5:1815
Douglas, W. O.
Function of democracy. BAP:275
Jefferson, T.
First inaugural: democracy defined. AND:116; ANN 1:143; BOORA 1:212; BREWE 7:2612; HURH:48; LINS:140; OLIS:28; USINAU:13; USINAUG:13
Johnson, J. W.
Our democracy and the ballot. FON:757
Jordan, B. C.
Keynote address to the Democratic National Convention. BA 1976-77:11; JAM:7; LINRST:334
Lilienthal, D. E.
My faith in democracy. ALA:111
Lowe, R.
Coming of democracy. MCB:138
Monroe, J.
Federal experiments in history. BREWE 8:3041
Parker, T.
Present crisis in American affairs. ANN 8:372
Pickens, W.
Kind of democracy the Negro race expects. FON:601
Razak, T. A.
Crucial cross-roads of history. MONS:64
Democracy and development in Malaysia. MONS:80
Roosevelt, F. D.
Address at University of Pennsylvania, September 20, 1940. FRIP:324
Address to White House

Correspondents' Association dinner, March 15, 1941. CROCK:11
Fireside chat on party primaries, June 24, 1938. FRIP:324
Third inaugural address. USINAU:244
Stevenson, A. E.
Prospects for democracy around the world. LINS:350
Tyndall, J.
Democracy and higher intellect. BREWE 9:3668
Willkie, W. L.
Loyal opposition. GRG:63; HURH:243
Wilson, W.
Eighth annual message. STAT 3:2608
The nature of democracy in the United States. FRIP:270

---- SINGAPORE
Lee Kuan Yew
Leaders' responsibility in sustaining a democratic system. MONSA:269

DEMOCRATIC CONVENTIONS
See Political Conventions, Democratic

DEMOCRATIC PARTY
Barkley, A. W.
Record of Democratic Party. BLY:233
Doolittle, J. R.
In favor of re-union. BREWE 5:1894
Jordan, B. C.
Keynote address to the Democratic National Convention. BA 1976-77:11; JAM:7; LINRST:334
Schwellenbach, L. B.
First seven years of the New Deal: let's view the record. BAD:47

Demosthenes
First Olynthiac oration. SAG:199
First Philippic. COG:40; SAG:188
For Megalopolis. Same as his Oration for the Megalopolitans
On the Chersoneus. SAG:235
On the crown. BREWE 5:1688; COG:151
Oration for the Megalopolitans. SAG:173
Oration on the liberty of the Rhodians. SAG:180
Oration on the peace. BREWE 5:1759; SAG:223
Second Olynthiac. BREWE 5:1754; COG:56; SAG:205
Second Philippic. BREWE 5:1763; SAG:228
Third Olynthiac. SAG:212
Third Philippic. COG:91; SAG:249

DEMOSTHENES
Aeschines
Against Ctesiphon. BREWE 1:114; COG:120
Dewey, O.
Genius of Demosthenes. BREWE 5:1822
Lytton, E. G. E. L.
Demosthenes and the nobility of the classics. BREWE 8:2869

Deniehy, Daniel Henry
On the Constitution Bill. MCA:26

Dennis, David Worth See Jordan, B. C., jt. auth.

DEOXYRIBONUCLEIC ACID
Hershey, A. D.
Idiosyncrasies of DNA structure. NOLM 4:417
Kornberg, A.
The biologic synthesis of deoxyribonucleic acid. NOLM 3:665

DEPARTMENT STORES
Wanamaker, J.
On the department store. BOORA 2:632

Depew, Chauncey M.
Columbian oration. BREWE 5:1769
England and America since the Spanish War. BREWE 5:1790
Liberty enlightening the world. Same as his Unveiling the Statue of Liberty
Military spirit in America. BREWE 5:1785
"A perfect woman, nobly planned,

to warm, to comfort, and command." Same as his Woman
Poetry and politics in Britain. BREWE 5:1796
Presents William Jennings Bryan. LYI:227
Unveiling the Statue of Liberty. BREWE 5:1782
Woman. (New York, Dec. 22, 1875). HURH:125

DEPRESSIONS, BUSINESS See Business cycles; United States - Economic conditions

Depta, Mark
Aims and purposes of the FFA. BREWW:157

Derby, Edward George Villiers Stanley, 17th Earl of
Emancipation of British Negroes. BREWE 5:1800

DERELICTS
Karos, P. A.
Haven of the defeated. ARS:148

Dering, Sir Edward
For the encouragement of learning. BREWE 5:1805
Religious controversy in Parliament. BREWE 5:1808

Deseze, Raymond
Defending Louis XVI. BREWE 5:1811

Desmoulins, Camille
Live free or die. BREWE 5:1815

De Sola Pool, David
Man's advocate. WALE:33

De Tuncq, Darlyne
UN: symbol or reality? SCHW:165

DEUTERIUM
Urey, H. C.
Some thermodynamic properties of hydrogen and deuterium. NOLC 2:339

DeVries, Calvin
Standards that stand. SCHW:15

D'Ewes, Sir Simon
Antiquity of Cambridge. BREWE 5:1818

Dewey, John
School and social progress. ANN 12:255

Dewey, Orville
Genius of Demosthenes. BREWE 5:1822
Rust of riches. BREWE 5:1823

Dewey, Thomas E.
Acceptance speech, Chicago, Illinois, June 28, 1944. SIN:205
Acceptance speech, Philadelphia, Pennsylvania, June 24, 1948. SIN:229
Campaign speech, Des Moines, Iowa, September 20, 1948. SIN:232
Campaign speech, Philadelphia, Pennsylvania, September 7, 1944. Same as his Opening campaign speech in Philadelphia
Corporate state not an American system (campaign speech, October 7, 1944). ROD:333
Opening campaign speech in Philadelphia (Sept. 7, 1944). SIN:210
Public service. ANN 16:471

Dexter, Samuel
"Higher law" of self-defense. BREWE 5:1825

DIABETES
Banting, F. G.
Diabetes and insulin. NOLM 2:50
Houssay, B. A.
The role of the hypophysis in carbohydrate metabolism and in diabetes. NOLM 3:210

DIAMONDS
Koblish, C. F.
Diamonds, their mining, selling, perfecting, and the determining of their quality. BAS:206 (outline only)

Diaz, Porfirio
Mexican progress.
BREWE 5:1832

Dickerson, Mahlon
Alien and Sedition Acts of the Adams administration.
BREWE 5:1836

Dickey, John Sloan
Betrayal of idealism (convocation address).
BA 1967-68:136

Dickinson, Daniel S.
Rebuking Senator Clemens of Alabama. BREWE 5:1844

DICKINSON, JACOB M.
Lewis, J. H.
Introduction of Jacob M. Dickinson. LYI:217

Dickinson, John
Before the Pennsylvania Assembly, March 24, 1764.
POC:182
Declaration of the Colonies on taking up arms.
BREWE 5:1849
Speech against independence.
ANN 2:438
Speech against the petition to change the form of government. Same as his Before the Pennsylvania Assembly, March 24, 1764

DICTATORS AND DICTATORSHIP
LaFollette, P. F.
Party of our time. BAD:120
Roosevelt, F. D.
Address to White House Correspondents' Association dinner, March 15, 1941.
CROCK:11
Message to Congress, January 4, 1939. STAT 3:2842

Didon, Henri
Christ and higher criticism.
BREWE 5:1856

Diels, Otto Paul Hermann
Description and importance of the aromatic basic skeleton of the steroids (Nobel Lecture, 1950). NOLC 3:259

DIELS, OTTO PAUL HERMANN
Fredga, A.
Presentation [of the Nobel Prize for Chemistry to Otto Paul Hermann Diels and Kurt Adler, Dec. 12, 1950]. NOLC 3:255

DIENE SYNTHESIS
Adler, K.
Diene synthesis and related reaction types. NOLC 3:267

Digby, Lord See Bristol, G. D.

DIGESTION
Pavlov, I. P.
Physiology of digestion.
NOLM 1:141

Dilke, Charles Wentworth
America. BREWE 5:1873
Omphalism. BREWE 5:1880

Dinwoodie, S. David
Inner city--our shame. ARS:216

Dirac, Paul Adrien Maurice
Theory of electrons and positrons (Nobel Lecture, Dec. 12, 1933).
NOLPH 2:320

DIRAC, PAUL ADRIEN MAURICE
Pleijel, H.
Presentation [of the Nobel Prize for Physics for 1932 to Werner Heisenberg and for 1933 to Erwin Schrodinger and Paul Adrien Maurice Dirac, Dec. 11, 1933].
NOLPH 2:283

Dirksen, Everett
Presents Robert A. Taft. LYI:210
Responds to introduction.
PRS:122

DISARMAMENT
Eisenhower, D. D.
First steps in disarmament.
ANN 17:330
Noel-Baker, P. J.
Peace and the arms race (Nobel Lecture, Dec. 11, 1959).
NOLP 3:186
Quidde, L.
Security and disarmament (Nobel Lecture, Dec. 10, 1927).
NOLP 2:47

DISCRIMINATION
Brockett, J. A.
Reply to Grady. ANN 11:250
Bunche, R. J.
Human relations in world perspective. FON:882
Deakin, A.
For a white Australia. MCA:88
Douglass, F.
Color line in America. ANN 10:584
Hains, J.
Lamp of freedom. SCHW:6
Hood, W. R.
Uncle Tom is dead! FON:843
Humphreys, B. G.
Justice but not equality for the Negro. ANN 9:626
Randolph, A. P.
Liberty, justice and democracy. SMHV:110
Rylaarsdam, J.
Undesirable one. SCHW:1
Wright, T. S.
Prejudice against the colored man. FON:61

DISCRIMINATION IN EMPLOYMENT
Bulkley, W. L.
Race prejudice as viewed from an economic standpoint. FON:680

DISCUSSIONS See Debates and debating

Disraeli, Benjamin See Beaconsfield, Benjamin Disraeli, 1st Earl of

DISSENTERS
Boorstin, D. J.
Dissent, dissension and the news. BA 1967-68:125; JEF:187; JEFF:181; LINR:203
Bronowski, J.
Protest-past and present. BA 1969-70:119
Griswold, E. N.
Dissent, protest, and disobedience. ANN 18:670; BA 1967-68:141; JEF:196
Smith, M. C.
Declaration of conscience--twenty years later. BA 1969-70:133

Ditzen, Lowell Russell
The right ticket but the wrong train (Washington). REID:404

DIVORCE
Rogers, J.
Day before Christmas. KEO:232; STOT:269
Stanton, E. C.
Address on the Divorce Bill, 1861. BOORA 1:367

Dix, John Adams
Christianity and politics. BREWE 5:1883

Dixon, Owen
Law and the scientific expert. MCA:176

Dod, Albert B.
Value of truth. BREWE 5:1885

DOGS
Vest, G. G.
Man's best friend--his dog. ALA:45; HURH:161

Dohrer, Jean
Our forgotten man. (Aberdeen, S.D., Feb. 1971). LINRS:269

Domack, Gerhard Johannes Paul
Further progress in chemotherapy of bacterial infections (Nobel Lecture for 1939, Dec. 12, 1947). NOLM 2:490

Domiano, Paul
Break down at United (Swimming Pool Company). REIR:38

DOMINICAN REPUBLIC
Grant, U. S.
For annexation (of Dominican Republic). ANN 10:231
Sumner, C.
Against annexation (of the Dominican Republic). ANN 10:233

---- See also United States - Foreign Relations - Dominican Republic

Dondero, George A.
Communism in our schools (1946). (Washington, June 14, 1946). DAVF:296
Modern art shackled to communism.

(Washington, August 16, 1949). DAVF:302

Donne, John
Man immortal, body and soul. BREWE 5:1888
Sermon preached at St. Paul's (Easter Day, 1625). BRYH:109

Donner, Frederic G.
Responds to an introduction. PRS:150

Donovan, Hedley
Presents Henry R. Luce. LYI:103

Donovan, William J.
Call for a Central Intelligence Agency. ANN 16:391

Doolittle, James R.
Attitude of the West in the Civil War. BREWE 5:1891
In favor of re-union. BREWE 5:1894

Dorr, Thomas
People's right to remake their constitution. ANN 7:56

Dorset, Edward Sackville, 4th Earl of
In favor of slitting Prynne's nose. BREWE 5:1899

Dougherty, Daniel
"Hancock the superb." BREWE 5:1904

Douglas, Lewis W.
Presents Lord Halifax. LYI: 222

Douglas, Paul H. See Russell, R., jt. auth.

DOUGLAS, PAUL H.
Burgess, W. R.
Presents Paul H. Douglas. LYI:231

Douglas, Stephen A.
Campaign speech for United States Senate--Chicago, July 9, 1858. Same as his Reply to Lincoln at Chicago, July 9, 1858
Defense of the Kansas-Nebraska Bill (January 30, 1854). ANN 8:254
"Expansion" and co-operation with England. BREWE 5:1918
Fifth joint debate at Galesburg, October 7, 1858. ANN 9:22
First debate with Lincoln. Same as his Reply to Lincoln at Chicago, July 9, 1858
Issues of 1861. BREWE 5:1929
John Brown raid. BREWE 5:1926
Kansas and "Squatter sovereignty." BREWE 5:1924
"Leave the people free to do as they please." Same as his Reply to Lincoln, Freeport, August 27, 1858
Lincoln-Douglas joint debate at Alton, October 15, 1858. ANN 9:30
Opening speech of Lincoln-Douglas debate, Ottawa, August 21, 1858. ANN 9:8
Reply to Lincoln at Chicago, July 9, 1858. ANN 9:4; BAS:45 (outline only); OLIS:133
Reply to Lincoln, Freeport, August 27, 1858. ANN 9:17; BREWE 5:1912; HURH:94
Reply to the Jonesboro speech. ANN 9:20

DOUGLAS, STEPHEN A.
Cox, S. S.
Stephen A. Douglas and his place in history. BREWE 4:1449
Trumbull, L.
Announcing the death of Douglas. BREWE 9:3654

Douglas, William O.
Function of democracy. BAP:275
Responds to an introduction. PRS:161

---- See also following jt. auths.
Brennan, W. J.; Jackson, R. H.

Douglass, Frederick
The abilities and possibilities of our race. (Baltimore, Oct. 1, 1865. Opening of the Douglass Institute). FON:326
Address for the unknown loyal dead. ALA:51
The claims of the Negro ethno-

logically considered. (Western Reserve College, July 12, 1854). FON:144
Color line in America (Louisville, Ky., Sept. 24, 1883). ANN 10:584; FON:491
Fourth of July. Same as his Slavery: speech at Rochester, July 5, 1852
Fourth of July oration. Same as his What to the slave is the Fourth of July?
I denounce the so-called emancipation as a stupendous fraud. (Washington, D.C., April 16, 1888). FON:520
If there is no struggle there is no progress. (Canandaigua, N.Y., August 4, 1857). FON:197
Lecture on slavery no. 1. Same as his Nature of slavery (speech at Rochester, New York, December 1, 1850)
The meaning of July fourth for the Negro. Same as his Slavery: speech at Rochester, July 5, 1852
"Men of color, to arms!" (March 2, 1863). OE:49
The mission of the war. (Cooper Institute, N.Y., January 13, 1864). FON:283
Nature of slavery (speech at Rochester, New York, December 1, 1850). BOSR:113; FRIP:222
Oration in memory of Abraham Lincoln (at unveiling of Freedmen's monument, Washington, D.C.). FRIP:242
Plea for free speech in Boston (Boston, Dec. 3, 1860). BREWE 5:1906; FON:244
Reception speech at Finsbury Chapel, Moorsfield, England. (May 12, 1846). OE:30; SMHV:31
Reception speech in England. Same as his Reception speech at Finsbury Chapel, Moorsfield, England
Slavery: speech at Rochester, July 5, 1852. FON:104; SMHR:125
Speech on the Declaration of Independence. Same as his What to the slave is the Fourth of July?
There is a better day coming. CUR:173
What is my duty as an anti-slavery voter? (April 25, 1856). FRIP:229
What the black man wants. (Mass. Anti-Slavery Society, 1865). MDT:175
What to the slave is the Fourth of July? (July 4, 1852). JAM:19; OE:41
Woman suffrage. (Washington, D.C. International Council of Women, April, 1888). FON:517

Douglass, H. Ford
I do not believe in the antislavery of Abraham Lincoln. (Framingham, Mass., July 4, 1860). FON:232

DOUGLASS INSTITUTE
Douglass, F.
The abilities and possibilities of our race. FON:326

Dow, Lorenzo, Jr.
Hope and despair. BREWE 5:1934
Improvement in America. BREWE 5:1933

Dowling, Alexander
Constitutionality of a compulsory school law: opinion for the court. ANN 12:417

Downing, George T.
May Hungary be free. (New York, Dec. 9, 1851). FON:102

DRAFT <u>See</u> Conscription

DRAFT RIOTS, 1863
Pennington, J. W. C.
The position and duties of the colored people. FON:271

Drake, Charles D.
Against "Copperheads." BREWE 5:1936

DRAMA - IRELAND
Yeats, W. B.
The Irish dramatic movement. NOL:201

Drayton, William Henry
Charge to the Grand Juries, November 5 & 15, 1774. POC:297

Drazin, Nathan
From the summit. WALE:34

DRED SCOTT DECISION
Breckenridge, J. C.
Dred Scott decision, December 1859. BREWE 2:615
Lincoln, A.
Dred Scott Decision. ANN 8:459
Taney, R. B.
Dred Scott Case: opinion for the Supreme Court. ANN 8:440

Dreier, Alex
Introduces the Honorable William Proxmire, United States Senator from Wisconsin. PRS:34

DRESS See Clothing and dress

Dreyfus, A. Stanley
Leo Baeck. WALE:207

DREYFUS, ALFRED
Labori, P.
Conspiracy against Dreyfus. BREWE 7:2684
Zola, E.
Appeal for Dreyfus. BAS:110 (outline only); BREWE 10:3931

Driberg, Tom See Sykes, C., jt. auth.

Drier, Alex
Introduces James T. Quirk. PRS:18

DRUGS
Rindo, J. P.
Life, librium, and the pursuit of happiness. LINRST:230

Drumm, Streuby L.
War on prosperity. CAPG:185

Drummond, Henry
Greatest thing in the world. BREWE 5:1941
Preparation for learning. BREWE 5:1959
Talk on books. BREWE 5:1964

Drummond, Roscoe
Responds to introduction. PRS:123

DuBois, W. E. Burghardt
Address to the National Negro Convention. (May 31, 1909). OE:88
Behold the land. (Columbia, S.C., Oct. 20, 1946). FON:837
The great migration north. (1918). FON:721
Politics and industry. (New York, May 31 and June 1, 1909). FON:673
Shall the negro be encouraged to seek cultural equality? (Chicago, March 17, 1929). FON:772
The value of agitation. (1906). FON:663

DUBOIS, W. E. BURGHARDT
King, M. L., Jr.
Honoring Dr. DuBois. SMHR:204

Dubos, René
Humanizing the earth. (December 29, 1972). BA 1972-73:149
Social attitudes and technological civilization (Harvard Univ., June 6, 1978). BA 1978-79:11
Theology of the earth. BA 1969-70:83

Ducommun, Elie
The futility of war demonstrated by history (Nobel Lecture for 1902, Oslo, May 16, 1904). NOLP 1:17

DUCOMMUN, ELIE
Løvland, J. G.
Toast to E. Ducommun. NOLP 1:15

DUELING
Against dueling. BREWE 1:199; BRYH:96

Duffey, Joseph D.
General education: the rule of the humanities (Univ. of Rhode Island, Oct. 24, 1977). BA 1977-78:146

DUFFIELD, EDWARD D.
Hedges, J. E.
Presents Edward D. Duffield. LYI:69

DuGard, Roger Martin
Acceptance [of the Nobel Prize for Literature, 1937]. NOB 14:9; NOL:348

DUGARD, ROGER MARTIN
Hallström, P.
Presentation [of the Nobel Prize for Literature to Roger Martin DuGard, 1937]. NOB 14:3; NOL:342

Dulles, John Foster
Containment or liberation? ANN 17:204
"The fact is that today any problem in any part of the world ramifies into almost every part of the world." Same as his Modern foreign policy
Modern foreign policy. (Washington, April 11, 1955). HURH:324
Peace through law. ANN 17:528
Strategy of massive retaliation. ANN 17:250
Why the Arbenz government was overthrown in Guatemala. LAA:117

DULUTH
Knott, J. P.
Glories of Duluth. BLY:135; BREWE 7:2653

Dumper, Anthony Charles
Church in a secular state. MONS:485

Dunbar, Roxanne
Women's liberation: where the movement is today and where it's going. (Nat. Org. for Women, May, 1970). STOT:311

DUNKIRK
Churchill, Sir W. L. S.
Dunkirk. MCB:498

Dunlap, David E.
The world needs our help. BREWW:98

Dunn, Oscar J.
We ask an equal chance in the race of life. (Louisiana, July 31, 1868). FON:355

DuPont, Henry B.
Greatest invention of them all. ANN 17:530

DURANT, WILLIAM J. (WILL)
Davis, C. R.
Presents Will Durant. LYI:56

Durfee, Job
Influence of scientific discovery and invention on social and political progress. ANN 7:128
Science and political progress. Same as his Influence of scientific discovery and invention on social and political progress

DuVall, W. O.
Presents Billy Graham. LYI:160

Dwight, Timothy
On the duty of Americans at the present crisis. ANN 4:33
Pursuit of excellence. BREWE 5:1968

- E -

Eagleton, Thomas F.
1977: year of opportunity in the Middle East? (Manhattan, Kan., Dec. 8, 1976). LINRST:124

EAR
Bekesy, G. V.
Concerning the pleasures of observing, and the mechanics of the inner ear. NOLM 3:722

EAST HARLEM
Dinwoodie, S. D.
Inner city-our shame. ARS:216

EAST INDIA BILL
Fox, C. J.
On the East India Bill.
BREWE 6:2189

EASTER
Aelfric
Sermon on the sacrifice on Easter-day. BRYH:14
Donne, J.
Sermon preached at St. Paul's (Easter Day, 1625).
BRYH:109
Prayer for Easter. BNH:76

Eban, Abba
Responds to an introduction.
PRS:159

Eccles, John Carew
The ionic mechanism of post-synaptic inhibition (Nobel Lecture, Dec. 11, 1963).
NOLM 4:6

ECCLES, JOHN CAREW
Granit, R.
Presentation [of the Nobel Prize for Physiology or Medicine to John Carew Eccles, Alan Lloyd Hodgkin, and Andrew Fielding Huxley, Dec. 11, 1963]. NOLM 4:3

Eccles, Marriner S.
Government spending is sound.
BAD:29

ECHEGARAY, JOSE DE
Wirsén, C. D. af
Presentation [of the Nobel Prize for Literature to Frédéric Mistral and José de Echegaray y Eizaguirre, 1904]. NOL:23; NOB 13:119

ECOLOGY
Dubos, R.
Theology of the earth.
BA 1969-70:83
Jones, A. L.
A question of ecology: the cries of wolf. LINRST:115
Muskie, E. S.
Environment: can man prosper and survive?
BA 1969-70:98

ECONOMIC ASSISTANCE, AMERICAN
Gaud, W. S.
Why foreign aid?
BA 1967-68:179
Truman, H. S.
Point Four Program.
ANN 16:595

ECONOMIC OPPORTUNITY ACT OF 1964
Wirtz, W. W.
Economic Opportunity Act of 1964. CAPG:165

ECONOMIC PLANNING See United States - Economic policy

ECONOMIC POLICY
Rogers, W.
Morgenthau's plan. GRG:55

ECONOMICS See Capitalism; Free trade and protection; Industry

Edberg, Rolf
Acceptance [of the Nobel Prize for Peace for Dag Hammarskjöld, Dec. 10, 1961].
NOLP 3:248

Eddy, Edward D., Jr.
Student involvement in educational policy. BA 1965-66:221; LINR:251

Edlén, B.
Presentation [of the Nobel Prize for Physics to Charles H. Townes, Nikolai G. Basov, and Alexander M. Prochorov, Dec. 11, 1964]. NOLPH 4:55

Edmunds, George F.
Constitution and the Electoral Commission. BREWE 5:1971

EDUCATION
Addams, J.
Foreign-born children in the primary grades. ANN 12:130
Brewster, K., Jr.
The decade of shortcuts.
BA 1972-73:176
Choate, R.
State and mental culture.
ANN 7:235
Clemens, S. L.
Public Education Association.

GRG:21
Conant, J. B.
Education for a classless society. ANN 16:22
Role of the state in education. CAPG:131
Danton, G. J.
Education, free and compulsory. BREWE 5:1629
Dewey, J.
School and social progress. ANN 12:255
Dowling, A.
Constitutionality of a compulsory school law: opinion for the court. ANN 12:417
Eliezer, C. J.
Ideology and education. MONSA:231
Euwema, B.
Excellence in teaching. ARS:18
Gardner, J. W.
Education. BA 1972-73:119
Geiman, C. K.
Are they really "unteachable"? LINR:94
Howe, H. II
Changing the pecking order. BA 1967-68:111
Public education for a humane society. BA 1972-73:161
Hutchins, R. M.
All our institutions are in disarray. BA 1974-75:117
The institutional illusion. BA 1971-72:161
Where do we go from here in education? CROCK:110
Irwin, H.
The true aim of education. CURM:167
Johnson, L. B.
Education opportunity message. CAPG:112
Lee Kuan Yew
Hong Kong and Singapore: a tale of two cities. MONSA:264
Lindsley, P.
Education of every child of the Republic. ANN 5:157
Macaulay, T. B.
Popular education. BREWE 8:2883
McElwee, R.
A plea for universal education in the South. FON:477
Mann, H.
The necessity of education in a Republican government. HOW:148
Montalembert, C. F. R.
For freedom of education. BREWE 8:3046
Myers, N. J.
Moppet manipulation. ARS:123
Rogers, W.
Education and wealth. HURH:200
Rosten, L.
Myths by which we live. KEO:240
Seward, W. H.
Prosperity and education. ANN 6:140
Shapp, M. J.
The educational process. VER:267
Spencer, S. R., Jr.
A call for new missionaries. BA 1971-72:172
Stevens, T.
Education as a public duty. ANN 6:136
Thio Chan Bee
Inspired education through inspired educators. MONS:463
Warren, P.
Bring forth the children. BRYF:485; MOPR:368
Wellington, J. K.
A look at the fundamental school concept. LINRST:314
White, R.
The educated man in the age of Aquarius. BAAE:271
Willkie, W. L.
Education determines civilization; the importance of liberal education policies. CROCK:93
Winter, R. A.
This I believe. SCHW:87
Wright, F.
Of existing evils and their remedy. ANN 5:290

---- See also Colleges and universities; Commencement addresses; Educators; Learning and scholarship; Religious education; Segregation in education; Students; Teachers; Veterans - Education. Also this subject with subheads Education, Adult; Education, Higher; Education of women

---- FINANCE
Chambers, M. M.
Higher education who should pay? CAPG:125

EDUCATION, ADULT
Coffman, L. D.
Adult education for the unemployed. ANN 15:98

---- HIGHER
Andelson, R. B.
Campus unrest; the erosion of excellence. LINRS:204
Barzun, J.
Place and the price of excellence. ARS:28
Benezet, L. T.
Acceleration or direction? BA 1966-67:105
The educator's leap of faith. HOR:107
Curtis, G. W.
Public duty of educated men. ALS:179
Eddy, E. D., Jr.
Student involvement in educational policy. BA 1965-66:221; LINR:251
Eliot, C. W.
Inaugural address as president of Harvard. ANN 10:201
Everett, E.
Plea for support of an Ohio college. ANN 6:26
State funds for Harvard. ANN 7:502
Fawcett, N. G.
Direction for destiny. BA 1970-71:106
Ferris, W. H.
Education and the Triple Revolution. MDV:216
Goheen, R. F.
Sorting it out. HOR:21
Griswold, A. W.
On conversation--chiefly academic. CROCK:75
Hesburgh, T. M.
Higher education begins the seventies. BA 1970-71:85; BAAE:277
Howard, J. A.
The innovation mirage. BA 1970-71:94
Hutchins, R. M.
Message to the younger generation. MDV:198
Kirk, G.
Responsibilities of the educated man (at centennial of University of Denver). LINR:143
McBath, J. H.
The vital university. BA 1974-75:127
McGill, W. J.
The public challenge and the campus response. BA 1971-72:182
Requiem for Joe College. BA 1969-70:139
Meyerson, M.
The ivory tower of Babel. HOR:99
Morgan, E. S.
What every Yale freshman should know. ARS:35
Nixon, R. M.
Campus revolutionaries. BAAGB:386
Peel, R.
Plea for higher education (installation speech as Lord Rector of University of Glasgow). BREWE 8:3153
Romney, G.
From the bottom to the top. CAPG:140
Shaw, G. B.
Universities and education. KEO:237
Syed Hussein Alatas
Primary aim of a university. MONS:475
Wentworth, W. C.
For the University Bill. MCA:17
Wilson, L.
Education for adequacy. HOR:16
Wong, L. K.
Intelligentsia in a nation of immigrants (Singapore). MONS:476

---- MALAYA
Thuraisingham, E. E. C.
Milestones in Malayan education. MONS:173
Spirit of teaching. MONS:169

---- MALAYSIA
Hamdan bin Sheikh Tahir, H.

Education for service--to society, the nation and our creator. MONSA:149
Problems of national education. MONSA:155 selections
Johari, M. K.
All schools are the same. MONS:145
Key to open the doors to all hearts and minds. MONS:141
Successful teacher. MONS:146
Lim Ching Yah
Teaching profession and nation building (Malaysia). MONS:317
Syed Hussein Alatas
Malaysia and its intellectual revolution. MONS:469
Tan Chee Khoon
The teachers' dilemma: the government gets the blame. MONSA:180

---- SINGAPORE
Ong Pang Boon
Educational pyramid. MONS:436
Wong, L. K.
Intelligentsia in a nation of immigrants (Singapore). MONS:476

EDUCATION AND STATE
Cobden, R.
Need for improved education. JAE:124
Conant, J. B.
Role of the state in education. CAPG:131
Johnson, L. B.
Education opportunity message. CAPG:112
Kennedy, J. F.
Federal aid to education. ANN 18:8
Romney, G.
From the bottom to the top. CAPG:140

EDUCATION DAY
Welcome to parents and ladies of the Woman's Missionary Society on Education Day. HNWM:21
Welcome to students on Education Day. HNWM:20
Welcome to teachers on Education Day. HNWM:18

EDUCATION OF WOMEN
Rush, B.
Thoughts on female education. ANN 3:207
Stevenson, A. E.
Trained intelligence: education and womanpower (Radcliffe College commencement address). MDV:205

EDUCATORS
Lim Chong Yah
Teaching profession and nation building (Malaysia). MONS:317
Welcome to a new educational director (2 examples). BNH:50

---- See also Inaugural addresses; Teachers

Edward VIII, King of England (abdicated)
Farewell of former King Edward VIII. BRYH:517
See also Baldwin, S. B., jt. auth.

EDWARD VIII, KING OF ENGLAND (ABDICATED)
Baldwin, S. B. and others
Debate in the House of Commons on the abdication of Edward VIII. BRYH:491

Edwards, George
Murder and gun control. (Washington, D.C., May 3-7, 1971). BA 1971-72:101

Edwards, Jonathan
Eternity of Hell torments. BREWE 5:1977
Farewell--sermon. POC:443
Sinners in the hands of an angry God (Enfield, Conn., July 8, 1741). ANN 1:423; BREWE 5:1982; HURH:21; LINS:121
Wrath upon the wicked to the uttermost. BREWE 5:1979
"You are thus in the hands of an angry God." Same as his Sinners in the hands of an angry God

Edwards, Ludy (Ludwika)
Libbing. BRYF:489

Edwin, King of Northumbria
On the flight of a sparrow and the life of man. BRYH:5

EFFICIENCY IN BUSINESS
See Business

EGYPT - FOREIGN RELATIONS - ISRAEL
Carter, J.
Announcing the Camp David accords. BA 1978-79:142

EGYPT AND SUDAN CAMPAIGNS, 1882-1900
Churchill, R. H. S.
Gladstone's Egyptian inconsistencies. BREWE 3:1148

Ehrlich, Paul
Partial cell functions (Nobel Lecture, Dec. 11, 1908). NOLM 1:304

EHRLICH, PAUL
Mörner, K. A. H.
Presentation [of the Nobel Prize for Physiology or Medicine to Elie Metchnikoff and Paul Ehrlich, Dec. 11, 1908]. NOLM 1:277

Eigen, Manfred
Immeasurably fast reactions (Nobel Lecture, Dec. 11, 1967). NOLC 4:170

EIGEN, MANFRED
Olander, H. A.
Presentation [of the Nobel Prize for Chemistry to Manfred Eigen, R. G. W. Norrish and George Porter Dec. 11, 1967]. NOLC 4:165

Eijkman, Christiaan
Antineuritic vitamin and beriberi (Nobel Lecture, Dec. 11, 1929). NOLM 2:199

EIJKMAN, CHRISTIAAN
Liljestrand, G.
Presentation [of the Nobel Prize for Physiology or Medicine to Christiaan Eijkman and Sir Frederick Gowland Hopkins, Dec. 11, 1929]. NOLM 2:193

Eilberg, Joshua See Jordan, B. C., jt. auth.

Einstein, Albert
Fundamental ideas and problems of the theory of relativity (Nobel Lecture for 1921, July 11, 1923). NOLPH 1:482

EINSTEIN, ALBERT
Arrhenius, S.
Presentation [of the Nobel Prize for Physics for 1921 to Albert Einstein, July 11, 1923]. NOLPH 1:482
My friend Albert. BURT:145
Nizer, L.
Presents Albert Einstein. LYI:176

Einthoven, Willem
The string galvanometer and the measurement of the action currents of the heart (Nobel Lecture for 1924, Dec. 11, 1925). NOLM 2:94

Eisenhower, Dwight D.
Acceptance speech, Chicago, Illinois, July 11, 1952. SIN:242
Acceptance speech, San Francisco, California, August 23, 1956. SIN:265
Atoms for peace. Same as his International control of atomic power for peaceful purposes
Campaign speech, Cleveland, Ohio, October 1, 1956. SIN:275
Campaign speech, Detroit, Michigan, October 24, 1952. Same as his Crusade for peace
Crisis in the Middle East. ANN 17:411
Crusade for peace (Detroit, October 24, 1952). ANN 17:199; SIN:245
Dangers of the military-industrial-university complex in America. Same as his Farewell address, January 17, 1961
Eighth annual message. STAT 3:3096
Faith in the individual. CAPG:31
Farewell address, January 17, 1961. ANN 18:1; JAM:36; LAA:209; MDV:132
Federal Court orders must be upheld. ANN 17:457
Fifth annual message.

STAT 3:3068
First annual message.
STAT 3:3012
First inaugural address. (Washington, Jan. 20, 1953).
HURH:304; USINAU:257; USINAUG:257
First steps in disarmament.
ANN 17:330
Fourth annual message.
STAT 3:3052
"History does not long entrust the care of freedom to the weak or the timid." Same as his First inaugural address
I shall go to Korea. Same as his Crusade for peace
International control of atomic power for peaceful purposes. ANN 17:211
Little Rock School crisis. Same as his Federal Court orders must be upheld
Ninth annual message.
STAT 3:3107
Open skies proposal to Russia. Same as his First steps in disarmament
Order of the day (June 6, 1944). Same as his Order of the Day to the Allied troops invading France
Order of the Day to Allied troops invading France.
GRG:74
Price of peace: second inaugural address.
USINAU:263; USINAUG:263
Responds to an introduction.
PRS:152
Second annual message.
STAT 3:3026
Second inaugural address. Same as his Price of Peace: second inaugural address
Seventh annual message.
STAT 3:3086
Sixth annual message. Same as his State of the Union (January 9, 1958)
Spirit of Geneva. BEN:136
State of the Union (January 9, 1958). STAT 3:3076
Third annual message.
STAT 3:3038
U-2 incident (May 25, 1960).
ANN 17:550
Veto of Natural Gas Bill.
ANN 17:370

EISENHOWER, DWIGHT D.
Reid, C. T.
Tribute to Dwight D. Eisenhower. BA 1968-69:165

Eisenhower, Milton S.
A new historical perspective, interdependence (Johns Hopkins Univ., June 13, 1967).
HOR:157

Ekstrand, A. G.
Presentation [of the Nobel Prize for Chemistry to Fritz Haber, 1918, June 2, 1920].
NOLC 1:321
Presentation [of the Nobel Prize for Physics to Charles-Edouard Guillaume, Dec. 11, 1920].
NOLPH 1:441
Presentation [of the Nobel Prize for Physics for 1919 to Johannes Stark, June 3, 1920].
NOLPH 1:423
Presentation [of the Nobel Prize for Physics for 1918 to Max Planck, June 2, 1920].
NOLPH 1:405

ELECTION - ACCEPTANCE See Offices - Acceptance

ELECTION DISTRICTS
Brennan, W. J., Jr.
Baker v. Carr: Opinion for the Supreme Court. ANN 18:130

ELECTION LAWS
Johnson, L. B.
Address to a Joint Session of Congress, March 15, 1965.
AND:81; BOORA 2:919; CROCK:164; MDV:144; REIR:143

ELECTIONS
Bayard, T. F.
Plea for conciliation in 1876.
BREWE 1:265
Curran, J. P.
Liberties of the indolent.
BREWE 4:1550
Davis, D.
On appeal from the caucus.
BREWE 5:1634

Jarrow, C.
Case for the non-voter. KEO:229
Johnson, J. W.
Our democracy and the ballot. FON:757
LaFollette, R. M.
Which shall rule, manhood or money? HURH:158
Macaulay, T. B.
Reform Bill. CLAYP:295; MCB:110
Root, E.
Invisible government: Short Ballot Amendment. ANN 13:528
Russell, J. R.
Reform of the franchise. MCB:87
Shepard, T.
Election sermon. POC:355
West, S.
Election sermon. POC:578

---- CORRUPT PRACTICES
Carpenter, M. H.
Louisiana Returning Board. BREWE 3:976

---- PRIMARY See Primaries

ELECTORAL COLLEGE
Lodge, H. C., Jr.
For abolishing the Electoral College. ANN 17:2

ELECTRIC WAVES
Kastler, A.
Optical methods for studying Hertzian resonances. NOLPH 4:186

ELECTRICITY
Thomson, J. J.
Carriers of negative electricity. NOLPH 1:145

ELECTROLYTES
Arrhenius, S. A.
Development of the theory of electrolytic dissociation. NOLC 1:45

ELECTRONS
Davisson, C. J.
The discovery of electron waves. NOLPH 2:387
De Broglie, L.
The wave nature of the electron. NOLPH 2:244
Dirac, P. A. M.
Theory of electrons and positrons. NOLPH 2:320
Franck, J.
Transformations of kinetic energy of free electrons into excitation energy of atoms by impacts. NOLPH 2:98
Kusch, P.
The magnetic moment of the electron. NOLPH 3:298
Lorentz, H. A.
The theory of electrons and the propagation of light. NOLPH 1:14
Millikan, R. A.
The electron and the light-quant from the experimental point of view. NOLPH 2:54
Thomson, G. P.
Electronic waves. NOLPH 2:397

ELECTROPHORESIS
Tiselius, A. W. K.
Electrophoresis and adsorption analysis as aids in investigations of large-molecular weight substances and their breakdown. NOLC 3:195

Eliezer, Christie Jayaratnam
Democratic societies and debating societies. MONS:262
Educated man with a sense of urgency (presenting Doctor of Laws degree). MONS:275
Ideology and education (Kuala Lumpur, Jan. 5, 1968). MONSA:231
Mathematics the queen of the arts. MONS:265
Toast to Oxford. MONS:271

Eliot, Charles W.
Elective curriculum. Same as his Inaugural address as president of Harvard
Harvard and Yale. (New York, Dec. 22, 1877). HURH:130
Inaugural address as president of Harvard. ANN 10:201
"You can not build a university on a sect at all; you must build it upon the nation." Same as his Harvard and Yale

Eliot, Sir John
On the Petition of Right.
BREWE 5:1986; BRYH:123

Eliot, Thomas Stearns
Acceptance [of the Nobel Prize for Literature, 1948].
NOB 5:267; NOL:435

ELIOT, THOMAS STEARNS
Österling, A.
Presentation [of the Nobel Prize for Literature to Thomas Stearns Eliot, 1948]. NOB 5:261; NOL:431
Trilling, L.
Presents T. S. Eliot.
LYI:35

Elizabeth I, Queen of England
Queen and the royal succession. BRYH:69
Speech at the dissolution of Parliament. BRYH:75
Speech at the proroguing of Parliament. BRYH:77
Speech on marriage and succession, to a delegation from the Lords and Commons. Same as her Queen and the royal succession

Elizabeth II, Queen of England
Toast to President Ford and to the American people (1976). JAM:22

ELIZABETH II, QUEEN OF ENGLAND
Ford, G. R.
Toast to Queen Elizabeth.
JAM:21
Garran, R. R.
Royal visit. MCA:191

Elleson, Jim
The imbalance of power (West Allis, Wisc., 1977).
LINRST:135

Elliott, Janice
There's always a mongoose.
MDYG:223

Elliott, Robert Browne
Civil Rights' Bill. (Washington, Jan. 6, 1874). FON:384; OE:55

Ellsworth, Oliver
Union and coercion.
BREWE 5:1993

El-Sadat, Anwar See Carter, J., jt. auth.

Elson, Edward L. R.
Freaks for Jesus' sake. (Washington, D.C., June 27, 1971).
BA 1971-72:151

Ely, Richard T.
Needs of the city. ANN 11:234

EMANCIPATION OF NEGROES See Slavery in the United States

EMANCIPATION PROCLAMATION
Bryant, M. E.
How shall we get our rights?
FON:510
Gibbs, J. C.
Freedom's joyful day. FON:262
Lincoln, A.
Third annual message.
ANN 9:473; STAT 2:1084
Phillips, W.
The proclamation, how to make it efficient. MDT:148
Purvis, R.
The good time is at hand.
FON:266

EMBARGO
Jefferson, T.
Eighth annual message.
STAT 1:94

EMBRYOLOGY
Spemann, H.
The organizer-effect in embryonic development.
NOLM 2:381

Emerson, Ralph Waldo
American scholar. ANN 6:367; ARS:39; BAS:156 (outline only); BOORA 1:283; BREWE 5:2003; LINS:162; OLIS:47
Greatness of a plain American.
BREWE 5:1999
Man the reformer.
BREWE 5:2008
Memory of Burns. (Boston, Jan. 25, 1859). HURH:106
On the Fugitive Slave Law.
ANN 8:261

"No man existed who could look down on Burns." Same as his Memory of Burns
Uses of great men. BREWE 5:2012
Young American. ANN 7:182

Emmet, Robert
Protest against sentence as a traitor. BREWE 6:2030

EMMET, ROBERT
Plunket, W. C.
Prosecuting Robert Emmet. BREWE 8:3213

EMPLOYMENT
Taft, R. A.
Should the government guarantee employment? ANN 16:263

Enche Arshad bin Ayub
The value of the English language--intensive study urged (Kuala Lumpur, April 7, 1970). MONSA:194 selections

Enders, John Franklin (and others)
The cultivation of the poliomyelitis viruses in tissue culture (Nobel Lecture, Dec. 11, 1954). NOLM 3:448

ENDERS, JOHN FRANKLIN
Gard, S.
Presentation [of the Nobel Prize for Physiology or Medicine to John Franklin Enders, Thomas Huckle Weller, and Frederick Chapman Robbins, Dec. 11, 1954]. NOLM 3:443

ENERGY CONSERVATION
Carter, J.
Energy problems. BA 1976-77:117

ENERGY CRISIS See Power resources

ENERGY INDUSTRIES
Sawhill, J. C.
Energy and the job market. BA 1975-76:102

ENERGY POLICY
Carter, J.
Energy address to the nation. EHN:327
Goodall, C. H.
Energy statement. TAC:219
Sawhill, J. C.
Energy and the job market. BA 1975-76:102
Wydler, J. W.
Science and the public trust. BA 1979-80:139

Engel, George
Address at trial, Chicago, October 7-9, 1886. ACC:43; PAF:37

ENGINEERING AND ENGINEERS
Holley, A. L.
Theory and practice in industrial engineering. ANN 10:366
Macios, M. A.
Model studies of structural design and construction should be conducted prior to the building of structure rather than on the site studies made after the completion of the project. BAS:193 (outline only)

ENGLAND See Great Britain; World War, 1939-1945 - Great Britain

ENGLISH LANGUAGE
Abdul Rahman, T.
English language must continue. MONS:7
Enche Arshad bin Ayub
The value of the English language--intensive study urged. MONSA:194 selections

---- DIALECTS - BLACKS See Black-English dialects

Engman, Lewis A.
Federal Trade Commission (Detroit, April 29, 1974). TAC:214

Engström, A.
Presentation [of the Nobel Prize for Physiology or Medicine to Francis Harry Compton Crick, James Dewey Watson, and

Maurice Hugh Frederick Wilkins, Dec. 11, 1962]. NOLM 3:751

ENTERTAINMENT See Introductions; Music and musicians; Theater, Wit and humor

ENTERTAINMENT, SPEECHES OF See After-dinner speeches

ENTHUSIASM
Chauncy, C.
Caveat against enthusiasm. POC:488

ENVIRONMENT
Dubos, R. J.
Humanizing the earth. BA 1972-73:149
Mead, M.
The planetary crisis and the challenge to scientists. BA 1973-74:97
Muskie, E. S.
Environment: can man prosper and survive? BA 1969-70:98
Ransley, M.
The life and death of our lakes. LINRS:63
Ruckelshaus, W. D.
The environment revolution. BA 1971-72:125
Seaborg, G. T.
Positive power of science. BA 1969-70:108
Swearingen, J. E.
Environmental pollution: a national problem. BAAGB:392

ENVIRONMENTAL PROTECTION
Speth, G.
Environmental regulation and the immobilization of truth. BA 1979-80:145

ENZYMES
Northrop, J. H.
The preparation of pure enzymes and virus proteins. NOLC 3:124
Sumner, J. B.
The chemical nature of enzymes. NOLC 3:114
Theorell, A. H. T.
The nature and mode of action of oxidation enzymes. NOLM 3:480

EQUAL RIGHTS AMENDMENT
Buckley, J.
The Equal Rights Amendment: the legislative aspect. LINRST:271
Chisholm, S.
In support of the Equal Rights Amendment. BOST:243; EHN:364; MOPR:372
Furay, M.
Statement [before the] Subcommittee on Constitutional Amendments of the Committee on the Judiciary of the U.S. Senate. BOST:219
Goldman, E. and others
Statement [before the] Subcommittee on Constitutional Amendments of the Committee on the Judiciary of the U.S. Senate. BOST:215
Green, E.
Representative Edith Green speaks in support of the Equal Rights Amendment. BOST:237
Griffiths, M. W. and others
House debates the Equal Rights Amendment. BOST:230
Holtzman, E.
Women and equality under the law. BA 1976-77:80
Springen, P. J.
The dimensions of the oppression of women. LINRS:109; LINRST:130
Witter, J.
Statement [before the] Subcommittee on Constitutional Amendments of the Committee on the Judiciary of the U.S. Senate. BOST:203
Wolfe, H. B.
The backlash phenomenon. LINRST:85

EQUALITY
Norton, E. H.
In pursuit of equality in academe. BA 1976-77:65
Thibeault, M. L.
The hazards of equity. VERD:265

---- See also Democracy

Erickson, Donald J.
Presents W. E. Whitehead. LYI:63

Erlanger, Joseph
Some observations on the responses of single nerve fibers (Nobel Lecture for 1944, Dec. 12, 1947). NOLM 3:50

Erskine, Thomas
Against Paine's "The Age of Reason." Same as his Against Thomas Williams for the publication of Paine's Age of Reason
Against Thomas Williams for the publication of Paine's Age of Reason. BREWE 6:2038
"Dominion founded on violence and terror." Same as his Speech in behalf of John Stockdale
Free speech and fundamental rights: defense of Tom Paine (Court of King's Bench, Dec. 18, 1792). BREWE 6:2069; CLAYP:166
Homicidal insanity (J. Hadfield). BREWE 6:2058; BRYH:294
In behalf of Hadfield. Same as his Homicidal insanity (J. Hadfield)
Speech in behalf of John Stockdale. BREWE 6:2050
Speech in behalf of Thomas Paine. Same as his Free speech and fundamental rights: defense of Tom Paine

ESKIMOES
Sara, M. J.
Do not refuse us. BA 1969-70:148

ESPIONAGE
Donovan, W. J.
Call for a Central Intelligence Agency. ANN 16:391

Essrig, Harry
Lordly cedar. WALE:35

Estep, Phyllis M.
Apathy. ARS:164

Ethelbert
Coming of Christianity. BRYH:3
On Augustine's mission to England (597). Same as his Coming of Christianity

ETHICS
Acheson, D. G.
Ethics in international relations today. ARS:229
Chapin, E. H.
Rectitude higher than morality. BREWE 3:1040
DeVries, C.
Standards that stand. SCHW:15
Hoover, H. C.
Moral standard in an industrial era. ANN 14:428
Jeffrey, R. C.
Ethics in public discourse. BA 1973-74:119
Jones, J. L.
Who is tampering with the soul of America? LINR:211; LINRS:220
Lerner, D.
Comfort and fun: morality in a nice society. ARS:168
Lewis, C. S.
Social morality. ARS:177
Three parts of morality. ARS:175
Mount, A.
The Playboy philosophy--pro. LINRS:157; LINRST:181
Parson, M. J.
Idealism: what's wrong with it? BA 1975-76:166
Pinson, W. M., Jr.
The Playboy philosophy--con. LINRS:170
Powell, L. F., Jr.
The eroding authority. BA 1972-73:101
Spiritual patterns. BURT:124

---- See also Behavior; Character; Charities, Christian ethics; Courage; Crime and criminals; Friendship; Honesty; Justice; Liberty; Love; Patience; Patriotism; Peace; Sin; Social problems; Success; Truthfulness and falsehood

Ettelson, Harry W.
God be with thee. WALE:38

Look above and beyond! WALE:41
Parting is such sweet sorrow. WALE:44

Eucken, Rudolf
Naturalism or idealism? (Nobel Lecture, March 27, 1909). NOL:74

EUCKEN, RUDOLF CHRISTOPH
Hjärne, H.
Presentation [of the Nobel Prize for Literature to Rudolf Christoph Eucken, 1908]. NOB 6:3; NOL:67

Euler, Hans Von
Fermentation of sugars and fermentative enzymes (Nobel Lecture for 1929, May 23, 1930). NOLC 2:144

EULER, HANS VON
Söderbaum, H. G.
Presentation [of the Nobel Prize for Chemistry to Arthur Harden and Hans Karl August Simon von Euler-Chelpin, Dec. 12, 1929]. NOLC 2:127

EULOGIES
Adler, M.
Bare spirit. WALE:3
Teacher's spiritual dimensions. WALE:6
Arm, M.
Vial of fragrant ointment. WALE:13
Becker, A.
To make a commonplace wondrous. WALE:15
Beecher, H. W.
Effect of the death of Lincoln. BREWE 1:365
Belson, R. S.
What really counts. WALE:18
Besdin, A. R.
Life's struggle. WALE:20
Bial, M. D.
Light from the stones. WALE:21
Blaine, J. G.
Life and character of J. A. Garfield. BREWE 2:482; HURH:137
Brademas, J.
Eulogy for Robert Kennedy. JAM:43
Brooks, S. H.
God's grief. WALE:23
Buchanan, D.
Eulogy of Garibaldi. MCA:78
Burstein, A.
Power of memory. WALE:25
Califano, J. A.
A tribute to the man of the people. BA 1977-78:197
Carter, J.
My good friend Hubert Humphrey. BA 1977-78:200
Chaney, F. L.
Ben is going to take his big brother's place. FON:1017
Cheek, J. E.
A promise made, a promise to keep: Whitney Young and the nation. BA 1970-71:131
Chertoff, M. S.
Benjamin A. Lichter. WALE:205
Go thou in peace. WALE:27
Chiel, S.
Seder of life. WALE:29
Cleaver, E.
Meditation on the assassination of Martin Luther King, Jr. OE:229
Cronbach, A.
Of Earth, earthy and of Heaven, heavenly. WALE:30
Curtis, G. W.
Eulogy on Wendell Phillips. BREWE 4:1571
Davis, A.
The legacy of George Jackson. FON:1191
Davis, O.
Malcolm was our manhood, our living Black manhood. FON:1010
De Sola Pool, D.
Man's advocate. WALE:33
Drazin, N.
From the summit. WALE:34
Dreyfus, A. S.
Leo Baeck. WALE:207
Essrig, H.
Lordly cedar. WALE:35
Ettelson, H. W.
God be with thee. WALE:38
Look above and beyond! WALE:41
Parting is such sweet sorrow.

WALE:44
Eulogy delivered by an American Indian chief for a friend. JAM:45
Everett, E.
Adams and Jefferson. HURH:64
Farrar, F. W.
Funeral oration on General Grant. BREWE 6:2128
Fedder, A. H.
Three ways to mourn. WALE:47
Feibelman, J. B.
Life's victor. WALE:49
Finkle, J. J.
Brief sojourn. WALE:51
Freehof, S. B.
David Glick. WALE:210
Garsek, I.
Do not judge this violent death. WALE:52
Highest attainment. WALE:54
Sorrow but not tragedy. WALE:57
Gerstein, I.
Candle of the Lord. WALE:60
Man is a soldier. WALE:60
Gladstone, W. E.
On Lord Beaconsfield. BREWE 6:2291
Go on and prosper (outline of eulogistic speech). CUB:76
Goldfarb, S. D.
Art of reconstruction. WALE:61
Embers and cinders. WALE:67
My cup runneth over. WALE:70
Goldman, I. M.
Biography of an angel. WALE:72
Book of life. WALE:73
Let thy garments always be white. WALE:75
Man who walked with God. WALE:77
Gordis, R.
Latter-Day Joseph. WALE:81
Gordon, D. W.
Fruitful tears. WALE:83
Greenberg, S.
Henry Goody. WALE:214
We weep today. WALE:84
Gregory of Nazianzus
Eulogy on Basil of Caesarea. BREWE 6:2336
Grollman, E. A.
If we love, we must lose. WALE:87
Hammer, R. A.
Disciple of Aaron. WALE:89
Helman, L. A.
Risks of life. WALE:90
Hurwitz, J.
Crown of our head has fallen. WALE:93
Jung, L.
Mother's immortality. WALE:96
Kahn, A. D.
John F. Kennedy. WALE:218
Kahn, R. I.
Like water spilled on the ground. WALE:98
Kaplan, L.
Three basic questions. WALE:99
Kaplan, S. M.
Man's true measurements. WALE:102
Katz, R. M.
Psalm of life. WALE:103
Kestenbaum, J.
Live each day. WALE:106
Prescription for humanity. WALE:107
Standard of life. WALE:109
Klein, I.
Before her time. WALE:110
Klein, J. T.
Question most frequently asked. WALE:112
Kosman, M.
Eulogy for Irving Wolberg. JAM:44
Langer, E.
Instrument of revelation. LINR:301; LINRS:300; LINRST:370
Levenson, J.
Live hopefully! WALE:116
Servant of the Lord has died. WALE:118
Levine, E. B.
John F. Kennedy. WALE:221
Lipis, P. L.
Darkness at noon. WALE:120
Dreams fulfilled. WALE:122
Four good signs. WALE:124
Look beyond the shadows. WALE:128
Lipnick, B.
Family's tribute. WALE:130
McGowan, C.

Eulogy on Adlai E. Stevenson. BA 1965-66:227
Malcolm, G. A.
Judge Andres Borromeo did his duty! CURM:183
Mansfield, M. J.
Eulogy for John F. Kennedy. ANN 18:202
Mays, B. E.
Eulogy on Dr. Martin Luther King, Jr.
BA 1967-68:161; BAAGB:399; SMHV:296
Menzies, R. G.
Eulogy of Churchill. MCA:151
Milgrom, J.
He cannot be replaced. WALE:132
Minda, A. G.
He died climbing. WALE:134
Vision that looks beyond. WALE:137
Mondale, W. F.
A time to celebrate life. BA 1977-78:205
Nussbaum, M.
Al Jolson. WALE:225
Parker, T.
Discourse on the death of Daniel Webster. BREWE 8:3137
Pearl, C.
Seal of truth. WALE:140
Percy, C. H.
Eulogy for Robert Kennedy. JAM:42
Phillips, W.
Toussaint L'Ouverture. OLIS:170
Pollak, G.
Light from sorrow. WALE:143
Poplack, A. M.
Preparation for eternity. WALE:146
Rackovsky, I.
Loom of time. WALE:147
Rainey, J. H.
Eulogy on Charles Sumner. FON:403
Ransom, R. C.
William Lloyd Garrison: a centennial oration. SMHV:66
Raskas, B. S.
Physician's prayer. WALE:149
Roosevelt, T.
First annual message. ANN 12:433; STAT 2:2014
Rosenthal, N. L.
My son, my son. WALE:152
Routtenberg, M. J.
Crown of a good name. WALE:154
Rubel, C. M.
Beauties of Japheth and the glory of Shem. WALE:157
Rudin, J. P.
Shadows in the sun. WALE:160
Rusk, D.
Eulogy of Lyndon Baines Johnson. BA 1972-73:132
Salkowitz, S.
King's answer. WALE:163
Sevareid, E.
Eulogy for the astronauts. MOP:189; MOPR:165
Eulogy for Wernher Von Braun. EHN:373
Shtull, J.
Man of deed. WALE:164
Shulman, C. E.
Alfred S. Alschuler. WALE:229
Silver, S. M.
Come back. WALE:166
Simon, E. Y.
Heavenly glow. WALE:169
Two arks. WALE:172
Simon, R.
This was a man! WALE:174
Upward climb. WALE:175
Stanley, A. O.
Address in honor of Robert E. Lee. BLY:216
Stanley, J.
Tribute to a fallen Black soldier. FON:268
Stern, H. J.
Work of art. WALE:178
Stevenson, A. E.
Address at the memorial service for Sir Winston Churchill. LINR:305; LINRS:307; LINRST:373
Eulogy on Eleanor Roosevelt. BRP:230
Farewell to a friend (Lloyd Lewis). ALA:119
Stiskin, M. N.
Man is a soul. WALE:179
Suggestions for the preparation of eulogistic speeches. MILS:6

Swarensky, M. E.
Bridge of love. WALE:181
Spiritual portrait. WALE:183
Teller, M.
What the Lord requires. WALE:185
Thomson, T. J. B.
Brightness is darkened (eulogy on Tuanku Abdul Rahman Ibni Al-Marhum Tuanku Mohammed, first King of Malaysia). MONS: 281
Let these be his epitaph (eulogy on Sultan Hissamuddin Alam Shah Ibni-Marhum Sultan Ala'iddin Sulaiman Shah). MONS:283
Thoreau, H. D.
Plea for Captain John Brown. ANN 9:136
Tomsky, M. B.
Bitter and the sweet. WALE:187
Righteous shall flourish like the palm-tree. WALE:188
Symphony of life. WALE:190
Turitz, L. E.
Measure of greatness. WALE:192
Wallack, M. A.
And thou shalt choose life. WALE:197
Living presence. WALE:194
Wears, I. C.
The Ku Klux of the North. FON:378
Webster, D.
Eulogy on Adams and Jefferson. BREWE 10:3848
Weinberger, S.
Cheerful spirit. WALE:198
Weinstein, J. J.
One of the thirty-six. WALE:200
Whipper, W.
Eulogy on William Wilberforce. FON:49
Williams, P.
A tribute to Captain Paul Cuffe. FON:28
Wirt, W.
Death of Jefferson and Adams. BREWE 10:3905

EUROPE - HISTORY - 20TH CENTURY
Nansen, F.
The suffering people of Europe (Nobel Lecture, Dec. 19, 1922). NOLP 1:361

EUROPEAN WAR, 1914-1918
Johnson, J. W.
Africa at the Peace Table and the descendants of Africans in our American democracy. FON:730
La Follette, R. M., Sr.
Against war with Germany. ANN 14:104
Soldier's pay. GRG:36
Lloyd George, David
Appeal to the nation. MCB:483
Mannix, D.
Case against conscription. MCA:134
Norris, G. W.
Opposition to Wilson's War Message. ANN 14:101
Root, E.
European War and the preservation of America's ideals. ANN 14:70
Wilson, W.
"Eyes of the people opened." STAT 3:2580
Fourteen points (January 8, 1918). BOORA 2:773; FRIP:291; GRG:42; HURH:180; OLIS:228
Neutrality message to the Senate, August 19, 1914. ANN 13:491
Peace without victory. ANN 14:65; FRIP:286; HURH:173
Second annual message. STAT 3:2551
Sixth annual message. STAT 3:2587
Speech opening campaign for fourth liberty loan. FRIP:295
Third annual message. STAT 3:2560
War message to Congress, April 2, 1917. ANN 14:77; HURH:177; LINS:291

---- See also Peace; Peace Conference, 1919; Unknown soldier

---- NEW ZEALAND
Bell, F. H. D.
The defence of the Empire in the Great War. MACS:273

Euwema, Ben
Excellence in teaching. ARS:48

Evangelista, Teodora
The needs of a nation (Rizal, Dec. 3, 1933). CURM:160

EVANGELISTS See Clergy

Evans, Theodore H., Jr.
Application of love. VI:90

Evarts, William M.
Weakest spot in the American system (defense at impeachment of A. Johnson). BREWE 6:2082

Evatt, Herbert Vere
Australia and the United Nations charter. MCA:161

Everett, Edward
Adams and Jefferson. (Charlestown, Mass., Aug. 1, 1826). HURH:64
Circumstances favorable to the progress of literature in America. ANN 5:118
"The fabric of American freedom ... may crumble into dust. But the cause in which these our fathers shone is immortal." Same as his Adams and Jefferson
History of liberty. BREWE 6:2092
Moral forces which make American progress. BREWE 6:2112
Plea for support of an Ohio college. ANN 6:26
State funds for Harvard. ANN 7:502
Universal and uncoerced cooperation. BREWE 6:2115

Everheart, William E.
We hold these truths (Kansas City, Mo., Jan. 22, 1976). BA 1975-76:27

Evers, Charles
We are going to make it better for Blacks and Whites. (New York, May, 1969). FON:1167

EVIL See Sin

EVOLUTION
Müller, F. M.
Impassable barrier between brutes and man. BREWE 8:3086

EXCITATION
Huxley, A. F.
The quantitative analysis of excitation and conduction in nerve. NOLM 4:52

EXECUTIVE POWER - UNITED STATES
Polk, J. K.
Fourth annual address. STAT 1:731

EXECUTIVES
Business leaders of tomorrow. BURT:37
Executive. BURT:27

EXHIBITIONS
McKinley, W.
At the Pan-American Exposition. ANN 12:428
Washington, B. T.
Address at the opening of the Atlanta Exposition. ANN 12:9; BAPRR:255; BAS:77 (outline only); BRYF:492; FON:577; LINS:263; OE:82; SMHV:94

EXPLANATION AND INSTRUCTION, SPEECHES OF See Informative speeches

EXPUNGING RESOLUTION
Clay, H.
Expunging Resolution. BREWE 4:1233

EXTREMISM See Right and left (Political science)

EYE
Granit, R.
The development of retinal neurophysiology. NOLM 4:255
Gullstrand, A.
How I found the mechanism of intracapsular accommodation. NOLM 1:414
Hartline, H. K.
Visual receptors and retinal interaction. NOLM 4:269
Wald, G.
The molecular basis of visual excitation. NOLM 4:292

- F -

Fabunmi, Larry
Black and white keys.
SCHW:206

FAILURE See Success

FAITH
Bulkeley, P.
The gospel-covenant.
JON:30
Fosdick, H. E.
Power to see it through.
CROCK:58

---- See also Religion

Falkland, Lucius Cary, 2nd Viscount
Ship-money-impeaching Lord Keeper Finch.
BREWE 6:2123

FAME
Conwell, R. H.
Acres of diamonds.
ANN 11:271; BEN:159; HURH:202
Damiani, P.
Secret of true greatness.
BREWE 4:1605
Emerson, R. W.
Uses of great men.
BREWE 5:2012
Kane, A.
Glory of notoriety. REIR:223

FAMILY
Jones, J. L.
"Let's bring back Dad": a solid value system.
LINRST:254
Muench, A.
Rural families and welfare.
ANN 15:462

FAMINES
Brown, M.
Famine: a reality, not just a threat. BREWW:168
Price, S.
Agriculture--the real answer to starvation. BREWW:161

FANEUIL, PETER
Lovell, J.
Funeral oration. POC:138

Fannings, Helen See Brown, Joan

FAR EAST See Orient; United States - Foreign Relations - East (Far East)

Farber, Seymour M.
Why national concern for biomedical communication?
BA 1966-67:118

Farber, William O.
Changing concepts of public service. ARS:208

FAREWELL ADDRESSES
Aelred, Saint
Farewell. BREWE 1:110
Benjamin, J. P.
Farewell to the Union.
BREWE 1:399
Cleaver, E.
Farewell address. SMHV:284
Curran, J. P.
Farewell to the Irish Parliament. BREWE 4:1552
Edward VIII
Farewell of former King Edward VIII. BRYH:517
Edwards, J.
Farewell-sermon. POC:443
Eisenhower, D. D.
Farewell address, January 17, 1961. ANN 18:1; JAM:36; LAA:209; MDV:132
Hutchins, R. M.
Message to the younger generation. MDV:198
Jackson, A.
Farewell address, 1837.
ANN 6:298
Jones, H. M.
Farewell to the English Department. REIR:232
Lee, R. E.
To the Army of Northern Virginia. ECH:188
Lincoln, A.
Farewell to Springfield (outline of speech). REIR:232
MacArthur, D.
Farewell to the cadets (accepting Sylvanus Thayer award for service to his nation, West Point, May 12, 1962).
LINR:264; LINRS:283; LINRST:357; MDV:20; MUS:332
Parting word from the pastor's wife (2 examples). BNH:84

Roxas, M.
A farewell to the Assembly. CURM:282
Sevareid, E.
Parting thoughts. BA 1977-78:143
Washington, G.
Farewell address. ANN 3:606; BEN:18; BOORA 1:194; BREWE 10:3740; HURH:44
When a pastor has to say goodbye (2 examples). BNH:83
Words of farewell. BON:53

Farley, James A.
Responds to an introduction. PRS:145

Farmer, James
The "Movement" now. (American Studies Conference at Lincoln Univ., Pa., Feb. 25, 1967). FON:1040

---- and others (Malcolm X)
Debate at Cornell University, March 7, 1962. ROSC:59; OE:248
Debate on the solution to America's race problem. Same as his Debate at Cornell University, March 7, 1962

FARMERS
Gould, J. C.
My responsibility as an agricultural citizen. BREWW:147

---- See also Agriculture

---- NEW ZEALAND
Massey, W. F.
Repeal of income tax on farmers, 1923. MACS:304 sel.

FARMINGTON CANAL
Wolcott, O.
Address at state line between Southwick, Massachusetts and Granby, Connecticut, July 4, 1825. HAW:122

FARRAGUT, DAVID GLASGOW
Choate, J. H.
Farragut. BREWE 3:1109

Farrar, Frederick William
Funeral oration on General Grant. BREWE 6:2128

Farwell, Jane See Scott, Richard

FATHERS
Dear old Dad. BURT:172
Overhill, J.
Regular snob. MDYG:75

FATHERS AND SONS
Berson, A.
Open letter to my middle-aged father. REIR:215
Welcome to fathers at Father-Son banquet. HNWM:37
Welcome to sons at Father-Son banquet. HNWM:38

FATHER'S DAY
Boy and his Dad (welcome address on Father's Day). HNWM:12
Forgotten man (welcome address on Father's Day). HNWM:10
He's somebody special (welcome address on Father's Day). HNWM:11
What is in a name (welcome address on Father's Day)? HNWM:13

Faulkner, William
On accepting the Nobel Prize, exhorts the young writers of the world (Stockholm, Dec. 10, 1950). ALA:125; ANN 17:33; ARS:52; BOORA 2:988; GRG:86; HURH:291; MOPR:379; NOB 19:7; NOL:444
Writer's duty. Same as his On accepting the Nobel prize

FAULKNER, WILLIAM
Hellström, G.
Presentation [of the Nobel Prize for Literature for 1949 to William Faulkner]. NOB 19:3; NOL:440

Fawcett, Novice G.
Direction for destiny. (Ohio State University, March 13, 1971). BA 1970-71:106
Introduces E. W. Ingram, president, White Castle, Inc. PRS:6

Fazakerly, Nicholas See Walpole, R., jt. auth.

FEAR
Gaustad, E. S.
The beginning of wisdom. CAPB:370
Hall, R. O.
Fear and faith. VI:98

Featherston, Isaac
The demand for responsible government (Wellington, April 18, 1853). MACS:84 sel.

---- and others (William Fox)
"Provincialism" 1856 (New Zealand House of Representatives, May 2, 1856). MACS:96 sel.

Fedder, Abraham H.
Three ways to mourn. WALE:47

FEDERAL AID TO EDUCATION See Education and state

FEDERAL AID TO RESEARCH
Califano, J. A.
Federal support of science and medicine. BA 1977-78:99

FEDERAL GOVERNMENT
Atkinson, H.
The abolition of the provinces, 1876. MACS:111 sel.
Church, F.
Rediscovering America. BA 1975-76:124
Hamilton, A.
On an act granting to Congress certain imposts and duties. ALS:133
Hoover, H. C.
Reassuring touch: President Hoover speaks, 1931. ROD:15
Marshall, J.
McCulloch v. Maryland: opinion for the Supreme Court. ANN 4:530; BOORA 1:241

---- See also United States - Politics and government

Feibelman, Julian B.
Life's victor. WALE:49

Feldmann, Margaret
Eyes of the whole world. SCHW:156
Of mice and women. SCHW:64

FELLOWSHIP See Friendship

FEMINISM
Edwards, L.
Libbing. BRYF:489
Pogrebin, L. C.
Commencement address. TAC:242

---- See also Women

Fénelon, François de Salignac de la Mothe
Nature as a revelation. BREWE 6:2142
Simplicity and greatness. Same as his True and false simplicity
True and false simplicity. BREWE 6:2137

FENTON, WALTER S.
Simmons, D. A.
Presents Walter S. Fenton. LYI:131

Ferguson, Jane
Witch trials. (Baylor University, 1955). CAPB:377

Ferguson, Virginia
Women in agriculture. BREWW:122

FERMENTATION
Buchner, E.
Cell-free fermentation. NOLC 1:103
Euler, H. V.
Fermentation of sugars and fermentative enzymes. NOLC 2:144
Harden, A.
The function of phosphate in alcoholic fermentation. NOLC 2:131

Fermi, Enrico
Artificial radioactivity produced by neutron bombardment (Nobel

Lecture, Dec. 12, 1938).
NOLPH 2:414

FERMI, ENRICO
Pleijel, H.
Presentation [of the Nobel Prize for Physics to Enrico Fermi, Dec. 12, 1938].
NOLPH 2:409

Ferrell, Dianne
Young men with visions. (Baylor University, 1969).
CAPB:385

Ferris, W. H.
Education and the Triple Revolution. MDV:216

Feynman, Richard P.
The development of the space-time view of quantum electrodynamics (Nobel Lecture, Dec. 11, 1965).
NOLPH 4:155

FEYNMAN, RICHARD P.
Waller, I.
Presentation [of the Nobel Prize for Physics to Sin-Itiro Tomonaga, Julian Schwinger, and Richard P. Feynman, Dec. 11, 1965].
NOLPH 4:123

FFA See Future Farmers of America

Fibiger, Johannes Andreas Grib
Investigations on Spiroptera carcinoma and the experimental induction of cancer (Nobel Lecture, Dec. 12, 1927). NOLM 2:122

FIBIGER, JOHANNES ANDREAS GRIB
Wernstedt, W.
Presentation of the Nobel Prize for Physiology or Medicine for 1926 to Johannes Andreas Grib Fibiger, Dec. 12, 1927. NOLM 2:119

FICTION See Literature

Field, David Dudley
Cost of "Blood and Iron."
BREWE 6:2157
In re Milligan--martial laws as lawlessness. BREWE 6:2147
In the case of McCardle--necessity as an excuse for tyranny.
BREWE 6:2155

Field, Stephen J. See following jt. auths. Miller, S. F.; Terry, D. S.; Waite, M. R.

Fielden, Samuel
Address at trial, Chicago, October 7-9, 1886. ACC:49; PAF:41

Fillmore, Millard
First annual message. ANN 8:109; STAT 1:792
Golden rule for foreign affairs. Same as his First annual message
Second annual message.
STAT 1:808
Third annual message.
STAT 1:834

FINANCE - UNITED STATES
Coolidge, C.
Third annual message.
STAT 3:2669
Landon, A. M.
Federal and family finances.
BAD:62
Taft, W. H.
Fourth annual message: part II, December 6, 1912.
STAT 3:2511
Third annual message: part IV, December 21, 1911.
STAT 3:2469

---- See also Tariff; Annual messages under name of each President, i.e. Hayes, Rutherford B. First annual message

FINANCIERS See Banks and banking

Finch, Sir Heneage See Nottingham, H. F.

FINCH OF FORDWICH, JOHN FINCH, 1st BARON
Falkland, L. C.
Ship-money-impeaching Lord Keeper Finch. BREWE 6:2123

FINE ARTS See Art and artists

Finkle, Jesse J.
Brief sojourn. WALE:51

Finley, Charles O.
Responds to introduction.
PRS:115

FINSEN, NIELS RYBERG
Mörner, K. A. H.
Presentation [of the Nobel Prize for Physiology or Medicine to Niels Ryberg Finsen, 1903]. NOLM 1:123

FIREMEN
Welcome to a Fire Chief as speaker of a civic club.
HNWM:42

Fischer, Adolph
Address at trial, Chicago, October 7-9, 1886.
ACC:36; PAF:32

Fischer, G.
Presentation [of the Nobel Prize for Physiology or Medicine to Paul Hermann Müller, Dec. 11, 1948].
NOLM 3:227

Fischer, Hans
On haemin and the relationships between haemin and chlorophyll (Nobel Lecture, Dec. 11, 1930). NOLC 2:165

FISCHER, HANS
Söderbaum, H. G.
Presentation [of the Nobel Prize for Chemistry to Hans Fischer, Dec. 11, 1930].
NOLC 2:161

Fischer, Hermann Emil
Syntheses in the purine and sugar group (Nobel Lecture, Dec. 12, 1902).
NOLC 1:21

FISCHER, HERMANN EMIL
Théel, H.
Presentation [of the Nobel Prize for Chemistry to Hermann Emil Fischer, Dec. 12, 1902]. NOLC 1:17

Fischer-Hjalmars, Inga
Presentation [of the Nobel Prize for Chemistry to Robert S. Mulliken, Dec. 12, 1966].
NOLC 4:127

Fishburn, Phillip
Land of cattle, land of America.
BREWW:105

Fisher, Charles T., Jr.
Presents George C. Kenney.
LYI:150

Fisher, John
Jeopardy of daily life.
BREWE 6:2164

Fisk, Theophilus
War of capital against labor.
ANN 6:118

Fitch, Thomas
A fervent appeal for free silver (1889). (National Silver Convention at St. Louis, Nov. 1889). DAVF:190

Flack, Gene
Responds to an introduction.
PRS:191

FLAG DAY
Beecher, H. W.
Raising the flag over Fort Sumter. BREWE 1:347

FLAGS
Beveridge, A. J.
March of the flag. ANN 12:198; BOORA 2:622; GRG:14; LINS:276
Jackson, R. H.
Court broadens the rights of citizens: the Second Flag Salute Case, 1943. ROD:214
---- and others
West Virginia Board of Education et al v. Barnette et al: opinion for the court and dissenting opinion. ANN 16:148

Flaxman, John
Physical and intellectual beauty.
BREWE 6:2167

Flechier, Esprit
Death of Turenne.
BREWE 6:2174

Fleming, Sir Alexander
Penicillin (Nobel Lecture, Dec. 11, 1945). NOLM 3:83

FLEMING, SIR ALEXANDER
Liljestrand, G.
Presentation [of the Nobel Prize for Physiology or Medicine to Sir Alexander Fleming, Ernst Boris Chain, and Sir Howard Walter Florey, Dec. 11, 1945]. NOLM 3:77

Fleming, Mrs. Ian See Sykes, C., jt. auth.

Florence, Franklin
Meaning of Black power. SMHR:161

Florey, Sir Howard Walter
Penicillin (Nobel Lecture, Dec. 11, 1945). NOLM 3:96

FLOREY, SIR HOWARD WALTER
Liljestrand, G.
Presentation [of the Nobel Prize for Physiology or Medicine to Sir Alexander Fleming, Ernst Boris Chain, and Sir Howard Walter Florey, Dec. 11, 1945]. NOLM 3:77

Flowers, Walter See Jordan, B. C., jt. auth.

FLYING SAUCERS
Sonberg, H. A.
Unidentified flying objects; their history, and various explanations which have been given concerning their nature. BAS:203 (outline only)

FOCH, FERDINAND
Pepper, G. W.
Introducing Ferdinand Foch. LYI:145

FOLK LITERATURE
Buchan, J.
Novel and the fairy tale. ARS:54

FOOD
Boyd Orr, J.
Science and peace (Nobel Lecture, Dec. 12, 1949). NOLP 2:415
Butz, E. L.
Feast or famine: the key to peace. BA 1974-75:81
Hannah, J. A.
Meeting world food news. BA 1976-77:103
Hatfield, M. O.
Global interdependence: "Life, Liberty, and the Pursuit of Happiness" in today's world. BA 1974-75:89
Kissinger, H. A.
Address before the World Food Conference. BA 1974-75:62

FOOD SUPPLY
Bark, D. R.
World food crisis. BREWW:219
Borlaug, N. E.
The green revolution, peace, and humanity (Nobel Lecture, Dec. 11, 1970). NOLP 3:454
Brown, M.
Famine: a reality, not just a threat. BREWW:168
Carpenter, E.
We are involved in the world food crisis. BREWW:223
Dunlap, D. E.
The world needs our help. BREWW:98
Grappe, A.
The age of food. BREWW:112
Kubicek, K.
Global crisis. BREWW:128
Rush, W.
Feeding the hungry world. BREWW:91
Stratton, R. D.
Food: a world crisis. BREWW:81
Sullivan, J. H.
The United States and the coming world food crisis. BA 1979-80:46
Trafton, C.
The moral dimensions of the world food problem. BREWW:206

FOOTE'S RESOLUTIONS See Foot's Resolution

FOOT'S RESOLUTION
Hayne, R. Y.

On Foot's Resolution (January 21, 1830). BREWE 7:2441
Webster, D.
Reply to Hayne. ANN 5:347; BEN:35; BREWE 10:3758; BRR:23; HOW:53

Forbes, George W.
The Public Safety Conservation Bill, 1932. (New Zealand House of Representatives, April 19, 1932). MACS:314 sel.

FORCED LABOR
White, W. F.
"Work or fight" in the South. FON:724

Ford, Gerald R.
Acceptance speech. (Washington, D.C., Dec. 6, 1973). BA 1973-74:193
First presidential address. (Washington, Aug. 9, 1974). BA 1974-75:50
Presidential remarks with question-and-answer session (Peoria, Ill., March 5, 1976). BA 1975-76:133
Republican National Convention acceptance speech (Kansas City, Mo., Aug. 19, 1976). LINRST:349
State of the Union address (Jan. 15, 1975). JAM:31
Toast to Queen Elizabeth (1976). JAM:21

---- and others (Jimmy Carter)
The third presidential debate (Williamsburg, Va., Oct. 22, 1976). BA 1976-77:30

---- See Burger, W. E., jt. auth.

FORD, GERALD R.
Elizabeth II, Queen of England
Toast to President Ford and to the American people. JAM:22
Kaunda, K.
Toast to President Ford. JAM:23
Nelson, G. A.
Against the nomination of Gerald R. Ford. BA 1973-74:188
Percy, C. H.
For the nomination of Gerald R. Ford. BA 1973-74:189

Ford, Guy Stanton
Presents Christopher Morley. LYI:55

Ford, Henry, II
Presents Elmo Roper. LYI:73

Ford, James W.
The right of revolution for the Negro people (Harlem, 1935). FON:800

FOREFATHERS' DAY
Prentiss, S. S.
On New England's Forefathers' Day. BREWE 8:3233

FOREIGN AID PROGRAM See Economic assistance, American; World War, 1939-1945 - United States - Aid to Great Britain

FOREIGN POPULATION See Immigration and emigration

FOREIGN TRADE See Commerce

Forman, James
Black manifesto. (Detroit, April 25, 1969). FON:1156; OE:235

Forssmann, Werner Theodor Otto
The role of heart catheterization and angiocardiography in the development of modern medicine (Nobel Lecture, Dec. 11, 1956). NOLM 3:506

FORSSMANN, WERNER THEODOR OTTO
Liljestrand, G.
Presentation [of the Nobel Prize for Physiology or Medicine to André Frederic Cournand, Werner Theodor Otto Forssmann, and Dickinson Woodruff Richards Jr., Dec. 11, 1956]. NOLM 3:501

Forten, James and others (R. Perrott)
Address to the humane and benev-

olent inhabitants of the city and county of Philadelphia. (Philadelphia, Aug. 10, 1817). OE:14
An appeal against the colonization movement.... Same as his Address to the humane and benevolent inhabitants of the city and county of Philadelphia

Fortune, T. Thomas
It is time to call a halt. (Chicago, Jan., 1890). FON:556
The present relations of labor and capital. (Brooklyn, April 20, 1886). FON:506

FORTUNES See Wealth

Fosdick, Harry Emerson
Christian conscience about war. OLIS:237
Fundamentalist controversy. Same as his Shall the Fundamentalists win?
Power to see it through. CROCK:58
Shall the Fundamentalists win? ANN 14:325
Unknown soldier. LINS:312

FOSDICK, HARRY EMERSON
Gossett, W. T.
Presents Harry Emerson Fosdick. LYI:157

FOUNDERS' DAY See Anniversaries

FOUR-H CLUBS
Welcome to Four H club members. HNWM:49

FOURTH OF JULY
Adams, J. Q.
Fourth of July oration, 1828. HAW:94
Bacon, L.
Plea for Africa. HAW:60
Sermon from Mark XII, 34. HAW:57
Bancroft, G.
Fourth of July oration, 1826. HAW:75
Barlow, J.
Unfinished revolution. ANN 3:90
Boudinot, E.
Mission of America. BREWE 2:581
Burger, W. E.
Bicentennial of American independence. BA 1976-77:185
Cadwell, D.
Oration. HAW:319
Carson, H. L.
American liberty. BREWE 3:985
Choate, R.
On American nationality (82nd anniversary of American independence). ANN 9:54
Clinton, D.
Address at the Licking Summit near Newark, Ohio. HAW:119
Cook, J.
Ultimate America. BREWE 4:1381
Cox, A.
Can the dream survive? BA 1979-80:157
Crockett, D.
Fourth of July oration, 1834. HAW:136
Douglass, F.
I do not believe in the anti-slavery of Abraham Lincoln. FON:232
Slavery: speech at Rochester, July 5, 1852. FON:104; SMHR:125
What to the slave is the Fourth of July? JAM:19; OE:41
Dwight, T.
On the duty of Americans at the present crisis. ANN 4:33
Everett, E.
History of liberty. BREWE 6:2092
Garrison, W. L.
Dangers of slavery. ANN 5:303; MDT:26
Hecker, F. K. F.
Liberty in the New Atlantis. BREWE 7:2457
King, T. S.
Fourth of July oration, 1860. HAW:231
The two declarations of independence: 1776 and 1861. HAW:260
McCorkle, S.
A sermon for the anniversary of American independence,

July 24th, 1786. HAW:292
Mack, E.
Fourth of July oration, 1838. HAW:164
Mason, J., Jr.
Oration delivered on the 4th of July, 1818 at Williamsburg, Virginia. HAW:300
Meek, A. B.
Oration. HAW:307
Osborne, P.
It is time for us to be up and doing. FON:47
Phillips, W.
Fourth of July oration. HAW:223
Rantoul, R., Jr.
On the barbarity of the common law. ANN 6:262
Robbins, A.
Fourth of July oration, July 4, 1834. HAW:160
Robinson, F.
A Jacksonian attack on monopoly (1834). DAVF:69
Labor as the source of reform. ANN 6:69
Rush, R.
Fourth of July oration, 1812. HAW:16
Seward, W. H.
Fourth of July oration, 1840. HAW:183
Sumner, C.
True grandeur of nations. BREWE 9:3548
Thoreau, H. D.
Fourth of July oration, 1854. HAW:200
Wallace, G. C.
Civil Rights Bill: fraud, sham, and hoax. MDV:175
Webster, D.
Fourth of July oration, 1800. HAW:1
Whitney, A. G.
Oration. HAW:329
Williams, P.
Slavery and colonization. FON:43
Wolcott, O.
Address at state line between Southwick, Massachusetts and Granby, Connecticut, July 4, 1825. HAW:122

Fox, Charles James
Address on the King's speech (protesting the call-up of the militia). STRM:121
Against Warren Hastings. BREWE 6:2192
Character of the Duke of Bedford. BREWE 6:2182
In favor of Mr. Grey's motion for Parliamentary reform. BRYH:254
On electoral reform. Same as his In favor of Mr. Grey's motion for Parliamentary reform
On the East India Bill. BREWE 6:2189
On the rejection of Napoleon's overtures. (H. of Commons, Feb. 3, 1800). CLAYP:232
Speech in the debate in Parliament on the French overtures for peace, February 3, 1800. Same as his On the rejection of Napoleon's overtures

Fox, William See Featherston, Isaac, jt. auth.

France, Anatole
Acceptance [of the Nobel Prize for Literature, 1921]. NOB 6:93; NOL:181

FRANCE, ANATOLE
Karlfeldt, E. A.
Presentation [of the Nobel Prize for Literature to Anatole France, 1921]. NOB 6:85; NOL:174

FRANCE
Carnot, L. N. M.
Against imperialism in France. BREWE 3:967
DeGaulle, C.
France: the third world power. MDV:38
Hugo, V. M.
Liberty tree in Paris. BREWE 7:2548
Pitt, W., 1759-1806
Against French Republicanism. BREWE 8:3202
---- and others
Deliverance of Europe (contains his Against French Republicanism speech). BRYH:281

---- FOREIGN RELATIONS - AFRICA
Houphouet-Boigny, F.
French Africa and the French Union. EMP:73

---- ---- MEXICO
Theirs, L. A.
Mexico and Louis Napoleon's policies. BREWE 9:3610

---- HISTORY
Gambetta, L.
France after German conquest. BREWE 6:2217

---- ---- REVOLUTION, 1789-1799
Cambon, P. J.
Crisis of 1793. BREWE 3:931
Danton, G. J.
How can France be saved? BRN:56
Let France be free. BREWE 5:1626
To dare again, ever to dare. BREWE 5:1625
Dwight, T.
On the duty of Americans at the present crisis. ANN 4:33
Guadet, M. E.
Reply to Robespierre. BREWE 6:2244
Mackintosh, J.
In behalf of free speech: on the trial of Jean Peltier accused of libelling Napoleon Bonaparte. BREWE 8:2919
Mirabeau, H. G. R.
Defying the French aristocracy. BREWE 8:3033
Justifying revolution. BREWE 8:3038
On Necker's project "And yet you deliberate." BREWE 8:3024
Reason immutable and sovereign. BREWE 8:3036
Robespierre, M.
Defense from the charge of tyranny. BREWE 9:3341
Demanding the King's death. BREWE 9:3338
His defense of terrorism. BREWE 9:3331
Moral ideas and Republican principles. BREWE 9:3334
Sheridan, R. B.
On the French Revolution. BREWE 9:3438
Patriotism and perquisites. BREWE 9:3439
Tappan, D.
A warning to Harvard seniors against world revolution (1798). DAVF:49
Vergniaud, P. V.
Reply to Robespierre. BREWE 10:3692
To the camp. BREWE 10:3690

---- ---- REVOLUTION, 1848
Lamartine, A. M. L.
Revolution of 1848. BREWE 7:2702

---- POLITICS AND GOVERNMENT
Barnave, A. P. J. M.
Representative democracy against majority absolutism. BREWE 1:218

FRANCHISE See Citizenship; Elections; Suffrage; Woman suffrage

Francis, Hal
Our three goals. BREWW:131

Franck, James
Transformations of kinetic energy of free electrons into excitation energy of atoms by impacts (Nobel Lecture for 1925, Dec. 11, 1926). NOLPH 2:98

FRANCK, JAMES
Oseen, C. W.
Presentation [of the Nobel Prize for Physics for 1925 to James Franck and Gustav Hertz, Dec. 11, 1926]. NOLPH 2:95

Frank, Il'ja Michajlovič
Optics of light sources moving in refractive media (Nobel Lecture, Dec. 11, 1958). NOLPH 3:442

FRANK, IL'JA MICHAJLOVIC
Siegbahn, K.
Presentation [of the Nobel Prize for Physics to Pavel Alekseievič Cerenkov, Il'ja Michajlovič Frank and Igor' Evgen'evič Tamm, Dec. 11, 1958]. NOLPH 3:423

Frankfurter, Felix
John Marshall and the judicial function, September 22, 1955. (Conf. on Govt. under Law--Harvard Law School in commemoration of the 200th anniversary of John Marshall's birth). FRIP:353
The judicial process and the Supreme Court, April 22, 1954. (American Philosophical Society). FRIP:345
The Zeitgeist and the Judiciary. (25th anniversary dinner of the Harvard Law Review in 1912). FRIP:340

---- See following jt. auths. Black, H. L.; Jackson, R. H.

Franklin, Barbara Hackman
Consumer safety and health (Boston, Mass., Nov. 29, 1978). BA 1978-79:133

Franklin, Benjamin
Address to the Federal Convention. Same as his Disapproving and accepting the Constitution
Dangers of a salaried bureaucracy. BREWE 6:2199
Disapproving and accepting the Constitution (Philadelphia, Sept. 17, 1787). ALA:13; AND:99; BOORA 1:78; BREWE 6:2197; HURH:34; REID:393
"The older I grow, the more apt I am to doubt my own judgment of others." Same as his Disapproving and accepting the Constitution
On signing the Constitution. Same as his Disapproving and accepting the Constitution
On the Constitution. Same as his Disapproving and accepting the Constitution
Plea to the Constitutional Convention. Same as his Disapproving and accepting the Constitution

FRANKLIN, BENJAMIN
Mirabeau, H. G. R.
Announcing the death of Franklin. BREWE 8:3035

Franklin, John Hope
America's window to the world: her race problem. (New York, Oct. 26, 1956). FON:907
Martin Luther King and American traditions. BA 1968-69:45

Franks, Brian See Sykes, C., jt. auth.

Fraser, Leon
Presents James F. Byrnes. LYI:218

Fraser, Peter
Universal collective security--amendments to the United Nations Charter, 1945 (San Francisco, May 3, 1945). MACS:378 sel.

---- and others
The adoption of the Statute of Westminster (New Zealand House of Representatives, Nov. 7 and 11, 1947). MACS:286 sel.

FRATERNITY See Brotherliness

Fredga, A.
Presentation [of the Nobel Prize for Chemistry to Derek H. R. Barton and Odd Hassel, Dec. 11, 1969]. NOLC 4:295
Presentation [of the Nobel Prize for Chemistry to Hermann Staudinger, Dec. 11, 1953]. NOLC 3:393
Presentation [of the Nobel Prize for Chemistry to Karl Ziegler and Giulio Natta, Dec. 12, 1963]. NOLC 4:3
Presentation [of the Nobel Prize for Chemistry to Otto Paul Hermann Diels and Kurt Adler, Dec. 12, 1950]. NOLC 3:255
Presentation [of the Nobel Prize for Chemistry to Robert Burns Woodward, Dec. 11, 1965]. NOLC 4:97
Presentation [of the Nobel Prize for Chemistry to Sir Alexander Robertus Todd, Dec. 11, 1957]. NOLC 3:519
Presentation [of the Nobel Prize

for Chemistry to Sir Robert Robinson, Dec. 12, 1947]. NOLC 3:166
Presentation [of the Nobel Prize for Chemistry to Vincent du Vigneaud, Dec. 12, 1955]. NOLC 3:443

FREE PRESS See Liberty of the press

FREE SPEECH
Constant, B.
Free speech necessary for good government. BREWE 4:1376
Curran, J. P.
England and English liberties --in the case of Rowan. BREWE 4:1546
For Peter Finnerty and free speech. BREWE 4:1537
Douglass, F.
Plea for free speech in Boston. BREWE 5:1906; FON:244
Erskine, T.
Against Thomas Williams for the publication of Paine's Age of Reason. BREWE 6:2038
Free speech and fundamental rights: defense of Tom Paine. BREWE 6:2069; CLAYP:166
Speech in behalf of John Stockdale. BREWE 6:2050
Gallagher, W.
Free just free. BA 1973-74:132
Hamilton, A.
In the case of Zenger--for free speech in America. BREWE 6:2373
Holmes, O. W., Jr.
Dissenting opinion on Abrams v. United States. ANN 14:244; BOORA 2:666
Kennedy, R. F.
Fruitful tension. BA 1966-67:138
LaFollette, R. M., Sr.
Free speech in wartime. CUB:53 (outline only)
Mackintosh, J.
In behalf of free speech: on the trial of Jean Peltier accused of libelling Napoleon Bonaparte. BREWE 8:2919
Milton, J.
For the liberty of unlicensed printing. BREWE 8:3017
Phillips, W.
Murder of Lovejoy. ALS:161; HURH:74
Royer-Collard, P. P.
Against press censorship. BREWE 9:3347
Sanford, E. T. and others
Gitlow v. New York: opinion for the court and dissenting opinion. ANN 14:476

---- See also Dissenters

FREE TRADE AND PROTECTION
Beaconsfield, B. D.
Third reading of the Corn Importation Bill. MCB:211
Clay, H.
Free trade and seamen's rights. BREWE 4:1264
Cobden, R.
Effects of protection in agriculture. MCB:189; STRM:246
Free trade with all nations. BREWE 4:1326

---- See also Corn laws; Tariff

---- NEW ZEALAND
Marshall, J. R.
NAFTA, 1965. MACS:448 sel.

FREEDMEN'S BUREAU, 1865
Johnson, A.
Veto of Freedmen's Bureau Bill. ANN 10:3

FREEDOM See Liberty; Religious liberty; Teaching, Freedom of

FREEDOM OF INFORMATION
Krug, J. F.
In defense of liberty: extremism and other vices. BA 1975-76:193

FREEDOM OF SPEECH See Free speech

Frehof, Solomon B.
David Glick. WALE:210

FREEMASONS

Address of the United States Anti-Masonic Convention (1830). DAVF:73
An anti-Masonic call for perseverance (1834). DAVF:83
Armstrong, L.
Masonry proved to be a work of darkness (1830). DAVF:82
Debates at the Anti-Masonic Convention (1830). DAVF:79
Hall, P.
Pray God give us the strength to bear up under all our troubles. FON:13

Frelinghuysen, Theodore
The Cherokee lands. (Congress, April 9, 1830). HOW:189
In favor of universal suffrage. BREWE 6:2203
Revivalist sermon. ANN 1:344

FRIED, ALFRED HERMANN
Løvland, J. G.
Presentation [of the Nobel Prize for Peace to Alfred Hermann Fried, Dec. 10, 1911]. NOLP 1:238

Fried, Paul
Price of peace. SCHW:35

Friedman, Milton
The future of capitalism (Los Angeles, Feb. 9, 1977). LINRST:243

FRIENDS, SOCIETY OF
Backhouse, M. A.
The international service of the Society of Friends (Nobel Lecture, Dec. 12, 1947). NOLP 2:380
Cadbury, M. J.
Quakers and peace (Nobel Lecture, Dec. 12, 1947). NOLP 2:391
Jahn, G.
Presentation [of the Nobel Prize for Peace to the Friends Service Council and the American Friends Service Committee, Dec. 10, 1947]. NOLP 2:373

FRIENDSHIP
Beecher, H. W.
On fellowship. HURH:118
Welcome to old friends (2 examples). BNH:52

Friesen, S. Von
Presentation [of the Nobel Prize for Physics to Luis W. Alvarez, Dec. 11, 1968]. NOLPH 4:239

Fry, Franklin Clark <u>See</u> Sevareid, E., jt. auth.

FUGITIVE SLAVE BILL <u>See</u> Slavery in the United States

Fulbright, James William
Arrogance of power. ANN 18:362
Foreign policy--old myths and new realities (Washington, March 25, 1964). ANN 18:225; HURH:374
Great Society is a sick society. LAA:10
Intervention in Santo Domingo; we are much closer to being the most unrevolutionary nation on earth. LAA:165
"The neglect of the song." (National Press Club, Washington, D.C., Dec. 18, 1974). BA 1974-75:109
Old myths and new realities. Same as his Foreign policy--old myths and new realities
Press and politicians. ERP:159
Two Americas. BA 1965-66:115
Violence in the American character. ANN 18:206
"We are clinging to old myths in the face of new realities." Same as his Foreign policy--old myths and new realities

FULBRIGHT, JAMES WILLIAM
Ashmore, H. S.
Presents J. William Fulbright. LYI:205

Fuller, Melville Weston and others (J. M. Harlan)
United States v. E. C. Knight Company, 1895: opinion for the Supreme Court and dissenting opinion. ANN 12:23

Fuller, Zelotes
Tree of liberty (George Washington birthday address). ANN 5:355

FUNDAMENTALISM See Religion

FUNERAL SERMONS
Bossuet, J. B.
Funeral oration over the Prince Condé. BREWE 2:557
Brooks, P.
Character of Abraham Lincoln. BREWE 2:644
Emerson, R. W.
Greatness of a plain American. BREWE 5:1999
Flechier, E.
Death of Turenne. BREWE 6:2174
Hugo, V. M.
Oration on Honoré de Balzac. BREWE 7:2546
Hypereides
Funeral oration. COG:210
Ingalls, J. J.
Undiscovered country. BREWE 7:2574
Lee, H.
Funeral oration on Washington. BREWE 7:2744
Lovell, J.
Funeral oration. POC:138
Lysias
Funeral oration. COG:9
Morris, G.
Oration over Hamilton. BREWE 8:3075; HURH:54
Morton, P.
Oration at the reinternment of Warren. POC:320
Pericles
On those who died in the war. ARS:191; BAS:133 (outline only); BREWE 8:3169; SAG:33
Stanley, A. P.
Palmerston and the duty of England (funeral oration). BREWE 9:3506

Funston, G. Keith
Responds to an introduction. PRS:135

Furay, Mortimer
Statement [before the] Subcommittee on Constitutional Amendments of the Committee on the Judiciary of the U. S. Senate. BOST:219

Furuseth, Andrew
Work is worship. ANN 14:561

FUTURE
Brown, H. A.
Plea of the future. BREWE 2:686
Mather, L.
Discourse concerning the uncertainty of the times of men. POC:377

FUTURE FARMERS OF AMERICA
Depta, M.
Aims and purposes of the FFA. BREWW:157
Francis, H.
Our three goals. BREWW:131
Harrison, R.
Leadership--a goal for us all. BREWW:150
Herink, R.
A succession of goals. BREWW:141
Madrid, S.
I am proud to be a part of it. BREWW:153
Morelli, L.
Vocational agriculture, the FFA, and our free enterprise system. BREWW:78
Slabach, D.
Five hundred miles south. BREWW:208

- G -

Gage, Patty
The Oahe Project--yes or no? BREWW:191

Gaitskell, Hugh
Labour, politics and democratic socialism. (Blackpool, Nov. 28, 1959). MCB:250

Galamison, Milton A.
Integration must work--nothing else can. (New York, March 27, 1963). FON:959

Galbraith, John Kenneth
On history, political economy, and

Vietnam (Memphis State University, May 30, 1975). BA 1975-76:78

Gale, James
Great American institution. REIR:161

Gallacher, William See Baldwin, S. B., jt. auth.

Gallagher, Buell G.
Memorial convocation address (on Martin Luther King, Jr.). BA 1967-68:169

Gallagher, Wes
The credibility gap: argument by specific instances. Same as his Upon acceptance of the 1967 William Allen White Foundation Award for Journalistic Merit
Free just free. (Saint Bonaventure, N. Y., May 14, 1973). BA 1973-74:132
Upon acceptance of the 1967 William Allen White Foundation Award for Journalistic Merit. BA 1966-67:148; JEF:327; JEFF:311

Gallatin, Albert
Constitutional liberty and executive despotism. BREWE 6:2209

---- See also Allen, J., jt. auth.

Galloway, Joseph
Speech for the petition to change the form of government. POC:200

Gallup, George
Mass information or mass entertainment. ANN 17:215

GALSWORTHY, JOHN
Österling, A.
Presentation [of the Nobel Prize for Literature to John Galsworthy, 1932]. NOB 6:277; NOL:302

Gambetta, Leon
France after German conquest. BREWE 6:2217

GAMBLING
Thuraisingham, E. E. C.
Lotteries: Hell, Hitler, and Bernard Shaw. MONS:167

GANDHI, INDIRA
Hayes, A.
Presents Indira Gandhi. LYI:99

Gandhi, Mohandas Karamchand
I live under no illusion. Same as his Speech in London (1931)
Speech in London (1931) (Second Round Table Conference, London, Nov. 28, 1931). BRN:109

Gannon, Ann Ida
A Catholic college, yesterday and tomorrow (Ursuline College, Cleveland, May 22, 1972). HOR:78

Gard, S.
Presentation [of the Nobel Prize for Physiology or Medicine to François Jacob, André Lwoff, and Jacques Monod, Dec. 11, 1965]. NOLM 4:143
Presentation [of the Nobel Prize for Physiology or Medicine to John Franklin Enders, Thomas Huckle Weller, and Frederick Chapman Robbins, Dec. 11, 1954]. NOLM 3:443
Presentation [of the Nobel Prize for Physiology or Medicine to Max Delbrück, Alfred D. Hershey, and Salvador E. Luria, Dec. 10, 1969]. NOLM 4:401
Presentation [of the Nobel Prize for Physiology or Medicine to Sir Frank Macfarlane Burnet and Peter Brian Medawar, Dec. 12, 1960]. NOLM 3:685

GARDENS
Hirschler, P.
How to beautify your farm. BREWW:124

Gardiner, Robert K.
Citizenship and political liberalism. EMP:106

Gardner, Henry J.
New England nativism. ANN 8:484

Gardner, John William
Education. (Austin, Jan. 1972). BA 1972-73:119
In behalf of a troubled nation. BA 1967-68:102
People power. (New Orleans, April 3, 1975--Public Affairs Research Council). BA 1974-75:158

Garfield, James A.
Conflict of ideas in America. BREWE 6:2231
Inaugural address. USINAU:141; USINAUG:141
Revolution and the logic of coercion. BREWE 6:2226

GARFIELD, JAMES A.
Blaine, J. G.
Life and character of J. A. Garfield. BREWE 2:482; HURH:137

GARIBALDI, GIUSEPPE
Buchanan, D.
Eulogy of Garibaldi. MCA:78
Crispi, F.
At the unveiling of Garibaldi's statue. BREWE 4:1467

Garnet, Henry Highland
Address to the slaves of the United States of America. (Buffalo, N.Y., National Convention of Negro Citizens, August, 1843). FON:81; OE:20; SMHV:21
Let the monster perish. (Washington, D.C., Feb. 12, 1865). FON:307
A plea in behalf of the Cuban revolution. (New York, Dec. 13, 1872). FON:380

Garran, Robert Randolph
Royal visit. MCA:191

Garrison, William Lloyd
Address delivered before the Old Colony Anti-Slavery Society, July 4, 1839. Same as his Dangers of slavery
At Charleston, South Carolina, 1865. BREWE 6:2241
Beginning a revolution. BREWE 6:2237
Dangers of slavery (July 4, 1839). ANN 5:303; MDT:26
On the death of John Brown. BREWE 6:2238
Union and slavery. BREWE 6:2240

GARRISON, WILLIAM LLOYD
Mill, J. S.
A tribute to William Lloyd Garrison. REID:395 selections
Ransom, R. C.
William Lloyd Garrison: a centennial oration. SMHV:66

Garry, Charles R.
In defense of Huey Newton. ERP:161

Garsek, Isadore
Do not judge this violent death. WALE:52
Highest attainment. WALE:54
Sorrow but not tragedy. WALE:57

Garvey, Marcus
The principles of the Universal Negro Improvement Association. (New York, Nov. 25, 1922). FON:748; OE:103; SMHV:100
UNIA movement. Same as his The principles of the Universal Negro Improvement Association
We are mostly subject peoples all over the world. (7th International Convention of the Negro Peoples of the World, St. Andrew, Jamaica, August, 1935). FON:790

GASES
Norrish, R. G. W.
Some fast reactions in gases studied by flash photolysis and kinetic spectroscopy. NOLC 4:206
Ramsay, Sir W.
The rare gases of the atmosphere. NOLC 1:68
Rayleigh, J. W. S.
The density of gases in the air and the discovery of argon. NOLPH 1:90
Waals, J. D. V. D.
The equation of state for gases and liquids. NOLPH 1:254

Gasser, Herbert Spencer
Mammalian nerve fibers (Nobel Lecture for 1944, Dec. 12, 1945). NOLM 3:34

Gaud, William Steen
Why foreign aid?
BA 1967-68:179

Gaustad, Eddie S.
The beginning of wisdom. (Baylor University, 1947). CAPB:370

Geiman, Carolyn Kay
Are they really "unteachable"?
LINR:94

Gell-Mann, Murray
Symmetry and currents in particle physics (Nobel Lecture, 1969). NOLPH 4:299

GELL-MANN, MURRAY
Waller, I.
Presentation [of the Nobel Prize for Physics to Murray Gell-Mann, 1969].
NOLPH 4:295

GENERAL MOTORS CORPORATION
Curtice, H.
Automotive research at General Motors. ANN 17:379

GENERATION GAP See Youth-adult relationship

GENETIC ENGINEERING
McGill, W. J.
Science and the law.
BA 1977-78:83

GENETICS
Crick, F. H. C.
On the genetic code.
NOLM 3:811
Lederberg, J.
A view of genetics.
NOLM 3:615
Morgan, T. H.
The relation of genetics to physiology and medicine.
NOLM 2:313
Nirenberg, M. W.
The genetic code.
NOLM 4:370

GENEVA CONFERENCE, 1955
Eisenhower, D. D.
Spirit of Geneva. BEN:136

GENIUS
Reynolds, J.
Genius and imitation.
BREWE 9:3313
Wirt, W.
Genius as the capacity of work.
BREWE 10:3910

George III, King of Great Britain
Speech to Parliament (Nov. 11, 1800). JAM:32

George, Dan
Brotherhood and understanding.
MAES:393
My people, the Indians (Yakima, Washington). MAES:397

GEORGE, GRACE
Taylor, D.
Presents Grace George.
LYI:19

Geren, Paul
The lie of war. (Baylor University, 1935). CAPB:359

German, Obadiah
Unprepared for war with England.
ANN 4:319

GERMAN LANGUAGE
Clemens, S. L.
Horrors of the German language. BEN:204

GERMANY
Bismarck, O.
Plea for imperial armament.
BREWE 2:456
Stresemann, G.
The new Germany (Nobel Lecture for 1926, June 29, 1927).
NOLP 2:8

GERSHWIN, GEORGE
Nizer, L.
Presents George Gershwin.
LYI:15

Gerstein, Israel
Candle of the Lord. WALE:60
Man is a soldier. WALE:60

GETTYSBURG, BATTLE OF, 1863
Adams, C. F., Jr.
Battle of Gettysburg. BREWE 1:31

GETTYSBURG NATIONAL CEMETERY See Lincoln, A. Gettysburg address

Ghali, Waguih
Egyptian in Israel. MDYG:152

Giauque, William Francis
Some consequences of low-temperature research in chemical thermodynamics (Nobel Lecture, Dec. 12, 1949). NOLC 3:227

GIAUQUE, WILLIAM FRANCIS
Tiselius, A. W. K.
Presentation [of the Nobel Prize for Chemistry to William Francis Giauque, Dec. 12, 1949]. NOLC 3:221

Gibbons, James, Cardinal
Defense of the Knights of Labor. ANN 11:131
Progress of the Catholic Church in America. ANN 11:148
To the Parliament of Religions. BREWE 6:2248

Gibbs, Jonathan C.
Freedom's joyful day. (Philadelphia, Jan. 1, 1863). FON:262

Gibson, John Bannister
Against judicial review: dissenting opinion on Eakin v. Raub. ANN 5:174

Giddings, Joshua Reed
Slavery and the annexation of Cuba. BREWE 6:2258
Texas and slavery. ANN 7:201

---- See also Chase, S. P., jt. auth.

Gide, André
Acceptance [of the Nobel Prize for Literature, 1947]. NOB 7:7; NOL:426

GIDE, ANDRE
Österling, A.
Presentation [of the Nobel Prize for Literature to André Gide, 1947]. NOB 7:3; NOL:422

GIDEONSE, HARRY D.
Sellers, R. Z.
Presents Harry D. Gideonse. LYI:80

Gierow, Karl Ragnar
Presentation address [of the Nobel Prize for Literature to Aleksandr Solzhenitsyn, 1970]. NOB 18:3
Presentation address [of the Nobel Prize for Literature to Samuel Beckett, 1969]. NOB 3:3

GIFTS See Acceptance speeches - Gifts; Presentation speeches - Gifts

Ginna, Robert
Responds to an introduction at a Newcomen Society dinner. PRS:156

GIRARD COLLEGE
Reed, T. B.
Immortality and good deeds (semi-centennial of Girard College). BREWE 9:3307

GIRL SCOUTS
Welcome to Girl Scouts (or Pioneer Girls, etc). HNWM:50

Gittings, Robert
Exploring the known. MDYG:207

Gladstone, William Ewart
Campaign speech (at Perth, December 1, 1879). BRYH:415
Commercial value of artistic excellence. BREWE 6:2283
Destiny and individual aspiration. BREWE 6:2288
First Home Rule Bill. Same as his Home Rule, June 7, 1886
Fundamental error of English colonial aggrandizement. BREWE 6:2266

Home Rule, June 7, 1886. (H. of Commons). MCB:301
Home rule and autonomy. BREWE 6:2278
On domestic and foreign affairs. (West Calder, Nov. 27, 1879). MCB:39; STRM:316
On Lord Beaconsfield. BREWE 6:2291
Principles of foreign policy. Same as his On domestic and foreign affairs
Use of books. BREWE 6:2289

GLADSTONE, WILLIAM EWART
Churchill, R. H. S.
Gladstone's Egyptian inconsistencies. BREWE 3:1148
Laurier, W.
Character and work of Gladstone. BREWE 7:2732

Glaser, Donald Arthur
Elementary particles and bubble chambers (Nobel Lecture, Dec. 12, 1960). NOLPH 3:529

GLASER, DONALD ARTHUR
Siegbahn, K.
Presentation [of the Nobel Prize for Physics to Donald Arthur Glaser, Dec. 12, 1960]. NOLPH 3:525

Glass, Carter See Connally, T. T., jt. auth.

Glenn, John H.
Accepting the Distinguished Service Medal. (Outline of speech). CUB:65
Address before the Joint Meeting of Congress. (Washington, Feb. 26, 1962). HURH:362
"What we have done so far but small building blocks in a huge pyramid to come." Same as his Address before the Joint Meeting of Congress

GLENN, JOHN H.
Kennedy, J. F.
Presenting the Distinguished Service Medal to John Glenn (outline of speech). CUB:64

GLICK, DAVID
Freehof, S. B.
David Glick. WALE:210

GOALS See Success

Gobat, Charles Albert
The development of the Hague Conventions of July 29, 1899 (Nobel Lecture for 1902, Oslo, July 18, 1906). NOLP 1:30

GOBAT, CHARLES ALBERT
Løvland, J. G.
Toast to C. A. Gobat [presenting the Nobel Prize for Peace for 1902, Oslo, July 18, 1906]. NOLP 1:29

GOD
Drummond, H.
Greatest thing in the world. BREWE 5:1941
Lubbers, A. D.
God and Joe College. SCHW:69
Read, D. H. C.
Is God over thirty? Religion and the youth revolt. BA 1966-67:129
Religious science. BURT:180
Robespierre, M.
Festival of the Supreme Being. BREWE 9:3340
"If God did not exist, it would be necessary to invent him." BREWE 9:3330
Moral ideas and Republican principles. BREWE 9:3334
Whitefield, G.
Kingdom of God. BREWE 10:3885
Zellner, L. R.
What can we prove about God? ARN:337; ARS:187

---- See also Death of God theology

Godfrey, James L.
Presents Frank Borden Hanes. LYI:38

Godley, Robert
The demand for responsible government. (Wellington, Nov. 15, 1850). MACS:66 sel.

Goedhart, G. J. van Heuven
Refugee problems and their solutions (Nobel Lecture, Dec. 12, 1955). NOLP 3:97

GOETHALS, GEORGE W.
Willcox, W. R.
Introducing G. W. Goethals to the Economic Club of New York, March 5, 1914. LYI:183

Goh Keng Swee
Elite combat party (Communist Party). MONS:394
How Singapore's monetary system now works (Singapore, Sept. 20, 1969). MONSA:282
A remarkable phenomenon: why Singapore is different ... (March 29, 1968). MONSA:277
Some delusions of the decade of development. MONS:385

Goheen, Robert F.
Sorting it out. (Princeton Univ., June 4, 1972). HOR:21

Goldberg, Arthur J.
Human rights and détente (Belgrade, Oct. 6, 1977). BA 1977-78:71

Golden, James L.
Moments to remember (commencement address--John Glenn High School). BRP:236
Political speaking since the 1920's. LINR:167

Goldfarb, Solomon D.
Art of reconstruction. WALE:61
Embers and cinders. WALE:67
My cup runneth over. WALE:70

Goldhaber, Gerald M.
Organizational communication (Monterrey, Mexico, Oct. 29, 1975). LINRST:44

Goldman, Emma
Anarchy vs. patriotism. (New York, 1910). HURH:166
"Patriotism--a menace to liberty." Same as her Anarchy vs. patriotism

---- and others (Sarah and Angelina Grimké)
Statement [before the] Subcommittee on Constitutional Amendments of the Committee on the Judiciary of the U.S. Senate. BOST:215

Goldman, Israel M.
Biography of an angel. WALE:72
Book of life. WALE:73
Let thy garments be always white. WALE:75
Man who walked with God. WALE:77

Goldwater, Barry M.
Acceptance speech, San Francisco, California, July 17, 1964. Same as his Extremism in defense of liberty (accepting nomination for presidency)
Campaign speech, Washington, D.C., October 21, 1964. SIN:345
Extremism in defense of liberty (accepting nomination for presidency, July 17, 1964). MAC:251; MACR:292; MDV:115; SIN:337
I accept your nomination. Same as his Extremism in defense of liberty (accepting nomination for Presidency)
Nomination acceptance speech. Same as his Extremism in defense of liberty (accepting nomination for Presidency)
Total victory in the Cold War. ANN 18:42
Why we must be stronger militarily. BAS:92 (outline only); LAA:8
Will to be strong. Same as his Why we must be stronger militarily

Golgi, Camilio
The neuron doctrine--theory and facts (Nobel Lecture, Dec. 11, 1906). NOLM 1:189

GOLGI, CAMILIO
Mörner, K. A. H.

Presentation [of the Nobel Prize for Physiology or Medicine to Camilio Golgi and Santiago Ramon y Cajal, Dec. 12, 1906]. NOLM 1:185

GOOD AND EVIL
Graham, W. F.
Confusing evil with good. LINR:179

GOOD WILL SPEECHES
Nixon, R. M.
Radio-television address from Moscow. ARS:242
Theater begins with wonder (outline of speech). CUB:70

Goodall, Clifford H.
Energy statement. TAC:219

GOODFELLOWS See Brotherliness

Goodloe, Joseph W.
A Black-operated firm. (Afro-American Student Union, Harvard Univ. School of Business Administration, May 12, 1971). VER:253

Goodman, Julian B.
Broadcast journalism: serving the democratic process. (Ithaca, N.Y., Oct. 22, 1976). BA 1976-77:52
Community and communications. MOP:381

Goodman, Stanley J.
Raising the fallen image of business. (New York, January 7, 1974). BA 1973-74:160

GOODY, HENRY
Greenberg, S.
Henry Goody. WALE:214

Gordis, Robert
Latter-Day Joseph. WALE:81

Gordon, David W.
Fruitful tears. WALE:83

Gordon, John Brown
It was purely a peace police organization. CUR:98

Gossage, Howard Luck
Our fictitious freedom of the press. MDV:285

Gossett, William T.
Presents Harry Emerson Fosdick. LYI:157

GOSSIP
Barrow, I.
Slander. BREWE 1:224
Butler, J.
Government of the tongue. BREWE 3:842
Massillon, J. B.
Curse of a malignant tongue. BREWE 8:2980

Gottheil, Richard
Jews as a race and as a nation. BREWE 6:2294

Gould, Jeffrey C.
My responsibility as an agricultural citizen. BREWW:147

GOVERNMENT See Democracy; Industry and state; Municipal government; Political science; State, The; State rights; Suffrage. Also Name of country or state with subdivision Politics and government, e.g. Great Britain - Politics and government; United States - Politics and government

GOVERNMENT, RESISTANCE TO
Boucher, J.
Civil liberty and nonresistance. ANN 2:343; POC:552
Griswold, E. N.
Dissent, protest, and disobedience. ANN 18:670; BA 1967-68:141; JEF:196
Hubbard, W.
Happiness of a people in the wisdom of their rulers directing and in obedience of their brethren attending unto what Israel ought to do. ANN 1:248
King, M. L., Jr.
Love, law, and civil disobedience. FON:943; LINR:63; LINRS:70; LINRST:75; STOT:321
Nonviolence and social change. OE:157
Nonviolence: moral challenge

for peace and justice.
NOLP 3:333; THOMS:99
Sacks, M.
The value of disobedience.
LINRS:148; LINRST:152
Thoreau, H. D.
Civil disobedience.
BOORA 1:318

GOVERNMENT BANKING See Banks and banking; Independent treasury

GOVERNMENT REGULATION OF INDUSTRY See Industry and state

GOVERNMENT SPENDING POLICY
Brown, E. G., Jr.
Proposals for change: an inaugural address.
BA 1978-79:103

GOVERNORS See Public officials

Grady, Henry W.
New South (speech to the New England Society).
ANN 11:240; BAS:121 (outline only); BOORA 1:465; LINS:254
New South and the race problem. Same as his Race problem
Race problem (speech to the Boston Merchants' Association). BREWE 6:2299

GRAFT (IN POLITICS) See Elections - Corrupt practices

Graham, D. A.
Some facts about Southern lynchings. (Indianapolis, June 4, 1899). FON:613

Graham, Frank Porter
Presents Robert M. Hutchins.
LYI:96

Graham, William F. (Billy Graham)
Confusing evil with good.
LINR:179
"Learn the lesson of the worm." Same as his National humility
National humility. (New York, 1957). HURH:339
Our bicentennial (Dec. 31, 1975).
BA 1975-76:34

GRAHAM, WILLIAM F. (BILLY GRAHAM)
DuVall, W. O.
Presents Billy Graham.
LYI:160

Granit, Ragnar
The development of retinal neurophysiology (Nobel Lecture, Dec. 12, 1967). NOLM 4:255
Presentation [of the Nobel Prize for Physiology or Medicine to John Carew Eccles, Alan Lloyd Hodgkin, and Andrew Fielding Huxley, Dec. 11, 1963].
NOLM 4:3

GRANIT, RAGNAR
Bernhard, C. G.
Presentation [of the Nobel Prize for Physiology or Medicine to Ragnar Granit, Haldan Keffer Hartline, and George Wald, Dec. 12, 1967]. NOLM 4:251

Granqvist, G.
Presentation [of the Nobel Prize for Physics for 1914 to Max Von Laue, Nov. 12, 1915].
NOLPH 1:343

Grant, Ulysses Simpson
Eighth annual message.
STAT 2:1318
Fifth annual message.
STAT 2:1254
First annual message.
STAT 2:1188
First inaugural address.
USINAU:129; USINAUG:129
For annexation (of the Dominican Republic). ANN 10:231
Fourth annual message.
STAT 2:1233
Second annual message.
STAT 2:1203
Second inaugural address.
USINAU:132; USINAUG:132
Separation of church and school.
ANN 10:365
Seventh annual message.
STAT 2:1294
Sixth annual message.
STAT 2:1275

Third annual message.
STAT 2:1220

GRANT, ULYSSES SIMPSON
Conkling, R.
Nomination of U.S. Grant for a third term. BREWE 4:1366
Farrar, F. W.
Funeral oration on General Grant. BREWE 6:2128
McKinley, W.
Grant (at dedication of Grant monument in New York City). BREWE 8:2905

Grappe, Allen
The age of food. BREWW:112

Grass, Fonda
The sky's the limit.
BREWW:115

Grattan, Henry
Against English imperialism. Same as his Declaration of Irish rights, April 19, 1780
Declaration of Irish rights, April 19, 1780.
BREWE 6:2314; CLAYP:120
Free people. Same as his Making his second motion for a Declaration of Irish rights, April 16, 1782
Invective against Corry.
BREWE 6:2330
Making his second motion for a Declaration of Irish rights, April 16, 1782.
BRYH:244
Unsurrendering fidelity to country. BREWE 6:2333

Gray, William H.
Justice should recognize no color. (Arkansas Constitutional Convention, 1868).
FON:353

GREAT BRITAIN
Abdul Rahman, T.
What the Commonwealth means (response to welcome address by British Prime Minister). MONS:22
Beloff, M.
Americanisation of British intellectual life. MYDG:114
Bristol, G. D.
Grievances and oppressions under Charles I. BREWE 5:1861
Canning, G.
England in repose.
BREWE 3:941
Chamberlain, J.
Empire and home rule.
MCB:60; STRM:387
Cromwell, O.
Debating whether or not to become King of England.
BREWE 4:1485
Curran, J. P.
England and English liberties--in the case of Rowan.
BREWE 4:1546
Ethelbert
Coming of Christianity.
BRYH:3
Gladstone, W. E.
Fundamental error of English colonial aggrandizement.
BREWE 6:2266
On domestic and foreign affairs.
MCB:39; STRM:316
Hyde, E.
"Discretion" as despotism.
BREWE 7:2562
Laurier, W.
Canada, England and the United States in 1899. BREWE 7:2737
Lloyd George, D.
The budget. BRYH:461; JAE:170; MCB:233; STRM:407

---- ARMY
Bristol, G. D.
Army in domestic politics.
BREWE 5:1865
Fox, C. J.
Address on the King's speech (protesting the call-up of the militia). STRM:121
William I
Speech to his troops before the battle of Hastings. BRYH:27

---- COLONIES
Bell, F. H. D.
The defence of the Empire in the Great War. MACS:273 sel.
Berkeley, W.
Speech to the Virginia House of Burgesses. POC:169
Bernard, F.
Speech to the Council and House of Representatives.
POC:227

Lee Kuan Yew
The Rhodesian problem and the change of mood in Britain. MONSA:251
Mather, I.
Speech at the Boston Town Meeting. POC:172
Mulford, S.
Speech to the Assembly at New-York. POC:174
Seeley, J. R.
Tendency in English history. MCB:50
Symonds, W.
Britain's claim to a New World empire justified. ANN 1:32

---- See also Africa; Boston Massacre, 1770; Canada; United States - History - Revolution

---- ---- DEFENSES
Coates, J. G.
Support for the Singapore Naval Base, 1927. MACS:278 selections

---- COMMERCE
Tan Siew Sin
Commonwealth trade: an explosive situation. MONS:127

---- CONSTITUTION
Pitt, W., 1708-1778
English Constitution. BREWE 3:1077

---- ECONOMIC CONDITIONS
George III, King of Great Britain
Speech to Parliament. JAM:32
Skidelsky, R.
Grand alternatives. MDYG:142

---- ECONOMIC POLICY
Beaconsfield, B. D.
Third reading of the Corn Importation Bill. MCB:211
Cobden, R.
Effects of protection in agriculture. MCB:189

---- FOREIGN RELATIONS
Bright, J.
Morality and military greatness. BREWE 2:637; MCB:23
Churchill, W. L. S.
Government policy (October 5, 1938 speech). STRM:468
Gladstone, W. E.
On domestic and foreign affairs. MCB:39; STRM:316
Salisbury, R. A. T. G.
Speech to the Primrose League. STRM:375

---- ---- FRANCE
Fox, C. J.
On the rejection of Napoleon's overtures. CLAYP:232

---- ---- GREECE
Palmerston, H. J. T.
Affairs in Greece. MCB:5

---- ---- IRELAND
Canning, G.
Hate in politics. BREWE 3:946

---- ---- ---- See also Ireland

---- ---- UNITED STATES
Bright, J.
Trent affair. STRM:271
Depew, C. M.
England and America since the Spanish War. BREWE 5:1790
Eliot, J.
On the Petition of Right. BREWE 5:1986; BRYH:123
Pym, J.
On grievances in the reign of Charles I. BREWE 8:3252
Seeley, J. R.
Tendency in English history. MCB:50

---- NAVY
Allen, J.
The Naval Defence Bill, 1908. MACS:270 sel.
Jervois, Sir W.
New Zealand's defence and Royal Navy supremacy. MACS:245 sel.
Walpole, R.
Debate in 1741 on wages of sailors. BREWE 10:3717; BRYF:176
Ward, Sir J.
New Zealand support for the Royal Navy, 1891-1908. MACS:254 sel.

---- PARLIAMENT

Bacon, F.
Upon the motion of subsidy (November 15, 1598 speech). BRYH:90

Bradlaugh, C.
Appeal for justice. JAE:142

Churchill, W. L. S.
Parliament in the air raids (September 17, 1940 speech). STRM:481

Cromwell, O.
Address to Parliament, September 4, 1654. BRYH:144
On the dissolution of Parliament (First Protectorate Parliament). CLAYP:14

Dering, E.
Religious controversy in Parliament. BREWE 5:1808

Elizabeth I
Speech at the dissolution of Parliament. BRYH:75
Speech at the proroguing of Parliament. BRYH:77

Fox, C. J.
In favor of Mr. Grey's motion for Parliamentary reform. BRYH:254

Grimstone, H.
Projecting canker worms and caterpillars. BREWE 6:2341

Lenthall, W.
Opening the long Parliament under Charles I. BREWE 7:2767

Mansfield, W. M.
Reply to the Earl of Chatham against Parliamentary exemption from arrest for debt. BREWE 8:2947

Oxford and Asquith, H. H.
Parliament Bill, 1911. MCB:162

Wellesley, A.
Against Parliamentary reform. STRM:171

Wentworth, P.
Liberty of the Commons. BRYH:79; CLAYP:1

Wilkes, J.
Denies the right of the House of Commons to reject duly elected members. STRM:39

Wyndham, W.
Royal prerogative delegated from the people (Army Bill, 1734). BREWE 10:3927

---- POLITICS AND GOVERNMENT

Attlee, C. R.
The Labour programme. MCB:471

Beaconsfield, B. D.
Against democracy for England. BREWE 1:296
Meaning of conservatism. BREWE 1:309; BRYF:534; MCB:431
Tory democracy. JAE:139

Bristol, G. D.
Army in domestic politics. BREWE 5:1865

Burke, E.
Principle in politics: speech at Bristol, previous to the election, 1780 (defends his Parliamentary conduct). BREWE 2:812; BRYH:211

Churchill, R. H. S.
Administration of Chips. STRM:355
Age of action. BREWE 3:1144
Trust the people speech. MCB:441

Churchill, W. L. S.
The Conservative programme. MCB:464

Curran, J. P.
On government by attachment. BREWE 4:1557

Curzon of Kedleston, G.
Debate on the Parliament Bill. MCB:169

Depew, C. M.
Poetry and politics in Britain. BREWE 5:1796

Hardie, J. K.
Socialist Commonwealth. MCB:451

Keynes, J. M.
Am I a Liberal? MCB:456

Lowe, R.
Coming of democracy. MCB:138

Macaulay, T. B.
Consent or force in government. BREWE 8:2888
Reform Bill. CLAYP:295; MCB:110

Mill, J. S.
Representation of the people. MCB:154

Russell, J. R.

Reform of the franchise.
MCB:87
Sidney, A.
Governments for the people and not the people for governments (scaffold speech).
BREWE 9:3454
Smith, S.
"Wounds, shrieks, and tears" in government.
BREWE 9:3490

GREAT SOCIETY See United States - Social policy

GREATNESS See Fame

Grede, William J.
America, a frontier.
ANN 17:154

GREECE, ANCIENT
Demosthenes
First Olynthiac oration.
SAG:199
First Philippic. COG:40; SAG:188
On the Chersoneus.
SAG:235
On the crown.
BREWE 5:1688; COG:151
Oration on the peace.
BREWE 5:1759; SAG:223
Second Olynthiac.
BREWE 5:1754; COG:56; SAG:205
Second Philippic.
BREWE 5:1763; SAG:228
Third Olynthiac. SAG:212
Third Philippic. COG:91; SAG:249
Hypereides
Funeral oration. COG:210
Isocrates
Address to Philip.
COG:67; SAG:137
Areopagiticus--"A few wise laws wisely administered."
BREWE 7:2589
Lysias
Against Eratosthenes for murder (on the execution without trial of Polemarchus). BREWE 8:2851; SAG:39
Funeral oration. COG:9

GREECE, MODERN
Clay, H.
Greek Revolution.
BREWE 4:1268
Menzies, R. G.
Greece and the Anzac spirit.
MCA:138
Palmerston, H. J. T.
Affairs in Greece. MCB:5
Truman, H. S.
Aid to Greece and Turkey.
ANN 16:434; GRG:76; LAA:49
Webster, D. and others
Debate on the Greek Revolution.
ANN 5:108

GREEK LITERATURE
Seferis, G.
Some notes on modern Greek tradition. NOL:484

Green, Alfred M.
Let us take up the sword. (Philadelphia, April 20, 1861).
FON:249

Green, Edith
Representative Edith Green speaks in support of the Equal Rights Amendment. BOST:237

Green, John P.
These evils call loudly for redress. (Pittsburgh, May, 1884). FON:499

Green, William
Modern trade unionism. (Cambridge, Mass., 1925).
HURH:205
"... Trade unionism is not a discovery or a formula. It grew and evolved slowly out of the needs of human experience."
Same as his Modern trade unionism

Greenberg, Simon
Henry Goody. WALE:214
We weep today. WALE:84

Greener, Richard T.
Emigration of colored citizens from the southern states. (Saratoga, N.Y., Sept. 12, 1879). FON:466

Greenidge, Terence See Sykes, C., jt. auth.

GREETINGS See Welcoming addresses

Gregory, Dick
Let your son fight for freedom. (Selma, Ala., Sept. 1963). FON:981

Gregory of Nazianzus, Saint
Eulogy on Basil of Caesarea. BREWE 6:2336

Greve, Donald
The American Indian. (St. Louis, Mo., Dec. 9, 1969). LINRS:100

Grey, Sir George
A radical programme, 1877 (New Zealand House of Representatives, Aug. 17, 1877). MACS:181 sel.

---- and others (John Ballance)
A Liberal Party (New Zealand House of Representatives, Oct. 29, 1877). MACS:182 sel.

---- See Atkinson, H., jt. auth.

Griffin, Clare E.
Presents James Palmer. LYI:67

Griffin, Robert P.
Responds to an introduction. PRS:144
When freedom dies in its sleep (Kalamazoo, Mich., Aug. 18, 1978). BA 1978-79:60

Griffiths, Martha W. and others (Emanuel Celler)
House debates the Equal Rights Amendment (Aug. 10, 1970). BOST:230

Grignard, Victor
The use of organomagnesium compounds in preparative organic chemistry (Nobel Lecture, Dec. 11, 1912). NOLC 1:234

GRIGNARD, VICTOR
Söderbaum, H. G.
Presentation [of the Nobel Prize for Chemistry to Victor Grignard and Paul Sabatier, Dec. 11, 1912]. NOLC 1:217

Grimes, James See Sumner, C., jt. auth.

Grimké, Angelina See Goldman, Emma

Grimke, Francis J.
Equality of rights for all citizens, Black and white, alike. (Washington, Nov. 20, 1898). FON:668

Grimké, Sarah See Goldman, Emma

Grimstone, Sir Harbottle, Bart.
Projecting canker worms and caterpillars. BREWE 6:2341

Grisham, G. N.
The functions of the Negro scholar. (Kansas City, Mo., Dec. 28, 1897). FON:599

GRISSOM, VIRGIL
Sevareid, E.
Eulogy for the astronauts. MOP:189

Griswold, A. Whitney
On conversation--chiefly academic. CROCK:75
This tongue-tied democracy. Same as his On conversation--chiefly academic

Griswold, Erwin N.
Dissent--1968 style. Same as his Dissent, protest, and disobedience
Dissent, protest, and disobedience (Tulane University School of Law, April 16, 1968). ANN 18:670; BA 1967-68:141; JEF:196
Organization techniques in a speech on the moral and legal implications of dissent. Same as his Dissent, protest, and disobedience

Grollman, Earl A.
If we love, we must lose. WALE:87

Gronlund, Laurence See Jones, A., jt. auth.

Gronouski, John A.
Mail service. BRP:223

Gruening, Ernest
United States policy and actions in Vietnam. BA 1965-66:23

Gruenther, Alfred M.
"The competition is very tough, and in this contest, there is no prize for second best." Same as his NATO
NATO. (New York, Dec. 7, 1956). HURH:334

Grundy, Felix and others (R. M. Johnson and J. Randolph)
Debate over war with England. ANN 4:291

Guadet, Marguerite Elie
Reply to Robespierre. BREWE 6:2244

GUATEMALA
Dulles, J. F.
Why the Arbenz government was overthrown in Guatemala. LAA:117

GUIDED MISSILES - DEFENSES
Nixon, R. M.
Questions of survival; the antiballistic missile system. BA 1968-69:9
Wiesner, J. B.
Argument against the ABM. BA 1968-69:19

Guillaume, Charles-Edouard
Invar and clinvar (Nobel Lecture, Dec. 11, 1920). NOLPH 1:444

GUILLAUME, CHARLES-EDOUARD
Ekstrand, A. G.
Presentation [of the Nobel Prize for Physics to Charles-Edouard Guillaume, Dec. 11, 1920]. NOLPH 1:441

Guizot, Francois Pierre Guillaume
Civilization and the individual man. BREWE 6:2344

Gullberg, Hjalmar
Presentation [of the Nobel Prize for Literature to Gabriela Mistral, 1945]. NOB 14:167; NOL:405
Presentation [of the Nobel Prize for Literature to Juan Ramón Jiménez, 1956]. NOB 10:3; NOL:513

Gullstrand, Allvar
How I found the mechanism of intracapsular accommodation (Nobel Lecture, Dec. 11, 1911). NOLM 1:414
Presentation [of the Nobel Prize for Physics for 1924 to Karl Manne Georg Siegbahn, Dec. 11, 1925]. NOLPH 2:73
Presentation [of the Nobel Prize for Physics for 1923 to Robert Andrews Millikan, May 23, 1924]. NOLPH 2:51

GULLSTRAND, ALLVAR
Mörner, K. A. H.
Presentation [of the Nobel Prize for Physiology or Medicine to Allvar Gullstrand, Dec. 11, 1911]. NOLM 1:411

Gunsaulus, Frank W.
Healthy heresies. BREWE 6:2353

Gustafsson, T.
Presentation [of the Nobel Prize for Physics to Hannes Alfvén and Louis Néel, Dec. 11, 1970]. NOLPH 4:303

Gwinn, Joseph M.
Presents Charles Lindbergh. LYI:188

- H -

Haak, Jan F. W.
Responds to an introduction. PRS:140

HAAS, FRANCIS B.
Hill, H.
Presents Francis B. Haas. LYI:93

HABEAS CORPUS
Stephens, A. H.

Civil rights in the Confederacy. ANN 9:493

HABEAS CORPUS SUSPENSION BILL, 1817
Romilly, Sir S.
Habeas Corpus Suspension Bill. STRM:143

Haber, Fritz
The synthesis of ammonia from its elements (Nobel Prize for 1918, June 2, 1920). NOLC 1:326

HABER, FRITZ
Ekstrand, A. G.
Presentation [of the Nobel Prize for Chemistry to Fritz Haber, 1918, June 2, 1920]. NOLC 1:321

HADFIELD, JAMES
Erskine, T.
Homicidal insanity (J. Hadfield). BREWE 6:2058; BRYH:294

HAEMIN
Fischer, H.
On haemin and the relationships between haemin and chlorophyll. NOLC 2:165

HAEMOGLOBIN See Hemoglobin

Hageman, Marianne
Wisdom of the heart. SCHW:177

Hagerup, Georg Francis
The work of the Institute of International Law (Nobel Lecture for 1904, Aug. 24, 1912). NOLP 1:64

Hagg, G.
Presentation [of the Nobel Prize for Chemistry to Dorothy Crowfoot Hodgkin, Dec. 11, 1964]. NOLC 4:67
Presentation [of the Nobel Prize for Chemistry to Linus Carl Pauling, Dec. 11, 1954]. NOLC 3:425
Presentation [of the Nobel Prize for Chemistry to Max Ferdinand Perutz and John Cowdery Kendrew, Dec. 11, 1962]. NOLC 3:649

Häggquist, G.
Presentation [of the Nobel Prize for Physiology or Medicine to Hans Spemann, Dec. 12, 1935]. NOLM 2:377

HAGUE CONVENTIONS
Gobat, C. A.
The development of the Hague Conventions of July 29, 1899 (Nobel Lecture for 1902, Oslo, July 18, 1906). NOLP 1:30
Renault, L.
The work at the Hague in 1899 and in 1907 (Nobel Lecture for 1907, May 18, 1908). NOLP 1:143

Hahn, Otto
From the natural transmutations of uranium to its artificial fission (Nobel Lecture for 1944, Dec. 13, 1946). NOLC 3:51

HAHN, OTTO
Westgren, A.
Presentation [of the Nobel Prize for Chemistry for 1944 to Otto Hahn, Dec. 13, 1946]. NOLC 3:47

Haiman, Franklyn S.
Rhetoric of 1968: a farewell to rational discourse (Univ. of Kansas, June 28, 1968). LINR:153; LINRS:133; LINRST:156

Hains, John
Lamp of freedom. SCHW:6
New day dawns. SCHW:140

HAIR
Burton, S.
You (male) should wear long hair. BAS:200 (outline only)

HAITI
Butler, B. F. and others
Congressional debate on Haiti

and Santo Domingo, January 13, 1869. ANN 10:143
Holly, J. T.
The Negro race, self-government and the Haitian revolution. FON:169
Russwurm, J. B.
The condition and prospects of Haiti. FON:33

Hale, Edward Everett
Boston's place in history. BREWE 6:2355

HALIFAX, EDWARD FREDERICK LINDLEY WOOD, 3rd VISCOUNT
Douglas, L. W.
Presents Lord Halifax. LYI:222

Hall, Carl
A heap of trouble. EHN:316

Hall, Prince
Pray God give us the strength to bear up under all our troubles. (Menotomy, Mass., June 24, 1797). FON:13

Hall, Ronald O.
Fear and faith. VI:98

Hallett, Benjamin
Sovereignty of the people (Luther v. Borden case). ANN 7:410

Hallström, Per
Broadcast lecture [on Johannes Vilhelm Jensen, 1944]. NOL:393
Presentation [of the Nobel Prize for Literature to Eugene Gladstone O'Neill, 1936]. NOB 19:125; NOL:330
Presentation [of the Nobel Prize for Literature to Frans Eemil Sillanpää, 1939]. NOB 16:223; NOL:386
Presentation [of the Nobel Prize for Literature to George Bernard Shaw, 1925]. NOB 16:77; NOL:224
Presentation [of the Nobel Prize for Literature to Henri Bergson, 1927]. NOB 2:267; NOL:242
Presentation [of the Nobel Prize for Literature to Ivan Alekseevich Bunin, 1933]. NOB 3:285; NOL:309
Presentation [of the Nobel Prize for Literature to Jacinto Benavente, 1922]. NOB 2:179; NOL:186
Presentation [of the Nobel Prize for Literature to Luigi Pirandello, 1934]. NOB 20:71; NOL:320
Presentation [of the Nobel Prize for Literature to Pearl Buck, 1938]. NOB 3:149; NOL:354
Presentation [of the Nobel Prize for Literature to Roger Martin DuGard, 1937]. NOB 14:3; NOL:342
Presentation [of the Nobel Prize for Literature to Sigrid Undset, 1928]. NOB 18:163; NOL:251
Presentation [of the Nobel Prize for Literature to William Butler Yeats, 1923]. NOB 18:275; NOL:194

Halsbury, Hardinge Stanley Giffard, 1st Earl of See Curzon of Kedleston, George, jt. auth.

Hambro, Carl Joachim
Presentation [of the Nobel Prize for Peace to George Catlett Marshall, Dec. 10, 1953]. NOLP 3:65
Presentation [of the Nobel Prize for Peace to the International Committee of the Red Cross and the League of the Red Cross Societies, Dec. 10, 1963]. NOLP 3:295

Hamdan bin Sheikh Tahir, Haji
Education for service--to society, the nation and our creator (June 17, 1967). MONSA:149
Problems of national education (Univ. of Malaya, April 11, 1969). MONSA:155 selections

Hamilton, Adam and others (Michael Savage)
The economy under the Labour government (New Zealand

House of Representatives, July 21, 1938). MACS:334 sel.
The Social Security Bill, 1938 (New Zealand House of Representatives, Aug. 16, 1938). MACS:337 sel.

Hamilton, Alexander
Coercion of delinquent states. BREWE 6:2361
On an act granting to Congress certain imposts and duties. ALS:133
On the Federal Constitution, June 24, 1788. HURH:35
Report on manufactures. BOORA 1:178
"The states can never lose their powers until the whole people of the United States are robbed of their liberties." Same as his On the Federal Constitution, June 24, 1788

HAMILTON, ALEXANDER
Morris, G.
Oration over Hamilton. BREWE 8:3075; HURH:54
Otis, H. G.
Hamilton's influence on American institutions. BREWE 8:3111

Hamilton, Andrew
In the case of Zenger--for free speech in America. BREWE 6:2373

Hamilton, William
A defense of the Negro. (New York, January 2, 1809). FON:26
Why a Negro convention is necessary. (New York--4th Convention of the Colored People, June 2 to June 13, 1834). FON:56

Hammarskjöld, Dag
Values of nationalism and internationalism (Stanford University commencement address). HURS:206

HAMMARSKJÖLD, DAG
Edberg, R.
Acceptance [of the Nobel Prize for Peace for Dag Hammarskjöld, Dec. 10, 1961]. NOLP 3:248
Jahn, G.
Presentation [of the Nobel Prize for Peace to Dag Hammarskjöld, Dec. 10, 1961]. NOLP 3:239

Hammarsten, E.
Presentation [of the Nobel Prize for Physiology or Medicine to Albert Szent-Györgyi Von Nagyrapolt, Dec. 11, 1937]. NOLM 2:435
Presentation [of the Nobel Prize for Physiology or Medicine to Axel Hugo Theodor Theorell, Dec. 12, 1955]. NOLM 3:477
Presentation [of the Nobel Prize for Physiology or Medicine to Hans Adolf Krebs and Fritz Albert Lipmann, Dec. 11, 1953]. NOLM 3:395
Presentation [of the Nobel Prize for Physiology or Medicine to Otto Heinrich Warburg, Dec. 10, 1931]. NOLM 2:251

Hammarsten, O.
Presentation [of the Nobel Prize for Chemistry to Fritz Pregl, Dec. 11, 1923]. NOLC 2:25

Hammer, Robert A.
Disciple of Aaron. WALE:89

Hampden, John
Patriot's duty defined: against own impeachment. BREWE 6:2385

HAMPDEN, JOHN
Holborne, J.
In defense of John Hampden. BREWE 7:2524
Hyde, E.
In John Hampden's case. BREWE 7:2564

Hampton, Wade
Present hour in South Carolina (inaugural address of would-be governor). CUR:159

Hamsun, Knut Pedersen
Acceptance [of the Nobel Prize

for Literature, 1920]. NOB 9:123; NOL:170

HAMSUN, KNUT PEDERSEN
Hjärne, H.
Presentation [of the Nobel Prize for Literature to Knut Pedersen Hamsun, 1920]. NOB 9:119; NOL:167

Hamzah bin Dato Abu Samah
Challenging opportunity for the press in Malaysia (Kuala Lumpur, Sept. 6, 1969). MONSA:110
The most powerful instrument for social cohesion (Kuala Lumpur, Oct. 18, 1969). MONSA:115

Hamzah bin Sendut See Hamzah Sendut

Hamzah Sendut
Joint efforts urged for uniting various ethnic groups (Penang Hill, Dec. 16, 1969). MONSA:172
Some new approaches to university education (Kuala Lumpur). MONSA:168
Trends and problems of government (Malaysia). MONS:253

Hancher, Virgil Melvin
Art of contemplation. CROCK:132
Presents Eleanor Roosevelt. LYI:244
Presents Franklyn Bliss Snyder. LYI:99

Hancock, John
Boston Massacre. (Boston, Mass., March 5, 1774). BRN:26; HURH:24
Boston Massacre oration (third anniversary). BREWE 6:2393; POC:262
Fight and even die. Same as his Boston Massacre
Moving the adoption of the Federal Constitution. BREWE 6:2389
"We fear not death." Same as his Boston Massacre

HANCOCK, WINFIELD SCOTT
Dougherty, D.
"Hancock the superb." BREWE 5:1904

HAND, AUGUSTUS N.
Buchanan, J. B.
Presents Augustus N. Hand. LYI:133

Hand, Learned
Judge's freedom before the law. ANN 15:233
Meaning of liberty. BRR:46

Handy, Arthur W.
Nat Turner. (New York City College, 1889). FON:538

HANES, FRANK BORDEN
Godfrey, J. L.
Presents Frank Borden Hanes. LYI:38

Hanley, John W.
The day innovation died (Houston, Tex., Sept. 26, 1978). BA 1978-79:122

Hannah, John A.
Civil rights and the public universities. BA 1965-66:93
Meeting world food news (Honolulu, Jan. 10, 1977). BA 1976-77:103

HANOI
Reeves, R. A.
Journey to Hanoi. VI:83

Hansberger, Robert V.
Responds to an introduction. PRS:146

Hansberry, Lorraine
A challenge to artists. (New York, Oct. 27, 1962). FON:954

Hanson, C. W. D.
Introduces Benson Ford, vice president, Ford Motor Company. PRS:22
Introduces Gene Lockhart. PRS:51

Hansson, Michael
The Nansen International Office

for Refugees (Nobel Lecture, Dec. 10, 1938). NOLP 2:268

Harden, Arthur
The function of phosphate in alcoholic fermentation (Nobel Lecture, Dec. 12, 1929). NOLC 2:131

HARDEN, ARTHUR
Söderbaum, H. G.
Presentation [of the Nobel Prize for Chemistry to Arthur Harden and Hans Karl August Simon von Euler-Chelpin, Dec. 12, 1929]. NOLC 2:127

Hardie, J. Keir
Socialist Commonwealth. (H. of Commons, April 23, 1901). MCB:451

Hardin, Ben, 1784-1852
The Wilkinson and Murdaugh case. (Harrodsburg, Ky., March 15, 1839). BLY:48

Harding, Harold F.
Matter of doubt and grave concern. BA 1968-69:121

Harding, Warren G.
First annual message. STAT 3:2616
Inaugural address. USINAU:207; USINAUG:207
"It is our purpose to prosper America first." ANN 14:292
Presents Marie S. Curie. LYI:179
Return to normalcy. Same as his "It is our purpose to prosper America first"
Second annual message. STAT 3:2628

HARDY, THOMAS
Erskine, T.
In defense of Thomas Hardy. BREWE 6:2066

Hare, Julius Charles
Children of light. BREWE 6:2402

Harlan, John M. and others (O. W. Holmes, Jr.)
Northern Securities Company v. United States, 1904: opinion for the court and dissenting opinion. ANN 12:576

---- See also following jt. auths. Bradley, J. P.; Brown, H. B.; Fuller, M. W.; White, E. D.

Harmann, Z.
UNICEF: achievement and challenge (Nobel Lecture, Dec. 11, 1965). NOLP 3:365

Harnwell, Gaylord P.
Responds to an introduction. PRS:142

Harper, Frances Ellen Watkins
Address at the centennial anniversary of the Pennsylvania Society for Promoting the Abolition of Slavery. (Philadelphia, April 14, 1875). FON:430
The great problem to be solved. Same as her Address at the centennial anniversary of the Pennsylvania Society for Promoting the Abolition of Slavery

Harper, Paul C.
What's happening, baby? (Off-the-Street Club, Chicago, June 21, 1966). JEF:232; JEFF:202; KEO:252

Harper, Robert Goodloe
Defending Judge Chase. BREWE 6:2425

Harriman, W. Averell
Challenges to peace and freedom. ANN 18:328

Harris, James G.
The prayer amendment. (Fort Worth, Tex., Oct. 3, 1971). BA 1971-72:143

Harris, LaDonna
American Indian education and pluralism. MAES:96

Harrison, Benjamin
Controversy over Hawaii (for annexation). ANN 11:479
First annual message. STAT 2:1628
Fourth annual message. STAT 2:1708

Inaugural address.
BREWE 6:2408; USINAU:153; USINAUG:153
Second annual message.
STAT 2:1653
Third annual message.
STAT 2:1676

Harrison, Hubert H.
What socialism means to us. (1912). FON:698

Harrison, Richard
Leadership--a goal for us all. BREWW:150

Harrison, Thomas
Speech on the scaffold.
BREWE 6:2421

HARRISON, THOMAS
Nottingham, H. F.
Opening the prosecution for regicide under Charles II (trial of T. Harrison).
BREWE 6:2159

Harrison, William Henry
Inaugural address. (March 4, 1841). HOW:67; USINAU:71; USINAUG:71

Hart, Gary
Big government: real or imaginary? (Western Electronic Manufacturers' Association, April 20, 1976).
LINRST:100

Hartline, Haldan Keffer
Visual receptors and retinal interaction (Nobel Lecture, Dec. 12, 1967).
NOLM 4:269

HARTLINE, HALDAN KEFFER
Bernhard, C. G.
Presentation [of the Nobel Prize for Physiology or Medicine to Ragnar Granit, Haldan Keffer Hartline, and George Wald, Dec. 12, 1967]. NOLM 4:251

Hartzog, George B., Jr.
Finding America. (Tucson, 1973). BA 1972-73:194

HARVARD LAW REVIEW
Frankfurter, F.
The Zeitgeist and the Judiciary.
FRIP:340

HARVARD UNIVERSITY
Capp, A.
Is this your university?
STOT:297
Eliot, C. W.
Harvard and Yale. HURH:130
Inaugural address as president of Harvard. ANN 10:201
Everett, E.
State funds for Harvard.
ANN 7:502
Washington, B. T.
Address delivered at the Harvard alumni dinner in 1896.
HURH:144

Hassel, Odd
Structural aspects of interatomic charge-transfer bonding (Nobel Lecture, June 9, 1970).
NOLC 4:314

HASSEL, ODD
Fredga, A.
Presentation [of the Nobel Prize for Chemistry to Derek H. R. Barton and Odd Hassel, Dec. 11, 1969]. NOLC 4:295

Hasselberg, K. B.
Presentation [of the Nobel Prize for Chemistry to Ernest Rutherford, Dec. 11, 1908].
NOLC 1:125
Presentation [of the Nobel Prize for Physics to Albert Abraham Michelson, Dec. 12, 1907].
NOLPH 1:159
Presentation [of the Nobel Prize for Physics to Gabriel Lippmann, Dec. 14, 1908].
NOLPH 1:183

HASTINGS, WARREN
Fox, C. J.
Against Warren Hastings.
BREWE 6:2192
Sheridan, R. B.
Against Warren Hastings.
BREWE 9:3422

Hatch, Orrin G. See Hayakawa, S. I., jt. auth.

Hatcher, Richard Gordon
Which is the path of change? (N.A.A.C.P. Legal Defense Fund, May, 1968). FON:1110

HATE
Korf, J.
And old hate walked on through time. SCHW:189

Hatfield, Mark O.
The energy crisis. (Oregon, March 2, 1974). BA 1973-74:105
Global interdependence: "Life, Liberty, and the Pursuit of Happiness" in today's world. (Washington, Sept. 11, 1974). BA 1974-75:89
If we fall down in the land of peace (San Antonio, Tex., Sept. 30, 1979). BA 1979-80:67
Noise. (Noise Abatement Council of America, Oct. 8, 1969). LINRS:211
Reconciliation and peace. (Washington, Feb. 1, 1973). BA 1972-73:91
Response to introduction. PRS:92

Hauptmann, Gerhart Johann Robert
Acceptance [of the Nobel Prize for Literature, 1912]. NOB 8:7; NOL:122

HAUPTMANN, GERHART JOHANN ROBERT
Hildebrand, H.
Presentation [of the Nobel Prize for Literature to Gerhart Johann Robert Hauptmann, 1912]. NOB 8:3; NOL:118

Hausman, Louis
Older Americans: a natural resource (Syracuse, N.Y., Nov. 18, 1976). LINRST:36

HAWAIIAN ISLANDS
Cleveland, G.
Controversy over Hawaii (against annexation). ANN 11:480
Harrison, B.
Controversy over Hawaii (for annexation). ANN 11:479
Kalakaua, D.
His Majesty's address to the people of Lahaina. ALA:57
Malone, G. W. and others
Statehood for Hawaii. ANN 17:522
Scarborough, W. S.
The ethics of the Hawaiian question. FON:570

HAWLEY, JOSEPH B.
Clemens, S. L.
Presents Joseph B. Hawley. LYI:148

Haworth, Walter Norman
The structure of carbohydrates and of vitamin C (Nobel Lecture, Dec. 11, 1937). NOLC 2:414

HAWORTH, WALTER NORMAN
Palmaer, W.
Presentation [of the Nobel Prize for Chemistry to Walter Norman Haworth and Paul Karrer, Dec. 11, 1937]. NOLC 2:407

Hay, William <u>See</u> Walpole, R. jt. auth.

Hayakawa, Samuel I. and others (Orrin G. Hatch and Daniel P. Moynihan)
Senate debate over ratification of treaties concerning the Panama Canal. BA 1977-78:17

Hayden, Lewis
Deliver us from such a Moses. (Boston, Dec. 27, 1865). FON:334

Haydon, Harold
The testimony of sculpture (Chicago). EHN:375; MOP:384; MOPR:380

Hayes, A. J.
Responds to an introduction. PRS:153

Hayes, Alfred
Presents Indira Gandhi. LYI:199

Hayes, John W. See Jones, A., jt. auth.

Hayes, Kimble
Crossbreeding beef cattle: progress or regression? BREWW:214

Hayes, Patricia Ann
Madame Butterfly and the collegian (Indiana University, 1967). LINR:262; LINRS:265

Hayes, Rutherford B.
First annual message. STAT 2:1334
Fourth annual message. STAT 2:1395
Inaugural address. BREWE 7:2434; USINAU:135; USINAUG:135
Second annual message. STAT 2:1355
Third annual message. STAT 2:1371
Veto of the Army Appropriation Act. ANN 10:449

HAYES, RUTHERFORD B.
Lawson, J.
I protest against Hayes's Southern policy. FON:457

HAYMARKET SQUARE RIOTS
See Chicago Haymarket Square Riots

Hayne, Robert Young
On Foot's Resolution (January 21, 1830). BREWE 7:2441

Haynes, Roy A.
Success of prohibition. ANN 14:523

HAYS, WILL H.
Landis, F.
Witty after-dinner speech on Will Hays. LYI:224

Hazlitt, William
On wit and humor. BREWE 7:2449

HEALTH
Freedom from hunger (outline of speech to persuade that continued good health of American people requires easy access to pharmaceutical vitamins and food supplements). CUB:48

---- See also Mental health; National Health Association; Proteins; Sick. Also Names of illnesses i.e. Backaches; Blood-diseases; Insanity

HEALTH, DRINKING OF See Toasts

HEART
Einthoven, W.
The string galvanometer and the measurement of the action currents of the heart. NOLM 2:94

Hecker, Frederick Karl Franz
Liberty in the New Atlantis. BREWE 7:2457

Hedges, Job Elmer
Presents Edward D. Duffield. LYI:69

Hedrén, G.
Presentation [of the Nobel Prize for Physiology or Medicine to Karl Landsteiner, Dec. 11, 1930]. NOLM 2:229

Heisenberg, Werner
The development of quantum mechanics (Nobel Lecture for 1932, Dec. 11, 1933). NOLPH 2:290

HEISENBERG, WERNER
Pleijel, H.
Presentation [of the Nobel Prize for Physics for 1932 to Werner Heisenberg and for 1933 to Erwin Schrodinger and Paul Adrien Maurice Dirac, Dec. 11, 1933]. NOLPH 2:283

HEISER, VICTOR
Sumner, G. L.
Presents Victor Heiser. LYI:174

HELIUM
Onnes, H. K.
Investigations into the properties of substances at low temperatures, which have

led, amongst other things, to the preparation of liquid helium. NOLPH 1:306

HELL
Bede
Torments of hell. BREWE 1:344
Edwards, J.
Eternity of Hell torments. BREWE 5:1977

Hellström, Gustaf
Presentation [of the Nobel Prize for Literature to William Faulkner, 1949]. NOB 19:3; NOL:440

Helman, Leonard A.
Risks of life. WALE:90

Helmholtz, Hermann Ludwig Ferdinand von
Mystery of creation. BREWE 7:2465

Hemin See Haemin

Hemingway, Ernest
Acceptance [of the Nobel Prize for Literature, 1954]. NOB 9:7; NOL:501

HEMINGWAY, ERNEST
Österling, A.
Presentation [of the Nobel Prize for Literature to Ernest Miller Hemingway, 1954]. NOB 9:3; NOL:497

HEMOGLOBIN
Perutz, M. F.
X-ray analysis of haemoglobin. NOLC 3:653
Whipple, G. H.
Hemoglobin regeneration as influenced by diet and other factors. NOLM 2:346

HEMOPHILIA See Blood-diseases

Hench, Philip Showalter
The reversibility of certain rheumatic and non-rheumatic conditions by the use of cortisone or of the pituitary adrenocorticotropic hormone (Nobel Lecture, Dec. 11, 1950). NOLM 3:311

HENCH, PHILIP SHOWALTER
Liljestrand, G.
Presentation [of the Nobel Prize for Physiology or Medicine to Edward Calvin Kendall, Tadeus Reichstein, and Philip Showalter Hench, Dec. 11, 1950]. NOLM 3:263

Henderson, Arthur
Essential elements of a universal and enduring peace (Nobel Lecture, Dec. 11, 1934). NOLP 2:185

HENDERSON, ARTHUR
Mowinckel, J. L.
Presentation [of the Nobel Prize for Peace to Arthur Henderson, Dec. 10, 1934]. NOLP 2:179

Hennings, Thomas C. See Jenner, W. E., jt. auth.

Henry, David D.
Perceptions of the university (Univ. of Utah, June 6, 1969). HOR:70

Henry, Jacob
On religion and elective office. ANN 4:239; BOORA 1:220
Private belief and public office. Same as his On religion and elective office

Henry, Patrick
Against ratification. Same as his June 4th 1788 speech in the Virginia Ratifying Convention
Against the Federal Constitution, June 5, 1788. BREWE 7:2488
"... as for me, give me liberty, or give me death." Same as his Liberty or death
Bill of Rights, June 14, 1788. BREWE 7:2484
Call to arms. Same as his Liberty or death
"Give me liberty or give me death." Same as his Liberty or death
June 4th, 1788 speech in the Virginia Ratifying Convention. BREWE 7:2478; LINS:136
Liberty or death (Richmond, Va.,

March 23, 1775). ANN 2:321; BAS:39 (outline only); BEN:13; BREWE 7:2473; HURH:27; HURS:209; OLIS:22; POC:305
Liberty or empire? Same as his Against the Federal Constitution, June 5, 1788
Nation--not a Federation, June 14, 1788 (on eighth section of Federal Constitution). BREWE 7:2480
"We, the people" or "We, the states." Same as his June 4th, 1788 speech in the Virginia Ratifying Convention

---- See also Mason, G., jt. auth.

Henschen, F.
Presentation [of the Nobel Prize for Physiology or Medicine for 1928 to Charles Jules Henri Nicolle]. NOLM 2:175
Presentation [of the Nobel Prize for Physiology or Medicine for 1933 to Thomas Hunt Morgan, June 4, 1934]. NOLM 2:307

Hepburn, William P.
Regulation of railroad rates. ANN 13:40

Herder, Johann Gottfried von
Meaning of inspiration. BREWE 7:2497

Herink, Russel
A succession of goals. BREWW:141

Herndon, Angelo
Give the people bread. (Atlanta, Ga., 1932). FON:779

HEROES AND HEROISM
Carlyle, T.
Heroic in history. BREWE 3:962
Choate, R.
Puritan and Spartan heroism. BREWE 3:1135
Chrysostom, J.
Heroes of faith. BREWE 3:1139

Herron, George Davis
Christianity and the use of Private property. ANN 12:226

Hershey, Alfred D.
Idiosyncrasies of DNA structure (Nobel Lecture, Dec. 12, 1969). NOLM 4:417

HERSHEY, ALFRED D.
Gard, S.
Presentation [of the Nobel Prize for Physiology or Medicine to Max Delbrück, Alfred D. Hershey, and Salvador E. Luria, Dec. 10, 1969]. NOLM 4:401

Hertz, Gustav
The results of electron-impact tests in the light of Bohr's theory of atoms (Nobel Lecture for 1925, Dec. 11, 1926). NOLPH 2:112

HERTZ, GUSTAV
Oseen, C. W.
Presentation [of the Nobel Prize for Physics for 1925 to James Franck and Gustav Hertz, Dec. 11, 1926]. NOLPH 2:95

Hesburgh, Theodore M.
Higher education begins the seventies. (Univ. of Notre Dame, Oct. 5, 1970). BA 1970-71:85; BAAE:277
The problems and opportunities on a very interdependent planet (Bryn Mawr College, May 11, 1975). HOR:142
Service to others (Salt Lake City, June 9, 1979). BA 1979-80:180

Hess, Victor Franz
Unsolved problems in physics: tasks for the immediate future in cosmic ray studies (Nobel Lecture, Dec. 12, 1936). NOLPH 2:360

Hess, Walter Rudolf
The central control of the activity of internal organs (Nobel Lecture, Dec. 12, 1949). NOLM 3:247

HESS, WALTER RUDOLF
Olivecrona, H.
Presentation [of the Nobel Prize

for Physiology or Medicine to Walter Rudolf Hess and Antonio Caetano De Abreu Freire Egas Moniz, Dec. 12, 1949]. NOLM 3:243

HESSE, HERMANN
Österling, A.
Presentation [of the Nobel Prize for Literature to Hermann Hesse, 1946]. NOB 9:233; NOL:412
Vallotton, H.
Acceptance [of the Nobel Prize for Literature for Hermann Hesse, 1946]. NOB 9:237; NOL:416

Heuss, John
Introduction to baccalaureate sermon. PRS:55

Hevesy, George De
Some applications of isotopic indicators (Nobel Lecture for 1943, Dec. 12, 1944). NOLC 3:9

HEVESY, GEORGE DE
Westgren, A.
Presentation [of the Nobel Prize for Chemistry for 1943 to George De Hevesy, Dec. 12, 1944]. NOLC 3:5

Heymans, Corneille Jean Francois
The part played by vascular presso- and chemo-receptors in respiratory control (Nobel Lecture for 1938, Dec. 12, 1945). NOLM 2:460

Heyrovsky, Jaroslav
The trends of polarography (Nobel Lecture, Dec. 11, 1959). NOLC 3:564

HEYROVSKY, JAROSLAV
Olander, A.
Presentation of the Nobel Prize for Chemistry to Jaroslav Heyrovsky, Dec. 11, 1959. NOLC 3:561

HEYSE, PAUL JOHANN LUDWIG
Wirsén, C. D. af
Presentation [of the Nobel Prize for Literature to Paul Johann Ludwig Heyse, 1910]. NOB 7:279; NOL:100

Hiatt, Howard H.
Prevention of the last epidemic (Cambridge, Mass., Feb. 9, 1980). BA 1979-80:56

Hibben, Joseph W.
Introduces Bishop James A. Pike. PRS:69
Introduces Braj K. Nehru, Ambassador from India. PRS:26
Introduces Dr. Howard B. Sprague. PRS:61
Introduces Hobart Rowen of Newsweek Magazine. PRS:95
Introduces the Honorable Otto Kerner, governor of Illinois. PRS:29
Introduces Willy Brandt, mayor of West Bertlin. PRS:37

Higgins, Marguerite
Responds to introduction. PRS:107

HIGGINS, MARGUERITE
Coulter, T. H.
Introducing Marguerite (Maggie) Higgins to the Executives' Club of Chicago. LYI:113

HIGH PRESSURE (SCIENCE)
Bergius, F.
Chemical reactions under high pressure. NOLC 2:244

HIGHER EDUCATION See Education, Higher

Higinbotham, George
Against assisted immigration. MCA:52
For the annexation of New Guinea. MCA:43

Hildebert of Lavardin, Abp. of Tours
Rebecca at the well. BREWE 7:2502

Hildebrand, Hans
Presentation [of the Nobel Prize for Chemistry to Wilhelm Ostwald, Dec. 12, 1909]. NOLC 1:147
Presentation [of the Nobel Prize

for Literature to Gerhart Johann Robert Hauptmann, 1912]. NOB 8:3; NOL:118
Presentation [of the Nobel Prize for Physics to Guglielmo Marconi and Carl Ferdinand Braun, Dec. 11, 1909]. NOLPH 1:193

Hildebrandt, Thomas
Christian way. SCHW:198

Hill, Archibald Vivian
The mechanism of muscular contraction (Nobel Lecture for 1922, Dec. 12, 1923). NOLM 2:10

HILL, ARCHIBALD VIVIAN
Johannsson, J. E.
Presentation [of the Nobel Prize for Physiology or Medicine for 1922 to Archibald Vivian Hill and Otto Fritz Meyerhof, Dec. 12, 1923]. NOLM 2:3

Hill, Benjamin Harvey
Little personal history. BREWE 7:2507

HILL, BENJAMIN HARVEY
Ingalls, J. J.
Undiscovered country. BREWE 7:2574

Hill, Henry
Presents Francis B. Haas. LYI:93

Hill, James J.
Natural wealth of the land and its conservation. ANN 13:153

Hills, Lee
Presents Fred Sparks. LYI:115

Hines, Frank T.
G. I. Bill of Rights. ANN 16:215

Hinshelwood, Sir Cyril Norman
Chemical kinetics in the past few decades (Nobel Lectures, Dec. 11, 1956). NOLC 3:474

HINSHELWOOD, SIR CYRIL NORMAN
Olander, A.
Presentation of the Nobel Prize for Chemistry to Sir Cyril Norman Hinshelwood and Nikolai Nikolaevic Semenov, Dec. 11, 1956. NOLC 3:471

Hird, Peter
Suffer suffer Yeddy. MDYG:66

Hirschler, Paul
How to beautify your farm. BREWW:124

HISSAMUDDIN ALAM SHAH IBNI AL-MARHUM SULTAN ALA' IDDIN SULAIMAN SHAH
Thomson, T. J. B.
Let these be his epitaph (eulogy on Sultan Hissamuddin Alam Shah Ibni Al-Marhum Sultan Ala'iddin Sulaiman Shah). MONS:283

HISTORY
Kennedy, J. F.
History will be our judge. LINS:371
Schlegel, K. W. F.
Philosophy of history. BREWE 9:3377

Hjärne, Harald
Presentation [of the Nobel Prize for Literature to Carl Friedrich Spitteler, 1919]. NOB 17:267; NOL:161
Presentation [of the Nobel Prize for Literature to Knut Pedersen Hamsun, 1920]. NOB 9:119; NOL:167
Presentation [of the Nobel Prize for Literature to Rabindranath Tagore, 1913]. NOB 18:10; NOL:127
Presentation [of the Nobel Prize for Literature to Rudolf Christoph Eucken, 1908]. NOB 6:3; NOL:67

Hoar, George Frisbie
Great men of Massachusetts. BREWE 7:2516
Lust of empire. ANN 12:248

Hodgkin, Alan Lloyd
The ionic basis of nervous con-

duction (Nobel Lecture, Dec. 11, 1963). NOLM 4:32

HODGKIN, ALAN LLOYD
Granit, R.
Presentation [of the Nobel Prize for Physiology or Medicine to John Carew Eccles, Alan Lloyd Hodgkin, and Andrew Fielding Huxley, Dec. 11, 1963]. NOLM 4:3

Hodgkin, Dorothy Crowfoot
The x-ray analysis of complicated molecules (Nobel Lecture, Dec. 11, 1964). NOLC 4:71

HODGKIN, DOROTHY CROWFOOT
Hagg, G.
Presentation [of the Nobel Prize for Chemistry to Dorothy Crowfoot Hodgkin, Dec. 11, 1964]. NOLC 4:67

Hoff, Jacobus Henricus Van't
Osmotic pressure and chemical equilibrium. (Nobel Lecture, Dec. 13, 1901). NOLC 1:5

HOFF, JACOBUS HENRICUS VAN'T
Odhner, C. T.
Presentation [of the Nobel Prize for Chemistry to Jacobus Henricus Van't Hoff, Dec. 13, 1901]. NOLC 1:3

HOFFA, JAMES
James Hoffa (satiric speech). BURT:47

HOFFMAN, PAUL G.
Lamont, T. S.
Presents Paul G. Hoffman. LYI:71

Hofstadter, Robert
The electron-scattering method and its application to the structure of nuclei and nucleons (Nobel Lecture, Dec. 11, 1961). NOLPH 3:560

HOFSTADTER, ROBERT
Waller, I.
Presentation [of the Nobel Prize for Physics to Robert Hofstadter and Rudolf Ludwig Mossbauer, Dec. 11, 1961]. NOLPH 3:555

Holborne, Sir Robert
In defense of John Hampden. BREWE 7:2524

Holden, W. Sprague
Newspapers of the U.S.A.--an appraisal. ARS:107

Holland, H. E. See Massey, W. F., jt. auth.

Holland, Harry
The socialist objective of the labour movement (New Zealand House of Representatives, Oct. 30, 1918). MACS:232 sel.

---- and others (Sir Robert Stout)
The 1913 Waterside Strike (Wellington, April 29, 1914). MACS:230 sel.

Holland, Jerome H.
Options along the pathway of community involvement. (Hampton Institute, May 26, 1974). HOR:8

Holland, Sidney
Forward defence--from the Middle East to Malaya, 1955 (New Zealand House of Representatives, March 24, 1955). MACS:392 sel.
The Suez Crisis, 1956 (New Zealand House of Representatives, Aug. 7, 1956). MACS:397 sel.

Holley, Alexander Lyman
Theory and practice in industrial engineering. ANN 10:366

Holley, Robert W.
Alanine transfer RNA (Nobel Lecture, Dec. 12, 1968). NOLM 4:324

HOLLEY, ROBERT W.
Reichard, P.
Presentation [of the Nobel Prize for Physiology or Medicine to Robert W. Holley, Har Gobind Khorana, and Marshall W. Niren-

berg, Dec. 12, 1968]. NOLM 4:321

Hollis, Christopher See Sykes, C., jt. auth.

Holly, James T.
The Negro race, self-government and the Haitian revolution. (1855). FON:169

Holman, William Arthur
Against sending troops to South Africa. MCA:109

Holmes, Oliver Wendell
Dorothy Q. (Boston, May 23, 1884). HURH:139
Introduces Matthew Arnold. LYI:44
"There were tones in the voice that whispered then you may hear today in a hundred men." Same as his Dorothy Q.

Holmes, Oliver Wendell, Jr.
Dissenting opinion on Abrams vs. United States. ANN 14:244; BOORA 2:666
John Marshall. (Mass. Supreme Judicial Court, Feb. 4, 1901). FRIP:257
Law and the court. (Harvard Law School Association of New York, Feb. 15, 1913). FRIP:260
Lechner v. New York, 1905; dissenting opinion for the Supreme Court. BOORA 2:662
"Live--I am coming" response to birthday greeting (Washington, March 7, 1931). GRG:48; HURH:215
Nixon v. Herndon: opinion for the court. ANN 14:534
On his ninetieth birthday. Same as his "Live--I am coming:" response to birthday greeting
Path of the law. BOORA 2:593

---- See also following jt. auths. Harlan, J. M.; Sanford, E. T.; Sutherland, G.

Holmgren, I.
Presentation [of the Nobel Prize for Physiology or Medicine to George Hoyt Whipple, George Richards Minot, and William Parry Murphy, Dec. 12, 1934]. NOLM 2:335

Holt, Roger
The second dust bowl. BREWW:137

Holtzman, Elizabeth
In celebration of the inauguration of the Susan B. Anthony coin (Rochester, N.Y., July 2, 1979). BA 1979-80:174
Women and equality under the law (Madison, Wisc., March 26, 1977). BA 1976-77:80

Holyoake, Keith J.
A military contribution in Vietnam, 1965 (New Zealand House of Representatives, May 28, 1965). MACS:398 sel.
The National Development Conference, 1968 (Wellington, Aug. 27-29, 1968). MACS:455 sel.

HOME
Brunsting, L.
Kid dreams. SCHW:49
Dedication services of a Christian home. BNH:59

HOME RULE BILLS See Ireland

HOMESTEAD BILL, 1852
Sutherland, J.
Free land and the supply of labor. ANN 8:180

HONESTY
Be honest. BURT:122

HONG KONG
Lee Kuan Yew
Hong Kong and Singapore: a tale of two cities. MONSA:264

Hood, William R.
Uncle Tom is dead! (Cincinnati, Ohio, Oct. 27, 1951). FON:843

Hooker, Thomas
The soul's exaltation. JON:104
The soul's vocation, doctrine 3 (1637-8). JON:82
The soul's vocation, doctrine 7.

JON:93
Unbelievers preparing for Christ. POC:331

Hoover, Herbert C.
Acceptance speech, Constitution Hall, Washington, D.C., August 11, 1932. SIN:88
Acceptance speech, Stanford University Stadium, Palo Alto, California, August 11, 1928. Same as his Accepting the nomination for presidency
Accepting the nomination for presidency (Palo Alto, Aug. 11, 1928). SIN:4
Against the proposed New Deal (October 31, 1932). ANN 15:188
Bill of Rights. (San Diego, Calif., Sept. 15, 1935). HURH:229
Campaign speech, Madison Square Garden, New York City, October 31, 1932. SIN:103
Campaign speech, New York. Same as his Speech at New York City, October 22, 1928
First annual message. STAT 3:2746
Fourth annual message. STAT 3:2795
Holy crusade for liberty. BAD:53
"I suggest that the United Nations be reorganized without the Communist nations in it." Same as his United Nations
In defense of tradition (Detroit, 1932). ROD:39
Inaugural address. USINAU:225; USINAUG:225
Military policy for the Cold War. Same as his Our national policies in this crisis
Moral standards in an industrial era. ANN 14:428
New Deal and European collectivisim. Same as his Road to freedom
On American individualism. Same as his Speech at New York City, October 22, 1928
Our national policies in this crisis. ANN 17:46
Reassuring touch: President Hoover speaks, 1931. ROD:15
Road to freedom. ANN 15:384
Rugged individualism. Same as his Speech at New York City, October 22, 1928
Second annual message. STAT 3:2772
Speech at New York City, October 22, 1928. ANN 14:595; BOORA 2:803; SIN:21
Third annual message. STAT 3:2783
United Nations. (April 27, 1950). HURH:287
Veto of the Muscle Shoals Bill. ANN 15:79
War comes to Europe. GRG:61

Hoover, J. Edgar
Menace of the Communist Party. ANN 16:451
Responds to an introduction. PRS:140

Hope, John
We are struggling for equality. (Nashville, 1896). FON:594

HOPE
Dow, L., Jr.
Hope and despair. BREWE 5:1934

Hopkins, Sir Frederick Gowland
The earlier history of vitamin research (Nobel Lecture, Dec. 11, 1929). NOLM 2:211

HOPKINS, SIR FREDERICK GOWLAND
Liljestrand, G.
Presentation [of the Nobel Prize for Physiology or Medicine to Christiaan Eijkman and Sir Frederick Gowland Hopkins, Dec. 11, 1929]. NOLM 2:193

Hopkins, Harry L.
18,000,000 on relief. ANN 15:261
"... they are just like the rest of us." ROD:127

HORMONES
Reichstein, T.
Chemistry of the adrenal cortex

hormones. NOLM 3:291
Ružička, L. S.
Multimembered rings, higher terpene compounds, and male sex hormones. NOLC 2:468

Horn, Francis H.
The student revolt, a defense of the older generation (1968). HOR:49

Horner, Matina Souretis
Opportunity for educational innovation. (Cambridge, Mass., Nov. 16, 1972). BA 1972-73:184

HORSE-RACING
Thuraisingham, E. E. S. C.
The prince of sportsmen. MONSA:187

HOTELS
Lavenson, J.
Think strawberries. VERD:259

Houphouet-Boigny, Felix
French Africa and the French Union. EMP:73

HOURS OF LABOR
Black, H. L.
Need to share what we have. ROD:75
Holmes, O. W., Jr.
Lochner v. New York, 1905; dissenting opinion for the Supreme Court. BOORA 2:662
Parkes, H.
Eight-hours movement. MCA:33
Peckham, R. W. and others
Lochner v. New York, 1905; opinion for the court and dissenting opinion. ANN 13:8

HOUSE COMMITTEE ON UNAMERICAN ACTIVITIES
See United States - Congress - House of Representatives - Committee on UnAmerican Activities

HOUSING
Karos, P. A.
Haven of the defeated. ARS:148
Savage, J.
Slums as a common nuisance (Meeker v. Van Renssalaer case). ANN 6:279
Zwerling, J. C.
Federal Government should continue its present housing program for low-income groups rather than change to the proposed rent subsidy plan. BAS:196 (outline only)

Houssay, Bernardo Alberto
The role of the hypophysis in carbohydrate metabolism and in diabetes (Nobel Lecture, Dec. 12, 1947). NOLM 3:210

HOUSSAY, BERNARDO ALBERTO
Theorell, H.
Presentation [of the Nobel Prize for Physiology or Medicine to Carl Ferdinand Cori, Gerty Theresa Cori-Radnitz, and Bernardo Alberto Houssay, Dec. 11, 1947]. NOLM 3:179

Houston, Samuel
His defense at the Bar of the House. BREWE 7:2532
On his defeat as a Union candidate. BREWE 7:2530
Sam Houston's speech, at Independence, Texas, May 10. ECH:174

Houtman, Mary
Dangers of security. SCHW:54

Howard, John A.
The innovation mirage. (Rockford, Ill., Sept. 9, 1970). BA 1970-71:94
The new furies: skepticism, criticism, and coercion (Racine, Wisc., June 6, 1974). LINRST:146
"... our sacred honor" (Rockford College, Illinois, Sept. 10, 1975). BA 1975-76:9

HOWARD UNIVERSITY
Powell, A. C.
Can any good thing come out of Nazareth? FON:1027; SMHR:154

Howarth, Don
2S Draft deferment should be retained. REIR:130

Howe, Harold, II
The Brown decision, pluralism, and the schools in the 1980s (Jeffersonville, Vermont, Aug. 1, 1979). BA 1979-80:101
Changing the pecking order. BA 1967-68:111
Public education for a humane society. (New York, Nov. 20, 1972). BA 1972-73:161

Howell, Wes
A new century in agriculture. BREWW:211

Hubbard, William
Happiness of a people in the wisdom of their rulers directing and in obedience of their brethren attending unto what Israel ought to do. ANN 1:248

Huber, Max
Acceptance [of the Nobel Prize for Peace for the International Committee of the Red Cross, 1944, Dec. 10, 1945]. NOLP 2:293

Huffman, John A.
Retrospect '73--Biblical lessons we can learn from Watergate (Pittsburgh, Dec. 30, 1973). TAC:221

Huggins, Charles Brenton
Endocrine-induced regression of cancers (Nobel Lecture, Dec. 13, 1966). NOLM 4:235

HUGGINS, CHARLES BRENTON
Klein, G.
Presentation [of the Nobel Prize for Physiology or Medicine to Peyton Rous and Charles Brenton Huggins, Dec. 13, 1966]. NOLM 4:215

Hughes, Charles Evans
"In the great enterprise of making democracy workable we are all partners." Same as his 150th anniversary of the First Congress
National Labor Relations Board v. Jones and Laughlin Steel Corporation, 1937: opinion for the Supreme Court. ROD:207
New power of government accepted. Same as his National Labor Relations Board v. Jones and Laughlin Steel Corporation, 1937; opinion for the Supreme Court
150th anniversary of the First Congress. (Washington, March 4, 1939). HURH:237
Schechter Poultry Corporation v. United States, 1935: opinion for the Supreme Court. ANN 15:301; ROD:186
Small step toward racial equality: opinion for the Supreme Court on Mitchell case, 1941. ROD:224

HUGHES, CHARLES EVANS
Pepper, G. W.
Presents Charles Evans Hughes. LYI:127

Hughes, Langston
Negro writers have been on the blacklist all their lives. (National Assembly of the Authors' League of America, May, 1957). FON:916
Negroes speak of war. (Paris, July, 1934). FON:787

Hughes, Ted
Capturing animals. MDYG: 191

Hughes, Thomas
Highest manhood. BREWE 7:2539

Hughes, William Morris
Australian Judas. MCA:125

Hugo, Victor Marie, Comte de
Liberty tree in Paris. BREWE 7:2548
Moral force in world politics. BREWE 7:2553
On the centennial of Voltaire's death. BREWE 7:2550
Oration on Honoré de Balzac. BREWE 7:2546

Huitfeldt, Jennifer
The service of sex. (Madison, Wisc., 1971). LINRS:114

Hulett, John
We've decided to stop begging. (Los Angeles, May 22, 1966). FON:1019

HULL, CORDELL
Jahn, G.
Presentation [of the Nobel Prize for Peace to Cordell Hull, Dec. 10. 1945]. NOLP 2:311
Osborne, L.
Acceptance [of the Nobel Prize for Peace for Cordell Hull, Dec. 10, 1945]. NOLP 2:318

Hulthén, E.
Presentation [of the Nobel Prize for Physics to Emilio Gino Segrè and Owen Chamberlain, Dec. 11, 1959]. NOLPH 3:487
Presentation [of the Nobel Prize for Physics to Felix Bloch and Edward Mills Purcell, Dec. 11, 1952]. NOLPH 3:199
Presentation [of the Nobel Prize for Physics to Frits Zernike, Dec. 11, 1953]. NOLPH 3:237
Presentation [of the Nobel Prize for Physics to Sir Edward Victor Appleton, Dec. 12, 1947]. NOLPH 3:75

HUMAN NATURE
Bushnell, H.
Dignity of human nature. BREWE 3:825

HUMAN RIGHTS See Civil rights

HUMANITIES
Coles, R.
A "larger vision" of the humanities. BA 1977-78:163
Duffey, J. D.
General education: the rule of the humanities. BA 1977-78:146

HUMBOLDT, WILHELM FREIHERR VON
Challemel-Lacour, P. A.
Humboldt and the Teutonic intellect. BREWE 3:1018

HUMILITY
Graham, W. F.
National humility. HURH:339

HUMOR
Rice, G. P.
The comic spirit and the public speaker. EHN:283

HUMOROUS SPEECHES See After-dinner speeches

Humphrey, Hubert H., Jr.
Acceptance speech, Chicago, Illinois, August 29, 1968. SIN:372
American system. CAPG:21
Anniversary of war on poverty. CAPG:174
Campaign speech, Salt Lake City, Utah, September 30, 1968. SIN:380
Guns and butter are tied together. LAA:207
I am optimistic about America (Washington, Oct. 22, 1977). BA 1977-78:192
Impromptu audience; adaptation in a speech to a university audience. (April 9, 1965, Louisiana State University). JEF:192; JEFF:185
Open door (21st anniversary of Churchill's "Iron curtain" speech). LINR:236
Problem-solution division: a speech on the open-door policy. (Fulton, Missouri, March 5, 1967). JEF:238; JEFF:207

HUMPHREY, HUBERT H., JR.
Califano, J. A.
A tribute to the man of the people. BA 1977-78:197
Carter, J.
My good friend Hubert Humphrey. BA 1977-78:200
Mondale, W. F.
A time to celebrate life. BA 1977-78:205
Nomination of Hubert Horatio

Humphrey, Jr. (outline of speech). CUB:100

Humphreys, Benjamin G.
Justice but not equality for the Negro. ANN 9:626

HUNGARY
Downing, G. T.
May Hungary be free. FON:102

Hunt, Everett Lee
Lincoln's rhetorical triumph at Cooper Union (centennial speech). BA 1969-70:189

Hunter, Robert Mercer
A Northern party is seeking to convert the government into an instrument of warfare upon slavery (1850). (Washington, March 25, 1850). DAVF:144

HUNTLEY, CHESTER ROBERT
Cragg, R. T.
Presents Chet Huntley. LYI:109

Hurst, Charles G.
Immorality, racism, and survival. (Chicago-Annual Summer Conf. - Speech Communication Association, July 11, 1970). STOT:343

Hurwitz, Jacob
Crown of our head has fallen. WALE:93

HUSAIN, ZAKIR
Wang, G. W.
Tribute to Dr. Azkir Husain (presenting him with Doctor of Laws degree). MONS:277

Hutchins, Robert Maynard
All our institutions are in disarray. (Long Beach, Calif., May 20, 1974). BA 1974-75:117
America and the war. Same as his Drifting into suicide
Drifting into suicide. ANN 16:66
The institutional illusion. (Chicago, April 3, 1971). BA 1971-72:161
Message to the younger generation. MDV:198
Where do we go from here in education? CROCK:110

HUTCHINS, ROBERT MAYNARD
Graham, F. P.
Presents Robert M. Hutchins. LYI:96

Hutchinson, Thomas
Speech to both Houses. POC:280

Huxley, Andrew Fielding
The quantitative analysis of excitation and conduction in nerve (Nobel Lecture, Dec. 11, 1963). NOLM 4:52

HUXLEY, ANDREW FIELDING
Granit, R.
Presentation [of the Nobel Prize for Physiology or Medicine to John Carew Eccles, Alan Lloyd Hodgkin, and Andrew Fielding Huxley, Dec. 11, 1963]. NOLM 4:3

Huxley, Thomas Henry
Method of scientific investigation. ARS:264; BRYF:521
Science and culture. (Mason College, Birmingham, Oct. 1, 1880). MCB:376
Threefold unity of life. BREWE 7:2557

Hyde, Edward
"Discretion" as a despotism. BREWE 7:2562
In John Hampden's case. BREWE 7:2564

HYDROGEN
Lamb, W. E.
Fine structure of the hydrogen bomb. NOLPH 3:286
Urey, H. C.
Some thermodynamic properties of hydrogen and deuterium. NOLC 2:339

HYDROGENATION
Sabatier, P.
The method of direct hydrogenation by catalysis. NOLC 1:221

Hypereides
Funeral oration. COG:210

HYPOCHONDRIA See Sick

- I -

Ibrahim, Ahmad M.
Muslims must face modern challenges. MONS:441

ICE
Miller, J.
Why ice floats. MOP:20; MOPR:59

Ickes, Harold L.
"Americans fight joyously in a just cause." Same as his What constitutes an American?
What constitutes an American? (New York, May 18, 1941). HURH:260

IDEALISM
Dickey, J. S.
Betrayal of idealism (convocation address). BA 1967-68:136
Eucken, R.
Naturalism or idealism? NOL:74
Parson, M. J.
Idealism: what's wrong with it? BA 1975-76:166

IDEAS
Ascoli, M.
Scarcity of ideas. ARS:201
Chapin, E. H.
Sovereignty of ideas. BREWE 3:1036

IDEOLOGY
Eliezer, C. J.
Ideology and education. MONSA:231

ILLNESS See Medicine

ILLUMINATI
Morse, J.
The present dangers and consequent duties of the citizens. DAVF:45
Tappan, D.
A warning to Harvard seniors against world revolution (1798). DAVF:49
Welch, R.
More stately mansions (1964). DAVF:327

IMAGINATION
Ingersoll, R. G.
Imagination. BREWE 7:2585

IMMIGRATION AND EMIGRATION
Addams, J.
Foreign-born children in the primary grades. ANN 12:130
Gardner, H. J.
New England nativism. ANN 8:484
Levin, L. C.
Native Americans and the foreign-born. ANN 7:313
Lodge, H. C.
For immigration restrictions. ANN 12:88
McWhirter, A. J.
Appeal to European immigrants to come to the South. ANN 10:587
Meade, E. R.
Chinese immigration to the United States. ANN 10:386
Roosevelt, T.
Sixth annual message. STAT 3:2194
Truman, H. S.
Veto of the McCarran-Walter Immigration Act. ANN 17:131
Turner, H. M.
Justice or emigration should be our watchword. FON:561
Webster, D.
For reform of the naturalization laws. ANN 7:168

---- See also Migration, Internal

---- AUSTRALIA
Deakin, A.
For a white Australia. MCA:88
Higinbotham, G.
Against assisted immigration. MCA:52

IMMORTALITY
Carson, A.
Glories of immortality. BREWE 3:981

Castelar, E.
In the Campo Santo of Pisa. BREWE 3:1003
Donne, J.
Man immortal, body and soul. BREWE 5:1888
Leighton, R.
Immortality. BREWE 7:2761

IMMUNITY
Metchnikoff, E.
On the present state of the question of immunity in infectious diseases. NOLM 1:281

IMMUNOLOGY
Burnet, Sir F. M.
Immunological recognition of self. NOLM 3:689
Medawar, P. B.
Immunological tolerance. NOLM 3:704

IMPEACHMENTS
Jordan, B. C. (and others)
Hearings on articles of impeachment by the Committee of the Judiciary of the House of Representatives. BA 1974-75:15

---- See Names of individuals, e.g. Crawley, F.; Hampden, J.; Johnson, A.; Nixon, R. M.

IMPERIALISM
Beveridge, A. J.
March of the flag. ANN 12:198; BOORA 2:622; GRG:14; LINS:276
Philippine question. ANN 12:336; BRR:29
Bryan, W. J.
Imperialism (accepting Democratic nomination for Presidency, 1900). ANN 12:345
Naboth's Vineyard. GRG:11
Butler, B. F. and others
Congressional debate on Haiti and Santo Domingo, January 13, 1869. ANN 10:143
Carnot, L. N. M.
Against imperialism in France. BREWE 3:967
Hoar, G. F.
Lust of empire. ANN 12:248

IMPROMPTU SPEECHES See After-dinner speeches

INAUGURAL ADDRESSES
Adams, J.
Inaugural address. BREWE 1:39; USINAU:7; USINAUG:7
Adams, J. Q.
Inaugural address. ANN 5:138; USINAU:47; USINAUG:47
Andrus, C. D.
The inaugural address (Governor of Idaho). BA 1970-71:137
Arthur, C. A.
Inaugural address. BREWE 1:180
Bigelow, J.
Future of arts and sciences. ANN 4:449
Birenbaum, W. M.
Time for reconstruction. BA 1969-70:154
Brown, E. G., Jr.
Proposals for change: an inaugural address. BA 1978-79:103
Buchanan, J.
Inaugural address. BREWE 2:707; USINAU:111; USINAUG:111
Carlyle, T.
Inaugural address at Edinburgh. BREWE 3:951
Carter, J.
The inaugural address. BA 1976-77:18; JAM:38
Inauguration address. BA 1970-71:142
Chamberlain, D. H.
Present hour in South Carolina (inaugural address of would-be governor). CUR:158
Cleveland, G.
First inaugural address. BREWE 4:1301; USINAU:149; USINAUG:149
Second inaugural address. USINAU:163; USINAUG:163
Coolidge, C.
Inaugural address. USINAU:215; USINAUG:215
Davis, J.
Inaugural address in 1861.

ANN 9:238; BREWE 5:1656; ECH:137

Dunn, O. J.
We ask an equal chance in the race of life. FON:355

Eisenhower, D. D.
First inaugural address. HURH:304; USINAU:257; USINAUG:257
Price of peace: second inaugural address. USINAU:263; USINAUG:263

Eliot, C. W.
Inaugural address as president of Harvard. ANN 10:201

Gardner, H. J.
New England nativism. ANN 8:484

Garfield, J. A.
Inaugural address. USINAU:141; USINAUG:141

Grant, U. S.
First inaugural address. USINAU:129; USINAUG:129
Second inaugural address. USINAU:132; USINAUG:132

Hampton, W.
Present hour in South Carolina (inaugural address of would-be governor). CUR:159

Harding, W. G.
Inaugural address. USINAU:207; USINAUG:207

Harrison, B.
Inaugural address. BREWE 6:2408; USINAU:153; USINAUG:153

Harrison, W. H.
Inaugural address. HOW:67; USINAU:71; USINAUG:71

Hayes, R. B.
Inaugural address. BREWE 7:2434; USINAU:135; USINAUG:135

Hoover, H.
Inaugural address. USINAU:225; USINAUG:225

Jackson, A.
First inaugural address. USINAU:55; USINAUG:55
Second inaugural address--"State rights and Federal sovereignty." BREWE 7:2597; HURH:71; USINAU:58; USINAUG:58

Jefferson, T.
First inaugural address, democracy defined. AND:166; ANN 4:143; BOORA 1:212; BREWE 7:2612; HURH:48; LINS:150; OLIS:28; USINAU:13; USINAUG:13
Second inaugural address. USINAU:17; USINAUG:17

Johnson, A.
Inaugural address (1st speech after Lincoln's death). BREWE 7:2626

Johnson, L. B.
Inaugural address. USINAU:271; USINAUG:271

Kennedy, J. F.
Inaugural address. ALS:265; ANN 18:5; ARN:312; ARS:226; BAS:145 (outline only); BEN:143; BOORA 2:913; BRR:82; BRYF:437; BRYO:232; GRG:113; HURH:358; LINR:297; LINRS:296; LINRST:366; LINS:375; MAC:244; MACR:284; MDV:127; OLIS:282; THOMS:17; USINAU:267; USINAUG:267

Lincoln, A.
First inaugural address. ANN 9:250; BOSR:1; HOW:239; LINS:218; USINAU:119; USINAUG:119
Second inaugural address. AND:48; ANN 9:555; BEN:49; BOORA 1:423; BREWE 7:2795; BRR:80; CUB:86 (outline); HURH:114; LINS:226; USINAU:127; USINAUG:127

Lindsley, P.
Education of every child in the Republic. ANN 5:157

MacDonald, P.
Inaugural address, Window Rock, Navajo Nation, January 7, 1975. MAES:213

McKinley, W.
First inaugural address. USINAU:169; USINAUG:169
Second inaugural address. USINAU:178; USINAUG:178

Madison, J.
First inaugural address. USINAU:23; USINAUG:23
Second inaugural address. USINAU:26; USINAUG:26

Monroe, J.
First inaugural address. USINAU:29; USINAUG:29

Second inaugural address.
USINAU:37; USINAUG:37
Nixon, R. M.
Inaugural address.
BA 1968-1969:113; ERP:93; HURH:393; USINAU:275; USINAUG:275
Second inaugural address.
BA 1972-73:15; USINAUG:280
Pierce, F.
Inaugural address.
USINAU:103; USINAUG:103
Polk, J. K.
Inaugural address.
ANN 7:286; USINAU:89; USINAUG:89
Quezon, M. L.
Inaugural address.
CURM:16
Roosevelt, F. D.
First inaugural address.
ALS:207; AND:67; ANN 15:205; BEN:74; BOORA 2:839; GRG:50; HURH:219; LINS:321; ROD:63; USINAU:235; USINAUG:235
Fourth inaugural address.
USINAU:248; USINAUG:248
Second inaugural address.
USINAU:240; USINAUG:240
Third inaugural address.
USINAU:244; USINAUG:244
Roosevelt, T.
Inaugural address.
USINAU:183; USINAUG:183
Taft, W. H.
Inaugural address.
USINAU:187; USINAUG:187
Taylor, Z.
Inaugural address.
USINAU:99; USINAUG:99
Truman, H. S.
Inaugural address.
ANN 16:561; BOORA 2:891; USINAU:251; USINAUG:251
Van Buren, M.
Inaugural address.
USINAU:61; USINAUG:61
Walker, R. J.
Address to the people of Kansas. ANN 8:452
Washington, G.
First inaugural address.
ANN 3:344; BOORA 1:172; BREWE 10:3737; USINAU:1; USINAUG:1
Second inaugural address.
USINAU:5; USINAUG:5
Wilson, J.
Study of law in the United States. ANN 3:380
Wilson, W.
First inaugural address.
ANN 13:412; USINAU:199; USINAUG:199
Second inaugural address.
USINAU:203; USINAUG:203

---- See also Installation speeches; Offices - Acceptance

Inche Ahmad bin Mohamad Ibrahim
See Ibrahim, Ahmad M.

Inche Senu bin Abdul Rahman See Abdul Rahman, Tunku

Inche Yusof bin Ishak
Lest we forget (Singapore, Jan. 18, 1970). MONSA:348 selections

INCOME TAX See Taxation

INDEPENDENCE DAY See Fourth of July

INDEPENDENT TREASURY
Calhoun, J. C.
Replying to Henry Clay (from "Independent treasury debate").
BREWE 3:921
Clay, C. C., Sr.
Subtreasury Bill of 1837.
BREWE 3:1216
Van Buren, M.
Fourth annual message.
STAT 1:543
Third annual message.
STAT 1:517

INDIA
Gandhi, M. K.
Speech in London (1931).
BRN:109

INDIAN EDUCATION ACT
Barlow, E.
Education on Indian terms.
MAES:90

INDIAN EDUCATION RESOURCES CENTER, ALBUQUERQUE, N.M.
Benham, W. J.
An Indian education resources center. MAES:114

INDIAN HEALTH SERVICE
Blue Spruce, G.
Needed: Indian health professionals. MAES:171

INDIAN SELF-DETERMINATION AND EDUCATION ASSISTANCE ACT
MacDonald, P.
Statement of the implementation of P.L. 93-638 Indian Self-Determination and Education Assistance Act, Window Rock, Navajo Nation, April 3, 1975. MAES:189

INDIAN WIT AND HUMOR
Maestas, J. R.
The subtle use of humor by the great Indian chief Osceola. MAES:307

INDIANA
Webster, D.
Reception at Madison, Indiana. OLIS:36

---- SUPREME COURT
Dowling, A.
Constitutionality of a compulsory school law: opinion for the court. ANN 12:417

INDIANS, TREATMENT OF
Trimble, A.
Keynote address NCAI Convention, October 18, 1976. MAES:233

INDIANS IN SINGAPORE
Lee Kuan Yew
Tribute to India and Indians. MONSA:244

INDIANS OF NORTH AMERICA
Blue, B.
Thinking out loud. MAES:419
Bruce, B. K.
A call for a change in our Indian policy. FON:471
Chino, W.
Indian affairs--what has been done and what needs to be done. BA 1969-70:179
Cushing, C.
Extermination of the Indians. BREWE 4:1584
Dohrer, J.
Our forgotten man. LINRS:269
Frelinghuysen, T.
The Cherokee lands. HOW:189
Greve, D.
The American Indian. LINRS:100
Jackson, A.
Seventh annual message. ANN 6:164; STAT 1:415
Joseph, Chief
From where the sun now stands. ALA:63
Keeler, W. W.
Inaugural address of the chief of the Cherokees. BA 1971-72:74
Kidwell, C. S.
American Indian attitudes toward nature. MAES:277
Lee, G. P.
Effective "Indian leadership" color-blind, but not naive. MAES:183
Red Eagle
Indian rights. ANN 10:242
Red Jacket
Missionary effort. ANN 4:194; BREWE 7:2571; HURH:57
Spotted tail
We are young no longer. ALA:37
Ybarra, B.
The wheel of poverty. BAPR:356; BAPRR:266

---- See also Cherokee Indians; Navaho Indians; see also Names of Indians, e.g. Logan, J.; Old Tassel; Red Eagle; Red Jacket; Tecumseh; Weatherford, W. Also this subject with subhead - Government relations

---- AGED
Peaches, D.
Statement on the problems of the elderly American Indians at the Conference on Indian Elders, Albuquerque, New Mexico, July 17, 1975. MAES:179

---- CIVIL RIGHTS
Savilla, E. M.
Address to the Assembly of the National Congress of American

Indians at San Diego, California, October 1974. MAES:225

---- CIVILIZATION
Sawyer, T. E.
Assimilation versus self-identity. MAES:197
West, D.
Cultural differences: a base. MAES:120
Yazzie, E.
Navajo wisdom. MAES:261

---- CULTURAL ASSIMILATION
George, D.
Brotherhood and understanding. MAES:393
My people, the Indians. MAES:397
Trimble, C.
Harmony--from where the sun now stands. MAES:388

---- ECONOMIC CONDITIONS
MacDonald, P.
Statement of Chairman of Navajo Tribal Council, April 14, 1975. MAES:243

---- EDUCATION
Barlow, E. J.
Education on Indian terms. MAES:90
If a man loses something. MAES:343
Multicultural education: its effective management. MAES:110
Benham, W. J.
An Indian education resources center. MAES:114
Demmert, W. G.
Tribal chartered education. MAES:156
Harris, L.
American Indian education and pluralism. MAES:96
MacDonald, P.
Statement before the Conference on Financing of Public Schools on Indian Reservations, April 3, 1975. MAES:105
McKeag, J.
Testimony of Jana McKeag, Education Director, National Congress of American Indians, July 19, 1975. MAES:249
Maestas, J. R.
With a touch of the master's hand. MAES:130
Platero, D.
Discussions of critical issues affecting Navajo education programs and policies. MAES:149
Rainer, J. C.
Institute of American Indian Arts Commencement exercises, Friday, May 21, 1976. MAES:219
Testimony: hearings before the Senate Appropriations Subcommittee on the Interior and Related Agencies, May 13, 1975. MAES:255
Sockey, C. E.
Excellence in Indian education. MAES:141
West, D.
Cultural differences: a base. MAES:120

---- GOVERNMENT RELATIONS
Arthur, C. A.
First annual message. STAT 2:1424
Atcitty, W. R.
Remarks. MAES:38
Barlow, E. J.
If a man loses something. MAES:343
Bennett, R.
The fall and rise of Indian sovereignty. MAES:11
Cleveland, G.
First annual message (first term). STAT 2:1514
Harrison, B.
Third annual message. STAT 2:1676
Jackson, A.
First annual message. ANN 5:330; BOORA 1:264; STAT 1:294
Second annual address. ANN 5:418; STAT 1:314
MacDonald, P.
Statement before the Indian sovereignty Conference of American Indians, Harvard, February 22, 1975. MAES:22
Statement of the implementation of P.L. 93-638 Indian Self-Determination and Education Assistance Act, Window Rock,

Navajo Nation, April 3, 1975. MAES:189
Peaches, D.
Statement on the problems of the elderly American Indians at the Conference on Indian Elders, Albuquerque, New Mexico, July 17, 1975. MAES:179
Seneca, M.
Address delivered at Brigham Young University February, 1975. MAES:26
Thompson, M.
The BIA at work. MAES:57
Trimble, C.
Harmony--from where the sun now stands. MAES:388
Trudell, J.
Commitment. MAES:83
Van Buren, M.
First annual message. STAT 1:472
Second annual message. STAT 1:494
Washington, G.
Fourth annual address. STAT 1:12
Seventh annual address. STAT 1:27
Third annual address. STAT 1:7

---- HISTORY - STUDY & TEACHING
Barlow, E. J.
If a man loses something. MAES:343
Costo, R.
Indian history--fact or fiction. MAES:321

---- LAND TENURE
Wah-shee, J.
A land settlement--what does it mean? MAES:45

---- LANGUAGES - STUDY AND TEACHING
Beaudin, J. A.
Testimony to the Senate Education Committee May 6, 1975 at the State Capitol concerning Senate Bill 145. MAES:245

---- ORATORY
Momaday, N. S.
Oral tradition of the American Indian. MAES:294

---- RACE IDENTITY
Sawyer, T. E.
Assimilation versus self-identity. MAES:197

---- RELIGION AND MYTHOLOGY
Whitemen, H. V.
Spiritual roots of Indian success. MAES:377

---- RESERVATIONS
MacDonald, P.
Statement before the Conference on Financing of Public Schools on Indian Reservations, April 3, 1975. MAES:105

---- SCHOLARSHIPS, FELLOWSHIPS, ETC.
Rainer, J. C.
Testimony: hearings before the Senate Appropriations Subcommittee on the Interior and Related Agencies, May 13, 1975. MAES:255

---- SOCIAL CONDITIONS
Mills, B.
New Indian, new commitment, February, 1974. MAES:402

---- SOCIAL LIFE AND CUSTOMS
Mills, B.
New Indian, new commitment, February, 1974. MAES:402

---- TRIBAL GOVERNMENT
Demmert, W. G.
Tribal chartered education. MAES:156
Wilson, D.
Real Indian leaders condemn A.I.M. MAES:63

---- URBAN RESIDENCE
Bellecourt, V.
American Indian Movement. MAES:66

---- WISCONSIN
Beaudin, J. A.
Testimony to the Senate Education Committee May 6, 1975 at the State Capitol concerning Senate Bill 145. MAES:245

---- WOMEN
Wittstock, L. W.
Native American women in the feminist milieu. MAES:373
Yazzie, E.
Special problems of Indian women in education. MAES:360

---- WARS See Seminole War, 1st, Florida, 1817-1818

INDIVIDUALISM
Eisenhower, D. D.
Faith in the individual. CAPG:31
Kerr, C.
The independent spirit. HOR:114
Schell, G.
Shackled by stereotypes. CAPB:381

INDONESIA
May, D.
Djakarta style. MDYG:168

---- FOREIGN RELATIONS
Razak, T. A.
And then came peace (Peace Agreement between Malaysia and Indonesia). MONS:94

INDUCTION See Inaugural addresses; Installation speeches

INDUSTRIAL ARTS
Webster, D.
Progress of the mechanic arts. BREWE 10:3856

INDUSTRIAL RELATIONS
Brandeis, L. D.
Curse of bigness. BOORA 2:759
Fisk, T.
War of capital against labor. ANN 6:118
Fortune, T. T.
The present relations of labor and capital. FON:506
Lincoln, A.
First annual message. STAT 2:1054
Roosevelt, T.
Eighth annual message. STAT 3:2296
Sixth annual message. STAT 3:2194
Truman, H. S.
Second annual message. STAT 3:2939
Webster, D.
Technical progress and prosperity. ANN 6:266
White, W. A.
Speaking for the consumer. HURH:234

---- See also Industry; Labor unions

---- MALAYSIA
Suffian bin Hashim
Warning to the white-collar worker. MONSA:138

INDUSTRIAL WORKERS OF THE WORLD
De Leon, D.
Political power of labor. ANN 13:19

INDUSTRY
Baldwin, S. B.
Good will in industry. MCB:243
Carty, J. J.
Pure science and industrial research. ANN 14:9
Chapin, E. H.
Peaceful industry. BREWE 3:1037
Clay, H.
American industry, 1824. ANN 5:114
Hoover, H. C.
Moral standard in an industrial era. ANN 14:428

---- See also Business; Industrial relations; Laissez-faire

INDUSTRY AND SOCIETY
Eisenhower, D. D.
Faith in the individual. CAPG:31
Grede, W. J.
America, a frontier. ANN 17:154

INDUSTRY AND STATE
Carpenter, C. U.
Justification of big business. ANN 13:327

Champion, G.
Consensus complex vs. the free market. BA 1965-66:187
Drumm, S. L.
War on prosperity. CAPG:185
Friedman, M.
The future of capitalism. LINRST:243
Hanley, J. W.
The day innovation died. BA 1978-79:122
Hart, G.
Big government: real or imaginary? LINRST:100
Hoover, H. C.
Campaign speech, Madison Square Garden, New York City, October 31, 1932. SIN:103
Speech at New York City, October 22, 1928. ANN 14:595; BOORA 2:803
Veto of the Muscle Shoals Bill. ANN 15:79
Johari, M. K.
A national chamber needed. MONSA:103
Richey, H. S.
The real cause of inflation: government services. LINRST:108
Romney, G.
Our unique economic principles: the market place should determine price. CAPG:40
Roosevelt, F. D.
Fifth annual message. STAT 3:2883
Stanton, F.
Remarks on government regulation of broadcasting (accepting Printers' Ink gold medal). MDV:277
Sutherland, G. and others
New State Ice Company v. Liebmann: opinion for the court and dissenting opinion. ANN 15:140
Taft, R. A.
New problems of government. ANN 15:571
Should the government guarantee employment? ANN 16:263
Van Buren, M.
Against government aid for business losses. ANN 6:314
Waite, M. R. and others
Munn v. Illinois, 1876: opinion for the court and dissenting opinion. ANN 10:377
Willkie, W. L.
Private enterprise--we have gone far enough down the road to federal control. BAD:69

INFLATION (FINANCE)
Muskie, E. S.
Too many questions ... not enough answers. BA 1978-79:112
Richey, H. S.
The real cause of inflation: government services. LINRST:108

INFORMATIVE SPEECHES
Bragg, L.
Art of talking about science. MOP:358
Burton, S.
You (male) should wear long hair. BAS:200 (outline only)
King, M. L., Jr.
Love, law, and civil disobedience. FON:943; LINR:63; LINRS:70; LINRST:75; STOT:321
Klein, P. A.
Big things happen in small places (outline of speech explaining protein synthesis). CUR:34
Koblish, C. F.
Diamonds, their mining, selling, perfecting, and the determining of their quality. BAS:206 (outline only)
Menninger, K.
Healthier than healthy. LINR:54
Miller, J.
Why ice floats. MOP:20; MOPR:59
Peters, L.
What is totalitarianism? LINR:50
Ragan, D. O.
Backaches. MOP:366
Sonberg, H. A.
Unidentified flying objects; their history and various explanations which have been given concerning their nature. BAS:203 (outline only)

Suggestions for preparation of the informative speech. With examples of. BRP:46, 169

---- See also Reports

Ingalls, John James
Undiscovered country. BREWE 7:2574

Ingebretsen, Herman Smitt
Presentation [of the Nobel Prize for Peace to John Raleigh Mott, Dec. 10, 1946]. NOLP 2:354

Ingersoll, Charles Jared
Influence of America on the mind. ANN 5:95

Ingersoll, Robert Green
Absurdity of religion. ANN 11:267
At his brother's grave. ALA:69; BREWE 7:2580; HURH:156
Blaine, the plumed knight. Same as his Nominating Blaine
Grave of Napoleon. Same as his Liberty of man, woman, and child
Imagination. BREWE 7:2585
Liberty of man, woman, and child. BREWE 7:2583
Life. BREWE 7:2587
"Life is a narrow vale between the cold and barren peaks of two eternities." Same as his Nominating Blaine
Nominating Blaine. BREWE 7:2578: HURH:154

INHIBITION
Eccles, J. C.
The ionic mechanism of postsynaptic inhibition. NOLM 4:6
Sherrington, Sir C. S.
Inhibition as a coordinative factor. NOLM 2:278

INQUIRY, SPEECHES OF See Informative speeches

INSANE - CARE AND TREATMENT
Seward, W. H.
Providing for the indigent insane. ANN 8:283

INSANITY
Erskine, T.
Homicidal insanity (J. Hadfield). BREWE 6:2058; BRYH:294

INSECTICIDES
Müller, P. H.
Dichloro-diphenyl-trichloroethane and newer insecticides. NOLM 3:227

INSECTS, INJURIOUS AND BENEFICIAL - CONTROL
Klayton, R. J.
Bureau of Forests and Waters should control pests by biological means rather than pesticides. BAS:188 (outline only)

INSPIRATIONAL TALKS
Bunche, R. J.
Barriers of race can be surmounted. CAPG:66
Eisenhower, D. D.
Price of peace: second inaugural address. USINAU:263; USINAUG:263
Suggestions for preparation of inspirational talks. PAE:189

INSTALLATION SPEECHES
Abdul Rahman, T.
Our university: pledge to nation (installation speech as Chancellor of University of Malaya). MONS:28
Installation services for general officers. BNH:53; BOS:53
Installation services for men's organizations. BNH:56; BOS:56
Peel, R.
Plea for higher education (installation speech as Lord Rector of University of Glasgow). BREWE 8:3153
Suggestions for preparing installation speeches. PAE:186

---- See also Inaugural addresses

INSTITUTE OF INTERNATIONAL LAW
Hagerup, G. F.

The work of the Institute of International Law (Nobel Lecture for 1904, Aug. 24, 1912). NOLP 1:64
Irgens, J.
Welcome [presenting the Nobel Prize for Peace to the Institute of International Law for 1904, Aug. 24, 1912]. NOLP 1:61

INSTITUTIONS, SIZE OF
Babbidge, H. D.
On thinking big. HOR:121

INSTRUCTION, SPEECHES OF
See Informative speeches

INSULIN
Banting, F. G.
Diabetes and insulin. NOLM 2:50
Macleod, J. J. R.
The physiology of insulin and its source in the animal body. NOLM 2:71

INSURANCE - ACCIDENT
Clemens, S. L.
Accident insurance--etc. MUS:291

INSURANCE - LIFE
Eisenhower, D. D.
Faith in the individual. CAPG:31

INSURANCE - PROPERTY
Title insurance racket. BURT:136

INTEGRATION
Browne, R. S.
A case for separation. FON:1121
---- and others
Separation or integration: which way for America? BA 1968-69:143
Galamison, M. A.
Integration must work--nothing else can. FON:959
James, D.
"Given time we'll get it together." BA 1974-75:135

---- See also Segregation

INTELLECT
Beloff, M.
Americanisation of British intellectual life. MDYG:114
Campbell, A.
Mind the master force. BREWE 3:935
Everett, E.
Circumstances favorable to the progress of literature in America. ANN 5:118
Huxley, T. H.
Method of scientific investigation. ARS:264
Ingersoll, C. J.
Influence of America on the mind. ANN 5:95
Living or the dead. BURT:127

INTERNAL SECURITY - MALAYSIA
Rahman, D. I. B. A.
Commendable features of public-spiritedness and co-operation. MONSA:76
Government is determined to take drastic measures if.... MONSA:72
Security situation in Malaysia: a warning and pledge. MONSA:69

INTERNAL SECURITY ACT, 1950
Truman, H. S.
Veto of the Internal Security Act. ANN 17:35

INTERNATIONAL COOPERATION
Balch, E. G.
Toward human unity or beyond nationalism (Nobel Lecture for 1946, April 7, 1948). NOLP 2:333
Branting, K. H.
Fraternity among nations (Nobel Lecture for 1921, June 19, 1922). NOLP 1:324
Cremer, W. R.
The progress and advantages of international arbitration (Nobel Lecture for 1903, Jan. 15, 1905). NOLP 1:46
Fried, P.
Price of peace. SCHW:35
Hammarskjöld, D.
Values of nationalism and internationalism (Stanford University commencement address). HURS:206

Lange, C. L.
Internationalism (Nobel Lecture, Dec. 13, 1921). NOLP 1:336
McKeever, P.
The United States and the United Nations. BRYF:479
Roosevelt, T.
International peace (Nobel Lecture for 1906, May 5, 1910). NOLP 1:102
Stevenson, A. E.
Strengthening international developing institutions. ALS:281

INTERNATIONAL ECONOMIC RELATIONS
Stevenson, A., III
Economic interdependence: the world at a crossroads. BA 1978-79:178

INTERNATIONAL LABOR ORGANIZATION
Lionaes, A.
Presentation [of the Nobel Prize for Peace to the International Labor Organization, Dec. 10, 1969]. NOLP 3:415
Manickavasagam, V.
ILO represents the social conscience of the world. MONSA:106 selections
Morse, D. A.
ILO and the social infrastructure of peace (Nobel Lecture, Dec. 11, 1969). NOLP 3:424

INTERNATIONAL LAW See Law and lawyers

INTERNATIONAL RELATIONS
Acheson, D. G.
Ethics of international relations today. ARS:229
Chateaubriand, F. A. R.
Has one government the right to intervene in the internal affairs of another? BREWE 3:1060
Eisenhower, M. S.
A new historical perspective, interdependence. HOR:157
Hesburgh, T. M.
The problems and opportunities on a very interdependent planet. HOR:142
Hugo, V. M.
Moral forces in world politics. BREWE 7:2553
Lee Kuan Yew
Changes in values and concepts. MONS:348
Lubbers, A. D.
Road to right. SCHW:159
Worden, G. J.
Person to person. SCHW:174

INTERNATIONALISM See International cooperation; Nationalism

INTERSTATE COMMERCE
Roosevelt, T.
Seventh annual message. STAT 3:2240

---- See also Railroads and state

INTERVIEWING
Scott, R.
A job-seeking interview: a transcript. MOPR:381

INTOLERANCE See Religious liberty

INTRODUCTIONS
Ace of aces (outline of speech). CUB:62
Ashmore, H. S.
Presents J. William Fulbright. LYI:205
Bard, G. M.
Introduces Alexander Rorke, Jr. PRS:69
Introduces Arthur Godfrey. PRS:45
Introduces Dr. Deane W. Malott, president of Cornell University. PRS:115
Introduces Dr. Henry A. Kissinger. PRS:124
Introduces George Ratterman. PRS:62
Introduces Gilbert W. Fitzhugh. PRS:17
Introduces Walter W. Heller, chairman of the President's Council on Economic Advisers. PRS:33
Introduces William F. Buckley, Jr., columnist. PRS:57
Blakely, R. J.

Presents Stephen Hayes Bush. LYI:77
Blumenschein, C. M.
Introduces Smith Hempstone. PRS:23
Borsch, R. A.
Introduces Irish Prime Minister William Norton. PRS:41
Introduces Selwyn Lloyd, former British Secretary of State for Foreign Affairs. PRS:39
Brorby, M.
Introduces Arnold J. Toynbee, professor, author and historian of Great Britain. LYI:86
Buchanan, J. G.
Presents Augustus N. Hand. LYI:133
Bullock, H.
Presents Lester B. Pearson. LYI:207
Burgess, W. R.
Presents Paul H. Douglas. LYI:231
Butler, N. M.
Presents Wilbur L. Cross. LYI:97
Cavanagh, J. P.
Presents George Alfred Brown. LYI:203
Caveny, C. C.
Greets Joey Bishop, substituting for Sir Cedric Hardwicke. PRS:118
Introduces David E. Bell, director of the Bureau of the Budget. PRS:92
Introduces Dr. George W. Beadle, chancellor of the University of Chicago. PRS:50
Introduces Dr. Jonas E. Salk. PRS:88
Introduces Henry J. Taylor, former United States Ambassador to Switzerland. PRS:25
Introduces Leonard E. Read. PRS:98
Introduces Ogden Nash. PRS:106
Introduces Robert E. Brooker, president of Whirlpool Corporation. PRS:9
Introduces Senator John G. Tower of Texas. PRS:111
Introduces Senator Kenneth B. Keating. PRS:27
Chandler, M.
Introduces Roscoe Drummond. PRS:122
Choate, J. H.
Presents James Bryce. LYI:237
Clemens, S. L.
Presents Henry M. Stanley. LYI:117
Presents Joseph B. Hawley. LYI:148
Presents Winston Churchill. LYI:198
Coulter, T. H.
Introducing Marguerite (Maggie) Higgins to the Executives' Club of Chicago. LYI:113
Cragg, R. T.
Introduces Judge Lester H. Loble of Juvenile Court of Helena, Montana. PRS:38
Presents Cyril Northcote. LYI:45
Croarkin, W.
Presents Frank F. Rosenthal. LYI:165
Presents William David O'Brien. LYI:163
Cullman, H. S.
Presents Roger L. Stevens. LYI:29
Daniels, J.
Presents Sir Norman Birkett. LYI:135
Davis, C. R.
Presents Will Durant. LYI:56
Davis, J. W.
Presents Lester B. Pearson. LYI:220
Day, J. E.
Introduces G. Keith Funston, president New York Stock Exchange. PRS:10
Introduces John L. Lewis, American labor leader. LYI:61
Depew, C. M.
Presents William Jennings Bryan. LYI:227
Dirksen, E.
Presents Robert A. Taft. LYI:210
Donovan, H.
Presents Henry R. Luce. LYI:103

Douglas, L. W.
Presents Lord Halifax. LYI:222
Dreier, A.
Introduces James T. Quirk. PRS:18
Introduces the Honorable William Proxmire, United States Senator from Wisconsin. PRS:34
DuVall, W. O.
Presents Billy Graham. LYI:160
Erickson, D. J.
Presents W. E. Whitehead. LYI:63
Fawcett, N. G.
Introduces E. W. Ingram, president, White Castle, Inc. PRS:6
Fisher, C. T., Jr.
Presents George C. Kenney. LYI:150
Ford, G. S.
Presents Christopher Morley. LYI:55
Ford, H. II
Presents Elmo Roper. LYI:73
Fraser, L.
Presents James F. Byrnes. LYI:218
Godfrey, J. L.
Presents Frank Borden Hanes. LYI:38
Gossett, W. T.
Presents Harry Emerson Fosdick. LYI:157
Graham, F. P.
Presents Robert M. Hutchins. LYI:96
Griffin, C. E.
Presents James Palmer. LYI:67
Gwinn, J. M.
Presents Charles Lindbergh. LYI:188
Hancher, V. M.
Presents Eleanor Roosevelt. LYI:244
Presents Franklyn Bliss Snyder. LYI:99
Hanson, C. W. D.
Introduces Benson Ford, vice-president, Ford Motor Company. PRS:22
Introduces Gene Lockhart. PRS:51
Harding, W. G.
Presents Marie S. Curie. LYI:179
Hayes, A.
Presents Indira Gandhi. LYI:199
Hedges, J. E.
Presents Edward D. Duffield. LYI:69
Hibben, J. W.
Introduces Bishop James A. Pike. PRS:69
Introduces Braj K. Nehru, Ambassador from India. PRS:26
Introduces Dr. Howard B. Sprague. PRS:61
Introduces Hobart Rowen of Newsweek Magazine. PRS:95
Introduces the Honorable Otto Kerner, governor of Illinois. PRS:29
Introduces Willy Brandt, mayor of West Berlin. PRS:37
Hill, H.
Presents Francis B. Haas. LYI:93
Hills, L.
Presents Fred Sparks. LYI:115
Holmes, O. W.
Introduces Matthew Arnold. LYI:44
Introduction of speakers (12 examples). HNWSN:59
Introduction of the head of the Executive Committee of the Chicago Central Area Committee. PRS:21
Introductions for doctors. BOS:25; (6 examples) BNH:25
Introductions for evangelists (19 examples). BNH:13; BON:26; BOS:13
Introductions for housewives (5 examples). BNH:33; BOS:33
Introductions for literary persons (2 examples). BNH:18; BOS:18
Introductions for medical doctors. BON:29
Introductions for men in general (10 examples). BNH:19; BON:15; BOS:19
Introductions for ministers (16 examples). BNH:9; BOS:9
Introductions for mission society leaders (4 examples). BNH:35; BOS:35
Introductions for missionaries. BON:34

Introductions for mothers-in-law (4 examples). BNH:32; BOS:34
Introductions for nurses (4 examples). BNH:32; BOS:32
Introductions for politicians (3 examples). BNH:31; BOS:31
Introductions for prize winners. BON:32
Introductions for public officials. BON:23; BOS:27; (3 examples) BNH:27
Introductions for singers and musicians (12 examples). BNH:22; BOS:22
Introductions for teachers (10 examples). BNH:28; BON:20; BOS:28
Introductions for women. BON:38
Jessel, G.
Presents Groucho Marx. LYI:32
Presents Jack Benny. LYI:30
Kipke, H. G.
Introduces John K. Herbert, president of the Magazine Publishers Association. PRS:21
Knight, J. R.
Introduces Lieutenant Thomas A. Dooley, United States Navy. PRS:67
Knoch, W. G.
Introduces Robert Taft, Jr., Congressman-at-large from Ohio. PRS:32
Lamont, T. S.
Presents Paul G. Hoffman. LYI:71
Presents Eleanor Robson Belmont. LYI:23
Presents W. L. Mackenzie King. LYI:233
Landis, F.
Witty after-dinner speech on Will Hays. LYI:224
Langlie, A. B.
Presents Norman S. Marshall. LYI:155
Lewe, J. C.
Presents Thomas C. Clark (Attorney General of the United States). LYI:137
Lewis, J. H.
Introduction of Jacob M. Dickinson. LYI:217
Lowe, J. A.
Presents E. J. Pratt. LYI:49
Lusty, R.
Presents Sir Norman Birkett. LYI:54
McCloud, B. G.
Presents C. D. Jackson. PRS:23
McLain, H. O.
Presents David Seabury. LYI:98
Martin, C.
Presents McGeorge Bundy. LYI:88
Martin, J. W.
Introducing Speaker Sam Rayburn. LYI:195
Martin, T. W.
Presents Charles F. Kettering. LYI:181
Mason, W. C.
Presents George Wharton Pepper. LYI:129
Meloney, Mrs. W. B.
Introducing Dorothy Thompson. LYI:112
Merriam, J. C.
Presents Ray Lyman Wilbur. LYI:82
Milburn, J. G.
Presents James R. Day. LYI:90
Mulroy, T. R.
Presents Ilka Chase. LYI:17
Murphy, H. D.
Introduces Dr. Norman Vincent Peale. PRS:103
Introduces Dr. Ralph W. Sockman. PRS:117
Introduces Lee Wulff. PRS:67
Introduces Senator Hubert Humphrey from Minnesota. PRS:40
Nix, L.
Presents Edmon Low. LYI:40
Nizer, L.
Presents Albert Einstein. LYI:176
Presents George Gershwin. LYI:15
Presents Grover A. Whalen. LYI:65
Presents Harry Woodburn Chase. LYI:91
Presents Heywood Broun. LYI:105
Noonan, T. C.

Introduces the Very Reverend Theodore M. Hesburgh, president of Notre Dame University. PRS:48
Olney, R.
Presents Woodrow Wilson. LYI:215
Olson, H. S.
Introduces Admiral John S. McCain. PRS:56
Introduces Charles O. Finley, owner, Kansas City Athletics. PRS:114
Introduces Dr. Glenn T. Seaborg, chairman of the Atomic Energy Commission. PRS:47
Introduces Dr. Luther L. Terry, United States Surgeon General. PRS:42
Introduces Dr. Max Rafferty, State Superintendent of Public Instruction (California). PRS:53
Introduces Dr. Walter H. Judd. PRS:125
Introduces Earl B. Hathaway, president of Firestone Tire and Rubber Company. PRS:13
Introduces Harry Schwartz of the New York Times. PRS:60
Introduces Marguerite Higgins. PRS:107
Introduces Ronald Reagan. PRS:49
Introduces Senator Everett M. Dirksen. PRS:121
Introduces Senator Karl E. Mundt. PRS:108
Introduces the Honorable Herve Alphand, French Ambassador to the United States. PRS:35
Introduces William McChesney Martin, Jr., chairman, board of governors, Federal Reserve System. PRS:63
Pepper, G. W.
Introducing Ferdinand Foch. LYI:145
Presents Charles Evans Hughes. LYI:127
Presents Earl Warren. LYI:121
Phelps, W. L.
Presents André Chevrillon. LYI:52
Presents Sir William Llewellyn. LYI:26
Prochnow, H. V.
Introduces Clarence B. Randall as moderator of panel. PRS:12
Introduces Dr. David Horowitz, governor of the Bank of Israel. PRS:31
Introduces Peter G. Peterson, president of Bell and Howell Company. PRS:8
Presents James C. Downs, Jr., chairman of the board of the Real Estate Research Corporation. PRS:14
Presents Richard J. Daley, mayor of Chicago. PRS:28
Rogers, W.
Presents Franklin Delano Roosevelt. LYI:111
Root, E.
Introducing H. Watterson to New England Society of New York. LYI:111
Schnadig, E. L.
Presents Gerald Wendt. LYI:186
Seaman, Sir O.
Presents Stephen Leacock. LYI:47
Sellers, R. S.
Presents Harry D. Gideonse. LYI:80
Shaw, G. B.
Presents Major Barbara. LYI:50
Shull, M. A.
Presents Bruce Catton. LYI:42
Simmons, D. A.
Presents Walter S. Fenton. LYI:131
Spellman, F. J.
Presents Maxwell D. Taylor. LYI:143
Spencer, H. R.
Introducing Anne O'Hare McCormick. LYI:107
Stevenson, A. E.
Presents Lyndon B. Johnson. LYI:197
Presents Pandit Jawaharlal Nehru. LYI:242
Stipp, J. E.
Introduces Nathan M. Pusey,

President, Harvard University. LYI:83
Street, W. S.
Introduces Dr. Charles E. Odegaard, president of the University of Washington. PRS:46
Streeter, F. S.
Introducing an educator (Frederick S. Jones). LYI:85
Suggestions for preparation of an introduction. MILS:8
With examples of. PAE:176
Sumner, G. L.
Presents Gertrude Lawrence. LYI:22
Presents Victor Heiser. LYI:19
Taylor, D.
Presents Grace George. LYI:19
Trilling, L.
Presents T. S. Eliot. LYI:35
Trippe, J. T.
Presents Vannevar Bush. LYI:177
Truman, H. S.
Presents Winston Churchill. LYI:211
Tweed, H.
Presents Dillon Anderson. LYI:125
Presents Hartley Shawcross. LYI:123
Walbert, R. B.
Introduces Albert L. Cole, president of Reader's Digest Association. PRS:96
Introduces Bruce Catton, historian. PRS:87
Introduces Clinton S. Sanders, chairman of the American Trucking Association. PRS:89
Introduces Dr. Ernest L. Wilkinson, president Brigham Young University. PRS:44
Introduces Dr. Norman Vincent Peale. PRS:112
Introduces George Meany, president of the AFL-CIO. PRS:59
Introduces J. Paul Austin, president, the Coca-Cola Company. PRS:19
Introduces Jervis Langdon, Jr. PRS:16
Introduces Mark O. Hatfield, governor of Oregon. PRS:91
Introduces Senator Thurston B. Morton. PRS:97
Introduces William G. Cole, president of Lake Forest College. PRS:97
Introduces William W. Scranton, governor of Pennsylvania. PRS:109
Waller, H. H.
Presents Bertrand Russell. LYI:94
Presents Estes Kefauver. LYI:230
Watkins, F. C.
Introduces Cloud Wampler, chairman of the board, Carrier Air Conditioning. PRS:126
Watson, A. K.
Presents William W. Scranton. LYI:201
Weaver, W.
Presents Sir Charles Percy Snow. LYI:171
Webb, W. P.
Presents Harry S. Truman. LYI:193
Welcome and introduction of coach of athletic team at awards banquet. HNWM:34
Weyforth, B. S., Jr.
Introduces Barry Goldwater, Senator from Arizona. PRS:39
Introduces Boris Morros. PRS:66
Introduces Cornelia Otis Skinner. PRS:53
Introduces General Mark W. Clark, president of the Citadel. PRS:64
Introduces George A. Smathers, United States Senator from Florida. PRS:36
Introduces Mrs. Ivy Baker Priest, Treasurer of the United States. PRS:28
Introduces Mural Deusing. PRS:63
Introduces Nikolai Khokhlov, former Soviet intelligence officer. PRS:68

Introduces Robert C. Tyson, chairman of the finance committee, United States Steel Corporation. PRS:15
Willcox, W. R.
Introducing G. W. Goethals to the Economic Club of New York, March 5, 1914. LYI:183
Wilson, E. F.
Introduces Wilbur M. Brucker, then Secretary of the Army. PRS:41
Youle, C.
Introduces Charles B. Thornton. PRS:100
Introduces Don Whitehead, chief of the Washington bureau of the New York Herald Tribune. PRS:65
Introduces Percy Brundage, the director of the Federal Budget. PRS:31
Introduces Stanley C. Hope, president, National Association of Manufacturers. PRS:15
Introduces W. Randolph Burgess, United States permanent representative on the North Atlantic Council. PRS:30
Presents S. Clarke Beise, president of the Bank of America. PRS:15
Zumwalt, E.
Introduction to Edmund G. Brown, Jr. JAM:33

---- See also Responses to introductions; Welcoming addresses

INVENTIONS AND INVENTORS
DuPont, H. B.
Greatest invention of them all. ANN 17:530
Durfee, J.
Influence of scientific discovery and invention on social and political progress. ANN 7:128
Ziegler, K.
Consequences and development of an invention. NOLC 4:6

INVESTIGATION See Research

INVESTMENTS
Investors. BURT:133

IONOSPHERE
Appleton, Sir E. V.
The ionosphere. NOLPH 3:79

IONS
Onsager, L.
The motion of ions: principles and concepts. NOLC 4:272
Wilson, C. T. R.
On the cloud method of making visible ions and the tracks of ionizing particles. NOLPH 2:194

IRAN
Demosthenes
Oration on the liberty of the Rhodians. SAG:180

IRELAND
Canning, G.
Hate in politics. BREWE 3:946
Curran, J. P.
Liberties of the indolent. BREWE 4:1550
On government by attachment. BREWE 4:1557
Davitt, M.
Ireland a nation, self-chartered and self-ruled. BREWE 5:1666
Gladstone, W. E.
Home Rule, June 7, 1886. MCB:301
Home rule and autonomy. BREWE 6:2278
Grattan, H.
Declaration of Irish rights, April 19, 1780. BREWE 6:2314; CLAYP:120
Making his second motion for a Declaration of Irish rights, April 16, 1782. BRYH:244
Unsurrendering fidelity to country. BREWE 6:2333
Meagher, T. F.
Withering influence of provincial subjection. BREWE 8:2999
O'Connell, D.
Demand for justice to Ireland. BREWE 8:3107
On repeal of the Union. BREWE 8:3099; BRYH:358; MCB:288; STRM:198
Oxford and Asquith, H. H. A.

Debate on the Government of Ireland Bill. MCB:321
Palmerston, H. J. T.
Against war on Ireland. BREWE 8:3134
Parnell, C. S.
Against nonresident landlords. BREWE 8:3145
At Ennis (boycotting defined and defended). BRYF:544; MCB:296; STRM:346
Sheil, R. L.
Ireland's part in English achievement. BREWE 9:3413
Smith, S.
"Wounds, shrieks, and tears" in government. BREWE 9:3490

Irgens, Johannes
Welcome [presenting the Nobel Prize for Peace to the Institute of International Law for 1904, Aug. 24, 1912]. NOLP 1:61

IRRIGATION - SOUTH DAKOTA
Gage, P.
The Oahe Project--yes or no? BREWW:191

Irwin, Henry
The true aim of education. CURM:167

Ising, G.
Presentation [of the Nobel Prize for Physics to Patrick Maynard Stuart Blackett, Dec. 13, 1948]. NOLPH 3:93

Ismail bin Mohammed Ali
The central Bank--the "financial conscience" of the government (Kuala Lampur, Sept. 1970). MONSA:189

ISOLATIONISM See United States - Neutrality

ISOTOPES
Aston, F. W.
Mass spectra and isotopes. NOLC 2:7
Soddy, F.
The origins of the conceptions of isotopes. NOLC 1:371

ISOTOPIC INDICATORS See Radioactive tracers

ISRAEL
Ghali, W.
Egyptian in Israel. MDYG:152

---- FOREIGN RELATIONS - EGYPT
Carter, J.
Announcing the Camp David accords. BA 1978-79:142

ITALY
Cavour, C. B.
Rome and Italy. BREWE 3:1012
Mazzini, G.
To the young men of Italy. BREWE 8:2992
Roosevelt, F. D.
Italy enters this war. ANN 16:8

Ivens, Mike
I still believe in the future of farming. BREWW:195

IVY ORATIONS See Commencement addresses

- J -

Jackson, Andrew
Autonomy of the executive. ANN 6:58
Eighth annual message. STAT 1:445
Farewell address, 1837. ANN 6:298
Fifth annual message. STAT 1:373
First annual message. ANN 5:330; BOORA 1:264; STAT 1:294
First inaugural address. USINAU:55; USINAUG:55
Fourth annual message. STAT 1:350
Independence of Texas. ANN 6:293
On the Indian removal. Same as his Second annual message
Permanent habitation for the American Indians. Same as

his Seventh annual message
Second annual address. ANN 5:418; STAT 1:314
Second inaugural address--"State rights and Federal sovereignty." (Washington, March 4, 1833). BREWE 7:2597; HURH:71; USINAU:58; USINAUG:58
Seventh annual message. ANN 6:164; STAT 1:415
Sixth annual message. STAT 1:389
Third annual message. STAT 1:344
Veto message of July 10, 1832. ANN 5:524
Veto of Maysville Road Bill. ANN 5:374
"Without union, our independence and liberty would never have been achieved; without union they never can be maintained." Same as his Second inaugural address--"State rights and federal sovereignty."

JACKSON, ANDREW
Benton, T. H.
Political career of Andrew Jackson. BREWE 2:411
Calhoun, J. C.
Denouncing Andrew Jackson. BREWE 3:919
Clay, H.
Dictators in American politics. BLY:33; BREWE 4:1124
Crockett, D.
Fourth of July oration, 1834. HAW:136
Robbins, A.
Fourth of July oration, July 4, 1834. HAW:160

Jackson, Esther M.
American theatre and the speech profession. BA 1965-66:200

JACKSON, GEORGE
Davis, A.
The legacy of George Jackson. FON:1191

Jackson, Robert H.
The Communist Party is a secret conclave. American Communications Association, C.I.O. et al v. Charles T. Douds; United Steel Workers of America et al v. National Labor Relations Board. (1949). DAVF:292
Court broadens the rights of citizens: the Second Flag Salute Case, 1943. ROD:214
To secure the existing order against revolutionary radicalism (1950). (Eugene Dennis et al v. U.S.A.). DAVF:294

---- and others (H. L. Black; W. O. Douglas; F. Frankfurter)
West Virginia Board of Education et al v. Barnette et al: opinion for the court and dissenting opinion. ANN 16:148

---- See also Black, H. L., jt. auth.

Jacob, François
Genetics of the bacterial cell (Nobel Prize, Dec. 11, 1965). NOLM 4:148

JACOB, FRANÇOIS
Gard, S.
Presentation [of the Nobel Prize for Physiology or Medicine to François Jacob, André Lwoff, and Jacques Monod, Dec. 11, 1965]. NOLM 4:143

Jacobusse, K. Don
Big man. SCHW:204
Peace through patriotism. SCHW:168
Uncommon thought. SCHW:79

Jahn, Gunnar
Presentation [of the Nobel Prize for Peace to Albert John Luthuli for 1960, Dec. 10, 1961]. NOLP 3:209
Presentation [of the Nobel Prize for Peace for 1952 to Albert Schweitzer, Dec. 10, 1953]. NOLP 3:37
Presentation [of the Nobel Prize for Peace to Cordell Hull, Dec. 10, 1945]. NOLP 2:311

Presentation [of the Nobel Prize for Peace to Dag Hammarskjöld, Dec. 10, 1961]. NOLP 3:239
Presentation [of the Nobel Prize for Peace to Emily Greene Balch, Dec. 10, 1946]. NOLP 2:325
Presentation [of the Nobel Prize for Peace to the Friends Service Council and the American Friends Service Committee, Dec. 10, 1947]. NOLP 2:373
Presentation [of the Nobel Prize for Peace to Georges Pire, Dec. 10, 1958]. NOLP 3:151
Presentation [of the Nobel Prize for Peace to the International Committee of the Red Cross, 1944, Dec. 10, 1945]. NOLP 2:289
Presentation [of the Nobel Prize for Peace to Léon Jouhaux, Dec. 10, 1951]. NOLP 3:3
Presentation [of the Nobel Prize for Peace to Lester Bowles Pearson, Dec. 10, 1957]. NOLP 3:119
Presentation [of the Nobel Prize for Peace, 1962, to Linus Carl Pauling, Dec. 10, 1963]. NOLP 3:259
Presentation [of the Nobel Prize for Peace to Lord Boyd Orr of Brechin, Dec. 10, 1949]. NOLP 2:407
Presentation [of the Nobel Prize for Peace to Martin Luther King, Jr., Dec. 10, 1964]. NOLP 3:325
Presentation [of the Nobel Prize for Peace to the Office of the United Nations High Commissioner for Refugees, Dec. 10, 1955]. NOLP 3:89
Presentation [of the Nobel Prize for Peace to Philip John Noel-Baker, Dec. 10, 1959]. NOLP 3:175
Presentation [of the Nobel Prize for Peace to Ralph Johnson Bunche, Dec. 10, 1950]. NOLP 2:435

James, Daniel
"Given time we'll get it together." (Pensacola, Fla., Feb. 14, 1975). BA 1974-75:135

JAMES, WILLIAM
Santayana, G.
Genteel tradition in American philosophy. ANN 13:277

JAPAN
Tuohy, F.
Three windows on Japan. MDYG:161

JAPANESE IN THE UNITED STATES
Black, H. L. and others
Korematsu v. United States: opinion for the court and dissenting opinion. ANN 16:234
Mink, P. T.
Seeking a link with the past. BA 1971-72:59
Stone, H. F.
Fear and hysteria: the Japanese relocation, "Hirabayashi v. United States," 1943: opinion for the Supreme Court. ROD:316
Tardiff, V.
Americans with Japanese faces. SCHW:20

Jarrow, Charles
Case for the non-voter. KEO:229

Jay, John, 1745-1829
Protest against colonial government. BREWE 7:2601

Jay, Peter See Sanford, N., jt. auth.

JAY TREATY See Treaties

JAZZ MUSIC
Bernstein, L.
World of jazz. ARN:320; ARS:67

Jefferson, Thomas
Eighth annual message. STAT 1:94
Fifth annual message. STAT 1:77
First annual message. STAT 1:48
First inaugural: democracy

defined (Washington, March 4, 1801). AND:116; ANN 1:143; BOORA 1:212; BREWE 7:2612; HURH:48; LINS:140; OLIS:28; USINAU:13; USINAUG:13
Fourth annual message. STAT 1:73
Jeffersonian democracy defines. Same as his First inaugural: democracy defined
Lewis and Clark expedition. ANN 4:158
Second annual message. STAT 1:64
Second inaugural address. USINAU:17; USINAUG:17
Seventh annual message. STAT 1:89
Sixth annual message. STAT 1:83
Third annual message. STAT 1:68
"We are all Republicans; we are all Federalists." Same as his First inaugural: democracy defined

JEFFERSON, THOMAS
Aly, B.
Remarks on Jefferson Day. BAP:273
Chase, S. P.
Thomas Jefferson and the colonial view of manhood rights. BREWE 3:1044
Everett, E.
Adams and Jefferson. HURH:64
Peden, W.
Is Thomas Jefferson relevant? BA 1972-73:94
Roosevelt, F. D.
Undelivered Jefferson Day address. MDV:32
Smith, J. M.
On the fourteenth query of Thomas Jefferson's Notes on Virginia. FON:215
Webster, D.
Eulogy on Adams and Jefferson. BREWE 10:3848
Wirt, W.
Death of Jefferson and Adams. BREWE 10:3905

Jeffrey, Robert C.
Ethics in public discourse. (New York, Nov. 11, 1973). BA 1973-74:119

JEHOVAH WITNESSES
Jackson, R. H. and others
West Virginia Board of Education et al v. Barnette et al: opinion for the court and dissenting opinion. ANN 16:148

Jekyll, Sir Joseph
Resistance to unlawful authority (impeachment of H. Sacheverell). BREWE 7:2617

Jenner, William E. and others (T. C. Hennings, Jr.)
Proposal to limit the power of the Supreme Court. ANN 17:491

Jensen, J. Hans D.
Glimpses at the history of the nuclear structure theory (Nobel Lecture, Dec. 12, 1963). NOLPH 4:40

JENSEN, J. HANS D.
Waller, I.
Presentation [of the Nobel Prize for Physics to Eugene P. Wigner, Maria Goeppert Mayer and J. Hans D. Jensen, Dec. 12, 1963]. NOLPH 4:3

Jensen, Johannes Vilhelm
Acceptance [of the Nobel Prize for Literature, 1944]. NOB 8:263; NOL:400

JENSEN, JOHANNES VILHELM
Hallström, P.
Broadcast lecture [on Johannes Vilhelm Jensen, 1944]. NOL:393
Österling, A.
Presentation [of the Nobel Prize for Literature to Johannes Vilhelm Jensen, 1944]. NOB 8:259; NOL:397

Jervois, Sir William
New Zealand's defence and Royal Navy supremacy (New Zealand Institute, Oct. 4, 1884). MACS:245 sel.

Jessel, George
Presents Groucho Marx. LYI:32

Presents Jack Benny.
LYI:30

JESUS CHRIST
Aelred, Saint
On manliness. BREWE 1:113
Athanasius, Saint
Divinity of Christ.
BREWE 1:182
Bourdaloue, L.
Passion of Christ.
BREWE 2:590
Didon, H.
Christ and higher criticism.
BREWE 5:1856
Great Disturber (outline of speech to celebrate acceptance of Christ's offer of salvation through obedience to His Word). CUB:95

---- See also Crucifixion

JESUS FREAKS
Elson, E. L. R.
The Black and Jewish communities. VERD:273

JEWS
Gottheil, R.
Jews as a race and as a nation. BREWE 6:2294
Kamin, L.
Defense of the Jew.
CAPB:366
Macaulay, T. B.
Tribute to the Jews.
BREWE 8:2886
Rylaarsdam, J.
Undesirable one. SCHW:1
What makes Sammy laugh?
BURT:60

JEWS IN THE UNITED STATES
Brackenridge, H. M.
Vindication of civil rights for Jews. ANN 4:552
Henry, J.
On religion and elective office. ANN 4:239;
BOORA 1:220

JIMENEZ, JUAN RAMON
Benitez, J.
Acceptance [of the Nobel Prize for Literature for Juan Ramón Jiménez, 1956].
NOB 10:7; NOL:517
Gullberg, H.
Presentation [of the Nobel Prize for Literature to Juan Ramón Jiménez, 1956]. NOB 10:3;
NOL:513

JOBS See Business

Johansson, J. E.
Presentation [of the Nobel Prize for Physiology or Medicine for 1922 to Archibald Vivian Hill and Otto Fritz Meyerhof, Dec. 12, 1923]. NOLM 2:3
Presentation [of the Nobel Prize for Physiology or Medicine to August Krogh, Dec. 11, 1920].
NOLM 1:529

Johari, Mohammed Khir
All schools are the same.
MONS:145
Key to open the doors to all hearts and minds. MONS:141
Malaysian Brothers (diamond jubilee of Y.M.C.A. of Kuala Lumpur). MONS:150
Nation building and the four-way test (Kuala Lumpur, July 1-3, 1970). MONSA:100
A national chamber needed (Kuala Lumpur, March 26, 1970).
MONSA:103
Successful teacher. MONS:146

JOHN BIRCH SOCIETY
Welch, R.
More stately mansions (1964).
DAVF:327

JOHN PAUL II (POPE)
Sevareid, E.
Pope John Paul's message.
BA 1979-80:155

Johnsen, Anders
Remarks [presenting the Nobel Prize for Peace to Thomas Woodrow Wilson, 1919, Dec. 10, 1920]. NOLP 1:293

Johnson, Andrew
Against the radical Republicans.
ANN 10:8
Annual message to Congress, December 3, 1866. ANN 10:81;
STAT 2:1129
At Cleveland in 1866.

BREWE 7:2640
At St. Louis. BREWE 7:2628
End itself is evil (third annual message, 1867). CUR:61; STAT 2:1144
First annual message. Same as his Presidential plan of Reconstruction
First reconstruction veto. Same as his Veto of the first Reconstruction Act, 1867
Fourth annual message. STAT 2:1167
Inaugural address (1st speech after Lincoln's death). BREWE 7:2626
Presidential plan of Reconstruction. CUR:8; STAT 2:1112
Representation for all Southern states. Same as his Annual message to Congress, December 3, 1866
St. Louis speech for which he was impeached. Same as his At St. Louis
Second annual message. Same as his Annual message to Congress, December 3, 1866
Second reconstruction veto. ANN 10:98
Spirit of mutual conciliation. Same as his Presidential plan of Reconstruction
Third annual message. Same as his End itself is evil
Veto of Freedmen's Bureau Bill. ANN 10:3
Veto of Tenure of Office Act. ANN 10:90
Veto of the first Reconstruction Act, 1867. ANN 10:93

---- and others (L. Trumbull)
Debate on civil and states' rights. ANN 10:11

JOHNSON, ANDREW
Boutwell, G. S.
President Johnson's "High crimes and misdemeanors." BREWE 2:604
Butler, B. F.
"Article Ten"; (Impeaching A. Johnson). BREWE 3:832
Curtis, B. R.
Defense of President Johnson. BREWE 4:1563
Evarts, W. M.
Weakest spot in the American system (defense at impeachment of A. Johnson). BREWE 6:2082
Hayden, L.
Deliver us from such a Moses. FON:334
Sumner, C. and others
Impeachment of Andrew Johnson. ANN 10:126

Johnson, James Weldon
Africa at the Peace Table and the descendants of Africans in our American democracy. (N.A.A.C.P., Jan. 6, 1919). FON:730
Our democracy and the ballot. (New York, March 10, 1923). FON:757

Johnson, Lyndon Baines
Acceptance speech, Atlantic City, New Jersey, August 27, 1964. SIN:329
Address on voting rights. Same as his Address to a Joint Session of Congress, March 15, 1965
Address to a Joint Session of Congress, March 15, 1965. AND:81; BOORA 2:919; CROCK:164; MDV:144; REIR:143
As the days dwindle down. (Temple, Texas, Sept. 16, 1972). BA 1972-73:138
Campaign speech, Washington, D.C., October 7, 1964. SIN:334
Education opportunity message. CAPG:112
First annual message. Same as his State of the Union Message, January 8, 1964
Great Society (commencement address at University of Michigan). ANN 18:216; CAPG:15; MDV:108; MUS:135
Inaugural address. USINAU:271; USINAUG:271
Johnson doctrine; why the United States intervened in the Dominican Republic. LAA:160
Let us continue. Same as his Remarks to a Joint Session

of the Congress, November 27, 1963
Obligation of power. ANN 18:368
Our foreign policy must always be an extension of this nation's domestic policy. LAA:3
A president defends his policies by argument from authorities. (San Antonio, Tex., National Legislative Conference, Sept. 29, 1967). JEF:331; JEFF:316
Remarks to a Joint Session of the Congress, November 27, 1963. ANN 18:203
Remarks to the nation (declining nomination to Presidency). ANN 18:613; BA 1967-68:63
Right to vote. Same as his Address to a Joint Session of Congress, March 15, 1965
Second annual message. STAT 3:3161
Speech at a Joint Session of the Tennessee State Legislature. BA 1966-67:11
Speech before the National Legislative Conference. BA 1967-68:11
State of the Union Message, January 8, 1964. STAT 3:3156
Third annual message. STAT 3:3171
University of Michigan commencement address. Same as his Great Society
Vietnam: the struggle to be free (On accepting National Freedom Award). BA 1965-66:11
Voting Rights Law of 1965--a victory for freedom. CAPG:97
War on poverty. ANN 18:212
We shall overcome. Same as his Address to a Joint Session of Congress, March 15, 1965
Why must we take this painful road? LAA:185
Withdrawal speech. Same as his Remarks to the nation (declining nomination to Presidency)

JOHNSON, LYNDON BAINES
Rusk, D.
Eulogy of Lyndon Baines Johnson. BA 1972-73:132
Stevenson, A. E.
Presents Lyndon B. Johnson. LYI:197

Johnson, Mordecai W.
Faith of the American Negro (at Harvard commencement, June 22, 1922). FON:742

Johnson, Richard M. See Grundy, F., jt. auth.

Johnstone, Abraham
Address to the people of color. (July 8, 1797). FON:16

Joliot, Jean Frédéric
Chemical evidence of the transmutation of elements (Nobel Lecture, Dec. 12, 1935). NOLC 2:369

JOLIOT, JEAN FREDERIC
Palmaer, W.
Presentation [of the Nobel Prize for Chemistry to Jean Frédéric Joliot and Irène Joliot-Curie, Dec. 12, 1935]. NOLC 2:359

Joliot-Curie, Irène
Artificial production of radioactive elements (Nobel Lecture, Dec. 12, 1935). NOLC 2:366

JOLIOT-CURIE, IRENE
Palmaer, W.
Presentation [of the Nobel Prize for Chemistry to Jean Frédéric Joliot and Irène Joliot-Curie, Dec. 12, 1935]. NOLC 2:359

JOLSON, AL
Nussbaum, M.
Al Jolson. WALE:225

Jones, A. L.
A question of ecology: the cries of wolf (Cleveland, Dec. 14, 1971). LINRST:115

Jones, Aaron and others (B. R. Tucker; J. W. Hayes; L. Gronlund; C. Studebaker)
Trusts in America. ANN 12:279

JONES, FREDERICK S.
Streeter, F. S.
Introducing an educator (Frederick S. Jones). LYI:85

Jones, Howard Mumford
Farewell to the English Department. REIR:232

Jones, James C. See Cass, L., jt. auth.

Jones, Jenkin Lloyd
"Let's bring back Dad": a solid value system (Ohio Chamber of Commerce, March 14, 1973). LINRST:254
Who is tampering with the soul of America? (American Society of Newspaper Editors, Oct. 16, 1961). LINR:211; LINRS:220

Jones, William N.
Why Negroes should support the Communists. (Harlem, Oct. 2, 1932). FON:785

Jordan, Barbara C.
Keynote address to the Democratic National Convention (New York, July 12, 1976). BA 1976-77:11; JAM:7; LINRST:334

---- (and others) Joshua Eilberg, Walter Flowers
Hearings on articles of impeachment by the Committee of the Judiciary of the House of Representatives. (Washington, July 24-30, 1974). BA 1974-75:15

Jordan, David Starr
Moral aspect of the protective tariff. ANN 13:147

Jordan, Len
Opportunities in H.S.A. (Harvard Student Agencies). REIR:101 (outline)

Jordan, Vernon E., Jr.
The Black agenda for the 1980s (Chicago, July 22, 1979). BA 1979-80:87
The Black and Jewish communities. (American Jewish Committee, Atlanta Chapter, June 2, 1974). VERD:273
Blacks and the Nixon administration: the next four years. (Washington, D.C., March 16, 1973). BA 1972-73:39
Survival. (Cleveland, January 28, 1972). BA 1971-72:49
Under the hammer: freedom, justice, and dignity. (Washington, May 4, 1974). LINRST:215
Unfinished business (Columbia, S.C., March 10, 1976). BA 1975-76:88

Jordan, William Joseph
The League and the Spanish Civil War (League of Nations Council, May 28, 1937). MACS:361 sel.

Joseph, Chief, The Nez Perce
From where the sun now stands. ALA:63
Surrender speech. Same as his From where the sun now stands

Jouhaux, Léon
Fifty years of trade-union activity in behalf of peace (Nobel Lecture, Dec. 11, 1951). NOLP 3:10

JOUHAUX, LEON
Jahn, G.
Presentation of the Nobel Prize for Peace to Léon Jouhaux, Dec. 10, 1951. NOLP 3:3

JOURNALISM AND JOURNALISTS
Gallagher, W.
Upon acceptance of the 1967 William Allen White Foundation Award for Journalists Merit. BA 1966-67:148; JEF:327; JEFF:311
Goodman, J. B.
Broadcast journalism. BA 1976-77:52
Holden, W. S.
Newspapers of the U.S.A. ARS:107
Lippmann, W.
On understanding society.

BAAGB:412
Sevareid, E.
Parting thoughts.
BA 1977-78:143
Welcome to newspaper editor as speaker at a civic club.
HNWM:44

---- See also Newspapers; Press

---- MALAYSIA
Hamzah bin Dato Abu Samah
Challenging opportunity for the press in Malaysia.
MONSA:110

JOYCE, JAMES
Woolsey, J. M.
Opinion December 6, 1933 (Ulysses case--freedom of reading). ANN 15:236

JUBILEE CELEBRATIONS See Anniversaries

Judd, Walter H.
Responds to introduction.
PRS:126

JUDGES See Law and lawyers; United States - Supreme Court

JUDICIAL REVIEW
Gibson, J. B.
Against judicial review: dissenting opinion on Eakin v. Raub. ANN 5:174

Julian, George W.
The strength and weakness of the slave power
Cincinnati, 1852. DAVF:122

Jung, Leo
Mother's immortality.
WALE:96

JURIES
Marshall, D. S.
Why abolish the jury trial?
MONSA:324

JURISPRUDENCE See Law and lawyers

JURY
Drayton, W. H.
Charge to the Grand Juries, November 5 & 15, 1774.
POC:297

---- See also Trial by jury

JUSTICE
Bede
Meeting of mercy and justice.
BREWE 1:340
Bradlaugh, C.
Appeal for justice. JAE:142
Cicero, M. T.
Supernatural justice.
BREWE 3:1178
Clayton, J. M.
Justice the supreme law of nations. BREWE 4:1290
King, M. L., Jr.
Nonviolence: moral challenge for peace and justice.
NOLP 3:333; THOMS:99
Muhammad, E.
We must have justice.
FON:969
Osias, C.
Justice and separation of powers. CURM:190
Roosevelt, F. D.
Philosophy of social justice through social action (campaign speech in Detroit October 2, 1932). ARS:135
Taft, R. A.
Equal justice under law.
BEN:100

JUVENILE DELINQUENCY See Crime and criminals

- K -

Kahn, Arthur D.
John F. Kennedy. WALE:218

Kahn, I.
Like water spilled on the ground.
WALE:98
Vote against prayer and for God.
KEO:300

Kalakaua, David, King of Hawaii
His Majesty's address to the people of Lahaina. ALA:57

Kaler, Irving
The Ku Klux Klan as a subversive

conspiratorial organization. (Washington, 1966). DAVF:355

Kamin, Lester
Defense of the Jew. (Baylor University, 1941). CAPB:366

Kanapathy, V.
Technological change and management policies (Hyderabad, June, 1970). MONSA:202

Kane, Anthony
Glory of notoriety. REIR:223

KANSAS
Buchanan, J.
First annual message. STAT 1:942
Second annual message. STAT 1:969
Douglas, S. A.
Kansas and "Squatter sovereignty." BREWE 5:1924
Sumner, C.
Crime against Kansas. ANN 8:267; BREWE 9:3557; HURH:85
Walker, R. J.
Address to the people of Kansas. ANN 8:452

KANSAS-NEBRASKA BILL
Buchanan, J.
First annual message. STAT 1:942
Chase, S. P. and others
Opposition to the Kansas-Nebraska Bill (January, 1854). ANN 8:251
Douglas, S. A.
Defense of the Kansas-Nebraska Bill (January 30, 1854). ANN 8:254
Pierce, F.
Third annual message. STAT 1:895

Kaplan, Louis
Three basic questions. WALE:99

Kaplan, Solomon M.
Man's true measurements. WALE:102

Karenga, Maulana Ron
The Black community and the university: a community organizer's perspective. (Yale University, 1968). LINRS:255

Karlfeldt, Erik Axel
Presentation [of the Nobel Prize for Literature to Anatole France, 1921]. NOB 6:85; NOL:174
Presentation [of the Nobel Prize for Literature to Sinclair Lewis, 1930]. NOB 11:237; NOL:271

KARLFELDT, ERIK AXEL
Österling, A.
Presentation [of the Nobel Prize for Literature to Erik Axel Karlfeldt, 1931]. NOB 10:101; NOL:295

Karos, Peter A.
Haven of the defeated. ARS:148

Karrer, Paul
Carotenoids, flavins and vitamin A and B_2 (Nobel Lecture, Dec. 11, 1937). NOLC 2:433

KARRER, PAUL
Palmaer, W.
Presentation [of the Nobel Prize for Chemistry to Walter Norman Haworth and Paul Karrer, Dec. 11, 1937]. NOLC 2:407

Kastler, Alfred
Optical methods for studying Hertzian resonances (Nobel Lecture, Dec. 12, 1966). NOLPH 4:186

KASTLER, ALFRED
Waller, I.
Presentation [of the Nobel Prize for Physics to Alfred Kastler, Dec. 12, 1966]. NOLPH 4:183

Katz, Bernhard
On the quantal mechanism of neural transmitter release (Nobel Lecture, Dec. 12, 1970). NOLM 4:485

KATZ, BERNHARD
Uvnäs, B.

Presentation [of the Nobel Prize for Physiology or Medicine to Julius Axelrod, Ulf Von Euler, and Bernhard Katz, Dec. 12, 1970]. NOLM 4:441

Katz, Reuben M.
Psalm of life. WALE:103

Katzenbach, Nicholas de Belleville
Civil Rights Act of 1964: respect for law. CAPB:88

Kaunda, Kenneth
Toast to President Ford (April 9, 1975). JAM:23

Kawabata, Yasunari
Acceptance speech [for the Nobel Prize for Literature, 1968]. NOB 11:7

KAWABATA, YASUNARI
Österling, A.
Presentation address [of the Nobel Prize for Literature to Yasunari Kawabata, 1968]. NOB 11:3

Keating, Kenneth B.
Responds to an introduction. PRS:132

KEATS, JOHN
Gittings, R.
Exploring the known. MDYG:207

Kee, Robert See Ayer, A. J., jt. auth.

Keeler, William Wayne
Inaugural address of the chief of the Cherokees. (Tahlequah, Okl., Sept. 4, 1971). BA 1971-72:74

Keeney, Barnaby C.
Afterword: how to make a commencement speech (Brown Univ., May 28, 1964). HOR:165

KEFAUVER, ESTES
Waller, H. H.
Presents Estes Kefauver. LYI:230

Kelley, Clarence M.
Terrorism, the ultimate evil (Washington, Jan. 13, 1976). BA 1975-76:117

Kellogg, Frank Billings
Acceptance and banquet speech [for the Nobel Prize for Peace, 1929, Dec. 10, 1930]. NOLP 2:79

KELLOGG, FRANK BILLINGS
Mowinckel, J. L.
Presentation [of the Nobel Prize for Peace to Frank Billings Kellogg, 1929, Dec. 10, 1930]. NOLP 2:73

KELLY, EDWARD
Barry, R.
Sentencing of "Ned" Kelly. MCA:74

Kelly, William F.
Responds to an introduction. PRS:129

Kemeny, John G.
An optimist looks at America's future (Boston College, June 4, 1973). HOR:128
Valedictory to the graduates (Dartmouth, June 10, 1973). HOR:2

Kendall, Edward Calvin
The development of cortisone as a therapeutic agent (Nobel Lecture, Dec. 11, 1950). NOLM 3:270

KENDALL, EDWARD CALVIN
Liljestrand, G.
Presentation [of the Nobel Prize for Physiology or Medicine to Edward Calvin Kendall, Tadeus Reichstein, and Philip Shawalter Hench, Dec. 11, 1950]. NOLM 3:263

Kendrew, John Cowdery
Myoglobin and the structure of proteins (Nobel Lecture, Dec. 11, 1962). NOLC 3:676

KENDREW, JOHN COWDERY
Hagg, G.
Presentation of the Nobel Prize for Chemistry to Max Ferdi-

nand Perutz and John Cowdery Kendrew, Dec. 11, 1962. NOLC 3:649

Kennan, George Frost
Responds to an introduction. PRS:148
Statement on Vietnam. BA 1965-66:56

Kennedy, Edward M.
China policy for the seventies. BA 1968-69:73
Eulogy to Robert F. Kennedy. Same as his Tribute to Senator Robert F. Kennedy
La Raza and the law. (Washington, D.C., March 3, 1972). BA 1971-72:68
Statement to the people of Massachusetts. MACR:318
Tribute to Senator Robert F. Kennedy. BA 1967-68:174; LINRS:303

Kennedy, John Fitzgerald
Acceptance address, 1960. Same as his New frontier
Acceptance speech, Los Angeles, California, July 15, 1960. Same as his New frontier
Address to the Ministers of Houston. Same as his Religion in government
Address to the nation October 22, 1962. ANN 18:140; LAA:147; MUS:340
"Ask not what your country can do for you--ask what you can do for your country." Same as his Inaugural address
Berlin crisis. (July 25, 1961). THOMS:22
Campaign speech, Houston, Texas, September 12, 1960. Same as his Religion in government (to Greater Houston Ministerial Association)
Cuban missile crisis. Same as his Address to the nation October 22, 1962
Federal aid to education. ANN 18:8
First annual message. STAT 3:3122
History will be our judge. LINS:371
Ich bin ein Berliner (Berlin, June 26, 1963). ALA:129; AND:79; LINR:294; LINRS:293
Inaugural address (Washington, Jan. 20, 1961). ALS:265; ANN 18:5; ARN:312; ARS:226; BAS:145 (outline only); BEN:143; BOORA 2:913; BRR:82; BRYF:437; BRYO:232; GRG:113; HURH:358; LINR:297; LINRS:296; LINRST:366; LINS:375; MAC:244; MACR:284; MDV:127; OLIS:282; THOMS:17; USINAU:267; USINAUG:267
Intellectual and the politician. BAP:285; LINR:267
Long twilight struggle. ANN 18:54
Negro and the American promise. ANN 18:152
New frontier (Los Angeles, July 15, 1960). CAPG:8; HURH:353; SIN:298
Nuclear Test-Ban Treaty. Same as his Step toward peace
Presenting the Distinguished Service Medal to John Glenn (outline of speech). CUB:64
President Kennedy's televised report to the Nation on the Berlin crisis. Same as his Berlin crisis
Religion in government (to Greater Houston Ministerial Association). ANN 17:589; SIN:303
Second annual message. STAT 3:3132
Soviet missiles in Cuba. Same as his Address to the nation October 22, 1962
Soviets are building nuclear missile sites in Cuba. Same as his Address to the nation, October 22, 1962
Special message to the Congress on Civil Rights. (Feb. 28, 1963). THOMS:50
Special message to the Congress on the nation's youth. (Feb. 14, 1963). THOMS:34
Step toward peace. ANN 18:192
Strategy of peace. Same as his Toward a strategy of peace
Tax cut. STAT 3:3144
Third annual message. Same as his Tax cut

Toward a strategy of peace. KEO:312; MDV:2
Undelivered Dallas speech. ANN 18:197
"We stand today on the edge of a New Frontier." Same as his New frontier

---- See also Nixon, R. M., jt. auth.

KENNEDY, JOHN FITZGERALD
Johnson, L. B.
Remarks to a Joint Session of the Congress, November 27, 1963. ANN 18:203
Kahn, A. D.
John F. Kennedy. WALE:218
Levine, E. B.
John F. Kennedy. WALE:221
Macmillan, (M.) H.
Tribute to President Kennedy. ALA:135
Mansfield, M. J.
Eulogy for John F. Kennedy. ANN 18:202
Stevenson, A. E.
Tribute to John F. Kennedy at the General Assembly of the United Nations. GRG:122; HURH:371

Kennedy, Robert F.
Address to the Free University of Berlin. MDV:95
Civil rights. Same as his Law Day address, University of Georgia
Counterinsurgency. ANN 18:323
Fruitful tension. BA 1966-67:138
Kennedy's decision to seek Presidential nomination. THOMS:131
Law Day address--University of Georgia (Athens, Ga., May 6, 1961). CAPG:73; THOMS:120
Responds to introductions. PRS:135; 136
Vietnam--illusion and reality. ANN 18:599

KENNEDY, ROBERT F.
Brademas, J.
Eulogy for Robert Kennedy. JAM:43
Kennedy, E. M.
Tribute to Senator Robert F. Kennedy. BA 1967-68:174; LINRS:303
Percy, C. H.
Eulogy for Robert Kennedy. JAM:42

KENNEY, GEORGE C.
Fisher, C. T., Jr.
Presents George C. Kenney. LYI:150

Kenny, Anthony
Self out of season. MDYG:199

Kenrick, Francis Patrick
Episcopal rights and parish autonomy. ANN 5:437

KENTUCKY - ECONOMIC CONDITIONS
Chandler, A. B.
Address to the General Assembly, Frankfort, Kentucky, April 20, 1936. BLY:258

KENYON COLLEGE
Everett, E.
Plea for support of an Ohio college. ANN 6:26

Kermicle, John
Bridging the gap. BREWW:94

KERNER REPORT
Abernathy, R. D.
The Kerner report, promises and realities. FON:1145

Kerr, Clark
The independent spirit (Swarthmore College, June, 1952). HOR:114
Perspectives on the prophets of doom (Univ. of California, June 12, 1965). HOR:34
Urban-grant university (centennial meeting of City College). BA 1967-68:86

Kerr, Deborah See Murrow, E. R., jt. auth.

Kerry, John F.
John Kerry's speech before the Senate Foreign Relations Committee. Same as his

Vietnam veterans against the war
Vietnam veterans against the war (Washington, April 22, 1971). JAM:9; LINRS:244; LINRST:288

Kestenbaum, Jerome
Live each day. WALE:106
Prescription for humanity. WALE:107
Standard of life. WALE:109

KETTERING, CHARLES F.
Martin, T. W.
Presents Charles F. Kettering. LYI:181

Keynes, John Maynard
Am I a Liberal? (Liberal Summer School, Cambridge, Aug. 1, 1925). MCB:456

KEYNOTE SPEECHES See Campaign speeches

Khorana, Har Gobind
Nucleic acid synthesis in the study of the genetic code (Nobel Lecture, Dec. 12, 1968). NOLM 4:341

KHORANA, HAR GOBIND
Reichard, P.
Presentation [of the Nobel Prize for Physiology or Medicine to Robert W. Holley, Har Gobind Khorana, and Marshall W. Nirenberg, Dec. 12, 1968]. NOLM 4:321

Kidwell, Clara Sue
American Indian attitudes toward nature, a bicentennial perspective. MAES:277

Killens, John O.
White liberals and the Black revolution. (New York, June 15, 1964). FON:1001

King, Martin Luther, Jr.
The American dream. (Lincoln University, June 6, 1961). FON:933
Declaration of independence from the war in Vietnam. VI:115
Give us the ballot--we will transform the South. (Washington, D.C., May 17, 1957). FON:919
Honoring Dr. DuBois. SMHR:204
"I have a dream." (Washington, Aug. 28, 1963). AND:50; ANN 18:156; ARS:154; BRR:78; CAPG:83; FON:971; GRG:117; HURH:366; LINR:290; LINRS:289; LINRST:362; LINS:379; MAC:247; MACR:288; MDV:156; MUS:336; OE:152; OLIS:289; SMHV:182; THOMS:94
I see the promised land. (April 3, 1968, Memphis). FON:1108
A long way to go. SMHV:188
Love, law, and civil disobedience (Fellowship of the Concerned, Nov. 16, 1961). FON:943; LINR:63; LINRS:70; LINRST:75; STOT:321
Nonviolence and social change. (Nov., 1967). OE:157
Nonviolence: moral challenge for peace and justice (Nobel Lecture, Dec. 11, 1964). NOLP 3:333; THOMS:99
The philosophy of the student nonviolent movement. Same as his Love, law, and civil disobedience
The quest for peace and justice. Same as his Nonviolence: moral challenge for peace and justice
A time to break silence. (New York, April 4, 1967). FON:1048
Where do we go from here? (Atlanta, Ga., August 16, 1967--Tenth Anniversary Convention of the Southern Christian Leadership Conference). FON:1068

KING, MARTIN LUTHER, JR.
Carter, J.
Speech at the Martin Luther King, Jr. Hospital. JAM:25
Cleaver, E.
Meditation on the assassination of Martin Luther King, Jr. OE:229
Franklin, J. H.

Martin Luther King and American traditions. BA 1968-69:45
Gallagher, B. G.
Memorial convocation address (on Martin Luther King, Jr.). BA 1967-68:169
Jahn, G.
Presentation [of the Nobel Prize for Peace to Martin Luther King, Jr., Dec. 10, 1964]. NOLP 3:325
Mays, B. E.
Eulogy on Dr. Martin Luther King, Jr. BA 1967-68:161; BAAGB:399; SMHV:296

King, Mrs. Martin Luther, Jr.
We need to be united. (Atlantic City-Automobile Workers' Const. Conv., April 22, 1970). FON:1169

KING, RICHARD COREY
Go on and prosper (outline of eulogistic speech). CUB:76

King, Rufus
Against the extension of slavery to the new states. Same as his On the Missouri Bill
For federal government by the people. BREWE 7:2642
On the Missouri Bill. ANN 4:579

King, Thomas Starr
Fourth of July oration, 1860 (San Francisco). HAW:231
The two declarations of independence: 1776 and 1861. (Sacramento, July 4, 1861). HAW:260

KING, W. L. MACKENZIE
Lamont, T. W.
Presents W. L. Mackenzie King. LYI:233

Kingsbury, F. J.
In defense of the city. ANN 12:61

Kingsley, Charles
Human soot; address at Liverpool in behalf of the Kirkdale Ragged Schools. BREWE 7:2645
Massacre of the innocents. BRYH:392

Kinross, Lord See Sykes, C., jt. auth.

Kipke, Harry G.
Introduces John K. Herbert, president of the Magazine Publishers Association. PRS:21

KIPLING, RUDYARD
Wirsén, C. D. af
Presentation [of the Nobel Prize for Literature to Rudyard Kipling, 1907]. NOB 11:89; NOL:58

Kirk, Grayson
Responsibilities of the educated man (at centennial of University of Denver). LINR:143

Kirkpatrick, Lyman B.
Responds to an introduction. PRS:141

Kissinger, Henry Alfred
Address before the World Food Conference. (Rome, Nov. 5, 1974). BA 1974-75:62
America's permanent interests (Boston, March 11, 1976). BA 1975-76:48
Responds to introduction. PRS:124
A review of the foreign policy (Washington, April 19, 1980). BA 1979-80:9
Statement to the Senate Foreign Relations Committee. (Washington, Sept. 7, 1973). BA 1973-74:87

Kitslaar, John L.
Is busing the answer? (Madison, Wisc., 1976). LINRST:294

Klaaren, Mary Ann
Divine command. SCHW:96

Klason, P.
Presentation [of the Nobel Prize for Chemistry to Henri Moissan, 1906]. NOLC 1:91

Presentation [of the Nobel Prize for Physics to Joseph John Thomson, Dec. 11, 1906]. NOLPH 1:141

Klayton, Ronald J.
Bureau of Forests and Waters should control pests by biological means rather than pesticides. BAS:188 (outline only)

Klein, G.
Presentation [of the Nobel Prize for Physiology or Medicine to Peyton Rous and Charles Brenton Huggins, Dec. 13, 1966]. NOLM 4:215

Klein, Isaac
Before her time. WALE:110

Klein, Joel T.
Question most frequently asked. WALE:112

Klein, O. B.
Presentation [of the Nobel Prize for Physics to Chen Ning Yang and Tsung Dao Lee, Dec. 11, 1957]. NOLPH 3:389
Presentation [of the Nobel Prize for Physics to Hans Albrecht Bethe, Dec. 11, 1967]. NOLPH 4:211

Klein, Paul A.
Big things happen in small places (outline of speech explaining process of protein synthesis). CUB:94

Klemme, Diane
The age of Gerontion. (West Yellowstone, Montana, May, 1970). LINRS:152

Knight, Joseph R.
Introduces Lieutenant Thomas A. Dooley, United States Navy. PRS:67

KNIGHTS OF LABOR
Gibbons, J.
Defense of the Knights of Labor. ANN 11:131

Knoch, Win G.
Introduces Robert Taft, Jr., Congressman-at-large from Ohio. PRS:32

Knopwood, Robert
On the everpresent God. MCA:11

Knott, James Proctor
Glories of Duluth (Jan. 27, 1871). BLY:135; BREWE 7:2653

KNOWLEDGE, THEORY OF
Chapin, E. H.
Sovereignty of ideas. BREWE 3:1036
Drummond, H.
Preparation for learning. BREWE 5:1959
Young, O. D.
How we meet ourselves (semicentennial of Hendrix College). HURH:227

---- See also Learning and scholarship

Knox, Frank
Lend-lease and national defense. ANN 16:48

Knox, John
Against tyrants. BREWE 7:2665

Knudsen, G.
Presentation [of the Nobel Prize for Peace to Theodore Roosevelt, Dec. 10, 1906]. NOLP 1:97

Koblish, Cameron F.
Diamonds, their mining, selling, perfecting, and the determining of their quality. BAS:206 (outline only)

Koch, Robert
The current state of the struggle against tuberculosis (Nobel Lecture, Dec. 12, 1905). NOLM 1:169

KOCH, ROBERT
Mörner, K. A. H.
Presentation [of the Nobel Prize for Physiology or Medicine to Robert Koch, Dec. 12, 1905]. NOLM 1:163

Kocher, Emil Theodor
Concerning pathological manifestations in low-grade thyroid diseases (Nobel Lecture, Dec. 11, 1909). NOLM 1:330

KOCHER, EMIL THEODOR
Mörner, K. A. H.
Presentation [of the Nobel Prize for Physiology or Medicine to Emil Theodor Kocher, Dec. 11, 1909]. NOLM 1:327

Koht, Halvdan
Presentation [of the Nobel Prize for Peace to Jane Addams and Nicholas Murray Butler, Dec. 10, 1931]. NOLP 2:125

KOPECHNE, MARY JO
Kennedy, E. M.
Statement to the people of Massachusetts. MACR:318

KOREAN WAR, 1950-1953
Cornish, D. T.
A warrior against fate. BA 1975-76:207
Eisenhower, D. D.
Crusade for peace. ANN 17:199
MacArthur, D.
Defends his conduct of the war in Korea. ALS:243; ANN 17:79; ARS:279; BAS:82 (outline only); BEN:113; BOSR:22; GRG:88; HURH:293; HURS:214; LINS:337
McCarthy, J. R.
Annual Kansas Day Republican banquet speech. BOSR:53
Stevenson, A. E.
Campaign speech, Academy of Music, Brooklyn, New York, October 31, 1952. SIN:255
Truman, H. S.
Preventing a new world war. ANN 17:75; BAP:291
Sixth annual message. STAT 3:2976
State of the Union (1952). STAT 3:2984

Korf, James
And old hate walked on through time. SCHW:189

Kornberg, Arthur
The biologic synthesis of deoxyribonucleic acid (Nobel Lecture, Dec. 11, 1959). NOLM 3:665

KORNBERG, ARTHUR
Theorell, H.
Presentation [of the Nobel Prize for Physiology or Medicine to Severo Ochoa and Arthur Kornberg, Dec. 11, 1959]. NOLM 3:641

Korteling, Marian
Renascence. SCHW:39

Kosman, Morris
Eulogy for Irving Wolberg (July 29, 1976). JAM:44

Kossel, Albrecht
The chemical composition of the cell nucleus (Nobel Lecture, Dec. 12, 1910). NOLM 1:394

KOSSEL, ALBRECHT
Mörner, K. A. H.
Presentation [of the Nobel Prize for Physiology or Medicine to Albrecht Kossel, Dec. 12, 1910]. NOLM 1:389

Kossuth, Louis
Local self-government. BREWE 7:2672

KOSSUTH, LOUIS
Downing, G. T.
May Hungary be free. FON:102

Krebs, Hans Adolf
The citric acid cycle (Nobel Lecture, Dec. 11, 1953). NOLM 3:399

KREBS, HANS ADOLF
Hammarsten, E.
Presentation [of the Nobel Prize for Physiology or Medicine to Hans Adolf Krebs and Fritz Albert Lipmann, Dec. 11, 1953]. NOLM 3:395

KREBS CYCLE
Krebs, H. A.
The citric acid cycle. NOLM 3:399
Lipmann, F. A.
Development of the acetylation problem: a personal account. NOLM 3:413

Krogh, August
A contribution to the physiology of the capillaries (Nobel Lecture, Dec. 11, 1920). NOLM 1:536

KROGH, AUGUST
Johansson, J. E.
Presentation [of the Nobel Prize for Physiology or Medicine to August Krogh, Dec. 11, 1920]. NOLM 1:529

Krug, Judith F.
In defense of liberty: extremism and other vices (Baton Rouge, April 17, 1975). BA 1975-76:193

Kubicek, Kathryn
Global crisis. BREWW:128

Kuiper, Della Rae
"You're an American, aren't you?" SCHW:186

KU KLUX KLAN
Gordon, J. B.
It was purely a peace police organization. CUR:98
Grand dragon of the Ku Klux Klan. BURT:65
Kaler, I.
The Ku Klux Klan as a subversive, conspiratorial organization (1966). DAVF:355
Sherman, J.
It is essentially a Rebel organization. CUR:102

Kusch, Polykarp
The magnetic moment of the electron (Nobel Lecture, Dec. 12, 1955). NOLPH 3:298

KUSCH, POLYKARP
Waller, I.
Presentation [of the Nobel Prize for Physics to Willis Eugene Lamb and Polykarp Kusch, Dec. 12, 1955]. NOLPH 3:283

- L -

LABOR AND LABORING CLASSES
Berle, A. A., Jr.
Emerging common law of free enterprise. ANN 16:573
Brandeis, L. D.
Law and the laboring classes. ANN 13:23
De Leon, D.
Political power of labor. ANN 13:19
Everett, E.
Universal and uncoerced cooperation. BREWE 6:2115
Fisk, T.
War of capital against labor. ANN 6:118
Furuseth, A.
Work is worship. ANN 14:561
Olson, C. L.
Migratory labor and civil liberties. ANN 15:587
Roosevelt, T.
Annual message, December 6, 1904. STAT 2:2105
Fifth annual message. ANN 13:1; STAT 3:2144
Wheeler, A.
Product of labor. ANN 11:113

---- See also Capitalism; Child labor; Industrial relations; Labor unions; Strikes and lockouts; Work

---- AUSTRALIA
Parkes, H.
Eight-hours movement. MCA:33

LABOR DAY
Altgeld, J. P.
Children of toil. ANN 11:445
Furuseth, A.
Work is worship. ANN 14:561

LABOR LAWS AND LEGISLATION
Hughes, C. E.

National Labor Relations Board v. Jones and Laughlin Steel Corporation, 1937; opinion for the Supreme Court. ROD:207

---- TAFT HARTLEY LAW
Taft, R. A.
Analysis of the Taft-Hartley Act. ANN 16:414

LABOR PARTY - AUSTRALIA
Chifley, J. B.
Things worth fighting for. MCA:166

---- GREAT BRITAIN
Attlee, C. R.
The Labour programme. MCB:471
Gaitskell, H.
Labour politics and democratic socialism. MCB:250

---- See also Great Britain - Politics and government

---- NEW ZEALAND
Holland, H.
The socialist objective of the labour movement. MACS:232 sel.

LABOR UNIONS
Abdul Rahman, T.
Warming to trade unions. MONS:45
Baldwin, S. B.
Goodwill in industry. MCB:243; STRM:433
Bevin, E.
Testimony at the "Docker's Inquiry." STRM:423
Billings
United States v. Workingmen's Amalgamated Council of New Orleans, 1893. ANN 11:435
Crosswaith, F. R.
The Negro labor committee. FON:857
Gibbons, J.
Defense of the Knights of Labor. ANN 11:131
Green, W.
Modern trade unionism. HURH:205
Jouhaux, L.
Fifty years of trade-union activity in behalf of peace (Nobel Lecture, Dec. 11, 1951). NOLP 3:10
King, Mrs. M. L., Jr.
We need to be unified. FON:1169
Lee Kuan Yew
Unionism: rethinking is vital (opening National Trade Union Conference). MONS:366
Lewis, J. L.
Industrial unions. ANN 15:511
Labor and the nation. HURH:232
Moore, E.
Trade unions and the "mechanic" arts. ANN 6:17
Murray, P.
Collective bargaining and industrial democracy. ANN 16:15
Myers, I.
Finish the good work of uniting colored and white workingmen. FON:367
Nair, C. D.
The role of trade union research and documentation services. MONSA:334
Narayanan, P. P.
Role of trade unions in South-East Asia. MONS:295
Parry, D.
Organized labor as the "Great Muscle Trust." ANN 12:513
Robinson, F.
Labor as the source of reform. ANN 6:69
Savage, J.
People v. Fisher: opinion for the court. ANN 6:172
Shaw, L.
Commonwealth of Massachusetts v. Hunt: opinion for the court. ANN 6:172

---- See also Labor Day; Labor Laws and legislation; Strikes and lockouts

---- AGRICULTURE
Wright, T.
"Viva la Huelga." BREWW:174

---- MALAYSIA
Alatas, S. H.
Sheep and lions in trade unions. MONSA:179 selections

---- SINGAPORE
Lee Kuan Yew
Self respect is what our trade unions have and.... MONSA:255

Labori, Fernand
Conspiracy against Dreyfus. BREWE 7:2684

Labouisse, Henry R.
Acceptance [of the Nobel Prize for Peace, Dec. 10, 1965]. NOLP 3:362

Lacordaire, Jean Baptiste Henri
Rationalism and miracles. BREWE 7:2695
Sacred cause of the human race (Panegyric of Daniel O'Connell). BREWE 7:2692

LAFAYETTE, MARIE JOSEPH PAUL ROCH YVES GILBERT DE MOTIER, MARQUIS DE
Adams, J. Q.
Life and character of Lafayette. BREWE 1:79

LaFollette, Philip F.
Party of our time. BAD:120

La Follette, Robert Marion, Sr.
Against war with Germany. ANN 14:104
Free speech in wartime. CUB:53 (outline only)
Opposition to Wilson's War Message. Same as his Against war with Germany
"The right to cast the ballot is regarded as sacred. The right to make the ballot is equally sacred." Same as his Which shall rule, manhood or money?
A small group of men hold in their hands the business of this country. (Washington, March 17, 1908). DAVF:200
Soldier's pay. GRG:36
Which shall rule, manhood or money? (Milwaukee, 1902). HURH:158

LA FONTAINE, HENRI MARIE
Moe, R.
Presentation [of the Nobel Prize for Peace to Henri Marie La Fontaine, Dec. 10, 1913]. NOLP 1:269

Lagerkvist, Pär Fabian
Acceptance [of the Nobel Prize for Literature, 1951]. NOB 10:205; NOL:469

LAGERKVIST, PAR FABIAN
Österling, A.
Presentation [of the Nobel Prize for Literature to Pär Fabian Lagerkvist, 1951]. NOB 10:201; NOL:466

Lagerlöf, Selma Ottiliana Lovisa
Acceptance [of the Nobel Prize for Literature, 1909]. NOB 10:283; NOL:94

LAGERLÖF, SELMA OTTILIANA LOVISA
Annerstedt, C.
Presentation [of the Nobel Prize for Literature to Selma Ottiliana Lovisa Lagerlöf, 1909]. NOB 10:279; NOL:90

LAISSEZ-FAIRE
Crawford, F. C.
Jobs, freedom, and opportunity. ANN 16:132
Grede, W. J.
America, a frontier. ANN 17:154
Marcus, S.
Can free enterprise survive success? BA 1975-76:152
Morelli, L.
Vocational agriculture, the FFA, and our free enterprise system. BREWW:78
Romney, G.
Our unique economic principles: the market place should determine price. CAPG:40
Willkie, W. L.
Private enterprise--we have gone far enough down the road to federal control. BAD:69

LAKE OAHE
Gage, P.

The Oahe Project--yes or no? BREWW:191

Lamartine, Alphonse Marie Louis de
Revolution of 1848. BREWE 7:2702

Lamas, Carlos Saavedra See Saavedra Lamas, C.

Lamb, Willis Eugene
Fine structure of the hydrogen bomb (Nobel Lecture, Dec. 12, 1955). NOLPH 3:286

LAMB, WILLIS EUGENE
Waller, I.
Presentation [of the Nobel Prize for Physics to Willis Eugene Lamb and Polykarp Kusch, Dec. 12, 1955]. NOLPH 3:283

Lamont, Thomas S.
Presents Paul G. Hoffman. LYI:71

Lamont, Thomas William
Presents Eleanor Robson Belmont. LYI:23
Presents W. L. Mackenzie King. LYI:233

LAND SETTLEMENT - NEW ZEALAND
McKenzie, J.
Land for Settlements Bill, 1894. MACS:205 sel.
Massey, W. F.
Freehold tenure. MACS:216 sel.
Taylor, T. E.
Leasehold defended. MACS:219 sel.
Ward, J. G.
Advances to settlers, 1894. MACS:207 sel.

---- UNITED STATES
Wah-shee, J.
A land settlement--what does it mean? MAES:45

LAND TENURE - NEW ZEALAND
Taylor, T. E.
Leasehold defended. MACS:219 sel.

LAND USE, RURAL
Lipton, J.
Land preservation in the Northeast. BREWW:75

LAND USE, URBAN
Lucas, M.
The waste of our precious farmland. BREWW:102

LANDAU, LEV DAVIDOVIC
Waller, I.
Presentation [of the Nobel Prize for Physics to Lev Davidovic Landau, 1962]. NOLPH 3:607

Landis, Frederick
Presents Will H. Hays. Same as his Witty after-dinner speech on Will Hays
Witty after-dinner speech on Will Hays. LYI:224

Landon, Alfred M.
Acceptance speech, Topeka, Kansas, July 23, 1936. SIN:136
Action challenged. ROD:162
Campaign speech, New York City, October 29, 1936. SIN:145
Federal and family finances. BAD:62

Landsteiner, Karl
On individual differences in human blood (Nobel Lecture, Dec. 11, 1930). NOLM 2:234

LANDSTEINER, KARL
Hedrén, G.
Presentation [of the Nobel Prize for Physiology or Medicine to Karl Landsteiner, Dec. 11, 1930]. NOLM 2:229

Lang, John Dunmore
"Little While" of the Saviour's absence and the prospect of his speedy return. MCA:64

Lange, Christian Louis
Internationalism (Nobel Lecture, Dec. 13, 1921). NOLP 1:336
Presentation [of the Nobel Prize for Peace to Carlos Saavedra Lamas, Dec. 10, 1936].

NOLP 2:217
Presentation [of the Nobel Prize for Peace, 1933, to Norman Angell, Dec. 10, 1934]. NOLP 2:147
Presentation [of the Nobel Prize for Peace to Viscount Cecil of Chelwood, Dec. 10, 1937]. NOLP 2:235

Langer, Elizabeth
Instrument of revelation (Ripon, Wisc., 1957). LINR:301; LINRS:300; LINRST:370

Langlie, Arthur B.
Presents Norman S. Marshall. LYI:155

Langmuir, Irving
Surface chemistry (Nobel Lecture, Dec. 14, 1932). NOLC 2:287

LANGMUIR, IRVING
Söderbaum, H. G.
Presentation [of the Nobel Prize for Chemistry to Irving Langmuir, Dec. 14, 1932]. NOLC 2:283

Langston, Charles H.
Should colored men be subject to the pains and penalties of the Fugitive Slave Law? (1858). FON:208

Langston, John Mercer
Equality before the law (anniversary of adoption of Fifteenth Amendment). (Oberlin College, May 17, 1874). FON:409
The other phase of reconstruction (Jersey City, N.J., April 17, 1877). SMHV:46

LANGUAGE AND LANGUAGES
Aziz, U.
Languages: anguish and confusion. MONSA:167
Bacon, W. A.
Language and the lived world. BA 1976-77:174
Toh Chin Chye
The role of the university in a multi-racial society. MONSA:291

Lansdowne, Henry Charles Keith Petty Fitzmaurice, 5th Marquis See Curzon of Kedleston, G., jt. auth.

Lansing, John
Answering Alexander Hamilton. BREWE 7:2710

Lardner, Dionysius
Plurality of worlds. BREWE 7:2716

Latimer, Hugh
Duties and respect of judges. BREWE 7:2721
On the pickings of officeholders. BREWE 7:2729
Sermon on the ploughers. Same as his Sermon on the plow
Sermon on the plow. BREWE 7:2724; BRYH:47

LATTIMORE, OWEN J.
Youngdahl, L.
United States v. Lattimore. ANN 17:300

Laue, Max von
Concerning the detection of x-ray interferences (Nobel Lecture for 1914, Nov. 12, 1915). NOLPH 1:347

LAUE, MAX VON
Granqvist, G.
Presentation [of the Nobel Prize for Physics for 1914 to Max Von Laue, Nov. 12, 1915]. NOLPH 1:343

Laughlin, James Laurence
Against free coinage of silver. ANN 12:75

Laurance, John and others (J. Madison)
General welfare and the limits of government authority. ANN 3:491

Laurier, Sir Wilfrid
Canada, England and the United States in 1899. BREWE 7:2737
Character and work of Gladstone. BREWE 7:2732

Lavenson, James
Think strawberries. (American

Medical Association, Feb. 7, 1974). VERD:259

Laveran, Charles Louis Alphonse
Protozoa as causes of disease (Nobel Lecture, Dec. 11, 1907). NOLM 1:264

LAVERAN, CHARLES LOUIS ALPHONSE
Sundberg, C.
Presentation [of the Nobel Prize for Physiology or Medicine to Charles Louis Alphonse Laveran]. NOLM 1:259

LAW AND LAWYERS
Azmi, B. H. M.
Duty of a lawyer. MONS:97
Bayard, J. A.
Federal judiciary. BREWE 1:249
Brandeis, L. D.
Law and the laboring classes. ANN 13:23
Brewer, D. J.
Independent judiciary as the salvation of the nation. ANN 11:423
Brougham and Vaux, H. P. B.
Present state of the law, (1828). STRM:153
Burger, W. E.
State of the Judiciary. BA 1970-71:13
Choate, J. H.
Bench and the bar. HURH:133
Cousin, V.
Foundations of law. BREWE 4:1428
Cox, A.
Creativity in law and government. BA 1973-74:49
Crockett, G. W.
Racism in the law. FON:1131
Curtis, G. W.
Liberty under the law. BAS:141 (outline only); LINS:249
Davis, D.
Ex parte Milligan, 1866: opinion for the court. ANN 10:31
Dawson, M.
My profession. CAPB:363
Dixon, O.
Law and the scientific expert. MCA:176
Field, D. D.
In re Milligan--martial law as lawlessness. BREWE 6:2147
Frankfurter, F.
John Marshall and the judicial function, September 22, 1955. FRIP:353
The Zeitgeist and the Judiciary. FRIP:340
Griswold, E. N.
Dissent, protest, and disobedience. ANN 18:670; BA 1967-68:141; JEF:196
Hand, L.
Judge's freedom before the law. ANN 15:233
Holmes, O. W., Jr.
Path of the law. BOORA 2:593
Isocrates
Areopagiticus. "A few wise laws wisely administered." BREWE 7:2589
Katzenbach, N. de B.
Civil Rights Act of 1964: respect for law. CAPG:88
Kennedy, R. F.
Law Day address--University of Georgia. CAPG:73; THOMS:120
Latimer, H.
Duties and respect of judges. BREWE 7:2721
Lee Kuan Yew
Law and its disciples. MONS:374
McGill, W. J.
Science and the law. BA 1977-78:83
Mansfield, W. M.
In the case of John Wilkes. BREWE 8:2943
In the case of the Dean of St. Asaph. BREWE 8:2945
Marbury, W. L.
Of movers and immobilists. BA 1965-66:77
Marshall, J.
Speech in Virginia Convention on Ratification of the Constitution, June 20, 1788. FRIP:90
Moneta, E. T.
Peace and law in the Italian

tradition (Nobel Lecture, 1907, Aug. 25, 1909). NOLP 1:114
Pym, J.
Laws as the safeguard of liberty. BREWE 8:3253
Rantoul, R., Jr.
On the barbarity of the common law. ANN 6:262
Royer-Collard, P. P.
"Sacrilege" in law. BREWE 9:3345
Shaw, L.
Law as a restraint on power. ANN 5:217
Thurman, A. G.
Vested rights and the obligations of contracts. BREWE 9:3626
Welcome to a State Attorney General as speaker at a civic club. HNWM:42
Wilson, J.
Study of law in the United States. ANN 3:380
Yamzon, V.
The lawyer shall never retreat. CURM:323
Young, J.
Property under the common law (Coster v. Lorillard case). ANN 6:181

---- See also Courts; Defense, Speeches of; Judicial review; Jury; Justice; Law enforcement; United States - Supreme Court

LAW DAY
Kennedy, R. F.
Law Day address--University of Georgia. CAPG:73; THOMS:120

LAW ENFORCEMENT
Wallace, G. C.
Address on law enforcement. MAC:271; MACR:312

---- NEW ZEALAND
Forbes, G. W.
The Public Safety Conservation Bill, 1932. MACS:314 sel.

Lawrence, David L.
Speaker of the year award (1962). TAC:227

Lawrence, Ernest Orlando
The evolution of the cyclotron (Nobel Lecture for 1939, Dec. 11, 1951). NOLPH 2:430

LAWRENCE, GERTRUDE
Sumner, G. L.
Presents Gertrude Lawrence. LYI:22

Lawson, Jesse
I protest against Hayes's Southern policy. (Princeton, N.Y., August, 1877). FON:457
The remedy for anarchy. (Bethel Literary and Historical Association, Washington, D.C., Feb. 5, 1902). FON:639

LAWYERS See Law and lawyers

Laxness, Halldór Kiljan
Acceptance [of the Nobel Prize for Literature, 1955]. NOB 12:7; NOL:508

LAXNESS, HALLDOR KILJAN
Wessén, E.
Presentation [of the Nobel Prize for Literature to Halldór Kiljan Laxness, 1955]. NOB 12:3; NOL:505

LEACOCK, STEPHEN
Seaman, Sir O.
Presents Stephen Leacock. LYI:47

LEADERSHIP
Clark, C.
Courage of leadership. BREWE 3:1207
Harrison, R.
Leadership--a goal for us all. BREWW:150
Lee, G. P.
Effective "Indian leadership" color-blind, but not naive. MAES:183
Lee Kuan Yew
Problems of leadership. MONS:371

Meyer, S.
What leadership means to me. BREWW:171
Mott, J. R.
The leadership demanded in this momentous time (Nobel Lecture, Dec. 13, 1946). NOLP 2:362
Muskie, E. S.
The astronauts on the moon. BAAGB:409

LEAGUE OF NATIONS
Borah, W. E.
League of Nations. HURH:190
Cecil, R.
The future of civilization (Nobel Lecture for 1937, June 1, 1938). NOLP 2:246
Jordan, W. J.
The League and the Spanish Civil War. MACS:361 sel.
Lodge, H. C.
In opposition to the Proposed League of Nations. BOORA 2:783
---- and others
Senate and the League of Nations, November 19, 1919 debate. ANN 14:196
Nash, W.
Collective security and the League of Nations. MACS:356 sel.
Wilson, W.
Appeal for support of the League of Nations (Omaha, Nebraska speech). ANN 14:187
For the League of Nations (Des Moines, Iowa speech). LINS:300

---- See also Peace Conference, 1919

LEARNING AND SCHOLARSHIP
Barzun, J.
Place and price of excellence. ARS:28
Bowdoin, J.
Encouragement of knowledge. ANN 2:540
Bowen, W. G.
Commitment to scholarship and research. BA 1978-79:41
Curtis, G. W.
Duty of the American scholar. ANN 8:411
Emerson, R. W.
American scholar. ANN 6:367; ARS:39; BAS:156 (outline only); BOORA 1:283; BREWE 5:2003; LINS:162; OLIS:47
Everett, E.
Circumstances favorable to the progress of literature in America. ANN 5:118
Kennedy, J. F.
Intellectual and the politician. BAP:285; LINR:267
Kirk, G.
Responsibilities of the educated man (at centennial of University of Denver). LINR:143
Morgan, E. S.
What every Yale freshman should know. ARS:35
Phillips, W.
Scholar in a Republic. ANN 10:488
Thani Nayagam, X.
Age and learning. MONS:187

---- See also Education, Higher; Intellect; Knowledge, Theory of; Research

Lederberg, Joshua
A view of genetics (Nobel Lecture for 1958, May 29, 1959). NOLM 3:615

LEDERBERG, JOSHUA
Caspersson, T.
Presentation [of the Nobel Prize for Physiology or Medicine to George Wells Beadle, Edward Lawrie Tatum, and Joshua Lederberg, Dec. 11, 1958]. NOLM 3:583

Lee, George P.
Effective "Indian leadership" color-blind, but not naive. MAES:183

Lee, Henry
Funeral oration on Washington. BREWE 7:2744

Lee, Sir Henry Hau Shik
Great institution (Central Bank of Malaya). MONS:164

Lee, Irving G.
Four ways of looking at a speech. ARS:12

Lee, John A.
The Auckland Riot, 1932 (New Zealand House of Representatives, April 19, 1932). MACS:312 sel.

Lee, Richard Henry
Address to the people of England. BREWE 7:2752

Lee, Robert E.
Gen. R. E. Lee's address to his troops. Same as his To the Army of Northern Virginia
To the Army of Northern Virginia. (Headquarters Army of Northern Virginia, Oct. 2d, 1862). ECH:188

LEE, ROBERT E.
Stanley, A. O.
Address in honor of Robert E. Lee. BLY:216

Lee, Tsung Dao
Weak interactions and nonconservation of parity (Nobel Lecture, Dec. 11, 1957). NOLPH 3:406

LEE, TSUNG DAO
Klein, O. B.
Presentation [of the Nobel Prize for Physics to Chen Ning Yang and Tsung Dao Lee, Dec. 11, 1957]. NOLPH 3:389

Lee, W. Leonard
Through the looking glass. SCHW:106

Lee Kuan Yew
Aim: a more equal society. MONS:369
Brighter future for all peoples of Singapore if ... (Singapore, Feb. 6, 1969). MONSA:239
Changes in values and concepts. MONS:348
Democratic socialism under stress in Asia. MONS:345
First step in nation building (Singapore). MONS:358
Hong Kong and Singapore: a tale of two cities (Univ. of Hong Kong, Feb. 18, 1970). MONSA:264
Law and its disciples. MONS:374
Leaders' responsibility in sustaining a democratic system (Singapore, March 21, 1970). MONSA:269
Lesson we have to learn (opening new Science Tower at the University of Singapore). MONS:361
The moral for Commonwealth members and Britain (London, Jan. 9, 1969). MONSA:259
A new relevance and a fresh validity for Commonwealth (Singapore, Jan. 14, 1971). MONSA:272
Our future is at stake--crucial years ahead (Singapore, May 6, 1968). MONSA:247
Problems of leadership. MONS:371
The Rhodesian problem and the change of mood in Britain (London, Jan. 10, 1969). MONSA:251
Self respect is what our trade unions have and ... (Singapore, Nov. 16, 1969). MONSA:255
Tribute to India and Indians (Singapore, May 19, 1968). MONSA:244
Unionism: rethinking is vital (opening National Trade Union Conference). MONS:366

Leenhouts, Thelma
Men of conscience. SCHW:119

LEGISLATORS See Law and lawyers; Public officials; United States - Congress

Legum, Colin
Pan-Africanism, the Communists, and the West. ARS:255

Lehman, Herbert H.
Freedom and individual security. ANN 17:21

Leighton, Robert
Immortality. BREWE 7:2761

Leloir, Luis F.
Two decades of research on the biosynthesis of saccharides (Nobel Lecture, Dec. 11, 1970). NOLC 4:338

LELOIR, LUIS F.
Myrbäck, K.
Presentation [of the Nobel Prize for Chemistry to Luis F. Leloir, Dec. 11, 1970]. NOLC 4:335

Lemke, William
Introduction of the aims of the Union Party of the United States. BAD:117

Lenard, Philipp Eduard Anton von
On cathode rays (Nobel Lecture for 1905, May 28, 1906). NOLPH 1:105

LENARD, PHILIPP EDUARD ANTON VON
Lindstedt, A.
Presentation [of the Nobel Prize for Physics for 1905 to Philipp Eduard Anton von Lenard, May 28, 1906]. NOLPH 1:101

LEND LEASE LAW
Knox, F.
Lend-lease and national defense. ANN 16:48
Roosevelt, F. D.
Proposal for Lend-Lease. ANN 16:40
Wheeler, B. K.
Menace of Lend-Lease. ANN 16:46

Lenin, Nikolai
Advance or retreat. Same as his War, peace, and revolutionary democracy
War, peace and revolutionary democracy. (The First All-Russian Congress of Soviets, Tauride Palace, Leningrad, June 17, 1917). BRN:81

Lenoir, William
Interest of the few and the liberties of the people. ANN 3:300

Lenthall, William
Opening the long Parliament under Charles I. BREWE 7:2767

LEOPOLD, NATHAN
Darrow, C.
Defense of Richard Loeb and Nathan Leopold. HURH:196

Lerner, Daniel
Comfort and fun: morality in a nice society. ARS:168

Levai, Blase
Broken sword. SCHW:144

Levenson, Joseph
Live hopefully! WALE:116
Servant of the Lord has died. WALE:118

Levin, Lewis C.
Native Americans and the foreign-born. ANN 7:313

Levine, Etan B.
John F. Kennedy. WALE:221

Lew Sip Hon
Our stake in natural rubber. MONS:302

Lewe, John C.
Presents Thomas C. Clark (Attorney General of the United States). LYI:137

Lewis, C. S.
Social morality. ARS:177
Three parts of morality. ARS:175

Lewis, David
His speech on the scaffold. BREWE 7:2772

Lewis, Ellis
Mott v. Pennsylvania Railroad Company: opinion for the court. ANN 9:61

Lewis, James Hamilton
Introduction of Jacob M. Dickinson. LYI:217

Lewis, John
We are in a serious revolution. (Washington, D.C., August 28, 1963). FON:975

Lewis, John L.
Industrial unions. ANN 15:511
Labor and the nation. (Washington, Sept. 3, 1937). HURH:232
"Labor, like Israel, has many sorrows." Same as his Labor and the nation

LEWIS, JOHN L.
Day, J. E.
Introduces John L. Lewis, American labor leader. LYI:61

LEWIS, LLOYD
Stevenson, A. E.
Farewell to a friend (Lloyd Lewis). ALA:119

Lewis, Sinclair
The American fear of literature (Nobel Lecture, Dec. 12, 1930). ANN 15:62; BEN:208; BOORA 2:824; NOL:278

LEWIS, SINCLAIR
Karlfeldt, E. A.
Presentation [of the Nobel Prize for Literature to Sinclair Lewis, 1930]. NOB 11:237; NOL:271

Lewis, W. Deming
Founder's Day remarks. BAS:164 (outline only)

LEWIS AND CLARK EXPEDITION
Jefferson, T.
Lewis and Clark expedition. ANN 4:158

LIABILITIES See Success

LIARS See Truthfulness and falsehood

Libby, Willard Frank
Radiocarbon dating (Nobel Lecture, Dec. 12, 1960). NOLC 3:593

LIBBY, WILLARD FRANK
Westgren, A.
Presentation [of the Nobel Prize for Chemistry to Willard Frank Libby, Dec. 12, 1960]. NOLC 3:589

LIBERAL ARTS See Education, Higher

LIBERAL PARTY - GREAT BRITAIN
Keynes, J. M.
Am I a Liberal? MCB:456

---- See also Great Britain - Politics and government

---- NEW ZEALAND
Grey, Sir G.
A Liberal Party. MACS:182 sel.

LIBERALISM
Ascoli, M.
Scarcity of ideas. ARS:201
Hatcher, R. G.
Which is the path of change? FON:1110
Oglesby, C.
How can we continue to sack the ports of Asia and still dream of Jesus. LAA:15
Schlesinger, A. M., Jr.
Challenge of abundance. ARS:196

LIBERTY
Aly, B.
Remarks on Jefferson Day. BAP:273
Ball, J.
Bondmen and freemen: address to the rebels at Blackheath. BRYH:42
Boucher, J.
Civil liberty and nonresistance. ANN 2:343; POC:552
Calhoun, J. C.
Individual liberty. BREWE 3:925
Carson, H. L.
American liberty. BREWE 3:995
Cotton, J.
A treatise of the covenant of grace. JON:48
Cousin, V.
Liberty an inalienable right. BREWE 4:1426

Curran, J. P.
England and English liberties--in the case of Rowan. BREWE 4:1546
In the case of Justice Johnson--civil liberty and arbitrary arrests. BREWE 4:1499
Curtis, G. W.
Liberty under the law. BAS:141 (outline only); LINS:249
Depew, C. M.
Unveiling the Statue of Liberty. BREWE 5:1782
Dickinson, J.
Before the Pennsylvania Assembly, March 24, 1760. POC:182
Douglass, F.
If there is no struggle there is no progress. FON:197
Drayton, W. H.
Charge to the Grand Juries, November 5 & 15, 1774. POC:297
Everett, E.
History of liberty. BREWE 6:2092
Fuller, Z.
Tree of liberty (George Washington birthday address). ANN 5:355
Goldwater, B. M.
Extremism in defense of liberty (accepting nomination for presidency, July 17, 1964). MAC:251; MACR:292; MDV:115; SIN:337
Hand, L.
Meaning of liberty. BRR:46
Henry, P.
Liberty or death. ANN 2:231; BAS:39 (outline only); BEN:13; BREWE 7:2473; HURH:27; HURS:209; OLIS:22; POC:305
Howard, J. A.
"... our sacred honor." BA 1975-76:9
Hugo, V. M.
Liberty tree in Paris. BREWE 7:2548
Ingersoll, R. G.
Liberty of man, woman, and child. BREWE 7:2583
Jacobusse, K. D.
Uncommon thought. SCHW:79
Johnson, L. B.
Vietnam: the struggle to be free (on accepting National Freedom Award). BA 1965-66:11
Kennedy, J. F.
Ich bin ein Berliner. ALA:129; AND:79; LINR:294; LINRS:293
Kennedy, R. F.
Address to the Free University of Berlin. MDV:95
Lehman, H. H.
Freedom and individual security. ANN 17:21
Lubbers, A. D.
Road to right. SCHW:159
Montalembert, C. F. T.
Devotion to freedom. BREWE 8:3048
Ngwa, J.
Our common tradition in peril. SCHW:123
Pym, J.
Law as the safeguard of liberty. BREWE 8:3253
Romulo, C. P.
Bandung address. CROCK:141
Roosevelt, F. D.
Four human freedoms. ANN 16:42; ROD:278; STAT 3:2855
Rowan, C. T.
Commencement address (at Howard University, June 5, 1964). HURS:216
Sargent, F. W.
The computer and civil liberties. BA 1973-74:141
Schurz, C.
True Americanism. ANN 9:97
Smith, W.
Eulogium. POC:3
Wentworth, P.
Liberty of the Commons. BRYH:79; CLAYP:1
West, S.
Election sermon. POC:578
Winthrop, J.
Little speech on liberty. HURH:17; POC:135
Zubly, J. J.
Law of liberty. POC:611

---- See also Civil rights; Democracy; Fourth of July; Free speech; Liberty of the press;

Religious liberty; Teaching, Freedom of; United States - Constitution; United States - Economic policy

LIBERTY OF THE PRESS
Brennan, W. J., Jr.
Conciliation between the press and the law.
BA 1979-80:119
Gossage, H. L.
Our fictitious freedom of the press. MDV:285
Mathias, C. M.
The First Amendment: freedom and responsibility.
BA 1977-78:134
Royster, V. C.
What the people grant, they can take away.
BA 1978-79:191
Schorr, D.
In defense of privilege.
BA 1978-79:202
Shaw, R. M.
Danger of getting used to lies. LINR:191

LIBERTY PARTY
Smith, G.
On the character, scope and duties of the Liberty Party. MDT:93

LIBRARIES AND LIBRARIANS
Choate, R.
Books and civilization in America. BREWE 3:1120
Phelps, W. L.
Owning books. HURH:225

---- See also Dedication addresses - Libraries

LIBRARY OF CONGRESS See United States - Library of Congress

LIES See Truthfulness and Falsehood

LIFE
Arnold, T.
Realities of life and death.
BREWE 1:173
Chalmers, T.
Use of the living.
BREWE 3:1025
Dwight, T.
Pursuit of excellence.
BREWE 5:1968
Fisher, J.
Jeopardy of daily life.
BREWE 6:2164
Gladstone, W. E.
Destiny and individual aspiration.
BREWE 6:2288
Huxley, T. H.
Threefold unity of life.
BREWE 7:2557
Ingersoll, R. G.
Life. BREWE 7:2587
Live today. BURT:131
Our changing world. BURT:129
Tyndall, J.
Origin of life. BREWE 9:3664

---- See also Behavior

LIFE INSURANCE See Insurance - Life

LIGHT
Frank, I. M.
Optics of light sources moving in refractive media.
NOLPH 3:442
Lorentz, H. A.
The theory of electrons and the propagation of light.
NOLPH 1:14
Raman, Sir C. V.
The molecular scattering of light. NOLPH 2:267
Zeeman, P.
Light radiation in a magnetic field. NOLPH 1:33

Lilienthal, David E.
Democratic faith. Same as his My faith in democracy
My faith in democracy. ALA:111

Liljestrand, G.
Presentation [of the Nobel Prize for Physiology or Medicine to André Frederic Cournand, Werner Theodor Otto Forssmann, and Dickinson Woodruff Richards Jr., Dec. 11, 1956].
NOLM 3:501
Presentation [of the Nobel Prize for Physiology or Medicine to Christiaan Eijkman and Sir Frederick Gowland Hopkins, Dec. 11, 1929].

NOLM 2:193
Presentation [of the Nobel Prize for Physiology or Medicine to Edward Calvin Kendall, Tadeus Reichstein, and Philip Showalter Hench, Dec. 11, 1950]. NOLM 3:263
Presentation [of the Nobel Prize for Physiology or Medicine to Sir Alexander Fleming, Ernst Boris Chain, and Sir Howard Walter Florey, Dec. 11, 1945]. NOLM 3:77
Presentation [of the Nobel Prize for Physiology or Medicine to Sir Charles Scott Sherrington and Edgar Douglas Adrian, Dec. 12, 1932]. NOLM 2:273
Presentation [of the Nobel Prize for Physiology or Medicine to Sir Henry Hallett Dale and Otto Loewi, Dec. 12, 1936]. NOLM 2:397

Lillehei, C. Walton See Sevareid, E., jt. auth.

Lim, P. G. (Miss)
Women's role in national development. MONS:339

Lim Chong Eu
The message of Rukunegara (Penang, Nov. 1, 1970). MONSA:147

Lim Chong Yah
Teaching profession and nation building (Malaysia). MONS:317

Lim Kim San
Massive exercise for survival. MONS:408
Three major problems of developing countries. MONS:412
Youth leadership (May 25, 1968). MONSA:310

Lim Swee Aun
Doubting Thomases were wrong (opening of Chemical Company of Malaysian factory). MONS:153

Lincoln, Abraham
Against the extension of slavery. Same as his Speech at Peoria
Campaign speech for United States Senate--Chicago, July 10, 1858. Same as his Reply to Douglas at Chicago
Cooper Institute address (New York, Feb. 27, 1860). ANN 9:158; BREWE 7:2791; FRIP:204; LINS:201
Danger to our liberty. Same as his Perpetuation of our political institutions
Dred Scott Decision. ANN 8:459
Farewell to Springfield (outline of speech). CUB:78
First annual message. STAT 2:1054
First inaugural address. ANN 9:250; BOSR:1; HOW:239; LINS:281; USINAU:119; USINAUG:119
First joint debate at Ottawa, August 21, 1858. ANN 9:11
Fourth annual message. STAT 2:1097
Gettysburg address (Nov. 19, 1863). ALA:29; ANN 9:462; BAS:131 (outline only); BEN:47; BOORA 1:418; BREWE 7:2794; CUB:79; HURH:112
"A house divided against itself cannot stand." (Springfield, Ill., June 16, 1858). ANN 9:1; BAS:100 (outline only); BREWE 7:2777; FRIP:197; HURH:88
"I believe this government cannot endure permanently, half slave and half free." Same as his "A house divided against itself cannot stand"
Interrogating Douglas. Same as his Second joint debate at Freeport, August 27, 1858
Labor, education, and the American farmer. ANN 9:121
Last public address, April 11, 1865. Same as his Speech before death
Lincoln-Douglas joint debate at Alton, October 15, 1858. ANN 9:26
Message to Congress, July 5, 1861. ANN 9:268
On John Brown. Same as his Cooper Institute Address

Perpetuation of our political institutions (1837). ANN 6:424; MOP:368
Plea for compensated emancipation. ANN 9:328
Program for reconstruction. Same as his Third annual message
Reply to Douglas at Chicago. OLIS:150
Righteous and speedy peace. Same as his Speech before death, April 11, 1865
Second annual message to Congress. BOORA 1:396; STAT 2:1068
Second inaugural address (Washington, March 4, 1869). AND:48; ANN 9:555; BEN:49; BOORA 1:423; BREWE 7:2795; BRR:80; CUB:86 (outline); HURH:114; LINS:226; USINAU:127; USINAUG:127
Second joint debate at Freeport, August 27, 1858. ANN 9:15; BREWE 7:2785
Speech at Charleston, September 18, 1858. ANN 9:21
Speech at Galesburg, October 7, 1858. ANN 9:23
Speech at Jonesboro, September 15, 1858. ANN 9:19
Speech at Peoria, October 16, 1854. ANN 8:491; FRIP:165
Speech before death, April 11, 1865. ANN 9:573; BREWE 7:2796; CUR:4
Speech on repeal of the Missouri Compromise, October 16, 1854. Same as his Speech at Peoria, October 16, 1854
Third annual message. ANN 9:473; STAT 2:1084
War to preserve the Union. Same as his Message to Congress, July 5, 1861
"... we here highly resolve that these dead shall not have died in vain." Same as his Gettysburg address
"With malice toward none, with charity for all, with firmness in the right...." Same as his Second inaugural address
With malice toward none. Same as his Second inaugural address

LINCOLN, ABRAHAM
Beaconsfield, B. D.
Assassination of Lincoln. BREWE 1:295
Beecher, H. W.
Effect of the death of Lincoln. BREWE 1:365
Bingham, J. A.
Against the assassins of President Lincoln. BREWE 2:445
Brooks, P.
Character of Abraham Lincoln. BREWE 2:644
Douglass, F.
Oration in memory of Abraham Lincoln (at unveiling of Freedmen's Monument, Washington, D.C.). FRIP:242
Douglass, H. F.
I do not believe in the antislavery of Abraham Lincoln. FON:232
Emerson, R. W.
Greatness of a plain American. BREWE 5:1999
Hunt, E. L.
Lincoln's rhetorical triumph at Cooper Union (centennial speech). BA 1969-70:189
Jacobusse, K. D.
Big man. SCHW:204
McGill, R. E.
Meaning of Lincoln today (centennial of Lincoln's speech at Cooper Institute). LINS:360
Runkel, H. W.
Making Lincoln live. BAPR:351; BAPRR:259
Sandburg, C.
On Lincoln (at 150th anniversary of Lincoln's birth). GRG:101; HURH:347
Wise, S. S.
Abraham Lincoln, man and American. HURH:169

Lindbergh, Charles Augustus
America first. Same as his Independent policy
Dissident view: Charles Lindbergh argues against intervention. Same as his Independent policy
Independent policy. ANN 16:72; HURH:254; ROD:290
"Those of us who believe in an

independent America must band together and organize for strength." Same as his Independent policy

LINDBERGH, CHARLES AUGUSTUS
Gwinn, J. M.
Presents Charles Lindbergh. LYI:188

Lindh, A. E.
Presentation [of the Nobel Prize for Physics to Cecil Frank Powell, Dec. 11, 1950]. NOLPH 3:139
Presentation [of the Nobel Prize for Physics to Percy Williams Bridgman, Dec. 11, 1946]. NOLPH 3:53

Lindsay, John V.
A politician adapts his introduction and conclusion to an audience of students. (Harvard Republican Club, April 20, 1968). JEF:194
Reality and rhetoric. BA 1967-68:79
Vietnam moratorium address. (New York, Oct. 15, 1969). AND:153

Lindsley, Philip
Dangers of a sectarian college. ANN 5:310
Education for every child of the Republic. ANN 5:157

Lindstedt, A.
Presentation [of the Nobel Prize for Physics for 1905 to Philipp Eduard Anton von Lenard, May 28, 1906]. NOLPH 1:101

Lingg, Louis
Address at trial, Chicago, October 7-9, 1886. ACC:39; PAF:34

Linowitz, Sol M.
Let candles be brought (New York, March 8, 1977). BA 1976-77:149

Lionaes, Aase
Presentation [of the Nobel Prize for Peace to the International Labor Organization, Dec. 10, 1969]. NOLP 3:415
Presentation [of the Nobel Prize for Peace to Norman Ernest Borlaug, Dec. 10, 1970]. NOLP 3:445
Presentation [of the Nobel Prize for Peace to René-Samuel Cassin, Dec. 10, 1968]. NOLP 3:385
Presentation [of the Nobel Prize for Peace to the United Nations Children's Fund, Dec. 10, 1965]. NOLP 3:353

Lipis, Philip L.
Darkness at noon. WALE:120
Dreams fulfilled. WALE:122
Four good signs. WALE:124
Look beyond the shadows. WALE:128

Lipmann, Fritz Albert
Development of the acetylation problem: a personal account (Nobel Lecture, Dec. 11, 1953). NOLM 3:413

LIPMANN, FRITZ ALBERT
Hammarsten, E.
Presentation [of the Nobel Prize for Physiology or Medicine to Hans Adolf Krebs and Fritz Albert Lipmann, Dec. 11, 1953]. NOLM 3:395

Lipnick, Bernard
Family's tribute. WALE:130

Lippmann, Gabriel
Colour photography (Nobel Lecture, Dec. 14, 1908). NOLPH 1:186

LIPPMANN, GABRIEL
Hasselberg, K. B.
Presentation [of the Nobel Prize for Physics to Gabriel Lippmann, Dec. 14, 1908]. NOLPH 1:183

Lippman, Walter
On understanding society. (Columbia University, 1969). BAAGB:412
Our world today. MDV:26
Rise of personal government in the United States. BAD:97

Lipton, Jeffrey
Land preservation in the Northeast. BREWW:75

LIQUIDS
Waals, J. D. V. D.
The equation of state for gases and liquids. NOLPH 1:254

LIQUOR PROBLEM See Alcoholism; Prohibition

LITERARY PRIZES See Literature

LITERATURE
Andrić, I.
Acceptance [of the Nobel Prize for Literature, 1961]. NOB 1:121; NOL:565
Arnold, M.
Literature and science. MCB:388
Ashley, L. R. N.
A guided tour of gobbledygook. REID:408
Avebury, J. L.
Hundred best books. BREWE 7:2820
Bacon, W. A.
The seacoast of Bohemia: truth in literature. BA 1977-78:170
Buchan, J.
Novel and the fairy tale. ARS:54
Camus, A.
Acceptance [of the Nobel Prize for Literature, 1957]. NOB 4:7; NOL:524
Depew, C. M.
Poetry and politics in Britain. BREWE 5:1796
Drummond, H.
Talk on books. BREWE 5:1964
Elliott, J.
There's always a mongoose. MDYG:223
Everett, E.
Circumstances favorable to the progress of literature in America. ANN 5:118
Faulkner, W.
On accepting the Nobel Prize, exhorts the young writers of the world. ALA:125; ANN 17:33; ARS:52; BOORA 2:988; GRG:86; HURH:291; MOPR:379; NOB 19:7; NOL:444
Gittings, R.
Exploring the known. MDYG:207
Gladstone, W. E.
Use of books. BREWE 6:2289
Hemingway, E.
Acceptance [of the Nobel Prize for Literature, 1954]. NOB 9:7; NOL:501
Introductions for literary persons (2 examples). BNH:18
Lewis, S.
The American fear of literature. ANN 15:62; BEN:208; BOORA 2:824; NOL:278
Macaulay, T. B.
Literature of England. BREWE 8:2876
Marshall, A.
I first saw the light of day. MDYG:231
Montgomery, J.
Modern English literature. BREWE 8:3052
Russell, J. R.
Science and literature as modes of progress. BREWE 9:3359
Smith, G.
Lamps of fiction (at centenary of Sir Walter Scott). BREWE 9:3465
Steinbeck, J.
Acceptance [of the Nobel Prize for Literature, 1962]. NOB 19:205; NOL:575
Thackeray, W. M.
Authors and their patrons. BREWE 9:3604
Novelist's future labors. BREWE 9:3606
Reality of the novelist's creation. BREWE 9:3602
Whitehead, A. N.
Technical education and its relation to science and literature. MCB:403
Woolsey, J. M.
Opinion December 6, 1933 (Ulysses case--freedom of reading). ANN 15:236

---- See also Acceptance speeches - Rewards (Prizes); Black authors; Book reviews; Books and reading; Poetry and poets

Little, Malcolm
The ballot or the bullet (Cleveland, April 3, 1964). AND:135; FON:985; REIR:47; SMHV:214
Black revolution (April 8, 1964). SMHV:235
Prospects for freedom (New York, January 7, 1965). SMHV:250
To young people. (New York, Dec. 31, 1964). FON:1004

---- See also Farmer, J., jt. auth.

LITTLE, MALCOLM
Breitman, G.
Myths about Malcolm X: another view. LINR:120
Cleage, A.
Myths about Malcolm X. LINR:108
Davis, O.
Malcolm was our manhood, our living Black manhood. FON:1010

LIVESTOCK See AGRICULTURE

Livingston, Edward
Against the Alien Act. Same as his On the Alien Bill
On the Alien Bill. ANN 4:49

Livingston, Homer J.
Responds to an introduction and speaks briefly at the dedication of a new manufacturing plant. PRS:130

Livingston, P. R. See Sanford, N., jt. auth.

Livingston, Robert R.
Wealth and poverty, aristocracy and Republicanism. BREWE 7:2801

LLEWELLYN, SIR WILLIAM
Phelps, W. L.
Presents Sir William Llewellyn. LYI:26

Lloyd George, David
Appeal to the nation (London, Sept. 19, 1914). MCB:483
The Budget (Limehouse, London, July 30, 1909). BRYH:461; JAE:170; MCB:233; STRM:407
The Budget and the people. Same as his The budget
Speech at Limehouse, July 30, 1909. Same as his The budget

LOANS See Lend Lease Law

LOCAL GOVERNMENT - CITIZEN PARTICIPATION
Gardner, J. W.
People power. BA 1974-75:158

Lodge, Henry Cabot
For immigration restrictions. ANN 12:88
For intervention in Cuba. ANN 12:85
"If a man is going to be an American at all let him be so without any qualifying adjectives." Same as his Our forefathers
In opposition to the Proposed League of Nations. BOORA 2:783
Our forefathers. (Brooklyn, Dec. 21, 1888). HURH:141
Speech on the League of Nations. Same as his In opposition to the Proposed League of Nations

---- and others (J. T. Robinson)
Senate and the League of Nations, November 19, 1919 debate. ANN 14:196

Lodge, Henry Cabot, Jr.
For abolishing the Electoral College. ANN 17:2
"Man can improve his material and physical lot without sacrificing his civil rights." Same as his United Nations
United Nations. (Chicago, Ill., Sept. 2, 1958). HURH:344

LODGE SPEECHES See Club speeches

LOEB, RICHARD
Darrow, C.
Defense of Richard Loeb and Nathan Leopold. HURH:196

Loewi, Otto
The chemical transmission of

nerve action (Nobel Lecture, Dec. 12, 1936). NOLM 2:416

LOEWI, OTTO
Liljestrand, G.
Presentation [of the Nobel Prize for Physiology or Medicine to Sir Henry Hallett Dale and Otto Loewi, Dec. 12, 1936]. NOLM 2:397

Logan, John, Chief of the Mingoes
On the murder of his family. ALA:9; BOORA 1:62; BREWE 7:2569
Speech to Lord Dunmore. Same as his On the murder of his family

Loguen, J. W.
I won't obey the Fugitive Slave Law. (Syracuse, N.Y., Oct. 4, 1850). FON:97

LONDON - ARCHITECTURE
Banham, R.
Fourth monument. MDYG:216

Long, Huey P.
Every man a king. BEN:80
Sharing our wealth (January, 1935 radio speech). ANN 15:318; BAD:109

Lonnquist, Ken
Ghosts (Madison, Wisc., 1977). LINRST:176

LORD'S SUPPER See Communion

Lorentz, Hendrik Antoon
The theory of electrons and the propagation of light (Nobel Lecture, Dec. 11, 1902). NOLPH 1:14

LORENTZ, HENDRIK ANTOON
Theel, Hj.
Presentation [of the Nobel Prize for Physics to Hendrik Antoon Lorentz and Pieter Zeeman, 1902]. NOLPH 1:11

Lorge, Barry
Great auto rally (outline). REIR:93

LOTTERIES See Gambling

LOUIS VI, KING OF FRANCE
Deseze, R.
Defending Louis VI. BREWE 5:1811

LOUISIANA
Lincoln, A.
Speech before death, April 11, 1865. ANN 9:573; BREWE 7:2796; CUR:4
Quincy, J., 1772-1864
On the admission of Louisiana. ANN 4:283

LOUISIANA PURCHASE
Jefferson, T.
Third annual message. STAT 1:68
White, S.
Opposition to the Louisiana Purchase. ANN 4:175

Loula, Louise A.
Drunken orgy. SCHW:149

LOVE
Drummond, H.
Greatest thing in the world. BREWE 5:1941
Elliott, J.
There's always a mongoose. MDYG:223
Klaaren, M. A.
Divine command. SCHW:96
Power of love. BURT:149

Lovell, Sir Bernard
Our present knowledge of the universe. MDYG:239

Lovell, James
Boston Massacre oration. POC:231

Lovell, John
Funeral oration. POC:138

Løvland, Jørgen Gunnarsson
Banquet speech [presenting the Nobel Prize for Peace to Bertha von Suttner, 1905, April 18, 1906]. NOLP 1:82

Presentation [of the Nobel Prize for Peace to Alfred Hermann Fried, Dec. 10, 1911]. NOLP 1:238
Presentation [of the Nobel Prize for Peace to Auguste Marie François Beernaert, Dec. 10, 1909]. NOLP 1:211
Presentation [of the Nobel Prize for Peace to Baron d'Estournelles de Constant, Dec. 10, 1909]. NOLP 1:216
Presentation [of the Nobel Prize for Peace to Ernesto Teodoro Moneta, Dec. 10, 1907]. NOLP 1:113
Presentation [of the Nobel Prize for Peace to Fredrik Bajer, Dec. 10, 1908]. NOLP 1:188
Presentation [of the Nobel Prize for Peace to Klas Pontus Arnoldson, Dec. 10, 1908]. NOLP 1:173
Presentation [of the Nobel Prize for Peace to Louis Renault, Dec. 10, 1907]. NOLP 1:141
Presentation [of the Nobel Prize for Peace to the Permanent International Peace Bureau, Dec. 10, 1910]. NOLP 1:223
Presentation [of the Nobel Prize for Peace to Tobias Michael Carel Asser, Dec. 10, 1911]. NOLP 1:233
Toast to C. A. Gobat [presenting the Nobel Prize for Peace for 1902, Oslo, July 18, 1906]. NOLP 1:29
Toast to E. Ducommun [presenting the Nobel Prize for Peace for 1902, Oslo, May 16, 1904]. NOLP 1:15
Welcome [presenting the Nobel Prize for Peace, 1903, to William Randal Cremer, Jan. 15, 1905]. NOLP 1:45

LOW, EDMON
Nix, L.
Presents Edmon Low. LYI:40

Lowe, John Adams
Presents E. J. Pratt. LYI:49

Lowe, Robert, 1st Viscount Sherbrooke
Against the extension of democracy. Same as his Coming of democracy
Coming of democracy. (H. of Commons, March 13, 1866). MCB:138

Lowell, James Russell
Poetical and the practical in America. BREWE 7:2808
Pope and his times. BREWE 7:2815

LOYALTY See Patriotism

Lubbers, Arend D.
God and Joe College. SCHW:69
Road to right. SCHW:159

Lubbock, Sir John See Avebury, J. L.

Lucas, Marty
The waste of our precious farmland. BREWW:102

Luce, Claire Boothe
Optimism about the future (Washington, Oct. 10, 1979). BA 1979-80:168

LUCE, HENRY R.
Donovan, H.
Presents Henry R. Luce. LYI:103

Lundy, Robert F.
World divided by three (politics, science, and religion). MONS:489

Luria, Salvador E.
Phage, colicins and macroregulatory phenomena (Nobel Lecture, Dec. 10, 1969). NOLM 4:426

LURIA, SALVADOR E.
Gard, S.
Presentation [of the Nobel Prize for Physiology or Medicine to Max Delbrück, Alfred D. Hershey, and Salvador E. Luria, Dec. 10, 1969]. NOLM 4:401

Lusty, Robert
Presents Sir Norman Birkett. LYI:54

Luther, Martin
Before the Diet of Worms. BREWE 7:2829
Pith of Paul's chief doctrine. BREWE 7:2833

Luthuli, Albert John
Africa and freedom (Nobel Lecture for 1960, Dec. 11, 1961). MDV:79; NOLP 3:217

LUTHULI, ALBERT JOHN
Jahn, G.
Presentation [of the Nobel Prize for Peace to Albert John Luthuli for 1960, Dec. 10, 1961]. NOLP 3:209

Lwoff, André
Interaction among virus, cell, and organism (Nobel Lecture, Dec. 11, 1965). NOLM 4:186

LWOFF, ANDRE
Gard, S.
Presentation [of the Nobel Prize for Physiology or Medicine to François Jacob, André Lwoff, and Jacques Monod, Dec. 11, 1965]. NOLM 4:143

Lygon, Lady Mary See Sykes, C., jt. auth.

Lynch, James
Colored men standing in the way of their own race. (Philadelphia, May, 1865). FON:316

LYNCHING
Chapman, J. R.
Coatesville. ARS:163
Graham, D. A.
Some facts about Southern lynchings. FON:613
Wells-Barnett, I. M.
Lynching, our national crime. FON:687
White, G. H.
I raise my voice against one of the most dangerous evils in our country. FON:624

Lyndhurst, John Singleton Copley, 1st Baron
Russia and the Crimean War. BREWE 7:2842

Lynen, Feodor
The pathway from "activated acetic acid" to the terpenes and fatty acids (Nobel Lecture, Dec. 11, 1964). NOLM 4:103

LYNEN, FEODOR
Bergstrom, S.
Presentation [of the Nobel Prize for Physiology or Medicine to Konrad Bloch and Feodor Lynen, Dec. 11, 1964]. NOLM 4:75

Lysias
Against Eratosthenes for murder (on the execution without trial of Polemarchus). BREWE 3:2851; SAG:39
Funeral oration. COG:9

Lyttleton, George See Walpole, R., jt. auth.

Lytton, Edward George Earle Lytton Bulwer-Lytton, 1st Baron
Demosthenes and the nobility of the classics. BREWE 8:2869

- M -

MacArthur, Douglas
Address to the joint session of Congress. Same as his Defends his conduct of the war in Korea
Defends his conduct of the war in Korea (Washington, April 19, 1951). ALS:243; ANN 17:79; ARS:279; BAS:82 (outline only); BEN:113; BOSR:22; GRG:88; HURH:293; HURS:214; LINS:337
Duty, honor, country. Same as his Farewell to the cadets (accepting Sylvanus Thayer award for service to his nation)

Farewell address to Congress. Same as his Defends his conduct of the war in Korea
Farewell to the cadets (accepting Sylvanus Thayer award for service to his nation, West Point, May 12, 1962). LINR:264; LINRS:283; LINRST:357; MDV:20; MUS:332
Hope of all mankind. ALA:105
"Old soldiers never die; they just fade away." Same as his Defends his conduct of the war in Korea
Remarks and final speech at Japanese surrender. ANN 16:339
Today the guns are silent. Same as his Remarks and final speech at Japanese surrender

MACARTHUR, DOUGLAS
Truman, H. S.
Preventing a new world war. ANN 17:75; BAP:291

MacAulay, John A.
The Red Cross in a changing world (Nobel Lecture, Dec. 11, 1963). NOLP 3:311

Macaulay, Thomas B.
Consent or force in government. BREWE 8:2888
Literature of England. BREWE 8:2876
Parliamentary reform. Same as his Reform Bill
Popular education. BREWE 8:2883
Reform Bill. (H. of Commons, March 2, 1831). CLAYP:295; MCB:110
Reform Bill. JAE:52
Speech on Parliamentary reform, House of Commons, March 2, 1831. Same as his Reform Bill
Tribute to the Jews. BREWE 8:2886

McBath, James Harvey
The vital university. (Los Angeles, June 5, 1975). BA 1974-75:127

McCARRAN-WALTER IMMIGRATION ACT, 1952
Truman, H. S.
Veto of the McCarran-Walter Immigration Act. ANN 17:131

McCarthy, Eugene J.
Address on Viet Nam (February 1, 1967). REIR:117

McCarthy, Joseph Raymond
Annual Kansas Day Republican banquet speech. BOSR:53
Communists in the State Department. ANN 17:16
A conspiracy of blackest infamy (1951). (Washington, June 14, 1951). DAVF:304

McCARTHY, JOSEPH RAYMOND
Benton, W.
For the expulsion of Senator McCarthy. ANN 17:108
Ferguson, J.
Witch trials. CAPB:377
McGowan, E. D.
Stop the foes of Negro freedom. FON:860

McClafferty, John J. See Murrow, E. R., jt. auth.

McClellan, John L.
Responds to an introduction. PRS:161

McCloud, Bentley G.
Introduces C. J. Jackson. PRS:23

MacColl, Rene
Borrowed plumage. MDYG:174

McCorkle, Samuel
A sermon for the anniversary of American independence, July 24th, 1786. (Salisbury, N.C.). HAW:292

McCORMICK, ANNE O'HARE
Spencer, H. R.
Introducing Anne O'Hare McCormick. LYI:107

Macdonald, Sir John Alexander
On the treaty of Washington. BREWE 8:2891
Prerogative and public right. BREWE 8:2895

MacDonald, Peter
Exploring new energy frontiers (Albuquerque, New Mexico, February 20, 1975). MAES:165
Inaugural address, Window Rock, Navajo Nation, January 7, 1975. MAES:213
Statement before the Conference on Financing of Public Schools on Indian Reservations, April 3, 1975. MAES:105
Statement before the Indian sovereignty Conference of American Indians, Harvard, February 22, 1975. MAES:22
Statement of Chairman of Navajo Tribal Council, April 14, 1975. MAES:243
Statement of the implementation of P.L. 93-638 Indian Self-Determination and Education Assistance Act, Window Rock, Navajo Nation, April 3, 1975. MAES:189

McDuffie, George
Natural slavery of the Negro. ANN 6:191

McElwee, Robert
A plea for universal education in the South. (Nashville, Tenn., Jan. 23, 1883). FON:477

McGechan, R. O.
Legal arguments for adopting the Statute of Westminster, 1944 (Victoria Univ.). MACS:284 sel.

McGill, Ralph E.
Meaning of Lincoln today (centennial of Lincoln's speech at Cooper Institute). LINS:360

McGill, William J.
The public challenge and the campus response. (Berkeley, July 15, 1971). BA 1971-72:182
Requiem for Joe College. BA 1969-70:139
Requiem for the countercul-ture: problems of a new student generation (Columbia Univ., May 14, 1975). HOR:66
Science and the law (New York, Sept. 20, 1977). BA 1977-78:83
Simple justice and existential victims (Reno, Nev., Oct. 6, 1978). BA 1978-79:23

McGovern, George
Acceptance speech, Miami Beach, Florida, July 14, 1972. SIN:408
American politics: a personal view. BA 1972-73:22
Campaign speech, Washington, D.C., August 5, 1972. SIN:413
Ignorance curtain vs. the open door. BA 1966-67:48

McGowan, Carl
Eulogy on Adlai E. Stevenson. BA 1965-66:227

McGowan, Edward D.
Stop the foes of Negro freedom. (Detroit, April 30, 1953). FON:860

McGraw, Harold W.
Business's responsibility in an information society (Washington, Oct. 17, 1977). BA 1977-78:121

MACHINE AGE See Machinery

MACHINERY
Webster, D.
Technical progress and prosperity. ANN 6:266

McIntyre, Thomas J.
Keeping the Senate independent (Washington, March 1, 1978). BA 1977-78:44

Macios, Miguel Angel
Model studies of structural design and construction should be conducted prior to the building of structure rather than on the site studies made after the completion of the project. BAS:193 (outline only)

Mack, Enoch
Fourth of July oration, 1838 (Dover, New Hampshire). HAW:164

McKeag, Jana
Testimony of Jana McKeag, Education Director, National Congress of American Indians, July 19, 1975. MAES:249

McKeever, Porter
The United States and the United Nations (Los Angeles, May 19, 1972). BRYF:479

McKenna, J. and others (R. R. Day)
United States v. United States Steel Corporation et al: opinion for the court and dissenting opinion. ANN 14:258

McKenzie, John
Land for Settlements Bill, 1894 (New Zealand House of Representatives, July 20, 1894). MACS:205 sel.

McKinley, William
Alternatives in Cuba. Same as his First annual message
American patriotism (at dedication of Cuyahoga County Soldiers' and Sailors' monument in Cleveland). BREWE 8:2899
At the Pan-American Exposition. ANN 12:428
First annual message. ANN 12:161; STAT 2:1858
First inaugural address. USINAU:169; USINAUG:169
Fourth annual message. STAT 2:1971
Grant (at dedication of Grant monument in New York City). BREWE 8:2905
Last speech. Same as his At the Pan-American Exposition
Reciprocal trade agreements. Same as his At the Pan-American Exposition
Second annual message. STAT 2:1881
Second inaugural address. USINAU:178; USINAUG:178
Third annual message. STAT 2:1922
War message, April 11, 1898. ANN 12:173

McKINLEY, WILLIAM
Lawson, J.
The remedy for anarchy. FON:639
Roosevelt, T.
First annual message. ANN 12:433; STAT 2:2014

McKinney, Stanley M.
Soils--our basic natural resources --the key to man's survival. BREWW:187

Mackintosh, Sir James
Canada and the autonomy of British colonies. BREWE 8:2909
In behalf of free speech: on the trial of Jean Peltier accused of libeling Napoleon Bonaparte. BREWE 8:2919
Peltier and the French Revolution. Same as his In behalf of free speech: on the trial of Jean Peltier accused of libeling Napoleon Bonaparte

McKissick, Floyd B.
Speech at the National Conference on Black Power, July 21, 1967. BOSC:127; FON:1065
The student and the ghetto. (Coe College, Cedar Rapids, Iowa, May, 1969). OE:216
Why the Negro must rebel. Same as his Speech at the National Conference on Black Power, July 21, 1967

McLain, Harold O.
Presents David Seabury. LYI:98

McLaren, Moray <u>See</u> Sykes, C., jt. auth.

Macleod, John James Richard
The physiology of insulin and its source in the animal body (Nobel Lecture for 1923, May 26, 1925). NOLM 2:71

MACLEOD, JOHN JAMES RICHARD
Sjöquist, J.
Presentation [of the Nobel Prize for Physiology or Medicine for 1923 to Frederick Grant Banting and John James Richard Macleod, 1925]. NOLM 2:45

McMillan, Edwin Mattison
The transuranium elements: early history (Nobel Lecture, Dec. 12, 1951). NOLC 3:314

McMILLAN, EDWIN MATTISON
Westgren, A.
Presentation [of the Nobel Prize for Chemistry to Edwin Mattison McMillan and Glenn Theodore Seaborg, Dec. 12, 1951]. NOLC 3:309

Macmillan, Harold
Tribute to President Kennedy. ALA:135
"The wind of change." (Cape Town, Feb. 3, 1960). MCB:75

McNally, Joseph
"Terrible beauty is born" (golden jubilee of St. Joseph's Novitiate and silver jubilee of Rev. Brother Michael in Penang). MONS:334

McNAMARA, JOHN JOSEPH
Darrow, C.
To the jury; self-defense. GRG:31

McNamara, Robert S.
Address before the American Society of Newspaper Editors. BA 1966-67:160
Military hardware, economic assistance, and civic action. ANN 18:356
Nuclear strategy. ANN 18:527
Searching for new solutions to poverty (Boston, Jan. 14, 1977). BA 1976-77:91

McNARY-HAUGEN BILL
Coolidge, C.
Vetoing the farmer: nonplanning as a way of life. ANN 14:568

MACROMOLECULES
Natta, G.
From the stereospecific polymerization to the asymmetric autocatalytic synthesis of macromolecules. NOLC 4:27
Staudinger, H.
Macromolecular chemistry. NOLC 3:397

McWhirter, A. J.
Appeal to European immigrants to come to the South. ANN 10:587

Madison, James
Agriculture and conservation. ANN 4:503
Bill of Rights proposed. ANN 3:354
Civil and religious functions of government. ANN 4:287
Eighth annual message. STAT 1:140
Fifth annual message. STAT 1:122
First annual message. STAT 1:102
First inaugural address. USINAU:23; USINAUG:23
Fourth annual message. STAT 1:115
On the commerce clause. ANN 4:462
Second annual message. STAT 1:105
Second inaugural address. USINAU:26; USINAUG:26
Seventh annual message. STAT 1:133
Sixth annual message. STAT 1:129
State sovereignty and federal supremacy (Richmond, Va., June 6, 1788). BREWE 8:2926; HURH:40
Third annual message. STAT 1:111
War message. ANN 4:314
"Would it be possible for government to have credit, without having the power of raising money?" Same as His State sovereignty and federal supremacy

---- See also Laurance, J., jt. auth.

Madrid, Steve
I am proud to be a part of it. BREWW:153

Maestas, John R.
The subtle use of humor by the great Indian chief Osceola. MAES:307
With a touch of the master's hand. MAES:130

MAETERLINCK, MAURICE
Wauters, C. C. M. A.
Acceptance [of the Nobel Prize for Literature for Maurice Maeterlinck, 1911]. NOL:114
Wirsén, C. D. af
Presentation [of the Nobel Prize for Literature to Maurice Polydore Marie Bernhard Maeterlinck, 1911]. NOB 12:139; NOL:107

MAGNESIUM
Grignard, V.
The use of organomagnesium compounds in preparative organic chemistry. NOLC 1:234

MAGNETISM
Néel, L.
Magnetism and the local molecular field. NOLPH 4:318

MALACAÑAN
Quirino, E.
Commemorating a national event. CURM:239

MALARIA
Ross, Sir R.
Researches on malaria. NOLM 1:25

MALAYA
Muhammad Ghazali bin Shafie
Loyalty to the nation (Malaya). MONS:218
Sambanthan, V. T.
Basic objectives of M.I.C. (Malayan Indian Congress). MONS:135

MALAYA, FEDERATION OF
Muhammad Ghazali bin Shafie
Independent Malaya--our rights and obligations. MONS:211

MALAYAN LANGUAGE
Abdul Rahman, T.
Basis of our unity. MONS:41
English language must continue. MONS:7

MALAYSIA
Abdul Rahman, T.
Big challenges ahead. MONS:25
Concept of Malaysia becomes a reality. MONS:12
Fight for Merdeka. MONS:1
Soul of our nation. MONS:36
Goh Keng Swee
Some delusions of the decade of development. MONS:385
Johari, M. K.
A national chamber needed. MONSA:103
Lee, H. H. S.
Great institution (Central Bank of Malaya). MONS:164
Lim, P. G.
Women's role in national development. MONS:339
Manickavasagam, V.
Era of opportunity. MONS:162
Muhammad Ghazali bin Shafie
Malaysia and the Asian perspective. MONS:222
Power politics and nation building (Malaysia). MONS:232
Rahman, Dr. I. bin A.
Unexpected ally after independence. MONS:99
Razak, T. A.
Alliance policy for unity. MONS:47
Democracy and development in Malaysia. MONS:80
Putting life into development plans. MONS:86
UMNO's twentieth milestone (20th anniversary of United Malay National Organization). MONS:53
Vital issues must be resolved if we are to survive. MONSA:1
Senu bin Abdul Rahman
Let our voice be heard (New Year message). MONS:160

Pledge to newsmen. MONS:156
Stephens, D. A.
Spirit of Merdeka. MONS:322
Tan Siew Sin
Meeting place of cultures. MONS:115
Mission of the M.C.A. MONS:117

---- ATTORNEY-GENERAL
Abdul Kadir bin Yusof
The role of attorney-general, Malaysia. MONSA:354

---- COMMERCE
Tan Siew Sin
Commonwealth trade: an explosive situation. MONS:127

---- CONSTITUTION
Seenivasagam, D. R.
Frankenstein in the making. MONS:199
Tan Siew Sin
Our constitution: a fair compromise. MONS:109

---- DEFENSES
Razak, T. A.
The significance of Five-Power Defence Agreement. MONSA:29

---- DEPT. OF NATIONAL UNITY
Muhammad Ghazali bin Shafie
Guide-lines and strategies for achieving national unity. MONSA:124 selections

---- ECONOMIC CONDITIONS
Lim Swee Aun
Doubting Thomases were wrong (opening of Chemical Company of Malaysian factory). MONS:153

---- ECONOMIC POLICY
Razak, T. A.
The development strategy for success of second Malaysian plan. MONSA:4
A new strategy to provide more jobs. MONSA:36
Tan Siew Sin
The need for dedicated service by civil servants. MONSA:89 selections

---- EDUCATION See Education - Malaysia; University of Malaya

---- FOREIGN RELATIONS
Abdul Rahman, T.
Break with Singapore. MONS:19
Muhammad Ghazali bin Shafie
Elements of Malaysian foreign policy. MONSA:119
Rahman, Dr. I. bin A.
New era of regional cooperation. MONS:103
Ramani, R.
Malaysia's stand in Kashmir dispute. MONS:240
Razak, T. A.
And then came peace (Peace Agreement between Malaysia and Indonesia). MONS:94
Bridge of communication (on departure to America). MONS:59
Most unfortunate of conflicts. MONS:69
Suffian bin Hashim
The danger of living our lives in isolation. MONSA:137
Ungku Omar Ahmad
Two countries in one. MONS:331

---- OFFICIALS AND EMPLOYEES
Suffian bin Hashim
Important factors for ensuring efficient, loyal public service. MONSA:132

---- POLITICS AND GOVERNMENT
Abdul Kadir bin Yusof
We cannot afford to fail this time to meet aspirations of people. MONSA:361
Abdul Rahman, T.
Face the future with faith and without fear. MONSA:55
Hamzah bin Sendut
Trends and problems of government (Malaysia). MONS:253
Muhammad Ghazali bin Shafie
Let us not mimic the democracy of Westminster 1957. MONSA:131 selections
Razak, T. A.
The beginning of a new realism in Malaysia: the period ahead is challenging. MONSA:24

A call to UMNO leaders: time for slogan chanting is over. MONSA:20
The significance of Five-Power Defence Agreement. MONSA:29
We will uphold concepts of parliamentary democracy. MONSA:41 selections
Tan Chee Khoon
Monstrous piece of legislation (Internal Security Act--Malaysia). MONS:190

---- RELIGION
Tuan Haji Ali bin Munawar
Religion in Malay society. MONS:308

MALAYSIAN CHINESE ASSOCIATION
Tan Siew Sin
Malays and Chinese must co-exist. MONSA:85
The role of M.C.A. and the loyalty of Malaysian Chinese. MONSA:78

MALCOLM X See Little, Malcolm

Malcolm, George A.
Judge Andres Borromeo did his duty! CURM:183

Malone, George W. and others (F. A. Seaton)
Statehood for Hawaii. ANN 17:522

Malott, Deane W.
Responds to introduction. PRS:117

MAN
Aelred, Saint
On manliness. BREWE 1:113
Burton, S.
You (male) should wear long hair. BAS:200 (outline only)
Channing, W. E.
Man above the state. BREWE 5:1032
Hughes, T.
Highest manhood. BREWE 7:2539
Welcome to husbands at Ladies Civic Club. HNWM:45

MANAGEMENT See Business

MANCHESTER, WILLIAM
Crooks, J.
Defense of "The death of a President." REIR:182

Mandela, Nelson Rolihlahla
Indictment of South Africa. EMP:94

Manickavasagam, V.
Era of opportunity. MONS:162
ILO represents the social conscience of the world (Geneva, June, 1970). MONSA:106 selections

Manley, Albert E.
Charge to the graduates (Spelman College, May 18, 1975). HOR:6

Mann, Horace
The necessity of education in a Republican government. (ca. 1838). HOW:148
Slavery in the territories. ANN 8:7

Mann, Thomas
Acceptance [of the Nobel Prize for Literature, 1929]. NOB 12:225; NOL:263

MANN, THOMAS
Böök, F.
Presentation [of the Nobel Prize for Literature to Thomas Mann, 1929]. NOB 12:221; NOL:260

Manning, Henry Edward, Cardinal
Rome the eternal. BREWE 8:2934

Mannix, Daniel
Case against conscription. MCA:134

Mansfield, Michael J.
Assessment in Vietnam. BA 1967-68:49
Eulogy for John F. Kennedy. ANN 18:202
Pacific perspective. BA 1968-69:98

Mansfield, William Murray, 1st Earl of
In the case of John Wilkes. BREWE 8:2943
In the case of the Dean of St. Asaph. BREWE 8:2945
Reply to the Earl of Chatham against Parliamentary exemption from arrest for debt. BREWE 8:2947

MANUFACTURERS AND MANUFACTURING
Clay, H.
Manufacturing and a protective tariff. ANN 4:612
Coxe, T.
Prospects for American manufacturing. ANN 3:196
Hamilton, A.
Report on manufactures. BOORA 1:178

MAORIS
Tirikatene, E.
Maiden speech in Parliament. MACS:179

MARA INSTITUTE OF TECHNOLOGY
Suffian bin Hashim
Only Malays can initiate the institutional changes. MONSA:140

Marbury, William L.
Of movers and immobilists. BA 1965-66:77

MARCH ON WASHINGTON MOVEMENT
Randolph, A. P.
A call for mass action. FON:822

Marconi, Guglielmo
Wireless telegraphic communication (Nobel Lecture, Dec. 11, 1909). NOLPH 1:196

MARCONI, GUGLIELMO
Hildebrand, H.
Presentation [of the Nobel Prize for Physics to Guglielmo Marconi and Carl Ferdinand Braun, Dec. 11, 1909]. NOLPH 1:193

Marcus, Stanley
Can free enterprise survive success? (Omaha, Nov. 18, 1975). BA 1975-76:152

MARIE ANTOINETTE, CONSORT OF LOUIS XVI, KING OF FRANCE
Burke, E.
Age of chivalry. BREWE 2:817

MARRIAGE
Coleridge, J. D. C.
Sacredness of matrimony. BREWE 4:1355
Marriage ceremony. BNH:69

Marshall, Arthur
I first saw the light of day. MDYG:231

Marshall, David Saul
Duty of citizens. MONS:448
Fundamental and minority rights. MONS:450
History of Singapore's struggle for nationhood, 1945-1959 (Singapore, July 12, 1969). MONSA:313
What is academic freedom? MONS:453
Why abolish the jury trial? Warnings of danger ahead (Singapore, Dec. 16, 1969). MONSA:324

Marshall, George C.
Address at Harvard University (June 5, 1947). ANN 16:438; BOORA 2:884; GRG:82; HURH:283
Essentials of peace (Nobel Lecture, Dec. 11, 1953). NOLP 3:76
Marshall Plan. Same as his Address at Harvard University
"Our policy is directed not against any country or doctrine but against hunger, poverty, desperation and chaos." Same as his Address at Harvard University

MARSHALL, GEORGE C.
Hambro, C. J.
Presentation of the Nobel Prize for Peace to George Catlett Marshall, Dec. 10, 1953.

NOLP 3:65
Truman, H. S.
Presents George C. Marshall. LYI:41

Marshall, J. R.
NAFTA, 1965 (New Zealand House of Representatives, Aug. 17, 1965). MACS:448 sel.

Marshall, John
Address on constitutionality of Alien and Sedition Laws. (Dec., 1798). FRIP:99
Cherokee Nation v. State of Georgia: opinion for the Supreme Court. ANN 5:427
Cohens v. Virginia, 1821: opinion for the Supreme Court. ANN 5:1
Dartmouth College v. Woodward. Same as his Trustees of Dartmouth College v. Woodward: opinion for the Supreme Court
Gibbons v. Ogden, 1824: opinion for the Supreme Court. ANN 5:128
Justice and the Federal Constitution (Virginia Convention on Ratification of the Constitution, June 10, 1788). BREWE 8:2950; FRIP:76
McCulloch v. Maryland: opinion for the Supreme Court. ANN 4:530; BOORA 1:241
Marbury v. Madison: opinion for the Supreme Court. ANN 4:165
Opposing Patrick Henry. Same as his Justice and the Federal Constitution
Speech in Virginia Convention on Ratification of the Constitution, June 10, 1788. Same as his Justice and the Federal Constitution
Speech in Virginia Convention on Ratification of the Constitution, June 20, 1788. FRIP:90
Trustees of Dartmouth College v. Woodward: opinion for the Supreme Court. ANN 4:522

MARSHALL, JOHN
Frankfurter, F.
John Marshall and the judicial function, September 22, 1955. FRIP:353
Holmes, O. W., Jr.
John Marshall. FRIP:257
Vander Jagt, G.
John Marshall. SCHW:201

MARSHALL, NORMAN S.
Langlie, A. B.
Presents Norman S. Marshall. LYI:155

Marshall, Thomas R.
National power and the American peace policy (on public land sales, 1841). BREWE 8:2964

Marshall, Thurgood
In praise of the sit-in strikes. (Charlotte, N.C., March 20, 1960). FON:930
The legal attack to secure civil rights. (NAACP Wartime Conf., July 13, 1944). OE:123
Segregation and desegregation. (New Orleans-Dillard Univ., Spring, 1954). FON:866

MARSHALL ISLANDS
Anjain, J.
Speech before the Senate Committee on Energy and Natural Resources, June 16, 1977. JAM:12

MARSHALL PLAN See Reconstruction, 1939-1951

Martin, Alfonso
Responds to an introduction. PRS:139

Martin, Archer John Porter
The development of partition chromatography (Nobel Lecture, Dec. 12, 1952). NOLC 3:359

MARTIN, ARCHER JOHN PORTER
Tiselius, A. W. K.
Presentation [of the Nobel Prize for Chemistry to Archer John Porter Martin and Richard Laurence Millington Synge, Dec. 12, 1952]. NOLC 3:355

Martin, Charles
Presents McGeorge Bundy. LYI:88

Martin, David
Trouble in the university. MDYG:121

Martin, Douglas
A case for optimism. EHN:124; MOP:154; MOPR:130

Martin, Joseph W.
Introducing Speaker Sam Rayburn. LYI:195

Martin, Luther
Is the government federal or national? BREWE 8:2970
People versus the states. Same as his Portion of the report of the proceedings of the General Convention held at Philadelphia in 1787
Portion of the report of the proceedings of the General Convention held at Philadelphia in 1787. ANN 3:166

Martin, Thomas W.
Presents Charles F. Kettering. LYI:181

Marvin, Richard
Man's other society. MOP:377

MARX, GROUCHO
Jessel, G.
Presents Groucho Marx. LYI:32

Mason, George
Natural propensity of rulers to oppress. BREWE 8:2976

---- and others (P. Henry and E. Pendelton)
Debates in the Virginia Ratifying Convention. ANN 3:278

Mason, J. M.
Speech of J. M. Mason, at Richmond, Va., June 8, 1861. ECH:166

Mason, John, Jr.
Oration delivered on the 4th of July, 1818 at Williamsburg, Virginia. HAW:300

Mason, William Clarke
Presents George Wharton Pepper. LYI:129

MASS MEDIA
Gallup, G.
Mass information or mass entertainment. ANN 17:215
Goodman, J. B.
Community and communications. MOP:381
Hausman, L.
Older Americans: a natural resource. LINRST:36

---- See also Communication

MASS SPECTROMETRY
Aston, F. W.
Mass spectra and isotopes. NOLC 2:7

MASSACHUSETTS
Hoar, G. F.
Great men of Massachusetts. BREWE 7:2516
Kennedy, J. F.
History will be our judge. LINS:371

---- SUPREME COURT
Sumner, C.
Segregation and the common school (Sarah C. Roberts v. City of Boston case, 1849). ANN 7:507

Massey, William Ferguson
Freehold tenure (New Zealand House of Representatives, Nov. 16, 1909). MACS:216 sel.
The Meat Board, 1922 (Wellington, Jan. 10, 1922). MACS:301

---- and others (H. E. Holland)
Repeal of income tax on farmers, 1923 (New Zealand House of Representatives, Aug. 14, 1923). MACS:304

Massillon, Jean Baptiste
Curse of a malignant tongue. BREWE 8:2980

MATHEMATICS
Eliezer, C. J.
Mathematics the queen of the arts. MONS:265

Mather, Cotton
At the sound of the trumpet. BREWE 8:2986

"Bostonian Evenezer."
POC:395

Mather, Increase
Discourse concerning the uncertainty of the times of men. POC:377
Speech at the Boston Town Meeting. POC:172

Mathias, Charles M.
The First Amendment: freedom and responsibility (Bloomington, Minn., Oct. 26, 1977). BA 1977-78:134
Privacy on the ropes (Univ. of Minnesota, Oct. 20, 1978). BA 1978-79:70
Truth in government. (Washington, D.C., April 17, 1973). BA 1972-73:60

Mathias, Tim
Is agriculture on its way out? BREWW:64

MATTER
Perrin, J. B.
Discontinuous structure of matter. NOLPH 2:138

MATTER, KINETIC THEORY OF
Hinshelwood, Sir C. N.
Chemical kinetics in the past few decades. NOLC 3:474

Mauriac, François
Acceptance [of the Nobel Prize for Literature, 1952]. NOB 13:7; NOL:481

MAURIAC, FRANÇOIS
Österling, A.
Presentation [of the Nobel Prize for Literature to François Mauriac, 1952]. NOB 13:3; NOL:477

Maxton, James See Baldwin, S. B., jt. auth.

May, Catherine
The American farmer. (American Agricultural Editors Association, June 23, 1970). LINRS:117

May, Derwent
Djakarta style. MDYG:168

May, Samuel J.
Enfranchisement of women. ANN 7:342

Mayer, Maria Goeppert
The shell model (Nobel Lecture, Dec. 12, 1963). NOLPH 4:18

MAYER, MARIA GOEPPERT
Waller, I.
Presentation [of the Nobel Prize for Physics to Eugene P. Wigner, Maria Goeppert Mayer and J. Hans D. Jensen, Dec. 12, 1963]. NOLPH 4:3

Mayhew, Jonathan
Discourse on the anniversary of the death of Charles I. ANN 1:481; POC:508
On unlimited submission to rulers. Same as his Discourse on the anniversary of the death of Charles I
Unlimited submission and non-resistance to the Higher Powers. Same as his Discourse on the Anniversary of the death of Charles I

Maynard, Horace See Butler, B. F., jt. auth.

Mays, Benjamin E.
Eulogy on Dr. Martin Luther King, Jr. (Morehouse College, Atlanta, April 9, 1968). BA 1967-68:161; BAAGB:399; SMHV:296

MAYSVILLE ROAD BILL, 1830
Jackson, A.
Veto of Maysville Road Bill. ANN 5:374

Mazzini, Giuseppe
To the young men of Italy. BREWE 8:2992

Mead, Margaret
The planetary crisis and the challenge to scientists. (New York, Dec. 6, 1973). BA 1973-74:97

Meade, Edwin R.
Chinese immigration to the United States. ANN 10:386

Meagher, Thomas Francis
Withering influence of provincial subjection. BREWE 8:2999

Meany, George
Responds to an introduction. PRS:156

MEAT INDUSTRY AND TRADE - NEW ZEALAND
Massey, W. F.
The Meat Board, 1922. MACS:301 sel.

MEDALS See Presentation speeches - Medals

Medawar, Peter Brian
Immunological tolerance (Nobel Lecture, Dec. 12, 1960). NOLM 3:704

MEDAWAR, PETER BRIAN
Gard, S.
Presentation [of the Nobel Prize for Physiology or Medicine to Sir Frank Macfarlane Burnet and Peter Brian Medawar, Dec. 12, 1960]. NOLM 3:685

MEDICAL CARE
Blue Spruce, G.
Needed: Indian health professionals. MAES:171

MEDICINE
Farber, S. M.
Why national concern for bio-medical communication? BA 1966-67:118
Watson, T. J., Jr.
Medical care. BA 1970-71:115; BAPR:359; BAPRR:266

---- See also Mental health; Physicians

Meek, Alexander Beaufort
Oration (Tuscaloosa, July 4, 1833). HAW:307

Melanchthon, Philip
Safety of the virtuous. BREWE 8:3007

Meloney, Mrs. William Brown
Introducing Dorothy Thompson. LYI:112
Presents Dorothy Thompson. Same as her Introducing Dorothy Thompson

MEMBERSHIP DRIVES See Club speeches

MEMORIAL DAY
Coolidge, C.
Destiny of America. ANN 14:409

MEMORIAL SPEECHES
Franklin, J. H.
Martin Luther King and American traditions. BA 1968-69:45
Gallagher, B. G.
Memorial convocation address (On Martin Luther King, Jr.). BA 1967-68:169
Hugo, V. M.
On the centennial of Voltaire's death. BREWE 7:2550
Mather, I.
Discourse concerning the uncertainty of the times of men. POC:377
Palmerston, H. J. T.
On the death of Cobden. BREWE 8:3131
Stevenson, A. E.
Address at the memorial service for Sir Winston Churchill. LINR:305; LINRS:307; LINRST:373
Thatcher, P.
Boston Massacre oration, March 5, 1776. POC:272

---- See also Commemorative addresses; Eulogies; Tributes

Menefee, Richard Hickman, 1809-1841
Speech (House of Representatives, Jan. 8, 1838). BLY:84

Menninger, Karl
Healthier than healthy. LINR:54

Menninger, William C.
Responds to an introduction. PRS:135

MENTAL DEFICIENCY
Weisensel, K.
David: and a whole lot of other neat people. LINRST:71

MENTAL HEALTH
Menninger, K.
Healthier than healthy. LINR:54

Menzies, Robert Gordon
Eulogy of Churchill. MCA:151
Greece and the Anzac spirit. MCA:138
On the nationalisation of the Suez Canal. MCA:144

MERCY
Bede
Meeting of mercy and justice. BREWE 1:340
Wycliffe, J.
Mercy to damned men in Hell. BREWE 10:3922

Merriam, John Campbell
Presents Ray Lyman Wilbur. LYI:82

MESONS
Yukawa, H.
Meson theory in its developments. NOLPH 3:128

Metchnikoff, Elie
On the present state of the question of immunity in infectious diseases (Nobel Lecture, Dec. 11, 1908). NOLM 1:281

METCHNIKOFF, ELIE
Mörner, K. A. H.
Presentation [of the Nobel Prize for Physiology or Medicine to Elie Metchnikoff and Paul Ehrlich, Dec. 11, 1908]. NOLM 1:277

MEXICANS IN THE UNITED STATES
Ponce, F. V.
La causa. LINRS:66; LINRST:68
Rodriguez, A. M.
This is our quest: to fight for the right. BA 1968-69:129

MEXICO
Diaz, P.
Mexican progress. BREWE 5:1832

Meyer, Steve
What leadership means to me. BREWW:171

Meyerhof, Otto Fritz
Energy conversions in muscle (Nobel Lecture for 1922, Dec. 12, 1923). NOLM 2:27

MEYERHOF, OTTO FRITZ
Johansson, J. E.
Presentation [of the Nobel Prize for Physiology or Medicine for 1922 to Archibald Vivian Hill and Otto Fritz Meyerhof, Dec. 12, 1923]. NOLM 2:3

Meyerson, Martin
The ivory tower of Babel (Annapolis, October 16, 1971). HOR:99

Michelson, Albert Abraham
Recent advances in spectroscopy (Nobel Lecture, Dec. 12, 1907). NOLPH 1:166

MICHELSON, ALBERT ABRAHAM
Hasselberg, K. B.
Presentation [of the Nobel Prize for Physics to Albert Abraham Michelson, Dec. 12, 1907]. NOLPH 1:159

Middendorf, J. William
World sea power: United States vs. USSR. (San Francisco, Dec. 3, 1974). LINRST:234

MIGRATION, INTERNAL
DuBois, W. E. B.
The great migration north. FON:721
Greener, R. T.
Emigration of colored citizens from the southern states. FON:466

Milburn, John G.
Presents James R. Day. LYI:90

MILES, NELSON A.
Depew, C. M.

Military spirit in America. BREWE 5:1785

Milgrom, Jacob
He cannot be replaced. WALE:132

MILITARY ACADEMY
Washington, G.
Eighth annual message. ANN 3:604; STAT 1:31

---- See also West Point

MILITARY COMMISSIONS, ACCEPTANCE OF See Acceptance speeches - Military commissions

MILITARY SERVICE, COMPULSORY See Conscription

MILITARY TRAINING See United States - Army

Mill, John Stuart
Representation of the people. (H. of Commons, April 13, 1866). MCB:154
A tribute to William Lloyd Garrison. REID:395 selections

Miller, George F.
They are all heroes. (Brooklyn, May 14, 1918). FON:719

Miller, Hugh
Pledge science gives to hope. BREWE 8:3013

Miller, Joyce
Why ice floats. MOP:20; MOPR:59

Miller, Kelly
The Brownsville affair. (American Negro Academy, 1907). FON:654

Miller, Samuel F. and others (S. J. Field)
Slaughter house cases, 1875: opinion for the court and dissenting opinion. ANN 10:302

Miller, Thomas E.
A plea against the disfranchisement of the Negro. (South Carolina, Oct. 26, 1895). FON:582

Millikan, Robert Andrews
The electron and the light-quant from the experimental point of view (Nobel Lecture for 1923, May 23, 1924). NOLPH 2:54

MILLIKAN, ROBERT ANDREWS
Gullstrand, A.
Presentation [of the Nobel Prize for Physics for 1923 to Robert Andrews Millikan, May 23, 1924]. NOLPH 2:51

Mills, Billy
New Indian, new commitment, February, 1974. MAES:402

Milton, John
For the liberty of unlicensed printing. BREWE 8:3017

MIND See Intellect; Thought and thinking

Minda, Albert G.
He died climbing. WALE:134
Vision that looks beyond. WALE:137

MINDANAO
Alunan, R. R.
Mindanao, the land of promise. CURM:108

MINES AND MINERAL RESOURCES - PHILIPPINE ISLANDS
Uewaki, T.
Discovery of hidden mineral veins with the aid of plants and animals, etc. CURM:292

MINISTERIAL RESPONSIBILITY - NEW ZEALAND
Wakefield, E. G.
The demand for responsible government. MACS:86 sel.

MINISTERS See Religion

Mink, Patsy Takemoto
Seeking a link with the past. (Los Angeles, Nov. 6, 1971). BA 1971-72:59

Minot, George Richards
The development of liver therapy in pernicious anemia (Nobel Lecture, Dec. 12, 1934). NOLM 2:357

MINOT, GEORGE RICHARDS
Holmgren, I.
Presentation [of the Nobel Prize for Physiology or Medicine to George Hoyt Whipple, George Richards Minot, and William Parry Murphy, Dec. 12, 1934]. NOLM 2:335

Minow, Newton N.
Television: the vast wasteland. Same as his Television and the public interest
Television and the public interest. ANN 18:12; MDV:248
Vast wasteland. Same as his Television and the public interest

Mirabeau, Honoré Gabriel Riqueti, Comte de
Against the charge of treason. BREWE 8:3039
Against the establishment of religion. BREWE 8:3034
Announcing the death of Franklin. BREWE 8:3035
Defying the French aristocracy. BREWE 8:3033
His defense of himself. Same as his Against the charge of treason
Justifying revolution. BREWE 8:3038
On Necker's project--"And yet you deliberate." BREWE 8:3024
Reason immutable and sovereign. BREWE 8:3036

MIRACLES
Lacordaire, J. B. H.
Rationalism and miracles. BREWE 7:2695

MISSIONS AND MISSIONARIES
Girls' auxiliary (or similar girls' missionary group). HNWN:24
Introductions for mission society leaders (4 examples). BNH:35
McNally, J.
"Terrible beauty is born" (golden jubilee of St. Joseph's Novitiate and silver jubilee of Rev. Brother Michael in Penang). MONS:334
Red Jacket
Missionary effort. ANN 4:194; BREWE 7:2571; HURH:57
Welcome to missionary appointees (3 examples). HNWM:57
Welcome to parents and ladies of the Woman's Missionary Society on Education Day. HNWM:21
Welcome to returning missionary (3 examples). HNWM:55
Welcome to Royal Ambassadors (or similar Boys' Missionary group). HNWM:23

MISSOURI COMPROMISE See Slavery in the United States

MISTRAL, FREDERIC
Wirsén, C. D. af
Presentation [of the Nobel Prize for Literature to Frédéric Mistral and José de Echegaray y Eizaguirre, 1904]. HOL:23; NOB 13:119

Mistral, Gabriela
Acceptance [of the Nobel Prize for Literature, 1945]. NOB 14:170; NOL:408

MISTRAL, GABRIELA
Gullberg, H.
Presentation [of the Nobel Prize for Literature to Gabriela Mistral, 1945]. NOB 14:167; NOL:405

Mitchell, Don G.
Responds to an introduction. PRS:148

Mitchell, James P.
Responds to an introduction. PRS:143

Mitford, Nancy See Sykes, C., jt. auth.

Moe, Ragnvald
Presentation [of the Nobel Prize

for Peace to Elihu Root, 1912, Dec. 10, 1913]. NOLP 1:245
Presentation [of the Nobel Prize for Peace to Henri Marie La Fontaine, Dec. 10, 1913]. NOLP 1:269
Presentation [of the Nobel Prize for Peace to the International Committee of the Red Cross, Dec. 10, 1917]. NOLP 1:281

Mohamed Khir Johari See Johari, Mohammed Khir

MOISSAN, HENRI
Klason, P.
Presentation [of the Nobel Prize for Chemistry to Henri Moissan, 1906]. NOLC 1:91

MOLECULAR BEAMS
Stern, O.
The method of molecular rays. NOLPH 3:8

MOLECULES
Debye, P. J. W.
Methods to determine the electrical and geometrical structure of molecules. NOLC 2:383
Hodgkin, D. C.
The x-ray analysis of complicated molecules. NOLC 4:71

Momaday, N. Scott
Oral tradition of the American Indian (Brigham Young University, 1975). MAES:294

MOMMSEN, CHRISTIAN MATTHIAS THEODOR
Wirsén, C. D. af
Presentation [of the Nobel Prize for Literature to Christian Matthias Theodor Mommsen, 1902]. NOL:7; NOB 13:235

MONARCHY
Elizabeth I
Queen and the royal succession. BRYH:69
Sheridan, R. B.
Example of kings. BREWE 9:3440

Mondale, Walter F.
Strengthening Sino-American relations (Peking University, August 27, 1979). BA 1979-80:28
A time to celebrate life (Washington, Jan. 15, 1978). BA 1977-78:205

Moneta, Ernesto Teodoro
Peace and law in the Italian tradition (Nobel Lecture, 1907, Aug. 25, 1909). NOLP 1:114

MONETA, ERNESTO TEODORO
Løvland, J. G.
Presentation [of the Nobel Prize for Peace to Ernesto Teodoro Moneta, Dec. 10, 1907]. NOLP 1:113

MONETARY POLICY - SINGAPORE
Goh Keng Swee
How Singapore's monetary system now works. MONSA:282

MONEY
Church, F.
The yen to make a mark with the dollar. BA 1978-79:168
Crawford, W. H.
Issue and control of money under the Constitution. BREWE 4:1462
Morgenthau, H., Jr.
Roosevelt monetary program. BAD:23
Peel, R.
Bank charter--the currency. STRM:213
Ruskin, J.
Iscariot in modern England. BREWE 9:3354
Wesley, J.
Use of money. BRYH:191

---- See also Banks and banking; Credit; Silver; Wealth

MONIZ, EGAS
Olivecrona, H.
Presentation [of the Nobel Prize for Physiology or Medicine to Walter Rudolf Hess and Antonio Caetano De Abreu Freire Egas Moniz, Dec. 12, 1949]. NOLM 3:243

MONKEYS
Reynolds, V.

Chimpanzee worlds.
MDYG:259

Monod, Jacques
From enzymatic adaptation to allosteric transitions (Nobel Lecture, Dec. 11, 1965). NOLM 4:188

MONOD, JACQUES
Gard, S.
Presentation [of the Nobel Prize for Physiology or Medicine to François Jacob, André Lwoff, and Jacques Monod, Dec. 11, 1965]. NOLM 4:143

MONOPOLIES
Colepeper, J.
Against monopolies.
BREWE 4:1494
Fuller, M. W. and others
United States v. E. C. Knight Company, 1895; opinion for the Supreme Court and dissenting opinion.
ANN 12:23
Marshall, J.
Gibbons v. Ogden, 1824: opinion for the Supreme Court. ANN 5:128
Wilson, W.
Fear of monopoly.
ANN 13:356

Monroe, James
Eighth annual message.
STAT 1:214
Federal experiments in history.
BREWE 8:3041
Fifth annual message.
STAT 1:181
First annual message.
STAT 1:148
First inaugural address.
USINAU:29; USINAUG:29
Fourth annual message.
STAT 1:174
Monroe doctrine (Washington, Dec. 2, 1823). ANN 5:73; BOORA 1:256; HURH:59; STAT 1:202
Second annual message.
STAT 1:156
Second inaugural address.
USINAU:37; USINAUG:37
Seventh annual message.
Same as his Monroe Doctrine
Sixth annual message.
STAT 1:192
Third annual message.
STAT 1:165
"... we should consider any attempt on their part to extend their system to any portion of this hemisphere, as dangerous to our peace and safety." Same as his Monroe Doctrine

MONROE DOCTRINE
Monroe, J.
Monroe doctrine. ANN 5:73; BOORA 1:256; HURH:59; STAT 1:202
Polk, J. K.
First annual message.
ANN 7:301; STAT 1:634
Roosevelt, T.
Annual message, December 6, 1904. STAT 2:2105
Fifth annual message.
ANN 13:1; STAT 3:2144
Smith, G.
Liberty destroyed by national pride (Mexican Treaty and Monroe Doctrine).
BREWE 9:3459

Montalembert, Charles Forbes Rene de Tryon, Comte de
Deo et Caesari fidelis.
BREWE 8:3050
Devotion to freedom.
BREWE 8:3048
For freedom of education.
BREWE 8:3046

Montelius, O.
Presentation [of the Nobel Prize for Chemistry to Otto Wallach, Dec. 12, 1910]. NOLC 1:175
Presentation [of the Nobel Prize for Physics to Johannes Diderik Van der Waals, Dec. 12, 1910]. NOLPH 1:251

Montgomery, James
Modern English literature.
BREWE 8:3052

MONTGOMERY DECLARATION OF 1861
King, T. S.
The two declarations of independence: 1776 and 1861.
HAW:260

MONUMENTS See Dedication addresses - Monuments

Moody, Dwight Lyman
On Daniel and the value of character. BREWE 8:3057

Moore, Ely
Trade unions and the "mechanic" arts. ANN 6:17

MOORE, HENRY
Haydon, H.
Testimony of sculpture. MOP:384; MOPR:380

Moore, Paul
A biblical faith for a president (New York, Nov. 21, 1976). BA 1976-77:24

Moore, Sydenham
A Southern response to John Brown and black republicanism (1859). (Washington, Dec. 8, 1859). DAVF:146

Moorehead, J. R.
Plight of small business. ANN 13:322

Moos, Malcolm
Darkness over the Ivory Tower. BA 1968-69:55
Restoring the tidemarks of trust. (South Bend, Ind., May 20, 1973). BA 1973-74:148

MORAL RE-ARMAMENT
Abdul Rahman, T.
These truths to remember. MONSA:68

MORALS See Behavior; Ethics; Vietnamese War, 1957--Moral and religious aspects; War and morals

More, Sir Thomas
Speech when on trial for life. BREWE 8:3062

MORE, SIR THOMAS
Kenny, A.
Self out of season. MDYG:199

Morelli, Laurie
Vocational agriculture, the FFA, and our free enterprise system. BREWW:78

Morgan, Charles, Jr.
Time to speak. KEO:308
Who's to blame in Birmingham? Same as his Time to speak

Morgan, Edmund S.
What every Yale freshman should know. ARS:35

Morgan, Mike
Building a better rural community today for a better agriculture tomorrow. BREWW:198

Morgan, Thomas Hunt
The relation of genetics to physiology and medicine (Nobel Lecture for 1933, June 4, 1934). NOLM 2:313

MORGAN, THOMAS HUNT
Henschen, F.
Presentation [of the Nobel Prize for Physiology or Medicine for 1933 to Thomas Hunt Morgan, June 4, 1934]. NOLM 2:307

Morgenthau, Henry, Jr.
Roosevelt monetary program. BAD:23

MORLEY, CHRISTOPHER
Ford, G. S.
Presents Christopher Morley. LYI:55

Morley of Blackburn, John Morley, 1st Viscount
Golden art of truth-telling. BREWE 8:3068

---- See also Curzon of Kedleston, George, jt. auth.

Mörner, K. A. H.
Presentation [of the Nobel Prize for Chemistry to Eduard Buchner, Dec. 11, 1907]. NOLC 1:99
Presentation [of the Nobel Prize for Physiology or Medicine to Albrecht Kossel, Dec. 12, 1910]. NOLM 1:309

Presentation [of the Nobel Prize for Physiology or Medicine to Allvar Gullstrand, Dec. 11, 1911]. NOLM 1:411
Presentation [of the Nobel Prize for Physiology or Medicine to Camilio Golgi and Santiago Râmon Y Cajal, Dec. 12, 1906]. NOLM 1:185
Presentation [of the Nobel Prize for Physiology or Medicine to Elie Metchnikoff and Paul Ehrlich, Dec. 11, 1908]. NOLM 1:277
Presentation [of the Nobel Prize for Physiology or Medicine to Emil Adolf Von Behring, Dec. 12, 1901]. NOLM 1:3
Presentation [of the Nobel Prize for Physiology or Medicine to Emil Theodor Kocher, Dec. 11, 1909]. NOLM 1:327
Presentation [of the Nobel Prize for Physiology or Medicine to Ivan Petrovich Pavlov, Dec. 12, 1904]. NOLM 1:135
Presentation [of the Nobel Prize for Physiology or Medicine to Niels Ryberg Finsen, 1903]. NOLM 1:123
Presentation [of the Nobel Prize for Physiology or Medicine to Robert Koch, Dec. 12, 1905]. NOLM 1:163
Presentation [of the Nobel Prize for Physiology or Medicine to Sir Ronald Ross, Dec. 12, 1902]. NOLM 1:21

Morris, Charles S.
The Wilmington massacre. (Boston, Jan., 1899). FON:604

Morris, Gouverneur
"I charge you to protect his fame. It is all that he has left." Same as his Oration over Hamilton
Oration at the funeral of Alexander Hamilton. Same as his Oration over Hamilton
Oration over Hamilton (New York, July 14, 1804). BREWE 8:3075; HURH:54

Morris, William
Art, wealth, and riches. BRYH:422

Morrison, Howard C.
In the pursuit of excellence. BREWW:61

Morse, David A.
ILO and the social infrastructure of peace (Nobel Lecture, Dec. 11, 1969). NOLP 3:424

Morse, Doug
Lab farms in vocational agriculture. BREWW:144

Morse, Jedidiah
The present dangers and consequent duties of the citizens (1799). (Charlestown, Mass., April 25, 1799). DAVF:45

Morse, Wayne L.
Need for a bipartisan foreign policy. ANN 17:11
Rejoiner to Joseph Alsop's attack. BRR:72
Verbiage of defense and attack. BRR:71

Morton, Oliver Perry
Reasons for Negro suffrage. BREWE 8:3079

Morton, Perez
Oration at the reinterment of Warren. POC:320

Morton, Thurston B.
Responds to introduction. PRS:98

Mosley, Lady See Sykes, C., jt. auth.

Mossbauer, Rudolf Ludwig
Recoilless nuclear resonance absorption of gamma radiation (Nobel Lecture, Dec. 11, 1961). NOLPH 3:584

MOSSBAUER, RUDOLF LUDWIG
Waller, I.
Presentation [of the Nobel Prize for Physics to Robert Hofstadter and Rudolf Ludwig Mossbauer, Dec. 11, 1961]. NOLPH 3:555

Mote, Carl H.
The ruling oligarchy wants to engage in a foreign war (1941). (Washington, 1941). DAVF:255

MOTHERS
Introductions for mothers-in-law (4 examples). BNH:34
Jung, L.
Mother's immortality. WALE:96
Welcome to mothers on Children's Day. HNWM:7

MOTHERS AND DAUGHTERS
Welcome to daughters at Mother-Daughter banquet. HNWM:36
Welcome to mothers at Mother-Daughter banquet. HNWM:35

MOTHER'S DAY
Holy motherhood (welcome address on Mother's Day). HNWM:8
Love in search of a word (welcome address on Mother's Day). HNWM:6
Pictures of mother (welcome address on Mother's Day). HNWM:7
Welcome to mothers: Mother's Day, a day of remembrance. HNWM:5

MOTHER-IN-LAW See Mothers

Moton, Robert Russa
Some elements necessary to race development. (Tuskegee, May, 1912). FON:692

Mott, John Raleigh
The leadership demanded in this momentous time (Nobel Lecture, Dec. 13, 1946). NOLP 2:362

MOTT, JOHN RALEIGH
Ingebretsen, H. S.
Presentation [of the Nobel Prize for Peace to John Raleigh Mott, Dec. 10, 1946]. NOLP 2:354

Mount, Anson
The Playboy philosophy--pro. (Atlanta, March 16-18, 1970). LINRS:157; LINRST:181

MOVING PICTURES - CENSORSHIP
Murrow, E. R. and others.
Movies and censorship. ARS:127

Mowinckel, Johan Ludwig
Presentation [of the Nobel Prize for Peace to Arthur Henderson, Dec. 10, 1934]. NOLP 2:179
Presentation [of the Nobel Prize for Peace to Frank Billings Kellogg, 1929, Dec. 10, 1930]. NOPL 2:73
Presentation [of the Nobel Prize for Peace to Nathan Söderblom, Dec. 11, 1930]. NOLP 2:73

Moynihan, Daniel
The middle of the journey. (White House, Dec. 21, 1970). BA 1970-71:29
World wide amnesty for political prisoners (New York, Nov. 12, 1975). BA 1975-76:65

---- See also Hayakawa, S. I., jt. auth.

Muench, Alosius
Rural families and welfare. ANN 15:462

Muhammad, Elijah
We must have justice. (June 21, 1963). FON:969

Muhammad Ghazali bin Shafie
Elements of Malaysian foreign policy (March 23, 1969). MONSA:119
Guide-lines and strategies for achieving national unity (July 17, 1969). MONSA:124 selections
Independent Malaya--our rights and obligations. MONS:211
Let us not mimic the democracy of Westminster 1957 (March 5, 1971). MONSA:131 selections
Loyalty to the nation (Malaya). MONS:218
Malaysia and the Asian perspective. MONS:222
The most dramatic fact of international life (April 28, 1970). MONSA:130
Power politics and nation-building (Malaysia). MONS:232
Strategy for the future: role of youths in national development

(Kuala Lumpur, July 31, 1970). MONSA:129

Mulford, Samuel
Speech to the Assembly at New York. POC:174

Müller, Friedrich Max
Impassable barrier between brutes and man. BREWE 8:3086

Muller, Hermann Joseph
The production of mutations (Nobel Lecture, Dec. 12, 1946). NOLM 3:154

MULLER, HERMANN JOSEPH
Caspersson, T.
Presentation [of the Nobel Prize for Physiology or Medicine to Hermann Joseph Muller, Dec. 12, 1946]. NOLM 3:149

Müller, Paul Hermann
Dichloro-diphenyl-trichloroethane and newer insecticides (Nobel Lecture, Dec. 11, 1948). NOLM 3:227

MÜLLER, PAUL HERMANN
Fischer, G.
Presentation [of the Nobel Prize for Physiology or Medicine to Paul Hermann Müller, Dec. 11, 1948]. NOLM 3:227

Mulliken, Robert S.
Spectroscopy, molecular orbitals, and chemical bonding (Nobel Lecture, Dec. 12, 1966). NOLC 4:131

MULLIKEN, ROBERT S.
Fischer-Hjalmars, I.
Presentation [of the Nobel Prize for Chemistry to Robert S. Mulliken, Dec. 12, 1966]. NOLC 4:127

Mullins, James See Butler, B. J., jt. auth.

Mulroy, Thomas R.
Presents Ilka Chase. LYI:17

Mumford, Lewis
Human way out. MDV:13

Mundt, Karl E.
Responds to an introduction. PRS:109

MUNICH FOUR POWER AGREEMENT, 1938
Churchill, W. L. S.
On the Munich Agreement (October 5, 1938). BRYH:521

MUNICIPAL GOVERNMENT
Wilson, W.
Commission city government. ANN 13:269

MUNITIONS
Bismarck, O.
Plea for imperial armament. BREWE 2:456

Munoz-Marin, Luis
Future of Puerto Rico. ANN 16:312

MURDER
Hardin, B.
The Wilkinson and Murdaugh case. BLY:48

Murphy, Frank See Black, H. L., jt. auth.

Murphy, Howard D.
Introduces Dr. Norman Vincent Peale. PRS:103
Introduces Dr. Ralph W. Sockman. PRS:117
Introduces Lee Wulff. PRS:67
Introduces Senator Hubert H. Humphrey from Minnesota. PRS:40

Murphy, Patrick V.
What the police expect of the citizenry. (Washington, Dec. 7, 1970). BA 1970-71:122

Murphy, William Parry
Pernicious anemia (Nobel Lecture, Dec. 12, 1934). NOLM 2:369

MURPHY, WILLIAM PARRY
Holmgren, I.
Presentation [of the Nobel Prize

for Physiology or Medicine to George Hoyt Whipple, George Richards Minot, and William Parry Murphy, Dec. 12, 1934]. NOLM 2:335

Murray, Philip
Collective bargaining and industrial democracy. ANN 16:15

Murrow, Edward R.
Broadcaster talks to his colleagues. MDV:263

---- and others (D. Kerr, P. Preminger and J. J. McClafferty)
Movies and censorship. ARS:127

MUSCLE SHOALS BILL
Hoover, H. C.
Veto of the Muscle Shoals Bill. ANN 15:79

MUSCLES
Hill, A. V.
The mechanism of muscular contraction. NOLM 2:10
Meyerhof, O. F.
Energy conversions in muscle. NOLM 2:27

MUSCULAR DYSTROPHY
Bunting, J. E.
The pay is good. BAPR:364

MUSIC AND MUSICIANS
Bernstein, L.
American musical comedy. KEO:274
Dedication of a musical instrument. BNH:65
Introductions for singers and musicians (12 examples). BNH:22
Welcome to adult choir members. HNWM:31
Welcome to children's choir members. HNWM:31
Welcome to youth choir members. HNWM:32

---- See also Art and artists; Jazz music

Muskie, Edmund S.
The astronauts on the moon. (Jeffersonville, Indiana, July 25, 1969). BAAGB:409
Election eve address. (Television, Nov. 2, 1970). STOT:262
Environment: can man prosper and survive? BA 1969-70:98
Too many questions ... not enough answers (Washington, Feb. 13, 1979). BA 1978-79:112

MUSLIMS
Ibrahim, A. M.
Muslims must face modern challenges. MONS:441

MUTATION (BIOLOGY)
Muller, H. J.
The production of mutations. NOLM 3:154

Myers, Isaac
Finish the good work of uniting colored and white workingmen. (Philadelphia, August 18, 1869, National Labor Union-3rd National Convention). FON:367

Myers, Nancy Jeanne
Moppet manipulation. ARS:123

MYOGLOBIN
Kendrew, J. C.
Myoglobin and the structure of proteins. NOLC 3:676

Myrbäck, K.
Presentation [of the Nobel Prize for Chemistry to Luis F. Leloir, Dec. 11, 1970]. NOLC 4:335
Presentation [of the Nobel Prize for Chemistry to Melvin Calvin, Dec. 11, 1961]. NOLC 3:615

- N -

NAACP See National Association for the Advancement of Colored People

Nader, Ralph
Meet the press. (Washington, D.C., May 30, 1971). BA 1971-72:79

Nail, William A.
What did you say? (7th Indiana University Broadcasting Institute, Bloomington, Indiana, July 17, 1971). VER:272

Nair, C. Devan
Nation building and the jealous gods of the past (Singapore, Sept. 18, 1969). MONSA:342
Reflections on Rabindranath Tagore. MONS:190
The role of trade union research and documentation services. MONSA:334

Nansen, Fridtjof
The suffering people of Europe (Nobel Lecture, Dec. 19, 1922). NOLP 1:361
Speech at Award Ceremony [presenting the Nobel Prize for Peace to Joseph Austen Chamberlain and Charles Gates Dawes for 1925, Dec. 10, 1926]. NOLP 1:383
Speech at Award Ceremony [presenting Nobel Prize for Peace to Aristide Briand and Gustav Stresemann, Dec. 10, 1926]. NOLP 2:3

NANSEN, FRIDTJOF
Stang, F.
Presentation [of the Nobel Prize for Peace to Fridtjof Nansen, Dec. 10, 1922]. NOLP 1:353

NANSEN INTERNATIONAL OFFICE FOR REFUGEES
Hansson, M.
The Nansen International Office for Refugees (Nobel Lecture, Dec. 10, 1938). NOLP 2:268
Stang, F.
Presentation [of the Nobel Prize for Peace to the Nansen International Office for Refugees, Dec. 10, 1938]. NOLP 2:265

Narayanan, Palayil Pathazapulrayil
Role of trade unions in South-East Asia. MONS:295

Nash, Ogden
Responds to introduction. PRS:106

Nash, Walter
Collective security and the League of Nations (King's Theatre, Sept. 16, 1935). MACS:356 sel.

Nation, Carry A.
Spiritual authority for my Christian work. BLY:183 selections

NATIONAL ADVISORY COMMISSION ON CIVIL DISORDERS
Abernathy, R. D.
The Kerner report, promises and realities. FON:1145

NATIONAL AFRO-AMERICAN LEAGUE
Fortune, T. T.
It is time to call a halt. FON:556

NATIONAL ASSOCIATION FOR THE ADVANCEMENT OF COLORED PEOPLE
DuBois, W. E. B.
Address to the National Negro Convention. OE:88
Marshall, T.
The legal attack to secure civil rights. OE:123
Wilkins, R.
Keynote address to the NAACP annual convention, Los Angeles, July 5, 1966. AND:101; BOSC:89; OE:166

NATIONAL CHARACTERISTICS - AMERICAN
Depew, C. M.
Military spirit in America. BREWE 5:1785
Everett, E.
Moral forces which make American progress. BREWE 6:2112
Garfield, J. S.
Conflict of ideas in America. BREWE 6:2231
Ickes, H. L.
What constitutes an American? HURH:260
Lodge, H. C.
Our forefathers. HURH:141
Lowell, J. R.
Poetical and the practical in

America. BREWE 7:2808
Sinclair, G.
The Americans. REID:396 selections
Story, J.
Intellectual achievement in America. BREWE 9:3531

---- GERMAN
Challemel-Lacour, P. A.
Humboldt and the Teutonic intellect. BREWE 3:1018

NATIONAL COMMITTEE TO DEFEND NEGRO LEADERSHIP
McGowan, E. D.
Stop the foes of Negro freedom. FON:860

NATIONAL DEFENSES See North Atlantic Treaty Organization; World War, 1939-1945 - Civilian activities. See also Names of countries or hemispheres with subdivision Defenses, e.g. United States - Defenses

NATIONAL HEALTH SERVICE BILL
Bevan, A.
National Health Service Bill. STRM:445

NATIONAL LABOR RELATIONS BOARD See Labor laws and legislation

NATIONAL LABOR UNION
Myers, I.
Finish the good work of uniting colored and white workingmen. FON:367

NATIONAL LIBERTY PARTY
Taylor, G. E.
Revolution by the ballot. FON:647

NATIONAL NEGRO CONGRESS
Randolph, A. P.
The crisis of the Negro and the Constitution. FON:816
The task of the Negro people. FON:807

NATIONAL NEGRO LABOR COUNCIL
Hood, W. R.
Uncle Tom is dead! FON:843

NATIONAL PROGRESSIVES OF AMERICA
LaFollette, P. F.
Party of our time. BAD:120

NATIONAL RECOVERY ADMINISTRATION
Hughes, C. E.
Schechter Poultry Corporation v. United States, 1935; opinion for the Supreme Court. ANN 15:301; ROD:186
Roosevelt, F. D.
Fireside chat: AAA and NRA, July 24, 1933. ANN 15:210

NATIONAL STATE
Nair, C. D.
Nation building and the jealous gods of the past. MONSA:342

NATIONALISM
Hammarskjöld, D.
Values of nationalism and internationalism (Stanford University commencement address). HURS:206

---- See also Citizenship

---- ASIA
Rajaratnam, S.
Asia needs the spirit of Sisyphus to succeed. MONSA:303

---- UNITED STATES
Gardner, H. J.
New England nativism. ANN 8:484
Levin, L. C.
Native Americans and foreign-born. ANN 7:313
Schurz, C.
True Americanism. ANN 9:97

---- ---- See also National characteristics - American

NATO See North Atlantic Treaty Organization

Natta, Giulio
From the stereospecific polymerization to the asymmetric auto-

catalytic synthesis of macromolecules (Nobel Lecture, Dec. 12, 1963). NOLC 4:27

NATTA, GIULIO
Fredga, A.
Presentation [of the Nobel Prize for Chemistry to Karl Ziegler and Giulio Natta, Dec. 12, 1963]. NOLC 4:3

NATURAL GAS BILL
Eisenhower, D. D.
Veto of Natural Gas Bill. ANN 17:370

NATURAL PRODUCTS
Robinson, Sir R.
Some polycyclic natural products. NOLC 3:166
Woodward, R. B.
Recent advances in the chemistry of natural products. NOLC 4:100

NATURAL RESOURCES See Conservation of natural resources

NATURALISM
Eucken, R.
Naturalism or idealism? NOL:74

NATURALIZATION See Immigration and emigration

NATURE
Cyril, Saint
Infinite artifices of nature. BREWE 4:1594
Fénelon, F.
Nature as a revelation. BREWE 6:2142
Kidwell, C. S.
American Indian attitudes toward nature. MAES:277
Wigner, E. P.
Events, laws of nature, and invariance principles. NOLPH 4:6

NAVAHO INDIANS
MacDonald, P.
Inaugural address, Window Rock, Navajo Nation, January 7, 1975. MAES:213
Yazzie, E.
Navajo wisdom. MAES:261

---- EDUCATION
Atcitty, T. E.
The future is at hand. MAES:160
Platero, D.
Discussions of critical issues affecting Navajo education program and policies. MAES:149

---- OIL LEASES
MacDonald, P.
Exploring new energy frontiers. MAES:165

---- RELIGION AND MYTHOLOGY
Yazzie, E.
Navajo wisdom as found in Navajo oral history. MAES:263

NAVAJO COMMUNITY COLLEGE
Atcitty, T. E.
The future is at hand. MAES:160

Neal, Joanne
DDT: friend or foe? BREWW:183

NEAR EAST - 20TH CENTURY
Eagleton, T. F.
1977: year of opportunity in the Middle East? LINRST:124

Neebe, Oscar
Address at trial, Chicago, October 7-9, 1886. ACC:29; PAF:28

Néel, Louis
Magnetism and the local molecular field (Nobel Lecture, Dec. 11, 1970). NOLPH 4:318

NEEL, LOUIS
Gustafsson, T.
Presentation [of the Nobel Prize for Physics to Hannes Alfvén and Louis Néel, Dec. 11, 1970]. NOLPH 4:303

NEGRO LABOR COMMITTEE
Crosswaith, F. R.
The Negro labor committee. FON:857

NEGROES See Blacks

NEHRU, JAWAHARLAL
Stevenson, A. E.
Presents Pandit Jawaharlal Nehru. LYI:242

Neil, William C.
The triumph of equal school rights in Boston. (Boston, Dec. 17, 1855). FON:164

Nelson, Gaylord A.
Against the nomination of Gerald R. Ford. (Washington, D.C., Nov. 27, 1973). BA 1973-74:188

Nernst, Walther Hermann
Studies in chemical thermodynamics (Nobel Lecture for 1920, Dec. 12, 1921). NOLC 1:353

NERNST, WALTHER HERMANN
DeGeer, G.
Presentation [of the Nobel Prize for Chemistry to Walther Hermann Nernst, 1920, Dec. 12, 1921]. NOLC 1:349

NERVES
Dale, Sir H. H.
Some recent extensions of the chemical transmission of the effects of nerve impulses. NOLM 2:402
Hodgkin, A. L.
The ionic basis of nervous conduction. NOLM 4:32
Loewi, O.
The chemical transmission of nerve action. NOLM 2:416

Ness, Frederic W.
Freedom and the labyrinth (Millikin Univ., May 21, 1972). HOR:87

NEURAL TRANSMISSION
Katz, B.
On the quantal mechanism of neural transmitter release. NOLM 4:485
Von Euler, U.
Adrenergic neurotransmitter functions. NOLM 4:470

NEUROFIBRILS
Adrian, E. D.
The activity of the nerve fibres. NOLM 2:293
Erlanger, J.
Some observations on the responses of single nerve fibers. NOLM 3:50
Gasser, H. S.
Mammalian nerve fibers. NOLM 3:34

NEURONS
Golgi, C.
The neuron doctrine--theory and facts. NOLM 1:189
Ramon y Cajal, S.
The structure and connexions of neurons. NOLM 1:220

NEUROSPORA
Beadle, G. W.
Genes and chemical reactions in Neurospora. NOLM 3:587

NEUTRALITY See United States - Neutrality

NEUTRONS
Chadwick, J.
The neutron and its properties. NOLPH 2:339

NEW DEAL See Democratic Party; United States - Economic conditions

NEW ENGLAND
Clemens, S. L.
New England weather. HURH:128
Curtis, G. W.
Liberty under law. BAS:141 (outline only); LINS:249

NEW GUINEA
Higinbotham, G.
For the annexation of New Guinea. MCA:43

NEW LEFT See Right and Left (political science)

NEW YEAR
New Year prayer. BNH:74
Senu bin Abdul Rahman
Let our voice be heard (New Year message). MONS:160

NEW YORK (CITY)
Wood, F.
Proposal for the secession of New York City. ANN 9:233

---- CITY COLLEGE
Kerr, C.
Urban-grant university (centennial meeting of City College). BA 1967-68:86

NEW YORK (STATE)
Smith, A. E.
The cooing dove. BRYO:249

---- SUPREME COURT
Roesch, G. F.
Constitutionality of a New York child labor law: opinion for the court. ANN 13:571

NEW ZEALAND - CONSTITUTION
Atkinson, H.
The abolition of the provinces, 1876. MACS:111 sel.
Featherston, I.
The demand for responsible government. MACS:84 sel.
"Provincialism" 1856. MACS:96 sel.
Sewell, H.
"Centralist" interpretation of the Constitution. MACS:93 sel.
The 'compact of 1856.' MACS:99 sel.

---- DEFENSES
Allen, J.
The Naval Defence Bill, 1908. MACS:270 sel.
Holland, S.
Forward defence--from the Middle East to Malaya, 1955. MACS:392 sel.
Jervois, Sir W.
New Zealand's defence and Royal Navy supremacy. MACS:245 sel.
Ward, Sir J.
New Zealand support for the Royal Navy, 1891-1908. MACS:254 sel.

---- ECONOMIC POLICY
Holyoake, K. J.
The National Development Conference, 1968. MACS:455 sel.

---- HISTORY
Coates, D.
Missionary opposition to the New Zealand Company. MACS:4 sel.
Vogel, J.
Colonization by public works and immigration. MACS:42 sel.
Wakefield, E. G.
Extending the 'frontier' of New South Wales. MACS:3 sel.

---- POLITICS AND GOVERNMENT
Atkinson, H.
The abolition of the provinces, 1876. MACS:111 sel.
Ballance, J.
The 1890 election: the opposition case. MACS:201 sel.
Coates, J. G.
The 1925 election: the Coates campaign. MACS:307 sel.
Featherston, I.
The demand for responsible government. MACS:84 sel.
"Provincialism" 1856. MACS:96 sel.
Godley, R.
The demand for responsible government. MACS:66 sel.
McGechan, R. O.
Legal arguments for adopting the Statute of Westminster, 1944. MACS:284 sel.
Sewell, H.
"Centralist" interpretation of the Constitution. MACS:93 sel.
The 'compact' of 1856. MACS:99 sel.
Wakefield, E. G.
The demand for responsible government. MACS:86 sel.

NEW ZEALAND COMPANY
Coates, D.
Missionary opposition to the New England Company. MACS:4 sel.

Newman, John Henry, Cardinal
Christianity and scientific investigation. (Catholic University of Ireland, Dublin, 1855). MCB:361
Property as a disadvantage. BREWE 8:3093

NEWSPAPERS
Holden, W. S.
Newspapers of the U.S.A.
ARS:107

---- See also Free speech; Journalism and Journalists; Liberty of the Press

Newton, Huey P.
The transformation of the Black Panther Party. (Univ. of California, Berkeley, May 19, 1971). FON:1182

NEWTON, HUEY P.
Garry, C. R.
In defense of Huey Newton.
ERP:161
Seale, B.
Free Huey. SMHR:175

Ngwa, Jacob
Africa and the United States--partners for peace.
SCHW:192
Our common tradition in peril.
SCHW:123

NIAGARA MOVEMENT
DuBois, W. E. B.
The value of agitation.
FON:663

NICARAGUA
Coolidge, C.
Intervention in Nicaragua.
ANN 14:519

NICARAGUA CANAL
McKinley, W.
Second annual message.
STAT 2:1881
Third annual message.
STAT 2:1922

NICKEL STEEL
Guillaume, C. E.
Invar and clinvar.
NOLPH 1:444

Nicolle, Charles Jules Henri
Investigations on typhus (Nobel Lecture for 1928).
NOLM 2:180

NICOLLE, CHARLES JULES HENRI
Henschen, F.
Presentation [of the Nobel Prize for Physiology or Medicine for 1928 to Charles Jules Henri Nicolle]. NOLM 2:175

Nielson, Arthur C., Sr.
Responds to an introduction.
PRS:155

Nies, Nola
Warrior and the woman.
SCHW:10

NIGERIA
Akintola, S. L. and others
Nigeria debates self-government.
EMP:65
Gardiner, R. K.
Citizenship and political liberalism. EMP:106
Okpara, M. I.
Progress without tears: address at convocation, University of Nigeria. EMP:138

Niles, John and others (J. C. Calhoun)
Debate on the Yucatan Bill.
ANN 7:426

Ningkan, Stephen Kalong
Three problems of Sarawak.
MONS:326

Nirenberg, Marshall W.
The genetic code (Nobel Lecture, Dec. 12, 1968). NOLM 4:370

NIRENBERG, MARSHALL W.
Reichard, P.
Presentation [of the Nobel Prize for Physiology or Medicine to Robert W. Holley, Har Gobind Khorana, and Marshall W. Nirenberg, Dec. 12, 1968].
NOLM 4:321

NITROGEN - FIXATION
Virtanen, A. I.
The biological fixation of nitrogen and the preservation of fodder in agriculture, and their importance to human nutrition.
NOLC 3:74

Nix, Lucile
Presents Edmon Low. LYI:40

Nixon, Richard M.
Academic freedom: a force in human history. CAPG:148
Acceptance speech, Chicago, Illinois, July 28, 1960. Same as his It is time to speak up for America
Acceptance speech, Miami Beach, Florida, August 8, 1968. SIN:356
Acceptance speech, Miami Beach, Florida, August 23, 1972. SIN:392
Address to the Russian people. Same as his Radio-television address from Moscow
Apologia (Television, Sept. 23, 1952). MAC:258; MACR:269; REIR:191
Bridges to human dignity. LINR:255
Cambodia. (April 31, 1970). LINRS:236; LINRST:280
Campaign speech, radio broadcast, September 19, 1968. SIN:366
Campaign speech, Toledo, Ohio, October 27, 1960. SIN:319
Campaign speech, White House, Washington, D.C., November 2, 1972. SIN:402
Campus revolutionaries. (General Beadle State College, Madison, S.D., June 3, 1969). BAAGB:386
Checkers address. Same as his Apologia
Final address as president. Same as his Our long national nightmare is over--speech of resignation
Inaugural address (Washington, Jan. 20, 1969). BA 1968-69:113; ERP:93; HURH:393; USINAU:275; USINAUG:275
It is time to speak up for America (Chicago, July 28, 1960). SIN:307
A new economic policy. (Television, Washington, Aug. 15, 1971). BAAE:263
Our long national nightmare is over--speech of resignation. BA 1974-75:43; JAM:34
Press Conference (Watergate). (Washington, March 6, 1974). BA 1973-74:24
The pursuit of peace (Nov. 3, 1969). BA 1969-70:9; BRYF:457; ERP:145
Question of survival; the anti-ballistic missile system. BA 1968-69:9
Radio-television address from Moscow. ARS:242
Remarks at the White House Conference on Children. (Dec. 13, 1970). BA 1970-71:37
Second inaugural address. (Washington, January 20, 1973). BA 1972-73:15; USINAUG:275
State of the Union message, 1972. (Washington, D.C., Jan. 20, 1972). BA 1971-72:13
Vietnam plan. Same as his Pursuit of peace
The Watergate affair. Same as his The Watergate case
The Watergate case (Washington, April 30, 1973). BA 1972-73:50; LINRST:169
"We cannot learn from one another until we stop shouting at one another." Same as his Inaugural address

---- and others (J. F. Kennedy)
Opening statements: the fourth debate. GRG:106

NIXON, RICHARD M.
Moynihan, D. P.
The middle of the journey. BA 1970-71:29

Nizer, Louis
Presents Albert Einstein. LYI:176
Presents George Gershwin. LYI:15
Presents Grover A. Whalen. LYI:65
Presents Harry Woodburn Chase. LYI:91
Presents Heywood Broun. LYI:105

Nkrumah, Francis Nwia Kofie (Kwame)
African history through African eyes. EMP:22

Freedom and unity as Africa's salvation. EMP:145

NOBEL PRIZE FOR CHEMISTRY
Adler, K.
Diene synthesis and related reaction types. NOLC 3:267
Arrhenius, S. A.
Development of the theory of electrolytic dissociation. NOLC 1:45
Aston, F. W.
Mass spectra and isotopes. NOLC 2:7
Barton, D. H. R.
The principles of conformational analysis. NOLC 4:298
Bergius, F.
Chemical reactions under high pressure. NOLC 2:244
Bosch, C.
The development of the chemical high pressure method during the establishment of the new ammonia industry. NOLC 2:197
Buchner, E.
Cell-free fermentation. NOLC 1:103
Calvin, M.
The path of carbon in photosynthesis. NOLC 3:618
Cederblom, J. E.
Presentation [of the Nobel Prize for Chemistry to Sir William Ramsay, Dec. 12, 1904]. NOLC 1:65
Claesson, S.
Presentation [of the Nobel Prize for Chemistry to Lars Onsager, Dec. 11, 1968]. NOLC 4:269
Curie, M.
Radium and the new concepts in chemistry. NOLC 1:202
Dahlgren, E. W.
Presentation [of the Nobel Prize for Chemistry to Marie Sklodowska Curie, Dec. 11, 1911]. NOLC 1:199
Debye, P. J. W.
Methods to determine the electrical and geometrical structure of molecules. NOLC 2:383
DeGeer, G.
Presentation [of the Nobel Prize for Chemistry to Walther Hermann Nernst, 1920, Dec. 12, 1921]. NOLC 1:349
Diels, O. P. H.
Description and importance of the aromatic basic skeleton of the steroids. NOLC 3:259
Eigen, M.
Immeasurably fast reactions. NOLC 4:170
Ekstrand, A. G.
Presentation [of the Nobel Prize for Chemistry to Fritz Haber, 1918, June 2, 1920]. NOLC 1:321
Euler, H. V.
Fermentation of sugars and fermentative enzymes. NOLC 2:144
Fischer, H.
On haemin and the relationships between haemin and chlorophyll. NOLC 2:165
Fischer, H. E.
Syntheses in the purine and sugar group. NOLC 1:21
Fischer-Hjalmars, I.
Presentation [of the Nobel Prize for Chemistry to Robert S. Mulliken, Dec. 12, 1966]. NOLC 4:127
Fredga, A.
Presentation [of the Nobel Prize for Chemistry to Derek H. R. Barton and Odd Hassel, Dec. 11, 1969]. NOLC 4:295
Presentation [of the Nobel Prize for Chemistry to Hermann Staudinger, Dec. 11, 1953]. NOLC 3:393
Presentation [of the Nobel Prize for Chemistry to Karl Ziegler and Giulio Natta, Dec. 12, 1963]. NOLC 4:3
Presentation [of the Nobel Prize for Chemistry to Otto Paul Hermann Diels and Kurt Adler, Dec. 12, 1950]. NOLC 3:255
Presentation [of the Nobel Prize for Chemistry to Robert Burns Woodward, Dec. 11, 1965]. NOLC 4:97
Presentation [of the Nobel Prize for Chemistry to Sir Alexander Robertus Todd, Dec. 11, 1957]. NOLC 3:519
Presentation [of the Nobel Prize

for Chemistry to Sir Robert Robinson, Dec. 12, 1947]. NOLC 3:166
Presentation [of the Nobel Prize for Chemistry to Vincent du Vigneaud, Dec. 12, 1955]. NOLC 3:443
Giauque, W. F.
Some consequences of low-temperature research in chemical thermodynamics. NOLC 3:227
Grignard, V.
The use of organomagnesium compounds in preparative organic chemistry. NOLC 1:234
Haber, F.
The synthesis of ammonia from its elements. NOLC 1:326
Hagg, G.
Presentation [of the Nobel Prize for Chemistry to Dorothy Crowfoot Hodgkin, Dec. 11, 1964]. NOLC 4:67
Presentation [of the Nobel Prize for Chemistry to Linus Carl Pauling, Dec. 11, 1954]. NOLC 3:425
Presentation [of the Nobel Prize for Chemistry to Max Ferdinand Perutz and John Cowdery Kenrew, Dec. 11, 1962]. NOLC 3:649
Hahn, O.
From the natural transmutations of uranium to its artificial fission. NOLC 3:51
Hammersten, O.
Presentation [of the Nobel Prize for Chemistry to Fritz Pregl, Dec. 11, 1923]. NOLC 2:25
Harden, A.
The function of phosphate in alcoholic fermentation. NOLC 2:131
Hassel, O.
Structural aspects of interatomic charge-transfer bonding. NOLC 4:314
Hasselberg, K. B.
Presentation [of the Nobel Prize for Chemistry to Ernest Rutherford, Dec. 11, 1908]. NOLC 1:125
Haworth, W. N.
The structure of carbohydrates and of vitamin C. NOLC 2:414
Hevesy, G. D.
Some applications of isotopic indicators. NOLC 3:9
Heyrovsky, J.
The trends of polarography. NOLC 3:564
Hildebrand, H.
Presentation [of the Nobel Prize for Chemistry to Wilhelm Ostwald, Dec. 12, 1909]. NOLC 1:147
Hinshelwood, Sir C. N.
Chemical kinetics in the past few decades. NOLC 3:474
Hodgkin, D. C.
The x-ray analysis of complicated molecules. NOLC 4:71
Hoff, J. H. V.
Osmotic pressure and chemical equilibrium. NOLC 1:5
Joliot, J. F.
Chemical evidence of the transmutation of elements. NOLC 2:369
Joliot-Curie, I.
Artificial production of radioactive elements. NOLC 2:366
Karrer, P.
Carotenoids, flavins and vitamin A and B_2. NOLC 2:433
Kendrew, J. C.
Myoglobin and the structure of proteins. NOLC 3:676
Klason, P.
Presentation [of the Nobel Prize for Chemistry to Henri Moissan, 1906]. NOLC 1:91
Langmuir, I.
Surface chemistry. NOLC 2:287
Leloir, L. F.
Two decades of research on the biosynthesis of saccharides. NOLC 4:338
Libby, W. F.
Radiocarbon dating. NOLC 3:593
McMillan, Edwin Mattison
The transuranium elements: early history. NOLC 3:314
Martin, A. J. P.
The development of partition chromatography. NOLC 3:359

Montelius, O.
Presentation [of the Nobel Prize for Chemistry to Otto Wallach, Dec. 12, 1910]. NOLC 1:175
Mörner, K.A.H.
Presentation [of the Nobel Prize for Chemistry to Eduard Buchner, Dec. 11, 1907]. NOLC 1:99
Mulliken, R. S.
Spectroscopy, molecular orbitals, and chemical bonding. NOLC 4:131
Myrbäck, K.
Presentation [of the Nobel Prize for Chemistry to Luis F. Leloir, Dec. 11, 1970]. NOLC 4:335
Presentation [of the Nobel Prize for Chemistry to Melvin Calvin, Dec. 11, 1961]. NOLC 3:615
Natta, G.
From the stereospecific polymerization to the asymmetric autocatalytic synthesis of macromolecules. NOLC 4:27
Nernst, W. H.
Studies in chemical thermodynamics. NOLC 1:353
Nordström, T.
Presentation [of the Nobel Prize for Chemistry to Alfred Werner, Dec. 11, 1913]. NOLC 1:253
Norrish, R. G. W.
Some fast reactions in gases studied by flash photolysis and kinetic spectroscopy. NOLC 4:206
Northrop, J. H.
The preparation of pure enzymes and virus proteins. NOLC 3:124
Odhner, C. T.
Presentation [of the Nobel Prize for Chemistry to Jacobus Henricus Van't Hoff, Dec. 13, 1901]. NOLC 1:3
Olander, A.
Presentation [of the Nobel Prize for Chemistry to Jaroslav Heyrovsky, Dec. 11, 1959]. NOLC 3:561
Presentation [of the Nobel Prize for Chemistry to Manfred Eigen, R. G. W. Norrish and George Porter, Dec. 11, 1967]. NOLC 4:165
Presentation [of the Nobel Prize for Chemistry to Sir Cyril Norman Hinshelwood and Nikolai Nikolaevic Semenov, Dec. 11, 1956]. NOLC 3:471
Onsager, L.
The motion of ions: principles and concepts. NOLC 4:272
Ostwald, W.
On catalysis. NOLC 1:150
Palmaer, W.
Presentation [of the Nobel Prize for Chemistry for 1931 to Carl Bosch and Friedrich Bergius, May 21, 1932]. NOLC 2:189
Presentation [of the Nobel Prize for Chemistry for 1934 to Harold Clayton Urey, Feb. 14, 1935]. NOLC 2:333
Presentation [of the Nobel Prize for Chemistry to Jean Frédéric Joliot and Irène Joliot-Curie, Dec. 12, 1935]. NOLC 2:359
Presentation [of the Nobel Prize for Chemistry to Walter Norman Haworth and Paul Karrer, Dec. 11, 1937]. NOLC 2:407
Pauling, L. C.
Modern structural chemistry. NOLC 3:429
Perutz, M. F.
X-ray analysis of haemoglobin. NOLC 3:653
Porter, G.
Flash photolysis and some of its applications. NOLC 4:241
Pregl, F.
Quantitative micro-analysis of organic substances. NOLC 2:28
Ramsay, Sir W.
The rare gases of the atmosphere. NOLC 1:68
Richards, T. W.
Atomic weights. NOLC 1:280
Robinson, Sir R.
Some polycyclic natural products. NOLC 3:166
Rutherford, E.
The chemical nature of the alpha particles from radioactive substances. NOLC 1:129
Ružička, L. S.

Multimembered rings, higher terpene compounds, and male sex hormones. NOLC 2:468
Sabatier, P.
The method of direct hydrogenation by catalysis. NOLC 1:221
Sanger, F.
The chemistry of insulin. NOLC 3:544
Seaborg, G. T.
The transuranium elements: present status. NOLC 3:325
Semenov, N. N.
Some problems relating to chain reactions and to the theory of combustion. NOLC 3:487
Söderbaum, H. G.
Presentation [of the Nobel Prize for Chemistry to Arthur Harden and Hans Karl August Simon von Euler-Chelpin, Dec. 12, 1929]. NOLC 2:127
Presentation [of the Nobel Prize for Chemistry to Francis William Aston, Dec. 12, 1922]. NOLC 2:3
Presentation [of the Nobel Prize for Chemistry for 1921 to Frederick Soddy, Dec. 12, 1922]. NOLC 1:367
Presentation [of the Nobel Prize for Chemistry to Hans Fischer, Dec. 11, 1930]. NOLC 2:161
Presentation [of the Nobel Prize for Chemistry for 1927 to Heinrich Otto Wieland and for 1928 to Adolf Otto Reinhold Windaus, Dec. 12, 1928]. NOLC 2:89
Presentation [of the Nobel Prize for Chemistry to Irving Langmuir, Dec. 14, 1932]. NOLC 2:283
Presentation [of the Nobel Prize for Chemistry for 1925 to Richard Adolf Zsigmondy, Dec. 11, 1926]. NOLC 2:41
Presentation [of the Nobel Prize for Chemistry to Theodor Svedberg, 1926, May 19, 1927]. NOLC 2:63
Presentation [of the Nobel Prize for Chemistry to Victor Grignard and Paul Sabatier, Dec. 11, 1912]. NOLC 1:217
Soddy, F.
The origins of the conceptions of isotopes. NOLC 1:371
Stanley, W. M.
The isolation and properties of crystalline tobacco mosaic. NOLC 3:137
Staudinger, H.
Macromolecular chemistry. NOLC 3:397
Sumner, J. B.
The chemical nature of enzymes. NOLC 3:114
Svedberg, T.
The ultracentrifuge. NOLC 2:67
Synge, R. L. M.
Applications of partition chromatography. NOLC 3:374
Théel, H.
Presentation [of the Nobel Prize for Chemistry to Hermann Emil Fischer, Dec. 12, 1902]. NOLC 1:17
Tiselius, A. W. K.
Electrophoresis and adsorption analysis as aids in investigations of large-molecular weight substances and their breakdown. NOLC 3:195
Presentation [of the Nobel Prize for Chemistry to Archer John Porter Martin and Richard Laurence Millington Synge, Dec. 12, 1952]. NOLC 3:355
Presentation [of the Nobel Prize for Chemistry to Frederick Sanger, Dec. 11, 1958]. NOLC 3:541
Presentation [of the Nobel Prize for Chemistry to James Batcheller Sumner, John Howard Northrop, and Wendell Meredith Stanley, Dec. 12, 1946]. NOLC 3:109
Presentation [of the Nobel Prize for Chemistry to William Francis Giauque, Dec. 12, 1949]. NOLC 3:221
Todd, Sir A. R.
Synthesis in the study of nucleotides. NOLC 3:522
Törnebladh, H. R.
Presentation [of the Nobel Prize for Chemistry to Svante August

Arrhenius, Dec. 11, 1903]. NOLC 1:43
Urey, H. C.
Some thermodynamic properties of hydrogen and deuterium. NOLC 2:339
Vigneaud, V. D.
A trail of sulfur research: from insulin to oxytocin. NOLC 3:446
Virtanen, A. I.
The biological fixation of nitrogen and the preservation of fodder in agriculture, and their importance to human nutrition. NOLC 3:74
Wallach, O.
Alicyclic compounds. NOLC 1:178
Werner, A.
On the constitution and configuration of higher-order compounds. NOLC 1:256
Westgren, A.
Presentation [of the Nobel Prize for Chemistry to Arne Wilhelm Kaurin Tiselius, Dec. 13, 1948]. NOLC 3:191
Presentation [of the Nobel Prize for Chemistry to Artturi Ilmari Virtanen, Dec. 12, 1945]. NOLC 3:71
Presentation [of the Nobel Prize for Chemistry to Edwin Mattison McMillan and Glenn Theodore Seaborg, Dec. 12, 1951]. NOLC 3:309
Presentation [of the Nobel Prize for Chemistry for 1943 to George De Hevesy, Dec. 12, 1944]. NOLC 3:5
Presentation [of the Nobel Prize for Chemistry for 1944 to Otto Hahn, Dec. 13, 1946]. NOLC 3:47
Presentation [of the Nobel Prize for Chemistry to Petrus Josephus Wilhelmus Debye, Dec. 12, 1936]. NOLC 2:379
Presentation [of the Nobel Prize for Chemistry to Willard Frank Libby, Dec. 12, 1960]. NOLC 3:589
Wieland, H. O.
The chemistry of the bile acids. NOLC 2:94
Willstätter, R. M.
On plant pigments. NOLC 1:301
Windaus, A. O. R.
Constitution of sterols and their connection with other substances occurring in nature. NOLC 2:105
Woodward, R. B.
Recent advances in the chemistry of natural products. NOLC 4:100
Ziegler, K.
Consequences and development of an invention. NOLC 4:6
Zsigmondy, R. A.
Properties of colloids. NOLC 2:45

NOBEL PRIZE FOR LITERATURE
Agnon, S. Y.
Acceptance [of the Nobel Prize for Literature, 1966]. NOB 1:5; NOL:614
Andrić, I.
Acceptance [of the Nobel Prize for Literature, 1961]. NOB 1:121; NOL:565
Annerstedt, C.
Presentation [of the Nobel Prize for Literature to Selma Ottiliana Lovisa Lagerlöf, 1909]. NOB 10:279; NOL:90
Asturias, M. A.
Acceptance [of the Nobel Prize for Literature, 1967]. NOB 2:7; NOL:626
Benitez, J.
Acceptance [of the Nobel Prize for Literature for Juan Ramón Jiménez, 1956]. NOB 10:7; NOL:517
Bergson, H.
Acceptance [of the Nobel Prize for Literature, 1927]. NOB 2:273; NOL:246
Bjørnson, B. M.
Acceptance [of the Nobel Prize for Literature, 1903]. NOL:16; NOB 3:81
Böök, F.
Presentation [of the Nobel Prize for Literature to Thomas Mann, 1929]. NOB 12:221; NOL:260
Buck, P.
Acceptance [of the Nobel Prize for Literature, 1938].

NOB 3:157; NOL:359
The Chinese novel.
NOL:361
Bunin, I. A.
Acceptance [of the Nobel Prize for Literature, 1933]. NOB 3:291; NOL:314
Brown, J. E.
Acceptance [of the Nobel Prize for Literature for Eugene Gladstone O'Neill, 1936]. NOB 19:131; NOL:336
Camus, A.
Acceptance [of the Nobel Prize for Literature, 1957]. NOB 4:7; NOL:524
Churchill, Sir W. L. S.
Acceptance [of the Nobel Prize for Literature, 1953]. NOB 4:183; NOL:493
DuGard, R. M.
Acceptance [of the Nobel Prize for Literature, 1937]. NOB 14:9; NOL:348
Eliot, T. S.
Acceptance [of the Nobel Prize for Literature, 1948]. NOB 5:267; NOL:435
Eucken, R.
Naturalism or idealism? NOL:74
Faulkner, W.
On accepting the Nobel Prize, exhorts the young writers of the world. ALA:125; ANN 17:33; ARS:52; BOORA 2:988; GRG:86; HURH:291; MOPR:279; NOB 19:7; NOL:444
France, A.
Acceptance [of the Nobel Prize for Literature, 1921]. NOB 6:93; NOL:181
Gide, A.
Acceptance [of the Nobel Prize for Literature, 1947]. NOB 7:7; NOL:426
Gierow, K. R.
Presentation address [of the Nobel Prize for Literature to Aleksandr Solzhenitsyn, 1970]. NOB 18:3
Presentation address [of the Nobel Prize for Literature to Samuel Beckett, 1969]. NOB 3:3
Gullberg, H.
Presentation [of the Nobel Prize for Literature to Gabriela Mistral, 1945]. NOB 14:167; NOL:405
Presentation [of the Nobel Prize for Literature to Juan Ramón Jiménez, 1956]. NOB 10:3; NOL:513
Hallström, P.
Broadcast lecture [on Johannes Vilhelm Jensen, 1944]. NOL:393
Presentation [of the Nobel Prize for Literature to Eugene Gladstone O'Neill, 1936]. NOB 19:125; NOL:330
Presentation [of the Nobel Prize for Literature to Frans Eemil Sillanpää, 1939]. NOB 16:223; NOL:386
Presentation [of the Nobel Prize for Literature to George Bernard Shaw, 1925]. NOB 16:77; NOL:224
Presentation [of the Nobel Prize for Literature to Henri Bergson, 1927]. NOB 2:267; NOL:242
Presentation [of the Nobel Prize for Literature to Ivan Alekseevich Bunin, 1933]. NOB 3:285; NOL:309
Presentation [of the Nobel Prize for Literature to Jacinto Benavente, 1922]. NOB 2:179; NOL:186
Presentation [of the Nobel Prize for Literature to Luigi Pirandello, 1934]. NOB 20:71; NOL:320
Presentation [of the Nobel Prize for Literature to Pearl Buck, 1938]. NOB 3:149; NOL:354
Presentation [of the Nobel Prize for Literature to Roger Martin DuGard, 1937]. NOB 14:3; NOL:342
Presentation [of the Nobel Prize for Literature to Sigrid Undset, 1928]. NOB 18:163; NOL:251
Presentation [of the Nobel Prize for Literature to William Butler Yeats, 1923]. NOB 18:275; NOL:194
Presentation [of the Nobel Prize for Literature to William Faulkner, 1949]. NOB 19:3; NOL:440
Hamsun, K. P.

Acceptance [of the Nobel Prize for Literature, 1920]. NOB 9:123; NOL:170
Hauptmann, G. J. R.
Acceptance [of the Nobel Prize for Literature, 1912]. NOB 8:7; NOL:122
Hemingway, E.
Acceptance [of the Nobel Prize for Literature, 1954]. NOB 9:7; NOL:501
Hildebrand, H.
Presentation [of the Nobel Prize for Literature to Gerhart Johann Robert Hauptmann, 1912]. NOB 8:3; NOL:118
Hjärne, H.
Presentation [of the Nobel Prize for Literature to Carl Friedrich Spitteler, 1919]. NOB 17:267; NOL:161
Presentation [of the Nobel Prize for Literature to Knut Pedersen Hamsun, 1920]. NOB 9:199; NOL:167
Presentation [of the Nobel Prize for Literature to Rabindranath Tagore, 1913]. NOB 18:10; NOL:127
Presentation [of the Nobel Prize for Literature to Rudolf Christoph Eucken, 1908]. NOB 6:3; NOL:67
Jensen, J. V.
Acceptance [of the Nobel Prize for Literature, 1944]. NOB 8:263; NOL:400
Karlfeldt, E. A.
Presentation [of the Nobel Prize for Literature to Anatole France, 1921]. NOB 6:85; NOL:174
Presentation [of the Nobel Prize for Literature to Sinclair Lewis, 1930]. NOB 11:237; NOL:271
Kawabata, Y.
Acceptance speech [for the Nobel Prize for Literature, 1968]. NOB 11:7
Lagerkvist, P. F.
Acceptance [of the Nobel Prize for Literature, 1951]. NOB 10:205; NOL:469
Lagerlöf, S. O. L.
Acceptance [of the Nobel Prize for Literature, 1909]. NOB 10:283; NOL:94
Laxness, H. K.
Acceptance [of the Nobel Prize for Literature, 1955]. NOB 12:7; NOL:508
Lewis, S.
The American fear of literature. ANN 15:62; BEN:208; BOORA 2:824; NOL:278
Mann, T.
Acceptance [of the Nobel Prize for Literature, 1929]. NOB 12:225; NOL:263
Mauriac, F.
Acceptance [of the Nobel Prize for Literature, 1952]. NOB 13:7; NOL:481
Mistral, G.
Acceptance [of the Nobel Prize for Literature, 1945]. NOB 14:170; NOL:408
Österling, A.
Presentation [of the Nobel Prize for Literature to Albert Camus, 1957]. NOB 4:3; NOL:522
Presentation [of the Nobel Prize for Literature to André Gide, 1947]. NOB 7:3; NOL:422
Presentation [of the Nobel Prize for Literature to Bertrand Arthur William Russell, 1950]. NOB 15:255; NOL:449
Presentation [of the Nobel Prize for Literature to Erik Axel Karlfeldt, 1931]. NOB 10:101; NOL:295
Presentation [of the Nobel Prize for Literature to Ernest Miller Hemingway, 1954]. NOB 9:3; NOL:497
Presentation [of the Nobel Prize for Literature to François Mauriac, 1952]. NOB 13:3; NOL:477
Presentation [of the Nobel Prize for Literature to Giorgos Seferis, 1963]. NOB 17:3; NOL:580
Presentation [of the Nobel Prize for Literature to Hermann Hesse, 1946]. NOB 9:233; NOL:412
Presentation [of the Nobel Prize for Literature to Ivo Andrić, 1961]. NOB 1:117; NOL:562
Presentation [of the Nobel Prize

for Literature to Johannes Vilhelm Jensen, 1944].
NOB 8:259; NOL:397
Presentation [of the Nobel Prize for Literature to John Galsworthy, 1932].
NOB 6:227; NOL:302
Presentation [of the Nobel Prize for Literature to John Steinbeck, 1962].
NOB 19:201; NOL:572
Presentation [of the Nobel Prize for Literature to Pär Fabian Lagerkvist, 1951].
NOB 10:201; NOL:466
Presentation [of the Nobel Prize for Literature to Miguel Angel Asturias, 1967]. NOB 2:3; NOL:624
Presentation [of the Nobel Prize for Literature to Mikhail Alcksandrovich Sholokhov, 1965].
NOB 17:37; NOL:603
Presentation [of the Nobel Prize for Literature to Saint-John Perse, 1960].
NOB 20:3; NOL:553
Presentation [of the Nobel Prize for Literature to Salvatore Quasimodo, 1959].
NOB 20:281; NOL:534
Presentation [of the Nobel Prize for Literature to Shmuel Yosef Agnon and Leonie Nelly Sachs, 1966].
NOB 1:3; NOB 16:3; NOL:611
Presentation [of the Nobel Prize for Literature to Thomas Stearns Eliot, 1948].
NOB 5:261; NOL:431
Presentation address [of the Nobel Prize for Literature to Yasunari Kawabata, 1968]. NOB 11:3

Quasimodo, S.
Acceptance [of the Nobcl Prize for Literature, 1959].
NOB 20:285; NOL:537
The poet and the politician.
NOL:540

Perse, S.
Acceptance [of the Nobel Prize for Literature, 1960].
NOB 20:7; NOL:556

Pirandello, L.
Acceptance [of the Nobel Prize for Literature, 1934].
NOB 20:77; NOL:324

Russell, B. A. W.
What desires are politically important? NOL:452

Sachs, L. N.
Acceptance [of the Nobel Prize for Literature, 1966].
NOB 16:5; NOL:619

Schück, H.
Presentation [of the Nobel Prize for Literature to Grazia Deledda, 1926]. NOB 5:117; NOL:232

Seferis, G.
Acceptance [of the Nobel Prize for Literature, 1963].
NOB 17:5; NOL:582
Some notes on modern Greek tradition. NOL:484

Sienkiewicz, H.
Acceptance [of the Nobel Prize for Literature, 1905].
NOB 17:183; NOL:45

Siwertz, S.
Presentation [of the Nobel Prize for Literature to Sir Winston Leonard Spencer Churchill, 1953]. NOB 4:177; NOL:488

Steinbeck, J.
Acceptance [of the Nobel Prize for Literature, 1962].
NOB 19:205; NOL:575

Torata, Count de
Acceptance [of the Nobel Prize for Literature for Jacinto Benavente, 1922]. NOL:191

Undset, S.
Acceptance [of the Nobel Prize for Literature, 1928].
NOB 18:167; NOL:255

Vallotton, H.
Acceptance [of the Nobel Prize for Literature for Hermann Hesse, 1946]. NOB 9:237; NOL:416

Wauters, C. C. M. A.
Acceptance [of the Nobel Prize for Literature for Maurice Maeterlinck, 1911]. NOL:114

Wirsén, C. D. af
Presentation [of the Nobel Prize for Literature to Bjørnstjerne Martinus Bjørnson, 1903].
NOL:14; NOB 3:77
Presentation [of the Nobel Prize for Literature to Christian Matthias Theodor Mommsen, 1902]. NOL:7; NOB 13:235

Presentation [of the Nobel Prize for Literature to Frédéric Mistral and José de Echegaray y Eizaguirre, 1904]. NOL:23; NOB 13:119
Presentation [of the Nobel Prize for Literature to Giosue Carducci, 1906]. NOB 5:3; NOL:48
Presentation [of the Nobel Prize for Literature to Halldor Kiljan Laxness, 1955]. NOB 12:3; NOL:505
Presentation [of the Nobel Prize for Literature to Henryk Sienkiewicz, 1905]. NOL:36; NOB 17:173
Presentation [of the Nobel Prize for Literature to Maurice Polydore Marie Bernhard Maeterlinck, 1911]. NOB 12:139; NOL:107
Presentation [of the Nobel Prize for Literature to Paul Johann Ludwig Heyse, 1910]. NOB 7:279; NOL:100
Presentation [of the Nobel Prize for Literature to Rudyard Kipling, 1907]. NOB 11:89; NOL:58
Presentation [of the Nobel Prize for Literature to Sully Prudhomme, 1901]. NOL:2; NOB 16:303
Yeats, W. B.
Acceptance [of the Nobel Prize for Literature, 1923]. NOB 18:263; NOL:199
The Irish dramatic movement. NOL:201

NOBEL PRIZE FOR PEACE
Arnoldson, K. P.
World referendum (Nobel Lecture, Dec. 10, 1908). NOLP 1:175
Angell, N.
Peace and the public mind (Nobel Lecture for 1934, June 12, 1935). NOLP 2:153
Backhouse, M. A.
The international service of the Society of Friends (Nobel Lecture, Dec. 12, 1947). NOLP 2:380
Bajer, F.
The organization of the Peace Movement (Nobel Lecture, 1908, May 18, 1909). NOLP 1:190
Balch, E. G.
Toward human unity or beyond nationalism (Nobel Lecture for 1946, April 7, 1948). NOLP 2:333
Bjørnson, B.
Introduction [presenting the Nobel Prize for Peace to Bertha von Suttner, 1905, April 18, 1906]. NOLP 1:81
Boissier, L. L.
Some aspects of the mission of the International Committee of the Red Cross (Nobel Lecture, Dec. 11, 1963). NOLP 3:301
Borlaugh, N. E.
The green revolution, peace, and humanity (Nobel Lecture, Dec. 11, 1970). NOLP 3:454
Boyd Orr, J.
Science and peace (Nobel Lecture, Dec. 12, 1949). NOLP 2:415
Branting, K. H.
Fraternity among nations (Nobel Lecture for 1921, June 19, 1922). NOLP 1:324
Briand, A.
Acceptance of the Nobel Prize for Peace, Dec. 10, 1926. NOLP 2:3
Buen, A. J.
Remarks [presenting the Nobel Prize for Peace to Leon Victor Auguste Bourgeois, Dec. 10, 1920]. NOLP 1:304
Buisson, F. E.
Changes in concepts of war and peace (Nobel Lecture, 1927, May 31, 1928). NOLP 2:35
Bunche, R. J.
Some reflections on peace in our time (Nobel Lecture, Dec. 11, 1950). NOLP 2:443
Butler, N. M.
Radio address (Nobel Lecture, Dec. 12, 1931). NOLP 2:136
Cadbury, H. J.
Quakers and peace (Nobel Lecture, Dec. 12, 1947). NOLP 2:391
Cassin, R. S.
The charter of human rights (Nobel Lectures, Dec. 11, 1968). NOLP 3:304

Cecil, R.
The future of civilization (Nobel Lecture for 1937, June 1, 1938). NOLP 2:246
Chamberlain, J.
Acceptance [of the Nobel Prize for Peace for 1925, Dec. 10, 1926]. NOLP 1:394
Chapuisat, E.
The activity of the International Committee of the Red Cross during the war, 1939-1945 (Nobel Lecture for 1944, Dec. 11, 1945). NOLP 2:295
Cremer, W. R.
The progress and advantages of international arbitration (Nobel Lecture for 1903, Jan. 15, 1905). NOLP 1:46
Dawes, C. G.
Acceptance [of the Nobel Prize for Peace for 1925, Dec. 10, 1926]. NOLP 1:399
Ducommun, E.
The futility of war demonstrated by history (Nobel Lecture for 1902). NOLP 1:17
Edberg, R.
Acceptance of the Nobel Prize for Peace for Dag Hammarskjöld, Dec. 10, 1961. NOLP 3:248
Gobat, C. A.
The development of the Hague Conventions of July 22, 1899 (Nobel Lecture for 1902, Oslo, July 18, 1906). NOLP 1:30
Goedhart, G. J. v. H.
Refugee problems and their solutions (Nobel Lecture, Dec. 12, 1955). NOLP 3:97
Hagerup, G. F.
The work of the Institute of International Law (Nobel Lecture for 1904, Aug. 24, 1912). NOLP 1:64
Hambro, C. J.
Presentation [of the Nobel Prize for Peace to George Catlett Marshall, Dec. 10, 1953]. NOLP 3:65
Presentation [of the Nobel Prize for Peace to the International Committee of the Red Cross and the League of the Red Cross Societies, Dec. 10, 1963]. NOLP 3:295
Hansson, M.
The Nansen International Office for Refugees (Nobel Lecture, Dec, 10, 1938). NOLP 2:268
Harmann, Z.
UNICEF: achievement and challenge (Nobel Lecture, Dec. 11, 1965). NOLP 3:365
Henderson, A.
Essential elements of a universal and enduring peace (Nobel Lecture, Dec. 11, 1934). NOLP 2:185
Huber, M.
Acceptance [of the Nobel Prize for Peace, 1944, for the International Committee of the Red Cross, Dec. 10, 1945]. NOLP 2:293
Hull, C.
Acceptance [of the Nobel Prize for Peace to Cordell Hull, Dec. 10, 1945]. NOLP 2:318
Ingebretsen, H. S.
Presentation [of the Nobel Prize for Peace to John Raleigh Mott, Dec. 10, 1946]. NOLP 2:354
Irgens, J.
Welcome [presenting the Nobel Prize for Peace to the Institute of International Law for 1904, Aug. 24, 1912]. NOLP 1:61
Jahn, G.
Presentation [of the Nobel Prize for Peace to Albert John Luthuli for 1960, Dec. 10, 1961]. NOLP 3:209
Presentation [of the Nobel Prize for Peace for 1952 to Albert Schweitzer, Dec. 10, 1953]. NOLP 3:37
Presentation [of the Nobel Prize for Peace to Cordell Hull, Dec. 10, 1945]. NOLP 2:311
Presentation [of the Nobel Prize for Peace to Dag Hammarskjöld, Dec. 10, 1961]. NOLP 3:239
Presentation [of the Nobel Prize for Peace to Emily Greene Balch, Dec. 10, 1946]. NOLP 2:325
Presentation [of the Nobel Prize

for Peace to the Friends Service Council and the American Friends Service Committee, Dec. 10, 1947]. NOLP 2:373
Presentation [of the Nobel Prize for Peace to Georges Pire, Dec. 10, 1958]. NOLP 3:151
Presentation [of the Nobel Prize for Peace to the International Committee of the Red Cross, 1944, Dec. 10, 1945]. NOLP 2:289
Presentation [of the Nobel Prize for Peace to Léon Jouhaux, Dec. 10, 1951]. NOLP 3:3
Presentation [of the Nobel Prize for Peace to Lester Bowles Pearson, Dec. 10, 1957]. NOLP 3:119
Presentation [of the Nobel Prize for Peace for 1962 to Linus Carl Pauling, Dec. 10, 1963]. NOLP 3:259
Presentation [of the Nobel Prize for Peace to Lord Boyd Orr of Brechin, Dec. 10, 1949]. NOLP 2:407
Presentation [of the Nobel Prize for Peace to Martin Luther King, Jr., Dec. 10, 1964]. NOLP 3:325
Presentation [of the Nobel Prize for Peace to the Office of the United Nations High Commissioner for Refugees, Dec. 10, 1955]. NOLP 3:89
Presentation [of the Nobel Prize for Peace to Philip John Noel-Baker, Dec. 10, 1959]. NOLP 3:175
Presentation [of the Nobel Prize for Peace to Ralph Johnson Bunche, Dec. 10, 1950]. NOLP 2:435

Johnsen, A.
Remarks [presenting the Nobel Prize for Peace to Thomas Woodrow Wilson, 1919, Dec. 10, 1920]. NOLP 1:293

Jouhaux, L.
Fifty years of trade-union activity in behalf of peace (Nobel Lecture, Dec. 11, 1951). NOLP 3:10

Kellogg, F. B.
Acceptance and banquet speech [for the Nobel Prize for Peace, 1929 (Dec. 10, 1930)]. NOLP 2:79

King, M. L., Jr.
Nonviolence: moral challenge for peace and justice. NOLP 3:333; THOMS:99

Knudsen, G.
Presentation [of the Nobel Prize for Peace to Theodore Roosevelt, Dec. 10, 1906]. NOLP 1:97

Koht, H.
Presentation [of the Nobel Prize for Peace to Jane Addams and Nicholas Murray Butler, Dec. 10, 1931]. NOLP 2:125

Labouisse, H. R.
Acceptance [of the Nobel Prize for Peace, Dec. 10, 1965]. NOLP 3:362

Lange, C. L.
Internationalism (Nobel Lecture, Dec. 13, 1921). NOLP 1:336
Presentation [of the Nobel Prize for Peace to Carlos Saavedra Lamas, Dec. 10, 1936]. NOLP 2:217
Presentation [of the Nobel Prize for Peace, 1933, to Norman Angell, Dec. 10, 1934]. NOLP 2:147
Presentation [of the Nobel Prize for Peace to Viscount Cecil of Chelwood, Dec. 10, 1937]. NOLP 2:235

Lionaes, A.
Presentation [of the Nobel Prize for Peace to the International Labor Organization, Dec. 10, 1969]. NOLP 3:415
Presentation [of the Nobel Prize for Peace to Norman Ernest Borlaug, Dec. 10, 1970]. NOLP 3:445
Presentation [of the Nobel Prize for Peace to René-Samuel Cassin, Dec. 10, 1968]. NOLP 3:385
Presentation [of the Nobel Prize for Peace to the United Nations Children's Fund, Dec. 10, 1965]. NOLP 3:353

Løvland, J. G.
Banquet speech [presenting the

Nobel Prize for Peace to Bertha von Suttner, 1905, April 18, 1906]. NOLP 1:82
Presentation [of the Nobel Prize for Peace to Alfred Hermann Fried, Dec. 10, 1911]. NOLP 1:238
Presentation [of the Nobel Prize for Peace to Auguste Marie François Beernaert, Dec. 10, 1909]. NOLP 1:211
Presentation [of the Nobel Prize for Peace to Baron d'Estournelles de Constant, Dec. 10, 1909]. NOLP 1:216
Presentation [of the Nobel Prize for Peace to Ernesto Teodoro Moneta, Dec. 10, 1907]. NOLP 1:113
Presentation [of the Nobel Prize for Peace to Fredrik Bajer, Dec. 10, 1908]. NOLP 1:188
Presentation [of the Nobel Prize for Peace to Klas Pontus Arnoldson, Dec. 10, 1908]. NOLP 1:173
Presentation [of the Nobel Prize for Peace to Louis Renault, Dec. 10, 1907]. NOLP 1:141
Presentation [of the Nobel Prize for Peace to the Permanent International Peace Bureau, Dec. 10, 1910]. NOLP 1:223
Presentation [of the Nobel Prize for Peace to Tobias Michael Carel Asser, Dec. 10, 1911]. NOLP 1:233
Toast to E. Ducommun [presenting the Nobel Prize for Peace, 1902]. NOLP 1:15
Toast to C. A. Gobat [presenting the Nobel Prize for Peace for 1902, Oslo, July 18, 1906]. NOLP 1:29
Welcome [presenting the Nobel Prize for Peace, 1903 to William Randal Cremer, Jan. 15, 1905]. NOLP 1:45

Luthuli, A. J.
Africa and freedom. MDV:79; NOLP 3:209

MacAulay, J. A.
The Red Cross in a changing world (Nobel Lecture, Dec. 11, 1963). NOLP 3:311

Marshall, G. C.
Essentials of peace (Nobel Lecture, Dec. 11, 1953). NOLP 3:76

Moe, R.
Presentation [of the Nobel Prize for Peace to Elihu Root, 1912, Dec. 10, 1913]. NOLP 1:245
Presentation [of the Nobel Prize for Peace to Henri Marie La Fontaine, Dec. 10, 1913]. NOLP 1:269
Presentation [of the Nobel Prize for Peace to the International Committee of the Red Cross, Dec. 10, 1917]. NOLP 1:281

Moneta, E. T.
Peace and law in the Italian tradition (Nobel Lecture, 1907, Aug. 25, 1909). NOLP 1:114

Morse, D. A.
ILO and the social infrastructure of peace (Nobel Lecture, Dec. 11, 1969). NOLP 3:424

Mott, J. R.
The leadership demanded in this momentous time (Nobel Lecture, Dec. 13, 1946). NOLP 2:362

Mowinckel, J. L.
Presentation [of the Nobel Prize for Peace to Arthur Henderson, Dec. 10, 1934]. NOLP 2:179
Presentation [of the Nobel Prize for Peace to Frank Billings Kellogg, 1929, Dec. 10, 1930]. NOLP 2:73
Presentation [of the Nobel Prize for Peace to Nathan Söderblom, Dec. 11, 1930]. NOLP 2:73

Nansen, F.
Speech at Award Ceremony [presenting Nobel Prize for Peace to Aristide Briand and Gustav Stresemann, Dec. 10, 1926]. NOLP 2:3
Speech at Award Ceremony [presenting the Nobel Prize for Peace to Joseph Austen Chamberlain and Charles Gates Dawes for 1925, Dec. 10, 1926]. NOLP 1:383
The suffering people of Europe (Nobel Lecture, Dec. 19, 1922).

NOLP 1:361
Noel-Baker, P. J.
Peace and the arms race (Nobel Lecture, Dec. 11, 1959). NOLP 3:186
Pauling, L. C.
Science and peace (Nobel Lecture for 1962, Dec. 11, 1963). NOLP 3:271
Pearson, L. B.
The four faces of peace (Nobel Lecture, Dec. 11, 1957). NOLP 3:129
Peirce, H. H. D.
Acceptance [of the Nobel Prize for Peace for Theodore Roosevelt, Dec. 10, 1906]. NOLP 1:99
Pire, G.
Brotherly love: foundation of peace (Nobel Lecture, Dec. 11, 1958). NOLP 3:157
Quidde, L.
Security and disarmament (Nobel Lecture, Dec. 10, 1927). NOLP 2:47
Renault, L.
The work at the Hague in 1899 and in 1907 (Nobel Lecture for 1907, May 18, 1908). NOLP 1:143
Roosevelt, T.
International peace (Nobel Lecture for 1906, May 5, 1910). NOLP 1:102
Root, E.
Towards making peace permanent (Nobel Lecture for 1912). NOLP 1:247
Saavedra Lamas, C.
Radio address (Nobel Lecture, Nov. 29, 1936). NOLP 2:225
Schmedeman, A. G.
Acceptance [of the Nobel Prize for Peace for Woodrow Wilson, 1919, Dec. 10, 1920]. NOLP 1:294
Schweitzer, A.
The problem of peace (Nobel Lecture for 1952, Nov. 4, 1954). NOLP 3:46
Söderblom, N.
The role of the church in promoting peace (Nobel Lecture, Dec. 11, 1930). NOLP 2:93
Stang, F.
Presentation [of the Nobel Prize for Peace, 1935, to Carl Von Ossietzky, Dec. 10, 1936]. NOLP 2:207
Presentation [of the Nobel Prize for Peace to Ferdinand Edouard Buisson and Ludwig Quidde, Dec. 10, 1927]. NOLP 2:29
Presentation [of the Nobel Prize for Peace to Fridtjof Nansen, Dec. 10, 1922]. NOLP 1:353
Presentation [of the Nobel Prize for Peace to the Nansen International Office for Refugees, Dec. 10, 1938]. NOLP 2:265
Stresemann, G.
The new Germany (Nobel Lecture for 1926, June 29, 1927). NOLP 2:8
Suttner, B. V.
The evolution of the Peace Movement (Nobel Lecture for 1905, April 18, 1906). NOLP 1:84

NOBEL PRIZE FOR PHYSICS

Alfvén, H.
Plasma physics, space research and the origin of the solar system. NOLPH 4:306
Alvarez, L. W.
Recent developments in particle physics. NOLPH 4:241
Anderson, C. D.
The production and properties of positrons. NOLPH 2:365
Appleton, Sir E. V.
The ionosphere. NOLPH 3:79
Arrhenius, S. A.
Presentation [of the Nobel Prize for Physics for 1921 to Albert Einstein, July 11, 1923]. NOLPH 1:482
Presentation [of the Nobel Prize for Physics to Niels Bohr, Dec. 11, 1922]. NOLPH 2:3
Bardeen, J.
Semiconductor research leading to the point contact transistor. NOLPH 3:318
Barkla, C. G.
Characteristic Röntgen radiation. NOLPH 1:392
Basov, N. G.
Semiconductor lasers. NOLPH 4:89
Becquerel, A. H.
On radioactivity, a new property of matter. NOLPH 1:52

Bethe, H. A.
Energy production in stars. NOLPH 4:215
Blackett, P. M. S.
Cloud chamber researches in nuclear physics and cosmic radiation. NOLPH 3:97
Bloch, F.
The principle of nuclear induction. NOLPH 3:203
Bohr, N.
The structure of the atom. NOLPH 2:7
Born, M.
The statistical interpretation of quantum mechanics. NOLPH 3:256
Bothe, W.
The coincidence method. NOLPH 3:271
Bragg, W. L.
The diffraction of x-rays by crystals. NOLPH 1:370
Brattain, W. H.
Surface properties of semiconductors. NOLPH 3:377
Braun, C. F.
Electrical oscillations and wireless telegraphy. NOLPH 1:226
Bridgman, P. W.
General survey of certain results in the field of high-pressure physics. NOLPH 3:53
Cederblom, J. E.
Presentation [of the Nobel Prize for Physics to Lord Rayleigh, Dec. 12, 1904]. NOLPH 1:87
Cerenkov, P. A.
Radiation of particles moving at a velocity exceeding that of light, and some of the possibilities for their use in experimental physics. NOLPH 3:423
Chadwick, J.
The neutron and its properties. NOLPH 2:339
Chamberlain, O.
The early antiproton work. NOLPH 3:489
Cockcroft, Sir J. D.
Experiments on the interaction of high-speed nucleons with atomic nuclei. NOLPH 3:167
Compton, A. H.
X-rays as a branch of optics. NOLPH 2:174
Curie, P.
Radioactive substances, especially radium. NOLPH 1:73
Dahlgren, E. W.
Presentation [of the Nobel Prize for Physics to Wilhelm Wien, Dec. 11, 1911]. NOLPH 1:271
Davisson, C. J.
The discovery of electron waves. NOLPH 2:387
De Broglie, L.
The wave nature of the electron. NOLPH 2:244
Dirac, P. A. M.
Theory of electrons and positrons. NOLPH 2:320
Edlén, B.
Presentation [of the Nobel Prize for Physics to Charles H. Townes, Nikolai G. Basov, and Alexander M. Prochorov, Dec. 11, 1964]. NOLPH 4:55
Einstein, A.
Fundamental ideas and problems of the theory of relativity. NOLPH 1:482
Ekstrand, A. G.
Presentation [of the Nobel Prize for Physics to Charles-Edouard Guillaume, Dec. 11, 1920]. NOLPH 1:441
Presentation [of the Nobel Prize for Physics for 1919 to Johannes Stark, June 3, 1920]. NOLPH 1:423
Presentation [of the Nobel Prize for Physics for 1918 to Max Planck, June 2, 1920]. NOLPH 1:405
Fermi, E.
Artificial radioactivity produced by neutron bombardment. NOLPH 2:414
Feynman, R. P.
The development of the space-time view of quantum electrodynamics. NOLPH 4:155
Franck, J.
Transformations of kinetic energy of free electrons into excitation energy of atoms by impacts. NOLPH 2:98
Frank, I. M.
Optics of light sources moving

in refractive media.
NOLPH 3:442
Friesen, S. V.
Presentation [of the Nobel Prize for Physics to Luis W. Alvarez, Dec. 11, 1968].
NOLPH 4:239
Gell-Mann, M.
Symmetry and currents in particle physics.
NOLPH 4:299
Glaser, D. A.
Elementary particles and bubble chambers.
NOLPH 3:529
Granqvist, G.
Presentation [of the Nobel Prize for Physics for 1914 to Max Von Laue, Nov. 12, 1915]. NOLPH 1:343
Guillaume, C. E.
Invar and clinvar.
NOLPH 1:444
Gullstrand, A.
Presentation [of the Nobel Prize for Physics for 1924 to Karl Manne Georg Siegbahn, Dec. 11, 1925].
NOLPH 2:73
Presentation [of the Nobel Prize for Physics for 1923 to Robert Andrews Millikan, May 23, 1924]. NOLPH 2:51
Gustafsson, T.
Presentation [of the Nobel Prize for Physics to Hannes Alfvén and Louis Néel, Dec. 11, 1970]. NOLPH 4:303
Hasselberg, K. B.
Presentation [of the Nobel Prize for Physics to Albert Abraham Michelson, Dec. 12, 1907]. NOLPH 1:159
Presentation [of the Nobel Prize for Physics to Gabriel Lippmann, Dec. 14, 1908].
NOLPH 1:183
Heisenberg, W.
The development of quantum mechanics. NOLPH 2:290
Hertz, G.
The results of electron-impact tests in the light of Bohr's theory of atoms.
NOLPH 2:112
Hess, V. F.
Unsolved problems in physics: tasks for the immediate future in cosmic ray studies.
NOLPH 2:360
Hildebrand, H.
Presentation [of the Nobel Prize for Physics to Guglielmo Marconi and Carl Ferdinand Braun, Dec. 11, 1909].
NOLPH 1:193
Hofstadter, R.
The electron-scattering method and its application to the structure of nuclei and nucleons.
NOLPH 3:560
Hulthén, E.
Presentation [of the Nobel Prize for Physics to Emilio Gino Segrè and Owen Chamberlain, Dec. 11, 1959]. NOLPH 3:487
Presentation [of the Nobel Prize for Physics to Felix Bloch and Edward Mills Purcell, Dec. 11, 1952]. NOLPH 3:199
Presentation [of the Nobel Prize for Physics to Frits Zernike, Dec. 11, 1953]. NOLPH 3:237
Presentation [of the Nobel Prize for Physics to Sir Edward Victor Appleton, Dec. 12, 1947].
NOLPH 3:75
Ising, G.
Presentation [of the Nobel Prize for Physics to Patrick Maynard Stuart Blackett, Dec. 13, 1948].
NOLPH 3:93
Jensen, J. H. D.
Glimpses at the history of the nuclear structure theory.
NOLPH 4:40
Kastler, A.
Optical methods for studying Hertzian resonances.
NOLPH 4:186
Klason, J. P.
Presentation [of the Nobel Prize for Physics to Joseph John Thomson, Dec. 11, 1906].
NOLPH 1:141
Klein, O. B.
Presentation [of the Nobel Prize for Physics to Chen Ning Yang and Tsung Dao Lee, Dec. 11, 1957]. NOLPH 3:389
Presentation [of the Nobel Prize for Physics to Hans Albrecht Bethe, Dec. 11, 1967].
NOLPH 4:211
Kusch, P.
The magnetic moment of the

electron. NOLPH 3:298
Lamb, W. E.
Fine structure of the hydrogen bomb. NOLPH 3:286
Laue, M. V.
Concerning the detection of x-ray interference. NOLPH 1:347
Lawrence, E. O.
The evolution of the cyclotron. NOLPH 2:430
Lee, T. D.
Weak interactions and non-conservation of parity. NOLPH 3:406
Lenard, P. E. A. V.
On cathode rays. NOLPH 1:105
Lindh, A. E.
Presentation [of the Nobel Prize for Physics to Cecil Frank Powell, Dec. 11, 1950]. NOLPH 3:139
Presentation [of the Nobel Prize for Physics to Percy Williams Bridgman, Dec. 11, 1946]. NOLPH 3:53
Lindstedt, A.
[Presentation of the Nobel Prize for Physics for 1905 to Philipp Eduard Anton von Lenard, May 28, 1906]. NOLPH 1:101
Lippmann, G.
Colour photography. NOLPH 1:186
Lorentz, H. A.
The theory of electrons and the propagation of light. NOLPH 1:14
Marconi, G.
Wireless telegraphic communication. NOLPH 1:196
Mayer, M. G.
The shell model. NOLPH 4:18
Michelson, A. A.
Recent advances in spectroscopy. NOLPH 1:166
Millikan, R. A.
The electron and the light-quant from the experimental point of view. NOLPH 2:54
Montelius, O.
Presentation [of the Nobel Prize for Physics to Johannes Diderik Van der Waals, Dec. 12, 1910]. NOLPH 1:251
Mossbauer, R. L.
Recoilless nuclear resonance absorption of gamma radiation. NOLPH 3:584
Néel, L.
Magnetism and the local molecular field. NOLPH 4:318
Nordstrom, T.
Presentation [of the Nobel Prize for Physics to Heike Kamerlingh Omnes, Dec. 11, 1913]. NOLPH 1:303
Odhner, C. T.
Presentation [of the Nobel Prize for Physics to Wilhelm Conrad Röntgen, 1901]. NOLPH 1:3
Onnes, H. K.
Investigations into the properties of substances at low temperatures, which have led, amongst other things, to the preparation of liquid helium. NOLPH 1:306
Oseen, C. W.
Presentation [of the Nobel Prize for Physics for 1925 to James Franck and Gustav Hertz, Dec. 11, 1926]. NOLPH 2:95
Presentation [of the Nobel Prize for Physics to Jean Baptiste Perrin, Dec. 11, 1926]. NOLPH 2:135
Presentation [of the Nobel Prize for Physics to Louis-Victor De Broglie, Dec. 12, 1929]. NOLPH 2:241
Presentation [of the Nobel Prize for Physics for 1928 to Owen Willans Richardson, Dec. 12, 1929]. NOLPH 2:221
Pauli, W.
Exclusion principle and quantum mechanics. NOLPH 3:27
Perrin, J. B.
Discontinuous structure of matter. NOLPH 2:138
Pleijel, H.
Presentation [of the Nobel Prize for Physics to Clinton Joseph Davisson and George Paget Thomson, Dec. 13, 1937]. NOLPH 2:387
Presentation [of the Nobel Prize for Physics to Enrico Fermi, Dec. 12, 1938]. NOLPH 2:409
Presentation [of the Nobel Prize for Physics to James Chadwick,

Dec. 12, 1935]. NOLPH 2:333
Presentation [of the Nobel Prize for Physics to Sir Chandrasekhara Venkata Raman, Dec. 11, 1930]. NOLPH 2:263
Presentation [of the Nobel Prize for Physics for 1932 to Werner Heisenberg and for 1933 to Erwin Schrodinger and Paul Adrien Maurice Dirac, Dec. 11, 1933]. NOLPH 2:283

Planck, M.
The genesis and present state of development of the quantum theory. NOLPH 1:407

Powell, C. F.
The cosmic radiation. NOLPH 3:144

Prochorov, A. M.
Quantum electronics. NOLPH 4:110

Purcell, E. M.
Research in nuclear magnetism. NOLPH 3:219

Raman, Sir C. V.
The molecular scattering of light. NOLPH 2:267

Rayleigh, J. W. S.
The density of gases in the air and the discovery of argon. NOLPH 1:90

Richardson, O. W.
Thermionic phenomena and the laws which govern them. NOLPH 2:224

Rudberg, E. G.
Presentation [of the Nobel Prize for Physics to William Shockley, John Bardeen and Walter Houser Brattain, Dec. 11, 1956]. NOLPH 3:315

Schrodinger, E.
The fundamental idea of wave mechanics. NOLPH 2:305

Schwinger, J.
Relativistic quantum field theory. NOLPH 4:140

Segrè, E. G.
Properties of antinucleons. NOLPH 3:508

Shockley, W.
Transistor technology evokes new physics. NOLPH 3:344

Siegbahn, K. M. G.
Presentation [of the Nobel Prize for Physics to Arthur Holly Compton and Charles Thomson Rees Wilson, Dec. 12, 1927]. NOLPH 2:169
Presentation [of the Nobel Prize for Physics to Donald Arthur Glaser, Dec. 12, 1960]. NOLPH 3:525
Presentation [of the Nobel Prize for Physics to Pavel Alekse-jevič Cerenkov, Il'ja Michalj-lovič Frank and Igor' Evgen'evič Tamm, Dec. 11, 1958]. NOLPH 3:423
The x-ray spectra and the structure of the atoms. NOLPH 2:81

Söderbaum, H. G.
Presentation [of the Nobel Prize for Physics to Nils Gustaf Dalen, 1912]. NOLPH 1:293

Stark, J.
Structural and spectral changes of chemical atoms. NOLPH 1:427

Stern, O.
The method of molecular rays. NOLPH 3:8

Tamm, I. E.
General characteristics of radiations emitted by systems moving with super-light velocities with some applications to plasma physics. NOLPH 3:470

Theel, Hj.
Presentation [of the Nobel Prize for Physics to Hendrik Antoon Lorentz and Pieter Zeeman, 1902]. NOLPH 1:11

Thomson, G. P.
Electronic waves. NOLPH 2:397

Thomson, J. J.
Carriers of negative electricity. NOLPH 1:145

Tomonaga, S. I.
Development of quantum electrodynamics. NOLPH 4:126

Tönrebladh, H. R.
Presentation [of the Nobel Prize for Physics to Antoine Henri Becquerel, Pierre Curie and Marie Sklodowska-Curie, Dec. 11, 1903]. NOLPH 1:47

Townes, C. H.
Production of coherent radiation

by atoms and molecules.
NOLPH 4:58
Waals, J. D. V. D.
The equation of state for gases and liquids. NOLPH 1:254
Waller, I.
Presentation [of the Nobel Prize for Physics to Alfred Kastler, Dec. 12, 1966].
NOLPH 4:183
Presentation [of the Nobel Prize for Physics to Eugene P. Wigner, Maria Goeppert Mayer and J. Hans D. Jensen, Dec. 12, 1963].
NOLPH 4:3
Presentation [of the Nobel Prize for Physics to Hideki Yukawa, Dec. 12, 1949].
NOLPH 3:125
Presentation [of the Nobel Prize for Physics to Lev Davidovic Landau, 1962].
NOLPH 3:607
Presentation [of the Nobel Prize for Physics to Max Born and Walther Bothe, Dec. 11, 1954].
NOLPH 3:253
Presentation [of the Nobel Prize for Physics to Murray Gell-Mann, 1969].
NOLPH 4:295
Presentation [of the Nobel Prize for physics to Robert Hofstadter and Rudolf Ludwig Mossbauer, Dec. 11, 1961].
NOLPH 3:555
Presentation [of the Nobel Prize for Physics to Sin-Itiro Tomonaga, Julian Schwinger, and Richard P. Feynman, Dec. 11, 1965].
NOLPH 4:123
Presentation [of the Nobel Prize for Physics to Sir John Douglas Cockcroft and Ernest Thomas Sinton Walton, Dec. 11, 1951]. NOLPH 3:163
Presentation [of the Nobel Prize for Physics to Willis Eugene Lamb and Polykarp Kusch, Dec. 12, 1955].
NOLPH 3:283
Presentation [of the Nobel Prize for Physics for 1945 to Wolfgang Pauli, Dec. 13, 1946]. NOLPH 3:25
Walton, E. T. S.
The artificial production of fast particles. NOLPH 3:187
Wien, W.
On the laws of thermal radiation. NOLPH 1:275
Wigner, E. P.
Events, laws of nature, and invariance principles.
NOLPH 4:6
Wilson, C. T. R.
On the cloud method of making visible ions and the tracks of ionizing particles.
NOLPH 2:194
Yang, C. N.
The law of parity conservation and other symmetry laws of physics. NOLPH 3:393
Yukawa, H.
Meson theory in its developments. NOLPH 3:128
Zeeman, P.
Light radiation in a magnetic field. NOLPH 1:33
Zernike, F.
How I discovered phase contrast. NOLPH 3:239

NOBEL PRIZE FOR PHYSIOLOGY OR MEDICINE
Adrian, E. D.
The activity of the nerve fibers.
NOLM 2:293
Akerman, J.
Presentation [of the Nobel Prize for Physiology or Medicine to Alexis Carrel, Dec. 11, 1912]. NOLM 1:437
Axelrod, J.
Noradrenaline: fate and control of its biosynthesis.
NOLM 4:444
Banting, F. G.
Diabetes and insulin.
NOLM 2:50
Barany, R.
Some new methods for functional testing of the vestibular apparatus and the cerebellum.
NOLM 1:500
Beadle, G. W.
Genes and chemical reactions in Neurospora. NOLM 3:587
Behring, E. A. V.
Serum therapy in therapeutics and medical science.
NOLM 1:6

Bekesy, G. V.
Concerning the pleasures of observing, and the mechanisms of the inner ear. NOLM 3:722
Bergstrand, H.
Presentation [of the Nobel Prize for Physiology or Medicine to Max Theiler, Dec. 11, 1951]. NOLM 3:347
Bergstrom, S.
Presentation [of the Nobel Prize for Physiology or Medicine to Konrad Bloch and Feodor Lynen, Dec. 11, 1964]. NOLM 4:75
Bernhard, C. G.
Presentation [of the Nobel Prize for Physiology or Medicine to Georg Von Bekesy, Dec. 11, 1961]. NOLM 3:719
Presentation [of the Nobel Prize for Physiology or Medicine to Ragnar Granit, Haldan Keffer Hartline, and George Wald, Dec. 12, 1967]. NOLM 4:251
Bloch, K.
The biological synthesis of cholesterol. NOLM 4:78
Bovet, D.
The relationships between isosterism and competitive phenomena in the field of drug therapy of the autonomic nervous system and that of the neuromuscular transmission. NOLM 3:552
Burnet, Sir F. M.
Immunological recognition of self. NOLM 3:689
Carrel, A.
Suture of blood-vessels and transplantation of organs. NOLM 1:442
Caspersson, T.
Presentation [of the Nobel Prize for Physiology or Medicine to George Wells Beadle, Edward Lawrie Tatum, and Joshua Lederberg, Dec. 11, 1958]. NOLM 3:583
Presentation [of the Nobel Prize for Physiology or Medicine to Hermann Joseph Muller, Dec. 12, 1946]. NOLM 3:149
Chain, E. B.
The chemical structure of the penicillins. NOLM 3:110
Cori, C.
Polysaccharide phosphorylase. NOLM 3:186
Cournand, A. F.
Control of the pulmonary circulation in man with some remarks on methodology. NOLM 3:529
Crick, F. H. C.
On the genetic code. NOLM 3:811
Dale, Sir H. H.
Some recent extensions of the chemical transmission of the effects of nerve impulses. NOLM 2:402
Dam, H.
The discovery of vitamin K, its biological functions and therapeutical application. NOLM 3:8
Delbrück, M.
A physicist's renewed look at biology--twenty years later. NOLM 4:404
Domack, G. J. P.
Further progress in chemotherapy of bacterial infections. NOLM 2:490
Eccles, J. C.
The ionic mechanism of postsynaptic inhibition. NOLM 4:6
Ehrlich, P.
Partial cell functions. NOLM 1:304
Eijkman, C.
Antineuritic vitamin and beriberi. NOLM 2:199
Einthoven, W.
The string galvanometer and the measurement of the action currents of the heart. NOLM 2:94
Enders, J. F.
The cultivation of the poliomyelitis viruses in tissue culture. NOLM 3:448
Engström, A.
Presentation [of the Nobel Prize for Physiology or Medicine to Francis Harry Compton Crick, James Dewey

Watson, and Maurice Hugh Frederick Wilkins, Dec. 11, 1962]. NOLM 3:751
Erlanger, J.
Some observations on the responses of single nerve fibers. NOLM 3:50
Fibiger, J. A. G.
Investigations on Spiroptera carcinoma and the experimental induction of cancer. NOLM 2:122
Fischer, G.
Presentation [of the Nobel Prize for Physiology or Medicine to Paul Hermann Müller, Dec. 11, 1948]. NOLM 3:227
Fleming, Sir A.
Penicillin. NOLM 3:83
Florey, Sir H. W.
Penicillin. NOLM 3:96
Forssmann, W. T. O.
The role of heart catheterization and angiocardiography in the development of modern medicine. NOLM 3:506
Gard, S.
Presentation [of the Nobel Prize for Physiology or Medicine to François Jacob, André Lwoff, and Jacques Monod, Dec. 11, 1965]. NOLM 4:143
Presentation [of the Nobel Prize for Physiology or Medicine to John Franklin Enders, Thomas Huckle Weller, and Frederick Chapman Robbins, Dec. 11, 1954]. NOLM 3:443
Presentation [of the Nobel Prize for Physiology or Medicine to Max Delbrück, Alfred D. Hershey, and Salvador E. Luria, Dec. 10, 1969]. NOLM 4:401
Presentation [of the Nobel Prize for Physiology or Medicine to Sir Frank Macfarlane Burnet and Peter Brian Medawar, Dec. 12, 1960]. NOLM 3:685
Gasser, H. S.
Mammalian nerve fibers. NOLM 3:34
Golgi, C.
The neuron doctrine--theory and facts. NOLM 1:189
Granit, R.
The development of retinal neurophysiology. NOLM 4:255
Presentation [of the Nobel Prize for Physiology or Medicine to John Carew Eccles, Alan Lloyd Hodgkin, and Andrew Fielding Huxley, Dec. 11, 1963]. NOLM 4:3
Gullstrand, A.
How I found the mechanism of intracapsular accommodation. NOLM 1:414
Häggquist, G.
Presentation [of the Nobel Prize for Physiology or Medicine to Hans Spemann, Dec. 12, 1935]. NOLM 2:377
Hammarsten, E.
Presentation [of the Nobel Prize for Physiology or Medicine to Albert Szent-Györgyi Von Nagyrapolt, Dec. 11, 1937]. NOLM 2:435
Presentation [of the Nobel Prize for Physiology or Medicine to Axel Hugo Theodor Theorell, Dec. 12, 1955]. NOLM 3:477
Presentation [of the Nobel Prize for Physiology or Medicine to Hans Adolf Krebs and Fritz Albert Lipmann, Dec. 11, 1953]. NOLM 3:395
Presentation [of the Nobel Prize for Physiology or Medicine to Otto Heinrich Warburg, Dec. 10, 1931]. NOLM 2:251
Hartline, H. K.
Visual receptors and retinal interaction. NOLM 4:269
Hedrén, G.
Presentation [of the Nobel Prize for Physiology or Medicine to Karl Landsteiner, Dec. 11, 1930]. NOLM 2:229
Hench, P. S.
The reversibility of certain rheumatic and nonrheumatic conditions by the use of cortisone or of the pituitary adrenocorticotropic hormone. NOLM 3:311
Henschen, F.
Presentation [of the Nobel Prize for Physiology or Medicine for

1928 to Charles Jules Henri Nicolle]. NOLM 2:175
Presentation [of the Nobel Prize for Physiology or Medicine for 1933 to Thomas Hunt Morgan, June 4, 1934]. NOLM 2:307
Hershey, A. D.
Idiosyncrasies of DNA structure. NOLM 4:417
Hess, W. R.
The central control of the activity of internal organs. NOLM 3:247
Heymans, C. J. F.
The part played by vascular presso- and chemoreceptors in respiratory control. NOLM 2:460
Hill, A. V.
The mechanism of muscular contraction. NOLM 2:10
Hodgkin, A. L.
The ionic basis of nervous conduction. NOLM 4:32
Holley, R. W.
Alanine transfer RNA. NOLM 4:324
Holmgren, I.
Presentation [of the Nobel Prize for Physiology or Medicine to George Hoyt Whipple, George Richards Minot, and William Parry Murphy, Dec. 12, 1934]. NOLM 2:335
Hopkins, Sir F. G.
The earlier history of vitamin research. NOLM 2:211
Houssay, B. A.
The role of the Hypophysis in carbohydrate metabolism and in diabetes. NOLM 3:210
Huggins, C. B.
Endocrine-induced regression of cancers. NOLM 4:235
Huxley, A. F.
The quantitative analysis of excitation and conduction in nerve. NOLM 4:52
Jacob, F.
Genetics of the bacterial cell. NOLM 4:148
Johansson, J. E.
Presentation [of the Nobel Prize for Physiology or Medicine for 1922 to Archibald Vivian Hill and Otto Fritz Meyerhof, Dec. 12, 1923]. NOLM 2:3
Presentation [of the Nobel Prize for Physiology or Medicine to August Krogh, Dec. 11, 1920]. NOLM 1:529
Katz, B.
On the quantal mechanism of neural transmitter release. NOLM 4:485
Kendall, E. C.
The development of cortisone as a therapeutic agent. NOLM 3:270
Khorana, H. G.
Nucleic acid synthesis in the study of the genetic code. NOLM 4:341
Klein, G.
Presentation [of the Nobel Prize for Physiology or Medicine to Peyton Rous and Charles Brenton Huggins, Dec. 13, 1966]. NOLM 4:215
Koch, R.
The current state of the struggle against tuberculosis. NOLM 1:169
Kocher, E. T.
Concerning pathological manifestations in low-grade thyroid diseases. NOLM 1:330
Kornberg, A.
The biologic synthesis of deoxyribonucleic acid. NOLM 3:665
Kossel, A.
The chemical composition of the cell nucleus. NOLM 1:394
Krebs, H. A.
The citric acid cycle. NOLM 3:399
Krogh, A.
A contribution to the physiology of the capillaries. NOLM 1:536
Landsteiner, K.
On individual differences in human blood. NOLM 2:234
Laveran, C. L. A.
Protozoa as causes of disease. NOLM 1:264
Lederberg, J.
A view of genetics. NOLM 3:615

Liljestrand, G.
Presentation [of the Nobel Prize for Physiology or Medicine to André Frederic Cournand, Werner Theodor Otto Forssmann, and Dickinson Woodruff Richards Jr., Dec. 11, 1956]. NOLM 3:501
Presentation [of the Nobel Prize for Physiology or Medicine to Christiaan Eijkman and Sir Frederick Gowland Hopkins, Dec. 11, 1929]. NOLM 2:193
Presentation [of the Nobel Prize for Physiology or Medicine to Edward Calvin Kendall, Tadeus Reichstein, and Philip Showalter Hench, Dec. 11, 1950]. NOLM 3:263
Presentation [of the Nobel Prize for Physiology or Medicine to Sir Alexander Fleming, Ernst Boris Chain, and Sir Howard Walter Florey, Dec. 11, 1945]. NOLM 3:77
Presentation [of the Nobel Prize for Physiology or Medicine to Sir Charles Scott Sherrington and Edgar Douglas Adrian, Dec. 12, 1932]. NOLM 2:273
Presentation [of the Nobel Prize for Physiology or Medicine to Sir Henry Hallett Dale and Otto Loewi, Dec. 12, 1936]. NOLM 2:397
Lipmann, F. A.
Development of the acetylation problem: a personal account. NOLM 3:413
Loewi, O.
The chemical transmission of nerve action. NOLM 2:416
Luria, S. E.
Phage, colicins and macroregulatory phenomena. NOLM 4:426
Lwoff, A.
Interaction among virus, cell, and organism. NOLM 4:186
Lynen, F.
The pathway from "activated acetic acid" to the terpenes and fatty acids. NOLM 4:103
Macleod, J. J. R.
The physiology of insulin and its source in the animal body. NOLM 2:71
Medawar, P. B.
Immunological tolerance. NOLM 3:704
Metchnikoff, E.
On the present state of the question of immunity in infectious diseases. NOLM 1:281
Meyerhof, O. F.
Energy conversions in muscle. NOLM 2:27
Minot, G. R.
The development of liver therapy in pernicious anemia. NOLM 2:357
Monod, J.
From enzymatic adaptation to allosteric transitions. NOLM 4:188
Morgan, T. H.
The relation of genetics to physiology and medicine. NOLM 2:313
Mörner, K. A. H.
Presentation [of the Nobel Prize for Physiology or Medicine to Albrecht Kossel, Dec. 12, 1910]. NOLM 1:389
Presentation [of the Nobel Prize for Physiology or Medicine to Allvar Gullstrand, Dec. 11, 1911]. NOLM 1:411
Presentation [of the Nobel Prize for Physiology or Medicine to Camilio Golgi and Santiago Ramon y Cajal, Dec. 12, 1906]. NOLM 1:185
Presentation [of the Nobel Prize for Physiology or Medicine to Elie Metchnikoff and Paul Ehrlich, Dec. 11, 1908]. NOLM 1:277
Presentation [of the Nobel Prize for Physiology or Medicine to Emil Adolf Von Behring, Dec. 12, 1901]. NOLM 1:3
Presentation [of the Nobel Prize for Physiology or Medicine to Emil Theodor Kocher, Dec. 11, 1909]. NOLM 1:327
Presentation [of the Nobel Prize for Physiology or Medi-

cine to Ivan Petrovich Pavlov, Dec. 12, 1904].
NOLM 1:135
Presentation [of the Nobel Prize for Physiology or Medicine to Niels Ryberg Finsen, 1903]. NOLM 1:123
Presentation [of the Nobel Prize for Physiology or Medicine to Robert Koch, Dec. 12, 1905].
NOLM 1:163
Presentation [of the Nobel Prize for Physiology or Medicine to Sir Ronald Ross, Dec. 12, 1902]. NOLM 1:21

Muller, H. J.
The production of mutations.
NOLM 3:154

Müller, P. H.
Dichloro-diphenyl-trichloroethane and newer insecticides.
NOLM 3:227

Murphy, W. P.
Pernicious anemia.
NOLM 2:369

Nicolle, C. J. H.
Investigations on typhus.
NOLM 2:180

Nirenberg, M. W.
The genetic code.
NOLM 4:370

Ochoa, S.
Enzymatic synthesis of ribonucleic acid.
NOLM 3:645

Olivecrona, H.
Presentation [of the Nobel Prize for Physiology or Medicine to Walter Rudolf Hess and Antonio Caetano De Abreu Freire Egas Moniz, Dec. 12, 1949].
NOLM 3:243

Pavlov, I. P.
Physiology of digestion.
NOLM 1:141

Petterson, A.
Presentation [of the Nobel Prize for Physiology or Medicine to Jules Bordet, 1919]. NOLM 1:519

Ramon y Cajal, S.
The structure and connexions of neurons.
NOLM 1:220

Reichard, P.
Presentation [of the Nobel Prize for Physiology or Medicine to Robert W. Holley, Har Gobind Khorana, and Marshall W. Nirenberg, Dec. 12, 1968].
NOLM 4:321

Reichstein, T.
Chemistry of the adrenal cortex hormones. NOLM 3:291

Richards, D. W.
The contributions of right heart catheterization to physiology and medicine, with some observations on the physiopathology of pulmonary heart disease. NOLM 3:513

Richet, C. R.
Anaphylaxis. NOLM 1:473

Ross, Sir R.
Researches on malaria.
NOLM 1:25

Rous, P.
The challenge to man of the neoplastic cell. NOLM 4:220

Sherrington, Sir C. S.
Inhibition as a coordinative factor. NOLM 2:278

Sjöquist, J.
Presentation [of the Nobel Prize for Physiology or Medicine for 1923 to Frederick Grant Banting and John James Richard Macleod, 1925].
NOLM 2:45

Spemann, H.
The organizer-effect in embryonic development.
NOLM 2:381

Sundberg, C.
Presentation [of the Nobel Prize for Physiology or Medicine to Charles Louis Alphonse Laveran, Dec. 11, 1907].
NOLM 1:259
Presentation [of the Nobel Prize for Physiology or Medicine to Charles Robert Richet, Dec. 11, 1913].
NOLM 1:469

Szent-Györgyi, A.
Oxidation, energy transfer, and vitamins. NOLM 2:440

Tatum, E. L.
A case history in biological research. NOLM 3:602

Theiler, M.
The development of vaccines against yellow fever.
NOLM 3:351

Theorell, A. H. T.
The nature and mode of action of oxidation enzymes. NOLM 3:480
Presentation [of the Nobel Prize for Physiology or Medicine to Carl Ferdinand Cori, Gerty Theresa Cori-Radnitz, and Bernardo Alberto Houssay, Dec. 11, 1947]. NOLM 3:179
Presentation [of the Nobel Prize for Physiology or Medicine to Severo Ochoa and Arthur Kornberg, Dec. 11, 1959]. NOLM 3:641
Uvnäs, B.
Presentation [of the Nobel Prize for Physiology or Medicine to Daniel Bovet, Dec. 11, 1957]. NOLM 3:549
Presentation [of the Nobel Prize for Physiology or Medicine to Julius Axelrod, Ulf Von Euler, and Bernhard Katz, Dec. 12, 1970]. NOLM 4:441
Von Euler, U.
Adrenergic neurotransmitter functions. NOLM 4:470
Wagner-Jauregg, J.
The treatment of dementia paralytica by malaria inoculation. NOLM 2:159
Waksman, S. A.
Streptomycin: background, isolation, properties, and utilization. NOLM 3:370
Wald, G.
The molecular basis of visual excitation. NOLM 4:292
Wallgren, A.
Presentation [of the Nobel Prize for Physiology or Medicine to Selman Abraham Waksman, Dec. 12, 1952]. NOLM 3:365
Warburg, O. H.
The oxygen-transferring ferment of respiration. NOLM 2:254
Watson, J. D.
The involvement of RNA in the synthesis of proteins. NOLM 3:785
Wernstedt, W.
Presentation [of the Nobel Prize for Physiology or Medicine for 1926 to Johannes Andreas Grib Fibiger, Dec. 12, 1927]. NOLM 2:119
Presentation [of the Nobel Prize for Physiology or Medicine to Julius Wagner-Jauregg, Dec. 12, 1927]. NOLM 2:155
Whipple, G. H.
Hemoglobin regeneration as influenced by diet and other factors. NOLM 2:346
Wilkins, M. H. F.
The molecular configuration of nucleic acids. NOLM 3:754
Yalow, R. S.
"Let us join hands, hearts and minds." BA 1977-78:181

Noel-Baker, Philip John
Peace and the arms race (Nobel Lecture, Dec. 11, 1959). NOLP 3:186

NOEL-BAKER, PHILIP JOHN
Jahn, G.
Presentation [of the Nobel Prize for Peace to Philip John Noel-Baker, Dec. 10, 1959]. NOLP 3:175

NOISE
Hatfield, M. O.
Noise. LINRS:211

NOMINATIONS
Conkling, R.
Nomination of U.S. Grant for a third term. BREWE 4:1366
Dougherty, D.
"Hancock the superb." BREWE 5:1904
Ingersoll, R. G.
Nominating Blaine. BREWE 7:2578; HURH:154
Johnson, L. B.
Remarks to the nation (declining nomination to Presidency). ANN 18:613; BA 1967-68:63
Lincoln, A.
"A house divided against itself cannot stand." ANN 9:1; BAS:100 (outline only); BREWE 7:2777; FRIP:197; HURH:88
Nomination of Hubert Horatio Humphrey, Jr. (outline of

speech). CUB:100
Nomination of someone for an office (3 examples). BNH:94
Rogers, W.
Nominating Calvin Coolidge. BAP:298; BAPR: 366
Suggestions for nomination or speech of praise. With examples of. PAE:185

---- See also Acceptance speeches - Nominations; Candidates

NONVIOLENCE
King, M. L., Jr.
Nonviolence: moral challenge for peace and justice. NOLP 3:333; THOMS:99

Noonan, T. Clifford
Introduces the Very Reverend Theodore M. Hesburgh, president of Notre Dame University. PRS:48

NORADRENALIN METABOLISM
Axelrod, J.
Noradrenaline: fate and control of its biosynthesis. NOLM 4:444

Nordmeyer, Arnold
The 'Black budget' 1958 (June 26, 1958). MACS:434 sel.

Nordström, T.
Presentation [of the Nobel Prize for Chemistry to Alfred Werner, Dec. 11, 1913]. NOLC 1:253
Presentation [of the Nobel Prize for Physics to Heike Kamerlingh Onnes, Dec. 11, 1913]. NOLPH 1:303

Norris, George W.
Opposition to Wilson's War Message. ANN 14:101

Norrish, R. G. W.
Some fast reactions in gases studied by flash photolysis and kinetic spectroscopy (Nobel Lecture, Dec. 11, 1967). NOLC 4:206

NORRISH, R. G. W.
Olander, H. A.
Presentation [of the Nobel Prize for Chemistry to Manfred Eigen, R. G. W. Norrish and George Porter, Dec. 11, 1967]. NOLC 4:165

NORTH ATLANTIC PACT See North Atlantic Treaty Organization

NORTH ATLANTIC TREATY ORGANIZATION
Acheson, D. G.
North Atlantic Pact. ANN 16:587
Gruenther, A. M.
NATO. HURH:334
Taft, R. A.
Against the treaty (North Atlantic Pact). ANN 16:591

Northcote, Cyril See Parkinson, Cyril Northcote

Northrop, John Howard
The preparation of pure enzymes and virus proteins (Nobel Lecture, Dec. 12, 1946). NOLC 3:124

NORTHROP, JOHN HOWARD
Tiselius, A. W. K.
Presentation [of the Nobel Prize for Chemistry to James Batcheller Sumner, John Howard Northrop, and Wendell Meredith Stanley, Dec. 12, 1946]. NOLC 3:109

Norton, Eleanor Holmes
In pursuit of equality in academe: new themes and dissonant chords (Chicago, March 7, 1976). BA 1976-77:65

Nottingham, Heneage Finch, 1st Earl of
Opening the prosecution for regicide under Charles II (trial of T. Harrison). BREWE 6:2159

NRA See National Recovery Administration

NUCLEAR INDUCTION
Bloch, F.
The principle of nuclear induction. NOLPH 3:203

NUCLEAR MAGNETISM
Purcell, E. M.
Research in nuclear magnetism. NOLPH 3:219

NUCLEAR PHYSICS
Jensen, J. H. D.
Glimpses at the history of the nuclear structure theory. NOLPH 4:40

NUCLEAR SHELL THEORY
Mayer, M. G.
The shell model. NOLPH 4:18

NUCLEAR WARFARE See Atomic warfare

NUCLEIC ACIDS
Khorana, H. G.
Nucleic acid synthesis on the study of the genetic code. NOLM 4:341
Wilkins, M. H. F.
The molecular configuration of nucleic acids. NOLM 3:754

NUCLEOTIDES
Todd, Sir A. R.
Synthesis in the study of nucleotides. NOLC 3:522

NURENBURG TRIALS See World War, 1939-1945 - War criminals

NURSES AND NURSING
Introductions for nurses (4 examples). BNH:32

Nussbaum, Max
Al Jolson. WALE:225

NUTRITION
Pyke, M.
Man eats dog. MDYG:280

NUTRITION POLICY
Hannah, J. A.
Meeting world food news. BA 1976-77:103

NYE, GERALD P., JR.
Connally, T. T. and others
Censure of Senator Nye. BRR:69

- O -

OATHS
Cox, S. S.
Against the ironclad oath. BREWE 4:1436

O'BRIEN, WILLIAM DAVID
Croarkin, W.
Presents William David O'Brien. LYI:163

OBSCENITY
Brennan, W. J., Jr. and others
Ginzburg et al v. United States: opinion for the court and dissenting opinion. ANN 18:350

OCCUPATIONS
Scott, R.
A job-seeking interview: a transcript. MOPR:381

Ochoa, Severo
Enzymatic synthesis of ribonucleic acid (Nobel Lecture, Dec. 11, 1959). NOLM 3:645

OCHOA, SEVERO
Theorell, H.
Presentation [of the Nobel Prize for Physiology or Medicine to Severo Ochoa and Arthur Kornberg, Dec. 11, 1959]. NOLM 3:641

Ockenga, Harold J.
Evangelical Christianity. ANN 16:115

O'Connell, Daniel
Catholic rights in Ireland (Dublin, Feb. 23, 1814). CLAYP:281
Demand for justice to Ireland. BREWE 8:3107
Ireland worth dying for. Same as his On repeal of the Union
On repeal of the Union (Tara Hill, Ireland, Aug. 15, 1843). BREWE 8:3099; BRYH:358; MCB:288; STRM:198
Speech at Tara. Same as his On repeal of the Union
Speech at a meeting to recover Catholic rights. Same as his Catholic rights in Ireland

Speech at Tara. Same as his On repeal of the Union

O'CONNELL, DANIEL
Lacordaire, J. B. H.
Sacred cause of the human race (panegyric of Daniel O'Connell). BREWE 7:2692

O'Connell, James T.
Responds to an introduction. PRS:138

Odegaard, Charles E.
Bridging the generation gap, the march downtown (Univ. of Washington, June 13, 1970). HOR:42
Responds to an introduction. PRS:155

Odhner, C. T.
Presentation [of the Nobel Prize for Chemistry to Jacobus Henricus Van't Hoff, Dec. 13, 1901]. NOLC 1:3
Presentation [of the Nobel Prize for Physics to Wilhelm Conrad Röntgen, 1901]. NOLPH 1:3

OFFICE - ACCEPTANCE
Accepting an office (2 examples). BNH:87
Coolidge, C.
Have faith in Massachusetts (on being elected President of Massachusetts Senate). BOORA 2:752

OFFICERS See Acceptance speeches - Nominations; Candidates; Educators; Executives; Inaugural addresses; Installation speeches; Nominations; Offices - Acceptance; Public officials; Presidents - United States. Also subheads under this subject

OFFICERS, PRESIDING
Suggestions for a presiding officer. PAE:195

OFFICERS, RETIRING
Suggestions for preparation of a speech for a retiring officer. PAE:187

Oglesby, Carl
How can we continue to sack the ports of Asia and still dream of Jesus. LAA:15

OHIO CANAL
Clinton, D.
Address at the Licking Summit near Newark, Ohio. HAW:119

Okpara, Michael Iheonukara
Progress without tears; address at convocation, University of Nigeria. EMP:138

Olander, A.
Presentation [of the Nobel Prize for Chemistry to Jaroslav Heyrovsky, Dec. 11, 1959]. NOLC 3:561
Presentation [of the Nobel Prize for Chemistry to Manfred Eigen, R. G. W. Norrish and George Porter, Dec. 11, 1967]. NOLC 4:165
Presentation [of the Nobel Prize for Chemistry to Sir Cyril Norman Hinshelwood and Nikolai Nikolaovic Semenov, Dec. 11, 1956]. NOLC 3:471

OLD AGE
Hausman, L.
Older Americans: a natural resource. LINRST:36
Klemme, D.
The age of Gerontion. LINSR:152
Spotted Tail
We are young no longer. ALA:37
Thani Nayagam, X.
Age and learning. MONS:187

Old Tassel, Indian chief
Plea for his home. BREWE 7:2569

Olivecrona, H.
Presentation [of the Nobel Prize for Physiology or Medicine to Walter Rudolf Hess and Antonio Caetano De Abreu Freire Egas Moniz, Dec. 12, 1949]. NOLM 3:243

Oliver, Robert T.
Culture and communication.

ARS:19
Responds to an introduction. PRS:152

Olmsted, Frederick Law
Unplanned growth of cities. ANN 10:224

Olney, Richard
Presents Woodrow Wilson. LYI:215

Olson, Culbert L.
Migratory labor and civil liberties. ANN 15:587

Olson, Harvey S.
Introduces Admiral John S. McCain. PRS:56
Introduces Charles O. Finley, owner, Kansas City Athletics. BRS:114
Introduces Dr. Glenn T. Seaborg, chairman of the Atomic Energy Commission. PRS:47
Introduces Dr. Luther L. Terry, United States Surgeon General. PRS:42
Introduces Dr. Max Rafferty, State Superintendent of Public Instruction (California). PRS:53
Introduces Dr. Walter H. Judd. PRS:125
Introduces Earl B. Hathaway, president of Firestone Tire and Rubber Company. PRS:13
Introduces Harry Schwartz of the New York Times. PRS:60
Introduces Marguerite Higgins. PRS:107
Introduces Ronald Reagan. PRS:49
Introduces Senator Everett M. Dirksen. PRS:121
Introduces Senator Karl E. Mundt. PRS:108
Introduces the Honorable Hervé Alphand, French Ambassador to the United States. PRS:35
Introduces William McChesney Martin, Jr., chairman, board of governors, Federal Reserve System. PRS:63

O'NEILL, EUGENE GLADSTONE
Brown, J. E.
Acceptance [of the Nobel Prize for Literature for Eugene Gladstone O'Neill, 1936]. NOB 19:131; NOL:336
Hallström, P.
Presentation [of the Nobel Prize for Literature to Eugene Gladstone O'Neill, 1936]. NOB 19:125; NOL:330

Ong Pang Boon
Educational pyramid. MONS:436

ONN BIN JAFFIR
Abdul Rahman, T.
Dato Onn--a great leader. MONS:33

Onnes, Heike Kamerlingh
Investigations into the properties of substances at low temperatures, which have led, amongst other things, to the preparation of liquid helium (Nobel Lecture, Dec. 11, 1913). NOLPH 1:306

ONNES, HEIKE KAMERLINGH
Nordstrom, T.
Presentation [of the Nobel Prize for Physics to Heike Kamerlingh Onnes, Dec. 11, 1913]. NOLPH 1:303

Onsager, Lars
The motion of ions: principles and concepts (Nobel Lecture, Dec. 11, 1968). NOLC 4:272

ONSAGER, LARS
Claesson, S.
Presentation [of the Nobel Prize for Chemistry to Lars Onsager, Dec. 11, 1968]. NOLC 4:269

OPENING ADDRESSES
Boorstin, D. J.
Beginnings. BA 1976-77:138
Douglass, F.
The abilities and possibilities of our race. FON:326
Lee Kuan Yew
Unionism: rethinking is vital (opening National Trade Union

Conference). MONS:366
Lim See Aun
Doubting Thomases were wrong (opening of Chemical Company of Malaysian factory). MONS:153
Thomson, T. J. B.
Spirit of humanity (opening of Federal Court of Malaysia). MONS:285
Trimble, A.
Keynote address NCAI Convention, October 18, 1976. MAES:233
Webster, D.
Railroad in New Hampshire (opening Northern Railroad). ANN 7:388

---- See also Club speeches; Dedication addresses; Welcoming addresses

Oppenheimer, J. Robert
Prospect in the arts and sciences (at Columbia University bicentennial anniversary celebration). New York, Dec. 26, 1954. HURH:319; HURS:211
"We know too much for one man to know much." Same as his Prospect in the arts and sciences

OPPORTUNITY
Manickavasagam, V.
Era of opportunity. MONS:162

OPTIMISM
Martin, D.
A case for optimism. EHN:124; MOP:154; MOPR:130

OREGON
Calhoun, J. C.
On territorial expansion. ANN 7:87
Cobb, H.
"Fifty-four forty or right." BREWE 4:1317
Winthrop, R. C.
Oregon question. ANN 7:317

ORGANIC COMPOUNDS
Pregl, F.
Quantitative micro-analysis of organic substances. NOLC 2:28

ORGANIZATION
Goldhaber, G. M.
Organizational communication. LINRST:44

ORGANIZED LABOR See Labor Unions

ORGANS (ANATOMY)
Hess, W. R.
The central control of the activity of internal organs. NOLM 3:247

ORIENT
Dean, V. M.
Minds of the non-western world. ARS:234

Orr, John Boyd See Boyd Orr, John

Osborne, Lithgow
Acceptance [of the Nobel Prize for Peace for Cordell Hull, Dec. 10, 1945]. NOLP 2:318

Osborne, Peter
It is time for us to be up and doing. (New Haven African Church, July 5, 1832). FON:47

Osceola See Maestas, J. R.

Oseen, C. W.
Presentation [of the Nobel Prize for Physics for 1925 to James Franck and Gustav Hertz, Dec. 11, 1926]. NOLPH 2:95
Presentation [of the Nobel Prize for Physics to Jean Baptiste Perrin, Dec. 11, 1926]. NOLPH 2:135
Presentation [of the Nobel Prize for Physics to Louis-Victor De Broglie, Dec. 12, 1929]. NOLPH 2:241
Presentation [of the Nobel Prize for Physics for 1928 to Owen Willans Richardson, Dec. 12, 1929]. NOLPH 2:221

Osgood, David
An American Thanksgiving for

divine favor. (Medford, Mass., Feb. 19, 1795). DAVF:42

Osias, Camilo
Justice and separation of powers (National Assembly, May 23, 1938). CURM:190

Osmeña, Sergio
The National Assembly, its aims and accomplishments (Bulacan, May 7, 1910). CURM:50

OSSIETZKY, CARL VON
Stang, F.
Presentation [of the Nobel Prize for Peace, 1935, to Carl Von Ossietzky, Dec. 10, 1936]. NOLP 2:207

Österling, Anders
Presentation [of the Nobel Prize for Literature to Albert Camus, 1957]. NOB 4:3; NOL:522
Presentation [of the Nobel Prize for Literature to André Gide, 1947]. NOB 7:3; NOL:422
Presentation [of the Nobel Prize for Literature to Bertrand Arthur William Russell, 1950]. NOB 15:255; NOL:449
Presentation [of the Nobel Prize for Literature to Erik Axel Karlfeldt, 1931]. NOB 10:101; NOL:295
Presentation [of the Nobel Prize for Literature to Ernest Miller Hemingway, 1954]. NOB 9:3; NOL:497
Presentation [of the Nobel Prize for Literature to François Mauriac, 1952]. NOB 13:3; NOL:477
Presentation [of the Nobel Prize for Literature to Giorgos Seferis, 1963]. NOB 17:3; NOL:580
Presentation [of the Nobel Prize for Literature to Hermann Hesse, 1946]. NOB 9:233; NOL:412
Presentation [of the Nobel Prize for Literature to Ivo Andrić, 1961]. NOB 1:117; NOL:562
Presentation [of the Nobel Prize for Literature to Johannes Vilhelm Jensen, 1944]. NOB 8:259; NOL:397
Presentation [of the Nobel Prize for Literature to John Galsworthy, 1932]. NOB 6:227; NOL:302
Presentation [of the Nobel Prize for Literature to John Steinbeck, 1962]. NOB 19:201; NOL:572
Presentation [of the Nobel Prize for Literature to Miguel Angel Asturias, 1967]. NOB 2:3; NOL:624
Presentation [of the Nobel Prize for Literature to Mikhail Aleksandrovich Sholokhov, 1965]. NOB 17:37; NOL:603
Presentation [of the Nobel Prize for Literature to Pär Fabian Lagerkvist, 1951]. NOB 10:201; NOL:466
Presentation [of the Nobel Prize for Literature to Saint-John Perse, 1960]. NOB 20:3; NOL:553
Presentation [of the Nobel Prize for Literature to Salvatore Quasimodo, 1959]. NOB 20:281; NOL:534
Presentation [of the Nobel Prize for Literature to Shmuel Yosef Agnon and Leonie Nelly Sachs, 1966]. NOB 1:3; NOB 16:3; NOL:611
Presentation [of the Nobel Prize for Literature to Thomas Stearns Eliot, 1948]. NOB 5:261; NOL:431
Presentation address [of the Nobel Prize for Literature to Yasunari Kawabata, 1968]. NOB 11:3

Ostwald, Wilhelm
On catalysis (Nobel Lecture, Dec. 12, 1909). NOLC 1:150

OSTWALD, WILHELM
Hildebrand, H.
Presentation [of the Nobel Prize for Chemistry to Wilhelm Ostwald, Dec. 12, 1909]. NOLC 1:147

Otis, Harrison Gray
Abolitionism is equivalent to

revolution (1835) (Faneuil Hall, Boston, Aug. 22, 1835). DAVF:138
Hamilton's influence on American institutions. BREWE 8:3111

Otis, James
Against Writs of Assistance. Same as his Writs of Assistance, February, 1761
For individual sovereignty and against "Writs of Assistance." Same as his Writs of Assistance, February, 1761
Speech against the Writs of Assistance. Same as his Writs of Assistance, February, 1761
Writs of Assistance, February, 1761. ANN 2:74; BREWE 8:3125; POC:90

OUTLINES (SPEECH) See Speeches - Outlines of

Overhill, Jack
Regular snob. MDYG:75

Oxford and Asquith, Herbert Henry, 1st Earl of
"The Commons and constitutional change. Same as his Parliament Bill, 1911
Parliament Bill, 1911. (H. of Commons, July 24, 1911). MCB:162

---- and others (Sir Edward Carson and John E. Redmond)
Debate on the Government of Ireland Bill. (H. of Commons, April 11, 1912). MCB:321

OXFORD UNIVERSITY
Eliezer, C. J.
Toast to Oxford. MONS:271

- P -

PACIFIC See Orient

PACIFISM
Walker, A.
Why I am a Christian pacifist. MCA:204

PAINE, THOMAS
Erskine, T.
Against Thomas Williams for the publication of Paine's Age of Reason. BREWE 6:2038
Free speech and fundamental rights: defense of Tom Paine. BREWE 6:2069; CLAYP:166

PAINTERS See Art and artists

PAINTING See Art and artists

Palewski, Gaston See Sykes, C., jt. auth.

Palmaer, W.
Presentation [of the Nobel Prize for Chemistry, 1931 to Carl Bosch and Friedrich Bergius, May 21, 1932]. NOLC 2:189
Presentation [of the Nobel Prize for Chemistry for 1934 to Harold Clayton Urey, Feb. 14, 1935]. NOLC 2:333
Presentation [of the Nobel Prize for Chemistry to Jean Frédéric Joliot and Irène Joliot-Curie, Dec. 12, 1935]. NOLC 2:359
Presentation [of the Nobel Prize for Chemistry to Walter Norman Haworth and Paul Karrer, Dec. 11, 1937]. NOLC 2:407

PALMER, JAMES
Griffin, C. E.
Presents James Palmer. LYI:67

Palmer, Joseph
Africa: continent of change. (Chicago Council on Foreign Relations, Dec. 5, 1968. Speech in 2nd ed. given at Brandeis Univ. in 1966). LINRS:33
New Africa: continent of change. LINR:32

Palmerston, Henry John Temple, 3d Viscount
Against war on Ireland. BREWE 8:3134
"Civis Romanus sum speech." Same as his On affairs in Greece
On affairs in Greece (H. of Commons, June 25, 1850). MCB:5

On the death of Cobden.
BREWE 8:3131

PALMERSTON, HENRY JOHN TEMPLE, 3d VISCOUNT
Stanley, A. P.
Palmerston and the duty of England (funeral oration).
BREWE 9:3506

Palovesik, Susan
Ripples of hope. BREWW:179

PANAMA CANAL
Hayakawa, S. I.
Senate debate over ratification of treaties concerning the Panama Canal.
BA 1977-78:17
Roosevelt, T.
"I took the Canal Zone."
STAT 2:2073
Rusk, D.
For ratification of treaties with Panama. BA 1977-78:9

PANAMA CANAL TREATIES, 1977
Hayakawa, S. I.
Senate debate over ratification of treaties concerning the Panama Canal.
BA 1977-78:17
McIntyre, T. J.
Keeping the Senate independent.
BA 1977-78:44
Rusk, D.
For ratification of treaties with Panama. BA 1977-78:9

PANAMA CONGRESS, 1826
Adams, J. Q.
On participating in a congress of American nations.
ANN 5:188

Pandora, Gary See Andino, Judy

Pankhurst, Mrs. Emmeline (Goulden)
Importance of the vote.
DRYH:442
Speech at the Bow Street Police Court (Oct. 24, 1908).
BRYF:499; BRYH:455

Paredes, Quintin
A brief sketch of the Philippines--past, present and future (Baltimore, April 4, 1938). CURM:214

PARENT AND CHILD
Welcome to parents and ladies of the Woman's Missionary Society on Education Day.
HNWM:21

PARIS
Buckley, F. R.
La Folle epoque. MDYG:181

PARITY NONCONSERVATION
Lee, T. D.
Weak interactions and nonconservation of parity.
NOLPH 3:406
Yang, C. N.
The law of parity conservation and other symmetry laws of physics. NOLPH 3:393

Parker, Theodore
Critique of American churches.
ANN 7:486
Discourse on the death of Daniel Webster. BREWE 8:3137
On Daniel Webster after the Compromise of 1850. Same as his Discourse on the death of Daniel Webster
Present crisis in American affairs. ANN 8:372
State of the nation (1850).
ANN 8:114
Transient and permanent in Christianity. LINS:178

Parkes, Henry
Eight-hour movement. MCA:33
New constellation. MCA:37

PARKINSON, CYRIL NORTHCOTE
Cragg, R. T.
Presents Cyril Northcote.
LYI:45

PARKS See Dedication addresses - Parks

PARLIAMENT ACT, 1911
Curzon of Kedleston, G. and others
Debate on the Parliament Bill.
MCB:169
Oxford and Asquith, H. H.
Parliament Bill, 1911.
MCB:162

PARLIAMENTARY FORM OF GOVERNMENT See Great Britain - Parliament

Parnell, Charles Stewart
Against nonresident landlords. BREWE 8:3145
At Ennis (boycotting defined and defended) (Ennis, Ireland, Sept. 19, 1880). BRYF:544; MCB:296; STRM:346
His first speech in America. BREWE 8:3143
The Irish land question. Same as his At Ennis (boycotting defined and defended)

Parry, David
Organized labor as the "Great Muscle Trust." ANN 12:513

Parry, William Edward
New Zealand citizenship, 1948 (New Zealand House of Representatives, Aug. 17, 1948). MACS:294 sel.

Parson, Mary Jean
Idealism: what's wrong with it? (New York, July 14, 1975). BA 1975-76:166

Parsons, Albert R.
Address at trial, Chicago, October 7-9, 1886. ACC:90; PAF:65

Parsons, Theodore and others (E. Pearson)
Disputation on "The Legality of Enslaving the Africans." POC:27

PARTICLES
Alvarez, L. W.
Recent developments in particle physics. NOLPH 4:241
Gell-Mann, M.
Symmetry and currents in particle physics. NOLPH 4:299

PARTICLES (NUCLEAR PHYSICS)
Cerenkov, P. A.
Radiation of particles moving at a velocity exceeding that of light, and some of the possibilities for their use in experimental physics. NOLPH 3:423
Cockcroft, Sir J. D.
Experiments on the interaction of high-speed nucleons with atomic nuclei. NOLPH 3:167
Glaser, D. A.
Elementary particles and bubble chambers. NOLPH 3:529
Hofstadter, R.
The electron-scattering method and its application to the structure of nuclei and nucleons. NOLPH 3:560
Walton, E. T. S.
The artificial production of fast particles. NOLPH 3:187

PASSION
Saurin, J.
Effect of passion. BREWE 9:3371

PATIENCE
Tertullian, Q. S. F.
Beauty of patience. BREWE 9:3597

PATRIOTISM
Abdul Rahman, T.
Soul of our nation. MONS:36
Bocobo, J. C.
Love of country. CURM:149
Bolingbroke, H. S.-J.
Patriotism. BREWE 2:550
Clay, H.
Noblest public virtue. BREWE 4:1271
Goldman, E.
Anarchy vs. patriotism. HURH:166
Grattan, H.
Unsurrendering fidelity to country. BREWE 6:2333
Hampden, J.
Patriot's duty defined: against own impeachment. BREWE 6:2385
Jacobusse, K. D.
Peace through patriotism. SCHW:168
King, T. S.
Fourth of July oration, 1860. HAW:231
McKinley, W.
American patriotism (at dedi-

cation of Cuyahoga County Soldiers' and Sailors' Monument in Cleveland). BREWE 8:2899
Muhammad Ghazali bin Shafie
Loyalty to the nation (Malaya). MONS:218
Sheridan, R. B.
Patriotism and perquisites. BREWE 9:3439
Walpole, R.
On patriots (at motion to dismiss him from Council). BREWE 10:3724

Patterson, Morehead
Responds to an introduction. PRS:160

Patterson, William L.
"Free by '63." (Civil Rights Congress, 1960). FON:924

Patton, George S.
"Flanks are something for the enemy to worry about." (France, July 31, 1944). HURH:274

Paul VI (Giovanni Battista Montini - Pope)
Address before United Nations. BA 1965-66:67; OLIS:297
Key to peace. BAS:150 (outline only)

Paul, Nathaniel
The abolition of slavery. (Albany, N.Y., July 5, 1827). FON:37

Pauli, Wolfgang
Exclusion principle and quantum mechanics (Nobel Lecture for 1945, Dec. 13, 1946). NOLPH 3:27

PAULI, WOLFGANG
Waller, I.
Presentation [of the Nobel Prize for Physics for 1945 to Wolfgang Pauli, Dec. 13, 1946]. NOLPH 3:25

Pauling, Linus Carl
Modern structural chemistry (Nobel Lecture, Dec. 11, 1954). NOLC 3:429
Science and peace (Nobel Lecture for 1962, Dec. 11, 1963). NOLP 3:271

PAULING, LINUS CARL
Hagg, G.
Presentation [of the Nobel Prize for Chemistry to Linus Carl Pauling, Dec. 11, 1954]. NOLC 3:425
Jahn, G.
Presentation [of the Nobel Prize for Peace for 1962 to Linus Carl Pauling, Dec. 10, 1963]. NOLP 3:259

Pavlov, Ivan Petrovich
Physiology of digestion (Nobel Lecture, Dec. 12, 1904). NOLM 1:141

PAVLOV, IVAN PETROVICH
Mörncr, K. A. H.
Presentation [of the Nobel Prize for Physiology or Medicine to Ivan Petrovich Pavlov, Dec. 12, 1904]. NOLM 1:135

Payne, Daniel A.
Slavery brutalizes man. (Fordsboro, N.Y., June, 1839). FON:66

Payne, James R.
Australia and the Vietnam War. VI:75

PEACE
Angell, N.
Peace and the public mind (Nobel Lecture for 1934, June 12, 1935). NOLP 2:153
Arnoldson, K. P.
World referendum (Nobel Lecture, Dec. 10, 1908). NOLP 1:175
Aubert, J.
Vietnam and world peace. VI:104
Bennett, J. C.
Issue of peace: the voice of religion. BA 1965-66:142
Blake, E. C.
Ecumenism and peace. VI:132
Borlaug, N. E.
The green revolution, peace, humanity (Nobel Lecture, Dec.

11, 1970). NOLP 3:454
Buisson, F. E.
Changes in concepts of war and peace (Nobel Lecture, 1927, May 31, 1928). NOLP 2:35
Bunche, R. J.
Some reflections on peace in our time (Nobel Lecture, Dec. 11, 1950). NOLP 2:443
Butler, N. M.
Radio address (Nobel Lecture, Dec. 12, 1931). NOLP 2:136
Cadbury, H. J.
Quakers and peace (Nobel Lecture, Dec. 12, 1947). NOLP 2:391
Chandler, R.
Quest for peace. SCHW:180
Churchill, W. L. S.
Sinews of peace (speech at Fulton, Missouri). ANN 16:365; MCB:541
Cremer, W. R.
The progress and advantages of international arbitration (Nobel Lecture for 1903, Jan. 15, 1905). NOLP 1:46
Demosthenes
Oration on the peace. BREWE 5:1759; SAG:223
Dulles, J. F.
Peace through law. ANN 17:528
Eisenhower, D. D.
Crusade for peace. ANN 17:199
Price of peace: second inaugural address. USINAU:263; USINAUG:263
Field, D. D.
Cost of "Blood and Iron." BREWE 6:2157
Fosdick, H. E.
Unknown soldier. LINS:312
Garfield, J. A.
Revolution and the logic of coercion. BREWE 6:2226
Gobat, C. A.
The development of the Hague Conventions of July 29, 1899 (Nobel Lecture for 1902, Oslo, July 18, 1906). NOLP 1:30
Henderson, A.
Essential elements of a universal and enduring peace (Nobel Lecture, Dec. 11, 1934). NOLP 2:185
Hildebrandt, T.
Christian way. SCHW:198
Inozemstev, N. N.
Alternative to war. MDV:69
Jacobusse, K. D.
Peace through patriotism. SCHW:168
Jouhaux, L.
Fifty years of trade-union activity in behalf of peace (Nobel Lecture, Dec. 11, 1951). NOLP 3:10
Kellogg, F. B.
Acceptance and banquet speech [for the Nobel Prize for Peace, 1929 (Dec. 10, 1930)]. NOLP 2:79
Kennedy, J. F.
Step toward peace. ANN 18:192
Toward a strategy of peace. KEO:312; MDV:2
Korf, J.
And old hate walked on through time. SCHW:189
Loula, L. A.
Drunken orgy. SCHW:149
Marshall, G. C.
Essentials of peace (Nobel Lecture, Dec. 11, 1953). NOLP 3:76
Moneta, E. T.
Peace and law in the Italian tradition (Nobel Lecture, 1907, Aug. 25, 1909). NOLP 1:114
Nixon, R. M.
Pursuit of peace. BA 1969-70:9; ERP:145
Noel-Baker, P. J.
Peace and the arms race (Nobel Lecture, Dec. 11, 1959). NOLP 3:186
Paul VI
Key to peace. BAS:150 (outline only)
Pearson, L. B.
The four faces of peace (Nobel Lecture, Dec. 11, 1957). NOLP 3:129
Pire, G.
Brotherly love: foundation of peace (Nobel Lecture, Dec. 11, 1958). NOLP 3:157
Razak, T. A.

And then came peace (Peace Agreement between Malaysia and Indonesia). MONS:94
Roosevelt, F. D.
Quarantining the aggressors. ANN 15:502; BEN:93; BOORA 2:847; BRYF:474; ROD:263
Root, E.
Towards making peace permanent (Nobel Lecture for 1912). NOLP 1:247
Saavedra Lamas, C.
Radio address (Nobel Lecture, Nov. 29, 1936). NOLP 2:225
Schweitzer, A.
The problem of peace (Nobel Lecture for 1952, Nov. 4, 1954). NOLP 3:46
Söderblom, N.
The role of the church in promoting peace (Nobel Lecture, Dec. 11, 1930). NOLP 2:93
Swets, P.
Bootstraps and moonshots. SCHW:183
Vander Jagt, G.
Price of the best. SCHW:59
Van Engen, B.
Casual approach to war. SCHW:195
Wallace, H. A.
Is American foreign policy leading to war? ANN 16:370
Wilson, W.
Peace without victory. ANN 14:65; FRIP:286; HURH:173

---- See also League of Nations; United Nations

PEACE CONFERENCE, 1919
Trotter, W. M.
How I managed to reach the Peace Conference. FON:470

---- SESSION JANUARY 25
Wilson, W.
Peace Conference at Paris: Session, January 25, 1919. HURH:185

---- SESSION, FEBRUARY 15
Wilson, W.
Speech at Peace Conference at Paris (Session February 15, 1919). ANN 14:180

PEACE MOVEMENT
Bajer, F.
The organization of the Peace Movement (Nobel Lecture, 1908, May 18, 1909). NOLP 1:190
Suttner, B. V.
The evolution of the Peace Movement (Nobel Lecture for 1905, April 18, 1906). NOLP 1:84

Peaches, Daniel
Statement on the problems of the elderly American Indians at the Conference on Indian Elders, Albuquerque, New Mexico, July 17, 1975. MAES:179

Peale, Norman Vincent
Responds to introductions. PRS:104; 113

Pearl, Chaim
Seal of truth. WALE:140

PEARL HARBOR See World War, 1939-1945 - United States

Pearson, Eliphalet See Parsons, T., jt. auth.

Pearson, Lester B.
The four faces of peace (Nobel Lecture, Dec. 11, 1957). NOLP 3:129

PEARSON, LESTER B.
Bullock, H.
Presents Lester B. Pearson. LYI:207
Davis, J. W.
Presents Lester B. Pearson. LYI:220
Jahn, G.
Presentation [of the Nobel Prize for Peace to Lester Bowles Pearson, Dec. 10, 1957]. NOLP 3:119

Peckham, Rufus William and others (J. M. Harlan and O. W. Holmes, Jr.)
Lochner v. New York, 1905:

opinion for the court and dissenting opinion. ANN 13:8

Peden, William
Is Thomas Jefferson relevant? (Columbia, Mo., April 13, 1972). BA 1972-73:94

Peel, Sir Robert, Bart.
Bank charter--the currency. STRM:213
On the repeal of the Corn Laws. BREWE 8:3148; JAE:102
Plea for higher education (installation speech as Lord Rector of University of Glasgow). BREWE 8:3153

Peirce, Herbert H. D.
Acceptance [of the Nobel Prize for Peace for Theodore Roosevelt, Dec. 10, 1906]. NOLP 1:99

Pelham, Henry See Walpole, R., jt. auth.

PELTIER, JEAN
Mackintosh, J.
In behalf of free speech: on the trial of Jean Peltier accused of libelling Napoleon Bonaparte. BREWE 8:2919

PENAL COLONIES
Higinbotham, G.
For the annexation of New Guinea. MCA:43

PENANG UNIVERSITY See University of Penang

Pendleton, Edmund
Liberty and government in America. BREWE 8:3156

---- See also Mason, G., jt. auth.

PENICILLIN
Chain, E. B.
The chemical structure of the penicillins. NOLM 3:110
Fleming, Sir A.
Penicillin. NOLM 3:83
Florey, Sir H. W.
Penicillin. NOLM 3:96

Penn, William
Golden rule against tyranny. BREWE 8:3162

Pennings, Burrell
New men for a new world. SCHW:153

Pennington, J. W. C.
The position and duties of the colored people. (Poughkeepsie, N.Y., August 24, 1863). FON:271

PENNSYLVANIA - SUPREME COURT
Gibson, J. B.
Against judicial review: dissenting opinion on Eakin v. Raub. ANN 5:174

PENSIONS
Curran, J. P.
Against pensions. BREWE 4:1543

---- MILITARY
Cleveland, G.
Skeptical view of pension legislation. ANN 11:90

Pepper, George Wharton
Introducing Ferdinand Foch. LYI:145
Presents Charles Evans Hughes. LYI:127
Presents Earl Warren. LYI:121

PEPPER, GEORGE WHARTON
Mason, W. C.
Presents George Wharton Pepper. LYI:129

Percy, Charles H.
Chicagoan goes South. BA 1965-66:106
Eulogy for Robert Kennedy (July 30, 1968). JAM:42
For the nomination of Gerald R. Ford. (Washington, D.C., Nov. 27, 1973). BA 1973-74:189
Responds to an introduction. PRS:147

Pericles
Funeral oration. Same as his On those who died in the war

On those who died in the war. ARS:191; BAS:133 (outline only); BREWE 8:3169; SAG:33
On the cause of Athenian greatness. Same as his On those who died in the war
Pericles' funeral speech. Same as his On those who died in the war

Perkins, James A.
Bridging the generation gap, how the New Deal became today's establishment (Univ. of Notre Dame, June 2, 1968). HOR:56

PERMANENT COURT OF INTERNATIONAL JUSTICE
Coughlin, C. E.
The menace of the World Court (1935). DAVF:249

PERMANENT INTERNATIONAL PEACE BUREAU
Løvland, J. G.
Presentation [of the Nobel Prize for Peace to the Permanent International Peace Bureau, Dec. 10, 1910]. NOLP 1:223

PERNICIOUS ANEMIA
Minot, G. R.
The development of liver therapy in pernicious anemia. NOLM 2:357
Murphy, W. P.
Pernicious anemia. NOLM 2:369

Perrin, Jean Baptiste
Discontinuous structure of matter (Nobel Lecture, Dec. 11, 1926). NOLPH 2:138

PERRIN, JEAN BAPTISTE
Oseen, C. W.
Presentation [of the Nobel Prize for Physics to Jean Baptiste Perrin, Dec. 11, 1926]. NOLPH 2:135

Perrott, Russell See Forten, J., jt. auth.

Perry, Micajah See Walpole, R., jt. auth.

Perse, Saint-John
Acceptance [of the Nobel Prize for Literature, 1960]. NOB 20:7; NOL:556

PERSE, SAINT-JOHN
Österling, A.
Presentation [of the Nobel Prize for Literature to Saint-John Perse, 1960]. NOB 20:3; NOL:553

PERSIA See Iran

PERSUASIVE SPEECHES
Beecher, L.
A plea for the West. HOW:133
Crary, D. R.
Plague of people. LINR:220
Crittenden, T. T.
Trade and commerce for the southwestern states. ANN 11:16
Davies, S.
Curse of cowardice. ANN 2:23; POC:534
Demosthenes
First Olynthiac oration. SAG:199
First Philippic. COG:40; SAG:188
On the Chersoneus. SAG:235
Oration on the peace. BREWE 5:1759; SAG:223
Second Olynthiac. BREWE 5:1754; COG:56; SAG:205
Second Philippic. BREWE 5:1763; SAG:228
Third Olynthiac. SAG:212
Third Philippic. COG:91; SAG:249
Freedom from hunger (outline of speech to persuade that continued good health of American people requires easy access to pharmaceutical vitamins and food supplements). CUB:48
Geiman, C. K.
Are they really "unteachable"? LINR:94
Hall, C.
A heap of trouble. EHN:316
Hardin, B.
The Wilkinson and Murdaugh case. BLY:48
Isocrates
Panogyric. COG:27; SAG:99

Jones, J. L.
Who is tampering with the soul of America? LINR:211; LINRS:220
Kennedy, J. F.
Inaugural address. ALS:265; ANN 18:5; ARN:312; ARS:226; BAS:145 (outline only); BEN:143; BOORA 2:913; BRR:82; BRYF:437; BRYO:232; GRG:113; HURH:358; LINR:297; LINRS:296; LINRST:366; LINS:375; MAC:244; MACR:284; MDV:127; OLIS:282; THOMS:17; USINAU:267; USINAUG:267
Intellectual and the politician. BAP:285; LINR:267
King, M. L., Jr.
"I have a dream." AND:50; ANN 18:156; ARS:154; BRR:78; CAPG:83; FON:971; GRG:117; HURH:366; LINR:290; LINRS:289; LINRST:362; LINS:379; MAC:247; MACR:288; MDV:156; MUS:336; OE:152; OLIS:289; SMHV:182; THOMS:94
Kirk, G.
Responsibilities of the educated man (at centennial of University of Denver). LINR:143
Lilienthal, D. E.
My faith in democracy. ALA:111
Lodge, H. C.
For intervention in Cuba. ANN 12:85
MacArthur, D.
Defends his conduct of the war in Korea. ALS:243; ANN 17:79; ARS:279; BAS:82 (outline only); BEN: 113; BOSR:22; GRG:88; HURH:293; HURS:214; LINS:337
Farewell to the cadets (accepting Sylvanus Thayer award for service to his nation, West Point, May 12, 1962). LINR:264; LINRS:283; LINRST:357; MDV:20; MUS:332
McWhirter, A. J.
Appeal to European immigrants to come to the South. ANN 10:587
Mason, J. M.
Speech of J. M. Mason, at Richmond, Va., June 8, 1861. ECH:166
Oliver, R. T.
Culture and communication. ARS:19
Roosevelt, F. D.
War address (December 8, 1941). ANN 16:103; CUB:88 (outline); GRG:71; HURH:265; LINS:327; MAC:242; MACR:282; ROD:306
Rush, R.
Fourth of July oration, 1812. HAW:16
Sampson, E. S.
Choose one of five. MOP:386
Stevens, T.
Education as a public duty. ANN 6:136
Stowe, L.
Children, peanuts--and you. MOP:263
Suggestions for preparation of the persuasive speech. With examples of. BRP:52, 194
Symonds, W.
Britain's claim to a New World empire justified. ANN 1:32
Wayman, M. K.
Unmentionable diseases. LINR:224
Webster, D.
Reply to Hayne. HOW:53
Why go second class? (Outline of speech to persuade City of Del Norte it should establish a Juvenile Court.) CUB:42
Wilkinson, H. C.
How separate should government and God be? LINR:98
Wilson, W.
Appeal to the voters to return a Democratic Congress. ANN 14:166
Woodmason, C.
You are to take these free booters and desperadoes. POC:548
Zimmerman, R.
Mingled blood. ARS:98; LINR:199

---- See also Inspirational talks; Sales talks and salesmanship

Perutz, Max Ferdinand
X-ray analysis of haemoglobin (Nobel Lecture, Dec. 11, 1962). NOLC 3:653

PERUTZ, MAX FERDINAND
Hagg, G.
Presentation [of the Nobel Prize for Chemistry to Max Ferdinand Perutz and John Cowdery Kendrew, Dec. 11, 1962]. NOLC 3:649

PESTS See Insects, Injurious and beneficial - Control

Peters, A. D. See Sykes, C., jt. auth.

Peters, Lauralee
What is totalitarianism? LINR:50

Peterson, Martha
In these present crises. (Univ. of Nebraska, June 17, 1970). BA 1970-71:73

PETITION OF RIGHT, 1628
Eliot, J.
On the Petition of Right. BREWE 5:1986; BRYH:123

PETROV, VLADIMIR
Ward, E. J.
Petrov case. MCA:196

Petterson, A.
Presentation [of the Nobel Prize for Physiology or Medicine to Jules Bordet, 1919]. NOLM 1:519

PHAGE
Luria, S. E.
Phage, colicins and macro-regulatory phenomena. NOLM 4:426

PHASE TRANSFORMATIONS
Zernike, F.
How I discovered phase contrast. NOLPH 3:239

Phelps, William Lyon
Owning books. (New Haven, Conn., April 6, 1933). HURH:225
Presents André Chevrillon. LYI:52
Presents Sir William Llewellyn. LYI:26
"You should own no book that you are afraid to mark up." Same as his Owning books

PHILANTHROPY See Charities

PHILIP II, KING OF MACEDONIA, 382-336 B.C.
Demosthenes
First Olynthiac oration. SAG:199
First Philippic. COG:40; SAG:188
On the crown. BREWE 5:1688; COG:151
Oration on the peace. BREWE 5:1759; SAG:223
Second Olynthiac. BREWE 5:1754; COG:56; SAG:205
Second Philippic. BREWE 5:1763; SAG:228
Third Olynthiac. SAG:212
Third Philippic. COG:91; SAG:249
Isocrates
Address to Philip. COG:67; SAG:137
On the Chersoneus. SAG:235

PHILIPPINE ISLANDS
Beveridge, A. J.
Philippine question. ANN 12:336; BRR:29
Bocobo, J. C.
Love of country. CURM:149
Evangelista, T.
The needs of a nation. CURM:160
McKinley, W.
Fourth annual message. STAT 2:1971
Quezon, M. L.
On Spain's contribution to the Philippines. CURM:24
Romulo, C. P.
Bandung address. CROCK:141
Roosevelt, T.
First annual message. ANN 12:433; STAT 2:2014

---- ARMY
Vargas, J. B.
The role of the army. CURM:98

---- CONSTITUTION
Recto, C. M.
The preparation of the Constitution. CURM:250
Vinzone, W. Q.
Defects in the draft of the Constitution. CURM:304

---- FOREIGN RELATIONS - UNITED STATES
Paredes, Q.
A brief sketch of the Philippines--past, present and future. CURM:214

---- HISTORY
Paredes, Q.
A brief sketch of the Philippines--past, present and future. CURM:214

---- NATIONAL ASSEMBLY
Osmeña, S.
The National Assembly, its aims and accomplishments. CURM:50

---- POLITICS AND GOVERNMENT
Osmeña, S.
The National Assembly, its aims and accomplishments. CURM:50
Quezon, M. L.
Filipinos of today and Filipinos of yesterday. CURM:29
Inaugural address. CURM:16
Quirino, E.
Commemorating a national event. CURM:239
Romulo, C. P.
The mind of a new commonwealth. CURM:267
Roxas, M.
A farewell to the Assembly. CURM:282

Phillips, Charles
Dinas Island speech on Washington. BREWE 8:3176

Phillips, Wendell
John Brown and the spirit of "59". BREWE 8:3181
Fourth of July oration (Boston, July 4, 1854). HAW:23
Murder of Lovejoy (Boston, Dec. 8, 1837). ALS:161; HURH:74
On the philosophy of the Abolition Movement. (January 27, 1853). MDT:35
The proclamation, how to make it efficient. (Music Hall, Boston, Jan. 4, 1863). MDT:148
Scholar in a Republic. ANN 10:488
Toussaint L'Ouverture. OLIS:170
Under the flag. Boston's Music Hall, April 21, 1861). MDT:119
"When he fell, civil authority was trampled under foot." Same as his Murder of Lovejoy

PHILLIPS, WENDELL
Curtis, G. W.
Eulogy on Wendell Phillips. BREWE 4:1571

PHILOSOPHY
Ayers, A. J. and others
What are philosophers for? MDYG:101
Santayana, G.
Genteel tradition in American philosophy. ANN 13:277

PHOTOCHEMISTRY
Porter, G.
Flash photolysis and some of its applications. NOLC 4:241

PHOTOSYNTHESIS
Calvin, M.
The path of carbon in photosynthesis. NOLC 3:618

PHYSICIANS
Introductions for doctors (6 examples). BNH:25
Raskas, B. S.
Physician's prayer. WALE:149
Skinner, C. O.
"Bottoms up" (toast to gynecologists). HURH:311

PHYSICS
Bothe, W.
The coincidence method. NOLPH 3:271
Bridgman, P. W.
General survey of certain results in the field of high-pressure physics. NOLPH 3:53

PICASSO, PABLO
Carlat, J.
Green parrot. LINR:46; LINRS:59

Pickens, William
Kind of democracy the Negro race expects. (WWI, 1917). FON:601

Pierce, Franklin
First annual message. STAT 1:856
Fourth annual message. STAT 1:918
Inaugural address. USINAU:103; USINAUG:103
Military academy. ANN 6:273
Second annual message. STAT 1:875
Third annual message. STAT 1:895

PILGRIM FATHERS
Adams, J. Q.
Oration at Plymouth (commemoration of the landing of the Pilgrims). BREWE 1:65
Webster, D.
Plymouth oration. BREWE 10:3846

Pinchback, Pinkney Benton Stewart
The whole race must protest. (1897). FON:596

Pinkney, William
Missouri question. BREWE 8:3195
On the first issues of Civil War. Same as his Missouri question

Pinson, William M., Jr.
The Playboy philosophy--con. (Atlanta, 1970). LINRS:170; LINRST:193

PIONEER GIRLS
Welcome to Girl Scouts (or Pioneer Girls, etc.). HNWM:50

Pirandello, Luigi
Acceptance [of the Nobel Prize for Literature, 1934]. NOB 20:77; NOL:324

PIRANDELLO, LUIGI
Hallström, P.
Presentation [of the Nobel Prize for Literature to Luigi Pirandello, 1934]. NOB 20:71; NOL:320

Pire, Georges
Brotherly love: foundation of peace (Nobel Lecture, Dec. 11, 1958). NOLP 3:157

PIRE, GEORGES
Jahn, G.
Presentation [of the Nobel Prize for Peace to Georges Pire, Dec. 10, 1958]. NOLP 3:151

Pitt, William, 1st Earl of Chatham, 1708-1778
Address to the throne concerning affairs in America, November 18, 1777. ALS:105; BREWE 3:1067; BRYH:201
Attempt to subjugate America. Same as his Address to the throne concerning affairs in America, November 18, 1777
Chatham's last speech. BREWE 3:1086
Debate in 1741 on wages of sailors. See Walpole, R., jt. auth.
English Constitution. BREWE 3:1077
On American policy. (January 20, 1775). (House of Lords, Jan. 20, 1775). CLAYP:40
On an address to the throne. Same as his Address to the throne concerning affairs in America, November 18, 1777
On restoring peace with America (speech on his Amendment to the Address of Thanks). Same as his Address to the throne concerning affairs in America, November 18, 1777
On the right to tax America. STRM:11
Speech on the government policy in America. Same as his On American policy, January 20, 1775

Pitt, William, 1759-1806
Abolition of the slave-trade.

Same as his Indicts the slave trade and foresees a liberated Africa
Against French Republicanism. BREWE 8:3202
England's share in the slave trade. Same as his Indicts the slave trade and foresees a liberated Africa
Indicts the slave trade and foresees a liberated Africa (House of Commons, April 2, 1792). BREWE 8:3208; CLAYP:138; JAE:12; STRM:91
Iniquity of slavery. Same as his Indicts the slave trade and foresees a liberated Africa
Speech on the slave trade. Same as his Indicts the slave trade and foresees a liberated Africa

---- and others (G. Tierney)
Deliverance of Europe (contains his Against French Republicanism speech). BRYH:281

Planck, Max
The genesis and present state of development of the quantum theory (Nobel Lecture for 1918, June 2, 1920). NOLPH 1:407

PLANCK, MAX
Ekstrand, A. G.
Presentation [of the Nobel Prize for Physics for 1918 to Max Planck, June 2, 1920]. NOLPH 1:405

PLANNED ECONOMY See United States - Economic policy

PLANNING, ECONOMIC See Economic policy

PLANT PIGMENTS
Willstätter, R. M.
On plant pigments. NOLC 1:301

PLANTATIONS
Cardozo, F. L.
Break up the plantation system. FON:350

PLASMA PHYSICS
Alfvén, H.
Plasma physics, space research and the origin of the solar system. NOLPH 4:306
Tamm, I. E.
General characteristics of radiations emitted by systems moving with super-light velocities with some applications to plasma physics. NOLPH 3:470

Platero, Dillon
Discussions of critical issues affecting Navajo education program and policies presented at the Seminar for Navajo Reservation School Administrators, July 26, 1976. MAES:149

PLAYBOY
Mount, A.
The Playboy philosophy--pro. LINRS:157
Pinson, W. M., Jr.
The Playboy philosophy--con. LINRS:170; LINRST:193

Pleijel, H.
Presentation [of the Nobel Prize for Physics to Clinton Joseph Davisson and George Paget Thomson, Dec. 13, 1937]. NOLPH 2:387
Presentation [of the Nobel Prize for Physics to Enrico Fermi, Dec. 12, 1938]. NOLPH 2:409
Presentation [of the Nobel Prize for Physics to James Chadwick, Dec. 12, 1935]. NOLPH 2:333
Presentation [of the Nobel Prize for Physics for 1932 to Werner Heisenberg and for 1933 to Erwin Schrodinger and Paul Adrien Maurice Dirac, Dec. 11, 1933]. NOLPH 2:283
Presentation [of the Nobel Prize for Physics to Sir Chandrasekhara Venkata Raman, Dec. 11, 1930]. NOLPH 2:263

Plumer, William
State control of Dartmouth College. ANN 4:420

Plunket, William Conyngham, 1st Baron
Prosecuting Robert Emmet. BREWE 8:3213

PLURALISM (SOCIAL SCIENCE)
Harris, L.
American Indian education and pluralism. MAES:96
Howe, H., II
The Brown decision, pluralism, and the schools in the 1980s. BA 1979-80:101

Poe, Edgar Allan
Love for the beautiful in speech. BREWE 8:3222

POETRY AND POETS
Eliot, T. S.
Acceptance [of the Nobel Prize for Literature, 1948]. NOB 5:267; NOL:435
Lowell, J. R.
Poetical and the practical in America. BREWE 7:2808
Perse, S.
Acceptance [of the Nobel Prize for Literature, 1960]. NOB 20:7; NOL:556
Poe, E. A.
Love for the beautiful in speech. BREWE 8:3222
Quasimodo, S.
The poet and the politician. NOL:540
Robertson, F. W.
Highest form of expression. BREWE 9:3319

Pogrebin, Letty Cottin
Commencement address (Rutgers Univ.) TAC:242

POLAROGRAPH AND POLAROGRAPHY
Heyrovsky, J.
The trends of polarography. NOLC 3:564

POLICE
Police. BURT:32
Warren, E. and others
Miranda v. Arizona: opinion for the court and dissenting opinion. ANN 18:427
Welcome to Chief of Police as speaker at a civic club. HNWM:41
Wilson, O. W.
Police arrest privileges in a free society. ANN 18:36

POLIOMYELITIS
Enders, J. F.
The cultivation of the poliomyelitis viruses in tissue culture. NOLM 3:448

POLITICAL CONVENTIONS
Gale, J.
Great American institution. REIR:161

---- See also Acceptance speeches - Nominations; Candidates; Congresses and conventions; Democratic Party; Republican Party. Also Subheads under this subject

---- DEMOCRATIC
Bryan, W. J.
Cross of gold. ANN 12:100; BAS:50 (outline only); BEN:52; BOORA 2:575; BREWE 2:694; HURH:147; LINS:268; OLIS:207
Voorhees, D. W.
Speech in the Tilden convention. BREWE 10:3697

---- REPUBLICAN
Curtis, G. W.
His sovereignty under his hat. BREWE 4:1570

POLITICAL PARTIES
Brooke, E. W.
Crisis in the two-party system. BA 1965-66:170

---- See also Names of parties, e.g. Conservative Party - Great Britain; Democratic Party; Labor Party - Great Britain; Liberal Party - Great Britain; Liberty Party; Republican Party; Union Party

---- NEW ZEALAND
Stout, R.
A call for liberal and conservative parties, 1876. MACS:180 sel.

POLITICAL PRISONERS
Borah, W. E.

Release of political prisoners. ANN 14:405
Moynihan, D. P.
World wide amnesty for political prisoners. BA 1975-76:65

POLITICAL SCIENCE
Cousin, V.
True politics. BREWE 4:1431
Dix, J. A.
Christianity and politics. BREWE 5:1883
Kennedy, J. F.
Intellectual and the politician. BAP:285; LINR:267
Religion in government. ANN 17:589; SIN:303
Kossuth, L.
Local self-government. BREWE 7:2672
LaFollette, R. M., Sr.
Which shall rule, manhood or money? HURH:158
Marshall, D. S.
Fundamental and minority rights. MONS:450
Monroe, J.
Federal experiments in history. BREWE 8:3041
Root, E.
Invisible government: Short Ballot Amendment. ANN 13:528
Russell, B. A. W.
What desires are politically important? NOL:452
Schurz, C.
Public offices as private perquisites. BREWE 9:3384
Smith, A. E.
Religion and politics. HURH:209
Weicker, L. P.
Televised debates. BA 1976-77:61
Willkie, W. L.
Loyal opposition. GRG:63; HURH:243

---- See also Communism; Right and left (political science); Socialism; United States - Politics and government

POLITICIANS
Introductions for politicians (3 examples). BNH:31

POLITICS See Campaign speeches; Candidates; Civil service; Political Science; World politics, 1945- . Also names of countries with subdivision Politics and government, e.g. Great Britain - Politics and government

POLITICS, PRACTICAL
Fulbright, J. W.
Press and politicians. ERP:159

Polk, James K.
Annexation of Texas and Oregon. Same as his Inaugural address
California and Mexico. Same as his Third annual message
First annual message. ANN 7:301; STAT 1:634
Fourth annual message. STAT 1:731
Inaugural address. ANN 7:286; USINAU:89; USINAUG:89
Reaffirmation of the Monroe Doctrine. Same as his First annual message
Second annual message. STAT 1:664
Third annual message. ANN 7:374; STAT 1:699

POLK, JAMES K.
Dayton, W. L.
Arraigning President Polk. BREWE 5:1676

Pollak, George
Light from sorrow. WALE:143

POLLUTION
Jones, A. L.
A question of ecology: the cries of wolf. LINRST:115

POLYSACCHARIDES
Cori, C.
Polysaccharide phosphorylase. NOLM 3:186

Ponce, Felipe V.
La causa (Indiana University, 1971). LINRS:66; LINRST:68

Pontier, Glenn
Plea for understanding. SCHW:136

POPE, ALEXANDER
Lowell, J. R.
Pope and his time.
BREWE 7:2815

Poplack, Alvin M.
Preparation for eternity.
WALE:146

POPULATION
Crary, D. R.
Plague of people. LINR:220
Stratton, R. D.
Food: a world crisis.
BREWW:81

POPULATION POLICY - MALAYSIA
Razak, T. A.
Devastating consequences of excessive population growth.
MONSA:9

Porter, George
Flash photolysis and some of its applications (Nobel Lecture, Dec. 11, 1967).
NOLC 4:241

PORTER, GEORGE
Olander, H. A.
Presentation [of the Nobel Prize for Chemistry to Manfred Eigen, R. G. W. Norrish and George Porter, Dec. 11, 1967]. NOLC 4:165

POSITRONS
Anderson, C. D.
The production and properties of positrons.
NOLPH 2:365

POST WAR PLANNING See Reconstruction, 1939-1951

POSTAL SERVICE
Gronouski, J. A.
Mail service. BRP:223

Potter, Henry Codman
Washington and American aristocracy (100th anniversary of Washington's first inauguration).
BREWE 8:3225

POVERTY
Drumm, S. L.
War on prosperity. CAPG:185
Humphrey, H. H., Jr.
Anniversary of war on poverty. CAPG:174
Johnson, L. B.
War on poverty. ANN 18:212
McNamara, R. S.
Searching for new solutions to poverty. BA 1976-77:91
Shriver, S.
Address at the Chicago Anti-poverty Conference. CAPG:180
Wirtz, W. W.
Economic Opportunity Act of 1964. CAPG:165
Ybarra, B.
The wheel of poverty.
BAPR:356; BAPRR:266
Young, W. M.
Crisis of the cities: the danger of the ghetto.
BA 1966-67:82; OE:177; SMHV:160

---- MALAYSIA
Suffian bin Hashim
Only Malays can initiate the institutional changes.
MONSA:140

Powell, Adam Clayton
Can any good thing come out of Nazareth? (Howard University, May 29, 1966).
FON:1027; SMHR:154

Powell, Cecil Frank
The cosmic radiation (Nobel Lecture, Dec. 11, 1950).
NOLPH 3:144

POWELL, CECIL FRANK
Lindh, A. E.
Presentation [of the Nobel Prize for Physics to Cecil Frank Powell, Dec. 11, 1950].
NOLPH 3:139

Powell, Lewis Franklin, Jr.
The eroding authority. (San Francisco, August 13, 1972).
BA 1972-73:101

Power, Donald C.
Responds to an introduction.
PRS:147

POWER
Russell, B. A. W.

What desires are politically important? NOL:452

POWER RESOURCES
Carter, J.
Energy and the national goals. BA 1979-80:76
Energy problems. BA 1976-77:117
Hatfield, M. O.
The energy crisis. BA 1973-74:105
MacDonald, P.
Exploring new energy frontiers. MAES:165
Mead, M.
The planetary crisis and the challenge to scientists. BA 1973-74:97

---- RESEARCH
Root, T. C.
The failure of scientists to communicate. BA 1977-78:110

PRAISE, SPEECHES OF See Eulogies; Tributes

PRATT, E. J.
Lowe, J. A.
Presents E. J. Pratt. LYI:49

Pray, Francis C.
Public relations in education (Pittsburgh, Oct. 27, 1955). TAC:209

PRAYERS
Augustine, Saint
On our Lord's prayer. BREWE 1:188
Christmas prayer. BNH:75
New Year prayer. BNH:74
Prayer at a time of doubt or sorrow. BNH:73
Prayer for commitment day. BNH:74
Prayer for Easter. BNH:76
Prayer for Thanksgiving. BNH:76

PREACHERS See Clergy

Pregl, Fritz
Quantitative micro-analysis of organic substances (Nobel Lecture, Dec. 11, 1923). NOLC 2:28

PREGL, FRITZ
Hammarsten, O.
Presentation [of the Nobel Prize for Chemistry to Fritz Pregl, Dec. 11, 1923]. NOLC 2:25

PREJUDICE See Discrimination

Preminger, Otto See Murrow, E. R., jt. auth.

Prentiss, Seargent Smith
On New England's Forefathers' Day. BREWE 8:3233

PREPAREDNESS, MILITARY See Names of countries or hemispheres with subdivision Defenses, e.g. United States - Defenses

PRESENTATION SPEECHES
Suggestions for preparation of speeches of presentation. With examples of. PAE:181

---- DEGREES, ACADEMIC
Eliezer, C. J.
Educated man with a sense of urgency (presenting Doctor of Laws degree). MONS:275
Wang, G. W.
Tribute to Dr. Azkir Husain (presenting him with Doctor of Laws degree). MONS:277

---- GIFTS
Presenting a gift (5 examples). BNH:86
Suggestions for the preparation of a speech presenting a gift or award. MILS:10

---- MEDALS
Kennedy, J. F.
Presenting the Distinguished Service Medal to John Glenn (outline of speech). CUB:64
Lamont, T. W.
Presents Eleanor Robson Belmont. LYI:23
Smith, W.
Eulogium. POC:3
Truman, H. S.

Presents George C. Marshall. LYI:141

---- REWARDS (PRIZES)
Akerman, J.
Presentation [of the Nobel Prize for Physiology or Medicine to Alexis Carrel, Dec. 11, 1912]. NOLM 1:437
Annerstedt, C.
Presentation [of the Nobel Prize for Literature to Selma Ottiliana Louisa Lagerlöf, 1909]. NOB 10:279; NOL:90
Arrhenius, S. A.
Presentation [of the Nobel Prize for Physics for 1921 to Albert Einstein, July 11, 1923]. NOLPH 1:482
Presentation [of the Nobel Prize for Physics to Niels Bohr, Dec. 11, 1922]. NOLPH 2:3
Bergstrand, H.
Presentation [of the Nobel Prize for Physiology or Medicine to Max Theiler, Dec. 11, 1951]. NOLM 3:347
Bergstrom, S.
Presentation [of the Nobel Prize for Physiology or Medicine to Konrad Bloch and Feodor Lynen, Dec. 11, 1964]. NOLM 4:75
Bernhard, C. G.
Presentation [of the Nobel Prize for Physiology or Medicine to Georg Von Bekesy, Dec. 11, 1961]. NOLM 3:719
Presentation [of the Nobel Prize for Physiology or Medicine to Ragnar Granit, Haldan Keffer Hartline, and George Wald, Dec. 12, 1967]. NOLM 4:251
Bjørnson, B.
Introduction [presenting the Nobel Prize for Peace to Bertha von Suttner, 1905, April 18, 1906]. NOLP 1:81
Böök, F.
Presentation [of the Nobel Prize for Literature to Thomas Mann, 1929]. NOB 12:221; NOL:260
Buen, A. J.
Remarks [presenting the Nobel Prize for Peace to Leon Victor Auguste Bourgeois, Dec. 10, 1920]. NOLP 1:304
Caspersson, T.
Presentation [of the Nobel Prize for Physiology or Medicine to George Wells Beadle, Edward Lawrie Tatum, and Joshua Lederberg, Dec. 11, 1958]. NOLM 3:583
Presentation [of the Nobel Prize for Physiology or Medicine to Hermann Joseph Muller, Dec. 12, 1946]. NOLM 3:149
Cederblom, J. E.
Presentation [of the Nobel Prize for Chemistry to Sir William Ramsay, Dec. 12, 1904]. NOLC 1:65
Presentation [of the Nobel Prize for Physics to Lord Rayleigh, Dec. 12, 1904]. NOLPH 1:87
Claesson, S.
Presentation [of the Nobel Prize for Chemistry to Lars Onsager, Dec. 11, 1968]. NOLC 4:269
Dahlgren, E. W.
Presentation [of the Nobel Prize for Chemistry to Marie Sklodowska Curie, Dec. 11, 1911]. NOLC 1:199
Presentation [of the Nobel Prize for Physics to Wilhelm Wien, Dec. 11, 1911]. NOLPH 1:271
DeGeer, G.
Presentation [of the Nobel Prize for Chemistry to Walther Hermann Nernst, 1920, Dec. 12, 1921]. NOLC 1:349
Edlén, B.
Presentation [of the Nobel Prize for Physics to Charles H. Townes, Nikolai G. Basov, and Alexander M. Prochorov, Dec. 11, 1964]. NOLPH 4:55
Ekstrand, A. G.
Presentation [of the Nobel Prize for Chemistry to Fritz Haber, 1918, June 2, 1920].

NOLC 1:321
Presentation [of the Nobel Prize for Physics to Charles-Edouard Guillaume, Dec. 11, 1920].
NOLPH 1:441
Presentation [of the Nobel Prize for Physics for 1919 to Johannes Stark, June 3, 1920]. NOLPH 1:423
Presentation [of the Nobel Prize for Physics for 1918 to Max Planck, June 2, 1920]. NOLPH 1:405
Engström, A.
Presentation [of the Nobel Prize for Physiology or Medicine to Francis Harry Compton Crick, James Dewey Watson, and Maurice Hugh Frederick Wilkins, Dec. 11, 1962].
NOLM 3:751
Fischer, G.
Presentation [of the Nobel Prize for Physiology or Medicine to Paul Hermann Müller, Dec. 11, 1948].
NOLM 3:227
Fischer-Hjalmars, I.
Presentation [of the Nobel Prize for Chemistry to Robert S. Mulliken, Dec. 12, 1966]. NOLC 4:127
Fredga, A.
Presentation [of the Nobel Prize for Chemistry to Derek H. R. Barton and Odd Hassel, Dec. 11, 1969].
NOLC 4:295
Presentation [of the Nobel Prize for Chemistry to Hermann Staudinger, Dec. 11, 1953]. NOLC 3:393
Presentation [of the Nobel Prize for Chemistry to Karl Ziegler and Giulio Natta, Dec. 12, 1963].
NOLC 4:3
Presentation [of the Nobel Prize for Chemistry to Otto Paul Hermann Diels and Kurt Adler, Dec. 12, 1950]. NOLC 3:255
Presentation [of the Nobel Prize for Chemistry to Robert Burns Woodward, Dec. 11, 1965]. NOLC 4:97
Presentation [of the Nobel Prize for Chemistry to Sir Alexander Robertus Todd, Dec. 11, 1957]. NOLC 3:519
Presentation [of the Nobel Prize for Chemistry to Sir Robert Robinson, Dec. 12, 1947]. NOLC 3:166
Presentation [of the Nobel Prize for Chemistry to Vincent du Vigneaud, Dec. 12, 1955]. NOLC 3:443
Friesen, S. V.
Presentation [of the Nobel Prize for Physics to Luis W. Alvarez, Dec. 11, 1968].
NOLPH 4:239
Gard, S.
Presentation [of the Nobel Prize for Physiology or Medicine to François Jacob, André Lwoff, and Jacques Monod, Dec. 11, 1965].
NOLM 4:143
Presentation [of the Nobel Prize for Physiology or Medicine to John Franklin Enders, Thomas Huckle Weller, and Frederick Chapman Robbins, Dec. 11, 1954].
NOLM 3:443
Presentation [of the Nobel Prize for Physiology or Medicine to Max Delbrück, Alfred D. Hershey, and Salvador E. Luria, Dec. 10, 1969].
NOLM 4:401
Presentation [of the Nobel Prize for Physiology or Medicine to Sir Frank Macfarlane Burnet and Peter Brian Medawar, Dec. 12, 1960].
NOLM 3:685
Gierow, K. R.
Presentation address [of the Nobel Prize for Literature to Aleksandr Solzhenitsyn, 1970].
NOB 18:3
Presentation address [of the Nobel Prize for Literature to Samuel Beckett, 1969].
NOB 3:3
Granit, R.
Presentation [of the Nobel Prize for Physiology or Medicine to John Carew Eccles, Alan Lloyd Hodgkin, and Andrew Fielding Huxley,

Dec. 11, 1963]. NOLM 4:3
Grandqvist, G.
Presentation [of the Nobel Prize for Physics for 1914 to Max Von Laue, Nov. 12, 1915]. NOLPH 1:343
Gullberg, H.
Presentation [of the Nobel Prize for Literature to Gabriela Mistral, 1945]. NOB 14:167; NOL:405
Presentation [of the Nobel Prize for Literature to Juan Ramón Jiménez, 1956]. NOB 10:3; NOL:513
Gullstrand, A.
Presentation [of the Nobel Prize for Physics for 1924 to Karl Manne Georg Siegbahn, Dec. 11, 1925]. NOLPH 2:73
Presentation [of the Nobel Prize for Physics for 1923 to Robert Andrews Millikan, May 23, 1924]. NOLPH 2:51
Gustafsson, T.
Presentation [of the Nobel Prize for Physics to Hannes Alfvén and Louis Néel, Dec. 11, 1970]. NOLPH 4:303
Hagg, G.
Presentation [of the Nobel Prize for Chemistry to Dorothy Crowfoot Hodgkin, Dec. 11, 1964]. NOLC 4:67
Presentation [of the Nobel Prize for Chemistry to Linus Carl Pauling, Dec. 11, 1954]. NOLC 3:425
Presentation [of the Nobel Prize for Chemistry to Max Ferdinand Perutz and John Cowdery Kendrew, Dec. 11, 1962]. NOLC 3:649
Häggquist, G.
Presentation [of the Nobel Prize for Physiology or Medicine to Hans Spemann, Dec. 12, 1935]. NOLM 2:377
Hallström, P.
Broadcast lecture [on Johannes Vilhelm Jensen, 1944]. NOL:393
Presentation [of the Nobel Prize for Literature to Eugene Gladstone O'Neill, 1936]. NOB 19:125; NOL:330
Presentation [of the Nobel Prize for Literature to Frans Eemil Sillanpää, 1939]. NOB 16:223; NOL:386
Presentation [of the Nobel Prize for Literature to George Bernard Shaw, 1925]. NOB 16:77; NOL:224
Presentation [of the Nobel Prize for Literature to Henri Bergson, 1927]. NOB 2:267; NOL:242
Presentation [of the Nobel Prize for Literature to Ivan Alekseevich Bunin, 1933]. NOB 3:285; NOL:309
Presentation [of the Nobel Prize for Literature to Jacinto Benavente, 1922]. NOB 2:179; NOL:186
Presentation [of the Nobel Prize for Literature to Luigi Pirandello, 1934]. NOB 20:71; NOL:320
Presentation [of the Nobel Prize for Literature to Pearl Buck, 1938]. NOB 3:149; NOL:354
Presentation [of the Nobel Prize for Literature to Roger Martin DuGard, 1937]. NOB 14:3; NOL:342
Presentation [of the Nobel Prize for Literature to Sigrid Undset, 1928]. NOB 18:163; NOL:251
Presentation [of the Nobel Prize for Literature to William Butler Yeats, 1923]. NOB 18:275; NOL:194
Presentation [of the Nobel Prize for Literature to William Faulkner, 1949]. NOB 19:3; NOL:440
Hambro, C. J.
Presentation [of the Nobel Prize for Peace to George Catlett Marshall, Dec. 10, 1953]. NOLP 3:65
Presentation [of the Nobel Prize for Peace to the International Committee of the Red Cross and the League of the Red Cross Societies, Dec. 10, 1963]. NOLP 3:295

Hammersten, O.
Presentation [of the Nobel Prize for Chemistry to Fritz Pregl, Dec. 11, 1923]. NOLC 2:25
Presentation [of the Nobel Prize for Physiology or Medicine to Albert Szent-Györgyi Von Nagyrapolt, Dec. 11, 1937]. NOLM 2:435
Presentation [of the Nobel Prize for Physiology or Medicine to Axel Hugo Theodor Theorell, Dec. 12, 1955]. NOLM 3:477
Presentation [of the Nobel Prize for Physiology or Medicine to Hans Adolf Krebs and Fritz Albert Lipmann, Dec. 11, 1953]. NOLM 3:395
Presentation [of the Nobel Prize for Physiology or Medicine to Otto Heinrich Warburg, Dec. 10, 1931]. NOLM 2:251
Hasselberg, K. B.
Presentation [of the Nobel Prize for Chemistry to Ernest Rutherford, Dec. 11, 1908]. NOLC 1:125
Presentation [of the Nobel Prize for Physics to Albert Abraham Michelson, Dec. 12, 1907]. NOLPH 1:159
Presentation [of the Nobel Prize for Physics to Gabriel Lippmann, Dec. 14, 1908]. NOLPH 1:183
Hedrén, G.
Presentation [of the Nobel Prize for Physiology or Medicine to Karl Landsteiner, Dec. 11, 1930]. NOLM 2:229
Henschen, F.
Presentation [of the Nobel Prize for Physiology or Medicine for 1928 to Charles Jules Henri Nicolle]. NOLM 2:175
Presentation [of the Nobel Prize for Physiology or Medicine for 1933 to Thomas Hunt Morgan, June 4, 1934]. NOLM 2:307
Hildebrand, H.
Presentation [of the Nobel Prize for Chemistry to Wilhelm Ostwald, Dec. 12, 1909]. NOLC 1:147
Presentation [of the Nobel Prize for Literature to Gerhart Johann Robert Hauptmann, 1912]. NOB 8:3; NOL:118
Presentation [of the Nobel Prize for Physics to Guglielmo Marconi and Carl Ferdinand Braun, Dec. 11, 1909]. NOLPH 1:193
Hjärne, H.
Presentation [of the Nobel Prize for Literature to Carl Friedrich Spitteler, 1919]. NOB 17:267; NOL:161
Presentation [of the Nobel Prize for Literature to Knut Pedersen Hamsun, 1920]. NOB 9:119; NOL:167
Presentation [of the Nobel Prize for Literature to Rabindranath Tagore, 1913]. NOB 18:10; NOL:127
Presentation [of the Nobel Prize for Literature to Rudolf Christoph Eucken, 1908]. NOB 6:3; NOL:67
Holmgren, I.
Presentation [of the Nobel Prize for Physiology or Medicine to George Hoyt Whipple, George Richards Minot, and William Parry Murphy, Dec. 12, 1934]. NOLM 2:335
Hulthén, E.
Presentation [of the Nobel Prize for Physics to Emilio Gino Segrè and Owen Chamberlain, Dec. 11, 1959]. NOLPH 3:487
Presentation [of the Nobel Prize for Physics to Felix Bloch and Edward Mills Purcell, Dec. 11, 1952]. NOLPH 3:199
Presentation [of the Nobel Prize for Physics to Frits Zernike, Dec. 11, 1953]. NOLPH 3:237
Presentation [of the Nobel Prize for Physics to Sir Edward Victor Appleton, Dec. 12, 1947]. NOLPH 3:75
Ingebretsen, H. S.
Presentation [of the Nobel

Prize for Peace to John Raleigh Mott, Dec. 10, 1946]. NOLP 2:354
Irgens, J.
Welcome [presenting the Nobel Prize for Peace to the Institute of International Law for 1904, Aug. 24, 1912]. NOLP 1:61
Ising, G.
Presentation [of the Nobel Prize for Physics to Patrick Maynard Stuart Blackett, Dec. 13, 1948]. NOLPH 3:93
Jahn, G.
Presentation [of the Nobel Prize for Peace to Albert John Luthuli for 1960, Dec. 10, 1961]. NOLP 3:209
Presentation [of the Nobel Prize for Peace for 1952 to Albert Schweitzer, Dec. 10, 1953]. NOLP 3:37
Presentation [of the Nobel Prize for Peace to Cordell Hull, Dec. 10, 1945]. NOLP 2:311
Presentation [of the Nobel Prize for Peace to Dag Hammarskjöld, Dec. 10, 1961]. NOLP 3:239
Presentation [of the Nobel Prize for Peace to Emily Greene Balch, Dec. 10, 1946]. NOLP 2:325
Presentation [of the Nobel Prize for Peace to the Friends Service Council and the American Friends Service Committee, Dec. 10, 1947]. NOLP 2:373
Presentation [of the Nobel Prize for Peace to Georges Pire, Dec. 10, 1958]. NOLP 3:151
Presentation [of the Nobel Prize for Peace to the International Committee of the Red Cross, 1944, Dec. 10, 1945]. NOLP 2:289
Presentation [of the Nobel Prize for Peace to Léon Jouhaux, Dec. 10, 1951]. NOLP 3:3
Presentation [of the Nobel Prize for Peace to Lester Bowles Pearson, Dec. 10, 1957]. NOLP 3:119
Presentation [of the Nobel Prize for Peace for 1962 to Linus Carl Pauling, Dec. 10, 1963]. NOLP 3:259
Presentation [of the Nobel Prize for Peace to Lord Boyd Orr of Brechin, Dec. 10, 1949]. NOLP 2:407
Presentation [of the Nobel Prize for Peace to Martin Luther King, Jr., Dec. 10, 1964]. NOLP 3:325
Presentation [of the Nobel Prize for Peace to the Office of the United Nations High Commissioner for Refugees, Dec. 10, 1955]. NOLP 3:89
Presentation [of the Nobel Prize for Peace to Philip John Noel-Baker, Dec. 10, 1959]. NOLP 3:175
Presentation [of the Nobel Prize for Peace to Ralph Johnson Bunche, Dec. 10, 1950]. NOLP 2:435
Johansson, J. E.
Presentation [of the Nobel Prize for Physiology or Medicine for 1922 to Archibald Vivian Hill and Otto Fritz Meyerhof, Dec. 12, 1923]. NOLM 2:3
Presentation [of the Nobel Prize for Physiology or Medicine to August Krogh, Dec. 11, 1920]. NOLM 1:529
Johnsen, A.
Remarks [presenting the Nobel Prize for Peace to Thomas Woodrow Wilson, 1919, Dec. 10, 1920]. NOLP 1:293
Karlfeldt, E. A.
Presentation [of the Nobel Prize for Literature to Anatole France, 1921]. NOB 6:85; NOL:174
Presentation [of the Nobel Prize for Literature to Sinclair Lewis, 1930]. NOB 11:237; NOL:271
Klason, P.
Presentation [of the Nobel Prize for Chemistry to Henri Moissan, 1906]. NOLC 1:91
Presentation [of the Nobel Prize for Physics to Joseph John Thomson, Dec. 11,

1906]. NOLPH 1:141
Klein, G.
Presentation [of the Nobel Prize for Physiology or Medicine to Peyton Rous and Charles Brenton Huggins, Dec. 13, 1966]. NOLM 4:215
Klein, O. B.
Presentation [of the Nobel Prize for Physics to Chen Ning Yang and Tsung Dao Lee, Dec. 11, 1957]. NOLPH 3:389
Presentation [of the Nobel Prize for Physics to Hans Albrecht Bethe, Dec. 11, 1967]. NOLPH 4:211
Knudsen, G.
Presentation [of the Nobel Prize for Peace to Theodore Roosevelt, Dec. 10, 1906]. NOLP 1:97
Koht, H.
Presentation [of the Nobel Prize for Peace to Jane Addams and Nicholas Murray Butler, Dec. 10, 1931]. NOLP 2:125
Lange, C. L.
Presentation [of the Nobel Prize for Peace to Carlos Saavedra Lamas, Dec. 10, 1936]. NOLP 2:217
Presentation [of the Nobel Prize for Peace, 1933, to Norman Angell, Dec. 10, 1934]. NOLP 2:147
Presentation [of the Nobel Prize for Peace to Viscount Cecil of Chelwood, Dec. 10, 1937]. NOLP 2:235
Liljestrand, G.
Presentation [of the Nobel Prize for Physiology or Medicine to André Frederic Cournand, Werner Theodor Otto Forssmann, and Dickinson Woodruff Richards, Jr., Dec. 11, 1956]. NOLM 3:501
Presentation [of the Nobel Prize for Physiology or Medicine to Christiaan Eijkman and Sir Frederick Gowland Hopkins, Dec. 11, 1929]. NOLM 2:193
Presentation [of the Nobel Prize for Physiology or Medicine to Edward Calvin Kendall, Tadeus Reichstein, and Philip Showalter Hench, Dec. 11, 1950]. NOLM 3:263
Presentation [of the Nobel Prize for Physiology or Medicine to Sir Alexander Fleming, Ernst Boris Chain, and Sir Howard Walter Florey, Dec. 11, 1945]. NOLM 3:77
Presentation [of the Nobel Prize for Physiology or Medicine to Sir Charles Scott Sherrington and Edgar Douglas Adrian, Dec. 12, 1932]. NOLM 2:273
Presentation [of the Nobel Prize for Physiology or Medicine to Sir Henry Hallett Dale and Otto Loewi, Dec. 12, 1936]. NOLM 2:397
Lindh, A. E.
Presentation [of the Nobel Prize for Physics to Cecil Frank Powell, Dec. 11, 1950]. NOLPH 3:139
Presentation [of the Nobel Prize for Physics to Percy William Bridgman, Dec. 11, 1946]. NOLPH 3:53
Lindstedt, A.
Presentation [of the Nobel Prize for Physics for 1905 to Philipp Eduard Anton von Lenard, May 28, 1906]. NOLPH 1:101
Lionaes, A.
Presentation [of the Nobel Prize for Peace to the International Labor Organization, Dec. 10, 1969]. NOLP 3:415
Presentation [of the Nobel Prize for Peace to Norman Ernest Borlaug, Dec. 10, 1970]. NOLP 3:445
Presentation [of the Nobel Prize for Peace to René-Samuel Cassin, Dec. 10, 1968]. NOLP 3:385
Presentation [of the Nobel Prize for Peace to the United Nations Children's Fund, Dec. 10, 1965]. NOLP 3:353

Løvland, J. G.
Banquet speech [presenting the Nobel Prize for Peace to Bertha von Suttner, 1905, April 18, 1906]. NOLP 1:82
Presentation [of the Nobel Prize for Peace to Alfred Hermann Fried, Dec. 10, 1911]. NOLP 1:238
Presentation [of the Nobel Prize for Peace to Auguste Marie François Beernaert, Dec. 10, 1909]. NOLP 1:211
Presentation [of the Nobel Prize for Peace to Baron d'Estournelles de Constant, Dec. 10, 1909]. NOLP 1:216
Presentation [of the Nobel Prize for Peace to Ernesto Teodoro Moneta, Dec. 10, 1907]. NOLP 1:113
Presentation [of the Nobel Prize for Peace to Fredrik Bajer, Dec. 10, 1908]. NOLP 1:188
Presentation [of the Nobel Prize for Peace to Klas Pontus Arnoldson, Dec. 10, 1908]. NOLP 1:173
Presentation [of the Nobel Prize for Peace to Louis Renault, Dec. 10, 1907]. NOLP 1:141
Presentation [of the Nobel Prize for Peace to the Permanent International Peace Bureau, Dec. 10, 1910]. NOLP 1:223
Presentation [of the Nobel Prize for Peace to Tobias Michael Carel Asser, Dec. 10, 1911]. NOLP 1:233
Welcome [presenting the Nobel Prize for Peace, 1903, to William Randal Cremer, Jan. 15, 1905]. NOLP 1:45
Moe, R.
Presentation [of the Nobel Prize for Peace to Elihu Root, 1912, Dec. 10, 1913]. NOLP 1:245
Presentation [of the Nobel Prize for Peace to Henri Marie La Fontaine, Dec. 10, 1913]. NOLP 1:269
Presentation [of the Nobel Prize for Peace to the International Committee of the Red Cross, Dec. 10, 1917]. NOLP 1:281
Montelius, O.
Presentation [of the Nobel Prize for Chemistry to Otto Wallach, Dec. 12, 1910]. NOLC 1:175
Presentation [of the Nobel Prize for Physics to Johannes Diderik Van der Waals, Dec. 12, 1910]. NOLPH 1:251
Mörner, K. A. H.
Presentation [of the Nobel Prize for Chemistry to Eduard Buchner, Dec. 11, 1907]. NOLC 1:99
Presentation [of the Nobel Prize for Physiology or Medicine to Albrecht Kossel, Dec. 12, 1910]. NOLM 1:389
Presentation [of the Nobel Prize for Physiology or Medicine to Allvar Gullstrand, Dec. 11, 1911]. NOLM 1:411
Presentation [of the Nobel Prize for Physiology or Medicine to Camilio Golgi and Santiago Ramon y Cajal, Dec. 12, 1906]. NOLM 1:185
Presentation [of the Nobel Prize for Physiology or Medicine to Elie Metchnikoff and Paul Ehrlich, Dec. 11, 1908]. NOLM 1:277
Presentation [of the Nobel Prize for Physiology or Medicine to Emil Adolf Von Behring, Dec. 12, 1901]. NOLM 1:3
Presentation [of the Nobel Prize for Physiology or Medicine to Emil Theodor Kocher, Dec. 11, 1909]. NOLM 1:327
Presentation [of the Nobel Prize for Physiology or Medicine to Ivan Petrovich Pavlov, Dec. 12, 1904]. NOLM 1:135
Presentation [of the Nobel Prize for Physiology or Medicine to Niels Ryberg Finsen, 1903]. NOLM 1:123
Presentation [of the Nobel Prize for Physiology or Medicine to Robert Koch, Dec. 12, 1905]. NOLM 1:163
Presentation [of the Nobel

Prize for Physiology or Medicine to Sir Ronald Ross, Dec. 12, 1902]. NOLM 1:21
Mowinckel, J. L.
Presentation [of the Nobel Prize for Peace to Arthur Henderson, Dec. 10, 1934]. NOLP 2:179
Presentation [of the Nobel Prize for Peace to Frank Billings Kellogg, 1929, Dec. 10, 1930]. NOLP 2:73
Presentation [of the Nobel Prize for Peace to Nathan Söderblom, Dec. 11, 1930]. NOLP 2:73
Myrbäck, K.
Presentation [of the Nobel Prize for Chemistry to Melvin Calvin, Dec. 11, 1961]. NOLC 3:615
Presentation [of the Nobel Prize for Chemistry to Luis F. Leloir, Dec. 11, 1970]. NOLC 4:335
Nansen, F.
Speech at Award Ceremony [presenting Nobel Prize for Peace to Aristide Briand and Gustav Stresemann, Dec. 10, 1926]. NOLP 2:3
Speech at Award Ceremony [presenting the Nobel Prize for Peace to Joseph Austen Chamberlain and Charles Gates Dawes for 1925, Dec. 10, 1926]. NOLP 1:383
Nordström, T.
Presentation [of the Nobel Prize for Chemistry to Alfred Werner, Dec. 11, 1913]. NOLC 1:253
Presentation [of the Nobel Prize for Physics to Heike Kamerlingh Onnes, Dec. 11, 1913]. NOLPH 1:303
Odhner, C. T.
Presentation [of the Nobel Prize for Chemistry to Jacobus Henricus Van't Hoff, Dec. 13, 1901]. NOLC 1:3
Presentation [of the Nobel Prize for Physics to Wilhelm Conrad Röntgen, 1901]. NOLPH 1:3
Olander, A.
Presentation [of the Nobel Prize for Chemistry to Jaroslav Heyrovsky, Dec. 11, 1959]. NOLC 3:561
Presentation [of the Nobel Prize for Chemistry to Manfred Eigen, R. G. W. Norrish and George Porter, Dec. 11, 1967]. NOLC 4:165
Presentation [of the Nobel Prize for Chemistry to Sir Cyril Norman Hinshelwood and Nikolai Nikolaevic Semenov, Dec. 11, 1956]. NOLC 3:471
Olivecrona, H.
Presentation [of the Nobel Prize for Physiology or Medicine to Walter Rudolf Hess and Antonio Caetano De Abreu Freire Egas Moniz, Dec. 12, 1949]. NOLM 3:243
Oseen, C. W.
Presentation [of the Nobel Prize for Physics for 1925 to James Franck and Gustav Hertz, Dec. 11, 1926]. NOLPH 2:95
Presentation [of the Nobel Prize for Physics to Jean Baptiste Perrin, Dec. 11, 1926]. NOLPH 2:135
Presentation [of the Nobel Prize for Physics to Louis-Victor de Broglie, Dec. 12, 1929]. NOLPH 2:241
Presentation [of the Nobel Prize for Physics for 1928 to Owen Willans Richardson, Dec. 12, 1929]. NOLPH 2:221
Österling, A.
Presentation [of the Nobel Prize for Literature to Albert Camus, 1957]. NOB 4:3; NOL:522
Presentation [of the Nobel Prize for Literature to André Gide, 1947]. NOB 7:3; NOL:422
Presentation [of the Nobel Prize for Literature to Bertrand Arthur William Russell, 1950]. NOB 15:255; NOL:449
Presentation [of the Nobel Prize for Literature to Erik Axel Karlfeldt, 1931]. NOB 10:101; NOL:295
Presentation [of the Nobel

Prize for Literature to Ernest Miller Hemingway, 1954]. NOB 9:3; NOL:497
Presentation [of the Nobel Prize for Literature to François Mauriac, 1952]. NOB 13:3; NOL:477
Presentation [of the Nobel Prize for Literature to Giorgos Seferis, 1963]. NOB 17:3; NOL:580
Presentation [of the Nobel Prize for Literature to Hermann Hesse, 1946]. NOB 9:233; NOL:412
Presentation [of the Nobel Prize for Literature to Ivo Andrić, 1961]. NOB 1:117; NOL:562
Presentation [of the Nobel Prize for Literature to Johannes Vilhelm Jensen, 1944]. NOB 8:259; NOL:397
Presentation [of the Nobel Prize for Literature to John Galsworthy]. NOB 6:227; NOL:302
Presentation [of the Nobel Prize for Literature to John Steinbeck, 1962]. NOB 19:201; NOL:572
Presentation [of the Nobel Prize for Literature to Miguel Angel Asturias, 1967]. NOB 2:3; NOL:624
Presentation [of the Nobel Prize for Literature to Mikhail Aleksandrovich Sholokhov, 1965]. NOB 17:37; NOL:603
Presentation [of the Nobel Prize for Literature to Pär Fabian Lagerkvist, 1951]. NOB 10:201; NOL:466
Presentation [of the Nobel Prize for Literature to Saint-John Perse, 1960]. NOB 20:3; NOL:553
Presentation [of the Nobel Prize for Literature to Salvatore Quasimodo, 1959]. NOB 20:281; NOL:534
Presentation [of the Nobel Prize for Literature to Shmuel Yosef Agnon and Leonie Nelly Sachs, 1966]. NOB 1:3; NOB 16:3; NOL:611
Presentation [of the Nobel Prize for Literature to Thomas Stearns Eliot, 1948]. NOB 5:261; NOL:431
Presentation address [of the Nobel Prize for Literature to Yasunari Kawabata, 1968]. NOB 11:3

Palmaer, W.
Presentation [of the Nobel Prize for Chemistry for 1931 to Carl Bosch and Friedrich Bergius, May 21, 1932]. NOLC 2:189
Presentation [of the Nobel Prize for Chemistry for 1934 to Harold Clayton Urey, Feb. 14, 1935]. NOLC 2:333
Presentation [of the Nobel Prize for Chemistry to Jean Frédéric Joliot and Irène Joliot-Curie, Dec. 12, 1935]. NOLC 2:359
Presentation [of the Nobel Prize for Chemistry to Walter Norman Haworth and Paul Karrer, Dec. 11, 1937]. NOLC 2:407

Petterson, A.
Presentation [of the Nobel Prize for Physiology or Medicine to Jules Bordet, 1919]. NOLM 1:519

Pleijel, H.
Presentation [of the Nobel Prize for Physics to Clinton Joseph Davisson and George Paget Thomson, Dec. 13, 1937]. NOLPH 2:387
Presentation [of the Nobel Prize for Physics to Enrico Fermi, Dec. 12, 1938]. NOLPH 2:409
Presentation [of the Nobel Prize for Physics to James Chadwick, Dec. 12, 1935]. NOLPH 2:333
Presentation [of the Nobel Prize for Physics to Sir Chandrasekhara Venkata Raman, Dec. 11, 1930]. NOLPH 2:263
Presentation [of the Nobel Prize for Physics for 1932 to Werner Heisenberg and for 1933 to Erwin Schrodinger and Paul Adrien Maurice Dirac, Dec. 11, 1933]. NOLPH 2:283

Reichard, P.

Presentation [of the Nobel Prize for Physiology or Medicine to Robert W. Holley, Har Gobind Khorana, and Marshall W. Nirenberg, Dec. 12, 1968]. NOLM 4:321
Rudberg, E. G.
Presentation [of the Nobel Prize for Physics to William Shockley, John Bardeen and Walter Houser Brattain, Dec. 11, 1956]. NOLPH 3:315
Schück, H.
Presentation [of the Nobel Prize for Literature to Grazia Deledda, 1926]. NOB 5:117; NOL:232
Siegbahn, K. M. G.
Presentation [of the Nobel Prize for Physics to Arthur Holly Compton and Charles Thomson Rees Wilson, Dec. 12, 1927]. NOLPH 2:169
Presentation [of the Nobel Prize for Physics to Donald Arthur Glaser, Dec. 12, 1960]. NOLPH 3:525
Presentation [of the Nobel Prize for Physics to Pavel Aleksejevič Cerenkov, Il'ja Michajlovič Frank and Igor' Evgen'evič Tamm, Dec. 11, 1958]. NOLPH 3:423
Siwertz, S.
Presentation [of the Nobel Prize for Literature to Sir Winston Leonard Spencer Churchill, 1953]. NOB 4:177; NOL:488
Sjöquist, J.
Presentation [of the Nobel Prize for Physiology or Medicine for 1923 to Frederick Grant Banting and John James Richard Macleod, 1925]. NOLM 2:45
Söderbaum, H. G.
Presentation [of the Nobel Prize for Chemistry to Arthur Harden and Hans Karl August Simon von Euler-Chelpin, Dec. 12, 1929]. NOLC 2:127
Presentation [of the Nobel Prize for Chemistry to Frederick Soddy, 1921, Dec. 12, 1922]. NOLC 1:367
Presentation [of the Nobel Prize for Chemistry to Francis William Aston, Dec. 12, 1922]. NOLC 2:3
Presentation [of the Nobel Prize for Chemistry to Hans Fischer, Dec. 11, 1930]. NOLC 2:161
Presentation [of the Nobel Prize for Chemistry for 1927 to Heinrich Otto Wieland and for 1928 to Adolf Otto Reinhold Windaus, Dec. 12, 1928]. NOLC 2:89
Presentation [of the Nobel Prize for Chemistry to Irving Langmuir, Dec. 14, 1932]. NOLC 2:283
Presentation [of the Nobel Prize for Chemistry to Richard Adolf Zsigmondy, 1925, Dec. 11, 1926]. NOLC 2:41
Presentation [of the Nobel Prize for Chemistry to Theodor Svedberg, 1926, May 19, 1927]. NOLC 2:63
Presentation [of the Nobel Prize for Chemistry to Victor Grignard and Paul Sabatier, Dec. 11, 1912]. NOLC 1:217
Presentation [of the Nobel Prize for Physics to Nils Gustaf Dalen, 1912]. NOLPH 1:293
Stang, F.
Presentation [of the Nobel Prize for Peace, 1935, to Carl Von Ossietzky, Dec. 10, 1936]. NOLP 2:207
Presentation [of the Nobel Prize for Peace to Fridtjof Nansen, Dec. 10, 1922]. NOLP 1:353
Presentation [of the Nobel Prize for Peace to the Nansen International Office for Refugees, Dec. 10, 1938]. NOLP 2:265
Suggestions for preparation of a speech presenting a gift or award. MILS:10
Sundberg, C.
Presentation [of the Nobel Prize for Physiology or Medicine to Charles Louis Alphonse

Laveran]. NOLM 1:259
Presentation [of the Nobel Prize for Physiology or Medicine to Charles Robert Richet, Dec. 11, 1913]. NOLM 1:469
Taylor, D.
Presents Grace George. LYI:19
Théel, H.
Presentation [of the Nobel Prize for Chemistry to Hermann Emil Fischer, Dec. 12, 1902]. NOLC 1:17
Presentation [of the Nobel Prize for Physics to Hendrik Antoon Lorentz and Pieter Zeeman, 1902]. NOLPH 1:11
Theorell, H.
Presentation [of the Nobel Prize for Physiology or Medicine to Carl Ferdinand Cori, Gerty Theresa Cori-Radnitz, and Bernardo Alberto Houssay, Dec. 11, 1947]. NOLM 3:179
Presentation [of the Nobel Prize for Physiology or Medicine to Severo Ochoa and Arthur Kornberg, Dec. 11, 1959]. NOLM 3:641
Tiselius, A. W. K.
Presentation [of the Nobel Prize for Chemistry to Archer John Porter Martin and Richard Laurence Millington Synge, Dec. 12, 1952]. NOLC 3:355
Presentation [of the Nobel Prize for Chemistry to Frederick Sanger, Dec. 11, 1958]. NOLC 3:541
Presentation [of the Nobel Prize for Chemistry to James Batcheller Sumner, John Howard Northrop, and Wendell Meredith Stanley, Dec. 12, 1946]. NOLC 3:109
Presentation [of the Nobel Prize for Chemistry to William Francis Giauque, Dec. 12, 1949]. NOLC 3:221
Törnebladh, H. R.
Presentation [of the Nobel Prize for Chemistry to Svante August Arrhenius, Dec. 11, 1903]. NOLC 1:43
Presentation [of the Nobel Prize for Physics to Antoine Henri Becquerel, Pierre Curie and Marie Sklodowska-Curie, Dec. 11, 1903]. NOLPH 1:47
Uvnäs, B.
Presentation [of the Nobel Prize for Physiology or Medicine to Daniel Bovet, Dec. 11, 1957]. NOLM 3:549
Presentation [of the Nobel Prize for Physiology or Medicine to Julius Axelrod, Ulf Von Euler, and Bernhard Katz, Dec. 12, 1970]. NOLM 4:441
Waller, I.
Presentation [of the Nobel Prize for Physics to Alfred Kastler, Dec. 12, 1966]. NOLPH 4:183
Presentation [of the Nobel Prize for Physics to Eugene P. Wigner, Maria Goeppert Mayer and J. Hans D. Jensen, Dec. 12, 1963]. NOLPH 4:3
Presentation [of the Nobel Prize for Physics to Hideki Yukawa, Dec. 12, 1949]. NOLPH 3:125
Presentation [of the Nobel Prize for Physics to Lev Davidovic Landau, 1962]. NOLPH 3:607
Presentation [of the Nobel Prize for Physics to Max Born and Walther Bothe, Dec. 11, 1954]. NOLPH 3:253
Presentation [of the Nobel Prize for Physics to Murray Gell-Mann, 1969]. NOLPH 4:295
Presentation [of the Nobel Prize for Physics to Robert Hofstadter and Rudolf Ludwig Mossbauer, Dec. 11, 1961]. NOLPH 3:555
Presentation [of the Nobel Prize for Physics to Sin-Itiro Tomonaga, Julian Schwinger, and Richard P. Feynman, Dec. 11, 1965]. NOLPH 4:123
Presentation [of the Nobel Prize for Physics to Sir John Douglas Cockcroft and Ernest Thomas Sinton Walton, Dec.

11, 1951]. NOLPH 3:163
Presentation [of the Nobel Prize for Physics to Willis Eugene Lamb and Polykarp Kusch, Dec. 12, 1955]. NOLPH 3:283
Presentation [of the Nobel Prize for Physics for 1945 to Wolfgang Pauli, Dec. 13, 1946]. NOLPH 3:25

Wallgren, A.
Presentation [of the Nobel Prize for Physiology or Medicine to Selman Abraham Waksman, Dec. 12, 1952]. NOLM 3:365

Wernstedt, W.
Presentation [of the Nobel Prize for Physiology or Medicine for 1926 to Johannes Andreas Grib Fibiger, Dec. 12, 1927]. NOLM 2:119
Presentation [of the Nobel Prize for Physiology or Medicine to Julius Wagner-Jauregg, Dec. 12, 1927]. NOLM 2:155

Wessén, E.
Presentation [of the Nobel Prize for Literature to Halldor Kiljan Laxness, 1955]. NOB 12:3; NOL:505

Westgren, A.
Presentation [of the Nobel Prize for Chemistry to Arne Wilhelm Kaurin Tiselius, Dec. 13, 1948]. NOLC 3:191
Presentation [of the Nobel Prize for Chemistry to Artturi Ilmari Virtanen, Dec. 12, 1945]. NOLC 3:71
Presentation [of the Nobel Prize for Chemistry to Edwin Mattison McMillan and Glenn Theodore Seaborg, Dec. 12, 1951]. NOLC 3:309
Presentation [of the Nobel Prize for Chemistry for 1943 to George De Hevesy, Dec. 12, 1944]. NOLC 3:5
Presentation [of the Nobel Prize for Chemistry for 1944 to Otto Hahn, Dec. 13, 1946]. NOLC 3:47
Presentation [of the Nobel Prize for Chemistry to Petrus Josephus Wilhelmus Debye, Dec. 12, 1936]. NOLC 2:379
Presentation [of the Nobel Prize for Chemistry to Willard Frank Libby, Dec. 12, 1960]. NOLC 3:589

Wirsen, C. D. af
Presentation [of the Nobel Prize for Literature to Bjørnstjerne Martinus Bjørnson, 1903]. NOL:14; NOB 3:77
Presentation [of the Nobel Prize for Literature to Christian Matthias Theodor Mommsen, 1902]. NOL:7; NOB 13:235
Presentation [of the Nobel Prize for Literature to Frédéric Mistral and José de Echegaray y Eizaguirre, 1904]. NOL:23; NOB 13:119
Presentation [of the Nobel Prize for Literature to Giosué Carducci, 1906]. NOB 5:3; NOL:48
Presentation [of the Nobel Prize for Literature to Henryk Sienkiewicz, 1905]. NOL:36; NOB 17:173
Presentation [of the Nobel Prize for Literature to Maurice Polydore Marie Bernhard Maeterlinck, 1911]. NOB 12:139; NOL:107
Presentation [of the Nobel Prize for Literature to Paul Johann Ludwig Heyse, 1910]. NOB 7:279; NOL:100
Presentation [of the Nobel Prize for Literature to Rudyard Kipling, 1907]. NOB 11:89; NOL:58
Presentation [of the Nobel Prize for Literature to Sully Prudhomme, 1901]. NOL:2; NOB 16:303

PRESIDENTIAL PRIMARIES See Primaries

PRESIDENTS See Educators; Executives; Inaugural addresses; Installation speeches;

Nominations; Officers; Offices - Acceptance; Presidents - United States; Public officials

---- UNITED STATES
Bayard, T. F.
Plea for conciliation in 1876. BREWE 1:265
Clay, H.
Against the growing power of the executive. ANN 6:565
Bank and the power of the executive. ANN 6:46
Ford, G. R.
The third presidential debate. BA 1976-77:30
Fulbright, J. W.
Arrogance of power. ANN 18:362
Jackson, A.
Autonomy of the executive. ANN 6:58
Johnson, A.
Veto of Tenure of Office Act. ANN 10:90
Johnson, L. B.
Obligation of power. ANN 18:368
Kennedy, R. F.
Kennedy's decision to seek Presidential nomination. THOMS:131
Moore, P.
A biblical faith for a president. BA 1976-77:24
Nixon, R. M.
Campaign speech, radio broadcast, September 19, 1968. SIN:366
Randolph, J., 1773-1833
"Blifil and Black George--Puritan and blackleg" (from debate on Executive patronage). BREWE 9:3292
Taft, W. H.
Limited presidential power. ANN 14:41
Thurman, A. G.
Tilden-Hayes election. BREWE 9:3621
Truckman, B.
Presidential eligibility. REIR:107 (outline)
Truman, H. S.
Powers of the President. HURH:316

---- See also Inaugural addresses

---- ELECTION
Lawson, J.
I protest against Hayes's Southern policy. FON:457

---- ---- See Electoral College

PRESIDING OFFICERS See Officers, Presiding

PRESS
Agnew, S.
Address before the Midwest Regional Republican Committee. BA 1969-70:59
Berryer, P. A.
Censorship of the press. BREWE 2:443
Clark, T. C.
Sheppard v. Maxwell, warden: opinion for the court. ANN 18:402
Fulbright, J. W.
"The neglect of the song." BA 1974-75:109
Press and the politicians. ERP:159
Kennedy, R. F.
Fruitful tension. BA 1966-67:138
Royer-Collard, P. P.
Against press censorship. BREWE 9:3347
Senu bin Abdul Rahman
Pledge to newsmen. MONS:156
Shaw, R. M.
Danger of getting used to lies. LINR:191
Stanton, F.
Address before the International Radio and Television Society. BA 1969-70:71
Stewart, P.
Or of the press. BA 1974-75:97
Sulzberger, A. O.
Business and the press: is the press anti-business? EHN:387

Price, Joseph C.
The race problem stated. SMHV:78

Price, Steven
Agriculture--the real answer to starvation. BREWW:161

PRIMARIES
Roosevelt, F. D.
Fireside chat on party primaries, June 24, 1938. FRIP:324

PRIMROSE LEAGUE
Salisbury, R. A. T. G.
Speech to the Primrose League. STRM:375

PRIVACY, RIGHT OF
Mathias, C. M.
Privacy on the ropes. BA 1978-79:70

PRIZES See Acceptance speeches - Rewards (Prizes); Presentation speeches - Rewards (Prizes)

Prochnow, Herbert V.
Introduces Clarence B. Randall as moderator of panel. PRS:12
Introduces Dr. David Horowitz, governor of the Bank of Israel. PRS:31
Introduces Peter G. Peterson, president of Bell and Howell Company. PRS:8
Presents James C. Downs, Jr., chairman of the board of the Real Estate Research Corporation. PRS:14
Presents Richard J. Daley, mayor of Chicago. PRS:28
Toast to the mayor of Copenhagen. PRS:56

Prochorov, Alexander M.
Quantum electronics (Nobel Lecture, Dec. 11, 1964). NOLPH 4:110

PROCHOROV, ALEXANDER M.
Edlén, B.
Presentation [of the Nobel Prize for Physics to Charles H. Townes, Nikolai G. Basov, and Alexander M. Prochorov, Dec. 11, 1964]. NOLPH 4:55

PRODIGAL SON (PARABLE)
Ditzen, L. R.
The right ticket but the wrong train. REID:404

PROFESSIONS
Dawson, M.
My profession. CAPB:363

PROGRESS
Brown, H. A.
One century's achievement (Valley Forge centennial). BREWE 2:683
Cass, L.
American progress and foreign oppression. BREWE 3:989
Chapin, E. H.
Source of modern progress. BREWE 3:1038
Dewey, J.
School and social progress. ANN 12:255
Durfee, J.
Influence of scientific discovery and invention on social and political progress. ANN 7:128
Russell, J.
Science and literature as modes of progress. BREWE 9:3359
Smith, G.
Origin and causes of progress. BREWE 9:3471
Webb, J. E.
From Runnymede to Ganymede. BA 1967-68:194
Wilson, Woodrow
What is progress? BEN:62

PROHIBITION
Haynes, R. A.
Success of prohibition. ANN 14:523

PROLETARIAT See Labor and laboring classes

PROMOTION See Sales talks and salesmanship

PROPAGANDA, ANTI-AMERICAN
Bray, C. W.
De-mystifying anti-Americanism. BA 1979-80:38

PROPERTY
Sanford, N. and others
Debate on property and suffrage. ANN 5:4
Sutherland, J.
Free land and the supply of labor. ANN 8:180

---- See also Real estate

PROPHECIES
Brown, B. G.
Prophecy. BREWE 2:675

PROSECUTION
Aeschines
Against Ctesiphon. BREWE 1:114; COG:120
Bingham, J. A.
Against the assassins of President Lincoln. BREWE 2:445
Cicero, M. T.
First oration against Catiline. BREWE 3:1159
First oration against Verres. BREWE 3:1174
Fourth Philippic. BREWE 3:1201
Second oration against Catiline. BREWE 3:1171
Coke, E.
Prosecuting Sir Walter Raleigh. BREWE 4:1348
Connally, T. T. and others
Censure of Senator Nye. BRR:69
Dorset, E. S.
In favor of slitting Prynne's nose. BREWE 5:1899
Erskine, T.
Against Thomas Williams for the publication of Paine's Age of Reason. BREWE 6:2038
Lysias
Against Eratosthenes for murder (on the execution without trial of Polemarchus). BREWE 8:2851; SAG:39
Nottingham, H. F.
Opening the prosecution for regicide under Charles II (trial of T. Harrison). BREWE 6:2159
Plunket, W. C.
Prosecuting Robert Emmet. BREWE 8:3213
Sheridan, R. B.
Against Warren Hastings. BREWE 9:3422
Webster, D.
Knapp White murder case. BREWE 10:3865

PROSTITUTION
Huitfeldt, J.
The service of sex. LINRS:114

PROTECTION See Free trade and protection

PROTEINS
Kendrew, J. C.
Myoglobin and the structure of proteins. NOLC 3:676
Klein, P. A.
Big things happen in small places (outline of speech explaining protein synthesis). CUB:34

PROTESTANT DISSENTERS See Church

PROTON AND ANTIPROTON ANNIHILATION
Chamberlain, O.
The early antiproton work. NOLPH 3:489
Segrè, E. G.
Properties of antinucleons. NOLPH 3:508

PROTOZOA
Laveran, C. L. A.
Protozoa as causes of disease. NOLM 1:264

PRUDHOMME, SULLY
Wirsén, C. D. af
Presentation [of the Nobel Prize for Literature to Sully Prudhomme, 1901]. NOL:2; NOB 16:303

PRUSSIA See Germany

PRYNNE, WILLIAM
Dorset, E. S.
In favor of slitting Prynne's nose. BREWE 5:1899

PUBLIC FINANCE See Finance - United States

PUBLIC LANDS See United States - Public lands

PUBLIC OFFICIALS
Dewey, T. E.
Public service. ANN 16:471
Introductions for public officials (3 examples). BNH:27
Lewe, J. C.
Presents Thomas C. Clark (Attorney General of the United States). LYI:137
Welcome to public official speaker at a civic club. HNWM:41

---- See also Law and lawyers

---- INTRODUCTION OF See Introductions

PUBLIC OPINION
Buchanan, C.
Planning and public opinion. MDYG:130
Lippmann, W.
On understanding society. BAAGB:412
Lodge, H. C., Jr.
United Nations. HURH:344

PUBLIC RELATIONS
Barton, B.
Which knew not Joseph. BRYF:554; BRYO:228
Wagner, R. B.
Public relations. ANN 16:285

---- AGRICULTURE
Kermicle, J.
Bridging the gap. BREWW:94
Spray, C.
Consumer education: the farmer's responsibility. BREWW:67

---- SCHOOLS
Pray, F. C.
Public relations in education. TAC:209

PUBLIC RELATIONS AND POLITICS - MALAYSIA
Hamzah bin Dato Abu Samah
The most powerful instrument for social cohesion. MONSA:115

PUBLIC SERVICE See Citizenship; Public officials

PUBLIC SPEAKING
Arnold, C. C.
Speech as a liberal study. ARS:2
Braden, W. W.
Has TV made the public speaker obsolete? EHN:309; MOPR:360
Caird, J.
Art of eloquence. BREWE 3:855
Carleton, W. G.
Effective speech in a democracy. ARS:5
Cousin, V.
Eloquence and the fine arts. BREWE 4:1419
Golden, J. L.
Political speaking since the 1920's. LINR:167
Haiman, F. S.
Rhetoric of 1968: a farewell to rational discourse. LINR:153
Hunt, E. L.
Lincoln's rhetorical triumph at Cooper Union (centennial speech). BA 1969-70:189
Jackson, E. M.
American theatre and the speech profession. BA 1965-66:200
Lawrence, D. L.
Speaker of the year award. TAC:227
Lee, I. G.
Four ways of looking at a speech. ARS:12
Schrier, W.
Address at Hope College Alumni banquet, May 31, 1958. SCHW:236
Address to the 60th Anniversary Oratorial Banquet, March 1, 1957. SCHW:226
Behind the scenes in oratory. SCHW:231
Coaching oratory. SCHW:239
Wigglesworth, M.
Prayse of eloquence. POC:8
Witherspoon, J.
On eloquence. POC:44

---- See also Debates and debating; Speeches - Outlines of. Also types of speeches; e.g. After-dinner speeches; Introductions; Responses

PUBLIC WELFARE
tenBroek, J.
Today's challenge in public welfare. MDV:233

PUERTO RICO
Munoz-Marin, L.
Future of Puerto Rico. ANN 16:312

PUERTO RICANS IN THE UNITED STATES
Zimbardo, P.
Puerto Ricans and the neighborhood: a persuasive interview. STOT:305

PULMONARY CIRCULATION
Cournand, A. F.
Control of the pulmonary circulation in man with some remarks on methodology. NOLM 3:529

Pulteney, William
Against standing armies. BREWE 8:3244

Purcell, Edward Mills
Research in nuclear magnetism (Nobel Lecture, Dec. 11, 1952). NOLPH 3:219

PURCELL, EDWARD MILLS
Hulthén, E.
Presentation [of the Nobel Prize for Physics to Felix Bloch and Edward Mills Purcell, Dec. 11, 1952]. NOLPH 3:199

PURITANS
Bulkeley, P.
City set upon a hill. ANN 1:211
Curtis, G. W.
Liberty under the law. BAS:141 (outline only); LINS:249

Pursley, Jerry See Andino, Judy

Purvis, Robert
The American government and the Negro. (New York, May 8, 1860). FON:227
The good time is at hand. (New York, May 12, 1863). FON:266

Pusey, Nathan M.
Thanksgiving and entreaty, a President's valedictory. (Harvard, June 15, 1971). HOR:26

PUSEY, NATHAN M.
Stipp, J. E.
Introduces Nathan M. Pusey, President, Harvard University. LYI:83

Putnam, Frank
The Negro's part in new national problems. (1900). FON:629

Pyke, Magnus
Man eats dog. MDYG:280

Pym, John
Law as the safeguard of liberty. BREWE 8:3253
On grievances in the reign of Charles I. BREWE 8:3252

- Q -

QUAKERS See Friends, Society of

QUALITY OF LIFE
Kemeny, J. G.
An optimist looks at America's future. HOR:128

QUANTUM ELECTRODYNAMICS
Feynman, R. P.
The development of the space-time view of quantum electrodynamics. NOLPH 4:155
Tomonaga, S. I.
Development of quantum electrodynamics. NOLPH 4:126

QUANTUM ELECTRONICS
Prochorov, A. M.
Quantum electronics. NOLPH 4:110

QUANTUM FIELD THEORY
Schwinger, J.

Relativistic quantum field theory. NOLPH 4:140

QUANTUM THEORY
Born, M.
The statistical interpretation of quantum mechanics. NOLPH 3:256
Heisenberg, W.
The development of quantum mechanics. NOLPH 2:290
Pauli, W.
Exclusion principle and quantum mechanics. NOLPH 3:27
Planck, M.
The genesis and present state of development of the quantum theory. NOLPH 1:407

Quasimodo, Salvatore
Acceptance [of the Nobel Prize for Literature, 1959]. NOB 20:285; NOL:537
The poet and the politician (Nobel lecture, Dec. 11, 1959). NOL:540

QUASIMODO, SALVATORE
Österling, A.
Presentation [of the Nobel Prize for Literature to Salvatore Quasimodo, 1959]. NOB 20:281; NOL:534

Quezon, Manuel L.
Filipinos of today and Filipinos of yesterday (Aug. 19, 1938). CURM:29
Inaugural address (Manila, Nov. 15, 1935). CURM:16
On Spain's contribution to the Philippines (Manila, Jan. 11, 1936). CURM:24

Quidde, Ludwig
Security and disarmament (Nobel Lecture, Dec. 10, 1927). NOLP 2:47

QUIDDE, LUDWIG
Stang, F.
Presentation [of the Nobel Prize for Peace to Ferdinand Edouard Buisson and Ludwig Quidde, Dec. 10, 1927]. NOLP 2:29

Quincy, Josiah, 1744-1775
Defence of British soldiers, 1770. BREWE 9:3269; POC:95
Lenity of the law to human infirmity (Weem et al): British soldiers arraigned for the Boston Massacre. Same as his Defence of the British soldiers, 1770
"Let us look to the end." POC:295
Speech in defence of the soldier. Same as his Defence of British soldiers, 1770

Quincy, Josiah, 1772-1864
Against the admission of new states. Same as his On the admission of Louisiana
Against the conquest of Canada. BREWE 9:3274
At the second centennial of Boston. BREWE 9:3272
On the admission of Louisiana. ANN 4:283

Quinn, William F.
Responds to an introduction. PRS:157

Quirino, Elpidio
Commemorating a national event (Malacañan Palace, Nov. 15, 1936). CURM:239

- R -

RACE PREJUDICE See Discrimination; Racism; Segregation

RACE PROBLEMS
Barnett, F. L.
Race unity. FON:461
Bruce, J. E.
Negro plea for organized resistance to white men. ANN 11:214
Bulkley, W. L.
Race prejudice as viewed from an economic standpoint. FON:680
Bunche, R. J.
Barriers of race can be surmounted. CAPG:66
Farmer, J. and others

Debate at Cornell University, March 7, 1961. OE:248
Franklin, J. H.
American's window to the world: her race problem. FON:907
Grady, H. W.
Race problem (speech to the Boston Merchants' Association). BREWE 6:2299
McKissick, F. B.
The student and the ghetto. OE:216
Morgan, C., Jr.
Time to speak. KEO:308
Moton, R. R.
Some elements necessary to race development. FON:692
Price, J. D.
The race problem stated. SMHV:78
Romulo, C. P.
Bandung address. CROCK:141
Roosevelt, T.
Sixth annual message. STAT 3:2194
Rowan, C. T.
New frontiers in racial relations. OE:201
Seale, B.
Free Huey. MACR:322
Simmons, B.
As time runs out. LINRS:251

RACE RELATIONS - MALAYSIA
Abdul Rahman, T.
What Abraham Lincoln said: Tunku's pledge to people of Malaysia. MONSA:65
Hamzah Sendut
Joint efforts urged for uniting various ethnic groups. MONSA:172
Johari, M. K.
Nation building and the four-way test. MONSA:100
Razak, T. A.
A new strategy to provide more jobs. MONSA:36
A rightful place for everyone in Malaysia. MONSA:12
Sambanthan, V. T.
Be a harmonising factor. MONSA:95

Rachovsky, Isaiah
Loom of time. WALE:147

RACISM
Carmichael, S.
Power and racism. BOSC:101
Crockett, G. W.
Racism in the law. FON:1131
DuBois, W. E. B.
Shall the Negro be encouraged to seek cultural equality? FON:772
Forman, J.
Black manifesto. FON:1156; OE:235
Harrison, H. H.
What socialism means to us. FON:698
Hurst, C. G.
Immorality, racism, and survival. STOT:343
Wells-Barnett, I. M.
Lynching, our national crime. FON:687

RADIATION
Barkla, C. G.
Characteristic Röntgen radiation. NOLPH 1:392
Mossbauer, R. L.
Recoilless nuclear resonance absorption of gamma radiation. NOLPH 3:584
Townes, C. H.
Production of coherent radiation by atoms and molecules. NOLPH 4:58
Wien, W.
On the laws of thermal radiation. NOLPH 1:275

RADIO
Braun, C. F.
Electrical oscillations and wireless telegraphy. NOLPH 1:226
Marconi, G.
Wireless telegraphic communication. NOLPH 1:196

RADIO BROADCASTING
Shaw, G. B.
Truth by radio. JEF:396; JEFF:378

---- See also Television broadcasting

RADIOACTIVE POLLUTION
Pauling, L. C.
Science and peace (Nobel Lec-

ture for 1962, Dec. 11, 1963). NOLP 3:271

RADIOACTIVE SUBSTANCES
Curie, P.
Radioactive substances, especially radium. NOLPH 1:73
Joliot-Curie, I.
Artificial production of radioactive elements. NOLC 2:366
Rutherford, E.
The chemical nature of the alpha particles from radioactive substances. NOLC 1:129

RADIOACTIVE TRACERS
Hevesy, G. D.
Some applications of isotopic indicators. NOLC 3:9

RADIOACTIVITY
Becquerel, A. H.
On radioactivity, a new property of matter. NOLPH 1:52
Fermi, E.
Artificial radioactivity produced by neutron bombardment. NOLPH 2:414

RADIOCARBON DATING
Libby, W. F.
Radiocarbon dating. NOLC 3:593

RADIUM
Curie, M.
Radium and the new concepts in chemistry. NOLC 1:202

Ragan, Dennis Owen
Backaches. MOP:366; MOPR:358

RAHMAN, (PARAMOUNT RULER) ABDUL d. 1960
Thomson, T. J. B.
Brightness is darkened (eulogy on Tuanku Abdul Rahman Ibni Al-Marhum Tuanku Mohammed, first King of Malaysia). MONS:281

Rahman, Dr. Ismail bin Abdul
Commendable features of public-spiritedness and co-operation (July 7, 1969). MONSA:76
Government is determined to take drastic measures if ... (July 4, 1969). MONSA:72
New era of regional cooperation. MONS:103
Security situation in Malaysia: a warning and pledge by Tun Ismail (July 5, 1969). MONSA:69
Unexpected ally after independence. MONS:99

RAILROADS
Bell, J.
Trans-continental railroads. BREWE 1:390
Buchanan, J.
Second annual message. STAT 1:969
Hepburn, W. P.
Regulation of railroad rates. ANN 13:40
Roosevelt, T.
Fifth annual message. ANN 13:1; STAT 3:2144
Webster, D.
Railroad in New Hampshire (opening Northern Railroad). ANN 7:388
Whitney, A.
Railroad to the Pacific. ANN 7:272

RAILROADS AND STATE
Roosevelt, T.
Sixth annual message. STAT 3:2194

Rainer, John C.
Institute of American Indian Arts Commencement exercises, Friday, May 21, 1976. MAES:219
Testimony: hearings before the Senate Appropriations Subcommittee on the Interior and Related Agencies, May 13, 1975. MAES:255

Rainey, Joseph H.
Eulogy on Charles Sumner. (Washington, April 27, 1874). FON:403

Rajaratnam, S.
Asia needs the spirit of Sisyphus

to succeed (Manila, April 12, 1970). MONSA:303
Asia's unfinished revolution. MONS:425
Faith in United Nations charter (on admission of Singapore). MONS:421
Parliament of Religion. MONS:417
Urgency of real problems facing the less developed nations (New York, Oct. 7, 1969). MONSA:295

Raleigh, Sir Walter
Speech on the scaffold. BREWE 9:3280; BRYH:104

RALEIGH, SIR WALTER
Coke, E.
Prosecuting Sir Walter Raleigh. BREWE 4:1348

Raman, Sir Chandrasekhara Venkata
The molecular scattering of light (Nobel Lecture, Dec. 11, 1930). NOLPH 2:267

RAMAN, SIR CHANDRASEKHARA VENKATA
Pleijel, H.
Presentation [of the Nobel Prize for Physics to Sir Chandrasekhara Venkata Raman, Dec. 11, 1930]. NOLPH 2:263

Ramani, Radhakrishna
Malaysia's stand in Kashmir dispute. MONS:240
Man of clear vision (tribute to Adlai E. Stevenson). MONS:250
Twenty four days in May (expression of thanks as President of Security Council of United Nations). MONS:248

Ramon y Cajal, Santiago
The structure and connexions of neurons (Nobel Lecture, Dec. 12, 1906). NOLM 1:220

RAMON Y CAJAL, SANTIAGO
Mörner, K. A. H.
Presentation [of the Nobel Prize for Physiology or Medicine to Camilio Golgi and Santiago Ramon y Cajal, Dec. 12, 1906]. NOLM 1:185

Ramsay, Sir William
The rare gases of the atmosphere (Nobel Lecture, Dec. 12, 1904). NOLC 1:68

RAMSAY, SIR WILLIAM
Cederblom, J. E.
Presentation [of the Nobel Prize for Chemistry to Sir William Ramsay, Dec. 12, 1904]. NOLC 1:65

Ramsey, R. Paul
Counting the costs. VI:24

Randolph, A. Philip
A call for mass action (Detroit, Sept. 26-27, 1942). FON:822
The crisis of the Negro and the Constitution. (2nd National Negro Congress, 1937). FON:816
Liberty, justice and democracy (Detroit, Sept. 27, 1942). SMHV:110
March on Washington address. (1941). OE:113
The task of the Negro people. (Chicago, 1936). FON:807

Randolph, Edmund
In defence of Aaron Burr, 1807. BREWE 9:3284

Randolph, John
Japanese "Lunchbox" universities. REIR:15

Randolph, John, 1773-1833
Against a protective tariff (1816). ANN 4:427
Against protective tariffs. Same as his On the tariff (1824)
Against trade restrictions. ANN 4:248
"Blifil and black George--Puritan and blackleg" (from debate on Executive patronage). BREWE 9:3292
On the tariff (1824). BREWE 9:3305

---- See also following jt. auths. Grundy, F.; Webster, D.

Ransley, Marie
The life and death of our lakes. (Univ. of Wisconsin, 1971). LINRS:63

Ransom, Reverdy C.
William Lloyd Garrison: a centennial oration (Boston, Dec. 10, 1905). SMHV:66

Rantoul, Robert, Jr.
On the barbarity of the common law. ANN 6:262

Rapier, James T.
Civil Rights Bill. (Washington, Feb. 4, 1875). FON:418

Raskas, Bernard S.
Physician's prayer. WALE:149

Rawson, Edward
Thanksgiving. (Charlestown, Mass., June 20, 1676). HURH:20
"... that the Lord may behold us as a people, offering praise and thereby glorifying Him...." Same as his Thanksgiving

Rayburn, Samuel
Impressive accomplishments (75th Congress). BAD:83

RAYBURN, SAMUEL
Martin, J. W.
Introducing Speaker Sam Rayburn. LYI:195

Rayleigh, John William Strutt, Baron
The density of gases in the air and the discovery of argon (Nobel Lecture, Dec. 12, 1904). NOLPH 1:90

RAYLEIGH, JOHN WILLIAM STRUTT, BARON, 1842-1919
Cederblom, J. E.
Presentation [of the Nobel Prize for Physics to Lord Rayleigh, Dec. 12, 1904]. NOLPH 1:87

Razak, Tun Abdul
Alliance policy for unity. MONS:47
And then came peace (Peace agreement between Malaysia and Indonesia). MONS:94
The beginning of a new realism in Malaysia: the period ahead is challenging (June 13, 1969). MONSA:24
Bridge of communication (on departure to America). MONS:59
A call to UMNO leaders: time for slogan chanting is over.... (Sept. 22, 1970). MONSA:20
Correct words for a toast! MONS:91
Crucial cross-roads of history. MONS:64
Democracy and development in Malaysia. MONS:80
The development strategy for success of second Malaysian plan (Kuala Lumpur, Feb. 3, 1970). MONSA:4
Devastating consequences of excessive population growth (Kuala Lumpur, March 18, 1970). MONSA:9
Hopes and anxieties of the countries of Southeast Asia (Singapore, Jan. 15, 1971). MONSA:47
Most unfortunate of conflicts. MONS:69
A new strategy to provide more jobs. MONSA:36
Problems of war and peace (Lusaka, Sept. 10, 1970). MONSA:15
Putting life into development plans. MONS:86
A rightful place for everyone in Malaysia (Hotel Merlin, Aug. 20, 1970). MONSA:12
The significance of Five-Power Defence Agreement (Canberra, June 19-20, 1969). MONSA:29
UMNO's twentieth milestone (20th anniversary of United Malay National Organization). MONS:53
Vital issues must be resolved if we are to survive (National Consultative Council, Jan. 27, 1970). MONSA:1
We will uphold concepts of parliamentary democracy (Jan. 23, 1971). MONSA:41 selections

Read, David H. C.
Is God over thirty? Religion and the youth revolt. BA 1966-67:129

Read, Leonard E.
Responds to introduction. PRS:98

READING See Books and reading; Literature

Reagan, Ronald
Responds to an introduction. PRS:157
Time for choosing. CAPG:48

REAL ESTATE
Investor. BURT:175

REAL PROPERTY See Real Estate

REASON
Clevenger, T.
To have lived without reason. CAPB:373
Wesley, J.
Poverty of reason. BREWE 10:3874

RECOMBINANT DNA
McGill, W. J.
Science and the law. BA 1977-78:83

RECONSTRUCTION
Adams, E. J.
These are revolutionary times. FON:342
Blair, A.
Military government. BREWE 2:504
Brockett, J. A.
Reply to Grady. ANN 11:250
Cardozo, F. L.
Break up the plantation system. FON:350
Chamberlain, D. H.
Present hour in South Carolina (inaugural address of would-be governor). CUR:158
Conkling, R.
Stalwart standpoint. BREWE 4:1369
Davis, D.
Ex parte Milligan, 1866; opinion for the court. ANN 10:31
Davis, H. W.
Constitutional difficulties of reconstruction. BREWE 5:1647
DeBow, J. D. B.
That feeling of hostility. CUR:52
Dunn, O. J.
We ask an equal chance in the race of life. FON:355
Gordon, J. B.
It was purely a peace police organization. CUR:98
Grant, U. S.
First annual message. STAT 2:1188
Gray, W. H.
Justice should recognize no color. FON:353
Hampton, W.
Present hour in South Carolina (inaugural address of would-be governor). CUR:159
Hayden, L.
Deliver us from such a Moses. FON:334
Johnson, A.
Against the radical Republicans. ANN 10:8
Annual message to Congress, December 3, 1868. ANN 10:81; STAT 2:1129
At Cleveland in 1866. BREWE 7:2640
At St. Louis. BREWE 7:2628
End itself is evil (third annual message, 1867). CUR:61; STAT 2:1144
Fourth annual message. STAT 2:1167
Presidential plan of Reconstruction. CUR:8; STAT 2:1112
Second reconstruction veto. ANN 10:98
Veto of Freedmen's Bureau Bill. ANN 10:3
Veto of the first Reconstruction Act, 1867. ANN 10:93
---- and others
Debate on civil and states' rights. ANN 10:11
Langston, J. M.
The other phase of reconstruction. SMHV:46
Lincoln, A.
Speech before death, April 11,

1865. ANN 9:573; BREWE 7:2796; CUR:4
Third annual message. ANN 9:473; STAT 2:1084
Seward, W. H.
Reconciliation in 1865. BREWE 9:3408
Sherman, J.
It is essentially a Rebel organization. CUR:102
Stevens, T.
On reconstruction. CUR:13
Radical view of reconstruction. BREWE 9:3529; CUR:58
Rights of the conqueror. ANN 9:608
Sumner, C.
Proper guaranties for security. CUR:12
Turner, H. M.
I claim the rights of a man. FON:357

RECONSTRUCTION, 1939-1951
Acheson, D.
Marshall Plan; relief and reconstruction are chiefly matters of American self-interest. LAA:55
Marshall, G. C.
Address at Harvard University. ANN 16:438; BOORA 2:884; GRG:82; HURH:283

Recto, Claro M.
The preparation of the Constitution (House of Representatives, Feb. 8, 1935). CURM:250

RECYCLING (WASTE, ETC.)
Hirschler, P.
How to beautify your farm. BREWW:124
Howell, W.
A new century in agriculture. BREWW:211

RED CROSS
Boissier, L. L.
Some aspects of the mission of the International Committee of the Red Cross (Nobel Lecture, Dec. 11, 1963). NOLP 3:301
Chapuisat, E.
The activity of the International Committee of the Red Cross during the War, 1939-1945 (Nobel Lecture for 1944, Dec. 11, 1945). NOLP 2:295
Hambro, C. J.
Presentation [of the Nobel Prize for Peace to the International Committee of the Red Cross and the League of the Red Cross Societies, Dec. 10, 1963]. NOLP 3:295
Huber, M.
Acceptance [of the Nobel Prize for Peace for the International Committee of the Red Cross, 1944, Dec. 10, 1945]. NOLP 2:293
Jahn, G.
Presentation [of the Nobel Prize for Peace to the International Committee of the Red Cross, 1944, Dec. 10, 1945]. NOLP 2:289
MacAulay, J. A.
The Red Cross in a changing world (Nobel Lecture, Dec. 11, 1963). NOLP 3:311
Moe, R.
Presentation [of the Nobel Prize for Peace to the International Committee of the Red Cross, Dec. 10, 1917]. NOLP 1:281

Red Eagle, Chief of the Teton Sioux Nation
Indian rights. ANN 10:242

Red Jacket, Seneca chief
Against white missions among the Indians. Same as his Missionary effort
Missionary effort (Seneca, N.Y., 1805). ANN 4:194; BREWE 7:2571; HURH:57
"You have got our country ... you want to force your religion upon us." Same as his Missionary effort

Redmond, John E. See Oxford and Asquith, Herbert Henry Asquith, 1st Earl of, jt. auth.

Reed, Thomas Brackett
Immortality and good deeds (semi-centennial of Girard College). BREWE 9:3307

Reeves, Richard Ambrose
Journey to Hanoi. VI:83

REFORM
Emerson, R. W.
Man the reformer.
BREWE 5:2008
Wright, F.
Of existing evils and their remedy. ANN 5:290

---- See also Great Britain - Politics and government; Reform Act (1867); Reform Bills (1831, 1832); Social problems

REFORM ACT (1867)
Beaconsfield, B. D.
Reform Bill of 1867 (Edinburgh speech, October 29, 1867). STRM:296
Lowe, R.
Coming of democracy.
MCB:138
Mill, J. S.
Representation of the people.
MCB:154

REFORM BILLS (1831, 1832)
Brougham and Vaux, H. P. B.
Supports the Reform Bill.
BRYH:322
Macaulay, T. B.
Reform Bill. CLAYP:295; JAE:52; MCB:110
Russell, J. R.
Reform the franchise.
MCB:87
Smith, S.
Mrs. Partington in politics.
BREWE 9:3479
Reform and stomach troubles.
BREWE 9:3484

REFUGEES
Goedhart, G. J. v. H.
Refugee problems and their solutions (Nobel Lecture, Dec. 12, 1955). NOLP 3:97
Hansson, M.
The Nansen International Office for Refugees (Nobel Lecture, Dec. 10, 1938).
NOLP 2:268

REFUSE AND REFUSE DISPOSAL
Hall, C.
A heap of trouble. EHN:316

Reichard, P.
Presentation [of the Nobel Prize for Physiology or Medicine to Robert W. Holley, Har Gobind Khorana, and Marshall W. Nirenberg, Dec. 12, 1968].
NOLM 4:321

Reichstein, Tadeus
Chemistry of the adrenal cortex hormones (Nobel Lecture, Dec. 11, 1950). NOLM 3:291

REICHSTEIN, TADEUS
Liljestrand, G.
Presentation [of the Nobel Prize for Physiology of Medicine to Edward Calvin Kendall, Tadeus Reichstein, and Philip Showalter Hench, Dec. 11, 1950]. NOLM 3:263

Reid, Charlotte T.
Tribute to Dwight D. Eisenhower.
BA 1968-69:165

Reinert, Paul C.
America, America, how does your garden grow? (Loyola Univ., Chicago, June 10, 1972). HOR:82

Reischauer, Edwin O.
Statement before the Senate Foreign Relations Committee.
BA 1966-67:70

RELATIVITY
Einstein, A.
Fundamental ideas and problems of the theory of relativity. NOLPH 1:482

RELIEF See Unemployed

RELIGION
Bede
On the nativity of St. Peter and St. Paul. BRYH:9
Beecher, H. W.
On fellowship. HURH:118
Butcyn, D. P.
Invisible abutments. SCHW:44
Chrysostom, J.
Heroes of faith.
BREWE 3:1139
Cotton, J.
God's promise to his plantations. ANN 1:107

Cox, S. S.
Sermon on the mount.
BREWE 4:1446
Dering, E.
For the encouragement of learning. BREWE 5:1805
Religious controversy in Parliament. BREWE 5:1808
Edwards, J.
Sinners in the hands of an angry God. ANN 1:423; BREWE 5:1982; HURH:21; LINS:121
Fosdick, H. E.
Shall the Fundamentalists win? ANN 14:325
Gibbons, J.
To the Parliament of Religions. BREWE 6:2248
Graham, W. F.
National humility.
HURH:339
Ingersoll, R. G.
Absurdity of religion.
ANN 11:267
Kennedy, J. F.
Religion in government.
ANN 17:589; SIN:303
Korteling, M.
Renascence. SCHW:39
Latimer, H.
On the pickings of office-holders. BREWE 7:2729
Sermon on the plow.
BREWE 7:2724; BRYH:47
Luther, M.
Pith of Paul's chief doctrine. BREWE 7:2833
Mather, C.
At the sound of the trumpet.
BREWE 8:2986
"Boston Ebenezer." POC:395
Melanchthon, P.
Safety of the virtuous.
BREWE 8:3007
Mirabeau, H. G. R.
Against the establishment of religion. BREWE 8:3034
Our changing world. BURT:129
Rajaratnam, S.
Parliament of Religion.
MONS:417
Sheen, F. J.
Change of hearts. HURH:264
Smith, A. E.
Religion and politics.
HURH:209
Sunday, W. A.
Evangelism. HURH:170
Thio Chan Bee
Christian laymen and the world of politics. MONS:465
Tillich, P. J.
"What is truth?" ARS:180
Wycliffe, J.
Concerning a grain of corn.
BREWE 10:3924

---- See also Church; Church and State; Clergy; Faith; God; Prayers; Sermons; Sin

RELIGION AND SCIENCE
Conant, J. B.
Science and spiritual values.
ARS:88
Newman, J. H.
Christianity and scientific investigation. MCB:361
Sevareid, E. and others
Science and religion: who will play God? MOP:391

RELIGION AND STATE See Church and state

RELIGIOUS EDUCATION
Welcome to parents at vacation Bible school commencement.
HNWM:19

RELIGIOUS LIBERTY
Binney, B.
Valedictory oration. POC:51
Bradlaugh, C.
Appeal for justice. JAE:142
Chew, S.
Speech, &c. POC:77
Danton, G. J.
Freedom of worship.
BREWE 5:1631
Henry, J.
On religion and elective office.
ANN 4:239; BOORA 1:220
Jackson, R. H. and others
West Virginia Board of Education et al v. Barnette et al: opinion for the court and dissenting opinion. ANN 16:148
Sheil, R. L.
Religious toleration.
MCB:269
Smith, A. E.
Campaign speech, Oklahoma City, Sept. 20, 1928.
SIN:52

Remond, Charles Lenox
Rights of colored citizens in traveling. (Mass. H. of Rep., February, 1842). ANN 7:74; FON:72
Slavery and the Irish. SMHR:110
Slavery as it concerns the British (London, June 24, 1840). SMHV:16

Renault, Louis
The work at the Hague in 1899 and in 1907 (Nobel Lecture for 1907, May 18, 1908). NOLP 1:143

RENAULT, LOUIS
Løvland, J. G.
Presentation [of the Nobel Prize for Peace to Louis Renault, Dec. 10, 1907]. NOLP 1:141

REPARTEE See Responses

REPORTS
Benchley, R. C.
Treasurer's report. HURH:211
Suggestions for preparation or reports on conventions. PAE:188
You get what you ask for (outline of speech). CUB:31

---- See also Club speeches; Congresses and conventions

REPUBLICAN PARTY
Brooke, E. W.
Crisis in the two-party system. BA 1965-66:170
Hoover, H. C.
Road to freedom. ANN 15:384
Lincoln, A.
Lincoln-Douglas joint debate at Alton, October 15, 1858. ANN 9:26
Roosevelt, F. D.
Republican leadership and national defense. ANN 16:36
Taft, R. A.
Declaration of Republican principles--the New Deal is rapidly receding. BAD:74
Tilden, S. J.
Negro suffrage. ANN 10:122

REPUBLICS See Democracy

RESEARCH
Bowen, W. G.
Commitment to scholarship and research. BA 1978-79:41
Carty, J. J.
Pure science and industrial research. ANN 14:9
Huxley, T. H.
Method of scientific investigation. ARS:264
Rowland, H. A.
Appeal for pure scientific research in America. ANN 12:262

RESIGNATIONS
Nixon, R. M.
Our long national nightmare is over--speech of resignation. BA 1974-75:43

---- See Officers, Retiring

RESPIRATION
Heymans, C. J. F.
The part played by vascular presso- and chemo-receptors in respiratory control. NOLM 2:460
Warburg, O. H.
The oxygen-transferring ferment of respiration. NOLM 2:254

RESPONSES TO INTRODUCTION
Alphand, H.
Responds to introductions. PRS:159; 198
Alsop, J.
Responds to an introduction. PRS:154
Anspach, C. L.
Responds to an introduction. PRS:138
Appling, H., Jr.
Responds to an introduction. PRS:144
Bell, D. E.
Responds to introduction. PRS:94
Bishop, J.
Responds to introduction (when substituting for Sir Cedric

Harwicke). PRS:119
Blough, R. M.
Responds to an introduction on an occasion when he is given an award. PRS:129
Booth, A. N.
Responds to an introduction. PRS:146
Bourguiba, H.
Responds to an introduction. PRS:136
Burns, J. L.
Responds to an introduction. PRS:150
Catton, B.
Response to introduction. PRS:88
Clark, E. M.
Responds to an introduction. PRS:139
Cole, A. L.
Responds to introduction. PRS:97
Conant, J. B.
Responds to an introduction. PRS:153
Copley, J. S.
Responds to an introduction. PRS:152
Cordiner, R. J.
Responds to an introduction. PRS:137
Davenport, J.
Responds to an introduction. PRS:155
David, J. K.
Responds to an introduction at a Newcomen Society dinner. PRS:151
Dirksen, E.
Responds to introduction. PRS:122
Donner, F. G.
Responds to an introduction. PRS:150
Douglas, W. O.
Responds to an introduction. PRS:161
Drummond, R.
Responds to introduction. PRS:123
Eban, A.
Responds to an introduction. PRS:159
Eisenhower, D. D.
Responds to an introduction. PRS:152
Farley, J. A.
Responds to an introduction. PRS:145
Finley, C. O.
Responds to introduction. PRS:115
Flack, G.
Responds to an introduction. PRS:191
Funston, G. K.
Responds to an introduction. PRS:135
Ginna, R.
Responds to an introduction at a Newcomen Society dinner. PRS:156
Griffin, R. P.
Responds to an introduction. PRS:144
Haak, J. F. W.
Responds to an introduction. PRS:140
Hansberger, R. V.
Responds to an introduction. PRS:146
Harnwell, G. P.
Responds to an introduction. PRS:142
Hatfield, M. O.
Response to introduction. PRS:92
Hayes, A. J.
Responds to an introduction. PRS:153
Higgins, M.
Responds to introduction. PRS:107
Hoover, J. E.
Responds to an introduction. PRS:140
Judd, W. H.
Responds to introduction. PRS:126
Keating, K. B.
Responds to an introduction. PRS:132
Kelly, W. F.
Responds to introduction. PRS:129
Kennan, G. F.
Responds to an introduction. PRS:148
Kennedy, R. F.
Responds to introductions. PRS:135; 136
Kirkpatrick, L. B.
Responds to an introduction. PRS:141
Kissinger, H. A.

Responds to introduction. PRS:124
Livingston, H. J.
Responds to an introduction and speaks briefly at the dedication of a new manufacturing plant. PRS:130
McClellan, J. L.
Responds to an introduction. PRS:161
Malott, D. W.
Responds to introduction. PRS:117
Martin, A.
Responds to an introduction. PRS:139
Meany, G.
Responds to an introduction. PRS:156
Menninger, W. C.
Responds to introduction. PRS:135
Miner by choice (outline of speech in response to welcome). CUB:68
Mitchell, D. G.
Responds to an introduction. PRS:148
Mitchell, J. P.
Responds to an introduction. PRS:143
Morton, T. B.
Responds to introduction. PRS:98
Mundt, K. E.
Responds to introduction. PRS:109
Nash, O.
Responds to introduction. PRS:106
Nielson, A. C., Sr.
Responds to an introduction. PRS:155
O'Connell, J. T.
Responds to an introduction. PRS:138
Odegaard, C. E.
Responds to an introduction. PRS:155
Oliver, R. T.
Responds to an introduction. PRS:152
Patterson, M.
Responds to an introduction. PRS:160
Peale, N. V.
Responds to introductions. PRS:104; 113
Percy, C. H.
Responds to an introduction. PRS:147
Power, D. C.
Responds to an introduction. PRS:147
Quinn, W. F.
Responds to an introduction. PRS:157
Read, L. E.
Responds to introduction. PRS:98
Reagan, R.
Responds to an introduction. PRS:157
Replies to introduction (31 examples). BNH:36; BON:45; BOS:36
Reply to an introduction by a former Pastor (4 examples). BNH:82
Rockefeller, D.
Responds to an introduction. PRS:149
Rogers, W. P.
Responds to an introduction. PRS:142
Romulo, C. P.
Responds to an introduction. PRS:161
Rowen, H.
Responds to introduction. PRS:96
Salk, J. E.
Responds to introduction. PRS:89
Sanders, C. S.
Responds to introduction. PRS:90
Scranton, W. W.
Responds to introduction. PRS:110
Sevier, R.
Responds to an introduction. PRS:158
Sockman, R. W.
Responds to introduction. PRS:118
Suggestions for preparation of responses to introductions. With examples of. PAE:180
Thornton, C. B.
Responds to introduction. PRS:101
Tower, J. G.
Responds to introduction. PRS:101
Wampler, C.

Responds to introduction.
PRS:128
Weaver, A. T.
Responds to an introduction.
PRS:137

---- See also Responses to welcome

RESPONSES TO PRESENTATION
See Acceptance Speeches

RESPONSES TO SPEECHES OF BLAME See Defense, Speeches of

RESPONSES TO TOASTS
Carpenter, M. H.
Replying to the Grand Duke Alexis (response to Duke's toast "To the President of the United States").
BREWE 3:974

RESPONSES TO TRIBUTES
Holmes, O. W., Jr.
"Live-I am coming:" response to birthday greeting.
GRG:48; HURH:215

RESPONSES TO WELCOME
Abdul Rahman, T.
What the Commonwealth means (response to welcome address by British Prime Minister). MONS:22
Parnell, C. S.
His first speech in America.
BREWE 8:3143
Phillips, C.
Dinas Island speech on Washington. BREWE 8:3176
Suggestions for preparation of a response to a speech of welcome. MILS:12

RESPONSIBILITY, MINISTERIAL
See Ministerial responsibility

Reston, James
Remarks at the Centennial Charter Day Convocation, the Ohio State University, March 22, 1970. BAAE:285

RETAIL TRADE See Business

RETIREMENT See Officers, Retiring

REUNIONS, CLASS
Schrier, W.
Address at Hope College Alumni banquet, May 31, 1958.
SCHW:236
Washington, B. T.
Address delivered at the Harvard Alumni dinner in 1896.
HURH:144

Revels, Hiram R.
A plea for desegregated schools. (Washington, Feb. 8, 1871).
FON:371

REVOLUTION, AMERICAN See United States - History - Revolution

REVOLUTION, FRENCH See France - History - Revolution, 1789-1799; France - History - Revolution, 1848

REVOLUTIONISTS
Pusey, N. M.
Thanksgiving and entreaty, a President's valedictory.
HOR:26

REVOLUTIONS
Brown, H. R.
The Third World and the ghetto. FON:1088
Kennedy, R. F.
Counterinsurgency. ANN 18:323
Rustin, B.
A way out of the exploding ghetto. FON:1078
Tappan, D.
A warning to Harvard seniors against world revolution (1798).
DAVF:49

REWARDS (PRIZES) See Acceptance speeches - Rewards (Prizes); Presentation speeches - Rewards (Prizes)

Reynolds, Sir Joshua
Genius and imitation.
BREWE 9:3313

Reynolds, Vernon
Chimpanzee worlds. MDYG:259

RHETORIC
Haiman, F. S.

The rhetoric of 1968: a farewell to rational discourse. LINRS:133

RHODE ISLAND - CONSTITUTION
Dorr, T.
People's right to remake their constitution. ANN 7:56
Hallett, B.
Sovereignty of the people (Luther v. Borden case). ANN 7:410

RHODES
Demosthenes
Oration on the liberty of the Rhodians. SAG:180

RHODESIA
Lee Kuan Yew
The Rhodesian problem and the change of mood in Britain. MONSA:251

RIBONUCLEIC ACID
Holley, R. W.
Alanine transfer RNA. NOLM 4:324
Ochoa, S.
Enzymatic synthesis of ribonucleic acid. NOLM 3:645
Watson, J. D.
The involvement of RNA in the synthesis of proteins. NOLM 3:785

Rice, George P.
The comic spirit and the public speaker. (Indianapolis, Oct. 9, 1974). EHN:283

Richards, Dickinson Woodruff
The contributions of right heart catheterization to physiology and medicine, with some observations on the physiopathology of pulmonary heart disease (Nobel Lecture, Dec. 11, 1956). NOLM 3:513

RICHARDS, DICKINSON WOODRUFF
Liljestrand, G.
Presentation [of the Nobel Prize for Physiology or Medicine to André Frederic Cournand, Werner Theodor Otto Forssmann, and Dickinson Woodruff Richards Jr., Dec. 11, 1956]. NOLM 3:501

Richards, Theodore William
Atomic weights (Nobel Lecture for 1914, Dec. 6, 1919). NOLC 1:280

Richardson, Elliot L.
Vulnerability and vigilance. (New York, Dec. 11, 1973). BA 1973-74:13

Richardson, Owen Willans
Thermionic phenomena and the laws which govern them (Nobel Lecture for 1928, Dec. 12, 1929). NOLPH 2:224

RICHARDSON, OWEN WILLANS
Oseen, C. W.
Presentation [of the Nobel Prize for Physics for 1928 to Owen Willans Richardson, Dec. 12, 1929]. NOLPH 2:221

Richet, Charles Robert
Anaphylaxis (Nobel Lecture, Dec. 11, 1913). NOLM 1:473

RICHET, CHARLES ROBERT
Sundberg, C.
Presentation [of the Nobel Prize for Physiology or Medicine to Charles Robert Richet, Dec. 11, 1913]. NOLM 1:469

Richey, Herbert S.
The real cause of inflation: government services. (Columbus, Ohio, March 16, 1977). LINRST:108

RIGHT AND LEFT (POLITICAL SCIENCE)
McIntyre, T. J.
Keeping the Senate independent. BA 1977-78:44
Oglesby, C.
How can we continue to sack the ports of Asia and still dream of Jesus. LAA:15
Rockefeller, N. A.
Extremism. KEO:320; MAC:268; MACR:309

RIGHTS See Civil rights; Petition of Right, 1628; United States - Constitution

Rindo, John P.
Life, librium, and the pursuit of happiness (Gatlinburg, Tex., 1976). LINRST:230

RISK-TAKING (PSYCHOLOGY)
Wriston, W. B.
Risk and other four-letter words. BA 1979-80:191

Rittenhouse, David
Oration, &c. POC:142

ROADS
Crockett, D.
Raccoon in a bag. BREWE 4:1482

Robbins, Asher
Fourth of July oration, July 4, 1834 (Philadelphia). HAW:160

Robbins, Frederick Chapman
See also Enders, J. F.

ROBBINS, FREDERICK CHAPMAN
Gard, S.
Presentation [of the Nobel Prize for Physiology or Medicine to John Franklin Enders, Thomas Huckle Weller, and Frederick Chapman Robbins, Dec. 11, 1954]. NOLM 3:443

Roberts, James
Art of seduction. REIR:84

Robertson, Frederick W.
Highest form of expression. BREWE 9:3319

Robeson, Paul
Anti-imperialists must defend Africa. (New York, June 6, 1946). FON:833
The Negro artist looks ahead. (Conference for Equal Rights for Negroes in the Arts, Sciences and Professions, New York, Dec. 1951). FON:849

Robespierre, Maximilien
Against capital punishment. BREWE 9:3326
Defense from the charge of tyranny. BREWE 9:3341
Demanding the King's death. BREWE 9:3338
Festival of the Supreme Being. BREWE 9:3340
His defense of terrorism. BREWE 9:3331
"If God did not exist, it would be necessary to invent him." BREWE 9:3330
Last words. Same as his Defense from the charge of tyranny
Moral ideas and Republican principles. BREWE 9:3334

Robinson, Frederick
A Jacksonian attack on monopoly (1834) (Boston Trades Union, July 4, 1834). DAVF:69
Labor as the source of reform. ANN 6:69

Robinson, Sir Robert
Some polycyclic natural products (Nobel Lecture, Dec. 12, 1947). NOLC 3:166

ROBINSON, SIR ROBERT
Fredga, A.
Presentation [of the Nobel Prize for Chemistry to Sir Robert Robinson, Dec. 12, 1947]. NOLC 3:166

Robinson, William E. See Butler, B. F., jt. auth.

Rock, John S.
I will sink or swim with my race. (Boston, March 5, 1858). FON:203
Negro hopes for emancipation. ANN 9:318
We ask for our rights. (Abington, Mass., August 1, 1862). FON:257
What if the slaves are emancipated? (Massachusetts Anti-Slavery Society, Jan. 23, 1862). FON:250

Rockefeller, David
Responds to an introduction. PRS:149

Rockefeller, Nelson A.
Extremism. KEO:320; MAC:268; MACR:309

---- See also Burger, W. E., jt. auth.

Rodriguez, Armando M.
This is our quest: to fight for the right. BA 1968-69:129

Roesch, George F.
Constitutionality of a New York child labor law: opinion for the court. ANN 12:571

Rogers, Jack
Day before Christmas (Univ. of Nebraska, 1953). KEO:232; STOT:269

Rogers, Will
Education and wealth. (New York, Dec. 4, 1924). HURH:200
"I am here tonight representing poverty." Same as his Education and Wealth
Morgenthau's plan. GRG:55
Nominating Calvin Coolidge (1924). BAP:298; BAPR:366
Presents Franklin Delano Roosevelt. LYI:213

Rogers, William P.
Responds to an introduction. PRS:142

Rogers, William Pierce
A brief assessment of where we stand today. (Judicial Conf. of the 2nd Judicial Circuit of the U.S. Court of Appeals, Buck Hill Falls, Pa.). BA 1974-75:54

Rokeach, Milton
Images of the consumer's changing mind on and off Madison Avenue. ARS:115

ROMAN CATHOLIC CHURCH
Beecher, L.
A plea for the West. HOW:133
Gibbons, J.
Progress of the Catholic Church in America. ANN 11:148
Kenrick, F. P.
Episcopal rights and parish autonomy. ANN 5:437
Smith, S.
Results of oppression. BREWE 9:3482; JAE:40

ROMAN CATHOLICS IN IRELAND
O'Connell, D.
Catholic rights in Ireland. CLAYP:281
Sheil, R. L.
In defense of Irish Catholics. BREWE 9:3419

ROME
Cavour, C. B.
Rome and Italy. BREWE 3:1012
Manning, H. E.
Rome the eternal. BREWE 8:2934

Romilly, Sir Samuel
Habeas Corpus Suspension Bill. STRM:143

Romney, George
From the bottom to the top. CAPG:140
Our unique economic principles: the market place should determine price. CAPG:40

Romulo, Carlos P.
Bandung address. CROCK:141
The mind of a new commonwealth (Notre Dame Univ., Dec. 9, 1935). CURM:267
Responds to an introduction. PRS:161

RÖNTGEN, WILHELM CONRAD
Odhner, C. T.
Presentation [of the Nobel Prize for Physics to Wilhelm Conrad Röntgen, 1901]. NOLPH 1:3

Roosevelt, Eleanor Anna
Defense of American territorial policies. ANN 17:128
United Nations. (Chicago, July 2, 1952). HURH:297
"Without the United Nations our country would walk alone, ruled by fear, instead of

confidence and hope." Same as her United Nations

ROOSEVELT, ELEANOR ANNA
Hancher, V. M.
Presents Eleanor Roosevelt. LYI:244
Stevenson, A. E.
Eulogy on Eleanor Roosevelt. BRP:230

Roosevelt, Franklin Delano
Acceptance of renomination for the presidency, June 27, 1936. SIN:125
Acceptance speech, Chicago, Illinois, July 2, 1932. SIN:68
Acceptance speech, Philadelphia, Pennsylvania, June 27, 1932. Same as his Acceptance of renomination for the presidency, June 27, 1936
Acceptance speech via radio to convention, Washington, D.C., July 19, 1940. SIN:156
Acceptance speech on renomination for president, July 20, 1944. SIN:194
Acceptance speech, Radio broadcast, San Diego, California, July 20, 1944. Same as his Acceptance speech on renomination for president, July 20, 1944
Action defended (campaign speech, October 31, 1936). ROD:168
Address at the annual gathering of the White House Correspondents' Association, February 12, 1943. ANN 16:130
Address at University of Pennsylvania, September 20, 1940. FRIP:331
Address on Constitution Day, September 17, 1937. FRIP:317
Address to the Commonwealth Club, September 23, 1932. ANN 15:158; ROD:31; SIN:77
Address to the people. Same as his Broadcast address, March 9, 1937
Address to White House Correspondents' Association dinner, March 15, 1941. CROCK:11
Address to Young Democratic Clubs of America, August 24, 1935. FRIP:304
Aid to the Democracies; our country is going to play its part. Same as his Address to White House Correspondents' Association dinner, March 15, 1941
American business is moving ahead. BAD:1
Arsenal of democracy. Same as his Preservation of American independence
Battle with the Court. Same as his Broadcast address, March 9, 1937 (proposal for the reform of the Federal Judiciary)
Broadcast address, March 9, 1937 (proposal for the reform of the Federal Judiciary). ANN 15:431; FRIP:309; ROD:192
Call for federal responsibility (October 13, 1932). ANN 15:185
Campaign speech, Chicago, Illinois, October 14, 1936. SIN:129
Campaign speech, Cleveland, Ohio, November 2, 1940. SIN:164
Campaign speech, San Francisco, California, September 23, 1932. Same as his Address to the Commonwealth Club, September 23, 1932
Campaign speech, Washington, D.C., September 23, 1944. Same as his Opening campaign speech at dinner of International Brotherhood of Teamsters
Casablanca Conference. Same as his Address at the annual gathering of the White House Correspondents' Association, February 12, 1943
Casting the die: FDR requests a Declaration of War against Japan, 1941. Same as his War address (December 8, 1941)
Challenge and hope. Same as his Address to the Commonwealth Club, September 23, 1932
Challenge and promise. Same

as his First inaugural address
Declaration of war address. Same as his War address (December 8, 1941)
Economic Bill of Rights. Same as his Message to Congress, January 11, 1944
Eighth annual message. Same as his Four human freedoms
Eleventh annual message. Same as his Message to Congress, January 11, 1944
Facing Communism: the true conservative is liberal. BAD:15
Fifth annual message. STAT 3:2833
Fireside chat (December 9, 1941). ANN 16:105
Fireside chat: AAA and NRA, July 24, 1933. ANN 15:210
Fireside chat on party primaries, June 24, 1938. FRIP:324
Fireside chat on reorganization of Judiciary, March 9, 1937. Same as his Broadcast address, March 9, 1937
Fireside chat on the accomplishments of the New Deal. ANN 15:263
First annual message. STAT 3:2806
First inaugural (Washington, March 4, 1933). ALS:207; AND:67; ANN 15:205; BEN:74; BOORA 2:839; GRG:50; HURH:219; LINS:321; ROD:63; USINAU:235; USINAUG:235
First war address before Congress. (Jan. 6, 1942). HURH:269; STAT 3:2861
Four human freedoms. ANN 16:42; ROD:278; STAT 3:2855
Fourth annual message. STAT 3:2827
Fourth inaugural address. USINAU:248; USINAUG:248
Good neighbor policy. ANN 15:352
Halfway between peace and war: Roosevelt requests Lend-lease, 1941. Same as his Four human freedoms
Hand that held the dagger. Same as his Italy enters this war
Immigrants and revolutionists. ALA:93
Martin, Barton, and Fish. Same as his Republican leadership and national defense
Message to Congress, January 4, 1939. STAT 3:2842
Message to Congress, January 7, 1943. STAT 3:2867
Message to Congress, January 11, 1944. ANN 16:211; ROD:337; STAT 3:2875
Message to Congress on the state of the nation, January 6, 1945. STAT 3:2882
Navy Day address on the attack on the destroyer Kearney. ANN 16:90
New Bill of Rights. Same as his Message to Congress, January 11, 1944
Ninth annual message. Same as his First war address before Congress
"No compromise can end that conflict." Same as his First war address before Congress
"The only thing we have to fear is fear itself--nameless, unreasoning, unjustified terror which paralyzes needed efforts to convert retreat into advance." Same as his First inaugural
Opening campaign speech at dinner of International Brotherhood of Teamsters (Washington, Sept. 23, 1944). LINS:330; SIN:198
Philosophy of social justice through social action (campaign speech in Detroit October 2, 1932). ARS:135
Preservation of American independence. (Washington, Dec. 29, 1940). HURH:246; OLIS:249
The President asks Congress for tax revision. BAD:8
President reminds Congress of the Tennessee Valley Authority. BAD:21
Presidential remarks on the occasion of the signing of the Social Security Act. BAD:13
Program for social security. Same as his Right to security

Progress of the recovery program. Same as his Fireside chat: AAA and NRA, July 24, 1933
Proposal for Lend-Lease. ANN 16:40
The "Quarantine" speech. Same as his Quarantining the aggressors
Quarantining the aggressors (Chicago, Oct. 5, 1937). ANN 15:502; BEN:93; BOORA 2:847; BRYF:474; ROD:263
Relief, recovery, and reform. Same as his Fireside chat on the accomplishments of the New Deal
Republican leadership and national defense. ANN 16:36
Request for a Declaration of War. Same as his War address (December 8, 1941)
Restating American Foreign Policy: FDR's Chautauqua speech, 1936. ROD:252
Right to security. ANN 15:315
Second annual message. ANN 15:309; ROD:106; STAT 3:2811
Second inaugural address. USINAU:240; USINAUG:240
Second New Deal. Same as his Second annual message
Seventh annual message. STAT 3:2849
Sixth annual message. Same as his Message to Congress, January 4, 1939
Teamsters' Union speech. Same as his Opening campaign speech at dinner of International Brotherhood of Teamsters
Tentative trial balloon: the "Quarantine speech." Same as his Quarantining the aggressors
Tenth annual message. Same as his Message to Congress, January 7, 1943
Third annual message. STAT 3:2819
Third inaugural address. USINAU:244; USINAUG:244
This nation will remain neutral. ROD:274
Total national defense. Same as his Navy Day address on the attack on the destroyer Kearney
Turning point. Same as his Second annual message
Twelfth annual message. Same as his Message to Congress on the state of the nation, January 6, 1945
Undelivered Jefferson Day address. MDV:32
Undelivered last speech. Same as his Undelivered Jefferson Day address
War address (Washington, Dec. 8, 1941). ANN 16:103; CUB:88 (outline); GRG:71; HURH:265; LINS:327; MAC:242; MACR:282; MOPR:377; ROD:306
War in Europe: the President addresses the people, 1939. Same as his This nation will remain neutral
"We are going to win the war and we are going to win the peace that follows." Same as his War address (December 8, 1941)
What the New Deal has done for business (campaign speech in Chicago, October 14, 1936). ANN 15:379
"With absolute faith that our common cause will greatly succeed." Same as his Preservation of American independence

ROOSEVELT, FRANKLIN DELANO
Roger, W.
Presents Franklin Delano Roosevelt. LYI:213
Schlesinger, A., Jr.
Roosevelt's place in history. BA 1971-72:133

Roosevelt, Theodore
Annual message, December 6, 1905. STAT 2:2105
Conservation of public lands. Same as his Public domain: the people's heritage
Controlling the trusts. Same as his First annual message
Corollary to the Monroe Doctrine. Same as his Fifth annual message

Eighth annual message.
STAT 3:2296
Fifth annual message.
ANN 13:1; STAT 3:2144
First annual message.
ANN 12:433; STAT 2:2014
Fourth annual message.
Same as his Annual message
"I took the Canal Zone."
STAT 2:2073
"I wish to preach not the doctrine of ignoble ease but the doctrine of the strenuous life." Same as his Strenuous life
Inaugural address. USINAU:183
International peace (Nobel Lecture for 1906, May 5, 1910). NOLP 1:102
Issues of the coming election.
ANN 11:170
Man with the muck-rake (at dedication of Office Building of the House of Representatives, April 14, 1906).
ARS:102; GRG:24; HURH:291; LINS:283; OLIS:217
Message to Congress, December 5, 1905. Same as his Fifth annual message
New nationalism (at dedication of John Brown Memorial Park, Osawatomic, Kansas).
ANN 13:250; BOORA 2:711
Public domain: the people's heritage. ANN 13:161
Second annual message.
STAT 2:2053
Seventh annual message.
STAT 3:2240
Sixth annual message.
STAT 3:2194
Strenuous life (Chicago, April 10, 1899). BEN:189; HURH:150
Third annual message. Same as his "I took the Canal Zone"

ROOSEVELT, THEODORE
Knudsen, G.
Presentation [of the Nobel Prize for Peace to Theodore Roosevelt, Dec. 10, 1906].
NOLP 1:97
Miller, K.
The Brownsville affair.
FON:654
Peirce, H. D. D.
Acceptance [of the Nobel Prize for Peace for Theodore Roosevelt, Dec. 10, 1906].
NOLP 1:99

Root, Elihu
European War and the preservation of America's ideals.
ANN 14:70
Introducing H. Watterson to New England Society of New York.
LYI:111
Invisible government: Short Ballot Amendment.
ANN 13:528
Proper pace of political change.
ANN 13:436
Towards making peace permanent (Nobel Lecture for 1912).
NOLP 1:247

ROOT, ELIHU
Moe, R.
Presentation [of the Nobel Prize for Peace to Elihu Root, 1912, Dec. 10, 1913].
NOLP 1:245

Root, Trent C.
The failure of scientists to communicate (Tucson, Ariz., Oct. 25, 1977). BA 1977-78:110

Roper, Bruce
A fable come true. BREWW:201

ROPER, ELMO
Ford, H. II
Presents Elmo Roper.
LYI:73

Rosebery, Archibald Philip Primrose, 5th Earl of See Curzon of Kedleston, George, jt. auth.

ROSENTHAL, FRANK F.
Croarkin, W.
Presents Frank F. Rosenthal.
LYI:165

Rosenthal, Norbert L.
My son, my son. WALE:152

Ross, John See Sanford, N., jt. auth.

Ross, Sir Ronald
Researches on malaria (Nobel Lecture, Dec. 12, 1902). NOLM 1:25

ROSS, SIR RONALD
Mörner, K. A. H.
Presentation [of the Nobel Prize for Physiology or Medicine to Sir Ronald Ross, Dec. 12, 1902]. NOLM 1:21

Rosten, Leo
Myths by which we live. KEO:240

Rostow, Eugene V.
Choice in foreign policy. ANN 18:605

ROTARIANS
Sandosham, A. A.
He stood up and drank the toast and joined in the applause! MONSA:224

ROTARY CLUB
Yeang, C. H.
The building of peaceful bridge the rotary way. MONSA:218

ROTARY CLUB OF KUALA LUMPUR
Johari, M. K.
Nation building and the four-way test. MONSA:100

Rous, Peyton
The challenge to man of the neoplastic cell (Nobel Lecture, Dec. 13, 1966). NOLM 4:220

ROUS, PEYTON
Klein, G.
Presentation [of the Nobel Prize for Physiology or Medicine to Peyton Rous and Charles Brenton Huggins, Dec. 13, 1966]. NOLM 4:215

Routtenberg, Max J.
Crown of a good name. WALE:154

ROWAN, ARCHIBALD HAMILTON
Curran, J. P.
England and English liberties--in the case of Rowan. BREWE 4:1546

Rowan, Carl T.
New frontiers in racial relations. (Youngstown, State University, Oct. 24, 1968). OE:201

Rowe, James N.
An American prisoner of war in South Vietnam. (Leavenworth, Kansas). LINRS:45; LINRST:56

Rowen, Hobart
Responds to introduction. PRS:96

Rowland, Henry A.
Appeal for pure scientific research in America. ANN 12:262

Roxas, Manuel
A farewell to the Assembly (National Assembly, Aug. 15, 1938). CURM:282

Royer-Collard, Pierre Paul
Against press censorship. BREWE 9:3347
"Sacrilege" in law. BREWE 9:3345

Royster, Vermont C.
What the people grant, they can take away (Washington, Dec. 5, 1978). BA 1978-79:191

RUBBER
Lew Sip Hon
Our stake in natural rubber. MONS:302

Rubel, Charles M.
Beauties of Japheth and the glory of Shem. WALE:157

Ruckelshaus, Jill See Steinem, G., jt. auth.

Ruckelshaus, William D.
The environment revolution. (Williamsburg, Va., Jan. 29, 1972). BA 1971-72:125

Rudberg, E. G.
Presentation [of the Nobel Prize

for Physics to William Shockley, John Bardeen and Walter Houser Brattain, Dec. 11, 1956]. NOLPH 3:315

Rudin, Jacob P.
Shadows in the sun. WALE:160

RUKUNEGARA
Lim Chong Eu
The message of Rukunegara. MONSA:147

Rumbold, Richard
Against booted and spurred privilege. BREWE 9:3352

Runkel, Howard W.
Making Lincoln live. (Oregon State Legislature, Feb. 12, 1957). BAPR:351; BAPRR:259

RURAL DEVELOPMENT See Land use, Rural

RURAL LIFE
Morgan, M.
Building a better rural community today for a better agriculture tomorrow. BREWW:198
Wilson, W. H.
Interaction of country and city. ANN 14:4

Rush, Benjamin
Thoughts on female education. ANN 3:207

Rush, Richard
Fourth of July oration, 1812 (Washington, July 4, 1812). HAW:16

Rush, Wayne
Feeding the hungry world. BREWW:91

Rusk, Dean
Eulogy of Lyndon Baines Johnson. (Washington, D.C., Jan. 24, 1973). BA 1972-73:132
For ratification of treaties with Panama. (Washington, Oct. 14, 1977). BA 1977-78:9
Formulating foreign policy. ANN 18:20

Ruskin, John
Iscariot in modern England. BREWE 9:3354

Russell, Bertrand Arthur William
What desires are politically important? (Nobel lecture, Dec. 11, 1950). NOL:452

RUSSELL, BERTRAND ARTHUR WILLIAM
Österling, A.
Presentation [of the Nobel Prize for Literature to Bertrand Arthur William Russell, 1950]. NOB 15:255; NOL:449
Waller, H. H.
Presents Bertrand Russell. LYI:94

Russell, John Russell, 1st Earl of
Reform of Parliament. Same as his Reform of the franchise
Reform of the franchise. (Commons, March 1, 1831). MCB:87
Science and literature as modes of progress. BREWE 9:3359

Russell, Richard and others (P. H. Douglas)
Pro's and con's of civil rights. BRR:73

RUSSIA
Lenin, N.
War, peace and revolutionary democracy. BRN:81
Lyndhurst, J. S. C.
Russia and the Crimean War. BREWE 7:2842

---- FOREIGN RELATIONS
Churchill, W. L. S.
Sinews of peace (speech at Fulton, Missouri). ANN 16:365; MCB:541
Inozemstev, N. N.
Alternative to war. MDV:69

---- See also United States - Foreign relations - Russia

Russwurm, John Browne
The condition and prospects of

Haiti. (Brunswick, Maine, Sept. 6, 1826). FON:33

Rustin, Bayard
A way out of the exploding ghetto. (Detroit, 1967). FON:1078

---- See also Brown, R. S., jt. auth.

Rutherford, Ernest
The chemical nature of the alpha particles from radioactive substances (Nobel Lecture, Dec. 11, 1908). NOLC 1:129

RUTHERFORD, ERNEST
Hasselberg, K. B.
Presentation [of the Nobel Prize for Chemistry to Ernest Rutherford, Dec. 11, 1908]. NOLC 1:125

Rutledge, John
Speech in time of Revolution. BREWE 9:3368; POC:325
Speech to both Houses. Same as his Speech in time of Revolution

Ružička, Leopold Stephen
Multimembered rings, higher terpene compounds, and male sex hormones (Nobel Lecture for 1939, Dec. 12, 1945). NOLC 2:468

Ryder, Sir Dudley See Walpole, R., jt. auth.

Rylaarsdam, Jeannette
Undesirable one. SCHW:1

- S -

Saavedra Lamas, Carlos
Radio address (Nobel Lecture, Nov. 29, 1936). NOLP 2:225

SAAVEDRA LAMAS, CARLOS
Lange, C. L.
Presentation [of the Nobel Prize for Peace to Carlos Saavedra Lamas, Dec. 10, 1936]. NOLP 2:217

Sabatier, Paul
The method of direct hydrogenation by catalysis (Nobel Lecture, Dec. 11, 1912). NOLC 1:221

SABATIER, PAUL
Söderbaum, H. G.
Presentation [of the Nobel Prize for Chemistry to Victor Grignard and Paul Sabatier, Dec. 11, 1912]. NOLC 1:217

Sacco, Nicola
I am never guilty See Sacco, Nicola and Vanzetti, Bartolomeo Proclaim their innocence

---- and Vanzetti, Bartolomeo
Proclaim their innocence. ALA:85; ANN 14:527

SACHEVERELL, HENRY
Jekyll, J.
Resistance to unlawful authority (impeachment of H. Sacheverell). BREWE 7:2617

Sachs, Leonie Nelly
Acceptance [of the Nobel Prize for Literature, 1966]. NOB 16:5; NOL:619

SACHS, LEONIE NELLY
Österling, A.
Presentation [of the Nobel Prize for literature to Shmuel Yosef Agnon and Leonie Nelly Sachs, 1966]. NOB 1:3; NOB 16:3; NOL:611

Sacks, Marvin
The value of disobedience (Indiana University, 1971). LINRS:148; LINRST:152

SAFETY REGULATIONS
Franklin, B. H.
Consumer safety and health. BA 1978-79:133

SALES TALKS AND SALESMANSHIP
Domiano, P.
Break down at United (Swim-

ming Pool Company).
REIR:38
You, too, can be a millionaire.
BURT:118

Salisbury, Robert Arthur Talbot Gascoyne-Cecil, 3d Marquis of
Speech to the Primrose League.
STRM:375

Salk, Jonas E.
Responds to introduction.
PRS:89

Salkowitz, Selig
King's answer. WALE:163

Salm, Nell
Matter of time. SCHW:83

SALVATION
Hooker, T.
The soul's vocation, doctrine 3. JON:82
The soul's vocation, doctrine 7. JON:93

SALVATION ARMY
Karos, P. A.
Haven of the defeated.
ARS:148

Sambanthan, V. T.
Basic objectives of M.I.C. (Malayan Indian Congress).
MONS:135
Be a harmonising factor (Kuala Lumpur, Nov. 8, 1970).
MONSA:95

Sampson, B. K.
To my white fellow citizens. (Fairfield, Ohio, Thanksgiving Day, 1867).
FON:347

Sampson, Edith S.
Choose one of five (North Central College, Ill., May 30, 1965). MOP:386; REID:398

Sandburg, Carl
Abraham Lincoln. Same as his On Lincoln (at 150th anniversary of Lincoln's birth)
On Lincoln (at 150th anniversary of Lincoln's birth). (Washington, Feb. 12, 1959).
GRG:101; HURH:347
"On occasions he was seen to weep in a way that made weeping decent, appropriate and majestic." Same as his On Lincoln (at 150th anniversary of Lincoln's birth)

Sanders, Clinton S.
Responds to introduction.
PRS:90

Sandosham, A. A.
He stood up and drank the toast and joined in the applause.
MONSA:224

Sanford, E. T. and others (O. W. Holmes, Jr.)
Gitlow v. New York: opinion for the court and dissenting opinion. ANN 14:476

Sanford, Nathan and others (M. Van Buren; J. Kent; P. R. Livingston; J. Cramer; D. Buel, Jr.; J. Ross; P. Jay)
Debate on property and suffrage.
ANN 5:4

Sanford, Terry
After Vietnam, a new United States foreign policy (Southwestern, Memphis, May 31, 1971). HOR:132

Sanger, Frederick
The chemistry of insulin (Nobel Lecture, Dec. 11, 1958).
NOLC 3:544

SANGER, FREDERICK
Tiselius, A. W. K.
Presentation [of the Nobel Prize for Chemistry to Frederick Sanger, Dec. 11, 1958]. NOLC 3:541

SANITATION
Kingsley, C.
Massacre of the innocents.
BRYH:392

Santayana, George
Genteel tradition in American philosophy. ANN 13:277

SANTO DOMINGO
Butler, B. F. and others
Congressional debate on Haiti and Santo Domingo, January 13, 1869. ANN 10:143

Sara, Martha J.
Do not refuse us. BA 1969-70:148

SARAWAK
Ningkan, S. K.
Three problems of Sarawak. MONS:326

Sargent, Francis W.
The computer and civil liberties. (Boston University, Oct. 4, 1973). BA 1973-74:141

SATELLITES See Communications satellites

SATIRIC SPEECHES
Bolton, T.
Oration (burlesque of Warren's second Boston Massacre oration). POC:301
Buchwald, A.
Parody of political speeches. JAM:27
Grand dragon of the Ku Klux Klan. BURT:65
James Hoffa (satiric speech). BURT:47
Rogers, W.
Morgenthau's plan. GRG:55
Nominating Calvin Coolidge. BAP:298; BAPR:366

Saurin, Jacques
Effect of passion. BREWE 9:3371

Savage, John
People v. Fisher: opinion for the court. ANN 6:172
Slums as a common nuisance (Meeker v. Van Rensselaer case). ANN 6:279

Savage, Michael Joseph
New Zealand's war aims, 1939 (Sept. 5, 1939). MACS:365 sel.

---- See also Hamilton, A., jt. auth.

Savilla, Elmer M.
Address to the Assembly of the National Congress of American Indians at San Diego, California, October 1974. MAES:225

Sawhill, John C.
Energy and the job market (Champion, Pa., Sept. 29, 1975). BA 1975-76:102

Sawyer, Thomas E.
Assimilation versus self-identity: a modern native American perspective, an address to the Western Social Science Association Conference, Arizona State Univ., Tempe, Ariz., May 1, 1976. MAES:197

Sayre, Francis B.
The tall ships (Newport, R.I., June 27, 1976). BA 1976-77:181

SCAFFOLD SPEECHES See Defense, Speeches of

Scarborough, William Sanders
The ethics of the Hawaiian question. (Wilberforce Univ., March, 1894). FON:570

Schalliol, Charles
The strangler (Indiana Univ., March, 1967). LINR:246; LINRS:260; LINRST:298

Schell, George
Shackled by stereotypes. (Baylor University, 1962). CAPB:381

Schlegel, Karl Wilhelm F. Von
Philosophy of history. BREWE 9:3377

Schlesinger, Arthur M., Jr.
Challenge of abundance. ARS:196
Roosevelt's place in history. (New York, Jan. 30, 1972). BA 1971-72:133

Schmedeman, Albert G.
Acceptance [of the Nobel Prize

for Peace for Woodrow Wilson, 1919, Dec. 10, 1920]. NOLP 1:294

Schmitt, Harrison
New policy options through technology (Baltimore, March 19, 1980). BA 1979-80:133

Schnadig, Edgar L.
Presents Gerald Wendt. LYI:186

SCHOLARS See Learning and scholarship

SCHOOL INTEGRATION
Howe, H., II
The Brown decision, pluralism, and the schools in the 1980s. BA 1979-80:101
Kitslaar, J. L.
Is busing the answer? LINRST:294

Schorr, Daniel
In defense of privilege (San Francisco, Dec. 14, 1978). BA 1978-79:202

Schrier, William
Address at Hope College Alumni banquet, May 31, 1958. SCHW:236
Address to the 60th Anniversary Oratorical Banquet, March 1, 1957. SCHW:226
Behind the scenes in oratory. SCHW:231
Coaching oratory. SCHW:239

Schrodinger, Erwin
The fundamental idea of wave mechanics (Nobel Lecture, Dec. 12, 1933). NOLPH 2:305

SCHRODINGER, ERWIN
Pleijel, H.
Presentation [of the Nobel Prize for Physics for 1932 to Werner Heisenberg and for 1933 to Erwin Schrodinger and Paul Adrien Maurice Dirac, Dec. 11, 1933]. NOLPH 2:283

Schroeder, Patricia
You can do it. (Houston, Feb. 9, 1973). BA 1972-73:86

Schück, Henrik
Presentation [of the Nobel Prize for Literature to Grazia Deledda, 1926]. NOB 5:117; NOL:232

Schurz, Carl
Civil service reform. Same as his Necessity and progress of Civil Service reform
The irrepressible conflict (1860). DAVF:130
Necessity and progress of Civil Service reform. ANN 11:493
Need for a rational forest policy. ANN 11:200
Old world and the new. (New York, Nov. 5, 1881). HURH:135
Public offices as private perquisites. BREWE 9:3384
True Americanism. ANN 9:97

Schwab, Michael
Address at trial, Chicago, October 7-9, 1886. ACC:24; PAF:25

Schweitzer, Albert
The problem of peace (Nobel Lecture for 1952, Nov. 4, 1954). NOLP 3:46

SCHWEITZER, ALBERT
Hageman, M.
Wisdom of the heart. SCHW:177
Jahn, G.
Presentation [of the Nobel Prize for Peace for 1952 to Albert Schweitzer, Dec. 10, 1953]. NOLP 3:37

Schwellenbach, Lewis B.
First seven years of the New Deal: let's view the record. BAD:47

Schwinger, Julian
Relativistic quantum field theory (Nobel Lecture, Dec. 11, 1965). NOLPH 4:140

SCHWINGER, JULIAN
Waller, I.
Presentation [of the Nobel Prize for Physics to Sin-Itiro Tomonaga, Julian Schwinger, and Richard P. Feynman, Dec. 11, 1965]. NOLPH 4:123

SCIENCE AND CIVILIZATION
Tan Siew Sin
The big question before us. MONSA:93

SCIENCE AND RELIGION See Religion and science

SCIENCE AND SCIENTISTS
Arnold, M.
Literature and science. MCB:388
Bigelow, J.
Future of arts and sciences. ANN 4:449
Boyd Orr, J.
Science and peace (Nobel Lecture, Dec. 12, 1949). NOLP 2:415
Bragg, L.
Art of talking about science. MOP:358
Brown, H. S.
Science, technology, and world development. ARS:83
Social responsibility of science. BAP:280
Dixon, O.
Law and the scientific expert. MCA:176
Durfee, J.
Influence of scientific discovery and invention on social and political progress. ANN 7:128
Huxley, T. H.
Method of scientific investigation. ARS:264; BRYF:521
Science and culture. MCB:376
Lee Kuan Yew
Lesson we have to learn (opening new Science Tower at University of Singapore). MONS:361
Miller, H.
Pledge science gives to hope. BREWE 8:3013
Oppenheimer, J. R.
Prospect in the arts and sciences (at Colombia University bicentennial anniversary celebration). HURH:319; HURS:211
Russell, J. R.
Science and literature as modes of progress. BREWE 9:3359
Seaborg, G. T.
Positive power of science. BA 1969-70:108
Smith, G.
Secret beyond science. BREWE 9:3476
Urey, H. C.
Science and society (at 100th anniversary Academic Convocation of Cooper Union for the Advancement of Science and Art). ARS:78
Whitehead, A. N.
Technical education and its relation to science and literature. MCB:403
Wiesner, J. B.
Science in the affluent society (centennial celebration of National Academy of Sciences). ANN 18:186
Wydler, J. W.
Science and the public trust. BA 1979-80:139

---- See also Atomic energy

SCIENCE AND THE HUMANITIES
Snow, Sir C. P.
The two cultures. MCB:417

SCIENCE NEWS
Farber, S. M.
Why national concern for biomedical communication? BA 1966-67:118

SCOTLAND
Belhaven, J. H.
Plea for the national life of Scotland. BREWE 1:371

Scott, Richard and others (Jane Farwell)
A job-seeking interview: a transcript. MOPR:381

SCOTT, SIR WALTER
Smith, G.

Lamps of fiction (at centenary of Sir Walter Scott). BREWE 9:3465

Scranton, William W.
Responds to introduction. PRS:110

SCRANTON, WILLIAM W.
Watson, A. K.
Presents William W. Scranton. LYI:201

Seaborg, Glenn Theodore
Positive power of science. BA 1969-70:108
The transuranium elements: present status (Nobel Lecture, Dec. 12, 1951). NOLC 3:325

SEABORG, GLENN THEODORE
Westgren, A.
Presentation [of the Nobel Prize for Chemistry to Edwin Mattison McMillan and Glenn Theodore Seaborg, Dec. 12, 1951]. NOLC 3:309

SEABURY, DAVID
McLain, H. O.
Presents David Seabury. LYI:98

Seale, Bobby
Free Huey. (March 16, 1968). MACR:322; SMHR:175

Seaman, Sir Owen
Presents Stephen Leacock. LYI:47

Seaton, Fred A. See Malone, G. W., jt. auth.

SECESSION See Confederate States of America; State rights; United States - History - Civil War - Causes

SECRET SOCIETIES
Morse, Jedidiah
The present dangers and consequent duties of the citizens (1799). DAVF:45

Smith, G.
A voice from the past (1870). (Syracuse, N.Y., Nov. 1870). DAVF:154

SECTIONALISM (UNITED STATES)
Lincoln, A.
Second annual message to Congress. BOORA 1:396; STAT 2:1068
Pierce, F.
Fourth annual message. STAT 1:918
Turner, F. J.
Sectionalism and national unity. ANN 14:493

SECURITY See Internal Security Act, 1950; Social security

SECURITY, INTERNATIONAL - EUROPE
Goldberg, A. J.
Human rights and détente. BA 1977-78:71

Seddon, Richard John and others
The South African War contingent, 1899 (New Zealand House of Representatives, Sept. 28, 1899). MACS:260 sel.

SEDUCTION
Roberts, J.
Art of seduction. REIR:84

Seeley, John R.
Tendency in English history. (Cambridge University, 1882). MCB:50

Seenivasagam, Dharma Raja
Frankenstein in the making. MONS:199

Seferis, Giorgos
Acceptance [of the Nobel Prize for Literature, 1963]. NOB 17:5; NOL:582
Some notes on modern Greek tradition (Nobel lecture, Dec. 11, 1963). NOL:484

SEFERIS, GIORGOS
Österling, A.
Presentation [of the Nobel Prize for Literature to

Giorgos Seferis, 1963]. NOB 17:3; NOL:580

Segrè, Emilio Gino
Properties of antinucleons (Nobel Lecture, Dec. 11, 1959). NOLPH 3:508

SEGRE, EMILIO GINO
Hulthèn, E.
Presentation [of the Nobel Prize for Physics to Emilio Gino Segrè and Owen Chamberlain, Dec. 11, 1959]. NOLPH 3:487

SEGREGATION
Brown, H. B. and others
Plessy v. Ferguson: opinion for the court and dissenting opinion. ANN 12:92
Davis, B. J.
The Negro people on the march. FON:902
Farmer, J.
The "Movement" now. FON:1040
Feldmann, M. H.
Eyes of the whole world. SCHW:156
Green, J. P.
These evils call loudly for redress. FON:499
Hope, J.
We are struggling for equality. FON:594
Hughes, C. E.
Small step toward racial equality: opinion for the Supreme Court on Mitchell case, 1941. ROD:224
King, M. L., Jr.
The American dream. FON:933
Give us the ballot--we will transform the South. FON:919
Marshall, T.
Segregation and desegregation. FON:866
Pinchback, P. B. S.
The whole race must protest. FON:596
Randolph, A. P.
A call for mass action. FON:822
Trotter, W. M.
Segregation destroys fellowship and citizenship. FON:702

---- See also Civil rights; Discrimination; Negroes; Race problems; Segregation in education

---- RESISTANCE TO
King, M. L., Jr.
Love, law, and civil disobedience. FON:943; LINR:63; LINRS:70; LINRST:75; STOT:321
Nonviolence and social change. OE:157
Revels, H. R.
A plea for desegregated schools. FON:371

SEGREGATION IN EDUCATION
Nell, W. C.
The triumph of equal school rights in Boston. FON:164
Revels, H. R.
A plea for desegregated schools. FON:371
Sumner, C.
Segregation and the common school (Sarah C. Roberts v. City of Boston case, 1849). ANN 7:507
Warren, E.
Brown et al v. Board of Education of Topeka et al: opinion for the court. ANN 17:253; BOORA 2:904
Wilkins, R.
The conspiracy to deny equality. FON:892

---- See also Blacks, Civil rights

SELF DEFENSE See Defense, Speeches of

SELF GOVERNMENT
Akintola, S. L. and others
Nigeria debates self-government. EMP:65
Eddy, E. D., Jr.
Student involvement in educational policy. BA 1965-66:221; LINR:251
Gardiner, R. K.
Citizenship and political liberalism. EMP:106
Holly, J. T.
The Negro race, self-government and the Haitian revolution. FON:169

SELF-RESPECT
Manley, A. E.
Charge to the graduates.
HOR:6

Sellers, Rose Z.
Presents Harry D. Gideonse.
LYI:80

SELLING See Sales talks and salesmanship

Semenov, Nikolai Nikolaevic
Some problems relating to chain reactions and to the theory of combustion (Nobel Lecture, Dec. 11, 1956).
NOLC 3:487

SEMENOV, NIKOLAI NIKOLAEVIC
Olander, A.
Presentation [of the Nobel Prize for Chemistry to Sir Cyril Norman Hinshelwood and Nikolai Nikolaevic Semenov, Dec. 11, 1956].
NOLC 3:471

SEMICENTENNIAL CELEBRATIONS See Anniversaries

SEMICONDUCTOR LASERS
Basov, N. G.
Semiconductor lasers.
NOLPH 4:89

SEMICONDUCTORS
Bardeen, J.
Semiconductor research leading to the point contact transistor. NOLPH 3:318
Brattain, W. H.
Surface properties of semiconductors. NOLPH 3:377

SEMINOLE WAR, 1st, FLORIDA, 1817-1818
Clay, H.
On the Seminole War.
BREWE 4:1236
Monroe, J.
Second annual message.
STAT 1:156

Sendut, Hamzah See Hamzah Sendut

Seneca, Lucius Annaeus
Address to Nero.
BREWE 9:3390

Seneca, Martin
Address delivered at Brigham Young University February, 1975. MAES:26

Senu bin Abdul Rahman
Let our voice be heard. (New Year message). MONS:160
Pledge to newsmen. MONS:156

SEPARATION OF POWERS
Osias, C.
Justice and separation of powers. CURM:190

SERMONS
Aelfric
Sermon on the sacrifice on Easter-Day. BRYH:14
Aelred, Saint
Sermon after absence.
BREWE 1:111
Anonymous
Sermon for the third Sunday after Trinity (by an unknown Medieval preacher). BRYH:31
Arnold, T.
Realities of life and death.
BREWE 1:173
Bacon, L.
Sermon from Mark XII, 34.
HAW:57
Ball, J.
We have the pain and travail.
BRYH:42
Baxter, R.
Unwilllingness to improve.
BREWE 1:242
Bede
Sermon for any day.
BREWE 1:343
Beecher, H. W.
Success of American democracy (anniversary of attack on Fort Sumter). OLIS:191
Bonaventura, Saint
Life of service.
BREWE 2:552
Boucher, J.
Civil liberty and nonresistance.
ANN 2:343; POC:552
Bulkeley, P.
City set upon a hill.

ANN 1:211
The gospel-covenant.
JON:30
Bunyan, J.
Heavenly footman.
BREWE 2:716
Burrows, J. L.
Opposition to the theater in time of war. ANN 9:402
Cahill, D. W.
Last judgment. BREWE 3:851
Chauncy, C.
Caveat against enthusiasm.
POC:488
Chiu Ban It
Be strong and of good courage (enthronement sermon). MONS:456
Colman, B.
Piety and duty of rulers to comfort and encourage the ministry of Christ.
POC:412
Cotton, J.
God's promise to his plantations. ANN 1:107
A treatise of the covenant of grace. JON:48
Viall I: the powring out of the seven vials or An exposition, with an application of the 16th Chapter of Revelation. POC:363
The way of life. JON:121
Cyprian, Saint
Unshackled living.
BREWE 4:1588
Davenport, J.
The saint's anchor-hold.
JON:147
Davies, S.
Curse of cowardice.
ANN 2:23; POC:534
Ditzen, L. R.
The right ticket but the wrong train. REID:404
Donne, J.
Sermon preached at St. Paul's (Easter Day, 1625).
BRYH:109
Dumper, A. C.
Church in a secular state.
MONS:485
Dwight, T.
On the duty of Americans at the present crisis.
ANN 4:33
Pursuit of excellence.
BREWE 5:1968
Edwards, J.
Farewell-sermon. POC:443
Fisher, J.
Jeopardy of daily life.
BREWE 6:2164
Frelinghuysen, T.
Revivalist sermon. ANN 1:344
Graham, W. F.
Confusing evil with good.
LINR:179
Great Disturber (outline of speech to celebrate acceptance of Christ's offer of salvation through obedience to His Word). CUB:95
Gunsaulus, F. W.
Healthy heresies.
BREWE 6:2353
Hare, J. C.
Children of light.
BREWE 6:2402
Hatfield, M. O.
If we fall down in the land of peace. BA 1979-80:67
Herder, J. G.
Meaning of inspiration.
BREWE 7:2497
Hooker, T.
The soul's exaltation.
JON:104
The soul's vocation, doctrine 3. JON:82
The soul's vocation, doctrine 7. JON:93
Unbelievers preparing for Christ. POC:331
Hubbard, W.
Happiness of a people in the wisdom of their rulers directing and in obedience of their brethren attending unto what Israel ought to do.
ANN 1:248
Huffman, J. A.
Retrospect '73--Biblical lessons we can learn from Watergate. TAC:221
Knopwood, R.
On the everpresent God.
MCA:11
Knox, J.
Against tyrants.
BREWE 7:2665
Lang, J. D.
"Little While" of the Saviour's absence and the prospect of his speedy return. MCA:64

McCorkle, S.
A sermon for the anniversary of American independence, July 24th, 1786. HAW:292
Mather, I.
Discourse concerning the uncertainty of the times of men. POC:377
Mayhew, J.
Discourse on the anniversary of the death of Charles I. ANN 1:481; POC:508
Parker, T.
Transient and permanent in Christianity. LINS:178
Saurin, J.
Effect of passion. BREWE 9:3371
Sayre, F. B.
The tall ships. BA 1976-77:181
Shepard, T.
Election sermon. POC:355
The parable of the ten virgins. JON:133
The sound believer. JON:63
Spurgeon, C. H.
Everlasting oxydization. BREWE 9:3500
Stoddard, S.
Defects of preachers improved. POC:430
Stone, B. W.
"And I will gladly spend and be spent for you though the more abundantly I love you, the less I be loved." BLY:19
Symonds, W.
Britain's claim to a New World empire justified. ANN 1:32
Taylor, J.
Foolish exchange. BREWE 9:3590
Tennent, G.
Danger of an unconverted ministry. POC:469
Tillotson, J.
Sermon against evil speaking. BRYH:156
Tyndale, W.
Use and abuse of images and relics. BREWE 9:3660
Wesley, J.
Sacri fames auri. BREWE 10:3877
Use of money. BRYH:191
West, S.
Election sermon. POC:578
Whitefield, G.
Abraham's offering up his son Isaac. OLIS:6
Winthrop, J.
Modell of Christian charity. BOORA 1:10
Woodmason, C.
You are to take these free booters and desperadoes. POC:548
Wulfstan
Sermon of the Wolf to the English when the Danes persecuted them most, which was in the year 1014 from the incarnation of our Lord Jesus Christ. BRYH:21
Wycliffe, J.
Good lore for simple folk. BREWE 10:3920
Zubly, J. J.
Law of liberty. POC:611

---- See also Baccalaureate addresses; Church; Funeral sermons; Religion; also subject of sermons, e.g. Faith

SERUM THERAPY
Behring, E. A. V.
Serum therapy in therapeutics and medical science. NOLM 1:6

SERVICE See Citizenship

SERVICE MEN See Army; Pensions, Military; Soldiers; United States - Army - Veterans

SESQUICENTENNIAL CELEBRATIONS See Anniversaries

Sevareid, Eric
Eulogy for the astronauts. MOP:189; MOPR:165
Eulogy for Wernher Von Braun. (June 17, 1977). EHN:373
Parting thoughts (Washington, Nov. 30, 1977). BA 1977-78:143
Pope John Paul's message (CBS, Oct. 3, 1979). BA 1979-80:155

---- and others (C. W. Lillehei, J. Bonner, W. Sullivan, J. J.

Wright, H. Cox, F. C. Fry)
Science and religion: who will play God? MOP:391

Sevier, Randolph
Responds to an introduction. PRS:158

Seward, William Henry
Fourth of July oration, 1840 (Cherry Valley, N.Y.). HAW:183
Freedom in the new territories. (Senate, March 11, 1850). HOW:226
Higher law than the Constitution. Same as his On the admission of California to the Union
Irrepressible conflict (Rochester, N.Y., Oct. 25, 1858). ANN 9:32; BREWE 9:3394; HURH:99
On the admission of California to the Union. ANN 8:29
Promise of Alaska. ANN 10:193
Prosperity and education. ANN 6:140
Providing for the indigent insane. ANN 8:283
Reconciliation in 1865. BREWE 9:3408

Sewell, Henry
"Centralist" interpretation of the Constitution. (New Zealand House of Representatives, April 25, 1856). MACS:93

---- and others (Edward William Stafford)
The 'compact of 1856' (New Zealand House of Representatives, June 10, 1856). MACS:99

Shaftesbury, Anthony Ashley Cooper, 7th Earl of
Employment of Children. JAE:81

SHAME See Ethics

Shaw, George Bernard
Presents Major Barbara. LYI:50
Truth by radio. (BBC, 1939). JEF:396; JEFF:378
Universities and education. KEO:237

---- and others (G. K. Chesterton; H. Belloc)
Do we agree? BRYH:474

SHAW, GEORGE BERNARD
Dale, J.
Rehearsing with George Bernard Shaw. MDYG:44
Hallström, P.
Presentation [of the Nobel Prize for Literature to George Bernard Shaw, 1925]. NOB 16:77; NOL:224

Shaw, Lemuel
Commonwealth of Massachusetts v. Hunt: opinion for the court. ANN 7:61; BOORA 1:303
Law as a restraint on power. ANN 5:217

Shaw, Robert M.
Danger of getting used to lies. LINR:191

SHAWCROSS, HARTLEY
Tweed, H.
Presents Hartley Shawcross. LYI:123

Sheen, Fulton J., Bp.
Change of hearts. (Washington, March 23, 1941). HURH:264
"A revolution that will change your hearts." Same as his Change of hearts

Sheil, Richard Lalor
In defense of Irish Catholics. BREWE 9:3419
Ireland's part in English achievement. BREWE 9:3413
Religious toleration. (Penenden Heath, Kent, Oct. 24, 1828). MCB:269

Shellabarger, Samuel See Butler, B. F., jt. auth.

SHELLEY, PERCY BYSSHE
Talfourd, T. N.
Queen against Moxon-Shelley as a blasphemer. BREWE 9:3565

Shepard, Thomas
Election sermon. POC:355
The parable of the ten virgins (1636-1640). JON:133
The sound believer (1645). JON:63

SHEPPARD, SAMUEL
Clark, T. C.
Sheppard v. Maxwell, warden: opinion for the court. ANN 18:402

Sheridan, Richard Brinsley
Against Warren Hastings. BREWE 9:3422
Closing speech against Hastings--the Hoard of the Begums of Oude. Same as his Against Warren Hastings
Example of kings. BREWE 9:3440
On the French Revolution. BREWE 9:3438
Patriotism and perquisites. BREWE 9:3439

Sherman, John
General financial policy of the government. BREWE 9:3442
It is essentially a Rebel organization. CUR:102

Sherrington, Sir Charles Scott
Inhibition as a coordinative factor (Nobel Lecture, Dec. 12, 1932). NOLM 2:278

SHERRINGTON, SIR CHARLES SCOTT
Liljestrand, G.
Presentation [of the Nobel Prize for Physiology or Medicine to Sir Charles Scott Sherrington and Edgar Douglas Adrian, Dec. 12, 1932]. NOLM 2:273

Shockley, William
Transistor technology evokes new physics (Nobel Lecture, Dec. 11, 1956). NOLPH 3:344

SHOCKLEY, WILLIAM
Rudberg, E. G.
Presentation [of the Nobel Prize for Physics to William Shockley, John Bardeen and Walter Houser Brattain, Dec. 11, 1956]. NOLPH 3:315

SHOLOKHOV, MIKHAIL ALEKSANDROVICH
Österling, A.
Presentation [of the Nobel Prize for Literature to Mikhail Aleksandrovich Sholokhov, 1965]. NOB 17:37; NOL:603

Shriver, Sargent
Address at the Chicago Antipoverty Conference. CAPG:180

Shtull, Jacob
Man of deed. WALE:164

Shull, Martha A.
Presents Bruce Catton. LYI:42

Shulman, Charles E.
Alfred S. Alschuler. WALE:229

SICK
Hypochondriac. BURT:106
Sickness. BURT:7

Sidney, Algernon
Governments for the people and not the people for governments (scaffold speech). BREWE 9:3454

Siegbahn, Karl Manne Georg
Presentation [of the Nobel Prize for Physics to Arthur Holly Compton and Charles Thomson Rees Wilson, Dec. 12, 1927]. NOLPH 2:169
Presentation [of the Nobel Prize for Physics to Donald Arthur Glaser, Dec. 12, 1960]. NOLPH 3:525
Presentation [of the Nobel Prize for Physics to Pavel Alekseje vič Cerenkov, Il'ja Michajlovič Frank and Igor' Evgen'evič Tamm, Dec. 11, 1958]. NOLPH 3:423
The x-ray spectra and the structure of the atoms (Nobel Lecture for 1924, Dec. 11, 1925). NOLPH 2:81

SIEGBAHN, KARL MANNE GEORG
Gullstrand, A.
Presentation [of the Nobel Prize for Physics for 1924 to Karl Manne Georg Siegbahn, Dec. 11, 1925]. NOLPH 2:73

Sienkiewicz, Henryk
Acceptance [of the Nobel Prize for Literature, 1905]. NOL:45; NOB 17:183

SIENKIEWICZ, HENRYK
Wirsén, C. D. af
Presentation [of the Nobel Prize for Literature to Henryk Sienkiewicz, 1905]. NOL:36; NOB 17:173

SILANPÄÄ, FRANS EEMIL
Hallström, P.
Presentation [of the Nobel Prize for Literature to Frans Eemil Sillanpää, 1939]. NOB 16:223; NOL:386

Silver, Samuel M.
Come back. WALE:166

SILVER
Bland, R. P.
Parting of the ways. BREWE 2:530
Bryan, W. J.
Cross of gold. ANN 12:100; BAS:50 (outline only); BEN:52; BOORA 2:575; BREWE 2:694; HURH:147; LINS:268; OLIS:207
Fitch, T.
A fervent appeal for free silver (1889). DAVF:190
Laughlin, J. L.
Against free coinage of silver. ANN 12:75
Warner, A. J. and others
The British plot to enslave the world (1892). DAVF:192

Simmons, Brent
As time runs out (1969). LINRS:251

Simmons, David A.
Presents Walter S. Fenton. LYI:131

Simon, E. Yechiel
Heavenly glow. WALE:169
Two arks. WALE:172

Simon, Sir John See Baldwin, S. B., jt. auth.

Simon, Ralph
This was a man! WALE:174
Upward climb. WALE:175

SIMPLICITY
Fénelon, F.
True and false simplicity. BREWE 6:2137

SIN
Edwards, J.
Sinners in the hands of an angry God. ANN 1:423; BREWE 5:1982; HURH:21; LINS:121
Shepard, T.
The sound believer. JON:63
Tillotson, J.
Sermon against evil speaking. BRYH:156

Sinclair, Sir Archibald See Baldwin, S. B., jt. auth.

Sinclair, Gordon
The Americans (Toronto, June, 1973). REID:396

SINGAPORE
Goh Keng Swee
A remarkable phenomenon: why Singapore is different. MONSA:277
Some delusions of the decade of development. MONS:385
Inche Yusof bin Ishak
Lest we forget. MONSA:348
Lee Kuan Yew
Aim: a more equal society. MONS:369
Brighter future for all peoples of Singapore if.... MONSA:239
First step in nation building (Singapore). MONS:358
Hong Kong and Singapore: a tale of two cities. MONSA:264
Marshall, D. S.
Fundamental and minority rights. MONS:450

Rajaratnam, S.
Faith in United Nations charter (on admission of Singapore). MONS:421
Toh Chin Chye
The beginnings of the city state and its achievement. MONSA:288
Lesson of the Three Kingdoms. MONS:375
Singapore in the eye of the storm. MONS:377

---- ECONOMIC CONDITIONS
Lim Kim San
Massive exercise for survival. MONS:408
Three major problems of developing countries. MONS:412

---- EDUCATION See Education - Singapore

---- FOREIGN RELATIONS
Abdul Rahman, T.
Break with Singapore. MONS:19

---- HISTORY
Lee Kuan Yew
Tribute to India and Indians. MONSA:244
Marshall, D. S.
History of Singapore's struggle for nationhood, 1945-1959. MONSA:313

---- PARLIAMENT
Lee Kuan Yew
The future is at stake--crucial years ahead. MONSA:247

---- RELIGION
Dumper, A. C.
Church in a secular state. MONS:485

SINGAPORE NAVAL BASE
Coates, J. G.
Support for the Singapore Naval Base, 1927. MACS:278 selections

SIOUX INDIANS See Dakota Indians

Siwertz, S.
Presentation [of the Nobel Prize for Literature to Sir Winston Leonard Spencer Churchill, 1953]. NOB 4:177; NOL:488

SIZE OF INSTITUTIONS See Institutions, Size of

Sjöquist, J.
Presentation [of the Nobel Prize for Physiology or Medicine for 1923 to Frederick Grant Banting and John James Richard Macleod, 1925]. NOLM 2:45

SKEPTICISM
Howard, J. A.
The new furies: skepticism, criticism, and coercion. LINRST:146

Skidelsky, Robert
Grand alternatives. MDYG:142

Skinner, Cornelia Otis
"Bottoms up" (toast to gynecologists). (Lake Placid, N.Y., June, 1953). HURH:311
"A toast from the ladies of America ... Bottoms up!" Same as her "Bottoms up" (toast to gynecologists)

Slabach, David
Five hundred miles south. BREWW:208

SLANDER See Gossip

SLAUGHTER AND SLAUGHTERING HOUSES
Miller, S. F. and others
Slaughter house cases, 1875: opinion for the court and dissenting opinion. ANN 10:302

SLAVERY
Bacon, L.
Plea for Africa. HAW:60
Chapman, J. R.
Coatesville. ARS:163
Derby, E. G. V. S.
Emancipation of British Negroes. BREWE 5:1800
Garnet, H. H.
A plea in behalf of the Cuban

revolution. FON:380
Pitt, W., 1759-1806
Indicts the slave trade and foresees a liberated Africa. BREWE 8:3208; CLAYP:136; JAE:12; STRM:91
Price, J. C.
The race problem stated. SMHV:78
Remond, C. L.
Slavery and the Irish. SMHR:110
Slavery as it concerns the British. SMHV:16
Walker, D.
We must have unity. SMHV:11
Wilberforce, W.
Horrors of the British slave trade in the eighteenth century. BREWE 10:3891

SLAVERY IN THE UNITED STATES
Benjamin, J. P.
Slavery as established by law. BREWE 1:406
Brown, W. W.
Slavery as it is, and its influence upon the American people. FON:90
Buchanan, J.
Fourth annual message. ANN 9:209; STAT 1:1025
Third annual message. STAT 1:1001
Calhoun, J. C.
Danger of abolitionist petitions (February, 1837). ANN 6:346
On the slavery question. ANN 8:16; HURH:77; OLIS:93
Chase, S. P.
Thomas Jefferson and the colonial view of manhood rights. BREWE 3:1044
Three great eras. BREWE 3:1056
---- and others
Opposition to the Kansas-Nebraska Bill (January, 1854). ANN 8:251
Clay, H.
Compromise of 1850 (February 5 & 6, 1850 speech). ANN 8:1; BREWE 4:1273; HURH:83; OLIS:66
Slavery and expansion, May 13 and May 21, 1850. ANN 8:36
Davis, S. H.
We must assert our rightful claims and plead our own cause. FON:77
Dayton, W. L.
Issues against slavery forced by the Mexican War. BREWE 5:1679
Douglas, S. A.
Defense of the Kansas-Nebraska Bill (January 30, 1854). ANN 8:254
Fifth joint debate at Galesburg, October 7, 1858. ANN 9:22
Lincoln-Douglas joint debate at Alton, October 15, 1858. ANN 9:30
Opening speech of Lincoln-Douglas debate, Ottawa, August 21, 1858. ANN 9:8
Reply to Lincoln, Freeport, August 27, 1858. ANN 9:17; BREWE 5:1912; HURH:94
Reply to the Jonesboro speech. ANN 9:20
Douglass, F.
If there is no struggle there is no progress. FON:197
The mission of the war. FON:283
Nature of slavery (speech at Rochester, New York, December 1, 1850). BOSR:113; FRIP:222
Reception speech--at Finsbury Chapel, Moorsfield, England, May 12, 1846. OE:30
Slavery: speech at Rochester, July 5, 1852. FON:104; SMHR:125
What is my duty as an anti-slavery voter. FRIP:229
What to the slave is the Fourth of July? JAM:19; OE:41
Douglass, H. F.
I do not believe in the anti-slavery of Abraham Lincoln. FON:232
Emerson, R. W.
On the Fugitive Slave Law. ANN 8:261
Fillmore, M.
Second annual message. STAT 8:808
Forten, J. and others

Address to the humane and benevolent inhabitants of the city and county of Philadelphia. OE:14
Garnet, H. H.
Address to the slaves of the United States of America. FON:81; OE:20
Let the monster perish. FON:307
Garrison, W. L.
Beginning a revolution. BREWE 6:2237
Dangers of slavery. ANN 5:303; MDT:26
Union and slavery. BREWE 6:2240
Giddings, J. R.
Slavery and the annexation of Cuba. BREWE 6:2258
Texas and slavery. ANN 7:201
Hall, P.
Pray God give us the strength to bear up under all our troubles. FON:13
Hamilton, W.
Why a Negro convention is necessary. FON:56
Harper, F. E. W.
Address at the centennial anniversary of the Pennsylvania Society for Promoting the Abolition of Slavery. FON:430
Hunter, R. M.
A Northern party is seeking to convert the government into an instrument of warfare upon slavery (1850). DAVF:144
Johnstone, A.
Address to the people of color. FON:16
Julian, G. W.
The strength and weakness of the slave power (1852). DAVF:122
King, R.
On the Missouri Bill. ANN 4:579
Langston, C. H.
Should colored men be subject to the pains and penalties of the Fugitive Slave Law? FON:208
Lincoln, A.
Cooper Institute address. ANN 9:158; BREWE 7:2791; FRIP:204; LINS:201
First joint debate at Ottawa, August 21, 1858. ANN 9:11
Lincoln-Douglas joint debate at Alton, October 15, 1858. ANN 9:26
Plea for compensated emancipation. ANN 9:328
Reply to Douglas at Chicago. OLIS:150
Second annual message to Congress. BOORA 1:396; STAT 2:1068
Second joint debate at Freeport, August 27, 1858. ANN 9:15; BREWE 7:2785
Speech at Charleston, September 18, 1858. ANN 9:21
Speech at Galesburg, October 7, 1858. ANN 9:23
Speech at Jonesboro, September 15, 1858. ANN 9:19
Speech at Peoria, October 16, 1854. ANN 8:491; FRIP:165
Loguen, J. W.
I won't obey the Fugitive Slave Law. FON:97
McDuffie, G.
Natural slavery of the Negro. ANN 6:191
Mack, E.
Fourth of July oration, 1838. HAW:164
Mann, H.
Slavery in the territories. ANN 8:7
Osborne, P.
It is time for us to be up and doing. FON:47
Otis, H. G.
Abolitionism is equivalent to revolution. (1835). DAVF:138
Parsons, T. and others
Disputation on "The Legality of Enslaving the Africans." POC:27
Paul, N.
The abolition of slavery in New York. FON:37
Payne, D. A.
Slavery brutalizes man. FON:66
Phillips, W.
Fourth of July oration. HAW:223
On the philosophy of the

Abolition movement. MDT:35
The proclamation, how to make it efficient. MDT:148
Pinkney, W.
Missouri question. BREWE 8:3195
Purvis, R.
The American government and the Negro. FON:227
The good time is at hand. FON:266
Rock, J. S.
I will sink or swim with my race. FON:203
Negro hopes for emancipation. ANN 9:318
We ask for our rights. FON:257
What if the slaves are emancipated? FON:250
Schurz, C.
The irrepressible conflict (1860). DAVF:130
Seward, W. H.
Freedom in the new territories. HOW:226
On the admission of California to the Union. ANN 8:29
Smith, G.
On the character, scope and duties of the Liberty Party. MDT:93
Stevens, T.
Against Webster and northern compromisers. BREWE 9:3522
Sumner, C.
Antislavery duties of the Whig Party. HOW:218
A Republican appeal for unity (1855). DAVF:132
Resolutions on secession and reconstruction. ANN 9:323
Thoreau, H. D.
Fourth of July oration, 1854. HAW:200
Slavery in Massachusetts. OLIS:118
Tyler, J.
From the sinks of Europe a plotter has come (1835). DAVF:140
Walker, R. J.
Address to the people of Kansas. ANN 8:452
Ward, S. R.
Speech on the Fugitive Slave Bill. FON:93
Wears, I. C.
Lincoln's colonization proposal is anti-Christian. FON:259
Webster, D.
On the Clay Compromise. ANN 8:24
Supporting the Compromise of 1850. BREWE 10:3868
Whipper, W.
Eulogy on William Wilberforce. FON:49
Williams, F.
Duty of colored men in the present national crisis. FON:281
Williams, P.
Oration on the abolition of the slave trade. FON:20
Slavery and colonization. FON:43

---- See also Blacks, Dred Scott Decision; Emancipation Proclamation; United States - History - Civil War

SLUMS See Housing

Smith, Alfred Emanuel
Acceptance speech, Albany, New York, August 22, 1928. SIN:34
Campaign speech, Oklahoma City, Sept. 20, 1928. SIN:52
The cooing dove (Albany, Oct. 23, 1926). BRYF:548; BRYO:249
"I do not want any Catholic in the United States to vote for me because I am a Catholic." Same as his Religion and politics
Religion and politics. (Oklahoma City, Sept. 20, 1928). HURH:209

Smith, Charles Stewart
The fallacy of industrial education as the solution of the race problem (Nashville, Jan. 28, 1899). FON:607

Smith, Eric R.
United we stand, divided we fall. BREWW:134

Smith, Gerrit
Liberty destroyed by national

pride (Mexican Treaty and Monroe Doctrine). BREWE 9:3459
On the character, scope and duties of the Liberty Party. (1847). MDT:93
A voice from the past (1870). (Syracuse, N.Y., Nov. 1870). DAVF:154

Smith, Goldwin
Lamps of fiction (at centenary of Sir Walter Scott). BREWE 9:3465
Origin and causes of progress. BREWE 9:3471
Secret beyond science. BREWE 9:3476

Smith, James McCune
On the fourteenth query of Thomas Jefferson's Notes on Virginia. (1859). FON:215

Smith, Jonathan
On the Federal Constitution. (Massachusetts Convention, Jan. 24 or 25, 1788). ARN:385; ARS:272

Smith, Margaret Chase
Declaration of conscience--twenty years later. BA 1969-70:133

Smith, Sydney
Mrs. Partington in politics. BREWE 9:3479
Plea for Catholic emancipation. Same as his Results of oppression
Reform and stomach troubles. BREWE 9:3484
Results of oppression. BREWE 9:3482; JAE:40
"Wounds, shrieks, and tears" in government. BREWE 9:3490

Smith, William
Eulogium. POC:3

Snell, Bertrand
Bankruptcy and moral disintegration. BAD:90

Snow, Sir Charles Percy
The two cultures. (Cambridge Univ., May 7, 1959). MCB:417

SNOW, SIR CHARLES PERCY
Weaver, W.
Presents Sir Charles Percy Snow. LYI:171

SNYDER, FRANKLIN BLISS
Hancher, V. M.
Presents Franklyn Bliss Snyder. LYI:99

SOCIAL AND ECONOMIC SECURITY
See Insurance, Social

SOCIAL CHANGE
Howard, J. A.
The new furies: skepticism, criticism, and coercion. LINRST:146

SOCIAL CLASSES
Conant, J. B.
Education for a classless society. ANN 16:22

SOCIAL PROBLEMS
Dinwoodie, S. D.
Inner city--our shame. ARS:216
Gardner, J. W.
In behalf of a troubled nation. BA 1967-68:102
Roosevelt, F. D.
Philosophy of social justice through social action (campaign speech in Detroit October 2, 1932). ARS:135

---- See also Alcoholism; Child labor; Crime and criminals; Immigration and emigration; Poverty; Race problems; Unemployed

SOCIAL SECURITY
Eisenhower, D. D.
State of the Union (January 9, 1958). STAT 3:3076
Houtman, M.
Dangers of security. SCHW:54
Roosevelt, F. D.
Presidential remarks on the occasion of the signing of the Social Security Act. BAD:13
Right to security. ANN 15:315

---- NEW ZEALAND
Atkinson, H.
Proposal for a National Insurance scheme, 1882. MACS:186
Hamilton, A.
The Social Security Bill, 1938. MACS:337

SOCIAL SERVICE See Citizenship

SOCIAL VALUES
Jones, J. L.
"Let's bring back Dad": a solid value system. LINRST:254

SOCIALISM
Clark, P. H.
Socialism: the remedy for the evils of society. FON:451
Crispi, F.
Socialism and discontent. BREWE 4:1469
De Leon, D.
Aims of socialism. ANN 12:106
Engel, G.
Address at trial, Chicago, October 7-9, 1886. ACC:43; PAF:37
Fielden, S.
Address at trial, Chicago, October 7-9, 1886. ACC:49; PAF:41
Gaitskell, H.
Labour, politics and democratic socialism. MCB:250
Hardie, J. K.
Socialist Commonwealth. MCB:451
Harrison, H. H.
What socialism means to us. FON:698
Lee Kuan Yew
Democratic socialism under stress in Asia. MONS:345
Lehman, H. H.
Freedom and individual security. ANN 17:21
Randolph, A. P.
The task of the Negro people. FON:87
Spies, A.
Address at trial, Chicago, October 7-9, 1886. ACC:1; ANN 11:117; PAF:11

---- See also Industry and state; Labor and laboring classes; Labor unions; Socialist Party

---- NEW ZEALAND
Hamilton, A.
The economy under the Labour government. MACS:334
Holland, H.
The socialist objective of the labour movement. MACS:232

SOCIALIST PARTY
Debs, E. V.
The issue. ANN 13:137
Thomas, N.
Townsend Plan and cough drops. BOSR:92

Sockey, Clennon E.
Excellence in Indian education (Scottsdale, Ariz., Dec. 11-13, 1974). MAES:141

Sockman, Ralph W.
Responds to introduction. PRS:118

Socrates
Address to his judges after they had condemned him. Same as his On being declared guilty
On being declared guilty. BAS:67 (outline only); BREWE 9:3493
On his condemnation to death. Same as his On being declared guilty

Soddy, Frederick
The origins of the conceptions of isotopes (Nobel Lecture for 1921, Dec. 12, 1922). NOLC 1:371

SODDY, FREDERICK
Söderbaum, H. G.
Presentation [of the Nobel Prize for Chemistry to Frederick Soddy, 1921, Dec. 12, 1922]. NOLC 1:367

Söderbaum, H. G.
Presentation [of the Nobel Prize for Chemistry to Arthur Harden and Hans Karl August Simon von Euler-Chelpin, Dec. 12, 1929]. NOLC 2:127
Presentation [of the Nobel Prize

for Chemistry to Francis William Aston, Dec. 12, 1922]. NOLC 2:3
Presentation [of the Nobel Prize for Chemistry to Frederick Soddy, 1921, Dec. 12, 1922]. NOLC 1:367
Presentation [of the Nobel Prize for Chemistry to Hans Fischer, Dec. 11, 1930]. NOLC 2:161
Presentation [of the Nobel Prize for Chemistry to Heinrich Otto Wieland, 1927 and Adolf Otto Reinhold Windaus, 1828, Dec. 12, 1928]. NOLC 2:89
Presentation [of the Nobel Prize for Chemistry to Irving Langmuir, Dec. 14, 1932]. NOLC 2:283
Presentation [of the Nobel Prize for Physics to Nils Gustaf Dalen, 1912]. NOLPH 1:293
Presentation [of the Nobel Prize for Chemistry to Richard Adolf Zsigmondy, 1925, Dec. 11, 1926]. NOLC 2:41
Presentation [of the Nobel Prize for Chemistry to Theodor Svedberg, 1926, May 19, 1927]. NOLC 2:63
Presentation [of the Nobel Prize for Chemistry to Victor Grignard and Paul Sabatier, Dec. 11, 1912]. NOLC 1:217
The role of the church in promoting peace (Nobel Lecture, Dec. 11, 1930). NOLP 2:93

SÖDERBLOM, NATHAN
Mowinckel, J. L.
Presentation [of the Nobel Prize for Peace to Nathan Söderblom, Dec. 11, 1930]. NOLP 2:73

SOIL - EXHAUSTION
Bozeman, M.
Soil--America's lifeblood. BREWW:85

SOIL CONSERVATION
Bozeman, M.
Soil--America's lifeblood. BREWW:85
McKinney, S. M.
Soils--our basic natural resources--the key to man's survival. BREWW:187

SOIL EROSION
Holt, R.
The second dust bowl. BREWW:137

SOILS, SALTS IN
Holt, R.
The second dust bowl. BREWW:137

SOLDIERS
Brandli, W.
Taps and reveille. SCHW:30
Welcome to military personnel. HNWM:25

---- See also Army; United States - Army; Veterans

SOLDIERS' BONUS See Pensions, Military

SOLZHENITSYN, ALEKSANDR
Gierow, K. R.
Presentation address [of the Nobel Prize for Literature to Aleksandr Solzhenitsyn, 1970]. NOB 18:3

Sonberg, H. Alexander
Unidentified flying objects; their history, and various explanations which have been given concerning their nature. BAS:203 (outline only)

SONGS See Music and musicians

SONS See Fathers and sons; Parent and child

SOUL
Hooker, T.
The soul's exaltation. JON:104

SOUTH AFRICA
Mandela, N. R.
Indictment of South Africa. EMP:94
Ngwa, J.

Our common tradition in peril. SCHW:123

SOUTH AFRICAN WAR, 1899-1902
Holman, W. A.
Against sending troops to South Africa. MCA:109
Seddon, R. J.
The South African War contingent, 1899. MACS:260 sel.

SOUTH AMERICA
Adams, J. Q.
On participating in a congress of American nations. ANN 5:188
Clay, H.
Emancipation of South American Republics. ANN 4:488; BREWE 4:1240

SOUTH CAROLINA
Chamberlain, D. H.
Present hour in South Carolina (inaugural address of would-be governor). CUR:158
Hampton, W.
Present hour in South Carolina (inaugural address of would-be governor). CUR:159

SOUTHERN STATES
Crittenden, T. T.
Trade and commerce for the southwestern states. ANN 11:16
Grady, H. W.
New South (speech to the New England Society). ANN 11:240; BAS:121 (outline only); BOORA 1:465; LINS:254
Race problem (speech to the Boston Merchants' Association). ANN 11:240; BREWE 6:2299
Stephens, A. H.
South and the public domain. BREWE 9:3513

SOVEREIGNTY
MacDonald, P.
Statement before the Indian sovereignty Conference of American Indians, Harvard, February 22, 1975. MAES:22

SPACE FLIGHT
Armstrong, N.
Moon rendezvous. BAAGB:404
Glenn, J. H.
Address before the Joint Meeting of Congress. HURH:362
Muskie, E. S.
The astronauts on the moon. BAAGB:409
Von Braun, W.
Earth benefits from space and space technology. BA 1971-72:111
Webb, J. E.
From Runnymede to Ganymede. BA 1967-68:194

Spain, Jayne Baker
A woman could be President. (U.S.A.F. Academy Public Affairs Forum, Feb. 25, 1971). VER:249

SPAIN - HISTORY - CIVIL WAR, 1936-1939
Jordan, W. J.
The League and the Spanish Civil War. MACS:361

---- POLITICS AND GOVERNMENT
Castelar, E.
Plea for Republican institutions. BREWE 3:998

Spalding, Rufus Paine See Butler, B. F., jt. auth.

SPANISH AMERICAN WAR See United States - History - War of 1898

SPANISH IN THE PHILIPPINE ISLANDS
Quezon, M. L.
On Spain's contribution to the Philippines. CURM:24

SPANISH IN THE UNITED STATES
Kennedy, E. M.
La Raza and the law. BA 1971-72:68

SPARKS, FRED
Hills, L.

Presents Fred Sparks. LYI:115

SPEAKER, THANKING See Thanks

SPEAKING See Debates and debating; Public speaking

SPECTROSCOPY
Michelson, A. A.
Recent advances in spectroscopy. NOLPH 1:166

SPEECH, FREEDOM OF See Free speech; Liberty of the press

SPEECHES - OUTLINES OF
Ace of aces (outline of speech). CUB:62
Bernard, Saint
Why another crusade? BAS:43 (outline only)
Bryan, W. J.
Cross of gold. BAS:50 (outline only)
Burton, S.
You (male) should wear long hair. BAS:200 (outline only)
Cataline
To his soldiers. BAS:37 (outline only)
Constitution, right or wrong (outline of speech celebrating Constitution Day). CUB:80
Curtis, G. W.
Liberty under law. BAS:141 (outline only)
Davis, J.
On withdrawing from the Union. BAS:71 (outline only)
Douglas, S. A.
Reply to Lincoln at Chicago, July 9, 1858. BAS:45 (outline only)
Emerson, R. W.
American scholar. BAS:156 (outline only)
Freedom from hunger (outline of speech to persuade that continued good health of American people requires easy access to pharmaceutical vitamins and food supplements). CUB:48
Glenn, J. H.
Accepting the Distinguished Service Medal (outline of speech). CUB:65
Go on and prosper (outline of eulogistic speech). CUB:76
Goldwater, B. M.
Why we must be stronger militarily. BAS:92 (outline only)
Grady, H. W.
New South. BAS:121 (outline only)
Great Disturber (outline of speech to celebrate acceptance of Christ's offer of salvation through obedience to His word). CUB:95
Henry, P.
Liberty or death. BAS:39 (outline only)
Howdy, pardner (outline of speech to welcome Dr. Gifford Wingate as new Chairman of the Drama and Speech Department at Texas Western College). CUB:66
Jordan, L.
Opportunities in H.S.A. (Harvard Student Agencies). REIR:101 (outline)
Kennedy, J. F.
Inaugural address. BAS:146 (outline only)
Presenting the Distinguished Service Medal to John Glenn (outline of speech). CUB:64
Klayton, R. J.
Bureau of Forests and Waters should control pests by biological means rather than pesticides. BAS:188 (outline only)
Kobish, C. F.
Diamonds, their mining, selling, perfecting, and the determining of their quality. BAS:206 (outline only)
LaFollette, R. M., Sr.
Free speech in wartime. CUB:53 (outline only)
Lewis, W. D.
Founder's Day remarks. BAS:164 (outline only)
Lincoln, A.
Farewell to Springfield (outline of speech). CUB:78
"A house divided against itself cannot stand." BAS:100

(outline only)
Lorge, B.
Great auto rally (outline). REIR:93
MacArthur, D.
Defends his conduct of the war in Korea. BAS:82 (outline only)
Macios, M. A.
Model studies of structural design and construction should be conducted prior to the building of structure rather than on the site studies made after the completion of the project. BAS:193 (outline only)
Miner by choice (outline of speech in response to welcome). CUB:68
Nomination of Hubert Horatio Humphrey, Jr. (outline of speech). CUB:100
Paradox (outline of commencement speech). CUB:91
Paul VI
Key to peace. BAS:150 (outline only)
Pericles
On those who died in the war. BAS:133 (outline only)
Socrates
On being declared guilty. BAS:67 (outline only)
Sonberg, H. A.
Unidentified flying objects: their history and various explanations which have been given concerning their nature. BAS:203 (outline only)
Suggestions for organization and outlining a speech. BRP:54, 57
Textbooks and all that: an inquiry into the operation of the college bookstore (outline). CUB:28
Theater begins with wonder (Outline of speech). CUB:70
Truckman, B.
Presidential eligibility. REIR:107 (outline)
Washington, B. T.
Address at the opening of the Atlanta Exposition. BAS:77 (outline only)
Westmoreland, W. C.
Vietnam--the situation today (1967). BAS:59 (outline only)
Why go second class? (outline of speech to persuade City of Del Norte it should establish a Juvenile Court). CUB:42
You get what you ask for (outline of speech). CUB:31
Zola, E.
Appeal for Dreyfus. BAS:110 (outline only)
Zwerling, J. C.
Federal Government should continue its present housing program for low-income groups rather than change to the proposed rent subsidy plan. BAS:196 (outline only)

Spellman, Francis J.
Presents Maxwell D. Taylor. LYI:143

Spemann, Hans
The organizer-effect in embryonic development (Nobel Lecture, Dec. 12, 1935). NOLM 2:381

SPEMANN, HANS
Häggquist, G.
Presentation [of the Nobel Prize for Physiology or Medicine to Hans Spemann, Dec. 12, 1935]. NOLM 2:377

Spencer, Henry R.
Introducing Anne O'Hare McCormick. LYI:107

Spencer, Samuel Reid, Jr.
A call for new missionaries. (Due West, S.C., May 23, 1971). BA 1971-72:172

Speth, Gus
Environmental regulation and the immobilization of truth (Washington, Feb. 28, 1980). BA 1979-80:145

Spies, August
Address at trial, Chicago, October 7-9, 1886. ACC:1; ANN 11:117; PAF:11

SPITTELER, CARL FRIEDRICH
Hjärne, H.
Presentation [of the Nobel

Prize for Literature to Carl Friedrich Spitteler, 1919]. NOB 17:267; NOL:161

SPORTS
Welcome to All-sports church banquet. HNWM:33

Spotted Tail, Brule Chief
We are young no longer. ALA:37

Spottswood, Stephen G.
The Nixon administration's anti-negro policy. (Buck Hill Falls, Pa., 1970). LINRS:109

Spray, Charlie
Consumer education: the farmer's responsibility. BREWW:67
A new crisis in agriculture. BREWW:71

Springen, Phyllis Jones
The dimensions of the oppression of women (Buck Hill Falls, Pa., Dec., 1970). LINRS:109; LINRST:130

Spurgeon, Charles Haddon
Everlasting oxydization. BREWE 9:3500

Stafford, Edward William See Sewell, Henry, jt. auth.

STAGE See Theater

STAMP ACT, 1765
Chauncy, C.
Good news from a far country (repeal of Stamp Act). BREWE 3:1090

Stang, Fredrik
Presentation [of the Nobel Prize for Peace, 1935, to Carl Von Ossietzky, Dec. 10, 1936]. NOLP 2:207
Presentation [of the Nobel Prize for Peace to Ferdinand Edouard Buisson and Ludwig Quidde, Dec. 10, 1927]. NOLP 2:29
Presentation [of the Nobel Prize for Peace to Fridtjof Nansen, Dec. 10, 1922]. NOLP 1:353
Presentation [of the Nobel Prize for Peace to the Nansen International Office for Refugees, Dec. 10, 1938]. NOLP 2:265

Stanley, Arthur Penrhyn
Palmerston and the duty of England (funeral oration). BREWE 9:3506

Stanley, Augustus Owsley
Address in honor of Robert E. Lee. (Chicago, April 9, 1907). BLY:216

STANLEY, HENRY M.
Presents Henry M. Stanley. LYI:117

Stanley, J.
Tribute to a fallen Black soldier. (Chicago, Sept. 8, 1963). FON:268

Stanley, Wendell Meredith
The isolation and properties of crystalline tobacco mosaic (Nobel Lecture, Dec. 12, 1946). NOLC 3:137

STANLEY, WENDELL MEREDITH
Tiselius, A. W. K.
Presentation [of the Nobel Prize for Chemistry to James Batcheller Sumner, John Howard Northrop, and Wendell Meredith Stanley, Dec. 12, 1946]. NOLC 3:109

Stanmeyer, William A.
Urban crime: its causes and control. (Hillsdale, Mich., Oct. 26, 1972). LINRST:303

Stanton, Elizabeth Cady
Address on the Divorce Bill, 1861. BOORA 1:367
Natural rights of civilized women. ANN 9:151

Stanton, Frank
Address before the International Radio and Television Society. BA 1969-70:71
Remarks on government regulation of broadcasting (accept-

ing Printers' Ink gold medal). MDV:277
Reply to the Vice President. (New York--International Radio and Television Society, Nov. 25, 1969). STOT:282

Stark, Johannes
Structural and spectral changes of chemical atoms (Nobel Lecture for 1919, June 3, 1920). NOLPH 1:427

STARK, JOHANNES
Ekstrand, A. G.
Presentation [of the Nobel Prize for Physics for 1919 to Johannes Stark, June 3, 1920]. NOLPH 1:423

STARS
Bethe, H. A.
Energy production in stars. NOLPH 4:215

STARVATION
Wivell, C. A.
World hunger: a question of rights. BREWW:119

Stasheff, Edward
What will the satellites say? KEO:262

STATE, THE
Channing, W. E.
Man above the state. BREWE 3:1032

---- See also Church and state; Education and state; Industry and state

STATE GOVERNMENTS
Smith, A. E.
The cooing dove. BRYF:548; BRYO:249

STATE RIGHTS
Calhoun, J. C.
Force Bill. BREWE 3:866
Douglas, S. A.
Fifth joint debate at Galesburg, October 7, 1858. ANN 9:22
Opening speech of Lincoln-Douglas debate, Ottawa, August 21, 1858. ANN 9:8
Reply to Lincoln at Chicago, July 9, 1858. ANN 9:4; BAS:45 (outline only); OLIS:133
Hayne, R. Y.
On Foot's Resolution (January 21, 1830). BREWE 7:2441
Henry, P.
Against the Federal Constitution, June 5, 1788. BREWE 7:2488
Jackson, A.
Second inaugural address--"State rights and Federal sovereignty." BREWE 7:2597; HURH:71; USINAU:58; USINAUG:58
Johnson, A. and others
Debate on civil and state rights. ANN 10:11
Madison, J.
State sovereignty and federal supremacy. BREWE 8:2926; HURH:40
Martin, L.
Portion of the report of the proceedings of the General Convention held at Philadelphia in 1787. ANN 3:166

---- See also Foot's Resolution; United States - History - Civil War - Causes

STATUES See Dedication addresses - Statues

STATUTE OF WESTMINSTER
Fraser, P.
The adoption of the Statute of Westminster. MACS:286
McGechan, R. O.
Legal arguments for adopting the Statute of Westminster, 1944. MACS:284

Staudinger, Hermann
Macromolecular chemistry (Nobel Lecture, Dec. 11, 1953). NOLC 3:397

STAUDINGER, HERMANN
Fredga, A.
Presentation [of the Nobel Prize for Chemistry to Hermann Staudinger, Dec. 11, 1953]. NOLC 3:393

Steele, Harland
House that Sam built. SCHW:25

Steffens, Gretchen
Law of the land. SCHW:132

Steinbeck, John
Acceptance [of the Nobel Prize for Literature, 1962]. NOB 19:205; NOL:575

STEINBECK, JOHN
Österling, A.
Presentation [of the Nobel Prize for Literature to John Steinbeck, 1962]. NOB 19:201; NOL:572

Steinem, Gloria
Speech at the U.S. Naval Academy (May 12, 1972). JAM:46

---- and others (J. Ruckelshaus)
Meet the press. BA 1972-73:65

Stendahl, Krister
Faith that enlivens the mind (Hickory, N.C., Jan. 8, 1977). BA 1976-77:168

Stephen, Campbell See Baldwin, S. B., jt. auth.

Stephens, Alexander Hamilton
African slavery, the cornerstone of the Southern confederacy. Same as his On the Confederate Constitution
Against secession. Same as his Sanctity of the Union
Civil rights in the Confederacy. ANN 9:493
On the Confederate Constitution (Savannah, March 22, 1861). BREWE 9:3517; ECH:77
Sanctity of the Union. ANN 9:199
South and the public domain. BREWE 9:3513
Speech of Hon. A. H. Stephens, delivered in the hall of the House of Representatives of Georgia, Nov. 14, 1860. ECH:7
Speech of Hon. A. H. Stephens at Atlanta Ga., April 30, 1861. ECH:157
Speech of Hon. A. H. Stephens at Richmond, Va., April 22, 1861. ECH:191

Stephens, Donald A.
Spirit of Merdeka. MONS:322

Stern, Harry J.
Work of art. WALE:178

Stern, Otto
The method of molecular rays (Nobel Lecture for 1943, Dec. 12, 1946). NOLPH 3:8

STEROIDS
Diels, O. P. H.
Description and importance of the aromatic basic skeleton of the steroids. NOLC 3:259

STEROLS
Windaus, A. O. R.
Constitution of sterols and their connection with other substances occurring in nature. NOLC 2:105

STEVENS, ROGER L.
Cullman, H. S.
Presents Roger L. Stevens. LYI:29

Stevens, Thaddeus
Against Webster and northern compromisers. BREWE 9:3522
Ascendency of the Union Party. Same as his Radical view of reconstruction
Concerning wartime taxes in the North. ANN 9:335
Education as a public duty. ANN 6:136
Fruit of foul rebellion. Same as his On reconstruction
Issue against Andrew Johnson. Same as his Radical view of reconstruction
On reconstruction. CUR:13
Radical view of reconstruction. BREWE 9:3529; CUR:58
Rights of the conqueror. ANN 9:608

Stevenson, Adlai, III
Economic interdependence: the

world at a crossroads (New York, Dec. 13, 1978). BA 1978-79:178
Acceptance of nomination. Same as his Agrees to run for President
Acceptance speech, Chicago, Illinois, August 17, 1956. SIN:282
Acceptance speech, Chicago, Illinois, July 26, 1952. Same as his Agrees to run for President
Address at the memorial service for Sir Winston Churchill (Jan. 28, 1965). LINR:305; LINRS:307; LINRST:373
Agrees to run for President (Chicago, Ill., July 26, 1952). ANN 17:196; BEN:123; GRG:96; HURH:302; LINS:345; SIN:251
Bay of Pigs. ANN 18:25
Campaign speech, Academy of Music, Brooklyn, New York, October 31, 1952. SIN:255
Campaign speech, Minneapolis, Minnesota, September 29, 1956. SIN:288
City--a cause for statesmanship. ARS:219
Eulogy: John Fitzgerald Kennedy. Same as his Tribute to John F. Kennedy at the General Assembly of the United Nations
Eulogy on Eleanor Roosevelt. BRP:230
Farewell to a friend (Lloyd Lewis). ALA:119
Foreign policy: the shades of gray. MDV:56
Meaning of the United Nations. ANN 18:317
Nature of patriotism. Same as his Speech to the American Legion, August 27, 1952
"The ordeal of the twentieth century ... is far from over." Same as his Agrees to run for President
Premeditated attempt: the building of the sites (United Nations, 1962). LINR:87; LINRS:93
Presents Lyndon B. Johnson. LYI:197
Presents Pandit Jawaharlal Nehru. LYI:242
Prospects for democracy around the world. LINS:350
Sir Winston Churchill. Same as his Address at the memorial service for Sir Winston Churchill
The speaker seeks a favorable hearing. (Yale University, 1955). JEF:189; JEFF:182
Speech to the American Legion, August 27, 1952. BEN:129
Strengthening international developing institutions. ALS:281
Today's most fateful fact (accepting honorary degree of Doctor of Laws). OLIS:272
Trained intelligence: education and womanpower (Radcliffe College commencement address). MDV:205
Tribute to John F. Kennedy at the General Assembly of the United Nations (New York, Nov. 26, 1963). GRG:122; HURH:371
"We shall honor him in the best way that lies open to us--by getting on with the everlasting search for peace and justice for which all mankind is praying." Same as his Tribute to John F. Kennedy at the General Assembly of the United Nations

STEVENSON, ADLAI E.
McGowan, C.
Eulogy on Adlai E. Stevenson. BA 1965-66:227
Ramani, R.
Man of clear vision (tribute to Adlai E. Stevenson). MONS:250

Stewart, Potter
Or of the press. (New Haven, Conn., Nov. 2, 1974). BA 1974-75:97

Still, William
A defense of independent voting. (Philadelphia, March 10, 1874). FON:398

Stimson, Henry L.
United States and the Caribbean. ANN 15:72

Stipp, John E.
Introduces Nathan M. Pusey, President, Harvard University. LYI:83

Stirling, William See Sykes, C., jt. auth.

Stiskin, Maurice N.
Man is a soul. WALE:179

STOCK AND STOCK BREEDING
See Agriculture

STOCKDALE, JOHN
Erskine, T.
Speech in behalf of John Stockdale. BREWE 6:2050

Stoddard, Solomon
Defects of preachers reproved. POC:430

Stone, Barton W., 1772-1844
"And I will gladly spend and be spent for you though the more abundantly I love you, the less I be loved." BLY:19

Stone, Harlan Fiske
Fear and hysteria: the Japanese relocation, "Hirabayashi v. United States," 1943: opinion for the Supreme Court. ROD:316

Story, Joseph
Intellectual achievement in America. BREWE 9:3531

---- See also Taney, R. B., jt. auth.

Stout, Robert
A call for liberal and conservative parties, 1876 (New Zealand House of Representatives, Aug. 18, 1876). MACS:180

---- See also Holland, H., jt. auth.

Stowe, Leland
Children, peanuts--and you. MOP:263

Strafford, Thomas Wentworth, 1st Earl of
Defense before the House of Lords. BREWE 9:3540; BRYH:131
His defense when impeached for treason. Same as his Defense before the House of Lords
Speech at his trial for treason. Same as his Defense before the House of Lords

Stratton, Richard D.
Food: a world crisis. BREWW:81

Stratton, Thomas
Agriculture--America's greatest tool. BREWW:109

Street, William S.
Introduces Dr. Charles E. Odegaard, president of the University of Washington. PRS:46

Streeter, Frank S.
Introducing an educator (Frederick S. Jones). LYI:85

STREPTOMYCIN
Waksman, S. A.
Streptomycin: background, isolation, properties, and utilization. NOLM 3:370

Stresemann, Gustav
The new Germany (Nobel Lecture, 1926, June 29, 1927). NOLP 2:8

STRESEMANN, GUSTAV
Nansen, F.
Speech at Award Ceremony [presenting Nobel Prize for Peace to Aristide Briand and Gustav Stresemann, Dec. 10, 1926]. NOLP 2:3

STRIKES AND LOCKOUTS
Tan Chee Khoon
Intellectual elite and the worker. MONS:197

---- NEW ZEALAND
Holland, H.
The 1913 Waterside Strike. MACS:230 sel.
Lee, J. A.
The Auckland Riot, 1932. MACS:312 sel.

Strutt, John William See Rayleigh, John William Strutt, Baron, 1842-1919

Stuart, Julia Davis
What can I do that matters? (Detroit, Sept. 19, 1967). BRYF:512

Studebaker, Clement See Jones, A., jt. auth.

STUDENT DEMONSTRATIONS
Moos, M.
Darkness over the Ivory Tower. BA 1968-69:55

STUDENT MOVEMENTS
Horn, F. H.
The student revolt, a defense of the older generation. HOR:49
McGill, W. J.
Requiem for the counterculture: problems of a new student generation. HOR:66
Odegaard, C. E.
Bridging the generation gap, the march downtown. HOR:42
Perkins, J. A.
Bridging the generation gap, how the New Deal became today's establishment. HOR:56

STUDENTS
Bittner, J. R.
The news media and campus unrest. STOT:290
Brewster, K., Jr.
Due process radicalism. HOR:37
Bronowski, J.
Protest--past and present. BA 1969-70:1119
Bunting, M. I.
Their questions. HOR:93
Capp, A.
Is this your university? STOT:297
Cry on the campus. BURT:102
Damrin, D. E.
The James Scholars and the university. BRYF:528; BRYO:243
Eddy, E. D., Jr.
Student involvement in educational policy. BA 1965-66:221; LINR:251
Hayes, P. A.
Madame Butterfly and the collegian. LINR:262
Jordan, L.
Opportunities in H.S.A. (Harvard Student Agencies). REIR:101 (outline)
Kane, A.
Glory of notoriety. REIR:223
Kerr, C.
Perspectives on the prophets of doom. HOR:34
Lindsay, J. V.
A politician adapts his introduction and conclusion to an audience of students. JEF:194
Lubbers, A. D.
God and Joe College. SCHW:69
McGill, W. J.
Requiem for Joe College. BA 1969-70:139
McKissick, F. B.
The student and the ghetto. OE:216
Martin, D.
Trouble in the university. MDYG:121
Moos, M.
Darkness over the Ivory Tower. BA 1968-69:55
Nixon, R. M.
Campus revolutionaries. BAAGB:386
Pusey, N. M.
Thanksgiving and entreaty, a President's valedictory. HOR:26
Thani Nayagam, X.
Town versus gown. MONS:183
Wald, G.
Generation in search of a future. BA 1968-1969:33
Welcome to a delegation of foreign students. HNWM:48
Welcome to a freshman class. HNWM:50

---- See also Black students; Colleges and universities; Commencement addresses; Education, Higher; Learning and scholarship; Youth

STUDENTS, PARTICIPATION IN SCHOOL GOVERNMENT See Self government in education

SUBSIDY See Taxation

SUBSTITUTE SPEAKERS
Bishop, J.
Responds to introduction (when substituting for Sir Cedric Hardwicke). PRS:119
Caveny, C. C.
Greets Joey Bishop, substituting for Sir Cedric Hardwicke, PRS:118

SUBTREASURY BILL See Independent treasury

SUCCESS
Art of success. BURT:112
Fosdick, H. E.
Power to see it through. CROCK:58
You, too, can be a millionaire. BURT:118

---- See also Behavior; Fame; Inspiration talks

SUEZ CANAL
Eisenhower, D. D.
Crisis in the Middle East. ANN 17:411
Holland, S.
The Suez crisis, 1956. MACS:397 sel.
Menzies, R. G.
On the nationalisation of the Suez Canal. MCA:144

Suffian bin Hashim
The danger of living our lives in isolation (April 4, 1970). MONSA:137
Important factors for ensuring efficient, loyal public service (Oct. 4, 1969). MONSA:132
Only Malays can initiate the institutional changes (Petaling Jaya, Oct. 11, 1969). MONSA:140
University should slow down: call to education planners (Univ. of Malaya, June 20, 1970). MONSA:144
Warning to the white-collar worker (Kuala Lumpur, Jan. 25, 1970). MONSA:138

SUFFRAGE
Carpenter, M. H.
In favor of universal suffrage. BREWE 3:978
Chamberlain, J.
Megaphone and manhood suffrage. BREWE 3:1026
Frelinghuysen, F. T.
In favor of universal suffrage. BREWE 6:2203
Sanford, N. and others
Debate on property and suffrage. ANN 5:4
Still, W.
A defense of independent voting. FON:398

---- See also Blacks - Politics and suffrage; Elections; Woman - Suffrage

SUGARS
Fischer, H. E.
Syntheses in the purine and sugar group. NOLC 1:21
Leloir, L. F.
Two decades of research on the biosynthesis of saccharides. NOLC 4:338

SUICIDE
Hayes, P. A.
Madame Butterfly and the collegian. LINR:262; LINRS:265

SULFUR
Vigneaud, V. D.
A trail of sulfur research: from insulin to oxytocin. NOLC 3:446

Sullivan, John H.
The United States and the coming world food crisis (River Falls, Wisc., April 26, 1979). BA 1979-80:46

Sullivan, Louis
Characteristics and tendencies of

American architecture. ANN 11:40
Young architect. ANN 12:385

Sullivan, Walter See Sevareid, E., jt. auth.

Sulzberger, Arthur Ochs
Business and the press: is the press anti-business? (Detroit, March 14, 1977). EHN:387

Sumner, Charles
Against annexation (of the Dominican Republic). ANN 10:233
Antislavery duties of the Whig Party. (Boston-Whig State Convention, Sept. 23, 1846). HOW:218
Crime against Kansas (Washington, May, 1856). ANN 8:267; BREWE 9:3557; HURH:85
Denouncing Douglas and Butler. Same as his Crime against Kansas
"An essential wickedness that makes other public crimes seem like public virtues." Same as his Crime against Kansas
Naboth's vineyard. Same as his Against annexation (of the Dominican Republic)
Proper guaranties for security. CUR:12
A Republican appeal for unity (1855). (Nov. 2, 1855, Faneuil Hall). DAVF:132
Resolutions on secession and reconstruction. ANN 9:323
Segregation and the common school (Sarah C. Roberts v. City of Boston case, 1849). ANN 7:507
True grandeur of nations. BREWE 9:3548
War and the common law of Nations. Same as his War system of the Commonwealth of Nations
War system of the Commonwealth of Nations. ANN 7:548

---- and others (J. Grimes)
Impeachment of Andrew Johnson. ANN 10:126

SUMNER, CHARLES
Brooks, P. S.
Assault on Sumner. BREWE 2:654
Burlingame, A.
Massachusetts and the Sumner assault. BREWE 2:820
Conkling, R.
Against Senator Sumner. BREWE 4:1374
Rainey, J. H.
Eulogy on Charles Sumner. FON:403

Sumner, G. Lynn
Presents Gertrude Lawrence. LYI:22
Presents Victor Heiser. LYI:174

Sumner, James Batcheller
The chemical nature of enzymes (Nobel Lecture, Dec. 12, 1946). NOLC 3:114

SUMNER, JAMES BATCHELLER
Tiselius, A. W. K.
Presentation [of the Nobel Prize for Chemistry to James Batcheller Sumner, John Howard Northrop, and Wendell Meredith Stanley, Dec. 12, 1946]. NOLC 3:109

Sunday, William A. (Billy Sunday)
Evangelism. (New York, 1914). HURH:170
'I like to have a man have a definite experience in religion." Same as his Evangelism

SUNDAY LEGISLATION
Terry, D. S. and others
On Sunday closing laws: opinion for the court and dissenting opinion (Ex parte Newman case). ANN 9:85

SUNDAY SCHOOLS
Welcome to Sunday school officers. HNWM:28
Welcome to visitors in Sunday school (3 examples). HNWM:52

Sundberg, O.
Presentation [of the Nobel Prize for Physiology or Medicine to Charles Louis Alphonse Laveran, Dec. 11, 1907].

NOLM 1:259
Presentation [of the Nobel Prize for Physiology or Medicine to Charles Robert Richet, Dec. 11, 1913]. NOLM 1:469

SUPREME COURT OF THE UNITED STATES See United States - Supreme Court

SURFACE CHEMISTRY
Langmuir, I.
Surface chemistry. NOLC 2:287

SURRATT, MARY E.
Aiken, F. A.
Defense of Mrs. Mary E. Surratt. BREWE 1:120

Sutherland, George and others (W. H. Taft and O. W. Holmes, Jr.)
Adkins v. Children's Hospital: opinion for the court and dissenting opinion. ANN 14:391
---- (L. D. Brandeis)
(New State Ice Company v. Liebmann: opinion for the court and dissenting opinion. ANN 15:140

Sutherland, Josiah
Free land and the supply of labor. ANN 8:180

Sutro, John See Sykes, C., jt. auth.

Suttner, Bertha Von
The evolution of the Peace Movement (Nobel Lecture for 1905, April 18, 1906). NOLP 1:84

SUTTNER, BERTHA VON
Bjørnson, G.
Introduction [presenting the Nobel Prize for Peace to Bertha von Suttner, 1905, April 18, 1906]. NOLP 1:81
Løvland, J. G.
Banquet speech [presenting the Nobel Prize for Peace to Bertha von Suttner, 1905, April 18, 1906]. NOLP 1:82

Sutton, Preston M.
Liberal arts in an agricultural college. ANN 11:18

Svedberg, Theodor
The ultracentrifuge (Nobel Lecture for 1926, May 19, 1927). NOLC 2:67

SVEDBERG, THEODOR
Söderbaum, H. G.
Presentation [of the Nobel Prize for Chemistry to Theodor Svedberg, 1926, May 19, 1927]. NOLC 2:63

Swarensky, Manfred E.
Bridge of love. WALE:181
Spiritual portrait. WALE:183

Swearingen, John E.
Environmental pollution: a national problem. (Indiana State Chamber of Commerce, Indianapolis, Nov. 6, 1969). BAAGB:392

Swets, Paul
Bootstraps and moonshots. SCHW:183

Swimmer, Ross O.
Cherokee history. MAES:314

Syed Hussein Alatas
Malaysia and its intellectual revolution. MONS:469
Primary aim of a university. MONS:475

Sykes, Christopher and others
Evelyn Waugh--the man. MDYG:11

Symonds, William
Britain's claim to a New World empire justified. ANN 1:32

Synge, Richard Laurence Millington
Applications of partition chromatography (Nobel Lecture, Dec. 12, 1952). NOLC 3:374

SYNGE, RICHARD LAURENCE MILLINGTON
Tiselius, A. W. K.
Presentation [of the Nobel

Prize for Chemistry to Archer John Porter Martin and Richard Laurence Millington Synge, Dec. 12, 1952]. NOLC 3:355

Szent-Györgyi, Albert
Oxidation, energy transfer, and vitamins (Nobel Lecture, Dec. 11, 1937). NOLM 2:440

SZENT-GYÖRGYI, ALBERT
Hammarsten, E.
Presentation [of the Nobel Prize for Physiology or Medicine to Albert Szent-Györgyi Von Nagyrapolt, Dec. 11, 1937]. NOLM 2:435

- T -

Taft, Robert A.
Against the treaty (North Atlantic Pact). ANN 16:591
Analysis of the Taft-Hartley Act. ANN 16:414
Declaration of Republican principles--the New Deal is rapidly receding. BAD:74
Equal justice under law. BEN:100
New problems of government. ANN 15:571
Opposition to the Roosevelt war policies. ANN 16:94
Should the government guarantee employment? ANN 16:263

TAFT, ROBERT A.
Dirksen, E.
Presents Robert A. Taft. LYI:210

Taft, William Howard
Antitrust: "Mere size is no sin." Same as his Third annual message; part I, December 5, 1911
Cabinet and the Congress. Same as his Fourth annual message; part III, December 19, 1912
Defense of a high tariff. Same as his Tariff fiasco: the Winona address
Dollar diplomacy. Same as his Fourth annual message: part I, December 3, 1912
First annual message. STAT 3:2338
Fourth annual message: part I, December 3, 1912. ANN 13:369; STAT 3:2486
Fourth annual message: part II, December 6, 1912. STAT 3:2511
Fourth annual message: part III, December 19, 1912. ANN 13:366; STAT 3:2531
Inaugural address. USINAU:187
Limited presidential power. ANN 14:41
Second annual message. STAT 3:2369
Tariff fiasco: the Winona address. ANN 13:176
Third annual message: part I, December 5, 1911. STAT 3:2432
Third annual message: part II, December 7, 1911. STAT 3:2444
Third annual message: part III, December 20, 1911. STAT 3:2464
Third annual message: part IV, December 21, 1911. STAT 3:2469
Veto of Arizona Enabling Act. ANN 13:272

---- See also Sutherland, G., jt. auth.

TAFT-HARTLEY BILL See Labor law and legislation - Taft-Hartley Law

TAGORE, RABINDRANATH
Hjärne, H.
Presentation [of the Nobel Prize for Literature to Rabindranath Tagore, 1913]. NOB 18:10; NOL:127
Nair, C. V. D.
Reflections on Rabindranath Tagore. MONS:190

Talfourd, Thomas Noon
Queen against Moxon-Shelley as a blasphemer. BREWE 9:3565

Talmage, Thomas Dewitt
On Admiral Dewey and the

American Navy.
BREWE 9:3584

TAMIL LANGUAGE
Abdul Rahman, T.
"All the earth is my homeland." MONS:31

Tamm, Igor' Evgen'evič
General characteristics of radiations emitted by systems moving with super-light velocities with some applications to plasma physics (Nobel Lecture, Dec. 11, 1958). NOLPH 3:470

TAMM, IGOR' EVGEN'EVIC
Siegbahn, K.
Presentation [of the Nobel Prize for Physics to Pavel Aleksejevič Cerenkov, Il'ja Michajlovič Frank and Igor' Evgen'evič Tamm, Dec. 11, 1958]. NOLPH 3:423

Tan Chee Khoon
Intellectual elite and the worker. MONS:197
Monstrous piece of legislation (Internal Security Act--Malaysia). MONS:190
The teachers' dilemma: the government gets the blame (Univ. of Malaya, Jan. 4-5, 1968). MONSA:180

Tan Siew Sin
The big question before us. (Kuala Lumpur, March 28, 1968). MONSA:93
Commonwealth trade: an explosive situation. MONS:127
Malays and Chinese must coexist (July 24, 1969). MONSA:85
Meeting place of cultures. MONS:115
Mission of the M.C.A. MONS:117
The need for dedicated service by civil servants (Kuala Lumpur, Feb. 4, 1968). MONSA:89
Our constitution: a fair compromise. MONS:109
The role of M.C.A. and the loyalty of Malaysian Chinese (Kuala Lumpur, March 7, 1969). MONSA:78

Tan Sri Muhammed Ghazali See Muhammed Ghazali bin Shafie

Tan Sri V. T. Sambanthan See Sambanthan, V. T.

Taney, Roger Brooke
Dred Scott Case: opinion for the Supreme Court. ANN 8:440
Dred Scott V. Sandford. Same as his Dred Scott case

---- and others (J. Story)
Charles River bridge v. Warren bridge: opinion for the court and dissenting opinion. ANN 6:326

Tanner, B. T.
The Sioux's revenge. (Philadelphia, July 13, 1876). FON:443

Tappan, David
A warning to Harvard seniors against world revolution. (June 19, 1798). DAVF:49

Tappan, Henry P.
Call for a secularized university. ANN 9:79

Tardiff, Vivian
Americans with Japanese faces. SCHW:20

TARIFF
Borah, W. E.
Western farming and the tariff. ANN 15:28
Clay, H.
American industry, 1824. ANN 5:114
American system. BREWE 4:1249; HOW:32
Manufacturing and a protective tariff. ANN 4:612
System of real reciprocity. ANN 5:392
Cleveland, G.
Fourth annual message (first term). STAT 2:1598
On tariff revision. ANN 11:154; STAT 2:1587
Dallas, G. M.

Pennsylvania idea.
BREWE 4:1599
Dawes, H. L.
Tariff Commission of 1880.
BREWE 5:1671
Harrison, B.
Second annual message.
STAT 2:1653
Jordan, D. S.
Moral aspects of the protective tariff. ANN 13:147
McKinley, W.
At the Pan-American Exposition. ANN 12:428
Randolph, J., 1773-1833
Against a protective tariff.
ANN 4:427
On the tariff (1824).
BREWE 9:3305
Taft, W. H.
Tariff fiasco: the Winona address. ANN 13:176
Third annual message: part III, December 20, 1911.
STAT 3:2464

---- See also Commerce; Corn Laws; Free trade and protection

Tatum, Edward Lawrie
A case history in biological research (Nobel Lecture, Dec. 11, 1958).
NOLM 3:602

TATUM, EDWARD LAWRIE
Caspersson, T.
Presentation [of the Nobel Prize for Physiology or Medicine to George Wells Beadle, Edward Lawrie Tatum, and Joshua Lederberg, Dec. 11, 1958].
NOLM 3:583

TAXATION
Bacon, F.
Upon the motion of subsidy (November 15, 1598 speech). BRYH:90
Chesterfield, P. D. S.
Against revenues from drunkenness and vice.
BREWE 3:1095
Danton, G. J.
Squeezing the sponge.
BREWE 5:1631
Hamilton, A.
On an act granting to Congress certain imposts and duties. ALS:133
Income tax--legalized larceny.
BURT:50
Kennedy, J. F.
Tax cut. STAT 3:3144
Lewis, E.
Mott v. Pennsylvania Railroad Company: opinion for the court. ANN 9:61
Lloyd George, D.
The budget. BRYH:461; JAE:170; MCB:233; STRM:407
Mulford, S.
Speech to the Assembly at New-York. POC:174
Pitt, W., 1708-1778
On the right to tax America.
STRM:11
Roosevelt, F. D.
The President asks Congress for tax revision. BAD:8
Roosevelt, T.
Seventh annual message.
STAT 3:2240
Sherman, J.
General financial policy of the government. BREWE 9:3442
Stevens, T.
Concerning wartime taxes in the North. ANN 9:335

---- NEW ZEALAND
Ballance, J.
A land tax of a halfpenny in the pound on land exceeding £500 in value, 1878.
MACS:184 sel.
Grey, Sir G.
A radical programme, 1877.
MACS:181 sel.
Massey, W. F.
Repeal of income tax on farmers, 1923. MACS:304 sel.
Nordmeyer, A.
The "Black budget" 1958.
MACS:434 sel.

Taylor, Deems
Presents Grace George.
LYI:19

Taylor, Frederick W.
On scientific management.
BOORA 2:740

Taylor, George Edwin
Revolution by the ballot. (St. Louis, July 5, 1904). FON:647

Taylor, Jeremy
Foolish exchange. BREWE 9:3590

TAYLOR, MAXWELL D.
Spellman, F.J.
Presents Maxwell D. Taylor. LYI:143

Taylor, Orlando L.
African origins of Black English. (Univ. of Texas, Oct. 23, 1969). JEF:443

Taylor, Thomas E.
Leasehold defended (New Zealand House of Representatives Nov. 16, 1909). MACS:219 sel.

Taylor, Zachary
First annual message. STAT 1:774
Inaugural address. USINAU:99

TEACHER APPRECIATION DAY
Welcome to teachers on Teacher Appreciation Day. HNWM:17

TEACHERS
Introductions for teachers (10 examples). BNH:28
Johari, M. K.
Successful teacher. MONS:146
Welcome to teachers on Education Day. HNWM:18

---- See also Education; Educators

TEACHING, FREEDOM OF
Marshall, D. S.
What is academic freedom? MONS:453
Nixon, R. M.
Academic freedom: a force in human history. CAPG:148
Toh Chin Chye
Essentials of academic freedom. MONS:379

TECHNICAL EDUCATION
Whitehead, A. N.
Technical education and its relation to science and literature. MCB:403

TECHNOLOGY
Brown, H. S.
Science, technology, and world development. ARS:83
Kanapathy, V.
Technological change and management policies. MONSA:202

TECHNOLOGY AND CIVILIZATION
Dubos, R.
Social attitudes and technological civilization. BA 1978-79:11
Linowitz, S. M.
Let candles be brought. BA 1976-77:149

TECHNOLOGY AND STATE
Schmitt, H.
New policy options through technology. BA 1979-80:133

Tecumseh, Shawnee chief
To General Proctor. BREWE 7:2567

TELEVISION BROADCASTING
Agnew, Spiro
Television news coverage; network censorship. ARN:367; BRYF:467; ERP:153; LINRS:191; LINRST:221; MACR:331; STAT:274
Braden, W. W.
Has TV made the public speaker obsolete? EHN:309; MOPR:360
Gallup, G.
Mass information or mass entertainment. ANN 17:215
Goodman, J. B.
Broadcast journalism: serving the democratic process. BA 1976-77:52
Minow, N. N.
Television and the public interest. ANN 18:12; MDV:248
Murrow, E. R.
Broadcaster talks to his colleagues. MDV:263

Myers, N. J.
Moppet manipulation.
ARS:123
Stanton, F.
Address before the International Radio and Television Society. BA 1969-70:71
Remarks on government regulation of broadcasting (accepting Printers' Ink gold medal). MDV:277
Reply to the Vice President.
STOT:282

Teller, Morris
What the Lord requires.
WALE:185

tenBroek, Jacobus
Today's challenge in public welfare. MDV:233

Tennent, Gilbert
Danger of an unconverted ministry. POC:469

TENNESSEE VALLEY AUTHORITY See Dams

TENURE OF OFFICE ACT, 1867
Johnson, A.
Veto of Tenure of Office Act. ANN 10:90

Terrell, Mary Church
The progress of colored women. (1904). FON:643

TERRITORIAL EXPANSION See United States - Territorial expansion

TERRORISM
Kelley, C. M.
Terrorism, the ultimate evil. BA 1975-76:117

Terry, David Smith and others (S. J. Field)
On Sunday closing laws: opinion for the court and dissenting opinion (Ex parte Newman case).
ANN 9:85

Tertullian, Quintus Septimius Florens
Beauty of patience.
BREWE 9:3597

TEXAS
Giddings, J. R.
Texas and slavery.
ANN 7:201
Jackson, A.
Independence of Texas.
ANN 6:293
Tyler, J.
Fourth annual message.
STAT 1:613

Thackeray, William Makepeace
Authors and their patrons.
BREWE 9:3604
Novelist's future labors.
BREWE 9:3606
Reality of the novelist's creation.
BREWE 9:3602

Thani Nayagam, Xavier S.
Age and learning. MONS:187
Town versus gown. MONS:183

THANKS
Appreciation on a day of dedication. BOS:68
Nine examples of brief thanks to special committees.
BNH:46
Nineteen examples of short speeches of public appreciation. BNH:43
Public appreciation. BOS:43
Ramani, R.
Twenty four days in May (expression of thanks as President of Security Council of United Nations). MONS:248
Thanks to special committees.
BOS:46
Words of appreciation.
BON:61

---- See also Acceptance speeches; Responses to tributes

THANKSGIVING DAY
Osgood, D.
An American Thanksgiving for divine favor (1795). DAVF:42
Parker, T.
State of the nation (1850).
ANN 8:114
Prayer for Thanksgiving.
BNH:76
Rawson, E.
Thanksgiving. HURH:20
Sampson, B. K.

To my white fellow citizens. FON:347

Thant, U.
Future of the United Nations. MDV:45

Thatcher, Peter
Boston Massacre oration, March 5, 1776. POC:272

Thayer, Robert H.
America's cultural relations abroad. ANN 17:545

THEATER
Burrows, J. L.
Opposition to the theater in time of war. ANN 9:402
Jackson, E. M.
American theatre and the speech profession. BA 1965-66:200
Theater begins with wonder (outline of speech). CUB:70

---- See also Music and musicians

Théel, Hj.
Presentation [of the Nobel Prize for Physics to Hendrik Antoon Lorentz and Pieter Zeeman, 1902]. NOLPH 1:11
Presentation [of the Nobel Prize for Chemistry to Hermann Emil Fischer, Dec. 12, 1902]. NOLC 1:17

Theiler, Max
The development of vaccines against yellow fever (Nobel Lecture, Dec. 11, 1951). NOLM 3:351

THEILER, MAX
Bergstrand, H.
Presentation [of the Nobel Prize for Physiology or Medicine to Max Theiler, Dec. 11, 1951]. NOLM 3:347

Theorell, Axel Hugo Theodor
The nature and mode of action of oxidation enzymes (Nobel Lecture, Dec. 12, 1955). NOLM 3:480

THEORELL, AXEL HUGO THEODOR
Hammarsten, E.
Presentation [of the Nobel Prize for Physiology or Medicine to Axel Hugo Theodor Theorell, Dec. 12, 1955]. NOLM 3:477

Theorell, H.
Presentation [of the Nobel Prize for Physiology or Medicine to Carl Ferdinand Cori, Gerty Theresa Cori-Radnitz, and Bernardo Alberto Houssay, Dec. 11, 1947]. NOLM 3:179
Presentation [of the Nobel Prize for Physiology or Medicine to Severo Ochoa and Arthur Kornberg, Dec. 11, 1959]. NOLM 3:641

THERMIONIC EMISSION
Richardson, O. W.
Thermionic phenomena and the laws which govern them. NOLPH 2:224

THERMODYNAMICS
Giauque, W. F.
Some consequences of low-temperature research in chemical thermodynamics. NOLC 3:227

Thibeault, Mary Lou
The hazards of equity. (Commencement Address, Hartford Colleges for Women, June 1, 1974). VERD:265

Thiers, Louis Adolphe
Mexico and Louis Napoleon's policies. BREWE 9:3610

Thio Chan Bee
Christian laymen and the world of politics. MONS:465
Inspired education through inspired educators. MONS:463

Thomas, Dylan
Life among the culture vultures. ANN 17:239

Thomas, James B.
"Light of the world." SCHW:110

Thomas, Norman
America and the war. (New

York, June 29, 1941). HURH:261
Townsend Plan and cough drops. BOSR:92
"We have better work for our sons to do than to have them die." Same as his America and the war

Thompson, Dorothy
"Democracy and freedom face the bitterest of tests." Same as her Hitler's plans for Canada and the United States
Hitler's plans for Canada and the United States (Toronto, May 2, 1941). HURH:257

THOMPSON, DOROTHY
Meloney, Mrs. W. B.
Introducing Dorothy Thompson. LYI:112

Thompson, Morris
The BIA at work. MAES:57

Thomson, George Paget
Electronic waves (Nobel Lecture for 1937, June 7, 1938). NOLPH 2:397

THOMSON, GEORGE PAGET
Pleijel, H.
Presentation [of the Nobel Prize for Physics to Clinton Joseph Davisson and George Paget Thomson, Dec. 13, 1937]. NOLPH 2:387

Thomson, Joseph John
Carriers of negative electricity (Nobel Lecture, Dec. 11, 1906). NOLPH 1:145

THOMSON, JOSEPH JOHN
Klason, J. P.
Presentation [of the Nobel Prize for Physics to Joseph John Thomson, Dec. 11, 1906]. NOLPH 1:141

Thomson, Tun Sir James Beveridge
Brightness is darkened (eulogy on Tuanku Abdul Rahman Ibni Al-Marhum Tuanku Mohammed, first King of Malaysia). MONS:281
Let these be his epitaph (eulogy on Sultan Hissamuddin Alam Shah Ibni Al-Marhum Sultan Ala'Iddin Sulaiman Shah). MONS:283
Spirit of humanity (opening of Federal Court of Malaysia). MONS:285

Thoreau, Henry David
Civil disobedience. BOORA 1:318
Fourth of July oration, 1854 (Boston). HAW:200
Plea for Captain John Brown. ANN 9:136
Slavery in Massachusetts. OLIS:118
Walking westward. ANN 8:125

Thorne, Will <u>See</u> Baldwin, S. B., jt. auth.

Thornton, Charles B.
Responds to introduction. PRS:101

THOUGHT AND THINKING
Don't limit yourself. BURT:115
Hancher, V. M.
Art of contemplation. CROCK:132

Thuraisingham, Ernest Emmanual Sir Clough
Call to Ceylonese to have one and only loyalty to rulers of Malaysia MONSA:185
Lotteries: Hell, Hitler and Bernard Shaw. MONS:167
Milestones in Malayan education. MONS:173
The prince of sportsmen (Kuala Lumpur, Sept. 18, 1970). MONSA:187
Spirit of teaching. MONS:169

Thurman, Allen G.
Tilden-Hayes election. BREWE 9:3621
Vested rights and the obligations of contracts. BREWE 9:3626

THYROID GLAND - DISEASES
Kocher, E. T.
Concerning pathological manifestations in low-grade thyroid diseases. NOLM 1:330

Tierney, George See Pitt, W., 1759-1806

Tilden, Samuel Jones
Arraignment of the Republican Party. Same as his Negro suffrage
Negro suffrage. ANN 10:122

Tillich, Paul J.
"What is truth?" ARS:180

Tillotson, John
Sermon against evil speaking. BRYH:156

Tilton, Theodore
The Negro; a speech. (1863). MDT:161

TIME
Salm, N.
Matter of time. SCHW:83

Tirikatene, Eruera
Maiden speech in Parliament (Sept. 29, 1932). MACS:179 sel.

Tiselius, Arne Wilhelm Kaurin
Electrophoresis and adsorption analysis as aids in investigations of large-molecular weight substances and their breakdown (Nobel Lecture, Dec. 13, 1948). NOLC 3:195
Presentation [of the Nobel Prize for Chemistry to Archer John Porter Martin and Richard Laurence Millington Synge, Dec. 12, 1952]. NOLC 3:355
Presentation [of the Nobel Prize for Chemistry to Frederick Sanger, Dec. 11, 1958]. NOLC 3:541
Presentation [of the Nobel Prize for Chemistry to James Batcheller Sumner, John Howard Northrop, and Wendell Meredith Stanley, Dec. 12, 1946]. NOLC 3:109
Presentation [of the Nobel Prize for Chemistry to William Francis Giauque, Dec. 12, 1949]. NOLC 3:221

TISELIUS, ARNE WILHELM KAURIN
Westgren, A.
Presentation [of the Nobel Prize for Chemistry to Arne Wilhelm Kaurin Tiselius, Dec. 13, 1948]. NOLC 3:191

TOASTMASTERS
Frustrated toastmaster. BURT:160
Suggestions for the toastmaster. BURT:56, 151
Toastmaster's responsibilities. PRS:1

TOASTS
Eliezer, C. J.
Toast to Oxford. MONS:271
Elizabeth II, Queen of England
Toast to President Ford and to the American people. JAM:22
Ford, G. R.
Toast to Queen Elizabeth. JAM:21
Kaunda, K.
Toast to President Ford. JAM:23
Løvland, J. G.
Toast to C. A. Gobat [presenting the Nobel Prize for Peace for 1902, Oslo, July 18, 1906]. NOLP 1:29
Toast to E. Ducommun [presenting the Nobel Prize for Peace, 1902]. NOLP 1:15
Prochnow, H. V.
Toast to the mayor of Copenhagen. PRS:56
Razak, T. A.
Correct words for a toast! MONS:91
Skinner, C. O.
"Bottoms up" (toast to gynecologists). HURH:311

Todd, Sir Alexander Robertus
Synthesis in the study of nucleotides (Nobel Lecture, Dec. 11, 1957). NOLC 3:522

TODD, SIR ALEXANDER ROBERTUS
Fredga, A.
Presentation [of the Nobel Prize for Chemistry to Sir Alexander Robertus Todd,

Dec. 11, 1957].
NOLC 3:519

Todd, Oliver See Ayer, A. J., jt. auth.

Toh Chin Chye
The beginnings of the city state and its achievement (Singapore, Aug. 29, 1969).
MONSA:288
Essentials of academic freedom.
MONS:379
Lesson of the Three Kingdoms.
MONS:375
The role of the university in a multi-racial society (Singapore, Nov. 28, 1968).
MONSA:291
Singapore in the eye of the storm. MONS:377

Tomonaga, Sin-Itiro
Development of quantum electrodynamics (Nobel Lecture for 1965, May 6, 1966).
NOLPH 4:126

TOMONAGA, SIN-ITIRO
Waller, I.
Presentation [of the Nobel Prize for Physics to Sin-Itiro Tomonaga, Julian Schwinger, and Richard P. Feynman, Dec. 11, 1965].
NOLPH 4:123

Tomsky, Mervin B.
Bitter and the sweet.
WALE:187
Righteous shall flourish like the palm-tree. WALE:188
Symphony of life. WALE:190

Tooke, John Horne
On the "Murders at Lexington and Concord" (at his trial for libel). BREWE 9:3633

Toombs, Robert
For secession. Same as his "Let us depart in peace"
"Let us depart in peace."
ANN 9:192; BREWE 9:3646
Robert Toombs' address to the people of Georgia. (Washington, Dec. 23, 1860).
ECH:103
Territorial acquisition and Civil War. BREWE 9:3641

Torata, Count de
Acceptance [of the Nobel Prize for Literature for Jacinto Benavente, 1922]. NOL:191

TORIES - ENGLAND
Beaconsfield, B. D.
Tory democracy. JAE:139

Törnebladh, H. R.
Presentation [of the Nobel Prize for Chemistry to Svante August Arrhenius, Dec. 11, 1903].
NOLC 1:43
Presentation [of the Nobel Prize for Physics to Antoine Henri Becquerel, Pierre Curie and Marie Sklodowska-Curie, Dec. 11, 1903].
NOLPH 1:47

TORY PARTY (GREAT BRITAIN)
See Conservative Party (Great Britain)

TOSCANINI, ARTURO
Langer, E.
Instrument of revelation.
LINR:301; LINRS:300; LINRST:370

TOTALITARIANISM
Peters, L.
What is totalitarianism?
LINR:50

TOUSSAINT L'OUVERTURE, PIERRE DOMINIQUE
Phillips, W.
Toussaint L'Ouverture.
OLIS:170

Tower, John G.
Responds to introduction.
PRS:112

Townes, Charles R.
Production of coherent radiation by atoms and molecules (Nobel Lecture, Dec. 11, 1964).
NOLPH 4:58

TOWNES, CHARLES H.
Edlén, B.
Presentation [of the Nobel

Prize for Physics to Charles H. Townes, Nikolai G. Basov, and Alexander M. Prochorov, Dec. 11, 1964]. NOLPH 4:55

TOWNSEND PLAN
Thomas, N.
Townsend Plan and cough drops. BOSR:92

TOYNBEE, ARNOLD J.
Brorby, M.
Introduces Arnold J. Toynbee, professor, author and historian of Great Britain. LYI:86

TRADE See Business; Commerce

TRADE REGULATION
Marcus, S.
Can free enterprise survive success? BA 1975-76:152
Speth, G.
Environmental regulation and the immobilization of truth. BA 1979-80:145

TRADE UNION (POLITICAL FUND) BILL
Baldwin, S. B., 1st Earl of Bewdley
Good will in industry. MCB:243; STRM:433

TRADE UNIONS See Labor Unions

Trafton, Cathy
The moral dimensions of the world food problem. BREWW:206

TRAITORS See Treason

TRANQUILIZING DRUGS
Rindo, J. P.
Life, librium, and the pursuit of happiness. LINRST:230

TRANSISTORS
Bardeen, J.
Semiconductor research leading to the point contact transistor. NOLPH 3:318
Shockley, W.
Transistor technology evokes new physics. NOLPH 3:344

TRANSMUTATION
Joliot, J. F.
Chemical evidence of the transmutation of elements. NOLC 2:369

TRANSPLANTATION OF ORGANS, TISSUES, ETC.
Carrel, A.
Suture of blood-vessels and transplantation of organs. NOLM 1:442

TRANSPORTATION See Railroads; Roads

TRANSURANIUM ELEMENTS
McMillan, E. M.
The transuranium elements: early history. NOLC 3:314
Seaborg, G. T.
The transuranium elements: present status. NOLC 3:325

TRAVEL
Benton, T. H.
"There is East; there is India." BREWE 2:429

---- See also Railroads

TREASON
Erskine, T.
In defense of Thomas Hardy. BREWE 6:2066

TREATIES
Ames, F.
Jay Treaty. BREWE 1:156
Barbour, J.
Treaties as supreme laws. BREWE 1:209
Clayton, J. M.
Clayton-Bulwer treaty and expansion. BREWE 4:1283
Macdonald, J. A.
On the treaty of Washington. BREWE 8:2891

TRIAL BY JURY
Black, H. L.
United States v. Lovett, Watson, and Dodd: opinion for the court. ANN 16:404

TRIBUTES
Abdul Rahman, T.
Dato Onn--a great leader. MONS:33

Adams, J. Q.
Life and character of Lafayette. BREWE 1:79
Brooks, P.
Character of Abraham Lincoln. BREWE 2:644
Cox, S. S.
Stephen A. Douglas and his place in history. BREWE 4:1449
Dewey, O.
Genius of Demosthenes. BREWE 5:1822
Emerson, R. W.
Memory of Burns. HURH:106
Fox, C. J.
Character of the Duke of Bedford. BREWE 6:2182
Hageman, M.
Wisdom of the heart. SCHW:177
Holmes, O. W.
Dorothy Q. HURH:139
Holmes, O. W., Jr.
John Marshall. FRIP:257
Ingersoll, R. G.
At his brother's grave. ALA:69; BREWE 7:2580; HURH:156
Jacobusse, K. D.
Big man. SCHW:204
Johnson, L. B.
Remarks to a Joint Session of the Congress, November 27, 1963. ANN 18:203
Kennedy, E. M.
Tribute to Senator Robert F. Kennedy. BA 1967-68:174; LINRS:303
Laurier, W.
Character and work of Gladstone. BREWE 7:2732
Macmillan, H.
Tribute to President Kennedy. ALA:135
Mill, J. S.
A tribute to William Lloyd Garrison. REID:395
Nair, C. V. D.
Reflections on Rabindranath Tagore. MONS:190
Ramani, R.
Man of clear vision (tribute to Adlai E. Stevenson). MONS:250
Reid, C. T.
Tribute to Dwight D. Eisenhower. BA 1968-1969:165
Roosevelt, F. D.
Undelivered Jefferson Day address. MDV:32
Stanley, A. P.
Palmerston and the duty of England (funeral oration). BREWE 9:3506
Stevenson, A. E.
Tribute to John F. Kennedy at the General Assembly of the United Nations. GRG:122; HURH:371
Tribute to a pastor's wife (2 examples). BNH:77
Vander Jagt, G.
John Marshall. SCHW:201
Vest, G. G.
Man's best friend--his dog. ALA:45; HURH:161
Wang, G. W.
Tribute to Dr. Azkir Husain (presenting him with Doctor of Laws degree). MONS:277
Wise, S. S.
Abraham Lincoln, man and American. HURH:169

---- See also Commemorative addresses; Eulogies; Memorial speeches; Responses to tributes

Trilling, Lionel
Presents T. S. Eliot. LYI:35

Trimble, Al
Keynote address NCAI Convention, October 18, 1976. MAES:233

Trimble, Chuck
Harmony--from where the sun now stands (1974). MAES:388

Trippe, Juan T.
Presents Vannevar Bush. LYI:177

Trotter, Virginia Karp
A shift in the balance. (Kansas State University, Feb. 15, 1975). BA 1974-75:148

Trotter, William Monroe
How I managed to reach the Peace Conference. (Boston, July, 1919). FON:740
Segregation destroys fellowship

and citizenship. (Washington, 1914). FON:702

Truckman, Bill
Presidential eligibility. REIR:107 (outline)

Trudell, John
Commitment. MAES:83

Truman, Harry S.
Acceptance speech, Democratic Party National Convention (Philadelphia, July 15, 1948). OLIS:262; SIN:220
Aid to Greece and Turkey. ANN 16:434; GRG:76; LAA:49
Announcement of the dropping of an atomic bomb on Hiroshima. Same as his Announcement of the first use of the atomic bomb
Announcement of the first use of the atomic bomb. ANN 16:334
Campaign speech, Harlem, New York, October 29, 1948. SIN:226
Civil Rights (February 2, 1948). ANN 16:510
Eighth annual message. Same as his Fair Deal in retrospect, January 7, 1953
Fair Deal in retrospect, January 7, 1953. STAT 3:2993
Fifth annual message. Same as his State of the Union (1950)
First annual message. STAT 3:2900
Fourth annual message. STAT 3:2961
Inaugural address. ANN 16:561; BOORA 2:891; USINAU:251
Korea and the policy of containment. Same as his Preventing a new world war
Korean crisis. Same as his Preventing a new world war
Navy Day speech on foreign policy. ANN 16:393
"Our government cannot function properly unless the President is master in his own house." Same as his Power so the President
Point Four Program. ANN 16:595
Postwar foreign policy. Same as his Navy Day speech on foreign policy
Powers of the President. (New York, May 8, 1954). HURH:316
Presents George C. Marshall. LYI:141
Presents Winston Churchill. LYI:211
Preventing a new world war. ANN 17:75; BAP:291
Second annual message. STAT 3:2939
Seventh annual message. Same as his State of the Union (1952)
Sixth annual message. STAT 3:2976
State of the Union (1950). STAT 3:2967
State of the Union (1952). STAT 3:2984
Third annual message. STAT 3:2951
Truman doctrine. Same as his Aid to Greece and Turkey
Veto of the Internal Security Act. ANN 17:35
Veto of the McCarran-Walter Immigration Act. ANN 17:131

TRUMAN, HARRY S.
Clifford, C. M.
We must renew our confidence. BA 1972-73:109
Webb, W. P.
Presents Harry S. Truman. LYI:193

TRUMAN DOCTRINE See Reconstruction, 1939-1951

Trumbull, Lyman
Announcing the death of Douglas. BREWE 9:3654

---- See also Johnson, A., jt. auth.

TRUSTS, INDUSTRIAL
Brooks, T. J.
Antitrust laws as applied to farmers. ANN 13:331
Harlan, J. M. and others
Northern Securities Company v. United States, 1904: opinion for the court and

dissenting opinion.
ANN 12:576
Jones, A. and others
Trusts in America.
ANN 12:279
McKenna, J. and others
United States v. United States Steel Corporation et al: opinion for the court and dissenting opinion.
ANN 14:258
Roosevelt, T.
Eighth annual message.
STAT 3:2296
Fifth annual message.
ANN 13:1; STAT 3:2144
First annual message.
ANN 12:433; STAT 2:2014
"I took the Canal Zone."
STAT 2:2073
Second annual message.
STAT 2:2053
Seventh annual message.
STAT 3:2240
Taft, W. H.
Third annual message: part I, December 5, 1911.
STAT 3:2432
White, E. D. and others
Standard Oil Company of New Jersey v. United States, 1911; opinion for the court and dissenting opinion. ANN 13:310

---- See also Capitalism; Corporations; Monopolies

Truth, Sojourner
When woman gets her rights man will be right. (New York, May 9 and 10, 1867).
FON:345
Woman's rights. (Akron, Ohio, 1851. Woman's Rights Convention). FON:100

TRUTHFULNESS AND FALSEHOOD
Dod, A. B.
Value of truth.
BREWE 5:1885
Mathias, C. M.
Truth in government.
BA 1972-73:60
Morley of Blackburn, J. M.
Golden art of truth-telling.
BREWE 8:3068
Shaw, G. B.
Truth by radio. JEF:396; JEFF:378
Tillich, P. J.
"What is truth?" ARS:180

Tuan Haji Ali bin Munawar
Religion in Malay society.
MONS:308

Tuanku Abdul Rahman Ibni Al-Marhum Tuanku Mohammed See Rhaman, (Paramount Ruler) Abdul d. 1960

TUBERCULOSIS
Koch, R.
The current state of the struggle against tuberculosis.
NOLM 1:169

Tucker, Benjamin R. See Jones, A., jt. auth.

Tun Abdul Razak See Razak, Tun Abdul

Tun Dr. Ismail See Rahman, Dr. Ismail bin Abdul

Tun Sir Henry H. S. Lee See Lee, Sir Henry Hau Shik

Tunku Abdul Rahman See Abdul Rahman, Tunku

Tuohy, Frank
Three windows on Japan.
MDYG:161

TURENNE, HENRI
Flechier, E.
Death of Turenne.
BREWE 6:2174

Turitz, Leo E.
Measure of greatness. WALE:192

TURKEY
Hird, P.
Suffer suffer Yeddy.
MDYG:66
Truman, H. S.
Aid to Greece and Turkey.
ANN 16:434; GRG:76; LAA:49

Turner, Frederick Jackson
Sectionalism and national unity.
ANN 14:493

Turner, Henry McNeal
How long? How long, O Heaven? (Philadelphia, August 5, 1876). FON:445
I claim the rights of a man. (Georgia, Sept. 3, 1868). FON:357
Justice or emigration should be our watchword. (Cincinnati, Nov. 1893). FON:561
Reasons for a new political party. (Atlanta, Ga., Feb. 12, 1886). FON:504

Turner, Jonathan Baldwin
Industrial university for Illinois. ANN 8:157

TURNER, NAT
Handy, A. W.
Nat Turner. FON:538

Tweed, Harrison
Presents Dillon Anderson. LYI:125
Presents Hartley Shawcross. LYI:123

Tyler, John
First annual message. STAT 1:566
Fourth annual message. STAT 1:613
From the sinks of Europe a plotter has come. (Gloucester Courthouse, Va., 1835). DAVF:140
Second annual message. STAT 1:581
Third annual message. STAT 1:598

TYLER, JOHN
Clay, H.
Noblest public virtue. BREWE 4:1271

Tyndall, John
Democracy and higher intellect. BREWE 9:3668
Origin of life. BREWE 9:3664

Tyndale, William
Use and abuse of images and relics. BREWE 9:3660

TYPHUS FEVER
Nicolle, C. J. H.
Investigations on typhus. NOLM 2:180

TYRANNY
Fox, C. J.
On the East India Bill. BREWE 6:2189
Knox, J.
Against tyrants. BREWE 7:2665
Penn, W.
Golden rule against tyranny. BREWE 8:3162

- U -

Udall, Morris K.
United States and Vietnam--what lies ahead. BA 1967-68:21

Uewaki, T.
Discovery of hidden mineral veins with the aid of plants and animals, etc. (Los Baños, Laguna, March 1, 1935). CURM:292

UNAMERICAN ACTIVITIES See United States - Congress - House of Representatives - Committee on UnAmerican Activities

UNDERDEVELOPED AREAS
Muhammad Ghazali bin Shafie
The most dramatic fact of international life. MONSA:130
Rajaratnam, S.
Urgency of real problems facing the less developed nations. MONSA:295

---- FOREIGN RELATIONS
Razak, T. A.
Problems of war and peace. MONSA:15

Undset, Sigrid
Acceptance [of the Nobel Prize for Literature, 1928]. NOB 18:167; NOL:255

UNDSET, SIGRID
Hallström, P.
Presentation [of the Nobel Prize for Literature to Sigrid Undset, 1928]. NOB 18:163; NOL:251

UNEMPLOYED
Coffman, L. D.
Adult education for the unemployed. ANN 15:98
Herndon, A.
Give the people bread. FON:770
Hopkins, H.
"... they are just like the rest of us." ROD:127
Nixon, R. M.
A new economic policy. BAAE:263
Wagner, R. F.
To feed the hungry. ROD:77

---- BLACKS
Jordan, V. E.
Unfinished business. BA 1975-76:88

Ungku Omar Ahmad
Two countries in one. MONS:331

UNION PARTY
Coughlin, C. E.
Money changers in the temple. ANN 15:388
Lemke, W.
Introduction of the aims of the Union Party of the United States. BAD:117

UNIONS, TRADE See Labor unions

UNITED FARM WORKERS ORGANIZATION COMMITTEE
Wright, T.
"Viva la Huelga." BREWW:174

UNITED MALAY NATIONAL ORGANISATION
Razak, T. A.
We will uphold concepts of parliamentary democracy. MONSA:41 selections

UNITED NATIONAL ORGANIZATION
Razak, T. A.
UMNO's twentieth milestone (20th anniversary of United Malay National Organization). MONS:53

UNITED NATIONS
Attlee, C. R.
Speech in Commons on the United Nations Charter. MCB:536
Churchill, W. L. S.
Sinews of peace (speech at Fulton, Missouri). ANN 16:365; MCB:541
De Tuncq, D.
UN: symbol or reality? SCHW:165
Evatt, H. V.
Australia and the United Nations charter. MC:161
Fraser, P.
Universal collective security--amendments to the United Nations Charter, 1945. MACS:378 sel.
Hoover, H. C.
United Nations. HURH:287
Lodge, H. C., Jr.
United Nations. HURH:344
McKeever, P.
The United States and the United Nations. BRYF:479
Moynihan, D. P.
World wide amnesty for political prisoners. BA 1975-76:65
Paul VI
Address before United Nations. BA 1965-66:67; OLIS:297
Rajaratnam, S.
Faith in United Nations charter (on admission of Singapore). MONS:421
Urgency of real problems facing the less developed nations. MONSA:295
Ramani, R.
Twenty four days in May (expression of thanks as President of Security Council of United Nations). MONS:248
Roosevelt, E. A.
United Nations. HURH:297
Stevenson, A. E.
Meaning of the United Nations. ANN 18:317
Thant, U.
Future of the United Nations. MDV:45

Vandenberg, A. H.
Sovereignty and the United Nations. ANN 16:331

---- HIGH COMMISSIONER FOR REFUGEES
Jahn, G.
Presentation of the Nobel Prize for Peace to the Office of the United Nations High Commissioner for Refugees, Dec. 10, 1955. NOLP 3:89

UNITED NATIONS CHILDREN'S FUND
Harmann, Z.
UNICEF: achievement and challenge (Nobel Lecture, Dec. 11, 1965). NOLP 3:365
Lionaes, A.
Presentation of the Nobel Prize for Peace to the United Nations Children's Fund, Dec. 10, 1965. NOLP 3:353

UNITED PARTY - NEW ZEALAND
Ward, Sir J.
The 1928 election. MACS:311 sel.

UNITED STATES
Berrien, J. M.
Effect of the Mexican conquest. BREWE 2:439
Brownlow, W. G.
Value of the American Union. BREWE 2:690
Buteyn, D. P.
Invisible abutments. SCHW:44
Calhoun, J. C.
On the internal improvement, 1817. ANN 4:457
Carter, J.
Fireside chat: unity on U. S. goals. LINRST:340
The inaugural address. DA 1976-77:18; JAM:38
Choate, R.
On American nationality (82nd anniversary of American independence). ANN 9:54
Clay, C. M.
America as a moral force. BREWE 3:1213
Aspirations for the Union. BREWE 3:1212
Clay, H.
In favor of a paternal policy of internal improvements. BREWE 4:1260
Internal improvements and the powers of Congress. ANN 4:482
Clayton, J. M.
Clayton-Bulwer treaty and expansion. BREWE 4:1283
Clifford, C. M.
We must renew our confidence. BA 1972-73:109
Cobden, R.
Small states and great achievements. BREWE 4:1336
Coolidge, C.
Destiny of America. ANN 14:409
Cox, A.
Can the dream survive? BA 1979-80:157
Dilke, C. W.
America. BREWE 5:1873
Dow, L., Jr.
Improvement in America. BREWE 5:1933
Emerson, R. W.
Young American. ANN 7:182
Hains, J.
Lamp of freedom. SCHW:6
Harding, W. G.
"It is our purpose to prosper America first." ANN 14:292
Houtman, M.
Dangers of security. SCHW:54
Humphrey, H. H., Jr.
I am optimistic about America. BA 1977-78:192
Ingersoll, C. J.
Influence of America on the mind. ANN 5:95
Johnson, L. B.
State of the Union Message, January 8, 1964. STAT 3:3156
Jones, J. L.
Who is tampering with the soul of America? LINR:211; LINRS:220
Lee, W. L.
Through the looking glass. SCHW:106
Lippmann, W.

Our world today. MDV:26
McGill, R. E.
Meaning of Lincoln today (centennial of Lincoln's speech at Cooper Institute). LINS:360
Marshall, T. R.
National power and the American peace policy (on public land sales, 1841). BREWE 8:2964
Nixon, R. M.
State of the Union message, 1972. BA 1971-72:13
Parker, T.
State of the nation (1850). ANN 8:114
Pennings, B.
New men for a new world. SCHW:153
Roosevelt, F. D.
Immigrants and revolutionists. ALA:93
Schura, C.
True Americanism. ANN 9:97
Truman, H. S.
State of the Union (1950). STAT 3:2967
State of the Union (1952). STAT 3:2984
Van Voorst, B.
Clock. SCHW:74
Worden, G.
Publican. SCHW:92

---- See also New England; Sectionalism (United States); Southern States; West, The. Also Annual messages under name of each President i.e. Jackson, A. First annual message

---- ARMY
Depew, C. M.
Military spirit in America. BREWE 5:1785
LaFollette, R. M., Sr.
Soldier's pay. GRG:36
Nies, N.
Warrior and the woman. SCHW:10
Roosevelt, T.
Seventh annual message. STAT 3:2240
Washington, G.
Address to the officers of the army. ANN 2:598

---- See also Army Appropriation Act; Conscription; Veterans - Education

---- BUDGET
Muskie, E. S.
Too many questions ... not enough answers. BA 1978-79:112

---- BUREAU OF INDIAN AFFAIRS
Sockey, C. E.
Excellence in Indian education. MAES:141
Thompson, M.
The BIA at work. MAES:57

---- CONGRESS
Clay, H.
Internal improvements and the powers of Congress. ANN 4:482
Hughes, C. E.
150th anniversary of the First Congress. HURH:237
Marshall, J.
Marbury v. Madison: opinion for the Supreme Court. ANN 4:165
Rayburn, S.
Impressive accomplishments (75th Congress). BAD:83
Roosevelt, F. D.
Message to Congress, January 4, 1939. STAT 3:2842
Message to Congress on the state of the nation, January 6, 1945. STAT 3:2882
Taft, W. H.
Fourth annual message; part III, December 19, 1912. ANN 13:366; STAT 3:2531
Wilson, W.
Appeal to the voters to return a Democratic Congress. ANN 14:166

---- For Annual addresses of various Presidents to Congress See Names of Presidents e.g. Roosevelt, F. D. First annual message

---- ---- HOUSE OF REPRESENTATIVES - COMMITTEE ON UNAMERICAN ACTIVITIES
Bosman, R. A.
Witch hunt. SCHW:128

---- ---- SENATE
Breckinridge, J. C.
Removal of the United States Senate. BLY:122
Webster, D.
Basis of the Senate. ANN 4:634

---- CONSTITUTION
Adams, J. Q.
Jubilee of the Constitution. ANN 6:470; BREWE 1:85
Blair, F. P.
On the 15th Amendment. BREWE 2:516
Brooke, E. W.
Responsibilities inherent in a constitutional democracy. BA 1973-74:74
Burger, W. E.
Bicentennial of American independence. BA 1976-77:185
Constitution, right or wrong (outline of speech celebrating Constitution Day). CUB:80
Corbin, F.
Answering Patrick Henry. BREWE 4:1394
Edmunds, G. F.
Constitution and the Electoral Commission. BREWE 5:1971
Ellsworth, O.
Union and coercion. BREWE 5:1993
Franklin, B.
Dangers of a salaried bureaucracy. BREWE 6:2199
Disapproving and accepting the Constitution. ALA:13; AND:99; BOORA 1:78; BREWE 6:2197; HURH:34; REID:393
Gallatin, A.
Constitutional liberty and executive despotism. BREWE 6:2209
Garnet, H. H.
Let the monster perish. FON:307
Hamilton, A.
Coercion of delinquent states. BREWE 6:2361
On the Federal Constitution, June 24, 1788. HURH:35
Hancock, J.
Moving the adoption of the Federal Constitution. BREWE 6:2389
Henry, P.
Against the Federal Constitution, June 5, 1788. BREWE 7:2488
Bill of Rights, June 14, 1788. BREWE 7:2484
June 4th, 1788 speech in the Virginia Ratifying Convention. BREWE 7:2478; LINS:136
Nation--not a Federation, June 14, 1788 (on eighth section of Federal Constitution). BREWE 7:2480
Hoover, H. C.
Bill of Rights. HURH:229
Jackson, A.
Veto of Maysville Road Bill. ANN 5:374
King, R.
For federal government by the people. BREWE 7:2642
Langston, J. M.
Equality before the law (anniversary of adoption of Fifteenth Amendment). FON:409
Lansing, J.
Answering Alexander Hamilton. BREWE 7:2710
Laurance, J. and others
General welfare and the limits of government authority. ANN 3:491
Lenoir, W.
Interest of the few and the liberties of the people. ANN 3:300
Lincoln, A.
First joint debate at Ottawa, August 21, 1858. ANN 9:11
Livingston, R. R.
Wealth and poverty, aristocracy and Republicanism. BREWE 7:2801
Madison, J.
Bill of Rights proposed. ANN 3:354
On the commerce clause. ANN 4:462
State sovereignty and federal supremacy. BREWE 8:2926; HURH:40
Marshall, J.
Justice and the Federal Constitution. BREWE 8:2950; FRIP:76
Convention on Ratification of

the Constitution, June 20, 1788. FRIP:90
McCulloch v. Maryland: opinion for the Supreme Court. ANN 4:530; BOORA 1:241
Martin, L.
Is the government federal or national? BREWE 8:2970
Portion of the report of the proceedings of the General Convention held at Philadelphia in 1787. ANN 3:166
Mason, G.
Natural propensity of rulers to oppress. BREWE 8:2976
---- and others
Debates in the Virginia Ratifying Convention. ANN 3:278
Monroe, J.
Federal experiments in history. BREWE 8:3041
Pendleton, E.
Liberty and government in America. BREWE 8:3156
Randolph, A. P.
The crisis of the Negro and the Constitution. FON:816
Roosevelt, F. D.
Address on Constitution Day, September 17, 1937. FRIP:317
Message to Congress, January 11, 1944. ANN 16:211; ROD:337; STAT 3:2875
Root, E.
Invisible government: Short Ballot Amendment. ANN 13:528
Smith, J.
On the Federal Constitution. ARN:385; ARS:272

---- ---- See also State rights. Also names of Bills and Resolution e.g. Foot's Resolution

---- DECLARATION OF INDEPENDENCE
Burger, W. E.
Bicentennial of American independence. BA 1976-77:185
Everheart, W. E.
We hold these truths. BA 1975-76:27

---- ---- See also Fourth of July

---- DEFENSES
Dulles, J. F.
Strategy of massive retaliation. ANN 17:250
Eisenhower, D. D.
State of the Union (January 9, 1958). STAT 3:3076
Goldwater, B. M.
Why we must be stronger militarily. BAS:92 (outline only); LAA:8
Kennedy, J. F.
Address to the nation, October 22, 1962. ANN 18:140; LAA:147; MUS:340
Undelivered Dallas speech. ANN 18:197
McNamara, R. S.
Military hardware, economic assistance and civic action. ANN 18:356
Nuclear strategy. ANN 18:527
Nixon, R. M.
Question of survival; the antiballistic missile system. BA 1968-69:9
Roosevelt, F. D.
Republican leadership and national defense. ANN 16:36
Wiesner, J. B.
Argument against the ABM. BA 1968-1969:19

---- ECONOMIC CONDITIONS
Ameringer, O.
Overproduction and underconsumption. ANN 15:129
Brandeis, L. D.
Danger of inaction: dissenting opinion for the Supreme Court on New State Ice Co. v. Liebmann, 1931. ROD:73
Church, F.
The yen to make a mark with the dollar. BA 1978-79:168
Cleveland, G.
Third annual message (second term). STAT 2:1794
Connor, J. T.
Impact on the American economy of the Vietnamese program. BA 1969-70:47
Cram, R. A.
What is a free man? ANN 15:498
Eisenhower, D. D.

Third annual message.
STAT 3:3038
Ford, G. R.
State of the Union address. JAM:31
Friedman, M.
The future of capitalism.
LINRST:243
Herndon, A.
Give the people bread.
FON:779
Hoover, H. C.
Fourth annual message.
STAT 3:3038
Holy crusade for liberty.
BAD:53
In defense of tradition.
(Detroit, 1932). ROD:39
Reassuring touch: President Hoover speaks, 1931.
ROD:15
Road to freedom.
ANN 15:384
Second annual message.
STAT 3:2772
Third annual message.
STAT 3:2783
Hopkins, H. L.
18,000,000 on relief.
ANN 15:261
Humphrey, H. H., Jr.
Anniversary of war on poverty. CAPG:174
Johnson, L. B.
War on poverty.
ANN 18:212
LaFollette, P. F.
Party of our time.
BAD:120
Long, H. P.
Sharing our wealth (January, 1935 radio speech).
ANN 15:318; BAD:109
Muench, A.
Rural families and welfare.
ANN 15:462
Roosevelt, F. D.
Address to the Commonwealth Club, September 23, 1932. ANN 15:158; ROD:31; SIN:77
American business is moving ahead. BAD:1
Fifth annual message.
STAT 3:2833
Fireside chat on the accomplishments of the New Deal. ANN 15:263
First annual message.
STAT 3:2806
Fourth annual message.
STAT 3:2827
Second annual message.
ANN 15:309; ROD:106;
STAT 3:2811
What the New Deal has done for business (campaign speech in Chicago, October 14, 1936).
ANN 15:379
Schwellenbach, L. B.
First seven years of the New Deal: let's view the record.
BAD:47
Shriver, S.
Address at the Chicago Anti-poverty Conference.
CAPG:180
Snell, B.
Bankruptcy and moral disintegration. BAD:90
Taft, R. A.
Declaration of Republican principles--the New Deal is rapidly receding. BAD:74
New problems of government.
ANN 15:571
Truman, H. S.
Fair Deal in retrospect, January 7, 1953. STAT 3:2993
Van Buren, M.
Against government aid for business losses. ANN 6:314
Wagner, R. F.
To feed the hungry. ROD:77
Wallace, H. A.
Pigs and pig iron. ANN 15:336
Webster, D.
Reception at Madison, Indiana.
OLIS:36
Wirtz, W. W.
Economic Opportunity Act of 1964. CAPG:165

---- ---- See also Business cycles; National Recovery Administration; Also Annual messages under name of each President i.e. Arthur, C. A. Third annual address

---- ECONOMIC POLICY
Chisholm, S.
Economic injustice in America today. BA 1971-72:27
Eccles, M. S.
Government spending is sound.

BAD:29
Landon, A. M.
Action challenged. ROD:162
Nixon, R. M.
A new economic policy. BAAE:263
Romney, G.
Our unique economic principles: the market place should determine price. CAPG:40
Roosevelt, F. D.
Action defended (campaign speech, October 31, 1936). ROD:168
Wagner, R. F.
Pump-priming--it is necessary for business recovery. BAD:44
Wallace, H. A.
Economic bill of rights. ANN 16:268

---- ---- See also Laissez-faire; United States - Foreign Relations

---- FEDERAL TRADE COMMISSION
Engman, L. A.
Federal Trade Commission. TAC:214

---- FOREIGN POLICY
Goldwater, B. M.
Campaign speech, Washington, D.C., October 21, 1964. SIN:345

---- ---- See United States - Foreign Relations

---- FOREIGN RELATIONS
Acheson, D.
Marshall Plan; relief and reconstruction are chiefly matters of American self-interest. LAA:55
Strategy of freedom. ANN 17:42
Baldwin, R. S.
Executive prerogative in foreign policy. ANN 7:423
Bray, C. W.
De-mystifying anti-Americanism. BA 1979-80:38
Bush, G.
Views of US foreign policy in the future. BA 1978-79:159
Calhoun, J. C.
Against general resolutions on foreign affairs. ANN 7:336
Cass, L. and others
Suitability of moral declarations in foreign policy. ANN 8:167
Dulles, J. F.
Containment or liberation? ANN 17:204
Modern foreign policy. HURH:324
Eisenhower, D. D.
Price of peace: second inaugural address. USINAU:263; USINAUG:263
Fillmore, M.
First annual message. ANN 8:109; STAT 1:792
Fulbright, J. W.
Arrogance of power. ANN 18:362
Foreign policy--old myths and new realities. ANN 18:225; HURH:374
Two Americas. BA 1965-66:115
Goldwater, B. M.
Total victory in the Cold War. ANN 18:42
Hoover, H. C.
Our national policies in this crisis. ANN 17:46
Humphrey, H. H.
Problem-solution division: a speech on the open-door policy. JEF:238; JEFF:207
Johnson, L. B.
Obligation of power. ANN 18:368
Our foreign policy must always be an extension of this nation's domestic policy. LAA:3
Second annual message. STAT 3:3161
Kennedy, J. F.
Long twilight struggle. ANN 18:54
Kissinger, H. A.
America's permanent interests. BA 1975-76:48
A review of the foreign policy. BA 1979-80:9
Statement to the Senate Foreign Relations Committee. BA 1973-74:87
Lodge, H. C., Jr.

United Nations. HURH:344
MacArthur, D.
Defends his conduct of the war in Korea. ALS:243; ANN 17:79; ARS:279; BAS:82 (outline only); BEN:113; BOSR:22; GRG:88; HURH:293; HURS:214; LINS:337
McNamara, R. S.
Address before the American Society of Newspaper Editors. BA 1966-67:160
Military hardware, economic assistance, and civic action. ANN 18:356
Nuclear strategy. ANN 18:527
Morse, W. L.
Need for a bipartisan foreign policy. ANN 17:11
Mumford, L.
Human way out. MDV:13
Nixon, R. M. and others
Opening statements: the fourth debate. GRG:106
Roosevelt, A. E.
Defense of American territorial policies. ANN 17:128
Roosevelt, F. D.
First war address before Congress. HURH:269; STAT 3:2861
Four human freedoms. ANN 16:42; ROD:278; STAT 3:2855
Message to Congress, January 4, 1939. STAT 3:2842
Restating American foreign policy: FDR's Chautauqua speech, 1936. ROD:252
Seventh annual message. STAT 3:2849
Third annual message. STAT 3:2819
Root, E.
European War and the preservation of America's ideals. ANN 14:70
Rusk, D.
Formulating foreign policy. ANN 18:20
Sanford, T.
After Vietnam, a new United States foreign policy. HOR:132
Steele, H.
House that Sam built. SCHW:25
Stevenson, A. E.
Foreign policy: the shades of gray. MDV:56
Taft, W. H.
Fourth annual message: part I, December 3, 1912. ANN 13:369
Third annual message: part II, December 7, 1911. STAT 3:2444
Truman, H. S.
Fair Deal in retrospect, January 7, 1953. STAT 3:2993
First annual message. STAT 3:2900
Navy Day speech on foreign policy. ANN 16:393
State of the Union (1952). STAT 3:2984
Vance, C. R.
Human rights and the foreign policy. BA 1976-77:127
Wallace, H. A.
Is American foreign policy leading to war? ANN 16:370
Wilson, W.
Second annual message. STAT 3:2551

---- ---- See also Economic assistance, American; Monroe Doctrine; United States - Neutrality; World War, 1939-1945 - United States - Aid to Great Britain; See also Annual messages under name of each President, i.e. Jackson, A. Second annual message

---- ---- AFRICA
Fabunmi, L.
Black and white keys. SCHW:206
Kaunda, K.
Toast to President Ford. JAM:23
Ngwa, J.
Africa and the United States--partners for peace. SCHW:192

---- ---- BARBARY STATES
Jefferson, T.
First annual message. STAT 1:58

---- ---- CANADA
Bright, J.

Will the United States subjugate Canada?
BREWE 2:620
Laurier, W.
Canada, England and the United States in 1899.
BREWE 7:2737
Stevenson, A. E.
Today's most fateful fact (accepting honorary degree of Doctor of Laws). OLIS:272

---- ---- CHINA
Brzezinski, Z.
Our China policy in a wider context. BA 1978-79:150
Fulbright, J. W.
Two Americas.
BA 1965-66:115
Kennedy, E. M.
China policy for the seventies.
BA 1968-1969:73
McGovern, G.
Ignorance curtain vs. the open door. BA 1966-67:48
Mondale, W. F.
Strengthening Sino-American relations. BA 1979-80:28

---- ---- CUBA
Castro, F.
Cuba is no longer an American colony. LAA:127
Kennedy, J. F.
Address to the nation, October 22, 1962. ANN 18:140; LAA:147; MUS:340
Stevenson, A. E.
Bay of Pigs. ANN 18:25
Premeditated attempt: the building of the sites.
LINR:87; LINRS:93

---- ---- DOMINICAN REPUBLIC
Fulbright, J. W.
Intervention in Santo Domingo: we are much closer to being the most unrevolutionary nation on earth. LAA:165
Johnson, L. B.
Johnson doctrine; why the United States intervened in the Dominican Republic.
LAA:160

---- ---- EAST (FAR EAST)
Brooke, E. W.
Report on Vietnam and East Asia. BA 1966-67:23
Harriman, W. A.
Challenges to peace and freedom. ANN 18:328
McGovern, G.
Ignorance curtain vs. the open door. BA 1966-67:48
Mansfield, M. J.
Pacific perspective.
BA 1968-69:98
Reischauer, E. O.
Statement before the Senate Foreign Relations Committee.
BA 1966-67:70

---- ---- EUROPE
Humphrey, H. H., Jr.
Open door (21st anniversary of Churchill's "Iron Curtain" speech). LINR:236

---- ---- FRANCE
Adams, J.
Third annual address.
STAT 1:49
Jackson, A.
Seventh annual message.
ANN 6:164; STAT 1:415
Sixth annual message.
STAT 1:389

---- ---- GREAT BRITAIN
Depew, C. M.
England and America since the Spanish War. BREWE 5:1790
Douglas, S. A.
"Expansion" and co-operation with England. BREWE 5:1918
Laurier, W.
Canada, England, and the United States in 1899.
BREWE 7:2737
Madison, J.
Third annual message.
STAT 1:111
See also World War, 1939-1945 - United States - Aid to Great Britain

---- ---- GREECE
Truman, H. S.
Aid to Greece and Turkey.
ANN 16:434; GRG:76; LAA:49
Webster, D. and others
Debate on the Greek Revolution. ANN 5:108

---- ---- LATIN AMERICA
Fulbright, J. W.

Two Americas.
BA 1965-66:115
Roosevelt, F. D.
Good neighbor policy.
ANN 15:352
Stimson, H. L.
United States and the Caribbean. ANN 15:72

---- ---- MEXICO
Jackson, A.
Eighth annual message.
STAT 1:445
Independence of Texas.
ANN 6:293
Tyler, J.
Fourth annual message.
STAT 1:613
Third annual message.
STAT 1:598
Van Buren, M.
First annual message.
STAT 1:472
Wilson, W.
First annual message.
STAT 3:2544
Tampico incident.
ANN 13:468
Third annual message.
STAT 3:2560

---- ---- MIDDLE EAST
Eisenhower, D. D.
Crisis in the Middle East.
ANN 17:411

---- ---- NICARAGUA See Nicaragua

---- ---- PUERTO RICO
Munoz-Marin, L.
Future of Puerto Rico.
ANN 16:312

---- ---- RUSSIA
Eisenhower, D. D.
U-2 incident (May 25, 1960).
ANN 17:550
Elleson, J.
The imbalance of power.
LINRST:135
Middendorf, J. W.
World sea power: United States vs. USSR.
LINRST:234
Nixon, R. M.
Radio-television address from Moscow. ARS:242
Stevenson, A. E.
Premeditated attempt: the building of the sites.
LINR:87; LINRS:93

---- ---- SPAIN
Cleveland, G.
Fourth annual message (second term). ANN 12:119; STAT 2:1824
Clinton, D.
Against the military spirit.
BREWE 4:1309
McKinley, W.
First annual message.
ANN 12:161; STAT 2:1858
Monroe, J.
Second annual message.
STAT 1:156
Third annual message.
STAT 1:165

---- ---- TURKEY
Truman, H. S.
Aid to Greece and Turkey.
ANN 16:434; GRG:76; LAA:49

---- ---- VIETNAM (REPUBLIC)
See Vietnamese War, 1957-1975; Vietnamese War, 1957-1975 - Moral and religious aspects

---- ---- YUCATAN
Niles, J. and others
Debate on the Yucatan Bill.
ANN 7:426

---- HISTORY
Dabney, V.
Facts and the founding fathers.
BA 1974-75:168

---- ---- COLONIAL PERIOD
Berkeley, W.
Speech to the Virginia House of Burgesses. POC:169
Mather, I.
Speech at the Boston Town Meeting. POC:172
Mulford, S.
Speech to the Assembly at New-York. POC:174

---- ---- REVOLUTION
Adams, S.
American independence.
BREWE 1:94; HURH:31

Boucher, J.
Civil liberty and nonresistance. ANN 2:343; POC:552
Burke, E.
Conciliation with America. ALS:29 (with analysis); ANN 2:312; BREWE 2:806; CLAYP:50; STRM:39
Dickinson, J.
Before the Pennsylvania Assembly, March 24, 1760. POC:182
Declaration of the Colonies on taking up arms. BREWE 5:1849
Speech against independence. ANN 2:438
Galloway, J.
Speech for the petition to change the form of government. POC:200
Henry, P.
Liberty or death. ANN 2:321; BAS:39 (outline only); BEN:13; BREWE 7:2473; HURH:27; HURS:209; OLIS:22; POC:305
Howard, J. A.
"... our sacred honor." BA 1975-76:9
Hutchinson, T.
Speech to both Houses. POC:280
Jay, J.
Protest against colonial government. BREWE 7:2601
Lee, R. H.
Address to the people of England. BREWE 7:2752
Morton, P.
Oration at the reinterment of Warren. POC:320
Pitt, W., 1708-1778
Address to the throne concerning affairs in America, November 18, 1777. ALS:105; BREWE 3:1067; BRYH:201
On American policy, January 20, 1775. CLAYP:40
On the right to tax America. STRM:11
Quincy, J., 1744-1775
"Let us look to the end." POC:295
Rutledge, J.
Speech in time of revolution. BREWE 9:3368; POC:325
Tooke, J. H.
On the "Murders at Lexington and Concord" (at his trial for libel). BREWE 9:3633
Varnum, J. M. and others
Disputation on "Whether British America can under present circumstances consistent with good policy, affect to become an independent state." POC:14
Warren, J.
Constitutional liberty and arbitrary power. BREWE 10:3727
Washington, G.
Address to the officers of the army. ANN 2:598
West, S.
Election sermon. POC:578
Wilkes, J.
Warning and a prophecy. BREWE 10:3901
Wilson, J.
In vindication of the colonies. POC:308
Zubly, J. J.
Law of liberty. POC:611

---- ---- See also Boston Massacre, 1770; Boston Tea Party, 1773; Great Britain - Colonies

---- ---- CONFEDERATION
Barlow, J.
Unfinished revolution. ANN 3:90
Witherspoon, J.
Public credit under the Confederation. BREWE 10:3912

---- ---- WAR OF 1812
Brougham and Vaux, H. P. B.
Against Pitt and war with America. BREWE 2:661
Clay, H.
Free trade and seamen's rights. BREWE 4:1264
On the War of 1812. ANN 4:327
German, O.
Unprepared for war with England. ANN 4:319
Grundy, F. and others
Debate over war with England. ANN 4:291

Madison, J.
Fifth annual message.
STAT 1:122
Fourth annual message.
STAT 1:115
Seventh annual message.
STAT 1:133
Sixth annual message.
STAT 1:129
War message. ANN 4:314
Quincy, J., 1772-1864
Against conquest of Canada.
BREWE 9:3274
Rush, R.
Fourth of July oration, 1812. HAW:16
Webster, D.
Against conscription.
ANN 4:355

---- ---- WAR WITH MEXICO
Cadwell, D.
Oration. HAW:319
Corwin, T.
War with Mexico.
BREWE 4:1405; HOW:203
Dayton, W. L.
Arraigning President Polk.
BREWE 5:1676
Polk, J. K.
Fourth annual message.
STAT 1:731
Second annual message.
STAT 1:664
Third annual message.
ANN 7:374; STAT 1:699

---- ---- CIVIL WAR
Adams, C. F.
States and the Union.
BREWE 1:25
Adams, C. F., Jr.
Battle of Gettysburg.
BREWE 1:31
Allen, E.
Call to arms (1861).
BREWE 1:150
Beecher, H. W.
Liverpool speech, October 16, 1863. LINS:229
Raising the flag over Fort Sumter. BREWE 1:347
Success of American democracy (anniversary of attack on Fort Sumter). OLIS:191
Bell, J.
Against extremism, North and South. BREWE 1:384
Benjamin, J. P.
Farewell to the Union.
BREWE 1:399
Brownlow, W. G.
Grape shot and hemp.
BREWE 2:690
Campbell, J. P.
Give us equal pay and we will go to war. FON:300
Choate, R.
Preservation of the Union.
HURH:80
Cobb, H.
Speech of Howell Cobb, at Atlanta, Georgia, May 22.
ECH:182
Colfax, S.
Confiscation of rebel property.
BREWE 4:1361
Davis, H. W.
Reasons for refusing to part company with the South.
BREWE 5:1642
Davis, J.
Against Clay and compromise.
BREWE 5:1660
Final exhortation to the Confederate people. ANN 9:557
Speech of President Davis at Richmond, June 1st, 1861.
ECH:146
Dickinson, D. S.
Rebuking Senator Clemens of Alabama. BREWE 5:1844
Doolittle, J. R.
Attitude of the West in the Civil War. BREWE 5:1891
Douglas, S. A.
Issues of 1861.
BREWE 5:1929
John Brown raid.
BREWE 5:1926
Douglass, F.
"Men of color, to arms!"
OE:49
The mission of the war.
FON:283
Drake, C. D.
Against "Copperheads."
BREWE 5:1936
Garfield, J. A.
Revolution and the logic of coercion. BREWE 6:2226
Garrison, W. L.
At Charleston, South Carolina, 1865. BREWE 6:2241
Beginning a revolution.
BREWE 6:2237

Union and slavery.
BREWE 6:2240
Green, A. M.
Let us take up the sword.
FON:249
Hill, B. H.
Little personal history.
BREWE 7:2507
Houston, S.
Sam Houston's speech at Independence, Texas, May 10. ECH:174
Johnson, A.
Presidential plan of Reconstruction. CUR:8; STAT 2:1112
King, T. S.
The two declarations of independence: 1776 and 1861.
HAW:260
Lincoln, A.
First annual message.
STAT 2:1054
Fourth annual message.
STAT 2:1097
"A house divided against itself cannot stand."
ANN 9:1; BAS:100 (outline only); BREWE 7:2777; FRIP:197; HURH:88
Message to Congress, July 5, 1861. ANN 9:268
Second annual message to Congress. BOORA 1:396; STAT 2:1068
Third annual message.
ANN 9:473; STAT 2:1084
Mason, J. M.
Speech of J. M. Mason, at Richmond, Va., June 8, 1861. EDH:166
Phillips, W.
Under the flag. MDT:119
Schurz, C.
The irrepressible conflict (1860). DAVF:130
Seward, W. H.
Irrepressible conflict.
ANN 9:32; BREWE 9:3394; HURH:99
Stephens, A. H.
On the Confederate Constitution. ECH:77
Speech of Hon. A. H. Stephens at Atlanta, Ga., April 30, 1861. ECH:157
Speech of Hon. A. H. Stephens at Richmond, Va., April 22, 1861. ECH:191
Speech of Hon. A. H. Stephens, delivered in the hall of the House of Representatives of Georgia, Nov. 14, 1860. ECH:7
Stevens, T.
Concerning wartime taxes in the North. ANN 9:335
Toombs, R.
Robert Toombs' address, to the people of Georgia.
ECH:103
Territorial acquisition and Civil War. BREWE 9:3641
Vallandigham, C. L.
Centralization and the revolutionary power of federal patronage. BREWE 10:3674
Plea to stop the war.
ANN 9:409
Voorhees, D. W.
Opposition argument in 1862.
BREWE 10:3700
Wise, H. A.
Speech of ex-governor Henry A. Wise. ECH:150
Wood, F.
Proposal for the secession of New York City. ANN 9:233

---- ---- ---- See also Confederate States of America; Reconstruction; Slavery in the United States

---- ---- ---- CAUSES
Buchanan, J.
Fourth annual message.
ANN 9:209; STAT 1:1025
Crittenden, J. J.
On the Crittenden Compromise.
ANN 9:221
Union at any price.
ANN 9:246
Davis, J.
Inaugural address in 1861.
ANN 9:238; BREWE 5:1656; ECH:137
Message to Congress, April 29, 1861. ANN 9:259
On withdrawing from the Union. BAS:71 (outline only); BREWE 5:1651; ECH:72; HURH:109
Stephens, A. H.
Sanctity of the Union.
ANN 9:199

Toombs, R.
"Let us depart in peace."
ANN 9:192; BREWE 9:3646
Wade, B. F.
On secession and the state of the union. ANN 9:220

---- ---- WAR OF 1898
Clinton, D.
Against the military spirit.
BREWE 4:1309
McKinley, W.
Second annual message.
STAT 2:1881
Third annual message.
STAT 2:1922
War message, April 11, 1898. ANN 12:173
Putnam, F.
The Negro's part in new national problems. FON:629

---- ---- EUROPEAN WAR, 1914-1918 See European War, 1914-1918

---- ---- WORLD WAR, 1939-1945 See World War, 1939-1945 - United States

---- IMMIGRATION See Immigration and emigration

---- LIBRARY OF CONGRESS
Boorstin, D. J.
Beginnings. BA 1976-77:138

---- NATIONAL CHARACTERISTICS See National characteristics, American

---- NAVY
Bayard, J. A.
Commerce and naval power.
BREWE 1:262
Cheves, L.
In favor of a stronger navy.
BREWE 3:1101
Middendorf, J. W.
World sea power: United States vs. USSR.
LINRST:234
Roosevelt, F. D.
Navy Day address on the attack on the destroyer Kearney. ANN 16:90
Roosevelt, T.
Seventh annual message.
STAT 3:2240
Sixth annual message.
STAT 3:2194
Talmage, T. D.
On Admiral Dewey and the American Navy.
BREWE 9:3584
Truman, H. S.
Navy Day speech on foreign policy. ANN 16:393

---- NEUTRALITY
Hutchins, R. M.
Drifting into suicide.
ANN 16:66
Lindberg, C. A.
Independent policy.
ANN 16:72; HURH:254; ROD:290
Roosevelt, F. D.
This nation will remain neutral. ROD:274
Taft, R. A.
Opposition to the Roosevelt war policies. ANN 16:94
Thomas, N.
America and the war.
HURH:261
Thompson, D.
Hitler's plans for Canada and the United States. HURH:257
Wilson, W.
Neutrality message to the Senate, August 19, 1914.
ANN 13:491

---- ---- See also United States - Foreign Relations

---- POLITICS AND GOVERNMENT
Barnard, D. D.
American experiment in government. ANN 6:353
The social system. HOW:106
Blair, A.
Military government.
BREWE 2:504
Calhoun, J. C.
Self-government and civilization. BREWE 3:924
Choate, R.
Necessity of compromise in American politics.
BREWE 3:1127
Clay, H.
Dictators in American politics.
BREWE 4:1224
Cleaver, E.

Political struggle in America. SMHR:166
Clinton, D. W.
Federal power and local rights. BREWE 4:1306
Conkling, R.
Stalwart standpoint. BREWE 4:1369
Door, T.
People's right to remake their constitution. ANN 7:56
Eisenhower, D. D.
Faith in the individual. CAPG:31
Hoover, H. C.
Against the proposed New Deal (October 31, 1932). ANN 15:188
Humphrey, H. H., Jr.
American system. CAPG:21
Kennedy, J. F.
History will be our judge. LINS:371
Lincoln, A.
Perpetuation of our political institutions (1837). ANN 6:424; MOP:368
Lippmann, W.
Rise of personal government in the United States. BAD:97
McGovern, G. S.
American politics: a personal view. BA 1972-73:22
Mathias, C. M.
Truth in government. BA 1972-73:60
Moynihan, D. P.
The middle of the journey. BA 1970-71:29
Reagan, R.
Time for choosing. CAPG:48
Rogers, W. P.
A brief assessment of where we stand today. BA 1974-75:54
Roosevelt, F. D.
Call for federal responsibility (October 13, 1932). ANN 15:185
Root, E.
Proper pace of political change. ANN 13:436
Thoreau, H. D.
Civil disobedience. BOORA 1:318
Wriston, W. B.
Long view of the short run. BA 1968-1969:89

---- PUBLIC LANDS
Jackson, A.
Fourth annual message. STAT 1:358
Marshall, T. R.
National power and the American peace policy (on public land sales, 1841). BREWE 8:2964
Van Buren, M.
First annual message. STAT 1:472

---- SOCIAL CONDITIONS
Barnard, D. C.
The social system. HOW:106
Chisholm, S.
It is time to reassess our national priorities. BA 1968-69:68
Clark, K. B.
Beyond dilemma. BA 1969-70:168
Fulbright, J. W.
Great Society is a sick society. LAA:10
Johnson, L. B.
Great Society (commencement address at University of Michigan). ANN 18:216; CAPG:15; MDV:108; MUS:135
King, Mrs. M. L., Jr.
We need to be united. FON:1169
Long, H. P.
Every man a king. BEN:80
Smith, M. C.
Declaration of conscience--twenty years later. BA 1969-70:133
Wilson, Woodrow
What is progress? BEN:62
Wriston, W. B.
Long view of the short run. BA 1968-69:89

---- SOCIAL POLICY
Abernathy, R. D.
The Kerner Report, promises and realities. FON:1145
Humphrey, H. H., Jr.
American system. CAPG:21
Johnson, L. B.
Second annual message. STAT 3:3161

Third annual message.
STAT 3:3171
Spottswood, S. G.
The Nixon administration's anti-Negro policy.
FON:1173

---- SUPREME COURT
Black, H. L.
United States v. Lovett, Watson, and Dodd: opinion for the court. ANN 16:404
---- and others
Korematsu v. United States: opinion for the court and dissenting opinion.
ANN 16:234
Bradley, J. P. and others
Civil rights cases: opinion for the court and dissenting opinion. ANN 10:577
Brandeis, L. D.
Ashwander rules.
ANN 15:350
Danger of inaction: dissenting opinion for the Supreme Court on New State Ice Co., v. Liebmann, 1931. ROD:73
Brennan, W. J., Jr.
Baker v. Carr: opinion for the Supreme Court.
ANN 18:130
---- and others
Ginzburg et al v. United States: opinion for the court and dissenting opinion.
ANN 18:350
Brewer, D. J.
In Re Debs: opinion for the court. ANN 12:18
Brown, H. B. and others
Plessy v. Ferguson: opinion for the court and dissenting opinion. ANN 12:92
Burges, T.
Supreme Court.
BREWE 2:729
Clark, T. C.
Sheppard v. Maxwell, warden: opinion for the court.
ANN 18:402
Davis, D.
Ex parte Milligan, 1866; opinion for the court.
ANN 10:31
Field, D. D.
In re Milligan--martial law as lawlessness.
BREWE 6:2147
In the case of McCardle--necessity as an excuse for tyranny. BREWE 6:2155
Frankfurter, F.
The judicial process and the Supreme Court, April 22, 1954. FRIP:345
Fuller, M. W. and others
United States v. E. C. Knight Company, 1895: opinion for the Supreme Court and dissenting opinion.
ANN 12:23
Hallett, B.
Sovereignty of the people (Luther v. Borden case).
ANN 7:410
Harlan, J. M. and others
Northern Securities Company v. United States, 1904: opinion for the court and dissenting opinion. ANN 12:576
Holmes, O. W., Jr.
Dissenting opinion on Abrams v. United States.
ANN 14:244; BOORA 2:666
Lochner v. New York, 1905: dissenting opinion for the Supreme Court.
BOORA 2:662
Nixon v. Herndon: opinion for the court. ANN 14:534
Hughes, C. E.
National Labor Relations Board v. Jones and Laughlin Steel Corporation, 1937: opinion for the Supreme Court. ROD:207
Schechter Poultry Corporation v. United States, 1935: opinion for the Supreme Court. ANN 15:301; ROD:186
Small step toward racial equality: opinion for the Supreme Court on Mitchell case, 1941. ROD:224
Jackson, R. H.
Court broadens the rights of citizens: the Second Flag Salute Case, 1943. ROD:214
---- and others
West Virginia Board of Education et al v. Barnette et al: opinion for the court and dissenting opinion. ANN 16:148
Jenner, W. E. and others
Proposal to limit the power of

the Supreme Court.
ANN 17:491
McKenna, J. and others
United States v. United States Steel Corporation et al: opinion for the court and dissenting opinion.
ANN 14:258
Marshall, J.
Cherokee Nation v. State of Georgia: opinion for the Supreme Court. ANN 5:427
Cohens v. Virginia, 1821: opinion for the Supreme Court. ANN 5:1
Gibbons v. Ogden, 1824; opinion for the Supreme Court. ANN 5:128
McCulloch v. Maryland: opinion for the Supreme Court. ANN 4:530; BOORA 1:241
Marbury v. Madison: opinion for the Supreme Court.
ANN 4:165
Trustees of Dartmouth College v. Woodward: opinion for the Supreme Court.
ANN 4:522
Miller, S. F. and others
Slaughter house cases, 1875: opinion for the court and dissenting opinion.
ANN 10:302
Peckham, R. W. and others
Lochner v. New York, 1905: opinion for the court and dissenting opinion.
ANN 13:8
Roosevelt, F. D.
Broadcast address, March 9, 1937 (proposal for the reform of the Federal Judiciary). ANN 15:431; FRIP:309; ROD:192
Sanford, E. T. and others
Gitlow v. New York: opinion for the court and dissenting opinion. ANN 14:476
Stone, H. F.
Fear and hysteria: the Japanese relocation, "Hirabayashi v. United States," 1943: opinion for the Supreme Court. ROD:316
Sutherland, G. and others
Adkins v. Children's Hospital: opinion for the court and dissenting opinion. ANN 14:391
New State Ice Company v. Liebmann: opinion for the court and dissenting opinion.
ANN 15:140
Taney, R. B.
Dred Scott Case: opinion for the Supreme Court.
ANN 8:440
---- and others
Charles River Bridge v. Warren Bridge: opinion for the court and dissenting opinion. ANN 6:326
Waite, M. R. and others
Munn v. Illinois, 1876: opinion for the court and dissenting opinion. ANN 10:377
Warren, E.
Brown et al. v. Board of Education of Topeka et al: opinion for the court.
ANN 17:253; BOORA 2:904
Perez v. Brownell: dissenting opinion. ANN 17:499
---- and others
Miranda v. Arizona: opinion for the court and dissenting opinion. ANN 18:427
Webster, D.
Dartmouth College case.
ANN 4:477; BREWE 10:3860
White, E. D. and others
Standard Oil Company of New Jersey v. United States, 1911: opinion for the court and dissenting opinion. ANN 13:310

---- TERRITORIAL EXPANSION
Berrien, J. M.
Conquest and territorial organization. BREWE 2:436
Beveridge, A. J.
March of the flag.
ANN 12:198; BOORA 2:622; GRG:14; LINS:276
Philippine question.
ANN 12:336; BRR:29
Butler, B. F. and others
Congressional debate on Haiti and Santo Domingo, January 13, 1869.
ANN 10:143
Calhoun, J. C.
On territorial expansion.
ANN 7:87
Grant, U. S.
For annexation (of Dominican

Republic). ANN 10:231
Hoar, G. F.
Lust of empire. ANN 12:248
Sumner, C.
Against annexation (of the Dominican Republic). ANN 10:233

UNIVERSAL NEGRO IMPROVEMENT ASSOCIATION
Garvey, M.
The principles of the Universal Negro Improvement Association. FON:748; OE:103

UNIVERSE
Lardner, D.
Plurality of worlds. BREWE 7:2716
Lovell, B.
Our present knowledge of the universe. MDYG:239

UNIVERSITIES AND COLLEGES
See Colleges and universities, e.g. Harvard University

UNIVERSITY OF CALIFORNIA
Kerr, C.
Perspectives on the prophets of doom. HOR:34

UNIVERSITY OF MALAYA
Abdul Rahman, T.
Our university; pledge to nation (installation speech as Chancellor of University of Malaya). MONS:28
Tan Chee Khoon
Monstrous piece of legislation (Internal Security Act--Malaysia). MONS:190

UNIVERSITY OF PENANG
Hamzah Sendut
Some new approaches to university education. MONSA:168

UNKNOWN SOLDIER
Fosdick, H. E.
Unknown soldier. LINS:312

UNVEILING SPEECHES See Dedication speeches

URANIUM
Hahn, O.
From the natural transmutations of uranium to its artificial fission. NOLC 3:51

URBAN LEAGUE
Jordan, V. E., Jr.
Survival. BA 1971-72:49

URBANIZATION - MALAYSIA
Muhammad Ghazali bin Shafie
Strategy for the future: role of youths in national development. MONSA:129

Urey, Harold Clayton
Science and society (at 100th anniversary Academic Convocation of Cooper Union for the Advancement of Science and Art). ARS:78
Some thermodynamic properties of hydrogen and deuterium (Nobel Lecture for 1934, Feb. 14, 1935). NOLC 2:339

UREY, HAROLD CLAYTON
Palmaer, W.
Presentation [of the Nobel Prize for Chemistry for 1934 to Harold Clayton Urey, Feb. 14, 1935]. NOLC 2:333

URSULINE COLLEGE
Gannon, A. I.
A Catholic college, yesterday and tomorrow. HOR:78

UTAH
Buchanan, J.
First annual message. STAT 1:942
Second annual message. STAT 1:969

Uvnäs, B.
Presentation [of the Nobel Prize for Physiology or Medicine to Daniel Bovet, Dec. 11, 1957]. NOLM 3:549
Presentation of the Nobel Prize for Physiology or Medicine to Julius Azelrod, Ulf Von Euler, and Bernhard Katz, Dec. 12, 1970. NOLM 4:441

- V -

V-J DAY See World War, 1939-1945 - Japan - Surrender

VALEDICTORY ADDRESSES
Binney, B.
Valedictory oration. POC:51

Vallandigham, Clement L.
Centralization and the revolutionary power of federal patronage. BREWE 10:3674
Plea to stop the war. ANN 9:409

Vallotton, Henry
Acceptance [of the Nobel Prize for Literature for Hermann Hesse, 1946]. NOB 9:237; NOL:416

Van Buren, Martin
Against government aid for business losses. ANN 6:314
First annual message. STAT 1:472
Fourth annual message. STAT 1:543
Inaugural address. USINAU:61; USINAUG:61
Second annual message. STAT 1:494
Third annual message. STAT 1:517

---- See also Sanford, N., jt. auth.

Vance, Cyrus R.
Human rights and the foreign policy (Athens, Ga., April 30, 1977). BA 1976-77:127

Vandenberg, Arthur H.
Sovereignty and the United Nations. ANN 16:331

Vander Jagt, Guy
Bonn report. SCHW:162
John Marshall. SCHW:201
Price of the best. SCHW:59

Vander Werf, Nathan
Mistaken enemy. SCHW:171

Vane, Sir Henry
Against Richard Cromwell. BREWE 10:3684
At his trial for high treason. BREWE 10:3685
Speech for duty in contempt of death. Same as his At his trial for high treason

Van Engen, Bernice
Casual approach to war. SCHW:195

Van Tatenhove, Jane E.
Echo or a voice? SCHW:115

Van't Hoff, Jacobus Henricus See Hoff, Jacobus Henricus Van't

Van Voorst, Bruce
Clock. SCHW:74

Vanzetti, Bartolomeo
Last statement in court See Sacco, N. and Vanzetti, B. Proclaim their innocence

Vargas, Jorge B.
The role of the army (Baguio, March 13, 1937). CURM:98

Varnum, James Mitchell and others (W. Williams)
Disputation on "Whether British America can under present circumstances consistent with good policy, affect to become an independent state." POC:14

VENEREAL DISEASES
Bjorklund, J.
Nice people. EHN:158; MOPR:246
Wayman, M. K.
Unmentionable diseases. LINR:224; LINRS:200

Vergniaud, Pierre Victurnien
Reply to Robespierre. BREWE 10:3692
To the camp. BREWE 10:3690

VERRES, GAIUS
Cicero, M. T.

First oration against Verres.
BREWE 3:1174

Vest, George Graham
Eulogy to the dog. Same as his Man's best friend--his dog
"He guards the sleep of his pauper master as if he were a prince." Same as his Man's best friend--his dog
Man's best friend--his dog. (Washington, 1903).
ALA:45; HURH:161

VETERANS
Brandli, W.
Taps and reveille.
SCHW:30

---- See also Pensions, Military

---- EDUCATION
Hines, F. T.
G.I. Bill of Rights.
ANN 16:215

VETERANS' DAY
Willkie, W. L.
Loyal opposition. GRG:63; HURH:243

VETO - UNITED STATES See Executive power - United States

VIETNAMESE WAR, 1957-1975
Ball, G. W.
Issue in Vietnam.
BA 1965-66:43
Barger, R. N.
Theology and amnesty.
BA 1973-74:177
Bilheimer, R. S.
Christian conscience and the Vietnam War. VI:15
Brooke, E. W.
Report on Vietnam and East Asia. BA 1966-67:23
Church, F.
Foreign policy and the generation gap. BA 1970-71:49
War without end.
BA 1969-70:27
Connor, J. T.
Impact on the American economy of the Vietnamese program. BA 1969-70:47
Fulbright, J. W.
Arrogance of power.
ANN 18:362
Great Society is a sick society.
LAA:10
Two Americas.
BA 1965-66:115
Galbraith, J. K.
On history, political economy, and Vietnam. BA 1975-76:78
Gruening, E.
United States policy and action: in Vietnam. BA 1965-66:23
Hatfield, M. O.
Reconciliation and peace.
BA 1972-73:91
Humphrey, H. H., Jr.
Campaign speech, Salt Lake City, Utah, September 30, 1968. SIN:380
Guns and butter are tied together. LAA:207
Johnson, L. B.
A president defends his policies by argument from authorities.
JEF:331; JEFF:316
Remarks to the nation (declining nomination to Presidency).
ANN 18:613; BA 1967-68:63
Speech at a joint session of the Tennessee State Legislature.
BA 1966-67:11
Speech before the National Legislative Conference.
BA 1967-68:11
Third annual message.
STAT 3:3171
Vietnam: the struggle to be free (on accepting National Freedom Award).
BA 1965-66:11
Why must we take this painful road? LAA:185
Kennan, G. F.
Statement on Vietnam.
BA 1965-66:56
Kennedy, J. F.
Vietnam--illusion and reality.
ANN 18:599
Kerry, J. F.
Vietnam veterans against the war. LINRS:244
King, M. L., Jr.
A time to break silence.
FON:1048
Lindsay, J. V.
Vietnam moratorium address.
AND:153

McCarthy, E. J.
Address on Viet Nam (February 1, 1967). REIR:117
Mansfield, M. J.
Assessment in Vietnam. BA 1967-68:49
Nixon, R. M.
Cambodia. LINRS:236
Pursuit of peace. BA 1969-70:9; ERP:145
Paul VI
Key to peace. BAS:150 (outline only)
Rostow, E. V.
Choice in foreign policy. ANN 18:605
Rowe, J. N.
An American prisoner of war in South Vietnam. LINRS:45
Udall, M. K.
United States and Vietnam--what lies ahead. BA 1967-68:21
Wald, G.
Generation in search of a future. BA 1968-69:33
Westmoreland, W. C.
Vietnam--the situation today (1967). BAS:59 (outline only)

---- MORAL AND RELIGIOUS ASPECTS
Aubert, J.
Vietnam and world peace. VI:104
Blake, E. C.
Ecumenism and peace. VI:132
Coffin, W. S., Jr.
Vietnam: a sermon. VI:64
Davis, G. R.
Vietnam War: a Christian perspective. VI:46
Evans, T. H., Jr.
Application of love. VI:90
Hall, R. O.
Fear and faith. VI:98
King, M. L., Jr.
Declaration of independence from the war in Vietnam. VI:115
Payne, J. R.
Australia and the Vietnam War. VI:75
Ramsey, R. P.
Counting the costs. VI:24
Reeves, R. A.
Journey to Hanoi. VI:83

---- NEW ZEALAND
Holyoake, K. J.
A military contribution in Vietnam, 1965. MACS:398 sel.

Vigneaud, Vincent Du
A trail of sulfur research: from insulin to oxytocin (Nobel Lecture, Dec. 12, 1955). NOLC 3:446

VIGNEAUD, VINCENT DU
Fredga, A.
Presentation [of the Nobel Prize for Chemistry to Vincent du Vigneaud, Dec. 12, 1955]. NOLC 3:443

Vincent, John
Churchill's early achievements. MDYG:50

Vinzons, Wenceslao Q.
Defects in the draft of the Constitution (Manila, Nov. 10, 1934). CURM:304

VIOLENCE
Edwards, G.
Murder and gun control. BA 1971-72:101
Fulbright, J. W.
Violence in the American character. ANN 18:206

VIRGINIA
Marshall, J.
Cohens v. Virginia, 1821: opinion for the Supreme Court. ANN 5:1

Virtanen, Artturi Ilmari
The biological fixation of nitrogen and the preservation of fodder in agriculture, and their importance to human nutrition (Nobel Lecture, Dec. 12, 1945). NOLC 3:74

VIRTANEN, ARTTURI ILMARI
Westgren, A.
Presentation [of the Nobel Prize for Chemistry to Artturi Ilmari Virtanen, Dec. 12, 1945]. NOLC 3:71

VIRUSES
Lwoff, A.
Interaction among virus, cell, and organism. NOLM 4:186
Stanley, W. M.
The isolation and properties of crystalline tobacco mosaic. NOLC 3:137

VITAMIN C
Haworth, W. N.
The structure of carbohydrates and of vitamin C. NOLC 2:414

VITAMIN K
Dam, H.
The discovery of vitamin K, its biological functions and therapeutical application. NOLM 3:8

VITAMINS
Hopkins, Sir F. G.
The earlier history of vitamin research. NOLM 2:211
Karrer, P.
Carotenoids, flavins and vitamin A and B_2. NOLC 2:433
Szent-Györgyi, A.
Oxidation, energy transfer, and vitamins. NOLM 2:440

Vogel, Julius
Colonization by public works and immigration (Budget speech, June 28, 1870). MACS:42 sel.

VOLTAIRE, FRANÇOIS MARIE AROUET DE
Hugo, V. M.
On the centennial of Voltaire's death. BREWE 7:2550

Von Braun, Wernher
Earth benefits from space and space technology (Washington, D.C., March 13, 1972). BA 1971-72:111

VON BRAUN, WERNHER
Sevareid, E.
Eulogy for Wernher Von Braun. EHN:373

Von Euler, Ulf
Adrenergic neurotransmitter functions (Nobel Lecture, Dec. 12, 1970). NOLM 4:470

VON EULER, ULF
Uvnäs, B.
Presentation [of the Nobel Prize for Physiology or Medicine to Julius Axelrod, Ulf Von Euler, and Bernhard Katz, Dec. 12, 1970]. NOLM 4:441

Voorhees, Daniel W.
Opposition argument in 1862. BREWE 10:3700
Speech in the Tilden convention. BREWE 10:3697

VOTING See Elections; Blacks - Politics and suffrage; Woman Suffrage

VOTING RIGHTS LAW OF 1965
Johnson, L. B.
Voting Rights Law of 1965--a victory for freedom. CAPG:97

- W -

Waals, Johannes Diderik van der
The equation of state for gases and liquids (Nobel Lecture, Dec. 12, 1910). NOLPH 1:254

WAALS, JOHANNES DIDERIK VAN DER
Montelius, O.
Presentation [of the Nobel Prize for Physics to Johannes Diderik Van der Waals, Dec. 12, 1910]. NOLPH 1:251

Wade, Benjamin Franklin
On secession and the state of the union. ANN 9:220
Opposition to compromise. Same as his On secession and the state of the union

WAGES
Sutherland, G. and others
Adkins v. Children's Hospital: opinion for the court and dissenting opinion. ANN 14:391

Wagner, Ralph B.
Public relations. ANN 16:285

Pump-priming--it is necessary for business recovery. BAD:44
To feed the hungry. ROD:77

Wagner-Jauregg, Julius
The treatment of dementia paralytica by malaria inoculation (Nobel Lecture, Dec. 13, 1927). NOLM 2:159

WAGNER-JAUREGG, JULIUS
Wernstedt, W.
Presentation [of the Nobel Prize for Physiology or Medicine to Julius Wagner-Jauregg, Dec. 12, 1927]. NOLM 2:155

Wah-shee, James
A land settlement--what does it mean? (Ottawa, May 24, 1974). MAES:45

Waite, Morrison Remick and others (S. J. Field)
Munn v. Illinois, 1876: opinion for the court and dissenting opinion. ANN 10:377

Wakefield, Edward Gibbon
The demand for responsible government (Auckland, June 2, 1854). MACS:86
Extending the 'frontier' of New South Wales (Parliamentary Select Committee on the Disposal of Land in Colonies, June 27, 1836). MACS:3

Waksman, Selman Abraham
Streptomycin: background, isolation, properties, and utilization (Nobel Lecture, Dec. 12, 1952). NOLM 3:370

WAKSMAN, SELMAN ABRAHAM
Wallgren, A.
Presentation [of the Nobel Prize for Physiology or Medicine to Selman Abraham Waksman, Dec. 12, 1952]. NOLM 3:365

Walbert, Richard B.
Introduces Albert L. Cole, president of Reader's Digest Association. PRS:96
Introduces Bruce Catton, historian. PRS:87
Introduces Clinton S. Sanders, chairman of the American Trucking Association. PRS:89
Introduces Dr. Ernest L. Wilkinson, president of Brigham Young University. PRS:44
Introduces Dr. Norman Vincent Peale. PRS:112
Introduces George Meany, president of the AFL-CIO. PRS:59
Introduces J. Paul Austin, president, the Coca-Cola Company. PRS:19
Introduces Jervis Langdon, Jr. PRS:16
Introduces Mark O. Hatfield, governor of Oregon. PRS:91
Introduces Senator Thurston B. Morton. PRS:97
Introduces William G. Cole, president of Lake Forest College. PRS:51
Introduces William W. Scranton, governor of Pennsylvania. PRS:109

Wald, George
Generation in search of a future. BA 1968-69:33
The molecular basis of visual excitation (Nobel Lecture, Dec. 12, 1967). NOLM 4:292

WALD, GEORGE
Bernhard, C. G.
Presentation [of the Nobel Prize for Physiology or Medicine to Ragnar Granit, Haldan Keffer Hartline, and George Wald, Dec. 12, 1967]. NOLM 4:251

Walker, Alan
Why I am a Christian pacifist. MCA:204

Walker, David
We must have unity (Boston, 1828). SMHV:11

Walker, Harold Blake
The future of the past (Washington, D.C., Sept. 20, 1970). BA 1970-71:63

Walker, Robert J.
Address to the people of Kansas. ANN 8:452

Wallace, George C.
Address on law enforcement (Miami, Fla., Aug. 29, 1967). MAC:271; MACR:312
Civil Rights Bill: fraud, sham, and hoax. MDV:175

Wallace, Henry Agard
Declaration of interdependence. ANN 15:220
Economic bill of rights. ANN 16:268
Is American foreign policy leading to war? ANN 16:370
New Farm Act--balanced abundance for farm and city. BAD:37
Pigs and pig iron. ANN 15:336
Price of peace. Same as his Is American foreign policy leading to war

Wallach, Otto
Alicyclic compounds (Nobel Lecture, Dec. 12, 1910). NOLC 1:178

WALLACH, OTTO
Montelius, O.
Presentation [of the Nobel Prize for Chemistry to Otto Wallach, Dec. 12, 1910]. NOLC 1:175

Wallack, Morton A.
And thou shalt choose life. WALE: 197
Living presence. WALE:194

Waller, Edmund
Tyrant's plea, necessity (impeaching Justice Crawley). BREWE 10:3709

Waller, Helen H.
Presents Bertrand Russell. LYI:94
Presents Estes Kefauver. LYI:230

Waller, I.
Presentation [of the Nobel Prize for Physics to Alfred Kastler, Dec. 12, 1966]. NOLPH 4:183
Presentation [of the Nobel Prize for Physics to Eugene P. Wigner, Maria Goeppert Mayer and J. Hans D. Jensen, Dec. 12, 1963]. NOLPH 4:3
Presentation [of the Nobel Prize for Physics to Hideki Yukawa, Dec. 12, 1949]. NOLPH 3:125
Presentation [of the Nobel Prize for Physics to Lev Davidovic Landau, 1962]. NOLPH 3:607
Presentation [of the Nobel Prize for Physics to Max Born and Walther Bothe, Dec. 11, 1954]. NOLPH 3:253
Presentation [of the Nobel Prize for Physics to Murray Gell-Mann, 1969]. NOLPH 4:295
Presentation [of the Nobel Prize for Physics to Robert Hofstadter and Rudolf Ludwig Mossbauer, Dec. 11, 1961]. NOLPH 3:555
Presentation [of the Nobel Prize for Physics to Sin-Itiro Tomonaga, Julian Schwinger, and Richard P. Feynman, Dec. 11, 1965]. NOLPH 4:123
Presentation [of the Nobel Prize for Physics to Sir John Douglas Cockcroft and Ernest Thomas Sinton Walton, Dec. 11, 1951]. NOLPH 3:163
Presentation [of the Nobel Prize for Physics to Willis Eugene Lamb and Polykarp Kusch, Dec. 12, 1955]. NOLPH 3:283
Presentation [of the Nobel Prize for Physics for 1945 to Wolfgang Pauli, Dec. 13, 1946]. NOLPH 3:25

Wallgren, A.
Presentation [of the Nobel Prize for Physiology or Medicine to Selman Abraham Waksman, Dec. 12, 1952]. NOLM 3:365

Walpole, Horace, 4th Earl of Orford
Debate in 1741 on wages of sailors. BREWE 10:3717; BRYH:176
Debate with Pitt in 1741. Same as his Debate in 1741 on wages of sailors

---- See also Walpole, R., jt. auth.

Walpole, Sir Robert, 1st Earl of Orford
On patriots (at motion to dismiss him from Council). BREWE 10:3724
Remarkable debate in the House of Commons on the Bill for encouraging seamen and manning the fleet. Same as his Debate in 1741 on wages of sailors

---- and others
Debate in 1741 on wages of sailors. BRYH:176

WALPOLE, SIR ROBERT 1ST EARL OF ORFORD
Wyndham, W.
Attack on Sir Robert Walpole. BREWE 10:3925

Walters, Alexander and others (B. T. Washington)
Two contrasting Black voices (April, 1899). FON:611

Walton, Ernest Thomas Sinton
The artificial production of fast particles (Nobel Lecture, Dec. 11, 1951). NOLPH 3:187

WALTON, ERNEST THOMAS SINTON
Waller, I.
Presentation [of the Nobel Prize for Physics to Sir John Douglas Cockcroft and Ernest Thomas Sinton Walton, Dec. 11, 1951]. NOLPH 3:163

Wamper, Cloud
Responds to introduction. PRS:128

Wanamaker, John
On the department store. BOORA 2:632

Wang, Gung Wu
Tribute to Dr. Zakir Husain (presenting him with Doctor of Laws degree). MONS:277

WAR
Buisson, F. E.
Changes in concepts of war and peace (Nobel Lecture, 1927, May 31, 1928). NOLP 2:35
Chalmers, T.
War and truth. BREWE 3:1024
Crittenden, J. J.
Against warring on the weak. BREWE 4:1477
DeVries, C.
Standards that stand. SCHW:15
Ducommun, E.
The futility of war demonstrated by history (Nobel Lecture for 1902). NOLP 1:17
Fosdick, H. E.
Unknown soldier. LINS:312
Gaustad, E. S.
The beginning of wisdom. CAPG:370
Geren, P.
The lie of war. CAPG:359
Hains, J.
New day dawns. SCHW:140
Ingersoll, R. G.
Vision of war, 1876 speech. BREWE 7:2582
Inozemstev, N. N.
Alternative to war. MDV:69
Levai, B.
Broken sword. SCHW:144
Loula, L. A.
Drunken orgy. SCHW:149
Roosevelt, F. D.
Quarantining the aggressors. ANN 15:502; BEN:93; BOORA 2:847; BRYF:474; ROD:263
Sumner, C.
War system of the Commonwealth of Nations. ANN 7:548
Vander Jagt, G.
Bonn report. SCHW:162
Van Engen, B.
Casual approach to war. SCHW:195
Wallace, H. A.
Is American foreign policy leading to war? ANN 16:370

---- See also Army; Disarmament; Peace; United States - Neutrality. Also Names of wars, e.g. World War, 1914-1918; World War, 1939-1945

WAR AND EDUCATION See Veterans - Education

WAR AND MORALS
Bennett, J. C.
Issue of peace: the voice of religion. BA 1965-66:142
Fosdick, H. E.
Christian conscience about war. OLIS:237

---- See also Vietnamese War, 1957-1975 - Moral and religious aspects

WAR OF 1812 See United States - History - War of 1812

WAR ON POVERTY See Poverty

Warburg, Otto Heinrich
The oxygen-transferring ferment of respiration (Nobel Lecture, Dec. 10, 1931). NOLM 2:254

WARBURG, OTTO HEINRICH
Hammarsten, E.
Presentation [of the Nobel Prize for Physiology or Medicine to Otto Heinrich Warburg, Dec. 10, 1931]. NOLM 2:251

Ward, Edward John
Petrov case. MCA:196

Ward, Sir Joseph
Advances to settlers, 1894 (New Zealand House of Representatives, Sept. 14, 1894). MACS:207
New Zealand support for the Royal Navy, 1891-1908 (New Zealand House of Representatives, Dec. 8, 1909). MACS:254
The 1928 election (Auckland, Oct. 16, 1928). MACS:311

Ward, Samuel R.
Speech on the Fugitive Slave Bill (Boston, March 25, 1850). FON:93

Warner, A. J. and others (H. C. Baldwin)
The British plot to enslave the world (2nd National Silver Convention, Washington, May, 1892). DAVF:192

Warren, Earl
Brown et al v. Board of Education of Topeka et al: opinion for the court. ANN 17:253; BOORA 2:904
Federal court congestion. ANN 17:487
Perez v. Brownell: dissenting opinion. ANN 17:499

---- and others (B. R. White)
Miranda v. Arizona: opinion for the court and dissenting opinion. ANN 18:427

WARREN, EARL
Pepper, G. W.
Presents Earl Warren. LYI:121

Warren, Joseph
Against a British Army in the Colonies. Same as his Boston Massacre
Boston Massacre (March 5, 1772). ANN 2:211; POC:237
Constitutional liberty and arbitrary power. BREWE 10:3727
Oration on the Boston Massacre, March 5, 1775. POC:245

WARREN, JOSEPH
Morton, P.
Oration at the reinterment of Warren. POC:320

Warren, Patricia
Bring forth the children. BRYF:485; MOPR:368

Washington, Booker T.
Address at the opening of the Atlanta Exposition (Sept. 18, 1895). ANN 12:9; BAPRR:255; BAS:77 (outline only); BRYF:492; FON:577; LINS:263; OE:82; SMHV:94
Address delivered at the Harvard Alumni dinner in 1896 (Boston, Mass., June, 1896). HURH:144
"The country demands that every race measure itself by the American standard." Same as his Address at the Opening of the Atlanta Exposition
Road to Negro progress. Same as his Address at the opening of the Atlanta Exposition

Speech at the Cotton States exposition. Same as his Address at the Opening of the Atlanta Exposition
There is still much to be done (New Haven, Conn., Oct. 25, 1915). FON:707
We must be a law-abiding and law-respecting people (Afro-American Council in New York, Oct. 11, 1906). FON:652

---- See also Walters, A., jt. auth.

Washington, George
Acceptance of military commission. POC:164
Acceptance of the command of the Continental Armies. Same as his Acceptance of military commission
Address to the officers of the army. ANN 2:598
Eighth annual address. ANN 3:604; STAT 1:31
Farewell address (Philadelphia, Sept. 19, 1796). ANN 3:606; BEN:18; BOORA 1:194; BREWE 10:3740; HURH:44
Fifth annual address. STAT 1:17
First annual address. STAT 1:2
First inaugural address. ANN 3:344; BOORA 1:172; BREWE 10:3737; USINAU:1; USINAUG:1
Fourth annual address. STAT 1:12
National university. Same as his Eighth annual address
Second annual address. STAT 1:4
Second inaugural address. USINAU:5; USINAUG:5
Seventh annual address. STAT 1:27
Sixth annual address. STAT 1:21
Third annual address. STAT 1:7
"Tis our true policy to steer clear of permanent alliances with any portion of the foreign world." Same as his Farewell address

WASHINGTON, GEORGE
Addams, J.
Washington's birthday. HURH:163
Clay, C. M.
The man died, but his memory lives. BLY:109
Daniel, J. W.
Dedication of the Washington Monument. BREWE 4:1608
Fuller, Z.
Tree of liberty (George Washington birthday address). ANN 5:355
Lee, H.
Funeral oration on Washington. BREWE 7:2744
Phillips, C.
Dinas Island speech on Washington. BREWE 8:3176
Potter, H. C.
Washington and American aristocracy (100th anniversary of Washington's first inauguration). BREWE 8:3225

WATER - POLLUTION
Campbell, B.
On the banks of the Wabash. KEO:226; STOT:266
Palovesik, S.
Ripples of hope. BREWW:179
Ransley, M.
The life and death of our lakes. LINRS:63

WATERGATE
Aiken, G. D.
Either impeach ... or get off his back. BA 1973-74:66
Cox, A.
Creativity in law and government. BA 1973-74:49
Ford, G. R.
First presidential address. BA 1974-75:50
Gallagher, W.
Free just free. BA 1973-74:132
Huffman, J. A.
Retrospect '73--Biblical lessons we can learn from Watergate. TAC:221
Jordan, B. C. and others
Hearings on articles of impeachment by the Committee of the Judiciary of the House of Representatives. BA 1974-75:15

Nixon, R. M.
Our long national nightmare is over--speech of resignation. BA 1974-75:43
Press conference (Watergate). BA 1973-74:24
The Watergate case. BA 1972-73:50
Richardson, E. L.
Vulnerability and vigilance. BA 1973-74:13
Rogers, W. P.
A brief assessment of where we stand today. BA 1974-75:54
Sargent, F. W.
The computer and civil liberties. BA 1973-74:141
Weicker, L. P.
The Watergate investigation. BA 1973-74:40

WATERSIDE STRIKE, 1913, NEW ZEALAND
Holland, H.
The 1913 Waterside Strike. MACS:230 sel.

Watkins, Ferre C.
Introduces Cloud Wampler, chairman of the board, Carrier Air Conditioning. PRS:126

Watkins, William J.
Our rights as men (Boston, Legislative Committee on the Militia, Feb. 24, 1853). FON:130

Watson, Arthur K.
Presents William W. Scranton. LYI:201

Watson, James Dewey
The involvement of RNA in the synthesis of proteins (Nobel Lecture, Dec. 11, 1962). NOLM 3:785

WATSON, JAMES DEWEY
Engström, A.
Presentation [of the Nobel Prize for Physiology or Medicine to Francis Harry Compton Crick, James Dewey Watson, and Maurice Hugh Frederick Wilkins, Dec. 11, 1962]. NOLM 3:751

Watson, Thomas J., Jr.
Medical care (Rochester, Minn., Nov. 19, 1970). BA 1970-71:115; BAPR:359; BAPRR:266

Watterson, Henry
The compromises of life. BLY:158

WATTERSON, HENRY
Root, E.
Introducing H. Watterson to New England Society of New York. LYI:111

WAUGH, EVELYN
Sykes, C. and others
Evelyn Waugh--the man. MDYG:11

Wauters, Charles C. M. A.
Acceptance [of the Nobel Prize for Literature for Maurice Maeterlinck, 1911]. NOL:114

WAVE MECHANICS
Schrodinger, E.
The fundamental idea of wave mechanics. NOLPH 2:305

Way, Peggy <u>See</u> Brown, Joan

Wayman, Mary Katherine
Unmentionable diseases. LINR:224; LINRS:200

WEALTH
Dewey, O.
Rust of riches. BREWE 5:1823
Long, H. P.
Every man a king. BEN:80
Sharing our wealth (January, 1935 radio speech). ANN 15:318; BAD:109
Morris, W.
Art, wealth, and riches. BRYH:422
Newman, J. H.
Property as a disadvantage. BREWE 8:3093
Rogers, W.
Education and wealth. HURH:200
Young, J.
Property under the common law (Coster v. Lorillard case). ANN 6:181

---- See also Money

WEALTH, ETHICS OF See Ethics

Wears, Isaiah C.
The Ku Klux of the North (Philadelphia, 1871). FON:378
Lincoln's colonization proposal is anti-Christian (Philadelphia, Aug. 15, 1862). FON:259

WEATHER
Clemens, S. L.
New England weather. HURH:128

Weatherford, William, Creek chief
To General Jackson. BREWE 7:2570

Weaver, Andrew Thomas
Responds to an introduction. PRS:137

Weaver, Robert C.
Negro as an American. MDV:162; SMHV:129

Weaver, Warren
Presents Sir Charles Percy Snow. LYI:171

Webb, James E.
From Runnymede to Ganymede. BA 1967-68:194

Webb, Walter Prescott
Presents Harry S. Truman. LYI:193

Webster, Daniel
Against conscription. ANN 4:355
Basis of the Senate. ANN 4:634
Bunker Hill monument (Boston, June 17, 1825). BREWE 10:3828; HURH:62; LINS:145
Contracts and corporate charters. Same as his Dartmouth College case
Dartmouth College case. ANN 4:477; BREWE 10:3860
Dartmouth College versus Woodward--on the obligation of contracts. Same as his Dartmouth College case
Eulogy on Adams and Jefferson. BREWE 10:3848
Exordium in the Knapp murder case. Same as his Knapp White murder case
For a uniform bankruptcy law. ANN 6:561
For reform of the naturalization laws. ANN 7:168
For the Bank Renewal Bill. ANN 5:535
Fourth of July oration, 1800. (Dartmouth College, July 4, 1800). HAW:1
Knapp White murder case. BREWE 10:3865
Laying the corner-stone of Bunker Hill Monument. Same as his Bunker Hill Monument
Liberty and Union. Same as his Reply to Hayne
"Mind is the great lever of all things." Same as his Bunker Hill monument
On the Clay Compromise. ANN 8:24
Plea for harmony and peace. Same as his On the Clay Compromise
Plymouth oration. BREWE 10:3846
Progress of the mechanic arts. BREWE 10:3856
Property and political power. Same as his Basis of the Senate
Railroad in New Hampshire (opening Northern Railroad). ANN 7:388
Reception at Madison, Indiana. OLIS:36
Reply to Hayne (U. S. Senate, Jan. 26, 1830). ANN 5:347; BEN:35; BREWE 10:3758; BRR:23; HOW:53
Supporting the Compromise of 1850. BREWE 10:3868
Technical progress and prosperity. ANN 6:266

---- and others (J. Randolph)
Debate on the Greek Revolution. ANN 5:108

WEBSTER, DANIEL
Parker, T.
Discourse on the death of

Daniel Webster.
BREWE 8:3137

Weicker, Lowell P., Jr.
Be a flake ... on behalf of somebody or something (Greenwich, Conn., June 15, 1979). BA 1979-80:187
Televised debates (Washington, Sept. 10, 1976). BA 1976-77:61
The Watergate investigation (New Haven, Conn., Nov. 26, 1973). BA 1973-74:40

Weinberger, Solomon
Cheerful spirit. WALE:198

Weinstein, Jacob J.
One of the thirty-six. WALE:200

Weisensel, Kathy
David: and a whole lot of other neat people. LINRST:71

Welch, Robert
More stately mansions (Chicago, June 5, 1964). DAVF:327

WELCOMING ADDRESSES
Boy and his Dad (welcome address on Father's Day). HNWM:12
Children on Children's Day (welcome address). HNWM:15
Downing, G. T.
May Hungary be free. FON:102
Forgotten man (welcome address on Father's Day). HNWM:10
Four examples of short welcome speeches to a group. BNH:48
Garran, R. R.
Royal visit. MCA:191
Girls' auxiliary (or similar girls' missionary group). HNWM:24
He's somebody special (welcome address on Father's Day). HNWM:11
Holy motherhood (welcome address on Mother's Day). HNWM:8
Howdy, pardner (outline of speech to welcome Dr. Gifford Wingate as new Chairman of the Drama and Speech Department at Texas Western College). CUB:66
Love in search of a word (welcome address on Mother's Day). HNWM:6
Men's brotherhood (for laymen's group). HNWM:23
Pictures of mother (welcome address on Mother's Day). HNWM:7
Suggestions for preparation of speech of welcome. MILS:11
Suggestions for preparation of speeches of welcome. (Teacher welcoming two business men to her classroom). With examples of. PAE:180
Welcome and introduction of coach of athletic team at awards banquet. HNWM:34
Welcome to a delegation of foreign students. HNWM:48
Welcome to a Fire Chief as speaker to a civic club. HNWM:42
Welcome to a freshman class. HNWM:50
Welcome to a new educational director (2 examples). BNH:50
Welcome to a new pastor and family (2 examples). BNH:49
Welcome to a State Attorney General as speaker at a civic club. HNWM:42
Welcome to a visiting pastor's wife. BNH:51
Welcome to adult choir members. HNWM:30
Welcome to All-sports church banquet. HNWM:33
Welcome to Baptist Training Union officers (Christian Endeavor, etc.). HNWM:27
Welcome to Boy Scout troop (or Boys' Brigade). HNWM:49
Welcome to Chief of Police as speaker at a civic club. HNWM:41
Welcome to children's choir members. HNWM:31
Welcome to church officials (Deacons, Stewards, Elders, etc.). HNWM:26

Welcome to civic affairs (Arbor Day). HNWSN:53
Welcome to civic affairs (Chamber of Commerce). HNWSN:50
Welcome to civic affairs (Christmas Tree Lighting). HNWSN:52
Welcome to civic affairs (Civic Club). HNWSN:47
Welcome to civic affairs (Dedication of historical museum). HNWSN:58
Welcome to civic affairs (Dedication of park). HNWSN:55
Welcome to civic affairs (Dedication of the school). HNWSN:54
Welcome to civic affairs (Fourth of July). HNWSN:56
Welcome to civic affairs (Groundbreaking). HNWSN:46
Welcome to civic affairs (Inauguration of club officers). HNWSN:47
Welcome to civic affairs (Inauguration of public official). HNWSN:48
Welcome to daughters at Mother-Daughter banquet. HNWM:36
Welcome to fathers at Father-Son banquet. HNWM:37
Welcome to Four H Club members. HNWM:49
Welcome to Girl Scouts (or Pioneer Girls, etc.). HNWM:50
Welcome to guest speaker at a stewardship banquet (3 examples). HNWM:60
Welcome to guest speaker at a stewardship banquet (3 examples). HNWM:60
Welcome to husbands at Ladies Civic Club. HNWM:45
Welcome to military personnel. HNWM:25
Welcome to minister as speaker at a civic club (3 examples). HNWM:43
Welcome to missionary appointee (3 examples). HNWM:57
Welcome to mothers: Mother's Day, a day of remembrance. HNWM:5
Welcome to mothers at Mother-Daughter banquet. HNWM:35
Welcome to mothers on Children's Day. HNWM:7
Welcome to new Christians (3 examples). HNWM:62
Welcome to new church member by transfer. HNWM:63
Welcome to new church members (new Christians). HNWSN:11
Welcome to new church members (transfers from other churches). HNWSN:14
Welcome to new members in civic club (3 examples). HNWM:46
Welcome to new members of church staff and family. HNWM:64
Welcome to newspaper editor as speaker at a civic club. HNWM:44
Welcome to old friends (2 examples). BNH:52
Welcome to parents and ladies of the Woman's Missionary Society on Education Day. HNWM:21
Welcome to parents at vacation Bible school commencement. HNWM:19
Welcome to public official as speaker at a civic club. HNWM:41
Welcome to returning missionary (3 examples). HNWM:55
Welcome to Royal Ambassadors (or similar Boys' Missionary group). HNWM:23
Welcome to sons at Father-Son banquet. HNWM:38
Welcome to students on Education Day. HNWM:20
Welcome to Sunday school officers. HNWM:28
Welcome to teachers on Education Day. HNWM:18
Welcome to teachers on Teacher Appreciation Day. HNWM:17
Welcome to various new church members. HNWM:64
Welcome to visitors (Ladies' weekly meeting). HNWSN:22
Welcome to visitors (Men-of-the-Church dinner). HNWSN:23
Welcome to visitors (New church member class). HNWSN:24

Welcome to visitors (Sunday evening training session). HNWSN:22
Welcome to visitors (Sunday School). HNWSN:20
Welcome to visitors (worship services). HNWSN:18
Welcome to visitors at church service (3 examples). HNWM:52
Welcome to visitors at Men-of-the Church dinners (3 examples). HNWM:39
Welcome to visitors in Sunday school (3 examples). HNWM:52
Welcome to wives of civic club members (on Ladies Day). HNWM:44
Welcome to youth choir members. HNWM:32
Welcomes for special days (Children's Day). HNWSN:42
Welcomes for special days (Church Leader Appreciation Day). HNWSN:32
Welcomes for special days (Civic Club Day). HNWSN:27
Welcomes for special days (Father's Day). HNWSN:36
Welcomes for special days (Grandparents' Day). HNWSN:38
Welcomes for special days (Home Dedication Day). HNWSN:34
Welcomes for special days (Homecoming Day). HNWSN:27
Welcomes for special days (Labor Day). HNWSN:43
Welcomes for special days (Law Day). HNWSN:28
Welcomes for special days (Law Enforcement Day). HNWSN:31
Welcomes for special days (Library Day). HNWSN:28
Welcomes for special days (Medical Day). HNWSN:41
Welcomes for special days (Mother-in-Law's Day). HNWSN:37
Welcomes for special days (Mother's Day). HNWSN:35
Welcomes for special days (Pastor Appreciation Day). HNWSN:44
Welcomes for special days (Race Relations Day). HNWSN:40
Welcomes for special days (Retirees' Day). HNWSN:29
Welcomes for special days (Staff Appreciation Day). HNWSN:31
Welcomes for special days (World Day of Prayer). HNWSN:39
Welcomes for special days (Youth Appreciation Day). HNWSN:33
Welcomes to a group. BOS:48
Welcomes to a new educational director. BOS:50
Welcomes to a new pastor and family. BOS:49
Welcomes to a visiting pastor's wife. BOS:51
Welcomes to old friends. BOS:52
What is in a name (welcome address on Father's Day)? HNWM:13
Words of welcome for visitors. BON:7

---- See also Introduction; Opening addresses; Responses to welcome; Toastmasters; Toasts

Weller, Thomas Huckle See Enders, J. F.

WELLER, THOMAS HUCKLE
Gard, S.
Presentation [of the Nobel Prize for Physiology or Medicine to John Franklin Enders, Thomas Huckle Weller, and Frederick Chapman Robbins, Dec. 11, 1954]. NOLM 3:443

Wellesley, Sir Arthur, 1st Duke of Wellington
Against Parliamentary reform. STRM:171

Wellington, James K.
A look at the fundamental school concept (Tempe, Ariz., Nov. 20, 1976). LINRST:314

Wells, Herman B.
Charge to the graduates (Indiana University, June 16, 1952). HOR:3

Wells-Barnett, Ida M.
Lynching, our national crime

(National Negro Conference, May 31, 1909). FON:687

WENDT, GERALD
Schnadig, E. L.
Presents Gerald Wendt. LYI:186

Wentworth, Peter
Liberty of the Commons (House of Commons, Feb. 7, 1576). BRYH:79; CLAYP:1
Speech in behalf of the liberties of the Parliament. Same as his Liberty of the Commons

Wentworth, Thomas, 1st Earl of Strafford See Strafford, T. W.

Wentworth, William Charles
For the University Bill. MCA:17

Werner, Alfred
On the constitution and configuration of higher-order compounds (Nobel Lecture, Dec. 11, 1913). NOLC 1:256

WERNER, ALFRED
Nordström, T.
Presentation [of the Nobel Prize for Chemistry to Alfred Werner, Dec. 11, 1913]. NOLC 1:253

Wernstedt, W.
Presentation [of the Nobel Prize for Physiology or Medicine to Julius Wagner-Jauregg, Dec. 12, 1927]. NOLM 2:155
Presentation of the Nobel Prize for 1926 to Johannes Andreas Grib Fibiger, Dec. 12, 1927]. NOLM 2:119

Wesley, John
On dressing for display. BREWE 10:3880
Poverty of reason. BREWE 10:3874
Sacra fames auri. BREWE 10:3877
Use of money. BRYH:191

Wessén, E.
Presentation [of the Nobel Prize for Literature to Halldor Kiljan Laxness, 1955]. NOB 12:3; NOL:505

West, Dick
Cultural differences: a base. MAES:120

West, Samuel
Election--sermon. POC:578

WEST, THE
Beecher, L.
A plea for the West. HOW:133
Billington, R. A.
Cowboys, Indians, and the land of promise: the world image of the American frontier. BA 1975-76:176
Thoreau, H. D.
Walking westward. ANN 8:125

WEST POINT
MacArthur, D.
Farewell to the cadets (accepting Sylvanus Thayer award for service to his nation). LINR:264; MDV:20; MUS:332
Pierce, F.
Military academy. ANN 6:273

Westgren, A.
Presentation [of the Nobel Prize for Chemistry to Arne Wilhelm Kaurin Tiselius, Dec. 13, 1948]. NOLC 3:191
Presentation [of the Nobel Prize for Chemistry to Artturi Ilmari Virtanen, Dec. 12, 1945]. NOLC 3:71
Presentation [of the Nobel Prize for Chemistry to Edwin Mattison McMillan and Glenn Theodore Seaborg, Dec. 12, 1951]. NOLC 3:309
Presentation [of the Nobel Prize for Chemistry for 1943 to George De Hevesy, Dec. 12, 1944]. NOLC 3:5
Presentation [of the Nobel Prize for Chemistry for 1944 to Otto Hahn, Dec. 13, 1946]. NOLC 3:47
Presentation [of the Nobel Prize for Chemistry to Petrus Josephus Wilhelmus Debye, Dec. 12, 1936]. NOLC 2:379
Presentation [of the Nobel Prize

for Chemistry to Willard Frank Libby, Dec. 12, 1960]. NOLC 3:589

Westmoreland, William C.
Vietnam--the situation today (1967). BAS:59 (outline only)

Weyforth, B. Stuart, Jr.
Introduces Barry Goldwater, Senator from Arizona. PRS:39
Introduces Boris Morros. PRS:66
Introduces Cornelia Otis Skinner. PRS:53
Introduces General Mark W. Clark, president of the Citadel. PRS:64
Introduces George A. Smathers, United States Senator from Florida. PRS:36
Introduces Mrs. Ivy Baker Priest, Treasurer of the United States. PRS:28
Introduces Mural Deusing. PRS:63
Introduces Nikolai Khokhlov, former Soviet intelligence officer. PRS:68
Introduces Robert C. Tyson, chairman of the finance committee, United States Steel Corporation. PRS:15

WHALEN, GROVER A.
Nizer, L.
Presents Grover A. Whalen. LYI:65

Wheeler, Alfred
Product of labor. ANN 11:113

Wheeler, Burton K.
Menace of Lend-Lease. ANN 16:46

WHIG PARTY
Sumner, C.
Antislavery duties of the Whig Party. HOW:218

Whipper, William
Eulogy on William Wilberforce (Philadelphia, Dec. 6, 1833). FON:49

Whipple, George Hoyt
Hemoglobin regeneration as influenced by diet and other factors (Nobel Lecture, Dec. 12, 1934). NOLM 2:346

WHIPPLE, GEORGE HOYT
Holmgren, I.
Presentation [of the Nobel Prize for Physiology or Medicine to George Hoyt Whipple, George Richards Minot, and William Parry Murphy, Dec. 12, 1934]. NOLM 2:335

WHISKEY INSURRECTION, 1794
Washington, G.
Sixth annual address. STAT 1:21

White, Byron R. See Warren, E., jt. auth.

White, Edward Douglas and others (J. M. Harlan)
Standard Oil Company of New Jersey v. United States, 1911: opinion for the court and dissenting opinion. ANN 13:310

WHITE, EDWARD H.
Sevareid, E.
Eulogy for the astronauts. MOP:189

White, George H.
Defense of the Negro race (Washington, D.C., Jan. 29, 1901). FON:635
I raise my voice against one of the most dangerous evils in our country (Washington, Jan. 20, 1900). FON:624

White, Richard
The educated man in the age of Aquarius (Wabash College, June 7, 1970). BAAE:271

White, Samuel
Opposition to the Louisiana Purchase. ANN 4:175

White, Walter F.
"Work or fight" in the South (1918). FON:724

White, William Allen
Speaking for the consumer (Washington, Sept. 20, 1937). HURH:234

"This is a middle-class country and the middle-class will have its will and way." Same as his Speaking for the consumer

WHITE HOUSE CONFERENCE ON CHILDREN
Nixon, R. M.
Remarks at the White House Conference on Children. BA 1970-71:37

Whitefield, George
Abraham's offering up his son Isaac. OLIS:6
Kingdom of God. BREWE 10:3885

Whitehead, Alfred North
Technical education and its relation to science and literature (London, Jan. 5, 1917). MCB:403

WHITEHEAD, W. E.
Erickson, D. J.
Presents W. E. Whitehead. LYI:63

Whitemen, Henrietta V.
Spiritual roots of Indian success. MAES:377

Whitney, Andrew Griswold
Oration (Detroit, July 4, 1818). HAW:329

Whitney, Asa
Railroad to the Pacific. ANN 7:272

Whitney, Frank L.
Total redevelopment of cities. ANN 18:338

Wieland, Heinrich Otto
The chemistry of the bile acids (Nobel Lecture for 1927, Dec. 12, 1928). NOLC 2:94

WIELAND, HEINRICH OTTO
Söderbaum, H. G.
Presentation [of the Nobel Prize for Chemistry for 1927 to Heinrich Otto Wieland and for 1928 to Adolf Otto Reinhold Windaus, Dec. 12, 1928]. NOLC 2:89

Wien, Wilhelm
On the laws of thermal radiation (Nobel Lecture, Dec. 11, 1911). NOLPH 1:275

WIEN, WILHELM
Dahlgren, E. W.
Presentation [of the Nobel Prize for Physics to Wilhelm Wien, Dec. 11, 1911]. NOLPH 1:271

Wiesner, Jerome B.
Argument against the ABM. BA 1968-1969:19
Science in the affluent society (centennial celebration of National Academy of Sciences). ANN 18:186

Wigglesworth, Michael
Prayse of eloquence. POC:8

Wigner, Eugene P.
Events, laws of nature, and invariance principles (Nobel Lecture, Dec. 12, 1963). NOLPH 4:6

WIGNER, EUGENE P.
Waller, I.
Presentation [of the Nobel Prize for Physics to Eugene P. Wigner, Maria Goeppert Mayer and J. Hans D. Jensen, Dec. 12, 1963]. NOLPH 4:3

Wilberforce, William
Horrors of the British slave trade in the eighteenth century. BREWE 10:3891

WILBERFORCE, WILLIAM
Whipper, W.
Eulogy on William Wilberforce. FON:49

WILBUR, RAY LYMAN
Merriam, J. C.
Presents Ray Lyman Wilbur. LYI:82

Wilkes, John
Denies the right of the House of Commons to reject duly elected members. STRM:39
Motion to redress. Same as his Denies the rights of the House of Commons to reject duly

elected members
Warning and a prophecy. BREWE 10:3901

WILKES, JOHN
Mansfield, W. M.
In the case of John Wilkes. BREWE 8:2943

Wilkins, Maurice Hugh Frederick
The molecular configuration of nucleic acids (Nobel Lecture, Dec. 11, 1962). NOLM 3:754

WILKINS, MAURICE HUGH FREDERICK
Engström, A.
Presentation [of the Nobel Prize for Physiology or Medicine to Francis Harry Compton Crick, James Dewey Watson, and Maurice Hugh Frederick Wilkins, Dec. 11, 1962]. NOLM 3:751

Wilkins, Roy
The conspiracy to deny equality (National Association for the Advancement of Colored People, August, 1955). FON:892; SMHV:120
Keynote address to the NAACP annual convention, Los Angeles, July 5, 1966. AND:101; BOSC:89; OE:166
Sail our NAACP ship-keynote address. Same as his Keynote address to the NAACP annual convention, Los Angeles, July 5, 1966

Wilkinson, Howard C.
How separate should government and God be? LINR:98

Willcox, William R.
Introducing G. W. Goethals to the Economic Club of New York, March 5, 1914. LYI:183

William I (the Conqueror of England)
Speech to his troops before the battle of Hastings. BRYH:27

Williams, Francis
Duty of colored men in the present national crisis. (Allegheny City, Pa., 1864). FON:281

Williams, Peter
Abolition of the slave trade. Same as his Oration on the abolition of the slave trade
Oration on the abolition of the slave trade (New York, January 1, 1808). FON:20
Slavery and colonization (St. Philip's Protestant Episcopal Church, July 4, 1830). FON:43
A tribute to Captain Paul Cuffe (New York African Institution, Oct. 21, 1817). FON:28

Williams, William See Varnum, J. M., jt. auth.

Willkie, Wendell L.
Acceptance speech. ANN 16:27; SIN:171
Campaign speech, St. Louis, Missouri, October 17, 1940. SIN:183
Consensus established. ROD:174
Education determines civilization; the importance of liberal education policies. CROCK:93
Loyal opposition (National radio address, Nov. 11, 1940). GRG:63; HURH:243
"Our American unity must be forged between the ideas of the opposition and the practices and the policies of the administration." Same as his Loyal opposition
Private enterprise--we have gone far enough down the road to federal control. BAD:69

Willstätter, Richard Martin
On plant pigments (Nobel Lecture for 1915, June 3, 1920). NOLC 1:301

Wilson, Charles Thomson Rees
On the cloud method of making visible ions and the tracks of ionizing particles (Nobel Lecture, Dec. 12, 1927). NOLPH 2:194

WILSON, CHARLES THOMSON REES
Siegbahn, K. M. G.
Presentation [of the Nobel Prize for Physics to Arthur Holly Compton and Charles Thomson Rees Wilson, Dec. 12, 1927]. NOLPH 2:169

Wilson, Dick
Real Indian leaders condemn A. I. M. MAES:63

Wilson, Edward Foss
Introduces Wilbur M. Brucker, then Secretary of the Army. PRS:41

Wilson, James
In vindication of the colonies. POC:308
Speech to the convention of the Pronvince of Pennsylvania. Same as his In vindication of the colonies
Study of law in the United States. ANN 3:380

WILSON, JOSEPH
Stanley, J.
Tribute to a fallen Black soldier. FON:268

Wilson, Logan
Education for adequacy (Univ. of Houston, June 3, 1967). HOR:16

Wilson, Orlando W.
Police arrest privileges in a free society. ANN 18:36

Wilson, Warren H.
Interaction of country and city. ANN 14:4

Wilson, Woodrow
Appeal for neutrality. Same as his Neutrality message to the Senate, August 19, 1914
Appeal for support of the League of Nations (Omaha, Nebraska speech). ANN 14:187
Appeal to the voters to return a Democratic Congress. ANN 14:166
Commission city government. ANN 13:269
Eighth annual message. STAT 3:2608
"Eyes of the people opened." STAT 3:2580
Fear of monopoly. ANN 13:356
Fifth annual message. Same as his "Eyes of the people opened."
First annual message. STAT 3:2544
First inaugural address. ANN 13:412. USINAU:199; USINAUG:199
For the League of Nations (Des Moines, Iowa speech). LINS:300
Fourteen points (Washington, Jan. 8, 1918). BOORA 2:773; FRIP:291; GRG:42; HURH:180; OLIS:228
Fourth annual message. STAT 3:2575
League of Nations. Same as his Speech at Peace Conference at Paris (Session February 15, 1919)
The nature of democracy in the United States (Owl Club in Hartford, Conn., May 17, 1889). FRIP:270
Neutrality message to the Senate, August 19, 1914. ANN 13:491
New call to duty. ALA:77
"Only a peace between equals can last." Same as his Peace without victory
Peace Conference at Paris: Session, January 25, 1919. HURH:185
Peace without victory (Washington, D.C., Jan. 21, 1917). ANN 14:65; FRIP:286; HURH:173
"The program of the world's peace, therefore, is our program." Same as his Fourteen points
Responding to the new call of duty. Same as his New call to duty
Second annual message. STAT 3:2551
Second inaugural address. USINAU:203; USINAUG:203
Seventh annual message. STAT 3:2598
Sixth annual message. STAT 3:2587

Speech at Peace Conference at Paris (Session February 15, 1919). ANN 14:180
Speech opening campaign for fourth liberty loan (Sept. 27, 1918). FRIP:295
Tampico incident. ANN 13:468
Third annual message. STAT 3:2560
"... to make permanent arrangements that justice shall be rendered and peace maintained." Same as his Peace Conference at Paris: Session, January 25, 1919
War message to Congress, April 2, 1917. ANN 14:77; HURH:177; LINS:291
"... we will not choose the path of submission and suffer the most sacred rights of our nation and our people to be ignored and violated." Same as his War message to Congress
What is progress? BEN:62

WILSON, WOODROW
Connally, T. T. and others
Censure of Senator Nye. BRR:69
Johnsen, A.
Remarks [presenting the Nobel Prize for Peace to Thomas Woodrow Wilson, 1919, Dec. 10, 1920]. NOLP 1:293
Olney, R.
Presents Woodrow Wilson. LYI:215
Schmedeman, A. G.
Acceptance [of the Nobel Prize for Peace for Woodrow Wilson, 1919, Dec. 10, 1920]. NOLP 1:294

Windaus, Adolf Otto Reinhold
Constitution of sterols and their connection with other substances occurring in nature (Nobel Lecture, Dec. 12, 1928). NOLC 2:105

WINDAUS, ADOLF OTTO REINHOLD
Söderbaum, H. G.
Presentation [of the Nobel Prize for Chemistry for 1927 to Heinrich Otto Wieland and for 1928 to Adolf Otto Reinhold Windaus, Dec. 12, 1928]. NOLC 2:89

Winnington, Thomas See Walpole, R., jt. auth.

Winter, Robert A.
This I believe. SCHW:87

Winthrop, John
"Liberty is the proper end and object of authority." Same as his Little speech on liberty
Little speech on liberty (Plymouth Colony, 1645). HURH:17; POC:135
Modell of Christian charity. BOORA 1:10

Winthrop, Robert C.
Oregon question. ANN 7:317

Wirsén, C. D. af
Presentation [of the Nobel Prize for Literature to Bjørnstjerne Martinus Bjørnson, 1903]. NOL:14; NOB 3:77
Presentation [of the Nobel Prize for Literature to Christian Matthias Theodor Mommsen, 1902]. NOL:7; NOB 13:235
Presentation [of the Nobel Prize for Literature to Frédéric Mistral and José de Echegaray y Eizaguirre, 1904]. NOL:23; NOB 13:119
Presentation [of the Nobel Prize for Literature to Giosué Carducci, 1906]. NOB 5:3; NOL:48
Presentation [of the Nobel Prize for Literature to Henryk Sienkiewicz, 1905]. NOL:36; NOB 17:173
Presentation [of the Nobel Prize for Literature to Maurice Polydore Marie Bernhard Maeterlinck, 1911]. NOB 12:139; NOL:107
Presentation [of the Nobel Prize for Literature to Paul Johann Ludwig Heyse, 1910]. NOB 7:279; NOL:100
Presentation [of the Nobel Prize for Literature to Rudyard

Kipling, 1907]. NOB 11:89; NOL:58
Presentation [of the Nobel Prize for Literature to Sully Prudhomme, 1901]. NOL:2; NOB 16:303

Wirt, William
Burr and Blennerhasset (at trial of Burr). BREWE 10:3908
Death of Jefferson and Adams. BREWE 10:3905
Genius as the capacity of work. BREWE 10:3910

Wirtz, W. Willard
Address at the Catholic University of America. BA 1966-67:177
Economic Opportunity Act of 1964. CAPG:165

Wise, Henry A.
Speech of ex-Governor Henry A. Wise. ECH:150

Wise, Stephen Samuel
Abraham Lincoln, man and American (Springfield, Ill., Feb. 12, 1914). HURH:169
"Lincoln is become for us the test of human worth." Same as his Abraham Lincoln, man and American

WIT AND HUMOR
Hazlitt, W.
On wit and humor. BREWE 7:2449

---- See also After-dinner speeches; Satiric speeches

Witherspoon, John
On eloquence. POC:44
Public credit under the Confederation. BREWE 10:3912

Witter, Jean
Statement [before the] Subcommittee on Constitutional Amendments of the Committee on the Judiciary of the U. S. Senate. (May 5-7, 1970). BOST:203

Wittstock, Laura Waterman
Native American women in the feminist milieu. (Palo Alto, Calif., March 21-22, 1975). MAES:373

Wivell, Cathy A.
World hunger: a question of rights. BREWW:119

WOLBERG, IRVING
Kosman, M.
Eulogy for Irving Wolberg. JAM:44

Wolcott, Oliver
Address at state line between Southwick, Massachusetts and Granby, Connecticut, July 4, 1825. HAW:122

Wolfe, Helen B.
The backlash phenomenon (Middle Atlantic Regional Conference, June, 1976). LINRST:85

WOMEN
Abzug, B. S.
A new kind of Southern strategy. BA 1971-72:37
Bates, D.
Bride-price. MDYG:59
Burke, Y. B.
"Aspirations ... unrequited." BA 1974-75:143
Carpenter, L.
Faces and voices of American women. BA 1977-78:184
Chisholm, S.
Women in politics. BA 1972-73:79
Clemens, S. L.
"The ladies." BEN:201
Depew, C. M.
Woman. HURH:125
Dunbar, R.
Women's liberation: where the movement is today and where it's going. STOT:311
Feldmann, M.
Of mice and women. SCHW:64
Horner, M. S.
Opportunity for educational innovation. BA 1972-73:184
Introduction for housewives (5 examples). BNH:33
Lim, P. G.
Women's role in national development. MONS:339
Nies, N.
Warrior and the woman.

SCHW:10
Peterson, M.
In these present crises.
BA 1970-71:73
Schroeder, P.
You can do it.
BA 1972-73:86
Spain, J. B.
A woman could be President.
VER:249
Steinem, G. and others
Meet the press.
BA 1972-73:65
Steinem, G.
Speech at the U. S. Naval Academy. JAM:46
Thibeault, M. L.
The hazards of equity.
VERD:265
Tribute to a pastor's wife (2 examples). BNH:77
Trotter, V. Y.
A shift in the balance.
BA 1974-75:148
Truth, S.
When woman gets her rights man will be right. FON:345
Woman's rights. FON:100
Welcome to wives of civic club members (on Ladies Day).
HNWM:44

---- BLACK
Crummell, A.
The Black woman of the South: her neglects and her needs. FON:479
Davis, A.
I am a Black revolutionary woman. FON:1177
Terrell, M. C.
The progress of colored women. FON:643

---- EDUCATION See Education of women

---- EMPLOYMENT
Furay, M.
Statement before the Subcommittee on Constitutional Amendments of the Committee on the Judiciary of the U.S. Senate.
BOST:219

---- LEGAL STATUS, LAWS, ETC.
Clay, L.
Laws of the states affecting women. BLY:199
Pankhurst, E. G.
Speech at the Bow Street Police Court. BRYF:499; BRYH:455

---- SUFFRAGE
Anthony, S. B.
Enfranchisement of women.
HURH:123
Catt, C. C.
Political parties and women voters. BRYF:506
Douglass, F.
Woman suffrage. FON:517
May, S. J.
Enfranchisement of women.
ANN 7:342
Pankhurst, E. G.
Importance of the vote.
BRYH:442
Speech at the Bow Street Police Court. BRYF:499; BRYH:455
Stanton, E. C.
Natural rights of civilized women. ANN 9:151

WOMEN AUTHORS
Yalow, R. S.
"Let us join hands, hearts and minds." BA 1977-78:181

WOMEN IN AGRICULTURE
Ferguson, V.
Women in agriculture.
BREWW:122

WOMEN'S RIGHTS
Brown, J.
Liberation struggle generates tension on race, sex issues.
BOST:265
Buckley, J.
The Equal Rights Amendment: the legislative aspect.
LINRST:271
Chisholm, S.
In support of the Equal Rights Amendment. BOST:243; EHN:364; MOPR:372
Goldman, E. and others
Statement [before the] Subcommittee on Constitutional Amendments of the Committee on the Judiciary of the U.S. Senate.
BOST:215

Green, E.
Representative Edith Green speaks in support of the Equal Rights Amendment. BOST:237
Griffiths, M. W. and others
House debates the Equal Rights Amendment. BOST:230
Holtzman, E.
Women and equality under the law. BA 1976-77:80
Springen, P. J.
The dimensions of the oppression of women. LINRS:109; LINRST:130
Witter, J.
Statement [before the] Subcommittee on Constitutional Amendments of the Committee on the Judiciary of the U. S. Senate. BOST:203
Wolfe, H. B.
The backlash phenomenon. LINRST:85

Wong, Lin Ken
Intelligentsia in a nation of immigrants (Singapore). MONS:476

Wong Lin Ken See Wong, Lin Ken

Wood, Fernando
Proposal for the secession of New York City. ANN 9:233

Woodmason, Charles
You are to take these free booters and desperadoes. POC:548

Woodward, George W. See Butler, B. F., jt. auth.

Woodward, Robert Burns
Recent advances in the chemistry of natural products (Nobel Lecture, Dec. 11, 1965). NOLC 4:100

WOODWARD, ROBERT BURNS
Fredga, A.
Presentation of the Nobel Prize for Chemistry to Robert Burns Woodward, Dec. 11, 1965. NOLC 4:97

Woolsey, John M.
Opinion December 6, 1933 (Ulysses case--freedom of reading). ANN 15:236
United States v. One book called Ulysses. Same as his Opinion December 6, 1933 (Ulysses case--freedom of reading)

Worden, George J.
Publican. SCHW:92
Person to person. SCHW:174

WORK
Furuset, A.
Work is worship. ANN 14:561
Wirt, W.
Genius as the capacity of work. BREWE 10:3190

WORKINGMEN'S PARTY OF THE UNITED STATES
Clark, P. H.
Socialism: the remedy for the evils of society. FON:451

WORLD COURT See Permanent Court of International Justice

WORLD FOOD CONFERENCE, ROME, 1974
Kissinger, H. A.
Address before the World Food Conference. BA 1974-75:62

WORLD POLITICS, 1945-
McNamara, R. S.
Address before the American Society of Newspaper Editors. BA 1966-67:160

WORLD WAR, 1939-1945
Chapuisat, E.
The activity of the International Committee of the Red Cross during the War, 1939-1945 (Nobel Lecture for 1944, Dec. 11, 1945). NOLP 2:295
Churchill, W. L. S.
Address to the Congress, December 26, 1941. ALS:223; AND:120; ARN:301; BRR:51; CROCK:29; JEF:190; JEFF:184
Hoover, H. C.
War comes to Europe. GRG:61
Mote, C. H.
The ruling oligarchy wants to

engage in a foreign war (1941). DAVF:255
Randolph, A. P.
A call for mass action. FON:822
Roosevelt, F. D.
Acceptance speech via radio to convention, Washington, D.C., July 19, 1940. SIN:156
Taft, R. A.
Opposition to the Roosevelt war policies. ANN 16:94
Vander Jagt, G.
Price of the best. SCHW:59
Willkie, W. L.
Campaign speech, St. Louis, Missouri, October 17, 1940. SIN:183

---- AERIAL OPERATIONS
Churchill, W. L. S.
Parliament in the air raids (September 17, 1940 speech). STRM:481

---- AUSTRALIA
Curtin, J.
We are fighting mad. MCA:154

---- CAMPAIGNS - WESTERN FRONT
Eisenhower, D. D.
Order of the Day to the Allied troops invading France. GRG:74
Patton, G. S.
"Flanks are something for the enemy to worry about." HURH:274

---- CHINA
Chiang, Mei-Ling
Japan is first U.S. foe. CROCK:46

---- CIVILIAN ACTIVITIES
Roosevelt, F. D.
Message to Congress, January 7, 1943. STAT 3:2867

---- GREAT BRITAIN
Bevan, A.
Change the direction of the war. MCB:524
Churchill, Sir W. L. S.
Be ye men of valour. MCB:495
"Blood, sweat and tears." ALA:99; MCB:493
Dunkirk. MCB:498
Never in the field of human conflict. MCB:514
Solemn hour (May 19, 1940 broadcast). BRYH:534
"Their finest hour." MCB:506

---- GREECE
Menzies, R. G.
Greece and the Anzac spirit. MCA:138

---- ITALY
Roosevelt, F. D.
Italy enters this war. ANN 16:8

---- JAPAN
Chiang, Mei-Ling
Japan is first U.S. foe. CROCK:46

---- ---- SURRENDER
MacArthur, D.
Hope of all mankind. ALA:105
Remarks and final speech at Japanese surrender. ANN 16:339

---- NAVAL OPERATIONS
Roosevelt, F. D.
Navy Day address on the attack on the destroyer Kearney. ANN 16:90

---- NEW ZEALAND
Savage, M. J.
New Zealand's war aims, 1939. MACS:365 sel.

---- UNITED STATES
Chiang, Mei-Ling
Japan is first U.S. foe. CROCK:46
Roosevelt, F. D.
Address at the annual gathering of the White House Correspondents' Association, February 12, 1943. ANN 16:130
Fireside chat (December 9, 1941). ANN 16:105
First war address before

Congress. HURH:269; STAT 3:2861
Message to Congress, January 7, 1943. STAT 3:2867
Message to Congress, January 11, 1944. ANN 16:211; ROD:337; STAT 3:2875
Message to Congress on the state of the nation, January 6, 1945. STAT 3:2882
Navy Day address on the attack on the destroyer Kearney. ANN 16:90
Opening campaign speech at dinner of International Brotherhood of Teamsters. LINS:330
This nation will remain neutral. ROD:274
War address (Washington, Dec. 8, 1941). ANN 16:103; CUB:88 (outline); GRG:71; HURH:265; LINS:327; MAC:242; MACR:282; MOPR:377; ROD:306
Truman, H. S.
Announcement of the first use of the atomic bomb. ANN 16:334
First annual message. STAT 3:2900

---- ---- AID TO GREAT BRITAIN
Roosevelt, F. D.
Address to White House Correspondents' Association dinner, March 15, 1941. CROCK:11
Preservation of American independence. HURH:246; OLIS:249

---- WAR AIMS
Chiang, Mei-Ling
Japan is first U.S. foe. CROCK:46

---- WAR CRIMINALS
Taft, R. A.
Equal justice under law. BEN:100

WORSHIP
Tyndale, W.
Use and abuse of images and relics. BREWE 9:3660

WOUNDED KNEE
Bellecourt, V.
American Indian Movement. MAES:66
Wilson, D.
Real Indian leaders condemn A.I.M. MAES:63

Wright, Frances
Of existing evils and their remedy. ANN 5:290

Wright, Frank Lloyd
Art and the machine. ANN 12:409
"A new integrity of human life." Same as his On architecture
On architecture (London, May, 1939). HURH:241

Wright, John S. See Sevareid, E., jt. auth.

Wright, Theodore S.
Prejudice against the colored man (Utica, N.Y., New York State Anti-Slavery Society, Sept. 20, 1837). FON:61

Wright, Tom
"Viva la Huelga." BREWW:174

Wriston, Walter B.
Long view of the short run. BA 1968-1969:89
Risk and other four-letter words (Chicago, Oct. 25, 1979). BA 1979-80:191

WRITS OF ASSISTANCE
Otis, J.
Writs of Assistance, February, 1761. ANN 2:74; BREWE 8:3125; POC:90

Wulfstan
Sermon of the Wolf to the English when the Danes persecuted them most, which was in the year 1014 from the incarnation of our Lord Jesus Christ. BRYH:21

Wycliffe, John
Concerning a grain of corn. BREWE 10:3924
Good lore for simple folk. BREWE 10:3920

Mercy to damned men in Hell.
BREWE 10:3922
Rule for decent living.
BREWE 10:3918
Sermon for the Sunday within the week of the twelfth day after Christmas, January 6--on meaning.
BRYH:38

Wydler, John W.
Science and the public trust (Schenectady, N. Y., Oct. 18, 1979).
BA 1979-80:139

Wyndham, Sir William, Bart
Attack on Sir Robert Walpole.
BREWE 10:3925
Royal prerogative delegated from the people (Army Bill, 1734).
BREWE 10:3927

- X -

Xavier S. Thani Nayagam See Thani Nayagam, Xavier S.

X-RAYS
Bragg, W. L.
The diffraction of x-rays by crystals. NOLPH 1:370
Compton, A. H.
X-rays as a branch of optics.
NOLPH 2:174
Laue, M. V.
Concerning the detection of x-ray interferences.
NOLPH 1:347

- Y -

YALE UNIVERSITY
Eliot, C. W.
Harvard and Yale.
HURH:130

Yalow, Rosalyn S.
"Let us join hands, hearts and minds" (Stockholm, Dec. 10, 1977).
BA 1977-78:181

Yamzon, Victoriano
The lawyer shall never retreat (Manila, Oct. 22, 1937).
CURM:323

Yang, Chen Ning
The law of parity conservation and other symmetry laws of physics (Nobel Lecture, Dec. 11, 1957). NOLPH 3:393

YANG, CHEN NING
Klein, O. B.
Presentation [of the Nobel Prize for Physics to Chen Ning Yang and Tsung Dao Lee, Dec. 11, 1957]. NOLPH 3:389

YANKEES See National characteristics, American

Yazzie, Ethelou
Navajo wisdom, 4th International Conference, Tarrytown, N. Y., November 1975. MAES:261
Navajo wisdom as found in Navajo oral history. MAES:263
Special problems of Indian women in education (Window Rock, Ariz., Sept. 24-25, 1975).
MAES:360

Ybarra, Barry
The wheel of poverty (Chabot College, 1971). BAPR:356; BAPRR:266

Yeang, C. H.
The building of peaceful bridge the rotary way (Penang, Sept. 27, 1970). MONSA:218

Yeats, William Butler
Acceptance [of the Nobel Prize for Literature, 1923].
NOB 18:263; NOL:199
The Irish dramatic movement (Nobel Lecture, Dec. 15, 1923).
NOL:201

YEATS, WILLIAM BUTLER
Hallström, P.
Presentation [of the Nobel Prize for Literature to William Butler Yeats, 1923].
NOB 18:275; NOL:194

YELLOW FEVER
Theiler, M.
The development of vaccines against yellow fever. NOLM 3:351

Yonge, Sir William See Walpole, R., jt. auth.

Youle, Clinton
Introduces Charles B. Thornton. PRS:100
Introduces Don Whitehead, chief of the Washington bureau of the New York Herald Tribune. PRS:65
Introduces Percy Brundage, then director of the Federal Budget. PRS:31
Introduces Stanley C. Hope, president, National Association of Manufacturers. PRS:15
Introduces W. Randolph Burgess, United States permanent representative on the North Atlantic Council. PRS:30
Presents S. Clarke Beise, president of the Bank of America. PRS:15

Young, John
Property under the common law (Coster v. Lorillard case). ANN 6:181

Young, Owen D.
How we meet ourselves (semicentennial of Hendrix College, Conway, Ark., Nov. 20, 1934). HURH:227
"You must fuse at white heat the several particles of your learning." Same as his How we meet ourselves

Young, Whitney M., Jr.
Can the city survive? Same as his Crisis of the city: the danger of the ghetto
Crisis of the city: the danger of the ghetto (54th annual Fall Conference of the National Association of Bank Loan and Credit Officers, Oct. 28, 1968). BA 1966-67:82; OE:177; SMHV:160
The social revolution: challenge to the nation (National Urban League, 1963). FON:961
A strategy for the seventies: unity, coalition, negotiation (New York, National Urban League Conference, July 19, 1970). STOT:331

YOUNG, WHITNEY M., JR.
Cheek, J. E.
A promise made, a promise to keep: Whitney Young and the nation. BA 1970-71:131

YOUNG DEMOCRATIC CLUBS OF AMERICA
Roosevelt, F. D.
Address to Young Democratic Clubs of America, August 24, 1935. FRIP:304

YOUNG MEN'S CHRISTIAN ASSOCIATION
Johari, M. K.
Malaysian Brothers (diamond jubilee of Y.M.C.A. of Kuala Lumpur). MONS:150

Youngdahl, Luther
United States v. Lattimore. ANN 17:300

YOUTH
Abbott, R. S.
A message to youth. FON:778
Ferrell, D.
Young men with visions. CAPG:385
Harper, P. C.
What's happening, baby? JEF:232; JEFF:202; KEO:252
Hutchins, R. M.
Message to the younger generation. MDV:198
Kennedy, R. F.
Address to the Free University of Berlin. MDV:95
Special message to the Congress on the nation's youth. THOMS:34
Lee Kuan Yew
Problems of leadership. MONS:371
Lim Kim San
Youth leadership. MONSA:310
Little, M.

To young people. FON:1004
Pontier, G.
Plea for understanding. SCHW:136
Roosevelt, F. D.
Address to Young Democratic Clubs of America, August 24, 1935. FRIP:304

---- ADULT RELATIONSHIP
Berson, A.
Open letter to my middle-aged father. REIR:215
Church, F.
Foreign policy and the generation gap. BA 1970-71:49
Horn, F. H.
The student revolt, a defense of the older generation. HOR:49
Perkins, J. A.
Bridging the generation gap, how the New Deal became today's establishment. HOR:56
Read, D. H. C.
Is God over thirty? Religion and the youth revolt. BA 1966-67:129
Walker, H. B.
The future of the past. BA 1970-71:63

---- RELIGIOUS LIFE
Read, D. H. C.
Is God over thirty? Religion and the youth revolt. BA 1966-67:129

YOUTH WEEK
Youth for Youth Week. HNWM:16

YUCATAN
Niles, J. and others
Debate on the Yucatan Bill. ANN 7:426

Yukawa, Hideki
Meson theory in its developments (Nobel Lecture, Dec. 12, 1949). NOLPH 3:128

YUKAWA, HIDEKI
Waller, I.
Presentation [of the Nobel Prize for Physics to Hideki Yukawa, Dec. 12, 1949]. NOLPH 3:125

- Z -

Zeeman, Pieter
Light radiation in a magnetic field (Nobel Lecture for 1902, May 2, 1903). NOLPH 1:33

ZEEMAN, PIETER
Theel, Hj.
Presentation [of the Nobel Prize for Physics to Hendrik Antoon Lorentz and Pieter Zeeman, 1902]. NOLPH 1:11

Zellner, Leon R.
What can we prove about God? (Pennsylvania State University, March 7, 1965). ARN:337; ARS:187

Zernike, Frits
How I discovered phase contrast (Nobel Lecture, Dec. 11, 1953). NOLPH 3:239

ZERNIKE, FRITS
Hulthén, E.
Presentation [of the Nobel Prize for Physics to Frits Zernike, Dec. 11, 1953]. NOLPH 3:237

Ziegler, Karl
Consequences and development of an invention (Nobel Lecture, Dec. 12, 1963). NOLC 4:6

ZIEGLER, KARL
Fredga, A.
Presentation [of the Nobel Prize for Chemistry to Karl Ziegler and Giulio Natta, Dec. 12, 1963]. NOLC 4:3

Zimbardo, Philip
Puerto Ricans and the neighborhood: a persuasive interview. STOT:305

Zimmerman, Ralph
Mingled blood. ARS:98; LINR:199

Zola, Emile
Appeal for Dreyfus. BAS:110 (outline only); BREWE 10:3931
Honor of France. Same as his Appeal for Dreyfus

Zsigmondy, Richard Adolf
Properties of colloids (Nobel Lecture for 1925, Dec. 11, 1926). NOLC 2:45

ZSIGMONDY, RICHARD ADOLF
Söderbaum, H. G.
Presentation [of the Nobel Prize for Chemistry for 1925 to Richard Adolf Zsigmondy, Dec. 11, 1926]. NOLC 2:41

Zubly, John Joachim
Law of Liberty. POC:611

Zumwalt, Elmo
Introduction to Edmund G. Brown, Jr. (August 12, 1976). JAM:33

Zwerling, Jeffrey C.
Federal government should continue its present housing program for low-income groups rather than change to the proposed rent subsidy plan. BAS:196 (outline only)

SELECTED LIST OF TITLES

EXPLANATION

Titles listed in the Selected List of Titles can be located by referring back to the Speech Index proper under the name of the author which follows each title.

Included in this list are the titles which the compiler thought would be difficult to locate for the user who does not know the name of the author, or if the meaning in the title bears no resemblance to the topic discussed, or if there are no key words in the title to guide the user to the proper subject entry. Examples of such titles are: "Acres of diamonds"; "Green parrot"; and "The strangler."

This list does not include titles which obviously may be located readily by subject or type of speech. "Liberty or death" can be found under LIBERTY.

Many titles of war speeches delivered by war leaders or by civilians are included in this list because the entry is usually under the name of a specific war rather than WAR in general.

By excluding the numerous titles under such types of speeches as INTRODUCTIONS; RESPONSES; INAUGURAL ADDRESSES; ACCEPTANCE SPEECHES, etc., much repetition was avoided, and the list kept simple enough to be quickly scanned for vaguely remembered titles, variant titles, and titles of speeches where the author is not known.

SELECTED LIST OF TITLES

Abilities and possibilities of our race - Douglass, F.
Abolition of slavery - Paul, N.
Abolition of the provinces, 1876, The - Atkinson, H.
Abolitionism is equivalent to revolution - Otis, H. G.
Abraham's offering up his son Isaac - Whitefield, G.
Acceleration or direction - Benezet, L. T.
Acres of diamonds - Conwell, R. H.
Action challenged - Landon, A. M.
Action defended - Roosevelt, F. D.
Activity of the International Committee of the Red Cross during the War, 1939-1945, The - Chapuisat, E.
Activity of the nerve fibres, The - Adrian, E. D.
Adams and Jefferson - Everett, E.
Address at Harvard University - Marshall, G. C.
Address at the Catholic University of America - Wirtz, W. W.
Address at the centennial anniversary of the Pennsylvania Society for Promoting the Abolition of Slavery - Harper, F. E. W.
Address at the memorial service for Sir Winston Churchill - Stevenson, A. E.
Address at the opening of the Atlanta Exposition - Washington, B. T.
Address at University of Pennsylvania - Roosevelt, F. D.
Address before the American Society of Newspaper Editors - McNamara, R. S.
Address before the Midwest Regional Republican Committee - Agnew, S.
Address delivered at the Harvard Alumni dinner in 1896 - Washington, B. T.
Address in honor of Robert E. Lee - Stanley, A. O.
Address of the United States Anti-Masonic Convention (1830) - Freemasons
Address on Constitution Day - Roosevelt, F. D.
Address on constitutionality of Alien and Sedition Laws - Marshall, J.
Address on law enforcement - Wallace, G. C.
Address on the King's speech - Fox, C. J.
Address to Congress - Churchill, W. L. S.
Address to Nero - Seneca, L. A.
Address to the Free University of Berlin - Kennedy, R. F.
Address to the General Assembly, Frankfort, Kentucky, April 20, 1936 - Chandler, A. B.
Address to the Humane and benevolent inhabitants of the city and county of Philadelphia - Forten, J.
Address to the people of color - Johnstone, A.
Address to the people of England - Lee, R. H.
Address to the slaves of the United States of America - Garnet, H. H.
Address to the throne concerning affairs in America, November 18, 1777 - Pitt, W., 1708-1778
Address to the unknown loyal dead - Douglass, F.
Address to Young Democratic Clubs of America - Roosevelt, F. D.
Adkins v. Children's Hospital - Sutherland, G.
Administration of Chips - Churchill, R. H. S.
Adoption of the Statute of Westminster, The - Fraser, P.
Adrenergic neurotransmitter functions - Von Euler, U.

Advances to settlers, 1894 - Ward, J. G.
Advice to ex-slaves - Delany, M. R.
Advice to young men - Bernard, Saint
Africa - Palmer, J.
Africa and freedom - Lutuli, A. J.
Africa at the Peace Table and the descendants of Africans in our American democracy - Johnson, J. W.
African origins of Black English - Taylor, O. L.
African problem and the methods of its solution - Blyden, E. W.
After Vietnam, a new United States foreign policy - Sanford, T.
Afterword: how to make a commencement speech - Kenney, B. C.
Against booted and spurred privilege - Rumbold, R.
Against Clay and compromise - Davis, J.
Against coercing America - Burke, E.
Against "Copperheads" - Drake, C. D.
Against Ctesiphon - Aeschines
Against English imperialism - Grattan, H.
Against Eratosthenes for murder - Lysias
Against extremists, North and South - Bell, J.
Against general resolutions on foreign affairs - Calhoun, J. C.
Against nonresident landlords - Parnell, C. S.
Against Pitt and war with America - Brougham and Vaux, H. P. B.
Against revenues from drunkenness and vice - Chesterfield, P. D. S.
Against standing armies - Pulteney, W.
Against the accomplices of Catiline - Cato, M. P.
Against the admission of new states - Quincy, J., 1772-1864
Against the charge of treason - Mirabeau, H. G. R.
Against the growing power of the executive - Clay, H.
Against the military spirit - Clinton, D. W.
Against the nomination of Gerald R. Ford - Nelson, G. A.
Against the radical Republicans - Johnson, A.
Against trade restrictions - Randolph, J.
Against war with Germany - LaFollette, R. M., Sr.
Against warring on the weak - Crittenden, J. J.
Against Webster and northern compromisers - Stevens, T.
Age of action - Churchill, R. H. S.
Age of food, The - Grappe, A.
Age of Gerontion - Klemme, D.
Agrees to run for President - Stevenson, A. E.
Agriculture--America's greatest tool - Stratton, T.
Agriculture--the real answer to starvation - Price, S.
Aid to democracies - Roosevelt, F. D.
Aim: a more equal society - Lee Kuan Yew
Aims and purposes of the FFA - Depta, M.
Alanine transfer RNA - Holley, R. W.
All our institutions are in disarray - Hutchins, R. M.
"All the earth is my homeland" - Abdul Rahman, T.
Alliance policy for unity - Razak, T. A.
Am I a Liberal? - Keynes, J. M.
America, a frontier - Grede, W. J.
America, America, how does your garden grow? - Reinert, P. C.
America and the war - Hutchins, R. M.; Thomas, N.
America as a moral force - Clay, C. M.
America first - Lindbergh, C. A.
American business is moving ahead - Roosevelt, F. D.
American dream - King, M. L., Jr.
American dream is at the expense of the American Negro - Baldwin, J.
American experiment in government - Barnard, D. D.
American farmer - May, C.
American fear of literature, The - Lewis, S.
American government and the Negro - Purvis, R.

American independence - Adams, S.
American Indian - Greve, D.
American Indian attitudes toward nature - Kidwell, C. S.
American Indian education and pluralism - Harris, L.
American musical comedy - Bernstein, L.
American politics - McGovern, G.
American prisoner of war in South Vietnam - Rowe, J. N.
American progress and foreign oppression - Cass, L.
American scholar - Emerson, R. W.
American system - Clay, H.; Humphrey, H. H., Jr.
American Thanksgiving for divine favor - Osgood, D.
Americanisation of British intellectual life - Beloff, M.
Americans, The - Sinclair, G.
America's permanent interests - Kissinger, H. A.
America's window to the world - Franklin, J. H.
Anarchy vs. patriotism - Goldman, E.
And old hate walked on through time - Korf, J.
And thou shalt choose life - Wallack, M. A.
Annexation of Texas and Oregon - Polk, J. K.
Announcing the Camp David accords - Carter, J.
Annual Kansas Day Republican banquet speech - McCarthy, J. R.
Answer to William J. Bryan - Cockran, W. B.
Answering Alexander Hamilton - Lansing, J.
Answering Patrick Henry - Corbin, F.
Anti-imperialists must defend Africa - Robeson, P.
Anti-Masonic Call for perseverance (1834) - Freemasons
Antineuritic vitamin and beriberi - Eijkman, C.
Antiquity of Cambridge - D'Ewes, S.
Apologia - Nixon, R. M.
Application of love - Evans, T. H., Jr.
Applications of partition chromatography - Synge, R. L. M.
Aquaculture--an answer to the food crisis - Alconcel, D.
Are they really "unteachable" - Geiman, C. K.
Areopagiticus - Isocrates
Army in domestic politics - Bristol, G. D.
Arraigning President Polk - Dayton, W. L.
Arrogance of power - Fulbright, J. W.
Arsenal of democracy - Roosevelt, F. D.
Art of contemplation - Hancher, V. M.
Art of eloquence - Caird, J.
Art of reconstruction - Goldfarb, S. D.
Article Ten - Butler, B. F.
Artificial production of fast particles, The - Walton, E. T. S.
Artificial production of radioactive elements - Joliot-Curie, I.
Artificial radioactivity produced by neutron bombardment - Fermi, E.
As the days dwindle down - Johnson, L. B.
As time runs out - Simmons, B.
Ascendency of the Union Party - Stevens, T.
Ashwander rules - Brandeis, L. D.
Asia needs the spirit of Sisyphus to succeed - Rajaratnan, S.
Aspirations for the Union - Clay, C. M.
Aspirations ... unrequited - Burke, Y. B.
Assimilation versus self-identity - Sawyer, T. E.
Astronauts on the moon - Muskie, E. S.
At Charleston, South Carolina, 1865 - Garrison, W. L.
At Cleveland in 1866 - Johnson, A.
At Ennis (boycotting defined and defended) - Parnell, C. S.
At his brother's grave - Ingersoll, R. G.
At St. Louis - Johnson, A.
At the sound of the trumpet - Mather, C.
Attack on orthodox Calvinism - Channing, W. E.
Auckland Riot, 1932, The - Lee, J. A.

Authors and their patrons - Thackeray, W. M.
Autonomy of the executive - Jackson, A.
Avarice and usury - Chrysostom, J.

- B -

Backlash phenomenon, The - Wolfe, H. B.
Baker v. Carr - Brennan, W. J., Jr.
Ballot or the bullet - Little, M.
Bandung address - Romulo, C. P.
Bankruptcy and moral disintegration - Shell, B.
Barriers of race can be surmounted - Bunche, R. J.
Basic objectives of M.I.C. - Sambanthan, V. T.
Basis of our unity - Abdul Rahman, T.
Be a flake ... on behalf of somebody or something - Weicker, L. P., Jr.
Be a harmonising factor - Sambanthan, V. T.
Be strong and of good courage - Chiu Ban It
Be ye men of valour - Churchill, W. L. S.
"Beat" generation - Brown, J. M.
Beauties of Japheth and the story of Shem - Rubel, C. M.
Before her time - Klein, L.
Before the Diet of Worms - Luther, M.
Before the Pennsylvania Assembly, March 24, 1765 - Dickinson, J.
Beginning a revolution - Garrison, W. L.
Beginning of a new realism in Malaysia, The - Razak, T. A.
Beginning of wisdom - Gaustad, E. S.
Beginnings - Boorstin, D. J.
Beginnings of the city state and its achievement, The - Toh Chin Chye
Behind the scenes in oratory - Schrier, W.
Behold the land - DuBois, W. E. B.
Bench and bar - Choate, J. H.
Berlin crisis - Kennedy, J. F.
Beyond the dilemma - Clark, K. B.
BIA at work, The - Thompson, M.
A biblical faith for a president - Moore, P.
Bicentennial of American independence - Burger, W. E.
Big challenges ahead - Abdul Rahman, T.
Big government: real or imaginary? - Hart, G.
Big man - Jacobusse, K. D.
Big question before us, The - Tan Siew Sin
Bill of Rights - Hoover, H. C.
Biography of an angel - Goldman, I. M.
Biologic synthesis of deoxyribonucleic acid, The - Kornberg, A.
Biological fixation of nitrogen and the preservation of fodder in agriculture, and their importance to human nutrition, The - Virtanen, A. I.
Biological synthesis of cholesterol, The - Bloch, K.
Bitter and the sweet - Tomsky, M. B.
Black agenda for the 1980s, The - Jordan, V.
Black and Jewish communities - Jordan, V. E., Jr.
Black and white keys - Fabunmi, L.
'Black budget' 1958, The - Nordmeyer, A.
Black community and the university - Karenga, M. R.
Black manifesto - Forman, J.
Black-operated firm - Goodloe, J. W.
Black power - Carmichael, S.
Black revolution - Little, M.
Black woman of the South - Crummell, A.
Blacks and the Nixon administration - Jordan, V. E., Jr.
"Blifil and black George--Puritan and blacklet" - Randolph, J.
"Blood, sweat and tears" - Churchill, W. L. S.
Bondmen and freemen - Ball, J.
Bonn report - Vander Jagt, G.
Book of life - Goldman, I. M.
Books and civilization in America - Choate, R.
Bootstraps and moonshots - Swets, P.
Boston Massacre - Hancock, J.
"Bostonian Ebenezer" - Mather, C.
"Bottoms up" - Skinner, C. O.

Break up the plantation system - Cardozo, F. L.
Bride-price - Bates, D.
Bridge of communication - Razak, T. A.
Bridge of love - Swarensky, M. E.
Bridges to human dignity - Nixon, R. M.
Bridging the gap - Kermicle, J.
Bridging the generation gap, how the New Deal became today's establishment - Perkins, J. A.
Bridging the generation gap, the march downtown - Odegaard, C. E.
Brief assessment of where we stand today - Rogers, W. P.
A brief sketch of the Philippines--past, present and future - Paredes, Q.
Brief sojourn - Finkle, J. J.
Brighter future for all peoples of Singapore if ... - Lee Kuan Yew
Bring forth the children - Warren, P.
British plot to enslave the world - Warner, A. J.
Broadcast address, March 9, 1937 (Proposal for the reform of the Federal Judiciary) - Roosevelt, F. D.
Broadcast journalism: serving the democratic process - Goodman, J. B.
Broadcaster talks to his colleagues - Murrow, E. R.
Broken sword - Levai, B.
Brotherhood and understanding - George, D.
Brotherly love: foundation of peace - Pire, G.
Brown decision, pluralism, and the schools in the 1980s, The - Howe, H., II
Brown, et al. v. Board of Education of Topeka - Warren, E.
Brownsville affair - Miller, K.
Budget - Lloyd George, D.
Building a better rural community today for a better agriculture tomorrow - Morgan, M.
Building of peaceful bridge the rotary way, The - Yeang, C. H.
Bunker Hill monument - Webster, D.
Business and the press: is the press anti-business? - Sulzberger, A. O.
Business's responsibility in an information society - McGraw, H. W.

- C -

California and Mexico - Polk, J. K.
Call for a change in our Indian policy - Bruce, B. K.
Call for federal responsibility - Roosevelt, F. D.
A call for liberal and conservative parties, 1876 - Stout, R.
Call for mass action - Randolph, A. P.
Call for new missionaries - Spencer, S. R., Jr.
Call to arms - Allen, T.; Henry, P.
Call to Ceylonese to have one and only loyalty to rulers of Malaysia - Thuraisingham, E. E. S. C.
A call to UMNO leaders - Hazak, T. A.
Cambodia - Nixon, R. M.
Campus revolutionaries - Nixon, R. M.
Campus unrest - Andelson, R. V.
Can ASEAN meet the challenge of the 70's? - Abdul Rahman, T.
Can any good thing come out of Nazareth? - Powell, A. C.
Can free enterprise survive success? - Marcus, S.
Can the dream survive? - Cox, A.
Candle of the Lord - Gerstein, I.
Carotenoids, flavins and vitamin A and B_2 - Karrer, P.
Carriers of negative electricity - Thomson, J. J.
Case for separation - Browne, R. S.
Case for the non-voter - Jarrow, C.
Case history in biological research, A - Tatum, E. L.
Casting the die - Roosevelt, F.
Catholic college, yesterday and tomorrow, A - Gannon, A. I.
Catholic rights in Ireland - O'Connell, D.
La causa - Ponce, F. V.
Cause of civil rights - Brooke, E. W.
Cell-free fermentation - Buchner, E.
Central Bank, The--the "financial conscience" of the government - Ismail bin Mohammed Ali

Central control of the activity of internal organs, The - Hess, W. R.
"Centralist" interpretation of the Constitution - Sewell, H.
Centralization and the revolutionary power of federal patronage - Vallandigham, C. L.
Challenge and hope - Roosevelt, F. D.
Challenge and promise - Roosevelt, F. D.
Challenge of abundance - Schlesinger, A. M., Jr.
Challenge to artists - Hansberry, L.
Challenge to man of the neoplastic cell, The - Rous, P.
Challenges to peace and freedom - Harriman, W. A.
Challenging opportunity for the press in Malaysia - Hamzah bin Dato Abu Samah
Change of hearts - Sheen, F. J., Bp.
Change the direction of the war - Bevan, A.
Changes in concepts of war and peace - Buisson, F. E.
Changes in values and concepts - Lee Kuan Yew
Changing the pecking order - Howe, H. II
Character of the Duke of Bedford - Fox, C. J.
Characteristic Röntgen radiation - Barkla, C. G.
Charge to the graduates - Manley, A. E.; Wells, H. B.
Charles River bridge v. Warren bridge - Taney, R. B.
Charter of human rights, The - Cassin, R. S.
Checkers speech - Nixon, R. M.
Cheerful spirit - Weinberger, S.
Chemical composition of the cell nucleus, The - Kossel, A.
Chemical evidence of the transmutation of elements - Joliot, J. F.
Chemical kinetics in the past few decades - Hinshelwood, Sir C. N.
Chemical nature of enzymes, The - Sumner, J. B.
Chemical nature of the alpha particles from radioactive substances, The - Rutherford, E.
Chemical reactions under high pressure - Bergius, F.
Chemical structure of the penicillins, The - Chain, E. B.
Chemical transmission of nerve action, The - Loewi, O.
Chemistry of insulin, The - Sanger, F.
Chemistry of the adrenal cortex hormones - Reichstein, T.
Chemistry of the bile acids, The - Wieland, H. O.
Cherokee history - Swimmer, R. O.
Cherokee lands - Frelinghuysen, T.
Chicagoan goes South - Percy, C. H.
Children of light - Hare, J. C.
Children of toil - Altgeld, J. P.
Chimpanzee worlds - Reynolds, V.
Chinese novel, The - Buck, P.
Choice between the quick and the dead - Baruch, B. M.
Choice in foreign policy - Rostow, E. V.
Choose one of five - Sampson, E. S.
Christian way - Hildebrandt, T.
Christianity and scientific investigation - Newman, J. H.
Church and the State must never mix!, The - Aquino, B. S.
Church in a secular state - Dumper, A. C.
Citric acid cycle, The - Krebs, H. A.
City set upon a hill - Bulkeley, P.
Civil and religious functions of government - Madison, J.
Civil Rights Bill - Elliott, R. B.; Rapier, J. T.
Claims of the Negro ethnologically considered - Douglass, F.
Clayton-Bulwer treaty and expansion - Clayton, J. M.
Clock - Van Voorst, B.
Closing argument for Queen Caroline - Brougham and Vaux, H. P. B.
Cloud chamber researches in nuclear physics and cosmic radiation - Blackett, P. M. S.
Coaching oratory - Schrier, W.
Coatesville - Chapman, J. R.
Coercion of delinquent states - Hamilton, A.
Cohens v. Virginia, 1821 - Marshall, J.
Coincidence method, The - Bothe, W.

Collective bargaining and industrial democracy - Murray, P.
Collective security and the League of Nations - Nash, W.
Colonization by public works and immigration - Vogel, J.
Color line in America - Douglass, F.
Colored men standing in the way of their own race - Lynch, J.
Columbian oration - Depew, C. M.
Come back - Silver, S. M.
Comfort and fun - Lerner, D.
The comic spirit and the public speaker - Rice, G. P.
Coming of democracy - Lowe, R.
Commemorating a national event - Quirino, E.
Commendable features of public-spiritedness and co-operation - Rahman, D. I. B. A.
Commercial politics - Barnave, A. P. J. M.
Commercial value of artistic excellence - Gladstone, W. E.
Commitment to scholarship and research - Bowen, W. G.
Commonwealth of Massachusetts v. Hunt - Shaw, L.
Communism in our schools - Dondero, G. A.
Communist Party is a secret conclave - Jackson, R. H.
Community and communications - Goodman, J. B.
"Compact of 1856," The - Sewell, H.
Compromise of 1850 - Clay, H.
Compromises of life, The - Watterson, H.
Computer and civil liberties - Sargent, F. W.
Concerning a grain of corn - Wycliffe, J.
Concerning pathological manifestations in low-grade thyroid diseases - Kocher, E. T.
Concerning the detection of x-ray interferences - Laue, M. V.
Concerning the pleasures of observing, and the mechanics of the inner ear - Bekesy, G. V.
Conciliation between the press and the law - Brennan, W. J., Jr.
Conciliation with America - Burke, E.
Condition and prospects of Haiti - Russwurm, J. B.
Confiscation of rebel property - Colfax, S.
Conflict of ideas in America - Garfield, J. A.
Conquest and territorial organization - Berrien, J. M.
Consensus complex vs. the free market - Champion, G.
Consensus established - Willkie, W. L.
Consent or force in government - Macaulay, T. B.
Consequences and development of an invention - Ziegler, K.
Conservation of public lands - Roosevelt, T.
Conservative programme - Churchill, W. L. S.
Conspiracy of blackest infamy - McCarthy, J. R.
Conspiracy to deny equality - Wilkins, R.
Constitution of sterols and their connection with other substances occurring in nature - Windaus, A. O. R.
Constitutional liberty and arbitrary power - Warren, J.
Constitutional liberty and executive despotism - Gallatin, A.
Consumer education: the farmer's responsibility - Spray, C.
Consumer safety and health - Franklin, B. H.
Containment or liberation - Dulles, J. F.
Contracts and corporate charters - Webster, D.
Contribution to the physiology of the capillaries, A - Krogh, A.
Contributions of right heart catheterization to physiology and medicine, The - Richards, D. W.
Control of the pulmonary circulation in man with some remarks on methodology - Cournand, A. F.
Cooing dove, The - Smith, A. E.
Cooper Institute address - Lincoln, A.
Corporate state not an American system - Dewey, T. E.
Cosmic radiation, The - Powell, C. F.
Cost of "Blood and Iron" - Field, D. D.
Counterinsurgency - Kennedy, R. F.

Counting the costs - Ramsey, R. P.
Cowboys, Indians, and the land of promise - Billington, R. A.
Creativity in law and government - Cox, A.
Crime against Kansas - Sumner, C.
Crisis of 1793 - Cambon, P. J.
Crisis of the city - Young, W. M., Jr.
Crisis of the Negro and the Constitution - Randolph, A. P.
Cross of gold - Bryan, W. J.
Crossbreeding beef cattle: progress or regression? - Hayes, K.
Crown of a good name - Routtenberg, M. J.
Crown of our head has fallen - Hurwitz, J.
Crucial cross-roads of history - Razak, T. A.
Crucifixion of Gavius - Cicero, M. T.
Cultivation of the poliomyelitis viruses in tissue culture, The - Enders, J. F.
Cultural differences: a base - West, D.
Current state of the struggle against tuberculosis, The - Koch, R.
Curse of a malignant tongue - Massillon, J. B.

- D -

Danger of a salaried bureaucracy - Franklin, B.
Danger of abolitionist petitions - Calhoun, J. C.
Danger of getting used to lies - Shaw, R. M.
Danger of inaction - Brandeis, L. D.
Danger of living our lives in isolation, The - Suffian bin Hashim
Danger to our liberty - Lincoln, A.
Dangers of slavery - Garrison, W. L.
Dangers of the present - Brown, H. A.
Darkness at noon - Lipis, P. L.
Darkness over the Ivory Tower - Moos, M.
Dartmouth College case - Webster, D.
David: and a whole lot of other neat people - Weisensel, K.
Day before Christmas - Rogers, J.
Day innovation died, The - Hanley, J. W.
DDT: friend or foe? - Neal, J.
Debate in 1741 on wages of sailors - Walpole, H.
Debate on the crown - Aeschines
Debate over war with England - Grundy, F. and others
Debates in the Virginia Ratifying Convention - Mason, G.
Debating whether or not to become King of England - Cromwell, O.
Decade of shortcuts - Brewster, K., Jr.
Declaration of conscience--twenty years later - Smith, M. C.
Declaration of interdependence - Wallace, H. A.
Declaration of Irish rights - Grattan, H.
Declaration of the Colonies on taking up arms - Dickinson, J.
Declining the poll - Burke, E.
Defects in the draft of the Constitution - Vinzons, W. Q.
Defence of the Empire in the Great War, The - Bell, F. H. D.
Defends his conduct of the war in Korea - MacArthur, D.
Defense of American territorial policies - Roosevelt, E. A.
Defense of independent voting - Still, W.
Defense of Richard Loeb and Nathan Leopold - Darrow, C.
Defense of the Jew - Kamin, L.
Defense of the Negro - Hamilton, W.
Defense of the Negro race - White, G. H.
Defying the French aristocracy - Mirabeau, H. G. P.
Deliver us from such a Moses - Hayden, L.
Deliverance of Europe - Pitt, W., 1759-1806
Demand for responsible government, The - Featherston, I.; Godley, R.; Wakefield, E. G.
Demanding the King's death - Robespierre, M.
Democracies and subject colonies - Cleon
De-mystifying anti-Americanism - Bray, C. W.

Density of gases in the air and the discovery of argon, The - Rayleigh, J. W. S.
Deo et Caesari fidelis - Montalembert, C. F. R.
Description and importance of the aromatic basic skeleton of the steroids - Diels, O. P. H.
Destiny and individual aspiration - Gladstone, W. E.
Destiny of America - Coolidge, C.
Devastating consequences of excessive population growth - Razak, T. A.
Development of cortisone as a therapeutic agent, The - Kendall, E. C.
The development of liver therapy in pernicious anemia, The - Minot, G. R.
Development of partition chromatography, The - Martin, A. J. P.
Development of quantum electrodynamics - Tomonaga, S. I.
Development of quantum mechanics, The - Heisenberg, W.
Development of retinal neurophysiology, The - Granit, R.
Development of the acetylation problem - Lipmann, F. A.
Development of the chemical high pressure method during the establishment of the new ammonia industry, The - Bosch, C.
Development of the Hague Conventions of July 29, 1899, The - Gobat, C. A.
Development of the space-time view of quantum electrodynamics, The - Feynman, R. P.
Development of the theory of electrolytic dissociation - Arrhenius, S. A.
Development of vaccines against yellow fever, The - Theiler, M.
Development strategy for success of second Malaysian plan, The - Razak, T. A.
Devotion to Freedom - Montalembert, C. F. T.
Diabetes and insulin - Banting, F. G.
Dichloro-diphenyl-trichloroethane and newer insecticides - Müller, P. H.
Dictators in American politics - Clay, H.
Diene synthesis and related reaction types - Adler, K.
Diffraction of x-rays by crystals, The - Bragg, W. L.
Discontinuous structure of matter - Perrin, J. B.
Dimensions of the oppression of women, The - Springen, P. J.
Direction for destiny - Fawcett, N. G.
Disapproving and accepting the Constitution - Franklin, B.
Disciple of Aaron - Hammer, R. A.
Discourse concerning the uncertainty of the times of men - Mather, I.
Discovery of electron waves, The - Davisson, C. J.
Discovery of hidden mineral veins with the aid of plants and animals, etc. - Uewaki, T.
Discovery of vitamin K, The - Dam, H.
"Discretion" as despotism - Hyde, E.
Dissent, dissension and the news - Boorstin, D. J.
Dissent, protest, and disobedience - Griswold, E. N.
Dissenting opinion on Abrams v. United States - Holmes, O. W., Jr.
Dissident view - Lindbergh, C. A.
Diversions of a Marquis - Curran, J. P.
Divine command - Klaaren, M. A.
Divine right to occupy the land - Cotton, J.
Divine tragedy - Abelard, P.
Djakarta style - May, D.
Do not judge this violent death - Garsek, I.
Do not refuse us - Sara, M. J.
Do we agree - Shaw, G. B. and others
Dollar diplomacy - Taft, W. H.
"Dominion founded on violence and terror" - Erskine, T.
Don't terrorize--but organize - Brown, J.
Dorothy Q - Holmes, O. W.
Doubting Thomases were wrong - Lim Swee Aun
Dreams fulfilled - Lipis, P. L.
Drifting into suicide - Hutchins, R. M.
Drunken orgy - Loula, L. A.
Due process radicalism - Brewster, K., Jr.

Dunkirk - Churchill, W. L. S.
Duties and respect of judges - Latimer, H.
Duty, honor, country - MacArthur, D.
Duty of colored men in the present national crisis - Williams, F.
Duty of the American scholar - Curtis, G. W.

- E -

Earlier history of vitamin research, The - Hopkins, Sir F. G.
Early antiproton work, The - Chamberlain, O.
Earth benefits from space and space technology - Von Braun, W.
Echo or a voice? - Van Tatenhove, J. E.
Economic bill of rights - Roosevelt, F. D. and others
Economic injustice in America today - Chisholm, S.
Economic interdependence: the world at a crossroads - Stevenson, A., III
Economy under the Labour government, The - Hamilton, A.
Edinburgh address - Carlyle, T.
Educated man in the age of Aquarius - White, R.
Educated man with a sense of urgency - Eliezer, C. J.
Education and wealth - Rogers, W.
Education for adequacy - Wilson, L.
Education for service - Hamdan bin Sheikh Tahir, H.
Education on Indian terms - Barlow, E.
Educational process - Shapp, M. J.
Educator's leap of faith, The - Benezet, L. T.
Effect of the Mexican conquest - Berrien, J. M.
Effective "Indian leadership" colorblind, but not naive - Lee, G. P.
Effective speech in a democracy - Carleton, W. G.
Effects of protection in agriculture - Cobden, R.
1890 election: the opposition case, The - Ballance, J.
Election eve address - Muskie, E. S.
Elective curriculum - Eliot, C. W.
Electrical oscillations and wireless telegraphy - Braun, C. F.
Electron and the light-quant from the experimental point of view, The - Millikan, R. A.
Electron-scattering method and its application to the structure of nuclei and nucleons, The - Hofstadter, R.
Electronic waves - Thomson, G. P.
Electrophoresis and adsorption analysis as aids in investigations of large-molecular weight substances and their breakdown - Tiselius, A. W. K.
Elementary particles and bubble chambers - Glaser, D. A.
Elements of Malaysian foreign policy - Muhammad Ghazali bin Shafie
Elite combat party - Goh Keng Swee
Eloquence and the fine arts - Cousin, V.
Embers and cinders - Goldfarb, S. D.
Emerging common law of free enterprise - Berle, A. A., Jr.
Emigration of colored citizens from the southern states - Greener, R. T.
Empire and home rule - Chamberlain, J.
Encouragement of knowledge - Bowdoin, J.
End itself is evil - Johnson, A.
Endocrine-induced regression of cancers - Huggins, C. B.
Energy address to the nation - Carter, J.
Energy and the job market - Sawhill, J. C.
Energy and the national goals - Carter, J.
Energy conversions in muscle - Meyerhof, O. F.
Energy crisis - Hatfield, M. O.
Energy problems - Carter, J.
Energy production in stars - Bethe, H. A.
Energy statement - Goodall, C. H.
Enfranchisement of women - Anthony, S. B.; May, S. J.
England and America since the Spanish War - Depew, C. M.
Environment revolution - Ruckelshaus, W. D.
Environmental pollution - Swearingen, J. E.

Environmental regulation and the immobilization of truth - Speth, G.
Enzymatic synthesis of ribonucleic acid - Ochoa, S.
Episcopal rights and parish autonomy - Kenrick, F. P.
Equality before the law - Langston, J. M.
Equality of rights for all citizens, black and white, alike - Grimke, F. J.
Equation of state for gases and liquids, The - Waals, J. D. V. D.
Eroding authority - Powell, L. F., Jr.
Essential elements of a universal and enduring peace - Henderson, A.
Essentials of peace - Marshall, G. C.
Ethics in public discourse - Jeffrey, R. C.
Ethics of the Hawaiian question - Scarborough, W. S.
Eulogium - Smith, W.
Eulogy for Wernher Von Braun - Sevareid, E.
Eulogy of Lyndon Baines Johnson - Rusk, D.
Eulogy on Charles Sumner - Rainey, J. H.
Eulogy on Dr. Martin Luther King, Jr. - Mays, B. E.
Eulogy on William Wilberforce - Whipper, W.
Evangelism - Sunday, W. A.
Events, laws of nature, and invariance principles - Wigner, E. P.
Everlasting oxydization - Spurgeon, C. H.
Every man a king - Long, H. P.
Every man should stand equal before the law - Bertonneau, A.
Evolution of the cyclotron, The - Lawrence, E. O.
Evolution of the Peace Movement, The - Suttner, B. V.
Ex parte Milligan - Davis, D.
Example of kings - Sheridan, R. B.
Excellence in Indian education - Sockey, C. E.
Excellence in teaching - Euwema, B.
Exclusion principle and quantum mechanics - Pauli, W.
"Expansion" and co-operation with England - Douglas, S. A.
Experiments on the interaction of high-speed nucleons with atomic nuclei - Cockcroft, Sir J. D.
Exploring new energy frontiers - MacDonald, P.
Exploring the unknown - Gittings, R.
Extending the "frontier" of New South Wales - Wakefield, E. G.
Extremism - Rockefeller, N. A.
Extremism in defense of liberty - Goldwater, B. M.
"Eyes of the people opened" - Wilson, W.
Eyes of the whole world - Feldmann, M. H.

- F -

Fable come true, A - Roper, B.
Face the future with faith and without fear - Abdul Rahman, P.
Faces and voices of American women - Carpenter, L.
Factory Bill (1833) - Cobbett, W.
Facts and the founding fathers - Dabney, V.
Failure of scientists to communicate, The - Root, T. C.
Fair Deal in retrospect - Truman, H. S.
Faith in the individual - Eisenhower, D. D.
Faith of the American Negro - Johnson, M. W.
Faith that enlivens the mind - Stendahl, K.
Fall and rise of Indian sovereignty, The - Bennett, R.
Fallacy of industrial education as the solution of the race problem - Smith, C. S.
False pretenses - Chillingworth, W.
Family's tribute - Lipnick, B.
Famine--a reality, not just a threat - Brown, M.
Farewell address - Washington, G.
Farewell to the Assembly, A - Roxas, S.
Farewell to the cadets - MacArthur, D.
Farmer, heal thyself! - Davidson, G.

Fear and hysteria: the Japanese relocation, etc. - Stones, H. F.
Feast or famine: the key to peace - Butz, E. L.
Federal Court orders must be upheld - Eisenhower, D. D.
Federal experiments in history - Monroe, J.
Federal judiciary - Bayard, J. A.
Federal power and local rights - Clinton, D. W.
Federal support of science and medicine - Califano, J. A.
Feeding the hungry world - Rush, W.
Fermentation of sugars and fermentative enzymes - Euler, H. V.
Fervent appeal for free silver - Fitch, T.
Festival of the Supreme Being - Robespierre, M.
"Fifty-four forty or fight" - Cobb, H.
Fifty years of trade-union activity in behalf of peace - Jouhaux, L.
Fight for Merdeka - Abdul Rahman, T.
Filipinos of today and Filipinos of yesterday - Quezon, M. L.
Financial reform - Churchill, R. H. S.
Finding America - Hartzog, G. B., Jr.
Fine structure of the hydrogen bomb - Lamb, W. E.
Finish the good work of uniting colored and white workingmen - Myers, I.
Fireside chat on party primaries - Roosevelt, F. D.
Fireside chat: unity on U. S. goals - Carter, J.
First Amendment, The: freedom and responsibility - Mathias, C. M.
First Olynthiac oration - Demosthenes
First oration against Catiline - Cicero, M. T.
First oration against Verres - Cicero, M. T.
First Philippic - Demosthenes
First step in nation building - Lee Kuan Yew
First war address before Congress - Roosevelt, F. D.
Five hundred miles south - Slabach, D.
"Flanks are something for the enemy to worry about" - Patton, G. S.
Flash photolysis and some of its applications - Porter, F.
Folle epoque, La - Buckley, F. R.
Food--a world crisis - Stratton, R. D.
Foolish exchange - Taylor, J.
For a vigorous prosecution of the war - Clay, H.
For a white Australia - Deakin, A.
For federal government by the people - King, R.
For ratification of treaties with Panama - Rusk, D.
For the encouragement of learning - Dering, E.
For the Federal Constitution - Deakin, A.
For the nomination of Gerald R. Ford - Percy, C. H.
Force Bill - Calhoun, J. C.
Foreign-born children in the primary grades - Addams, J.
Foreign policy--old myths and new realities - Fulbright, J. W.
Forgiveness of injuries - Cranmer, T.
Forward defence--from the Middle East to Malaya, 1955 - Holland, S.
Four faces of peace, The - Pearson, L. B.
Four good signs - Lipis, P. L.
Four human freedoms - Roosevelt, F. D.
Four ways of looking at a speech - Lee, I. G.
Fourteen points - Wilson, W.
Fourth Philippic - Cicero, M. T.
Frankenstein in the making - Seenivasagam, D. R.
Fraternity among nations - Branting, K. H.
Freaks for Jesus' sake - Elson, E. L. R.
"Free by '63" - Patterson, W. L.
Free Huey - Seale, B.
Free just free - Gallagher, W.
Free land and the supply of labor - Sutherland, J.
Free people - Grattan, H.
Free speech and fundamental rights - Erskine, T.
Freedom and individual security - Lehman, H. H.

Freedom and the labyrinth - Ness, F. W.
Freedom in the new territories - Seward, W. H.
Freedom of worship - Danton, G. J.
Freedom's joyful day - Gibbs, J. C.
Freehold tenure - Massey, W. F.
From enzymatic adaptation to allosteric transitions - Monod, J.
From Runnymede to Ganymede - Webb, J. E.
From the natural transmutations of uranium to its artificial fission - Hahn, O.
From the sinks of Europe a plotter has come - Tyler, J.
From the stereospecific polymerization to the asymmetric autocatalytic synthesis of macromolecules - Natta, G.
From the bottom to the top - Romney, G.
From the summit - Drazin, N.
From where the sun now stands - Joseph, Chief
Fruit of foul rebellion - Stevens, T.
Fruitful tears - Gordon, D. W.
Fruitful tension - Kennedy, R. F.
Function of phosphate in alcoholic fermentation, The - Harden, A.
Functions of the Negro scholar - Grisham, G. N.
Fundamental and minority rights - Marshall, D. S.
Fundamental error of English colonial aggrandizement - Gladstone, W. E.
Fundamental idea of wave mechanics, The - Schrodinger, E.
Fundamental ideas and problems of the theory of relativity - Einstein, A.
Further progress in chemotherapy of bacterial infections - Domack, G. J. P.
Futility of war demonstrated by history, The - Ducommun, E.
Future is at hand, The - Atcitty, T. E.
Future is at stake, The - Lee Kuan Yew
Future of capitalism, The - Friedman, M.
Future of civilization, The - Cecil, R.
Future of the past - Walker, H. B.

- G -

General characteristics of radiations - Tamm, I. E.
General education: the rule of the humanities - Duffey, J. D.
General survey of certain results in the field of high-pressure physics - Bridgman, P. W.
General welfare and the limits of government - Laurance, J.
Generation in search of a future - Wald, G.
Genes and chemical reactions in Neurospora - Beadle, G. W.
Genesis and present state of development of the quantum theory, The - Planck, M.
Genetic code, The - Nirenberg, M. W.
Genetics of the bacterial cell - Jacob, F.
Gettysburg address - Lincoln, A.
Ghosts - Lonnquist, K.
G.I. Bill of Rights - Hines, F. T.
Gibbons v. Ogden, 1824 - Marshall, J.
Ginzburg et al v. United States - Brennan, W. J., Jr.
Gitlow v. New York - Sanford, E. T.
Give me liberty or give me death! - Castro, F.
Give the people bread - Herndon, A.
Give us equal pay and we will go to war - Campbell, J. P.
Give us the ballot--we will transform the South - King, M. L., Jr.
Given time we'll get it together - James, D.
Glimpses at the history of the nuclear structure theory - Jensen, J. H. D.
Global crisis - Kubicek, K.
Global interdependence - Hatfield, M. O.
Glory of notoriety - Kane, A.
Go thou in peace - Chertoff, M. S.
God and Joe College - Lubbers, A. D.
God be with thee - Ettelson, H. W.
God's grief - Brooks, S. H.

God's promise to his plantations - Cotton, J.
Golden rule for foreign affairs - Fillmore, M.
Good lore for simple folk - Wycliffe, J.
Good neighbor policy - Roosevelt, F. D.
Good news from a far country - Chauncy, C.
Good time is at hand - Purvis, R.
Goodwill in industry - Baldwin, S. B.
Gospel-covenant, The - Bulkeley, P.
Government is determined to take drastic measures if ... - Rahman, D. I. B. A.
Government of the tongue - Butler, J.
Government policy - Churchill, W. L. S.
Government spending is sound - Eccles, M. S.
Governments for the people and not the people for governments - Sidney, A.
Grand alternatives - Skidelsky, R.
Grape shot and hemp - Brownlow, W. G.
Great American institution - Gale, J.
Great institution - Lee, H. H. S.
Great migration north - DuBois, W. E. B.
Great society - Johnson, L. B.
Great society is a sick society - Fulbright, J. W.
Greatest thing in the world - Drummond, H.
Greatness of a plain American - Emerson, R. W.
Green parrot - Carlat, J.
Green revolution, peace, and humanity, The - Borlaug, N. E.
Grievances and oppressions under Charles I - Bristol, G. D.
Guided tour of gobbledygook, A - Ashley, L. R. N.
Guide-lines and strategies for achieving national unity - Muhammad Ghazali bin Shafie
Guns and butter are tied together - Humphrey, H. H., Jr.

- H -

Hand that held the dagger - Roosevelt, F. D.
Happiness of a people in the wisdom of their rulers directing and in obedience of their brethren attending unto what Israel ought to do - Hubbard, W.
Harmony--from where the sun now stands - Trimble, C.
Harvard and Yale - Eliot, C. W.
Has one government the right to intervene in the internal affairs of another - Chateaubriand, F. A. R.
Has TV made the public speaker obsolete? - Braden, W. W.
Hate in politics - Canning, G.
Have faith in Massachusetts - Coolidge, C.
Haven of the defeated - Karos, P. A.
Hazards of equity - Thibeault, M. L.
He cannot be replaced - Milgrom, J.
He died climbing - Minda, A. G.
He stood up and drank the toast and joined in the applause! - Sandosham, A. A.
Healthier than healthy - Menninger, K.
Healthy heresies - Gunsaulus, F. W.
Heap of trouble, A - Hall, C.
Heavenly footman - Bunyan, J.
Heavenly glow - Simon, E. Y.
Hemoglobin regeneration as influenced by diet and other factors - Whipple, G. H.
Heroes of faith - Chrysostom, J.
Heroic in history - Carlyle, T.
Higher education begins the seventies - Hesburgh, T. M.
Higher law than the Constitution - Seward, W. H.
Highest attainment - Garsek, I.
Highest form of expression - Robertson, F. W.
Highest manhood - Hughes, T.
His sovereignty under his hat - Curtis, G. W.
History of Singapore's struggle for nationhood, 1945-1959 - Marshall, D. S.
Hitler's plans for Canada and the United States - Thompson, D.
Holy crusade for liberty - Hoover, H. C.

Home Rule - Gladstone, W. E.
Home rule and autonomy - Gladstone, W. E.
Honor of France - Zola, E.
Honoring Dr. DuBois - King, M. L., Jr.
Hope of all mankind - MacArthur, D.
Hopes and anxieties of the countries of Southeast Asia - Hazak, T. A.
House divided against itself cannot stand - Lincoln, A.
House that Sam built - Steele, H.
How can France be saved? - Danton, G. J.
How can the government best protect the American consumer? - Andino, J.
How can we continue to sack the ports of Asia and still dream of Jesus - Oglesby, C.
How I discovered phase contrast - Zernike, F.
How I found the mechanism of intracapsular accommodation - Gullstrand, A.
How I managed to reach the Peace Conference - Trotter, W. M.
How long can we cope? - Burger, W. E.
How long? How long, O Heaven? - Turner, H. M.
How shall we get our rights? - Bryant, M. E.
How Singapore's monetary system now works - Goh Keng Swee
How to beautify your farm - Hirschler, P.
How we meet ourselves - Young, O. D.
Human relations in world perspective - Bunche, R. J.
Human rights and détente - Goldberg, A. J.
Human rights and the foreign policy - Vance, C. R.
Human soot - Kingsley, C.
Human way out - Mumford, L.
Humanizing the earth - Dubos, R.

- I -

I am a Black revolutionary woman - Davis, A.
I am never guilty - Sacco, N.
I am optimistic about America - Humphrey, H. H., Jr.
I am proud to be part of it - Madrid, S.
I claim the rights of a man - Turner, H. M.
I denounce the so-called emancipation as a stupendous fraud - Douglass, F.
I do not believe in the antislavery of Abraham Lincoln - Douglass, H. F.
I first saw the light of day - Marshall, A.
"I have a dream" - King, M. L., Jr.
I protest against Hayes's Southern policy - Lawson, J.
I raise my voice against one of the most dangerous evils in our country - White, G. H.
I see the promised land - King, M. L., Jr.
I still believe in the future of farming - Ivens, M.
I took the Canal Zone - Roosevelt, T.
I will sink or swim with my race - Rock, J. S.
I won't obey the Fugitive Slave Law - Loguen, J. R.
Ich bin ein Berliner - Kennedy, J. F.
Idealism: what's wrong with it? - Parson, M. J.
Ideology and education - Eliezer, C. J.
Idiosyncrasies of DNA structure - Hershey, A. D.
If a man loses something - Barlow, E. J.
If there is no struggle there is no progress - Douglass, F.
If we fall down in the land of peace - Hatfield, M. O.
If we love, we must lose - Grollman, E. A.
Ignorance curtain vs. the open door - McGovern, G.
Illuminations - Cutforth, R.
ILO and the social infrastructure of peace - Morse, D. A.
ILO represents the social conscience of the world - Manickavasagam, V.
Images of the consumer's changing mind on and off Madison Avenue - Rokeach, M.

Imbalance of power, The - Elleson, J.
Immeasurably fast reactions - Eigen, M.
Immigrants and revolutionists - Roosevelt, F. D.
Immorality, racism, and survival - Hurst, C. G.
Immortality and good deeds - Reed, T. B.
Immunological recognition of self - Burnet, Sir F. M.
Immunological tolerance - Medawar, P. B.
Impassable barrier between brutes and man - Müller, F. M.
Imperial union and tariff reform - Chamberlain, J.
Importance of race pride - Brown, E. E.
Importance of the vote - Pankhurst, E. G.
Important factors for ensuring efficient, loyal public service - Suffian bin Hashim
Impressive accomplishments - Rayburn, S.
In behalf of a troubled nation - Gardner, J. W.
In celebration of the inauguration of the Susan B. Anthony coin - Holtzman, E.
In defense of liberty: extremism and other vices - Krug, J. F.
In defense of privilege - Schorr, D.
In defense of tradition - Hoover, H. C.
In favor of a paternal policy of internal improvements - Clay, H.
In favor of a stronger navy - Cheves, L.
In favor of re-union - Doolittle, J. R.
In favor of slitting Prynne's nose - Dorset, E. S.
In praise of the sit-in strikes - Marshall, T.
In pursuit of equality in academe - Norton, E. H.
In re Milligan - Field, D. D.
In support of an American empire - Beveridge, A. J.
In support of the Equal Rights Amendment - Chisholm, S.
In the Campo Santo of Pisa - Castelar, E.
In the case of Justice Johnson--civil liberty and arbitrary arrests - Curran, J. P.
In the case of McCardle - Field, D. D.
In the case of the Dean of St. Asaph - Mansfield, W. M.
In the case of Zenger - Hamilton, A.
In the pursuit of excellence - Morrison, H. C.
In these present crises - Peterson, M.
In vindication of the colonies - Wilson, J.
Independent judiciary as the salvation of the nation - Brewer, D. J.
Independent policy - Lindbergh, C. A.
Independent spirit, The - Kerr, C.
Indian education resources center, An - Benham, W. J.
Indian history--fact or fiction - Costo, R.
Indicts the slave trade and foresees a liberated Africa - Pitt, W., 1759-1806
Industrial peace - Baldwin, S. B.
Influence of America on the mind - Ingersoll, C. J.
Inhibition as a coordinative factor - Sherrington, Sir C. S.
Innovation mirage - Howard, J. A.
Institutional illusion - Hutchins, R. M.
Instrument of revelation - Langer, E.
Integration must work--nothing else can - Galamison, M. A.
Intellectual achievement in America - Story, J.
Intellectual and the politician - Kennedy, J. F.
Intellectual elite and the worker - Tan Chee Khoon
Intelligentsia in a nation of immigrants - Wong, L. K.
Interaction among virus, cell, and organism - Lwoff, A.
Interest of the few and the liberties of the people - Lenoir, W.
Internal improvements and the powers of Congress - Clay, H.
International control of atomic energy - Baruch, B. M.
International peace - Roosevelt, T.
International service of the Society of Friends, The - Backhouse, M. A.

Internationalism - Lange, C. L.
Invar and clinvar - Guillaume, C. E.
Invective against Corry - Grattan, H.
Investigations into the properties of substances at low temperatures - Onnes, H. K.
Investigations on Spiroptera carcinoma and the experimental induction of cancer - Fibiger, J. A. G.
Investigations on typhus - Nicolle, C. J. H.
Invisible abutments - Buteyn, D. P.
Invisible government - Root, E.
Involvement of RNA in the synthesis of proteins, The - Watson, J. D.
Ionic basis of nervous conduction, The - Hodgkin, A. L.
Ionic mechanism of postsynaptic inhibition, The - Eccles, J. C.
Irish dramatic movement, The - Yeats, W. B.
Irish land question - Parnell, C. S.
Iron curtain - Churchill, W. L. S.
Irrepressible conflict - Schurz, C.; Seward, W. H.
Is agriculture on its way out? - Mathias, T.
Is busing the answer? - Kitslaar, J. L.
Is the government federal or national - Martin, L.
Is this your university? - Capp, A.
Is Thomas Jefferson relevant? - Peden, W.
Iscariot in modern England - Ruskin, J.
Isolation and properties of crystalline tobacco mosaic, The - Stanley, W. M.
Issue, The - Debs, E.
Issue against Andrew Johnson - Stevens, T.
Issues of 1861 - Douglas, S. A.
It is essentially a Rebel organization - Sherman, J.
"It is our purpose to prosper America first" - Harding, W. G.
It is time for a change - Chisholm, S.
It is time for us to be up and doing - Osborne, P.
It is time to call a halt - Fortune, T. T.
It is time to reassess our national priorities - Chisholm, S.
It is time to speak up for America - Nixon, R. M.
It was purely a peace police organization - Gordon, J. B.
Ivory tower of Babel, The - Meyerson, M.

- J -

Jacksonian attack on monopoly - Robinson, F.
James Scholars and the university, The - Damrin, D. E.
Jobs, freedom, and opportunity - Crawford, F. C.
Job-seeking interview, A: a transcript - Scott, R.
John Brown raid - Douglas, S. A.
John Marshall - Holmes, O. W., Jr.
John Marshall and the judicial function - Frankfurter, F.
Johnson doctrine - Johnson, L. B.
Joint efforts urged for uniting various ethnic groups - Hamzah Sendut
Judge Andres Borromeo did his duty! - Malcolm, G. A.
Judicial process and the Supreme Court - Frankfurter, F.
Justice and separation of powers - Osias, C.
Justice and the Federal Constitution - Marshall, J.
Justice or emigration should be our watchword - Turner, H. M.
Justice should recognize no color - Gray, W. H.
Justifying revolution - Mirabeau, H. G. R.

- K -

Keeping the Senate independent - McIntyre, T. J.
Kerner report - Abernathy, R. D.
Key to open the doors to all hearts and minds - Johari, M. K.
Keynote address - Jordan, B.

Keynote address to the Democratic National Convention - Jordan, B. C.
Keynote address to the NAACP annual convention, Los Angeles, July 5, 1966 - Wilkins, R.
Kid dreams - Brunsting, L.
Kind of democracy the Negro race expects - Pickens, W.
King's answer - Salkowitz, S.
Knapp White murder case - Webster, D.
Korematsu v. United States - Black, H. L.
Ku Klux Klan as a subversive conspiratorial organization - Kaler, I.
Ku Klux of the North - Wears, I. C.

- L -

Lab farms in vocational agriculture - Morse, D.
Labor and the nation - Lewis, J. L.
Labor, education, and the American farmer - Lincoln, A.
Labour, politics and democratic socialism - Gaitskell, H.
Labour programme - Attlee, C. R.
Lamp of freedom - Hains, J.
Lamps of fiction - Smith, G.
Land for Settlements Bill - McKenzie, J.
Land of cattle, land of America - Fishburn, P.
Land preservation in the Northeast - Lipton, J.
Land settlement, A--what does it mean? - Wah-shee, J.
Land tax of a halfpenny in the pound on land exceeding £500 in value, 1878, A - Ballance, J.
Language and the lived world - Bacon, W. A.
Languages: anguish and confusion - Aziz, U.
"Larger vision" of the humanities, A - Coles, R.
Last entry into Jerusalem - Abelard, P.
Last judgment - Cahill, D. W.
Last speech at Charleston, West Virginia - Brown, J.
Latter-Day Joseph - Gordis, R.
Law and the court - Holmes, O. W., Jr.
Law Day address - Kennedy, R. F.
Law of parity conservation and other symmetry laws of physics, The - Yang, C. N.
Law of the land - Steffens, G.
Laws of the states affecting women - Clay, L.
Lawyer shall never retreat, The - Yamzon, V.
Leaders' responsibility in sustaining a democratic system - Lee Kuan Yew
Leadership--a goal for us all - Harrison, R.
Leadership demanded in this momentous time, The - Mott, J. R.
League and the Spanish Civil War, The - Jordan, W. J.
League of Nations - Borah, W. E.
Leasehold defended - Taylor, T. E.
Lecture on slavery - Douglass, F.
Legacy of George Jackson - Davis, A.
Legal arguments for adopting the Statute of Westminster, 1944 - McGechan, R. O.
Legal attack to secure civil rights - Marshall, T.
Lenity of the law to human infirmity - Quincy, J., 1744-1775
Lesson of the Three Kingdoms - Toh Chin Chye
Lesson we have to learn - Lee Kuan Yew
Lest we forget - Abdul Rahman, T.; Inche Yasot bin Ishak
Let candles be brought - Linowitz, S. M.
Let France be free - Danton, G. J.
Let our voice be heard - Senu bin Abdul Rahman
Let the monster perish - Garnet, H. H.
Let thy garments be always white - Goldman, I. M.
Let us continue - Johnson, L. B.
Let us depart in peace - Toombs, R.
Let us go to the King - Ball, J.
"Let us join hands, hearts and minds" - Yalow, R. S.
"Let us look to the end" - Quincy, J., 1744-1775
Let us not mimic the democracy of Westminster 1957 - Muhammad Ghazali bin Shafie

Let us take up the sword - Green, A. M.
Let your son fight for freedom - Gregory, D.
"Let's bring back Dad": a solid value system - Jones, J. L.
Libbing - Edwards, L.
Liberal Party, A - Grey, Sir G.
Liberation struggle generates tension on race, sex issues - Brown, Joan
Liberties of the indolent - Curran, J. P.
Liberty and government in America - Pendleton, E.
Liberty and Union - Webster, D.
Liberty destroyed by national pride - Smith, G.
Liberty in the New Atlantis - Hecker, F. K. F.
Liberty, justice and democracy - Randolph, A. P.
Liberty tree in Paris - Hugo, V. M.
Lie of war - Geren, P.
Life and character of J. A. Garfield - Blaine, J. G.
Life and death of our lakes - Ransley, M.
Life, librium, and the pursuit of happiness - Rindo, J. P.
Life of service - Bonaventura, Saint
Life's struggle - Besdin, A. R.
Life's victor - Feibelman, J. B.
Light from sorrow - Pollak, G.
Light from the stones - Bial, M. D.
"Light of the world" - Thomas, J. B.
Light radiation in a magnetic field - Zeeman, P.
Like water spilled on the ground - Kahn, R. I.
Lincoln's colonization proposal is anti-Christian - Wears, I. C.
Literature and science - Arnold, M.
Little personal history - Hill, B. H.
Little Rock school crisis - Eisenhower, D. D.
Little speech on liberty - Winthrop, J.
"Little while" of the Saviour's absence and the prospect of his speedy return - Lang, J. D.
Live each day - Kestenbaum, J.
Live free or die - Desmoulins, C.
Live hopefully - Levenson, J.
"Live--I am coming" - Holmes, O. W., Jr.
Liverpool speech - Beecher, H. W.
Living presence - Wallack, M. A.
Local self-government - Kossuth, L.
Lochner v. New York, 1905 - Holmes, O. W., Jr. and others
Long twilight struggle - Kennedy, J. F.
Long way to go, A - King, M. L., Jr.
Look above and beyond - Ettelson, H. W.
Look at the fundamental school concept, A - Wellington, J. K.
Look beyond the shadows - Lipis, P. L.
Loom of time - Rackovsky, I.
Lordly cedar - Essrig, H.
Louisiana Returning Board - Carpenter, M. H.
Love of country - Bocobo, J. C.
Love for the beautiful in speech - Poe, E. A.
Love, law and civil disobedience - King, M. L., Jr.
Loyal opposition - Willkie, W. L.
Lust of empire - Hoar, G. F.

- M -

McCulloch v. Maryland - Marshall, J.
Macromolecular chemistry - Staudinger, H.
Madame Butterfly and the collegian - Hayes, P. A.
Magnetic moment of the electron, The - Kusch, P.
Magnetism and the local molecular field - Néel, L.
Mail service - Gronouski, J. A.
Making Lincoln live - Runkel, H. W.
Malaysian Brothers - Johari, M. K.
Malays and Chinese must co-exist - Tan Siew Sin
Malcolm was our manhood, our living Black manhood - Davis, O.
Mammalian nerve fibers - Gasser, H. S.
Man died, but his memory lives, The - Clay, C. M.
Man eats dog - Pyke, M.
Man is a soldier - Gerstein, I.
Man is a soul - Stiskin, M. N.

Man of clear vision - Ramani, R.
Man of deed - Shtull, J.
Man on the tower - Cobbett, W.
Man the reformer - Emerson, R. W.
Man who walked with God - Goldman, I. M.
Man with the muck-rake - Roosevelt, T.
Man's advocate - De Sola Pool, D.
Man's best friend--his dog - Vest, G. G.
Man's other society - Marvin, R.
Man's true measurements - Kaplan, S. M.
Marbury v. Madison - Marshall, J.
March of the flag - Beveridge, A. J.
March on Washington address - Randolph, A. P.
Martin, Barton, and Fish - Roosevelt, F. D.
Masonry proved to be a work of darkness - Armstrong, L.
Mass spectra and isotopes - Aston, F. W.
Massacre of the innocents - Kingsley, C.
Massive exercise for survival - Lim Kim San
Matter of doubt and grave concern - Harding, H. F.
May Hungary be free - Downing, G. T.
Meaning of Black history - Clarke, J. H.
Meaning of Black power - Florence, F.
Meaning of Conservatism - Beaconsfield, B. D.
Meaning of inspiration - Herder, J. G.
Measure of greatness - Turitz, L. E.
Meat Board, 1922, The - Massey, W. F.
Mechanism of muscular contraction, The - Hill, A. V.
Medical care - Watson, T. J., Jr.
Meditation on the assassination of Martin Luther King, Jr. - Cleaver, E.
Meet the press - Nader, R.
Meeting place of cultures - Tan Siew Sin
Meeting world food news - Hannah, J. A.
Megaphone and manhood suffrage - Chamberlain, J.
Memory of Burns - Emerson, R. W.
"Men of color, to arms!" - Douglass, F.
Men of conscience - Leenhouts, T.
Menace of the World Court - Coughlin, C. E.
Meson theory in its developments - Yukawa, H.
Message of Rukunegara, The - Lim Chong Eu
Message to the younger generation - Hutchins, R. M.
Message to youth - Abbott, R. S.
Method of direct hydrogenation by catalysis, The - Sabatier, P.
Method of molecular rays, The - Stern, O.
Method of scientific investigation, The - Huxley, T. H.
Methods to determine the electrical and geometrical structure of molecules - Debye, P. J. W.
Middle of the journey - Moynihan, D. P.
Military academy - Pierce, F.
Military contribution in Vietnam, 1965, A - Holyoake, K. J.
Military government - Blair, A.
Military hardware, economic assistance, and civic action - McNamara, R. S.
Military policy for the Cold War - Hoover, H. C.
Military spirit in America - Depew, C. M.
Mind of a new commonwealth, The - Romulo, C. P.
Mind--the master force - Campbell, A.
Minds of the non-western world - Dean, V. M.
Mingled blood - Zimmerman, R.
Miranda v. Arizona - Warren, E.
Misfortune and exile - Bolingbroke, H. S. J.
Mission of America - Boudinot, E.
Mission of the M.C.A. - Tan Siew Sin
Mission of the war - Douglass, F.
Missionary effort - Red Jacket
Missionary opposition to the New Zealand Company - Coates, D.
Missouri question - Pinkney, W.
Mistaken enemy - Vander Werf, N.

Mrs. Partington in politics - Smith, S.
Model studies of structural design and construction, etc. - Macios, M. A.
Modern art shackled to communism - Dondero, G. A.
Modern foreign policy - Dulles, J. F.
Modern structural chemistry - Pauling, L. C.
Modern trade unionism - Green, W.
Moments to remember - Golden, J. L.
Molecular basis of visual excitation, The - Wald, G.
Molecular configuration of nucleic acid, The - Wilkins, M. H. F.
Molecular scattering of light, The - Raman, Sir C. V.
Money changers in the temple - Coughlin, C. E.
Monroe Doctrine - Monroe, J.
Monstrous piece of legislation - Tan Chee Khoon
Moon rendezvous - Armstrong, N.
Moppet manipulation - Myers, N. J.
Moral dimensions of the world food problem, The - Trafton, C.
Moral for Commonwealth members and Britain, The - Lee Kuan Yew
Moral force in world politics - Hugo, V. M.
Moral forces which make American progress - Everett, E.
Moral ideas and Republican principles - Robespierre, M.
Morality and military greatness - Bright, J.
More stately mansions - Welch, R.
Morgenthau's plan - Rogers, W.
Most dramatic fact of international life, The - Muhammad Ghazali bin Shafie
Most powerful instrument for social cohesion, The - Hamzah bin Dato Abu Samah
Most unfortunate of conflicts - Razak, T. A.
Motion of ions, The - Onsager, L.
Motion to redress - Wilkes, J.
Mott v. Illinois, 1876 - Waite, M. R.
"Movement" now - Farmer, J.
Multicultural education: its effective management - Barlow, E.
Multimembered rings, higher terpene compounds, and male sex hormones - Ružička, L. S.
Murder and gun control - Edwards, G.
Murder of Lovejoy - Phillips, W.
My cup runneth over - Goldfarb, S. D.
My good friend Hubert Humphrey - Carter, J.
My people, the Indians - George, D.
My profession - Dawson, M.
My responsibility as an agricultural citizen - Gould, J. C.
My son, my son - Rosenthal, N. L.
Myoglobin and the structure of proteins - Kendrew, J. C.
Myths by which we live - Rosten, L.

- N -

Naboth's vineyard - Bryan, W. J. and others
NAFTA, 1965 - Marshall, J. R.
Nat Turner - Handy, A. W.
Nation building and the four-way test - Johari, M. K.
Nation building and the jealous gods of the past - Nair, C. D.
Nation, not a Federation - Henry, P.
National Assembly, its aims and accomplishments, The - Osmeña, S.
National chamber needed, A - Johari, M. K.
National Development Conference, 1968, The - Holyoake, K. J.
National humility - Graham, W. F.
National Labor Relations Board v. Jones and Laughlin Steel Corporation - Hughes, C. E.
National power and the American peace policy - Marshall, T. R.
Native American women in the feminist milieu - Wittstock, L. W.
Native Americans and the foreign born - Levin, L. C.
NATO - Gruenther, A. M.
Natural propensity of rulers to oppress - Mason, G.
Naturalism or idealism? - Eucken, R.

Nature and mode of action of oxidation enzymes, The - Theorell, A. H. T.
Nature of democracy in the United States - Wilson, W.
Nature of slavery - Douglass, F.
Navajo wisdom - Yazzie, E.
Navajo wisdom as found in Navajo oral history - Yazzie, E.
Naval Defence Bill, 1908, The - Allen, J.
Necessity of education in a Republican government - Mann, H.
Need for a rational forest policy - Schurz, C.
Need for dedicated service by civil servants, The - Tan Siew Sin
Need to share what we have - Black, H.
Needed: Indian health professionals - Blue Spruce, G.
Needs of a nation, The - Evangelista, T.
Neglect of the song - Fulbright, J. W.
Negro and the American promise - Kennedy, J. F.
Negro artist looks ahead - Robeson, P.
Negro labor committee - Crosswaith, F. R.
Negro people on the march - Davis, B. J.
Negro plea for organized resistance to white men - Bruce, J. E.
Negro race, self-government and the Haitian revolution - Holly, J. T.
Negro writers have been on the blacklist all their lives - Hughes, L.
Negroes speak of war - Hughes, L.
Negro's part in new national problems - Putnam, F.
Neuron doctrine--theory and facts, The - Golgi, C.
Neutron and its properties, The - Chadwick, J.
Never in the field of human conflict - Churchill, W. L. S.
New Bill of Rights - Roosevelt, F. D.
New call to duty - Wilson, W.
New century in agriculture, A - Howell, W.
New constellation - Parkes, H.
New crisis in agriculture, A - Spray, C.
New day dawns - Hains, J.
New economic policy - Nixon, R. M.
New England nativism - Gardner, H. J.
New England weather - Clemens, S. L.
New era of regional cooperation - Rahman, I. b. A.
New frontier - Kennedy, J. F.
New frontiers in racial relations - Rowan, C. T.
New furies, The: skepticism, criticism, and coercion - Howard, J. A.
New Germany, The - Stresemann, G.
New historical perspective, A, interdependence - Eisenhower, M. S.
New Indian, new commitment - Mills, B.
New kind of Southern strategy - Abzug, B. S.
New men for a new world - Pennings, B.
New nationalism - Roosevelt, T.
New policy options through technology - Schmitt, H.
New powers of government accepted - Hughes, C. E.
New problems of government - Taft, R. A.
New relevance and a fresh validity for Commonwealth, A - Lee Kuan Yew
New State Ice Company v. Liebmann - Sutherland, G.
New strategy to provide more jobs, A - Razak, T. A.
New Testament history as allegory - Damiani, P.
New Zealand citizenship, 1948 - Parry, W. E.
New Zealand support for the Royal Navy, 1891-1908 - Ward, Sir J.
New Zealand's defence and Royal Navy supremacy - Jervois, Sir W.
New Zealand's war aims, 1939 - Savage, M. J.
News media and campus unrest - Bittner, J. R.
Nice people - Bjorklund, J.
1913 Waterside Strike, The - Holland, H.
1925 election, The: the Coates campaign - Coates, J. G.
1928 election, The - Ward, Sir J.

1977: year of opportunity in the Middle East? - Eagleton, T. F.
Nixon administration's anti-negro policy - Spottswood, S. G.
Nixon v. Herndon - Holmes, O. W., Jr.
Noblest public virtue - Clay, H.
Nominating Blaine - Ingersoll, R. G.
Nominating Calvin Coolidge - Rogers, W.
Nonviolence - King, M. L., Jr.
Nonviolence and social change - King, M. L., Jr.
Noradrenaline: fate and control of its biosynthesis - Axelrod, J.
Northern party is seeking to convert the government into an instrument of warfare upon slavery - Hunter, R. M.
Northern Securities Company v. United States, 1904 - Harlan, J. M.
Not just a farmer - Blizzard, E.
Novelist's future labors - Thackeray, W. M.
Now is the era of real awakening in Southeast Asia - Abdul Kadir bin Yusof
Nuclear Test-Ban Treaty - Kennedy, J. F.
Nucleic acid synthesis in the study of the genetic Code - Khorana, H. B.

- O -

Oahe Project, The--yes or no? - Gage, P.
Obligation of power - Johnson, L. B.
Of earth, earthy and of Heaven, heavenly - Cronbach, A.
Of existing evils and their remedy - Wright, F.
Of mice and women - Feldmann, M.
Of movers and immobilists - Marbury, W. L.
Old myths and new realities - Fulbright, J. W.
Old soldiers never die - MacArthur, D.
Old world and the new - Schurz, C.
Older Americans - Hausman, L.
Omphalism - Dilke, C. W.
On a recreant nun - Basil the Great, Saint
On accepting the Nobel prize - Faulkner, W.
On affairs in Greece - Palmerston, H. J. T.
On American individualism - Hoover, H. C.
On American nationality Choate, R.
On American policy, January 20, 1775 - Pitt, W., 1708-1778
On an act granting to Congress certain imposts and duties - Hamilton, A.
On appeal from the caucus - Davis, D.
On architecture - Wright, F. L.
On Augustine's mission to England (597) - Ethelbert
On being declared guilty - Socrates
On catalysis - Ostwald, W.
On cathode rays - Lenard, P. E. A. V.
On declining the election at Bristol - Burke, E.
On domestic and foreign affairs - Gladstone, W. E.
On dressing for display - Wesley, J.
On electoral reform - Fox, C. J.
On eloquence - Witherspoon, J.
On fellowship - Beecher, H. W.
On government by attachment - Curran, J. P.
On grievances in the reign of Charles I - Pym, J.
On haemin and the relationships between haemin and chlorophyll - Fischer, H.
On his condemnation to death - Socrates
On history, political economy, and Vietnam - Galbraith, J. K.
On individual differences in human blood - Landsteiner, K.
On internal improvement, 1817 - Calhoun, J. C.
On Lincoln - Sandburg, C.
On manliness - Aelred, Saint
On Necker's project - Mirabeau, H. G. R.
On participating in a congress of American nations - Adams, J. Q.
On patriots - Walpole, R.
On plant pigments - Willstätter, R. M.

On punishment of death - Bright, J.
On radioactivity, a new property of matter - Becquerel, A. H.
On receiving sentence - Debs, E.
On religion and elective office - Henry, J.
On repeal of the Union - O'Connell, D.
On Spain's contribution to the Philippines - Quezon, M. L.
On territorial expansion - Calhoun, J. C.
On the banks of the Wabash - Campbell, B.
On the Canticles - Bernard, Saint
On the cause of Athenian greatness - Pericles
On the character, scope and duties of the Liberty Party - Smith, G.
On the Chersoneus - Demosthenes
On the cloud method of making visible ions and the tracks of ionizing particles - Wilson, C. T. R.
On the commerce clause - Madison, J.
On the Confederate Constitution - Stephens, A. H.
On the constitution and configuration of higher-order compounds - Werner, A.
On the Constitution Bill - Deniehy, D. H.
On the Crittenden Compromise - Crittenden, J. J.
On the crown - Demosthenes
On the dissolution of Parliament - Cromwell, O.
On the duty of Americans at the present crisis - Dwight, T.
On the everpresent God - Knopwood, R.
On the Federal Constitution - Hamilton, A.
On the 15th Amendment - Blair, F. P.
On the flight of a sparrow and the life of man - Edwin
On the fourteenth query of Thomas Jefferson's Note on Virginia - Smith, J. M.
On the genetic code - Crick, F. H. C.
On the grievances in the reign of Charles I - Pym, J.
On the laws of thermal radiation - Wien, W.
On the Missouri Bill - King, R.
On the murder of his family - Logan, J.
On the "Murders at Lexington and Concord" - Tooke, J. H.
On the mysteries - Andocides
On the nativity of St. Peter and St. Paul - Bede
On the philosophy of the Abolition Movement - Phillips, W.
On the pickings of officeholders - Latimer, H.
On the present state of the question of immunity in infectious diseases - Metchnikoff, E.
On the punishment of the Mytileneans - Cleon
On the quantal mechanism of neural transmitter - Katz, B.
On the rejection of Napoleon's overtures - Fox, C. J.
On the right to tax America - Pitt, W., 1708-1778
On the slavery question - Calhoun, J. C.
On thinking big - Babbidge, H. D.
On those who died in the war - Pericles
On understanding society - Lippmann, W.
On unlimited submission to rulers - Mayhew, J.
On withdrawing from the Union - Davis, J.
One century's achievement - Brown, H. A.
150th anniversary of the First Congress - Hughes, C. E.
One of the thirty-six - Weinstein, J. J.
Only Malays can initiate the institutional changes - Suffian bin Hashim
Open door - Humphrey, H. H., Jr.
Open skies proposal to Russia - Eisenhower, D. D.
Opening the prosecution for regicide under Charles II - Nottingham, H. F.
Opportunities in H. S. A. - Jordan, L.
Opportunity for educational innovation - Horner, M. S.
Opposition argument in 1862 - Voorhees, D. W.
Optical methods for studying Hertzian resonances - Kastler, A.
Optics of light sources moving in refractive media - Frank, I. M.

Optimism about the future - Luce, C. B.
Optimist looks at America's future, An - Kemeny, J. G.
Options along the pathway of community involvement - Holland, J. H.
Or of the press - Stewart, P.
Oral tradition of the American Indian - Momaday, N. S.
Oration delivered on the 4th of July, 1818 at Williamsburg, Virginia - Mason, J., Jr.
Oration, &c. - Rittenhouse, D.
Oration for the Megalopolitans - Demosthenes
Oration in memory of Abraham Lincoln - Douglass, F.
Oration on the abolition of the slave trade - Williams, P.
Oration on the liberty of the Rhodians - Demosthenes
Oration over Hamilton - Morris, G.
Order of the Day to the Allied troops invading France - Eisenhower, D. D.
Organization of the Peace Movement, The - Bajer, F.
Organizational communication - Goldhaber, G. M.
Organizer-effect in embryonic development, The - Spemann, H.
Origins of the conceptions of isotopes, The - Soddy, F.
Osmotic pressure and chemical equilibrium - Hoff, J. H. V.
Other phase of reconstruction, The - Langston, J. M.
Our bicentennial - Graham, W. F.
Our China policy in a wider context - Brzezinski, Z.
Our common responsibility and our common challenge - Carter, J.
Our common tradition in peril - Ngwa, J.
Our constitution: a fair compromise - Tan Siew Sin
Our democracy and the ballot - Johnson, J. W.
Our forefathers - Lodge, H. C.
Our forgotten man - Dohrer, J.
Our long national nightmare is over - Nixon, R. M.
Our national policies in this crisis - Hoover, H. C.
Our rights as men - Watkins, W. J.
"... our sacred honor" - Howard, J. A.
Our three goals - Francis, H.
Our unique economic principles - Romney, G.
Our university - Abdul Rahman, T.
Our world today - Lippmann, W.
Overproduction and underconsumption - Ameringer, O.
Owning books - Phelps, W. L.
Oxidation, energy transfer, and vitamins - Szent-Györgyi, A.
Oxygen-transferring ferment of respiration, The - Warburg, O. H.

- P -

Pacific perspective - Mansfield, M. J.
Panegyric - Isocrates
Parable of the ten virgins, The - Shepard, T.
Parliament Bill, 1911 - Oxford and Asquith, H. H.
Parliament in the air raids - Churchill, W. L. S.
Parody of political speeches - Buchwald, A.
Part played by vascular presso- and chemo-receptors in respiratory control, The - Heymans, C. J. F.
Partial cell functions - Ehrlich, P.
Parting is such sweet sorrow - Ettelson, H. W.
Parting of the ways - Bland, H. P.
Parting thoughts - Sevareid, E.
Party of our time - LaFollette, P. F.
Path of carbon in photosynthesis, The - Calvin, M.
Pathway from "activated acetic acid" to the terpenes and fatty acids, The - Lynen, F.
Pay is good - Bunting, J. E.
Peace and law in the Italian tradition - Moneta, E. T.
Peace and the arms race - Noel-Baker, P. J.
Peace and the public mind - Angell, N.
Peace Conference at Paris - Wilson, W.
Peace without victory - Wilson, W.

Pennsylvania idea - Dallas, G. M.
People power - Gardner, J. W.
People v. Fisher - Savage, J.
People's right to remake their constitution - Dorr, T.
Perceptions of the university - Henry, D. D.
Perez v. Brownell - Warren, E.
Perpetuation of our political institutions - Lincoln, A.
Person to person - Worden, G. J.
Perspectives on the prophets of doom - Kerr, C.
Phage, colicins and macroregulatory phenomena - Luria, S. E.
Physicist's renewed look at biology, A - Delbrück, M.
Physiology of digestion - Pavlov, I. P.
Physiology of insulin and its source in the animal body, The - Macleod, J. J. R.
Piety and duty of rulers to comfort and encourage the ministry of Christ - Colman, B.
Pigs and pig iron - Wallace, H. A.
Pith of Paul's chief doctrine - Luther, M.
Place and the price of excellence - Barzun, J.
Plague of people - Crary, D. H.
Plan for a defense movement - Costley, W.
Planetary crisis and the challenge to scientists - Mead, M.
Plasma physics, space research and the origin of the solar system - Alfvén, H.
Playboy philosophy--con - Pinson, W. M., Jr.
Playboy philosophy--pro - Mount, A.
Plea against the disfranchisement of the negro - Miller, T. E.
Plea for Africa - Bacon, L.
Plea for conciliation in 1876 - Bayard, T. F.
Plea for desegregated schools - Revels, H. R.
Plea for free speech in Boston - Douglass, F.
Plea for harmony and peace - Webster, D.
Plea for his home - Old Tassel
Plea for imperial armament - Bismarck, O.
Plea for Republican institutions - Castelar, E.
Plea for support of an Ohio college - Everett, E.
Plea for the national life of Scotland - Belhaven, J. H.
Plea for the West - Beecher, L.
Plea for understanding - Pontier, G.
Plea for universal education in the South - McElwee, R.
Plea in behalf of the Cuban revolution - Garnet, H. H.
Plea to stop the war - Vallandigham, C. L.
Plessay v. Ferguson - Brown, H. B.
Plurality of worlds - Lardner, D.
Plymouth oration - Webster, D.
Poet and the politician, The - Quasimodo, S.
Poetical and the practical in America - Lowell, J. R.
Point Four Program - Truman, H. S.
Policy for internal improvement - Adams, J. Q.
Political parties and women voters - Catt, C. C.
Political speaking since the 1920's - Golden, J. L.
Politics and industry - DuBois, W. E. B.
Polysaccharide phosphorylase - Cori, C.
Pope John Paul's message - Sevareid, E.
Position and duties of the colored people - Pennington, J. W. C.
Power of memory - Burstein, A.
Power over the lives of others - Brooks, P.
Power politics and nation-building - Muhammad Ghazali bin Shafie
Power to see it through - Fosdick, H. E.
Powers of the President - Truman, H. S.
Pray God give us the strength to bear up under all our troubles - Hall, P.
Prayer amendment - Harris, J. G.
Prayse of eloquence - Wigglesworth, M.
Prejudice against the colored man - Wright, T. S.
Premeditated attempt - Stevenson, A. E.
Preparation for eternity - Poplack, A. M.
Preparation for learning - Drummond, H.

Preparation of pure enzymes and virus proteins, The - Northrop, J. H.
Preparation of the Constitution, The - Recto, C. M.
Prerogative and public right - Macdonald, J. S.
Prescription for humanity - Kestenbaum, J.
Present crisis in American affairs - Parker, T.
Present dangers and consequent duties of the citizens - Morse, J.
Present dilemma of the Negro - Clark, K. B.
Present relations of labor and capital - Fortune, T. T.
Preservation of American independence - Roosevelt, F. D.
Preservation of the Union - Choate, R.
Presidential remarks with question-and-answer session - Ford, G. R.
Press conference (Watergate) - Nixon, R. M.
Preventing a new world war - Truman, H. S.
Prevention of the last epidemic - Hiatt, H. H.
Price of peace - Fried, P.
Price of the best - Vander Jagt, G.
Price supports and farm surpluses - Benson, E. T.
Primordial rights of the universal people - Cushing, C.
Prince of sportsmen, The - Thuraisingham, E. E. S. C.
Principle in politics - Burke, E.
Principle of nuclear induction, The - Bloch, F.
Principles of conformational analysis, The - Barton, D. H. R.
Principles of the Universal Negro Improvement Association - Garvey, M.
Privacy on the ropes - Mathias, C. M.
Private belief and public office - Henry, J.
Problem of peace, The - Schweitzer, A.
Problems and opportunities on a very interdependent planet, The - Hesburgh, T. M.
Problems of national education - Hamdan bin Sheikh Tahir, H.
Problems of war and peace - Razak, T. A.
Proclaim their innocence - Sacco, N. and Vanzetti, B.
Proclamation, how to make it efficient - Phillips, W.
Production and properties of positrons, The - Anderson, C. D.
Production of coherent radiation by atoms and molecules - Townes, C. H.
Production of mutations, The - Muller, H. J.
Progress and advantages of international arbitration, The - Cremer, W. R.
Progress of colored women - Terrell, M. C.
Progress of the mechanic arts - Webster, D.
Progress without tears - Okpara, M. I.
Projecting canker worms and caterpillars - Grimstone, H.
Promise made, a promise to keep - Cheek, J. E.
Proper guaranties for security - Sumner, C.
Proper pace of political change - Root, E.
Properties of antinucleons - Segrè, E. G.
Properties of colloids - Zsigmondy, R. A.
Property and political power - Webster, D.
Property as a disadvantage - Newman, J. H.
Property under the common law (Coster v. Lorillard case) - Jay, J. (1745-1829); Young, J.
Proposal for a National Insurance scheme, 1882 - Atkinson, H.
Proposals for change - Brown, E. G., Jr.
Prospect in the arts and sciences - Oppenheimer, J. R.
Prospects for freedom - Little, M.
Protest against sentence as a traitor - Emmet, R.
Protozoa as causes of disease - Laveran, C. L. A.
"Provincialism" 1856 - Featherston, I.
Psalm of life - Katz, R. M.
Public challenge and the campus response - McGill, W. J.

Public domain: the people's heritage - Roosevelt, T.
Public Education Association - Clemens, S. L.
Public education for a humane society - Howe, H.
Public offices as private perquisites - Schurz, C.
Public relations in education - Pray, F. C.
Public Safety Conservation Bill, 1932, The - Forbes, G. W.
Public service - Dewey, T. E.
Publican - Worden, G.
Puerto Ricans and the neighborhood - Zimbardo, P.
Pump-priming--it is necessary for business recovery - Wagner, R. F.
Puritan principle: liberty under law - Curtis, G. W.
Pursuit of excellence - Dwight, T.
Putting life into development plans - Razak, T. A.

- Q -

Quakers and peace - Cadbury, H. J.
Quantitative analysis of excitation and conduction in nerve, The - Huxley, A. F.
Quantitative micro-analysis of organic substances - Pregl, F.
Quarantining the aggressors - Roosevelt, F. D.
Queen against Moxon - Talfourd, T. N.
Queen and the royal succession - Elizabeth I
Quest for peace and justice, The - King, M. L., Jr.
Question most frequently asked - Klein, J. T.
Question of ecology, A - Jones, A. L.
Question of survival - Nixon, R. M.

- R -

Raccoon in a bag - Crockett, D.
Race prejudice as viewed from an economic standpoint - Bulkley, W. L.
Race problem - Grady, H. W.
Race problem stated, The - Price, J. C.
Race unity - Barnett, F. L.
Racism in the law - Crockett, G. W.
Radiation of particles moving at a velocity exceeding that of light - Cerenkov, P. A.
Radical programme, 1877, A - Grey, Sir G.
Radioactive substances, especially radium - Curie, P.
Radium and the new concepts in chemistry - Curie, M.
Raising the fallen image of business - Goodman, S. J.
Raising the flag over Fort Sumter - Beecher, H. W.
Rare gases of the atmosphere, The - Ramsay, Sir W.
Rare spirit - Adler, M.
Raza and the law, La - Kennedy, E. M.
Reaffirmation of the Monroe Doctrine - Polk, J. K.
Real cause of inflation, The: government services - Richey, H. S.
Real Indian leaders condemn A.I.M. - Wilson, D.
Reality and rhetoric - Lindsay, J. V.
Reality of the novelist's creation - Thackeray, W. M.
Reason immutable and sovereign - Mirabeau, H. G. R.
Reasons for a new political party - Turner, H. M.
Reasons for refusing to part company with the South - Davis, H. W.
Reasons why the colored American should go to Africa - Bruce, J. E.
Reassuring touch - Hoover, H. C.
Rebecca at the well - Hildebert of Lavardin
Rebuking Senator Clemens of Alabama - Dickinson, D. S.
Recent advances in spectroscopy - Michelson, A. A.
Recent advances in the chemistry of natural products - Woodward, R. B.
Recent developments in particle physics - Alvarez, L. W.
Reception at Madison, Indiana - Webster, D.
Reception speech at Finsbury Chapel - Douglass, F.

Recoilless nuclear resonance absorption of gamma radiation - Mossbauer, R. L.
Reconciliation and peace - Hatfield, M. O.
Reconciliation in 1865 - Seward, W. H.
Record of Democratic Party - Barkley, A. W.
Rectitude higher than morality - Chapin, E. H.
Red Cross in a changing world, The - MacAulay, J. A.
Rediscovering America - Church, F.
Reform Bill - Macaulay, T. B.
Reform of the franchise - Russell, J. R.
Refugee problems and their solutions - Goedhart, G. J. v. H.
Regular snob - Overhill, J.
Rejoiner to Joseph Alsop's attack - Morse, W. L.
Relation of genetics to physiology and medicine, The - Morgan, T. H.
Relationships between isosterism and competitive phenomena, The - Fovet, D.
Relativistic quantum field theory - Schwinger, J.
Religion and politics - Smith, A. E.
Religion in government - Kennedy, J. F.
Religious toleration - Sheil, R. L.
Remarkable phenomenon, A: why Singapore is different - Goh Keng Swee
Remarks at the Centennial Charter Day Convocation, the Ohio State University - Reston, J.
Remarks at the White House Conference on Children - Nixon, R. M.
Remarks in Chicago on urban imperatives - Benedict, D. L.
Remarks to the nation - Johnson, L. B.
Remedy for anarchy - Lawson, J.
Renascence - Korteling, M.
Repeal of income tax on farmers, 1923 - Massey, W. F.
Reply to Grady - Brockett, J. A.
Reply to Hayne - Webster, D.
Reply to Lincoln - Douglas, S. A.
Reply to Robespierre - Guadet, M. E.; Vergniaud, P. V.
Reply to the Earl of Chatham against Parliamentary exemption from arrest for debt - Mansfield, W. M.
Reply to the Vice President - Stanton, E.
Replying to Henry Clay - Calhoun, J. C.
Representation for all Southern states - Johnson, A.
Representation of the people - Mill, J. S.
Republican appeal for unity - Sumner, C.
Republican National Convention acceptance speech - Ford, G. R.
Requiem for Joe College - McGill, W. J.
Requiem for the counterculture: problems of a new student generation - McGill, W. J.
Research in nuclear magnetism - Purcell, E. M.
Researches on malaria - Ross, Sir R.
Resistance to unlawful authority - Jekyll, J.
Resolutions on secession and reconstruction - Sumner, C.
Responsibilities inherent in a constitutional democracy - Brooke, E. W.
Responsibilities of the educated man - Kirk, G.
Restoring the tidemarks of trust - Moos, M.
Results of electron-impact tests in the light of Bohr's theory of atoms, The - Hertz, G.
Results of oppression - Smith, S.
Resurrection of Lazarus - Abelard, P.
Retrospect '73--Biblical lessons we can learn from Watergate - Huffman, J. A.
Return to normalcy - Harding, W. G.
Reversibility of certain rheumatic and nonrheumatic conditions by the use of cortisone or of the pituitary adrenocorticotropic hormone, The - Hench, P. S.
Review of the foreign policy, A - Kissinger, H. A.
Revolution and the logic of coercion - Garfield, J. A.
Revolution by the ballot - Taylor, G. E.

Revolution in the white mother country and national liberation in the Black colony - Cleaver, E.
Revolution of 1848 - Lamartine, A. M. L.
Rhapsody - Clay, C. M.
Rhetoric of 1968 - Haiman, F. S.
Rhodesian problem and the change of mood in Britain, The - Lee Kuan Yew
Right of revolution for the Negro people - Ford, J. W.
Right ticket but the wrong train, The - Ditzen, L. R.
Right to vote - Johnson, L. B.
Righteous and speedy peace - Lincoln, A.
Righteous shall flourish like the palm-tree - Tomsky, M. B.
Rightful place for everyone in Malaysia, A - Razak, T. A.
Rights of colored citizens in traveling - Redmond, C. L.
Rights of the conqueror - Stevens, T.
Ripples of hope - Palovesik, S.
Risk and other four-letter words - Wriston, W. B.
Risks of life - Helman, L. A.
Road to freedom - Hoover, H. C.
Road to right - Lubbers, A. D.
Roadways and waterways - Calhoun, J. C.
Role of attorney-general, Malaysia, The - Abdul Kadir bin Yusof
Role of heart catheterization and angiocardiography in the development of modern medicine, The - Forssmann, W. T. O.
Role of M.C.A. and the loyalty of Malaysian Chinese, The - Tan Siew Sin
Role of the army, The - Vargas, J. B.
Role of the church in promoting peace, The - Söderblom, N.
Role of the hypophysis in carbohydrate metabolism and in diabetes, The - Houssay, B. A.
Role of the university in a multiracial society, The - Toh Chin Chye
Role of trade union research and documentation services, The - Nair, C. D.
Roosevelt's place in history - Schlesinger, A. M., Jr.
Rout the forces of hate - Collins, L.
Royal prerogative delegated from the people - Wyndham, W.
Royal visit - Garran, R. R.
Rugged individualism - Hoover, H. C.
Rule for decent living - Wycliffe, J.
Ruling oligarchy wants to engage in a foreign war - Mote, C. H.
Rural families and welfare - Muench, A.
Rust of riches - Dewey, O.

- S -

Sacra fames auri - Wesley, J.
Sacred cause of the human race - Lacordaire, J. B. H.
Sacredness of matrimony - Coleridge, J. D. C.
Safety of the virtuous - Melanchthon, P.
Saint's anchor-hold, The - Davenport, J.
Sanctity of the Union - Stephens, A. H.
Schechter Poultry Corporation v. United States - Hughes, C. E.
Scholar in a Republic - Phillips, W.
Science and culture - Huxley, T. H.
Science and peace - Boyd Orr, J.; Pauling, L. C.
Science and the law - McGill, W. J.
Science and the public trust - Wydler, J. W.
Scientia Liberatrix - Chapin, E. H.
Scientific concepts of external aid for agricultural education - Aziz, U.
Sea of life - Anselm, Saint
Seacoast of Bohemia, The: truth in literature - Bacon, W. A.
Seal of truth - Pearl, C.
Searching for new solutions to poverty - McNamara, R. S.
Second dust bowl, The - Holt, R.
Second Olynthiac - Demosthenes
Second oration against Catiline - Cicero, M. T.
Second Philippic - Demosthenes
Secretness of true greatness - Damiani, P.
Security and disarmament - Quidde, L.
Security situation in Malaysia - Rahman, D. I. B. A.

Seder of life - Chiel, S.
Seeking a link with the past - Mink, P. T.
Segregation and desegregation - Marshall, T.
Segregation destroys fellowship and citizenship - Trotter, W. M.
Self-government and civilization - Calhoun, J. C.
Self out of season - Kenny, A.
Self respect is what our trade unions have and ... - Lee Kuan Yew
Semiconductor research leading to the point contact transistor - Bardeen, J.
Senate debate over ratification of treaties concerning the Panama Canal - Hayakawa, S. I.
Sermon for the anniversary of American independence, July 24th, 1786, A - McCorkle, S.
Sermon from Mark XII, 34 - Bacon, L.
Sermon on the Mount - Cox, S. S.
Sermon on the plow - Latimer, H.
Serum therapy in therapeutics and medical science - Behring, E. A. V.
Servant of the Lord has died - Levenson, J.
Service of sex - Huitfeldt, J.
Service to others - Hesburgh, T. M.
Shackled by stereotypes - Schell, G.
Shadows in the sun - Rudin, J. P.
Shall the Fundamentalists win - Fosdick, H. E.
Shall the negro be encouraged to seek cultural equality? - DuBois, W. E. B.
Shame of America - Grimke, A. H.
Sheep and lions in trade unions - Alatas, S. H.
Shell model, The - Mayer, M. G.
Sheppard v. Maxwell - Clark, T. C.
Shift in the balance - Trotter, V. Y.
Ship-money--impeaching Lord Keeper Finch - Falkland, L. C.
Should colored men be subject to the pains and penalties of the Fugitive Slave Law? - Langston, C. H.
Significance of Five-Power Defence Agreement, The - Razak, T. A.
Simple justice and existential victims - McGill, W. J.
Sinews of peace - Churchill, W. L. S.
Sinners in the hands of an angry God - Edwards, J.
Sioux's revenge - Tanner, B. T.
Sixty years of sectionalism - Clay, H.
Sky's the limit, The - Grass, F.
Slander - Barrow, I.
Slavery and colonization - Williams, P.
Slavery as it concerns the British - Remond, C. L.
Slavery as it is, and its influence upon the American people - Brown, W. W.
Slavery brutalizes man - Payne, D. A.
Slums as a common nuisance (Meeker v. Van Rensselaer case) - Savage, J.
Small group of men hold in their hands the business of this country - LaFollette, R. M., Sr.
Small states and great achievements - Cobden, R.
Small step toward racial equality - Hughes, C. E.
Social attitudes and technological civilization - Dubos, R.
Social morality - Lewis, C. S.
Social responsibility of science - Brown, H. S.
Social revolution - Young, W. M.
Social Security Bill, 1938, The - Hamilton, A.
Socialism - Clark, P. H.
Socialist Commonwealth - Hardie, J. K.
Socialist objective of the labour movement, The - Holland, H.
Soil--America's lifeblood - Bozeman, M.
Soils--our basic natural resources--the key to man's survival - McKinney, S. M.
Soldier's pay - LaFollette, R. M., Sr.
Solemn hour - Churchill, W. L. S.
Some applications of isotopic indicators - Hevesy, G. D.
Some aspects of the mission of the International Committee of the Red Cross - Boissier, L. L.
Some consequences of low-temperature research in chemical thermodynamics - Giauque, W. F.
Some delusions of the decade of development - Goh Keng Swee

Some elements necessary to race development - Moton, R. R.
Some facts about Southern lynchings - Graham, D. A.
Some fast reactions in gases studied by flash photolysis and kinetic spectroscopy - Norrish, R. G. W.
Some new approaches to university education - Hamzah Sendut
Some notes on modern Greek tradition - Seferis, G.
Some observations on the responses of single nerve fibers - Erlanger, J.
Some of the new methods for functional testing of the vestibular apparatus and the cerebellum - Barany, R.
Some polycyclic natural products - Robinson, Sir R.
Some problems relating to chain reactions and to the theory of combustion - Semenov, N. N.
Some recent extensions of the chemical transmission of the effects of nerve impulses - Dale, Sir H. H.
Some reflections on peace in our time - Bunche, R. J.
Some thermodynamic properties of hydrogen and deuterium - Urey, H. C.
Sorrow but not tragedy - Garsek, I.
Sorting it out - Goheen, R. F.
Soul of our nation - Abdul Rahman, T.
Soul's exaltation, The - Hooker, T.
Soul's vocation, doctrine 3, The - Hooker, T.
Soul's vocation, doctrine 7, The - Hooker, T.
Sound believer, The - Shepard, T.
South African War continent, 1899, The - Seddon, R. J.
Southern response to John Brown and black republicanism - Moore, S.
Sovereignty of the people - Hallett, B.
Soviet missiles in Cuba - Kennedy, J. F.
Speaker of the year award - Lawrence, D. L.
Speaking for the consumer - White, W. A.
Special problems of Indian women in education - Yazzie, E.
Spectroscopy, molecular orbitals, and chemical bonding - Mulliken, R. S.
Speech against independence - Dickinson, J.
Speech at Peoria - Lincoln, A.
Speech at the Boston Town Meeting - Mather, I.
Speech at the Bow Street Police court - Pankhurst, E. G.
Speech at the Martin Luther King, Jr. Hospital - Carter, J.
Speech at the Peasants' Rising - Ball, J.
Speech at the stake - Cranmer, T.
Speech at the U. S. Naval Academy - Steinem, G.
Speech, &c. - Chew, S.
Speech for the petition to change the form of government - Galloway, J.
Speech in the Tilden convention - Voorhees, D. W.
Speech in time of revolution - Rutledge, J.
Speech in Virginia Convention on Ratification of the Constitution, June 20, 1788 - Marshall, J.
Speech on the Fugitive Slave Bill - Ward, S. R.
Speech on the scaffold - Harrison, T.; Raleigh, W.
Speech opening campaign for fourth liberty loan - Wilson, W.
Speech to both Houses - Hutchinson, T.; Rutledge, J.
Speech to his troops before the battle of Hastings - William I
Speech to Parliament - George III, King of Great Britain
Speech to the Assembly at New York - Mulford, S.
Speech to the Council and House of Representatives - Bernard, F.
Speech to the Primrose League - Salisbury, R. A. T. G-C.
Speech to the Virginia House of Burgesses - Berkeley, W.
Speech when on trial for life - More, T.
Spirit of humanity - Thomson, T. J. B.
Spirit of Merdeka - Stephens, D. A.
Spirit of mutual conciliation - Johnson, A.

Spiritual authority for my Christian work - Nation, C. A.
Spiritual portrait - Swarensky, M. E.
Spiritual roots of Indian success - Whitemen, H. V.
Squeezing the sponge - Danton, G. J.
Stalwart standpoint - Conkling, R.
Standard of life - Kentenbaum, J.
Standard Oil Company of New Jersey v. United States - White, E. D.
Standards that stand - DeVries, C.
State of the country from a Black man's point of view - Brown, D. P.
State of the judiciary - Burger, W. E.
State of the nation (1850) - Parker, T.
State of the state address - Brown, E. G.
State of the Union address - Ford, G. R.
State sovereignty and federal supremacy - Madison, J.
Statement before the Indian sovereignty Conference of American Indians, Harvard, February 22, 1975 - MacDonald, P.
Statement to the people of Massachusetts - Kennedy, E. M.
States and the Union - Adams, C. F.
Statistical interpretation of quantum mechanics, The - Born, M.
Stop the foes of Negro freedom - McGowan, E. D.
Strangler - Schalliol, C.
Strategy for the future - Muhammad Ghazali bin Shafie
Strategy for the seventies - Young, W. M., Jr.
Strategy of freedom - Acheson, D.
Strategy of mass retaliation - Dulles, J. F.
Strength and weakness of the slave power - Julian, G. W.
Strengthening international developing institutions - Stevenson, A. E.
Strengthening Sino-American relations - Mondale, W. F.
Strenuous life - Roosevelt, T.
Streptomycin: background, isolation, properties, and utilization - Waksman, S. A.
String galvanometer and the measurement of the action currents of the heart, The - Einthoven, W.
Structural and spectral changes of chemical atoms - Stark, J.
Structural aspects of interatomic charge-transfer bonding - Hassel, O.
Structure and connexions of neurons, The - Ramon Y Cajal, S.
Structure of carbohydrates and of vitamin C, The - Haworth, W. N.
Structure of the atom, The - Bohr, N.
Student and the ghetto - McKissick, F. B.
Student revolt, The, a defense of the older generation - Horn, F. H.
Studies in chemical thermodynamics - Nernst, W. H.
Subtle use of humor by the great Indian chief Osceola, The - Maestas, J. R.
Subtreasury Bill of 1837 - Clay, C. C., Sr.
Succession of goals, A - Herink, R.
Suez crisis, 1956, The - Holland, S.
Suffer suffer Yeddy - Hird, P.
Suffering people of Europe, The - Nansen, F.
Support for the Singapore Naval Base, 1927 - Coates, J. G.
Surface properties of semiconductors - Brattain, W. H.
Surrender speech - Joseph, Chief
Survival - Jordan, V. E., Jr.
Suture of blood-vessels and transplantation of organs - Carrel, A.
Symmetry and currents in particle physics - Gell-Mann, M.
Symphony of life - Tomsky, M. B.
Syntheses in the purine and sugar group - Fischer, H. E.
Synthesis in the study of nucleotides - Todd, Sir A. R.
Synthesis of ammonia from its elements, The - Haber, F.
System of real reciprocity - Clay, H.

- T -

Talk on books - Drummond, H.
Tall ships, The - Sayre, F. B.
Tampico incident - Wilson, W.
Taps and reveille - Brandli, W.

Task of the Negro people - Randolph, A. P.
Taste of empire - Beveridge, A. J.
Teachers' dilemma, The: the government gets the blame - Tan Chee Khoon
Teacher's spiritual dimension - Adler, M.
Teamsters' Union speech - Roosevelt, F. D.
Technical education and its relation to science and literature - Whitehead, A. N.
Technical progress and prosperity - Webster, D.
Technological change and management policies - Kanapathy, V.
Televised debates - Weicker, L. P.
Television news coverage - Agnew, S.
Tendency in English history - Seeley, J. R.
Tentative trial balloon - Roosevelt, F. D.
"Terrible beauty is born" - McNally, J.
Terrorism, the ultimate evil - Kelley, C. M.
Testimony at the "Docker's Inquiry" - Bevin, E.
Thanksgiving - Rawson, E.
Thanksgiving and entreaty, a President's valedictory - Pusey, N. M.
That feeling of hostility - DeBow, J. D. B.
"Their finest hour" - Churchill, W. L. S.
Their questions - Bunting, M. I.
Theology and amnesty - Barger, R. N.
Theology of the earth - Dubos, R.
Theory of electrons and positrons - Dirac, P. A. M.
Theory of electrons and the propagation of light, The - Lorentz, H. A.
There is a better day coming - Douglass, F.
"There is East; there is India." Benton, T. H.
There is still much to be done - Washington, B. T.
There's always a mongoose - Elliott, J.
Thermionic phenomena and the laws which govern them - Richardson, O. W.
These are revolutionary times - Adams, E. J.
These evils call loudly for redress - Green, J. P.
These truths to remember - Abdul Rahman, T.
They are all heroes - Miller, G. F.
"... they are just like the rest of us" - Hopkins, H.
Things worth fighting for - Chifley, J. B.
Think strawberries - Lavenson, J.
Thinking out loud - Blue, B.
Third Olynthiac - Demosthenes
Third Philippic - Demosthenes
Third World and the ghetto - Brown, H. R.
This I believe - Winter, R. A.
This is our quest - Rodriguez, A. M.
This nation will remain neutral - Roosevelt, F. D.
This tongue-tied democracy - Griswold, A. W.
This was a man - Simon, R.
Three basic questions - Kaplan, L.
Three great eras - Chase, S. P.
Three major problems of developing countries - Lim Kim San
Three parts of morality - Lewis, C. S.
Three ways to mourn - Fedder, A. H.
Through the looking glass - Lee, W. L.
Tilden-Hayes election - Thurman, A. G.
Time for choosing - Reagan, R.
Time for reconstruction - Birenbaum, W. M.
Time to break silence - King, M. L., Jr.
Time to celebrate life, A - Mondale, W. F.
Time to speak - Morgan, C., Jr.
To dare again, ever to dare - Danton, G. J.
To General Jackson - Weatherford, W.
To General Proctor - Tecumseh
To have lived without reason - Clevenger, T.
To his soldiers - Cataline
To make a commonplace wondrous - Becker, A.
To my white fellow citizens - Sampson, B. K.

To secure the existing order against revolutionary radicalism - Jackson, R. H.
To the Army of Northern Virginia - Lee, R. E.
To the camp - Verginiaud, P. V.
To the jury - Darrow, C.
To the young men of Italy - Mazzini, G.
To young people - Little, M.
Toast to President Ford - Kaunda, K.
Toast to President Ford and to the American people - Elizabeth II, Queen of England
Toast to Queen Elizabeth - Ford, G. R.
Today the guns are silent - MacArthur, D.
Today's most fateful fact - Stevenson, A. E.
Too many questions ... not enough answers - Muskie, E. S.
Total national defense - Roosevelt, F. D.
Total victory in the Cold War - Goldwater, B. M.
Toward human unity or beyond nationalism - Balch, E. G.
Towards making peace permanent - Root, E.
Trade and commerce for the southwestern states - Crittenden, T. T.
Trail of sulfur research, A - Vigneaud, V. D.
Trained intelligence - Stevenson, A. E.
Transformation of the Black Panther Party - Newton, H. P.
Transformations of kinetic energy of free electrons into excitation energy of atoms by impacts - Franck, J.
Transistor technology evokes new physics - Shockley, W.
Treasurer's report - Benchley, R. C.
Treatise of the covenant of grace, A - Cotton, J.
Treatment of dementia paralytica by malaria inoculation, The - Wagner-Jauregg, J.
Trends and problems of government - Hamzah bin Sendut
Trends of polarography, The - Heyrovsky, J.
Trent affair - Bright, J.
Tribal chartered education - Demmert, W. G.
Tribute to a fallen Black soldier - Stanley, J.
Tribute to Captain Paul Cuffe - Williams, P.
Tribute to India and Indians - Lee Kuan Yew
Tribute to John F. Kennedy at the General Assembly of the United Nations - Stevenson, A. E.
Tribute to the man of the people, A - Califano, J. A.
Tribute to William Lloyd Garrison, A - Mill, J. S.
Triumph of equal school rights in Boston - Neil, W. C.
Trouble in the university - Martin, D.
True aim of education, The - Irwin, H.
True Americanism - Schurz, C.
True grandeur of nations - Sumner, C.
True politics - Cousin, V.
"Trust the people" speech - Churchill, R. H. S.
Trustees of Dartmouth College v. Woodward - Marshall, J.
Truth by radio - Shaw, G. B.
Truth in government - Mathias, C. M.
Tunku's recipe for success: how to get things done - Abdul Rahman, T.
Turning point - Roosevelt, F. D.
Twenty four days in May - Ramani, R.
Two Americas - Fulbright, J. W.
Two arks - Simon, E. Y.
Two contrasting Black voices - Walters, A.
Two countries in one - Ungku Omar Ahmad
Two cultures - Snow, C. P.
Two decades of research on the biosynthesis of saccharides - Leloir, L. F.
Two declarations of independence, The: 1776 and 1861 - King, T. S.
Two myths and a paradox - Cole, E. N.
Tyrant's plea, necessity - Waller, E.

- U -

U-2 incident - Eisenhower, D. D.
Ultimate America - Cook, J.
Ultracentrifuge, The - Svedberg, T.
UMNO's twentieth milestone - Razak, T. A.
Uncle Tom is dead! - Hood, W. R.
Uncommon thought - Jacobusse, K. D.
Undelivered Dallas speech - Kennedy, J. F.
Under the flag - Phillips, W.
Under the hammer: freedom, justice, and dignity - Jordan, V. E., Jr.
Undesirable one - Rylaarsdam, J.
Undiscovered country - Ingalls, J. J.
Unexpected ally after independence - Rahman, I. b. A.
Unfinished business - Jordan, V. E.
Unfinished revolution - Barlow, J.
UNICEF: achievement and challenge - Harmann, Z.
Unidentified flying objects, etc. - Sonberg, H. A.
Union and coercion - Ellsworth, O.
Union at any price - Crittenden, J. J.
United Nations - Hoover, H. C.; Lodge, H. C., Jr.; Roosevelt, E. A.
United States and the Caribbean - Stimson, H. L.
United States and the coming world food crisis, The - Sullivan, J. H.
United States and the United Nations, The - McKeever, P.
United States v. E. C. Knight Company, 1895 - Fuller, M. W.
United States v. Lattimore - Youngdahl, L.
United States v. Lovett, Watson, and Dodd - Black, H. L.
United States v. One book called Ulysses - Woolsey, J. M.
United States v. United States Steel - McKenna, J.
United States v. Workingmen's Amalgamated Council of New Orleans - Billings
United we stand, divided we fall - Smith, E. R.
Universal collective security--amendments to the United Nations Charter, 1945 - Fraser, P.
Universal declaration of human rights - Carter, J.
Universities: discrepancy between ideal and reality takes alarming turn - Alatas, S. H.
University should slow down - Suffian bin Hashim
Unlimited submission and nonresistance to the Higher Powers - Mayhew, J.
Unmentionable diseases - Wayman, M. K.
Unprepared for war with England - German, O.
Unreasonable prejudices against people of color in Philadelphia - Barrett, B. F.
Unshackled living - Cyprian, Saint
Unsolved problems in physics - Hess, V. F.
Unsurrendering fidelity to country - Grattan, H.
Unwillingness to improve - Baxter, R.
Upon acceptance of the 1967 William Allen White Foundation Award for Journalistic Merit - Gallagher, W.
Upon the motion of subsidy - Bacon, F.
Upward climb - Simon, R.
Urban crime: its causes and control - Stanmeyer, W. A.
Urgency of real problems facing the less developed nations - Rajaratnan, S.
Use and abuse of images and relics - Tyndale, E.
Uses of great men - Emerson, R. W.
Use of organomagnesium compounds in preparative organic chemistry, The - Grignard, V.
Uses of adversity, The - Crosby, G. A.

- V -

Valedictory to the graduates - Kemeny, J. G.
Value of agitation - DuBois, W. E. B.

Value of disobedience - Sacks, M.
Value of the American Union - Brownlow, W. G.
Value of the English language, The - Enche Arshad bin Ayub
Vast wasteland - Minow, N. N.
Vested rights and the obligations of contracts - Thurman, A. G.
Vial of fragrant ointment - Arm, M.
Viall I: the powring out of the seven vials or An exposition with an application of the 16th Chapter of Revelation - Cotton, J.
Vietnam moratorium address - Lindsay, J. V.
Vietnam veterans against the war - Kerry, J. F.
View of genetics, A - Lederberg, J.
View of US foreign policy in the future - Bush, G.
Vision that looks beyond - Minda, A. G.
Visual receptors and retinal interaction - Hartline, H. K.
Vital issues must be resolved if we are to survive - Razak, T. A.
Vital university - McBath, J. H.
"Viva la Huelga" - Wright, T.
Vocational agriculture, the FFA, and our free enterprise system - Morelli, L.
Voice from the past - Smith, G.
Vote against prayer and for God - Kahn, R. I.
Vulnerability and vigilance - Richardson, E. L.

- W -

Walking westward - Thoreau, H. D.
War address (December 8, 1941) - Roosevelt, F. D.
War comes to Europe - Hoover, H. C.
War in Europe - Roosevelt, F. D.
War message to Congress - Wilson, W.
War on prosperity - Drumm, S. L.
War, peace and revolutionary democracy - Lenin, N.
War with Mexico - Corwin, T.
War without end - Church, F.
Warning and a prophecy - Wilkes, J.
Warning to Harvard seniors against world revolution - Tappan, D.
Warning to the white-collar worker - Suffian bin Hashim
Warrior and the woman - Nies, N.
Waste of our precious farmland, The - Lucas, M.
Watergate case - Nixon, R. M.
Watergate investigation - Weicker, L. P.
Wave nature of the electron, The - De Broglie, L.
Way of life, The - Cotton, J.
Way out of the exploding ghetto - Rustin, B.
We are fighting mad - Curtin, J.
We are going to make it better for Blacks and whites - Evers, O.
We are in a serious revolution - Lewis, J.
We are involved in the world food crisis - Carpenter, E.
We are mostly subject peoples all over the world - Garvey, M.
We are struggling for equality - Hope, J.
We ask an equal chance in the race of life - Dunn, O. J.
We ask for our rights - Rock, J. S.
We cannot afford to fail this time to meet aspirations of people - Abdul Kadir bin Yusof
We have the pain and travail - Ball, J.
We hold these truths - Everheart, W. E.
We must be a law-abiding and law-respecting people - Washington, B. T.
We must have justice - Muhammad, E.
We must have unity - Walker, D.
We need to be united - King, Mrs. M. L., Jr.
We shall overcome - Johnson, L. B.
"We, the people" or "We, the states" - Henry, P.
We weep today - Greenberg, S.
We will uphold concepts of parliamentary democracy - Razak, T. A.
Weak interactions and nonconservation of parity - Lee, T. D.
Weakest spot in the American system - Evarts, W. M.

Wealth and poverty, aristocracy and Republicanism - Livingston, R. R.
West Virginia Board of Education et al v. Barnette et al - Jackson, R. H.
We've decided to stop begging - Hulett, J.
What Abraham Lincoln said - Abdul Rahman, T.
What can I do that matters? - Stuart, J. D.
What can we prove about God? - Zellner, L. R.
What constitutes an American? - Ickes, H. L.
What desires are politically important? - Russell, B. A. W.
What did you say? - Nail, W. A.
What every Yale freshman should know - Morgan, E. S.
What if the slaves are emancipated? - Rock, J. S.
What is a free man? - Cram, R. A.
What is my duty as an anti-slavery voter? - Douglass, F.
What leadership means to me - Meyer, S.
What really counts - Belson, R. S.
What socialism means to us - Harrison, H. H.
What the Black man wants - Douglass, F.
What the Lord requires - Teller, M.
What the people grant, they can take away - Royster, V. C.
What the police expect of the citizenry - Murphy, P. V.
What to the slave is the Fourth of July? - Douglass, F.
What's happening, baby? - Harper, P. C.
Wheel of poverty - Ybarra, B.
When freedom dies in its sleep - Griffin, R. P.
When old things pass away - Chalmers, T.
When woman gets her rights man will be right - Truth, S.
Where do we go from here? - King, M. L., Jr.
Which is the path of change? - Hatcher, R. G.
Which knew not Joseph - Barton, B.
Which shall rule, manhood or money? - LaFollette, R. M., Sr.
White liberals and the Black revolution - Killens, J. O.
Who is tampering with the soul of America? - Jones, J. L.
Whole race must protest - Pinchback, P. B. S.
Who's to blame in Birmingham? - Morgan, C., Jr.
Why a Negro convention is necessary - Hamilton, W.
Why abolish the jury trial? - Marshall, D. S.
Why foreign aid? - Gaud, W. S.
Why must we take this painful road? - Johnson, L. B.
Why Negroes should support the Communists - Jones, W. N.
Why we must be stronger militarily - Goldwater, B. M.
Wilkinson and Murdaugh case, The - Hardin, B.
Will to be strong - Goldwater, B. M.
Wilmington massacre - Morris, C. S.
"The wind of change" - Macmillan, H.
Wireless telegraphic communication - Marconi, G.
Wisdom of the heart - Hageman, M.
Witch hunt - Bosman, R. A.
Witch trials - Ferguson, J.
With a touch of the master's hand - Maestas, J. R.
With malice toward none - Lincoln, A.
Withdrawal speech - Johnson, L. B.
Withering influence of provincial subjection - Meagher, T. F.
Woman - Depew, C. M.
Woman could be President - Spain, J. B.
Woman suffrage - Douglass, F.
Woman's rights - Truth, S.
Women and equality under the law - Holtzman, E.
Women in politics - Chisholm, S.
Women's liberation - Dunbar, R.
Work at the Hague in 1899 and in 1907, The - Renault, L.
Work of art - Stern, H. J.
Work of the Institute of International Law, The - Hagerup, G. F.
"Work or fight" in the South - White, W. F.
World divided by Three - Lundy, R. F.
World food crisis - Bark, D. R.

World hunger: a question of rights - Wivell, C. A.
World needs our help, The - Dunlap, D. E.
World of jazz - Bernstein, L.
World referendum - Arnoldson, K. P.
World sea power: United States vs. USSR - Middendorf, J. W.
World wide amnesty for political prisoners - Moynihan, D. P.
"Wounds, shrieks, and tears" in government - Smith, S.
Wrath upon the wicked to the uttermost - Edwards, J.
Writer's duty - Faulkner, W.

- X -

The x-ray analysis of complicated molecules - Hodgkin, D. C.
X-ray analysis of haemoglobin - Perutz, M. F.
X-ray spectra and the structure of the atoms, The - Siegbahn, K. M. G.
X-rays as a branch of optics - Compton, A. H.

- Y -

Yen to make a mark with the dollar, The - Church, F.
You are to take these free booters and desperadoes - Woodmason, C.
You can do it - Schroeder, P.
You (male) should wear long hair - Burton, S.
Young American - Emerson, R. W.
Young men with visions - Ferrell, D.
"You're an American, aren't you?" - Kuiper, D. R.
Youth leadership - Lim Kim San

- Z -

Zeitgeist and the Judiciary - Frankfurter, F.

JOHN TAGGART HINCKLEY LIBRARY
NORTHWEST COLLEGE
POWELL, WY 82435
WITHDRAWN